Before you leave, you might want to give Mother Nature a call.

Remove card and see instructions on back.

F r o m m e r's®
3 Free Minutes of Weather Information

THE WEATHER CHANNEL®

- **Current conditions and forecasts for over 1,500 locations worldwide**

- **Severe-weather information, including winter storm advisories and tropical storm updates**

- **Wake-up call, complete with forecast for city of your choice**

- **Special-interest forecasts, featuring ski resort, boating and other outdoor conditions**

Weather information provided by The Weather Channel. Network services provided by AT&T. All other services provided by ICN, Ltd. Offer valid only in the U.S.

Easy.
Convenient. Accurate.

During your free call, an automated operator will offer you an option to add $10, $20 or $30 to your phone card using any major credit card. Once a payment option is selected, five free minutes of long distance will be added to your phone card.

Use your card to:

• Save 20% on comprehensive weather information.

• Save up to 60% on long-distance calls to anywhere in the U.S., anytime.

• Save 20% on other helpful information, including lottery, sports and more.

Weather fans
you're not alone.

Travel Discount Coupon

This coupon entitles you to special discounts
when you book your trip through the

RESERVATION SERVICE

Hotels ♦ Airlines ♦ Car Rentals ♦ Cruises
All Your Travel Needs

Here's what you get: *

♦ A discount of $50 USD on a booking of $1,000** or
  more for two or more people!

♦ A discount of $25 USD on a booking of $500** or more
  for one person!

♦ Free membership for three years, and 1,000 free miles
  on enrollment in the unique Travel Network Miles-to-
  Go® frequent-traveler program. Earn one mile for
  every dollar spent through the program. Redeem
  miles for free hotel stays starting at 5,000 miles. Earn
  free roundtrip airline tickets starting at 25,000 miles.

♦ Personal help in planning your own, customized trip.

♦ Fast, confirmed reservations at any property
  recommended in this guide, subject to availability.***

♦ Special discounts on bookings in the U.S. and around
  the world.

♦ Low-cost visa and passport service.

♦ Reduced-rate cruise packages and special car rental
  programs worldwide.

Visit our website at http://www.travelnetwork.com/Frommer
or call us globally at 201-567-8500, ext. 55. In the U.S., call
toll-free at 1-888-940-5000, or fax 201-567-1838. In Canada,
call at 1-905-707-7222, or fax 905-707-8108. In Asia, call
60-3-7191044, or fax 60-3-7185415.

---

* To qualify for these travel discounts, at least a portion of your trip must
  include destinations covered in this guide. No more than one coupon discount
  may be used in any 12-month period, for destinations covered in this guide.
  Cannot be combined with any other discount or promotion.
**These are U.S. dollars spent on commissionable bookings.
*** A $10 USD fee, plus fax and/or phone charges, will be added to the cost of
  bookings at each hotel not linked to the reservation service. Customers must
  approve these fees in advance. If only hotels of this kind are booked, the traveler(s)
  must also purchase roundtrip air tickets from Travel Network for the trip.

Valid until December 31, 1998. Terms and conditions of the Miles-to-
Go® program are available on request by calling 201-567-8500, ext 55.

MAS234

"Amazingly easy to use. Very portable, very complete."

♦

"Complete, concise, and filled with useful information."

♦

"Hotel information is close to encyclopedic."

♦

"The only mainstream guide to list specific prices. The Walter Cronkite of guidebooks—with all that implies."

Frommer's® 98

Cape Cod, Nantucket & Martha's Vineyard

by Laura M. Reckford

Macmillan • USA

ABOUT THE AUTHOR

Laura M. Reckford is a writer and editor who lives on Cape Cod. Formerly the managing editor of *Cape Cod Life Magazine,* she has also been on the editorial staffs of *Good Housekeeping Magazine* and *Entertainment Weekly.*

MACMILLAN TRAVEL

A Simon & Schuster Macmillan Company
1633 Broadway
New York, NY 10019

Find us online at **www.frommers.com**

Copyright © 1998 by Simon & Schuster, Inc.
Maps copyright © by Simon & Schuster, Inc.

ISBN 0-02862093-3
ISSN 1042-8399

Editor: Neil E. Schlecht
Production Editor: Carol Sheehan
Production Team: Eric Brinkman, Toi Davis, Natalie Hollifield, Angel Perez, and Heather Pope
Design by Michele Laseau
Digital Cartography by Jim Moore and Ortelius Design

SPECIAL SALES

Bulk purchases (10+ copies) of Frommer's and selected Macmillan travel guides are available to corporations, organizations, mail-order catalogs, institutions, and charities at special discounts, and can be customized to suit individual needs. For more information, write to Special Sales, Macmillan General Reference, 1633 Broadway, New York, NY 10019.

Manufactured in the United States of America

Contents

List of Maps

AN INVITATION TO THE READER

In researching this book, we discovered many wonderful places—hotels, restaurants, shops, and more. We're sure you'll find others. Please tell us about them, so we can share the information with your fellow travelers in upcoming editions. If you were disappointed with a recommendation, we'd love to know that, too. Please write to:

Frommer's Cape Cod, Nantucket & Martha's Vineyard '98
Macmillan Travel
1633 Broadway
New York, NY 10019

AN ADDITIONAL NOTE

Please be advised that travel information is subject to change at any time—and this is especially true of prices. We therefore suggest that you write or call ahead for confirmation when making your travel plans. The authors, editors, and publisher cannot be held responsible for the experiences of readers while traveling. Your safety is important to us, however, so we encourage you to stay alert and be aware of your surroundings. Keep a close eye on cameras, purses, and wallets, all favorite targets of thieves and pickpockets.

WHAT THE SYMBOLS MEAN

✪ **Frommer's Favorites**

Our favorite places and experiences—outstanding for quality, value, or both.

The following abbreviations are used for credit cards:

AE	American Express	EURO	Eurocard
CB	Carte Blanche	JCB	Japan Credit Bank
DC	Diners Club	MC	MasterCard
DISC	Discover	V	Visa

MAP   Modified American Plan. Also called Half Board or Half Pension; breakfast and dinner included.

FIND FROMMER'S ONLINE

Arthur Frommer's Outspoken Encyclopedia of Travel (www.frommers.com) offers more than 6,000 pages of up-to-the-minute travel information—including the latest bargains and candid, personal articles updated daily by Arthur Frommer himself. No other Web site offers such comprehensive and timely coverage of the world of travel.

The Best of Cape Cod, Nantucket & Martha's Vineyard

The "arm" of the Cape has beckoned wayfarers since precolonial days. And little wonder. The fishing is still nearly as good as it was in the 16th century, but it's a whole lot less arduous. Although it's hard to fathom why the settlers waited nearly 3 centuries to go splashing in the surf, ever since the Victorians donned their bathing costumes, there's been no stopping the waves of sun-, sand-, and sea-worshippers who, every summer, religiously pour onto this peninsula and the islands beyond.

Narrowing down possible "bests" is a tough call, even for a native of the region. The selections in this chapter are intended merely as an introduction to some of the highlights. They're listed from closest to farthest along the Cape, followed by the Islands. A great many other outstanding resorts, hotels, inns, attractions, and destinations are described in the pages of this book. Once you start wandering, you're sure to discover bests of your own.

Basic contact information is given for the enterprises listed below. With a few exceptions, you'll find more information by referring to the appropriate chapters of the text.

1 The Best Beaches

It is difficult to identify the best beaches without specifying for whom: fearless surfers or timid toddlers, party types or incurable recluses? The bay-side and sound beaches, for instance, tend to be a lot more placid than those on the ocean, and thus preferable for little ones who only plan to splash and muck about.

- **Sandy Neck:** This relatively unpopulated, 6-mile barrier beach, extending from the eastern edge of Sandwich to shelter Barnstable Harbor, features pretty little dunes seldom seen on the bay side. Hike in far enough (but avoiding the nests of piping plovers), and you're sure to find a secluded spot. Adventurous types can even **camp** overnight, with permission (☎ 508/362-8300). See chapter 5.

- **Falmouth Heights:** On a clear day, you can almost see Martha's Vineyard from this hip beach in Falmouth's most picturesque neighborhood. Grand turn-of-the-century homes compete for the view with newer motels, and the beach stays rowdy with twentysomethings late into the night as crowds stream into **The Casino** (☎ 508/548-2772) for live music and victuals.

Off-season, this beach is virtually deserted, perfect for romantic arm-in-arm strolling. See chapter 5.

- **Nauset Beach:** Located along the outer "elbow" of the Cape, this barrier beach descends all the way from East Orleans to a point parallel to Chatham—about 9 miles in all, each increasingly deserted. The entry point, however, is a body squeeze: It's here that the young crowd convenes to strut their stuff. Administered by the town of Orleans, but still considered part of the Cape Cod National Seashore, Nauset Beach has paid parking, rest rooms, and a snack bar. See chapter 7.

- **Cahoon Hollow:** A Wellfleet favorite, cozy Cahoon Hollow boasts a most unusual music club housed in an 1897 life-saving station: the **Beachcomber,** referred to fondly as the 'Comber, or better yet, Coma (☎ 508/349-6055). Twenty-somethings are the primary patrons, but lingering families also enjoy the reggae and rock that start to leak out late in the afternoon on summer weekends. See chapter 8.

- **Race Point:** Free of the sexual politics that predominate the beaches closer to Provincetown (certain sections of Herring Cove Beach are tacitly reserved for gays of each sex), Race Point—another CCNS beach-cum-visitor-center (☎ 508/487-1256) at the northernmost tip of the Cape—is strictly nondenominational. Even whales are welcome—they can often be spotted with the bare eye, surging toward Stellwagen Bank. See chapter 8.

- **Gay Head:** These landmark bluffs on the western extremity of Martha's Vineyard (call the **Chamber of Commerce,** ☎ 508/693-0085, for directions) are threatened with erosion, so it's no longer politically correct to engage in multicolored mud baths, as hippies once did. Still, it's an incredibly scenic place to swim—come early to beat the crowds. See chapter 9.

- **Jetties Beach:** Nantucket's beaches as a rule have the best amenities of any beaches in the region; most have rest rooms, showers, lifeguards, and food concessions. For families and active types, Jetties Beach (just 1/2 mile from the center of town) can't be beat. There are boat and windsurfing rentals, tennis courts, volleyball nets, a playground, and great fishing (off the eponymous jetties). It's also scenic (those jetties again) with calm, warm water. See chapter 10.

2 The Best Bike Routes

Blessed with gently rolling hills (at most), the Cape and Islands are custom-made for a bike trek—whether as a way to get to the beach or an outing unto itself.

- **Cape Cod Canal:** On this 14-mile loop maintained by the **U.S. Army Corps of Engineers** (☎ 508/759-5991), you can race alongside the varied craft taking a shortcut through the world's widest sea-level canal. See chapter 5.

- **Shining Sea Bicycle Path** (☎ 508/548-8500): Connecting Falmouth to Woods Hole by way of the shore and the picturesque Nobska Lighthouse, this 3.6-mile path lets you dash to the ferry or dally at the beach of your choice. See chapter 5.

- **Cape Cod Rail Trail** (☎ 508/896-3491): Reclaimed by the Rails to Trails Conservancy, this paved railroad bed stretches some 25 miles—currently—from South Dennis all the way to Wellfleet, with innumerable detours that beckon en route. See chapters 6 through 8.

- **Province Lands Trail** (☎ 508/487-1256): Offering by far the most rigorous workout, this 7-mile network swoops among the parabolic dunes and stunted forests at the very tip of the Cape. Take your time enjoying this somewhat spooky moonscape, and be sure to stop off at Race Point Beach for a bracing dip and at the **Province Lands Visitor Center** (☎ 508/487-1256). See chapter 8.

- **Oak Bluffs to Edgartown** (☎ **508/693-0085**): All of Martha's Vineyard is easily accessible for two-wheel recreationalists. This 6-mile path hugs the water almost all the way, so you're never far from a refreshing dip. See chapter 9.
- **Chilmark to Gay Head** (Martha's Vineyard; ☎ **508/693-0085**): Awe-inspiring vistas of ponds, inlets, and ocean greet you at every turn as you bike along State Road and then turn on to the Moshup Trail, a road that takes you along the coast up to Gay Head. It's a strenuous ride with perhaps the best scenic views in the region. On the way back, treat yourself to a bike-ferry ride to the fishing village of Menemsha. See chapter 9.
- **Nantucket Town to Madaket** (☎ **508/228-1700**): Only 3 miles wide and 14 miles long, Nantucket is a snap to cover by bike. The 6-mile Madaket path crosses undulating moors to reach a beach with boisterous surf. See chapter 10.
- **Nantucket Town to Surfside** (☎ **508/228-1700**): An easy, flat few miles from town, Surfside Beach is a perfect miniexcursion for the whole family. There are even benches along the route if you'd like to stop and admire the scrub pine and beach plums. On the return trip, you'll want to pause at Brant Point Light to watch the yachts maneuver in and out of Nantucket Harbor. See chapter 10.

3 The Best Family Vacation Experiences

With wide-open beaches at every turn, and plenty of other kids to enjoy them with, there's no way a family could fail to have a fabulous time here. Even if the weather is iffy, there's always fun stuff to do, some of it subtly educational. For further recommendations, see "The Best Ways to Get Out on the Water," above, and the listings of "Family-Friendly Hotels & Restaurants" that accompany each chapter.

- **Renting a Cottage:** Younger kids will happily spend dawn to dusk wading into the waves and mucking about on the beach. Bring an umbrella and a doorstop novel and you'll be all set. To inquire about rentals, ask the local chamber of commerce (see the "Visitor Information" sections for each town listed in subsequent chapters) to refer you to a real-estate agency—preferably a year in advance.
- **Going for Ice Cream:** The Cape and Islands are home to some of the most charming and delectable ice cream parlors around. Most of these places are a mob scene in July and August, but that's all part of the fun. Some of the classic shops are Whistlestop in West Falmouth, Four Seas in Centerville, Sundae School in Dennisport and East Orleans, Mad Martha's on Martha's Vineyard, and Juice Bar and Yogurt Plus on Nantucket, all local brands, but you'll also find Ben & Jerry's in Eastham, Emack and Bolio's in Cataumet and Orleans, and the ubiquitous Friendly's. See chapters 5 through 10.
- **Beaching It:** The best beaches for families with young children are sound and bay beaches with gentle surf and, if you're lucky, boardwalks or playgrounds. Here are a few of my favorites: Old Silver Beach in North Falmouth, West Dennis Beach, Parker's River Beach in South Yarmouth, Bass Hole in Yarmouth Port, State Beach on Martha's Vineyard, Children's Beach on Nantucket. Lakes and ponds are also great for little ones. Favorites are Scargo Lake in Dennis; Gull, Great, and Long Ponds in Wellfleet; and Lake Tashmoo on Martha's Vineyard. See chapters 5 through 10.
- **Diving Into an Aquatic Adventure** (in Woods Hole): For junior oceanologists, this is the place to be. You can try the hands-on exhibits at the **Woods Hole Oceanographic Institute** (☎ **508/289-2252**), observe experiments at the **Marine Biological Laboratory** (☎ **508/548-7684**), explore the touch tanks at the

country's oldest **Aquarium** (☎ **508/548-7684**), and even collect crucial data with the **"Ocean Quest"** crew (☎ **800/376-2326** or 508/457-0508). See chapter 5.

- **Riding the Flying Horses Carousel** (in Oak Bluffs, Martha's Vineyard; ☎ **508/693-9481**): Some claim this is the oldest carousel in the country, but your kids might not notice the genuine horsehair, sculptural details, or glass eyes. They'll be too busy trying to grab the brass ring to win a free ride. After several rides on the carousel, stroll around the town of Oak Bluffs. Children will be enchanted by the clustered "gingerbread" houses, a carryover from the 19th-century revivalist movement. Community sings and concerts—some big-name—still take place at the open-air **Trinity Park Tabernacle** (☎ **508/693-0525**). See chapter 9.

- **Biking Nantucket:** Short flat trails crisscross the island, and every one leads to a beach. The shortest rides lead to Children's Beach (with its own playground) and Jetties Beach; older kids will be able to make the few miles to Surfside and Madaket. The rest of the vacation will be a big hit too. Looking like a toy town in all its preserved 19th-century primness, Nantucket has lots for tots. Story time at the Atheneum, a striped lighthouse, a turn-of-the-century movie house, and two old-fashioned soda fountains complete the idyll. See chapter 10.

- **Attending a Cape Cod Baseball League Game:** For more than 100 years, the highlights of a summer on Cape Cod have included attendance at a Cape Cod Baseball League game. Local families host the amateur players, many of whom are "pro" material being groomed for the majors. The league consists of 10 teams who play on natural grass diamonds before enthusiastic fans cheering for the home team. These games have all the excitement of a professional game without the long lines and high prices. Potential hall of famers like Carlton Fiske, Jeff Reardon, and Mike Greenwell all played in the Cape Cod League, which has developed an exceptional talent pool of unspoiled, soon to be professional athletes. For just a few dollars, you can treat the whole family to an evening of baseball, the way it was meant to be played. See chapters 5 through 7.

- **Exploring Chatham:** Still a stellar example of Main Street, USA, Chatham draws thousands Friday evenings in summer for its spirited **band concerts** (☎ **508/945-0342**). Also appealing is its Railroad Museum, overlooking the vast and imaginative Play-a-Round Park (free and open to the public). Well-heeled scions favor the **Chatham Bars Inn** (☎ **800/527-4884** or 508/945-0096), whose attractions include a private beach, full resort facilities, and supervised children's programs day and night. See chapter 7.

4 The Best Small Towns & Villages

The prettier towns of the Cape and Islands combine the austere traditionalism of New England—well-tended historic houses punctuated by modest white steeples—with a whiff of their own salty history.

- **Sandwich:** For a "gateway" town, Sandwich is remarkably composed and peaceful. Not-too-fussy preservation efforts have ensured the survival of many of this first settlement's attractions, such as the pond that feeds the 17th-century **Dexter Grist Mill** (☎ **508/888-1173**). Generous endowments fund an assortment of fascinating museums, including the multifaceted **Heritage Plantation** (☎ **508/888-3300**), which, with its splendid rhododendrons, doubles as a botanical garden. See chapter 5.

- **Yarmouth Port:** It may look somewhat staid on the surface (Hallet's, the local soda fountain, hasn't changed much since 1889, except to start renting videos), but a trio of unabashedly "grumpy old men"—author/illustrator Edward Gorey, restaurateur Jack Braginton-Smith (of the ultracasual Jack's Place), and vintage bookseller Ben Muse (of the gloriously jumbled Parnassus Books)—keep things interesting. Stop in at Inaho, all but hidden within an ordinary frame house, for the Cape's best sushi. See chapter 6.

- **Chatham:** Only Provincetown offers better strolling-and-shopping options, and Chatham's version is G-rated. In summer, Friday-night band concerts draw multigenerational crowds in the thousands. For a glimpse of nature's awesome forces at work (it's busy rearranging the shoreline, with little eye to local real-estate values), take an aerial tour with the **Cape Cod Flying Circus** (☎ **508/945-9000**): Loop-de-loops are optional. Look for the hordes of seals on uninhabited Monomoy Island. See chapter 7.

- **Wellfleet:** A magnet for creative artists (literary as well as visual), this otherwise classic New England town is a haven of good taste—from its dozens of shops and galleries to its premier restaurant, Aesop's Tables. All is not prissy, however: certainly not the iconoclastic offerings at the **Wellfleet Harbor Actors' Theatre** (☎ **508/349-6835**) or the goings-on at the 'Comber (see "The Best Beaches," above). See chapter 8.

- **Provincetown:** At the far tip of the Cape's curl, in intensely beautiful surroundings, is Provincetown. Provincetown's history goes back nearly 400 years, and in the last century it's been a veritable headquarters of bohemia—more writers and artists have holed up here than you could shake a stick at. It's also, of course, among the world's great gay and lesbian resorts—people come here for the pleasure of being "out" together, in great numbers. If you're discomfited by same-sex public displays of affection, do everyone a favor and stay home. Straights who are more open-minded will have a great time here—Provincetown has savory food, fun shopping, terrific company, and fascinating people-watching. See chapter 8.

- **Oak Bluffs,** Martha's Vineyard: This harbor town on Martha's Vineyard evolved from a Methodist campground that sprang up in the mid-19th century. Pleased with the scenic and refreshing ocean-side setting (and who wouldn't be?), the faithful started replacing their canvas tents with hundreds of tiny, elaborately decorated and gaudily painted "gingerbread" cottages. Still operated primarily as a religious community, the revivalist village is flanked by a commercial zone known for its rocking nightlife. See chapter 9.

- **Edgartown,** Martha's Vineyard: For many visitors, Edgartown *is* Martha's Vineyard, its regal captain's houses and manicured lawns a symbol of a more refined way of life. Roses climb white picket fences, and the tolling of the Whaling Church bell signals dinnertime. By July, gleaming pleasure boats fill the harbor passing Edgartown Lighthouse, and shops overflow with luxury goods and fine art. Edgartown's old-fashioned 4th of July parade harkens back to small-town America, as hundreds line Main Street cheering the loudest for the floats with the most heart. It's a picture-perfect little town, a slice of homemade apple pie to go with nearby Oak Bluff's hot fudge sundae. See chapter 9.

- **Nantucket Town:** It looks as though the whalers just left, leaving behind their grand houses, the cobbled streets, and a gamut of enticing shops offering luxury goods from around the world. Tourism may be rampant, but not its tackier side effects, thanks to stringent preservation measures. Time has not so much stood still here as vanished: You can relax and shift into island time, dictated purely by your desires. See chapter 10.

5 The Best Luxury Hotels & Inns

- **Chatham Bars Inn** (Chatham; ☎ 800/527-4884 or 508/945-0096): The last of the grand old oceanfront hotels, this is hands-down the most elegant place to stay on Cape Cod. A recent multimillion-dollar renovation has only added to the splendor of this resort. You can stay in one of the luxury suites for $1,500 a night or stay off-season in a regular room for under $100. Lunch at the Beach House Grill with sand underfoot is a delight, and by all means, have an evening cocktail on the majestic porch overlooking the Atlantic Ocean. The service throughout the hotel is impeccable, and the best part is that this is a family-friendly place; bring the kids and treat yourself. You only live once. See chapter 7.
- **The Wequassett Inn** (Chatham; ☎ 800/225-7125 or 508/432-5400): This Chatham institution occupies its own little peninsula on Pleasant Bay and offers excellent sailing and tennis clinics. You'll be tempted just to goof off, though—especially if you score one of the clapboard cottages, done up in an upscale country mode, right on the water. The restaurant, housed in the 18th-century Eben Ryder House, holds its own with the top Cape contenders. See chapter 7.
- **Captain's House Inn** (Chatham; ☎ 800/315-0728 or 508/945-0127): An elegant country inn that positively drips with good taste, this is among the best small inns in the region. Most rooms have fireplaces, elegant paneling, and antiques throughout; they're sumptuous yet cozy. This may be the ultimate spot to enjoy Chatham's Christmas Stroll festivities, but you may need to book your room a couple of years in advance. See chapter 7.
- **Brass Key Guesthouse** (Provincetown; ☎ 800/842-9858 or 508/487-9005): What do you get when you take a charming inn and add a couple million dollars plus a lot of good taste? The Brass Key Guesthouse, now a compound consisting of three historic buildings, has been transformed into *the* place to stay in Provincetown. With Ritz-Carlton–style amenities in mind, Michael MacIntyre and Bob Anderson have created a paean to luxury. These are the kind of innkeepers who think of everything: Pillows are goose down, showers have wall jets, and gratis iced tea is delivered poolside. See chapter 8.
- **Charlotte Inn** (Edgartown, Martha's Vineyard; ☎ 508/627-4751): Edgartown tends to be the most formal enclave on Martha's Vineyard, and this anglicized compound of exquisite buildings is by far the fanciest address in town. The rooms are distinctively decorated: One boasts a baby grand piano, another its own thematic dressing room. The conservatory restaurant, **l'étoile** (☎ 508/627-5187), is among the finest you'll find this side of the Atlantic. See chapter 9.
- **The Inn at Blueberry Hill** (Chilmark, Martha's Vineyard; ☎ 800/336-3322 or 508/645-3799): Rural sophistication is the rule at this country estate in Chilmark, Martha's Vineyard. The Shaker-like simplicity of the decor is refreshing, especially when combined with such sensual treats as down duvets and a festive restaurant, Theo's, which celebrates fresh regional fare. There's a tennis court, lap pool, and health club on the premises, and 56 acres of adjoining conservation land to roam. See chapter 9.
- **The Wauwinet** (Nantucket; ☎ 800/426-8718 or 508/228-0145): Far from the bustle of Nantucket Town, and nestled between a bay beach and an ocean beach, this opulently restored landmark proffers the ultimate retreat. Everything a summering sybarite could want is close at hand, including tennis courts, a launch to drop you off on your own secluded beach (part of a 1,100-acre wildlife refuge), and an outstanding New American restaurant, Topper's. See chapter 10.

6   The Best Hotel Buys

- **Simmons Homestead Inn** (Hyannisport; ☎ 800/637-1649 or 508/778-4999): Bill Putman may be the most personable and hospitable innkeeper on Cape Cod. He is determined that his guests have an excellent vacation, a factor that may make the Simmons Homestead Inn one of the best deals around. A former race-car driver/ad exec, Putman, who has filled his inn with a merry mishmash of animals, (stuffed, sculpted, or painted), has thoughtfully written up all his choices for the best things to see and do on Cape Cod. After you've toured around on his recommendations, join him for cocktails and tell him about your day. He'd love to hear about it. *Note:* This is one of the few local inns that allows smoking. See chapter 6.

- **Inn at the Mills** (Marstons Mills; ☎ 508/428-2967): Follow the graceful swans in the placid Mill Pond to this tiny estate anchored by a 1780 cheerful barn-red homestead. For such a pretty site, ideally located, the rates are quite reasonable. Rooms are charming and cozy with canopy beds made up with chenille bedspreads. From May to October, wedding parties tend to fill the property on weekends, but the inn is open year-round. You're sure to be able to book a spot midweek or during the "quiet" season. See chapter 6.

- **Isaiah Hall B&B Inn** (Dennis; ☎ 800/736-0160 or 508/385-9928): Fancy enough for the Broadway luminaries who star in summer stock at the nearby Cape Cod Playhouse, this former farmhouse in Dennis is the antithesis of glitz. The Great Room doubles as a green room—an actors' hangout—and breakfast is celebrated communally in the country kitchen. The more-plain rooms will set you back less than a pair of orchestra tix. See chapter 6.

- **The Lighthouse Inn** (West Dennis; ☎ 508/328-2244): A classic 1930s beachside resort, now run by the third generation of owners, this homey little complex has everything a family could require, at affordable prices: comfy cottages, a calm strip of beach, plus a pool, tennis and volleyball courts, miniature golf and other lawn games, and a game room. Kids can enroll in a structured play program, for a slight surcharge, and dinner is a communal feast, all the better to befriend other families. See chapter 6.

- **Nauset House Inn** (East Orleans; ☎ 508/255-2195): You half-expect to spot Heathcliff roaming the surrounding moors, so romantic is this 1810 inn in East Orleans. The turn-of-the-century conservatory is the perfect place in which to lose yourself in a novel while waiting for the sky to clear; Nauset Beach is a 10-minute, hand-in-hand walk away. See chapter 7.

- **Even'Tide Motel** (South Wellfleet; ☎ 800/368-0007 or 508/349-3410): A motel with rare style, this popular establishment in South Wellfleet embodies the best aspects of the 1960s: handsome blond oak furniture, a rather hedonistic 60-foot heated indoor pool, and a $3/4$-mile nature trail leading to the sea. It's a low-key, low-cost family haven. See chapter 8.

- **White Horse Inn** (Provincetown; ☎ 508/487-1790): Look for the bright-yellow door with the intriguing oval window. The very embodiment of Provincetown funkiness, this inn has been known to host such "downtown" celebrities as cult filmmaker John Waters and poet laureate Robert Pinsky. Rooms are short on amenities (no cable TV here) but long on kitschy style and artiness. Innkeeper Frank Schaefer has been in Provincetown for 30 years and can give you a quick history of art by pointing out the original works that grace the walls of the inn. See chapter 8.

7 The Best Restaurants

It wasn't long ago that "fancy" food in these parts began and ended with classic French. Several spots still uphold the old standards, but the New American revolution has sparked ever more inventive ways to highlight local delicacies. The best luxury hotels (see above) all maintain superlative restaurants, and soaring on a par with them are the following choices, some chef-owned, and all truly memorable.

- **Regatta of Falmouth-by-the-Sea** (Falmouth; ☎ **508/548-5400**): Perched over Falmouth Harbor, this dining room features exquisite nouvelle and fusion cuisine and atmosphere that's more relaxed than reverential. Signature dishes include a memorable crab-and-corn chowder, plus succulent lamb *en chemise*. See chapter 5.

- **The Regatta of Cotuit at the Crocker House** (Cotuit; ☎ **508/428-5715**): What most distinguishes the two Regattas from their competition is the sensational service, far exceeding most local establishments. In addition, the Regatta of Cotuit has a quintessential Olde Cape Cod setting; the building was once a stagecoach inn and the decor is formal Federal style. Food here is consistently excellent, with fresh ingredients, generous portions, and creative preparations. See chapter 6.

- **abbicci** (Yarmouth Port; ☎ **508/362-3501**): You'd expect to find this kind of sophisticated northern Italian restaurant in New York City, but it's a bit of a shock to find it tucked into an antique cape on the Old King's Highway. Those in-the-know have discovered abbicci, though, and it can be tough to get a reservation here on a summer weekend. Instead, go during the week when the skilled staff is a little more relaxed, and you can linger over this delicate cuisine and the fine wine that should accompany it. See chapter 6.

- **Bramble Inn Restaurant** (Brewster; ☎ **508/896-7644**): An elegantly established entry in the Lower Cape dining scene, this is a favorite for those who don't mind a rather steeply priced, four-course fixed-price dinner. The five intimate dining rooms are decorated with antique china and fresh flowers. Chef Ruth Manchester is a local favorite for her extraordinary evolving cuisine. See chapter 7.

- **High Brewster** (Brewster; ☎ **508/896-3636**): What could be more romantic than dinner in a dimly lit historic house, whimsically decorated, enjoying flavorful meals skillfully prepared and delightfully served? While slightly off the beaten track, High Brewster has developed a solid reputation as one of the finest restaurants in a town full of superior dining opportunities. After dinner, stroll under the stars over to the bluff's edge and watch the moonlight play over Mill Pond. See chapter 7.

- **Martin House** (Provincetown; ☎ **508/487-1327**): The Provincetown competition can be tough, but this captain's house (ca. 1750) has it all: atmosphere (with a fireplace flickering in each rustic room); friendly, intelligent service; and, most important, brilliantly conceived cuisine embracing a whole world's worth of cultural influences. See chapter 8.

- **La Cucina Ristorante at the Tuscany Inn** (Edgartown, Martha's Vineyard; ☎ **508/627-8161**): The dining buzz on the Vineyard begins and ends with this chic new restaurant in Edgartown. Owner Laura Sbrana-Scheuer is sort of an Italian Martha Stewart, with seemingly boundless energy, talent, and style. She also runs an acclaimed cooking school. At La Cucina, she's installed her talented son Marco as chef. Seating is outdoors under an arbor with candlelight twinkling or indoors in the tiled dining rooms. If you are unable to get over to Italy this year, La Cucina will tide you over just fine. See chapter 9.

- **The Summer House** (Siasconset, Nantucket; ☎ **508/257-4577**): Ruth and Tim Pitts are considered top chefs on Nantucket, an island with more than its share of culinary talent. Specialties of the house include fresh, locally caught seafood with island vegetables delicately prepared and stylishly presented. The atmosphere is classic Nantucket: wicker and wrought iron, roses and honeysuckle, Gershwin tunes from the pianist, and the Atlantic Ocean just over the bluff. See chapter 10.

8 The Best Clam Shacks

- **The Clam Shack** (Falmouth Harbor; ☎ 508/540-7758): The ultimate clam shack sits on the edge of the harbor and serves up reasonably priced fried seafood with all the fixings. Order the fried clams (with bellies, please!) and squeeze into the picnic tables beside the counter to await your feast. See chapter 5.
- **Mill Way** (Barnstable Harbor; ☎ 508/362-2760): Sort of a gourmet clam shack, Mill Way offers succulent specialties beyond the usual picnic-table fare. This is a seasonal joint (open May through mid-October), and when it's open, it's packed, so go early and hungry. See chapter 6.
- **Cap't Cass Rock Harbor Seafood** (Orleans; no phone): Take a photo of the family in front of this shack covered with colorful buoys, then go inside and chow down. Fresh fish, simply prepared, and hearty portions keep them coming back year after year. See chapter 7.
- **The Bite** (Menemsha, Martha's Vineyard; ☎ 508/645-9239): A travel writer once called it the best restaurant on Martha's Vineyard, perhaps in retaliation for a high-priced meal in Edgartown. Nevertheless, this is a top-shelf clam shack, tucked away in a picturesque fishing village. Order your meal to go and stroll over to the beach, which has the best sunset views on the island. The fried clams are succulent; some say the secret is the batter. Of course, the fish couldn't be fresher, unloaded just steps away. What more could you want? See chapter 9.
- **Moby Dick's Restaurant** (Wellfleet; ☎ 508/349-9795): Unfortunately, word has spread about this terrific family restaurant, and it can get pretty mobbed here around supper time. Still, it's a terrific place to bring the family, screaming kids and all. The clambake special is a $1^1/_4$-pound lobster, native Monomoy steamed clams, and corn on the cob. Perfect. See chapter 8.
- **Sayle's Seafood** (Nantucket; ☎ 508/228-4599): Just a 10-minute walk from town on Washington Street Extension and you'll arrive at this fish-store-cum-clam shack. Charlie Sayles is a local fisherman, and everything here is deliciously fresh. Get your fried clams to go and eat them picnic-style at the beach. See chapter 10.

9 The Best Shopping

No matter how spectacular the scenery or splendid the weather, certain towns have so many intriguing shops that you'll be lured away from the beach, at least temporarily. The inventory is so carefully culled or created that just browsing can be sufficient entertainment—but slip a credit card into your cutoffs just in case.

- **Osterville:** Old money and good taste go together here like ice cream and jimmies. Anyone wishing to decorate either house or self will be happily occupied here, what with a range of imaginative home-decor outfits and a cluster of traditionalist dress shops. See chapter 6.
- **Chatham:** Old-fashioned, tree-shaded Main Street is packed with inviting storefronts, including the **Spyglass** for nautical antiques (☎ 508/945-9686), **Pentimento** for casual clothing and curious gifts (☎ 508/945-0178), and gourmet treats-to-go at **Chatham Cookware** (☎ 508/945-1550). See chapter 7.

- **Wellfleet:** The commercial district is 2 blocks long, the art zone is twice that. Pick up a walking map to locate the galleries in town: **Cherry Stone** (☎ **508/349-3026**) tops the don't-miss list. Seekers of low-key chic will want to check out two designers, **Hannah** (☎ **508/349-9884**) and **Karol Richardson** (☎ **508/349-6378**). For designer produce and impeccable seafood, peruse the array at homey **Hatch's Fish & Produce Market** (☎ **508/349-2810**) behind Town Hall. See chapter 8.
- **Provincetown:** Overlooking the import junk that floods the center of town, the 3-mile gamut of Commercial Street is a shopoholic's dream. It's all here, seemingly direct from Soho: sensual, cutting-edge clothing (for every sex and permutation thereof), art, jewelry, antiques, antique jewelry, and more. And, whatever you really need but didn't know you needed can be found at **Marine Specialties** (☎ **508/487-1730**), a warehouse packed with surplus essentials. See chapter 8.
- **Vineyard Haven:** Though it's the dowdiest of Martha's Vineyard towns, this ferry port boasts the best shops, from **Bramhall & Dunn** for housewares (☎ **508/693-6437**) to **The Great Put On** for designer and contemporary women's wear (☎ **508/627-5495**). You might want to save some cash, though, for the multiethnic boutiques of Oak Bluffs or the pricey preppy redoubts of Edgartown. See chapter 9.
- **Nantucket:** Imagine Martha Stewart cloned a hundredfold, and you'll have some idea of the tenor of shops in this well-preserved 19th-century town. Centre Street—known as "Petticoat Row" in whaling days—still caters to feminine tastes, and the town's many esteemed antique stores would never deign to present anything less than the genuine article. See chapter 10.

10   The Best Bars & Clubs

- **Casino by the Sea** (Falmouth Heights; ☎ **508/548-0777**): On a clear night you can almost see Martha's Vineyard from this classic bar on Falmouth Heights Beach. If you show up early (5-ish), before the twentysomethings stagger in, you can have a cocktail and enjoy the view in peace. Or you may want to participate in the party hardy scene that erupts most summer nights. See chapter 5.
- **Roadhouse Cafe** (Hyannis; ☎ **508/775-2386**): Most consider this the best bar in town, and, even better, this one is for grown-ups. There is live music nightly in the new "Back Door Bistro," and a sizzling Monday night Jazz Series popular with locals and those in the know. See chapter 6.
- **Beachcomber** (Wellfleet; ☎ **508/349-6055**): Perched atop the towering dunes of Cahoon Hollow Beach, this bar and dance club is one of the most scenic watering holes on Cape Cod. Although the crowd tends to be on the young and rowdy side, the young at heart are also welcome. You *will* end up on the dance floor, so wear comfortable shoes. See chapter 8.
- **The Mews** (Provincetown; ☎ **508/487-1500**): This is a good place to go to have a drink and decide which outrageous nightclub performance to attend. Or maybe you'll just stay at The Mews, listening to piano stylings while watching the twinkling lights of Provincetown Harbor. See chapter 8.
- **Hot Tin Roof** (Martha's Vineyard; ☎ **508/693-1137**): Carly Simon's nightclub at the airport is the hottest after-dark scene on the Vineyard. It's a great space, particularly the outside area with its own funky bar. Be aware that cover prices can skyrocket depending on the act; also, some nights are reserved for comedy. See chapter 9.
- **Club Car** (Nantucket: ☎ **508/228-1101**): You'll love the red leather banquets in this antique railroad car left over from Nantucket's railroading days. The Club Car serves as the most sophisticated bar/restaurant on the island. You'll want to have one (expensive) drink in here just to absorb the atmosphere. See chapter 10.

Getting to Know Cape Cod & the Islands

Only 70 miles long, Cape Cod is a curling peninsula that encompasses hundreds of miles of beaches and more freshwater ponds than there are days in the year. The ocean's many moods rule this thin spit of land, and in summer it has a very sunny disposition indeed. More than 17 million visitors flock from around the world to enjoy nature's nonstop carnival, a combination of torrid sun and cool, salty air.

On the Cape, days have a way of unfurling aimlessly but pleasantly, with a round of inviolable rituals. First and foremost is a long, restful stint at the beach (you can opt for either the warmer, gently lapping waters of the bay side or the pounding Atlantic surf). The beach is generally followed by a stroll through the shops of the nearest town, with an obligatory ice-cream stop. After a desalinating shower and perhaps a nap (the pristine air has a way of inspiring impromptu snoozes), it's time for a fabulous dinner. There are few experiences quite so blissful as sitting at a picnic table overlooking a bustling harbor and feasting on a just-caught, butter-dripping, boiled lobster.

Be forewarned, however, that the Cape can be a bit too popular at full swing. Experienced travelers are beginning to discover the subtler appeal of the off-season, when the population—and prices—plummet. For some travelers, the prospect of sunbathing with the midsummer crowds on sizzling sand can't hold a candle to the chance to take long, solitary strolls on a windswept beach, with only the gulls as company. Come Labor Day (or Columbus Day, for stragglers) the crowds clear out, and the whole place hibernates till Memorial Day weekend, the official start again of "the season." It's in this downtime that you're most likely to experience the "real" Cape. For some it may take a little resourcefulness to see the beauty in the wintry, shuttered landscape (even the Pilgrims, who forsook this spot for Plymouth, didn't have quite the necessary mettle), but the people who do stick around are an interesting, independent-minded lot worth getting to know.

As alluring as it is on the surface, the region becomes all the more so the more you learn about it. One visit is likely to prompt a follow-up. Although you can "see" all of the Cape, and the Islands as well, in a matter of days, you could spend a lifetime exploring its many facets and still just begin to take it all in. Early Pilgrims saw

Cape Cod

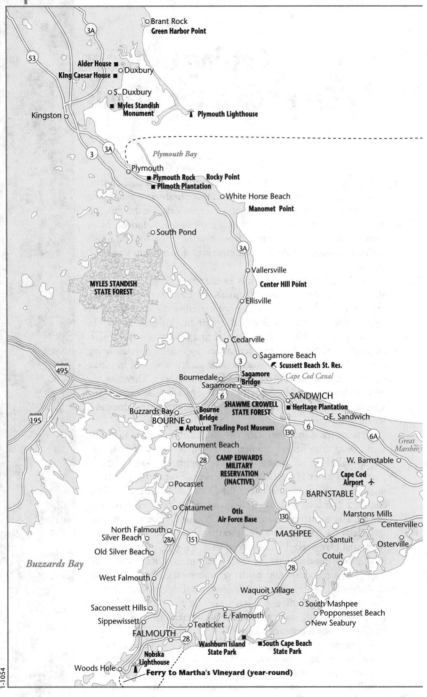

Brant Rock
Green Harbor Point

3A

53

Alder House ■
King Caesar House ■ ○ Duxbury

○ S. Duxbury

Kingston ○ ■ **Myles Standish Monument**

⚐ **Plymouth Lighthouse**

3 3A

Plymouth Bay

○ Plymouth
■ **Plymouth Rock** **Rocky Point**
■ **Plimoth Plantation**

○ **White Horse Beach**
Manomet Point

○ South Pond

3A

○ Vallersville
Center Hill Point

MYLES STANDISH STATE FOREST

○ Ellisville

○ Cedarville

495

3

○ Sagamore Beach
⚐ **Scussett Beach St. Res.**
Cape Cod Canal

Bournedale ○ **Sagamore Bridge**
Sagamore ○

195

6

SHAWME CROWELL STATE FOREST

SANDWICH

Buzzards Bay ○ **Bourne Bridge**
BOURNE ○
■ **Aptucxet Trading Post Museum**

■ **Heritage Plantation**
○ E. Sandwich

130 6 6A

Great Marshes

○ Monument Beach

28

CAMP EDWARDS MILITARY RESERVATION (INACTIVE)

W. Barnstable ○

Cape Cod Airport ✈

○ Pocasset

BARNSTABLE

○ Cataumet

Otis Air Force Base

130

Marstons Mills ○
Centerville ○

MASHPEE

North Falmouth ○
Silver Beach ○

28A 151

○ Santuit
Osterville ○

Old Silver Beach ○

Cotuit ○

Buzzards Bay

28

West Falmouth ○

Waquoit Village ○

Saconessett Hills ○
Sippewissett ○

E. Falmouth ○

○ South Mashpee
○ Popponesset Beach
○ New Seabury

FALMOUTH ○

○ Teaticket

28

Nobska Lighthouse
Woods Hole ○ ⚓ ⛴ **Ferry to Martha's Vineyard (year-round)**

■ **Washburn Island State Park**

■ **South Cape Beach State Park**

1-1054

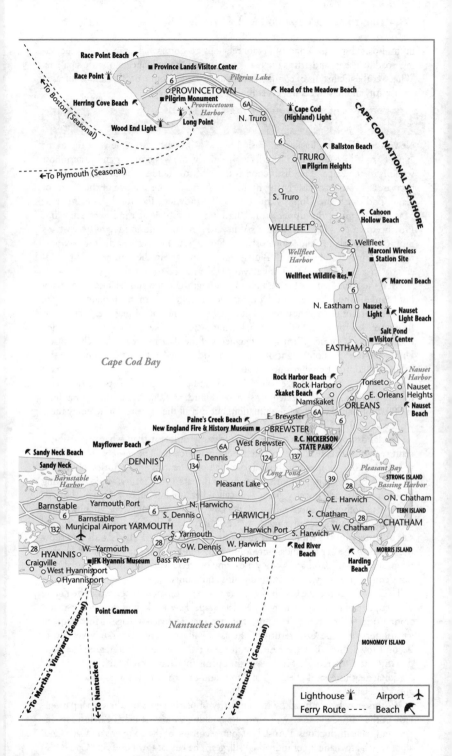

in this isolated spot the opportunity for religious freedom, whaling merchants the watery road to riches, and artists the path to capturing the brilliance of nature's palette. Whatever the incursions of commercialism and overdevelopment, the land is suffused with spirit, and it attracts seekers still.

1 The Lay of the Land

Newcomers—known locally as "wash-ashores"—invariably struggle with the terms "upper" and "lower," used to describe, respectively, the westernmost and easternmost sections of the Cape. The distinction is thought to allude to the longitude, which decreases as you head east. Many find it helpful to use the analogy of the "arm" of Cape Cod, with the Upper Cape towns of Sandwich, Falmouth, Bourne, and Mashpee forming the upper arm, Chatham the elbow of the lower arm, and Provincetown the "fist." In Martha's Vineyard, similar confusion reigns over what's meant by "up-island" and "down-island." Down-island consists of the touristy port towns of Vineyard Haven, Oak Bluffs, and Edgartown. In the summer months, locals try to stay up-island, avoiding down-island at all costs.

Even the term "land" may be a bit misleading; the Cape and Islands are actually just heaps of sand, sans bedrock. Described geologically as "terminal moraine," they're what remains of the grit heaved and dumped by the motion of massive glaciers that finally receded some 12,000 years ago, leaving a legacy of "kettle ponds"—steep-sided freshwater pools formed when sharp fragments of the glacier were left to melt in place. Under the relentless onslaught of storms and tides, the land mass's outlines are still subject to constant change and eventual erasure. The shoreline is known to have eroded about a full mile since colonial times, and current scientific predictions give the Cape and Islands a projected life span of as much as 5,000 more years—or as little as 500. Not to make light of the situation, but it is all the more reason to enjoy them while you can!

The landscape a modern visitor views is vastly different than what was visible a century ago. Virtually all the trees represent new growth. The settlers, in their rush to build not only houses but ships, and to fuel both hearths and factories, plundered all the lumber. Were it not for the recession of the late 19th century, you'd be looking at turnip fields and "poverty grass"—so-called because it will grow anywhere, needing next to nothing to survive. Instead, the Lower Cape and Mid Cape are now lushly forested, and if the tree cover tends to get spindly along the Outer Cape, it's the result of battery by salt winds rather than human depredation. The Islands also show the effects of the ocean winds—predominantly those out of the southwest. Harbor towns and down-island areas enjoy a canopy of trees, while the more exposed portions consist primarily of grassy sand plains and moors.

The 15 towns on Cape Cod in fact represent many different capes, with often quite distinct personalities to match the varied landscape. Few similarities exist, for instance, among rural Truro, rowdy Hyannis, and historic Sandwich Village. Most frequent vacationers to Cape Cod return to the same village every year, rarely venturing beyond town lines. But the resourceful visitor who explores the region, perhaps driving the Old King's Highway, shopping in Chatham, beaching it at the National Seashore, and checking out an island or two, will get a good idea of the area's diversity.

Visitors may be confused by the similarity of place names on the Cape, particularly in the Mid Cape area. When you are booking a room, it may be helpful to understand these distinctions. Barnstable County consists of the 15 towns on Cape Cod, all of which are made up of individual villages. The largest town on Cape Cod is also called Barnstable, and it is made up of the following eight villages: Cotuit, Osterville, Marstons Mills, Centerville, Hyannis, Hyannisport, West Barnstable, and (is there an echo in here?) Barnstable Village.

Despite the similar names, towns and even villages on the Cape retain their own distinct character. For instance, charming and historic Barnstable Village along Route 6A (the historic Old King's Highway) couldn't be more different from Hyannis (off Route 28; transportation hub and home of the mall). Both are villages in the town of Barnstable. In the same vein, the village of West Barnstable (off Route 6A; sleepy, rural, and historic) doesn't have much in common with Osterville (off Route 28 on the coast; wealthy and preppy). Other notable villages in Barnstable include Cotuit (off Route 28; historic and charming), Marstons Mills (off Route 28 but inland; mainly residential), Centerville (off Route 28; beachy, yet with some commercial sprawl), and Hyannisport (off Route 28 on the coast; a residential neighborhood made famous by the Kennedys).

A number of other villages and towns are notable for their unique characteristics. Woods Hole—where bohemians and scientists coexist in a bustling ferry port—is a village in the town of Falmouth, a historic but not musty town with a pleasant Main Street and picturesque town green. Chatham and Osterville both have main streets that are destinations for shoppers seeking expensive, quality wares. Provincetown's colorful main street boasts the best people-watching. Sandwich may well be the quaintest town; Wellfleet, the most artsy. West Barnstable, Barnstable, Yarmouth Port, Dennis, and Brewster are all prototypical New England villages along the historic Old King's Highway. Of these, Dennis Village has the most going on—with museum, cinema, and playhouse all in one historic complex. The outer Cape towns (Eastham, Wellfleet, Truro, and Provincetown) have the National Seashore beaches, but many families prefer the accessibility of villages like West Dennis and Harwich Port which have pretty beaches with calm surf and warmer water on Nantucket Sound. Many gay vacationers in particular are partial to the open, artistic, and anything-goes lifestyle in Provincetown.

On the islands, location is also an important factor. Most visitors to Nantucket will want to choose lodging in town, where everything is within walking distance. On Martha's Vineyard, down-island towns (Vineyard Haven, Oak Bluffs, Edgartown) have the majority of the action—shops, restaurants, and fellow tourists. If a serene escape from the grind is what you seek, you may want to be up-island (West Tisbury, Chilmark, including the village of Menemsha, or Gay Head), but you'll need a car—or a passion for biking—to enjoy these locations.

Socially, a parallel could be drawn between the slightly more conservative types that populate the older, more protected communities and the renegades who gravitate to the wilder extremes. Towns like Sandwich, Falmouth, and Edgartown will suit conventional visitors, while twentysomethings and adventurous types of all ages will probably feel more at home in an open-minded, forward-thinking setting such as Wellfleet or Provincetown. Families, in particular, are sure to have a fabulous time at whatever spot they choose, because all it takes is some splashing surf and an expanse of sand to keep kids happily absorbed.

Route 28 east of Hyannis, an eyesore of tacky strip-mall development, presents a warning of what lies in store unless residents continue to clamp down on zoning. Though the pressures of development are unrelenting, Cape-lovers have done a pretty good job, so far, of fending off more egregious offenders. The Cape Cod National Seashore—though hotly protested when it was instituted in 1961, especially by landowners—serves as a living reminder of the beauty that otherwise would have almost inevitably been lost or reserved for the enjoyment of the ultrarich.

Today the task of monitoring and, when necessary, curbing development falls to the Cape Cod Commission, a Cape-wide planning and land-use council with regulatory powers (Martha's Vineyard and Nantucket have comparable agencies). Though the CCC's actions also rouse the occasional squawk, even pro-growth proponents know that it wouldn't do to kill the golden goose—the unspoiled natural beauty and historical charm that attract visitors in the first place. Cape Cod draws more than 17 million visitors a year who infuse the region with more than $700 million in revenues. Tourism has been the leading business sector since the late 19th century and is likely to remain so for centuries to come.

2 History 101

Dateline

- 1614 Captain John Smith reconnoiters the New England coast and sends back glowing reports of fecund land and fabulous natural resources.

- 1617 Wampanoag natives, angered by the kidnapping of six men by Captain Smith's crew, board an unoccupied ship and there contract the plague, which all but wipes out the 40,000-member Algonquian tribe.

- 1620 In November, the Pilgrims touch down at what is now Provincetown. Finding the land and its inhabitants inhospitable, they cross the bay in December to settle an abandoned indigenous campsite in Plymouth.

- 1626 In the Cape's first recorded wreck (one of thousands to come), the Jamestown-bound *Sparrow-Hawk* founders off Nauset Beach.

- 1627 Having paid off their debt to the Merchant Adventurers, who funded their trip, the Pilgrims set up America's first trading post at Aptucxet, in what is now Bourne.

- 1637 Ten households of Puritan dissidents from a community north of Boston settle Sandwich, the first

continues

PRE-"DISCOVERY"   Compared to the rest of the continental United States, the Cape and Islands truly do represent a "new land." They're only some 12,000 to 15,000 years old and, from the archaeological evidence found to date, were only inhabited during the late Pleistocene (about 10,000 to 12,000 years ago), by nomadic hunter-gatherers. By the time the first European explorers arrived at the turn of the 17th century (a rumored ca. A.D. 1000 visit by Viking Leif Eriksson has yet to be substantiated), Algonquian tribes had set up permanent winter and summer camps and were farming, fishing, and hunting.

The interlopers proved deadly, not just because of their greed for land and resources (including human: long before the Pilgrims arrived, English scouts kidnapped several "Indians" to be displayed as curiosities in London), but because they bore diseases against which the natives had no immunity. From a population thought to number around 30,000 in the early 17th century, their numbers quickly plummeted to mere hundreds.

THE PILGRIMS' SPEEDY PROGRESS   The decimation of native tribes left the fields, quite literally, wide open to this band of 102 "saints and sinners" (religious dissidents and mercenary adventurers), who set anchor off what would become Provincetown on the morning of November 11, 1620. The *Mayflower* had been bound for the Hudson River, at that point part of the Virginia Colonies, and with no established government—in fact, nothing at all—awaiting them on shore, the Pilgrims paused to make a covenant intended to prevent anarchy. Stating the case for self-rule, as well as for the full participation of every citizen, the "Mayflower Compact" has since been heralded as a forerunner of the U.S. Constitution.

Though the Pilgrims were fairly lucky in their choice of harbor—a scouting party led by Captain

Miles Standish managed to steal some seed corn stored in what is now Truro and met with no hostility until reaching Eastham's "First Encounter Beach"—Provincetown's climate did not strike them as conducive to agriculture. They kept searching until they found "Plimoth," an ideal spot across the bay, with freshwater springs close at hand and a relatively safe vantage point overlooking the harbor. The Pilgrims dug in and, despite losing half their number that first harsh winter, stayed put.

However, just as the Puritans themselves had fled England in search of religious freedom, splinter groups soon tired of the Puritans' own intolerance and set off to forge their own destinies. The first such settlement on the Cape was Sandwich, settled in 1637. Colonization quickly spread along the bay, into Barnstable and Yarmouth, where the fringe of salt marsh proved an excellent source of hay.

Martha's Vineyard was also among the earliest settlements. In 1642, speculator Thomas Mayhew bought all the islands, including the Elizabeths, from an English noble for the grand sum of 40 pounds. His missionary son immediately set about converting the natives of Martha's Vineyard and succeeded in swaying some 1,600 within a few short years, before perishing at sea. In 1959, Mayhew, Sr. sold Nantucket to a group of settlers—some of them *non grata* on the mainland for having evidently sympathized with Quakers—for 30 pounds, plus "two Beaver Hatts."

Early peace treaties made in Plymouth and massive conversions sufficed to keep a wary peace with the Wampanoag tribe for over 50 years—until the 1675–76 uprising known as King Philip's War, a last-ditch effort by East Coast tribes to contain colonial expansion. Greatly outnumbered, the natives were crushed, and with them, in large part, their way of life.

ON THE WATERFRONT Among the useful skills passed on by natives to newcomers was the practice of feasting off the occasional beached whale—or better yet, canoeing in pursuit of the "right" whales, which, once speared, stayed afloat and could be towed into shore. Using sailboats instead, the settlers set off in pursuit, and in 1712 a Nantucket ship blown out to sea managed to harpoon a sperm whale, which boasted not only blubber but spermaceti, a waxy substance that turned out to be ideal for candle-making and lamp fuel. The hunt was on, and over the next 1 1/2 centuries—until kerosene supplanted whale oil in 1859—

town to be incorporated on the Cape.

- **1660** Missionary Richard Bourne persuades the Plymouth court to accord the decimated Wampanoag tribe 10,500 acres in Mashpee "in perpetuity"—a land grant that a 1976 court refused to recognize.

- **1675–76** Over half a century of carefully negotiated peace between the natives and settlers is undone during the bloody confrontations of "King Philip's War."

- **1690** Nantucketers hire Ichabod Paddock of Truro to instruct them in the art of hunting "right" whales—so-called because they stick close to shore and float once killed.

- **1712** Blown off course into deeper waters, Nantucket's Captain Christopher Hussey happens to harpoon a sperm whale, whose oil proves far superior to that of near-shore whales. The tiny island soon takes the lead in worldwide whaling.

- **1770** Bowing to Quaker beliefs, Nantucket abolishes slavery, 13 years before the state as a whole adopts the measure.

- **1776** As many disdain the Revolutionary cause as those who embrace it. As the outcome becomes increasingly clear, many Tories debark for Canada.

- **1779** The British attempt to land in Falmouth, but are repelled by the local militia.

- **1812** The British fire on Falmouth and Orleans and quash all seagoing ventures with a death-lock blockade.

- **1816** Henry Hall of Dennis notices that his wild cranberries flourish when covered with a light dusting of sand; his cultivation tips,

continues

and a favorable environment, eventually elevate Massachusetts to the largest cranberry-producer in the world.

- **1828** Boston merchant Deming Jarves introduces the Industrial Revolution to the Cape, in the form of the pioneering Boston & Sandwich Glass Company.
- **1846** The Great Fire levels the port of Nantucket, but the prosperous town quickly rebounds.
- **1849** Henry David Thoreau embarks on the first of several walking tours of Cape Cod, observing native customs with astringent wit.
- **1859** The introduction of kerosene, derived from petroleum discovered in Pennsylvania in 1836, sounds the death knell for the whaling industry.
- **1871** The U.S. Commission of Fish and Fisheries sets up a collection station in Woods Hole to support the study of oceanography.
- **1872** The first train reaches Woods Hole, and a summer colony is launched.
- **1888** Undercut by competition from coal-powered plants in the Midwest, the Boston & Sandwich Glass Company goes under, ending the Cape's brief flirtation with large-scale industrialism.
- **1892** President Grover Cleveland establishes the first "summer White House" at his mansion, Gray Gables, on Monument Beach in Bourne.
- **1899** New York artist Charles W. Hawthorne founds the Cape Cod School of Painting in the remote port of Provincetown, attracting Greenwich Village intelligentsia.
- **1907–10** The Pilgrim Monument is constructed

continues

Nantucket would remain in the forefront of the hugely lucrative whaling industry. Captains from the Cape and Islands tracked their quarry to the four corners of the earth, while initiating the China Trade in luxury goods like fine porcelain and dressing up their home towns with fine mansions.

Pro-independence forces along the coast were especially avid, either because they were a self-select band of dissidents to begin with or because they'd long been subject to excessive taxation. One of the revolution's most influential orators was lawyer James Otis of West Barnstable, who in 1761 quit his post as customs agent to protest writs authorizing British soldiers to conduct searches at will: "A man's home is his castle," Otis declaimed to a receptive crowd at Old South Meeting House in Boston. His outspokenness earned him a near-fatal beating at a Tory pub in 1769, and a year later, the Boston Massacre definitively turned the tide of public opinion. By the time the Continental Congress declared independence on July 4, 1776, most Tory sympathizers along the coast were quietly planning to decamp. Though most of the action was far removed, the Cape did see a few skirmishes: Falmouth's volunteer militia, for instance, fended off an invading British fleet in 1779—several houses still bear the mark of cannon fire. And the ocean itself accomplished one of the most significant victories of 1778 in sinking the warship *Somerset* (the very boat Paul Revere had quietly paddled past en route to his famous ride of April 17, 1775) off North Truro. Townspeople rounded up the 480 soldiers who managed to make it to shore and hustled them back to Boston as prisoners of war.

The shipping trade remained a dangerous one right through the War of 1812, as British ships continued to conscript any American crews unlucky enough to cross their path. Some dangers—such as the risk of shipwreck—never abated, but the valiant captains of the Cape and Islands pressed on, broadening both commercial and intellectual horizons.

A SOMEWHAT GOLDEN AGE   The early 18th century was a time of unprecedented prosperity. With shipping routes well established for the distribution of goods, the Cape caught a touch of the Industrial Revolution fever then sweeping the mainland. The largest local enterprise was the Boston & Sandwich Glass Company (1828–88), which successfully applied glassblowing techniques on a factory scale, rendering glassware accessible to the masses for the first time in history.

Although the mostly immigrant labor force was treated quite exploitatively, the newly emerging leisure class did feel an obligation to enlighten and instruct; hence, the proliferation of public libraries. Such was the mandate of the Nantucket Atheneum, whose brilliant young director, the amateur astronomer Maria Mitchell, drew to her remote island such eminent contemporary figures as Frederick Douglass, John James Audubon, and Melville, Emerson, and Thoreau. Mitchell's accomplishments (she discovered a comet at the age of 29 and later became the country's first female college professor) are fairly indicative of the de facto feminism operative in a region where a good portion of the men spent most of their time at sea. As for Thoreau, he was clearly smitten with the Cape, returning repeatedly in the 1850s to report with acerbic relish on this "wild, rank place."

FROM BACKWATER TO SPA   With the abrupt demise of whaling in the 1860s, recession-struck residents streamed northward to seek work in the factory towns surrounding Boston—or westward in search of gold. The population of the Cape and Islands declined steadily over the next 60 years, not recovering until the advent of the automobile.

Meanwhile, however, tourists had begun their gradual takeover. The first wave, in the 1830s, consisted of Methodist revivalists who camped in Eastham and Centerville before permanently pitching their tents—and later, gingerbread houses—in Oak Bluffs on Martha's Vineyard. Erected in the 1860s and 1870s, their colorful "Cottage City" survives as one of the earliest instances of successful urban planning. Another beneficiary of the region's long economic sleep is the beautiful port town of Nantucket. Preserved in near pristine condition, with minimal accommodation to modern amenities, it represents the largest concentration of pre-1850 structures in the United States. But for the cars and crowds, you'd swear that scarcely any time had passed.

Nantucket began bouncing back as a tourist destination in the 1870s (it even supported an actors' colony in rose-covered 'Sconset). Falmouth became another popular destination with the coming of the railroad. At the turn of the century, Provincetown, hitherto a hardscrabble fishing town, started attracting artists and writers from Greenwich Village. The radical theater movement that brought forth Eugene O'Neill also spawned more broadly appealing strawhat ventures, including Dennis's still-thriving

in Provincetown, with presidential visits—by Taft and Roosevelt—to mark the laying of its commencement and completion.

- **1914** The Cape Cod Canal, still the world's widest sea-level waterway, is completed 17 days before the Panama Canal.
- **1916** Attracted by rumors of a radical new theater enterprise at the tip of the Cape, Eugene O'Neill shyly offers his first works to the Provincetown Players.
- **1918** A German sub fires on Orleans while Chatham's Naval Air Station crew is otherwise engaged, playing baseball.
- **1926** Raymond Moore founds the Cape Playhouse in Dennis, attracting such raw talent as Bette Davis (an ambitious usherette), Humphrey Bogart, and others.
- **1935** Hans Hoffman revives the Cape Cod School of Art (dormant since Hawthorne's death in 1930) and turns Provincetown into a hotbed of abstract expressionism.
- **1950** Broadway star Gertrude Lawrence and her husband, Cape Playhouse manager Richard Aldrich, found the Cape Cod Melody Tent in Hyannis, still going strong today.
- **1961** Roughly 44,000 acres of the Outer Cape— a 30-mile swath of coast—is placed under National Park Service stewardship as the Cape Cod National Seashore.
- **1970** The Cape Cod Mall inaugurates an era of unbridled strip-mall development.
- **1973** Jaws is filmed on Martha's Vineyard, placing this moneyed hideaway on

continues

the hoi polloi's touristic hit list.

- 1975 Fishing captain Al Avellar of Provincetown comes up with the notion of "whaling" for sightseers.
- 1987 Local treasure-hunter Barry Clifford unearths the pirate ship *Whydah* off Wellfleet, where it has lain undisturbed since 1717. The federal government grants the Wampanoags of Gay Head on Martha's Vineyard a $4.5-million settlement with which to buy back approximately 475 acres of their ancestral land (and hatch plans for a gambling casino).
- 1989 After much debate, Cape Codders vote for a Cape Cod Commission, a regulatory agency that seeks to control development on Cape Cod.
- 1994 Stellwagen Bank, an underwater reef that serves as a primary feeding ground for migrating whales, is declared a National Marine Monument.
- 1995 With the backing of the Mashpee Wampanoags, senators Edward Kennedy and John Kerry successfully mobilize for the creation of the 5,871-acre Mashpee National Wildlife Refuge along Waquoit Bay.
- 1996 Within a few months of each other, both Highland (Cape Cod) Lighthouse in North Truro and Nauset Lighthouse in Eastham are moved back from their rapidly eroding cliffs, thus preserving the beacons for future generations.
- 1997 After a *Cape Cod Times* exposé about gross negligence regarding the cleanup of toxic waste at the Massachusetts Military Reservation in

continues

Cape Playhouse, where actors such as Bette Davis and Henry Fonda made their debuts.

The cast of characters may have changed over the years, but Provincetown—protectively encircled by the Cape Cod National Seashore preserve since 1961—still takes itself seriously as an art colony. In particular, the off-season residency program at the Fine Arts Work Center, founded in 1968 by such local luminaries as painter Robert Motherwell and poet Stanley Kunitz, continues to elicit emerging talent; the "scholars," visual and literary, often settle in for good. Seductively diffuse light, scintillating company, great stretches of unspoiled nature close at hand—the features that attracted the intelligentsia of the teens and twenties are every bit as potent today as they were back then. By toeing the fine line between progress and preservation, those who love the region—residents and visitors alike—hope to perpetuate its charms for as long as the land lasts.

3 Cape Architecture

The classic Cape cottage is a design with remarkable staying power. Hastily improvised by the first settlers of the New World, it made a hearty comeback 3 centuries later as attractive, affordable housing for the ever-expanding reaches of suburbia. In the meantime, several successive waves of architectural styles peaked and waned along the coast, as the moneyed merchants tried to keep up with the latest continental fashions.

Fashion was the furthest thing from the Pilgrims' minds when they landed at the start of winter in 1620. Survival was their sole concern. A few hardy types may have tossed up thatched huts, but most settlers remained huddled on the *Mayflower,* awaiting balmier days. When they did start to build in earnest, they tended to replicate the cottages of home: one-room post-and-beam structures measuring about 1 rod (16 ft.) square, centered on a fieldstone hearth. Glass was prohibitively expensive, so the casement windows were minimal. Wattle and daub provided insulation (later these interior walls would be finished with vertical boards), and steep roofs not only fended off fierce north winds but also kept snow from accumulating. A mighty beam called the summer beam, braced against the chimney, supported an attic used for the storage of grain or, in some cases, a communal bedroom for children.

The first such structures usually had a door with two windows to one side—what we'd now term a "half-Cape." A full Cape would have two windows on both sides; a three-quarter, two on one side and one on another. The beauty of the basic design was that the houses were easy to expand as a family's needs grew. Some houses grew vertically, into the "saltbox" style named for the slant-topped boxes in which that crucial substance was stored. Full Capes tended to be divided into rooms with specific purposes: a front parlor and master bedroom on either side of the (usually) south-facing door and, along the back of the house, a "keeping room" that served as kitchen, dining room, and catchall living room. With fires going all day to prepare food, the latter was the warmest room in the house. Sometimes a small portion of the western end of the keeping room would be portioned off as a "borning room," or small bedroom for the aged or infirm; the cooler, eastern end might be turned into a buttery or pantry. Sometimes a lean-to construction would extend the keeping room further, and specialized outbuildings—known as "warts"—were also common.

Bourne, the portion of the base used as a National Guard practice target range is closed until further notice. Cape Cod residents vigorously debate a Cape Cod Land Bank Bill that would tax real-estate purchases in order to purchase land for conservation. President Clinton and his family vacation on Martha's Vineyard for the third time during his presidency.

Early builders were cautious when it came to supporting the weight of a roof; some included "gun-stock" beams in the corners (they're thicker at the bottom, like a rifle stood on end) in the mistaken belief that they'd be sturdier. It wasn't until the mid-1600s that they were confident pitching roofs at a 45° angle and adding on a second story, thereby creating the "colonial mansion" style. A further refinement was the gambrel roof, which afforded more interior space. Glass, though still prohibitively expensive for all but the most prosperous, was more readily available from England, so the mansions began to sport double-hung windows, with 6-by-8-inch panes hung in multiples of four. The fanciest house in town, for instance, might boast very showy, light-enhancing windows of "12 over 16."

Doors, too, received more elaborate treatment—especially with the growing popularity of "Palladian" design, a classical style derived from Renaissance Italy that was all the rage in England. "Pattern books" enabled even country carpenters to emulate such decorative touches as pediments and pilasters. During England's Georgian period (1714–1830), many an austere colonial mansion got gussied up, and new buildings took advantage of the larger panes of glass now being made: multiples of three across typify the Georgian era. Whereas England built its classicist structures in sturdy brick or stone, however, the colonists used their seemingly inexhaustible supplies of wood to mimic the same effects. Look for "quoins," the decorative planks arranged to look like cornerstones, or massive "marble" columns that are merely skillfully worked lumber.

It was in the Federal period (1775–1820) that American builders really came into their own, creating a spare, handsome style that has held up beautifully over the centuries. Greek Revival leanings predominated between 1820 and 1860, resulting in grand public edifices and modest homes alike adorned by a colonnade topped with a pediment, à la the Parthenon. Carpenter's Gothic—its elaborate "gingerbread" trim made possible by the invention of the jigsaw—blossomed in the 1860s, especially in the revivalist stronghold of Oak Bluffs on Martha's Vineyard. In fact, the entire Victorian era, whose repercussions were felt well into the 20th century, was big on architectural froufrou. Meanwhile, a countermovement was afoot in the form of an indigenous Shingle style, characterized by simple, shingled exteriors concealing cool, spacious rooms refreshed by the seaside breezes. Fitting well within their setting, the

Summer's Bounty: From Pick-Your-Own to Farmers Markets

Summer on the Cape and Islands means fresh produce in abundance. Farms that offer "pick-your-own" are great family outings: Kids go home tired; parents go home virtuous; all go home with eats. Strawberry season is from early June through early July, while blueberry season kicks in toward the end of July and lasts through August. Throughout the summer and fall, there's also a variety of locally grown fresh produce available. Farms are scattered all over the region, and in the summer roadside farm stands are ubiquitous.

In the Upper Cape, you'll want to go to **Tony Andrews Farm** at 398 Old Meetinghouse Rd. in East Falmouth (☎ **508/548-5257**). He offers pick-your-own strawberries, as well as tomatoes, peas, and beans. **Peach Tree Circle,** at 881 Palmer Ave. in Falmouth (☎ **508/548-2354**), is a small farm stand with a cheerful little restaurant attached. **Crow Farm,** along Route 6A in Sandwich (☎ **508/888-0690**), is, at 68 years young, the oldest business in town and somewhat of a local institution. Owned and managed by the Crowell family, it specializes in apples and peaches, but also features homemade cider, vegetables, pies, and specialty items. Crow Farm is open from May to December from 9am to 5pm; in the summer, it's closed on Sundays. Fall is the big season at **Windstar Farm** on Country Farm Road in Forestdale, Sandwich (☎ **508/477-0051**). They have the largest pick-your-own pumpkin patch in Massachusetts: 70 acres of gourds of every imaginable color and size. Capturing the complete autumn experience, there are also apples, mums, and hayrides here. Fall hours are Monday to Friday from noon to 6pm and Saturday and Sunday from 10am to 6pm.

In the Mid-Cape, **Blueberry Hill Farm,** 820 Rte. 6A in Barnstable Village (☎ **508/362-3781**), offers pick-your-own blueberries on Monday and Thursday in season. **Holbrook House,** at 252 Union St. in Yarmouth Port (☎ **508/362-3348**), offers pick-your-own blueberries and raspberries in season. These days, **Tobey Farm,** 352 Main St. (Route 6A) in Dennis Village (☎ **508/385-2930**), is mainly a nursery with annuals in the spring and mums in the fall; fresh native corn is available in season, while October is festive with spooky hayrides. There's a lot of history here: This is Cape Cod's oldest family farm, dating back to a land grant

Shingle-style mansions and grand hotels that survive to this day look impressive yet unostentatious—little wonder they're often copied in new construction.

The lean years of the Great Depression not only popularized the scaled-down bungalow style (borrowed from India) but resuscitated the practical Capes, and, in fact, spread them all across the country. With the exception of a few precious, cohesive enclaves of a particular style, most communities along the Cape and on the Islands represent a hodgepodge of every significant era to date. A simple stroll around town can offer the chance to time-travel through the architectural enthusiasms of the past several centuries.

4 A Taste of the Cape

SEAFOOD GALORE   Cape Cod, of course, was named for the quantities of **cod** that explorer Bartholomew Gosnold encountered in its waters in 1602. Salted cod was a mainstay of the colonial diet and still turns up in the Portuguese specialty *bacalao* (check out Provincetown's Portuguese restaurants). The Pilgrims would have from Charles II in 1681. Tobey Farm is open from May through Christmas daily from 9:30am to 6pm.

In the Lower Cape, **Namskaket Farm,** Route 6A in Brewster (☎ **508/896-7290**), offers pick-your-own strawberries in season. The place for produce in the Outer Cape is **Hatch's Market,** 310 Main St. in Wellfleet (next to Town Hall; ☎ **508/349-6734**). In addition to fresh produce and seafood, they carry specialty items, prepared foods, and flowers. In season, Hatch's is open Monday to Thursday from 9am to 6pm and Friday to Sunday from 9am to 7pm.

On Nantucket, **Bartlett's Ocean View Farm,** on 100 acres off Hummock Pond Road (☎ **508/228-9403**), sells vegetables, annuals, perennials, and pick-your-own strawberries. Most summer mornings, the Bartlett truck can be found parked on Main Street, overflowing with colorful fresh vegetables and flowers. Locals and visitors alike flock to buy produce right off the truck. On Martha's Vineyard, **Morning Glory Farm,** on Edgartown–West Tisbury Road (☎ **508/627-9003**), sells produce as well as baked goods, cheese, honey, flowers, and beef. It's open from 9am to 6pm daily from Memorial Day until Thanksgiving. Also on Martha's Vineyard, **Thimble Farm,** on Edgartown–Vineyard Haven Road (☎ **508/693-6396**), offers pick-your-own raspberries and strawberries. They are open June through October Tuesday to Sunday from 10am to 5pm. Martha's Vineyard also boasts the region's best farmers market; the **West Tisbury Farmers Market** takes place every Wednesday from 3 to 6pm and Saturday from 9am to noon at the old Ag Hall (near Alley's General Store) in West Tisbury (☎ **508/696-0100**).

For the freshest and most complete selection of produce on the Cape, head over to **Lambert's Rainbow Fruit,** 1000 W. Main St. in Centerville (☎ **508/778-4066**) and 325 Rte. 28 in West Yarmouth (☎ **508/790-5954**). Matt Lambert buys daily from the Boston produce market, bringing the world's best fruits and vegetables to Cape Cod. Another popular local market is **Fancy's,** located in East Orleans at 199 Main St. (☎ **508/255-1949**) and in Chatham at 1291 Main St. in The Cornfield shopping plaza (☎ **508/945-1949**). Fancy's specializes in a variety of fresh produce, including native corn.

---

turned up their noses, however, at what most tourists consider New England's ultimate delicacy: **lobster.** In fact, they considered these curious arachnids (yes, they belong to the spider family) fodder fit for pigs, and what the pigs spurned was used as fertilizer. In the mid-19th century, you could buy a shipload for a penny, and prisoners rioted when force-fed too many lobster dinners. Today, lobster is a coveted "last meal."

With a "chicken lobster" (the smallest size legal to harvest, about 1¼ lb.) fetching more than $10 cooked and larger sizes exponentially priced at "market rates," these days you're more likely to find tourists complaining of feasting on too few. Do tackle at least one, whether at a no-frills lobster shack or a four-star restaurant. Lobsters are delicious just boiled, ripped asunder, and dipped in butter, and a sumptuous experience when rendered as a mild, creamy **bisque** or infused, for example, with champagne beurre blanc and deshelled. The chronically inept might want to opt for such a deconstructed "lazy man's lobster." If you're doing the dismantling yourself, though, there's no shame in donning a plastic bib; they're slippery devils and liable to spurt.

Start by wrenching off the claws, and use a nutcracker to free the meat (it may take some poking and prodding). Then grab the whole tail and bend it backwards till it snaps off; after you do the same with the flippers, it's easy to pull or push out the tail, where the bulk of the meat is. Pry open the chest cavity: The greenish tomalley (liver) is especially tasty, and if you're lucky, you might run into some roe (eggs). Some people claim to be able to suck tiny morsels from the spinnerets—good luck! The claws are the tastiest treat; you might want to save them for last.

Lobsters are the main event in a **"New England shore dinner,"** which usually comes with "steamers" as a preamble, plus a baked potato and corn on the cob. **Steamers**—soft-shell, long-neck clams—are another sloppy proposition. You pry open the shell (discard any that won't easily open), peel off the tough membrane covering the neck like a turtleneck, and dunk it first in brine, then butter.

Shore dinners were originally prepared *within* the shore, in a heated sandpit, and it's still possible to arrange such a supper, or make one yourself. WPA writer Josef Berger outlines the basic procedure in his 1937 classic, *Cape Cod Pilot*. The idea, essentially, is to dig a 6-foot circle and line it with large stones; get a driftwood fire going for about an hour (on most beaches today, you'd need a permit); rake the embers and pile on more wood, topped with masses of rinsed seaweed, the foodstuffs to be steamed, another thick layer of seaweed, and an old sailcloth (surely everyone keeps one handy); then cover the whole shebang with sand. Wait patiently for at least 45 minutes, and *voilà*—an authentic shore dinner.

Mollusks turn up in other enticing guises as well. Smaller-sized **clams,** known as cherrystones and littlenecks, are usually served chilled with lemon, horseradish, or a cocktail or mignonette sauce, or, less typically, baked (as, for instance, clams casino); they're at their height of flavor when freshly shucked. The same is true of **oysters,** and the Cape has two world-class oyster beds, those of Wellfleet and Cotuit. Many restaurants feature a **raw bar,** where you can order these delicacies by the piece, fresh off the boat.

Fried clams are a beloved, if caloric, coastal staple; if given a choice, opt for whole "bellied" clams, which have a richer taste and less rubbery texture. In the local lexicon, large hard-shell clams are known as **quahogs** ("*ko*-hogs"): Being tough, they're usually served diced, breaded, and baked, or camouflaged in a chowder. The latter is the only use for giant sea clams. **Chowder** itself—the milk- or cream-based kind— is another renowned New England specialty, and towns often mount chowder contests so that you can taste the infinite variations, involving varying amounts of potatoes, onions, bacon, seasonings, and secret ingredients.

Mussels are a relative newcomer to Cape menus, but following the European lead, they're now treated to delicious preparations—steamed with white wine and garlic, for example, or stewed in a spicy tomato sauce. **Scallops** have always been a treat, especially the tender bay type. Now they're being farmed offshore, and a few adventurous restaurants have taken to serving them whole, instead of using just the muscle portion. As with bellied clams, whole scallops offer a much fuller taste and more interesting texture.

Though local fishing stocks are becoming dangerously depleted (certain restrictions are already in place), there appears to be no shortage of **bluefish**—a rather oily but delicious fish fairly easy to catch from shore. **Tuna** still turns up, and contemporary chefs know to undercook it so that, when seared, it retains a tender pink core. Though not yet as numerous as raw bars, sushi bars are on the rise; there's no better way to enjoy fresh Cape seafood.

REGIONAL PRODUCE   The **cranberry,** one of only three fruits exclusive to the New World (the others are blueberries and Concord grapes), proved a godsend to the colonists, who found in it a ready source of a substance they didn't know they needed: vitamin C. The Native Americans called the ruby fruits of this creeping evergreen vine "bitter berries" and used them as a dye, as a poultice for treating wounds, and as food, sweetened with maple sap and pounded with venison to make pemmican. It was Dutch settlers who named them cranberries, noting that the plant's delicate pink blossom resembles the head of a crane. Following the natives' example, the English settlers were soon making cranberry sauce (boiled, with sugar) to accompany meat, and they noticed that it tended to keep scurvy at bay. Later, the whalers would pack along a barrel of cranberries to fend off scurvy on their long journeys.

In 1816, a Dennis native, Henry Hall, figured out how to cultivate the wild vines commercially. Today, cranberries are Massachusetts's foremost crop, and the state is the nation's premier producer. Some 12,000 acres yield hundreds of millions of dollars' worth a year, the great bulk of it converted into juice. Local chefs are always on the lookout for creative uses, so you're apt to encounter—beyond the ubiquitous cranberry muffins—waffles, cookies, relishes, and even salsa. Because cranberry bogs need to quadruple their area in wetlands to support them, they're even serving to preserve the pastoral landscape.

The Pilgrims were right: The Cape's sandy soil is not the most arable in the world. But it's ideal for certain crops. Falmouth, for instance, long reigned as the strawberry capital of the world, and Eastham held the same title for asparagus and turnips. Though land is now too costly, as a rule, to be devoted to large-scale agriculture, a good number of commercial gardens and, more recently, aqua farms produce a wide variety of greens and vegetables destined for farmers markets and the finer restaurants.

The terrain is also proving, amazingly enough, conducive to cultivation of **wine grapes,** thanks to its relatively moderate climate, warmed by the Gulf Stream, and fast-draining soil. Among the half-dozen vinicultural enterprises launched in recent decades, the most successful is **Chicama Vineyards** on Martha's Vineyard (☎ **508/ 693-0309**). They offer entertaining summertime tours, followed by a commendable tasting.

3

Planning a Trip to Cape Cod & the Islands

Once you've made it over one of the bridges guarding the Cape Cod Canal, getting around is relatively easy—and you can bypass the bridges, of course, by flying or boating in. The Cape is really many capes: tacky in spots, ordinary in others, as well as a nature-lover's dream, a living historical treasure, and a hotbed of creativity. The town-by-town chapters should help you to zone in on the area that will suit you best, and this broader introduction should steer you there smoothly.

1 Visitor Information & Money

VISITOR INFORMATION

For the free *Getaway Guide*, which covers the whole state, contact the **Massachusetts Office of Travel and Tourism,** 100 Cambridge St., 13th floor, Boston, MA 02202 (☎ **800/447-MASS** or 617/727-3201).

The **Cape Cod Chamber of Commerce,** Routes 6 and 132, Hyannis, MA 02601 (☎ **508/362-3225;** fax 508/362-3698; Web site www.capecod.com), **Martha's Vineyard Chamber of Commerce,** Beach Road, Vineyard Haven, MA 02568 (☎ **508/693-0085;** fax 508/693-7589; Web site www.mvy.com), and **Nantucket Island Chamber of Commerce,** 48 Main St., Nantucket, MA 02554 (☎ **508/228-1700;** fax 508/325-4925), can provide more localized information and answer any questions that may arise. In addition, most towns on the Cape have their own chambers of commerce, which are listed in the relevant chapters that follow.

If you're a member of the **American Automobile Association (AAA)** (☎ **800/222-8252**), they'll provide a complimentary map and guide covering the area.

Additional useful Web sites are the following: Cape Cod Life Magazine, www.capecodlife.com; and the Nantucket Chamber of Commerce, www.nantucketchamber.org.

HOSTEL INFORMATION Hostelling International/American Youth Hostels (☎ **202/783-6161**) offers low-cost dorm accommodations in five sites on the Cape and Islands. Rates are $15 per person per night for nonmembers; members ($25 a year for adults, $15 for adults over 54, $10 for children under 18) pay somewhat less. Note that there's a "lockout" period (typically, 10am to

5pm daily), and, likely, a limit on the length of stay. HI/AYH properties are located on the outskirts of Hyannis; in Eastham, just off the bike trail; in a former Coast Guard station overlooking Ballston Beach in Truro; adjoining 4,000-acre Manuel F. Correllus State Forest in West Tisbury on Martha's Vineyard; and in an 1874 life-saving station on Surfside Beach on Nantucket. For details, see "Where to Stay" in the relevant chapters.

SPORTS INFORMATION   Cape Cod Chamber of Commerce (☎ 508/ 362-3225; fax 508/362-3698; Web site www.capecod.com) offers a "Sportsman's Guide" outlining fishing and hunting options. Those interested in outdoor activities will find reams of info through the **World Wide Web's Great Outdoor Recreation Pages** (www.gorp.com). Birders should call the **Cape Cod Museum of Natural History** (☎ 508/896-3867) for info about the Cape Cod Bird Club or call the **Birdwatchers General Store** in Orleans (☎ 508/255-6974) for top spots and the latest sightings. Many of the Cape's **golf clubs** are open to the public; for an anno-tated listing and advice, call ☎ **800/TEE-BALL,** "the chamber of golf."

MONEY

Though the Cape and Islands—especially the Islands—might seem pricey compared to nontourist areas, visitors used to city prices will find costs quite reasonable. Basi-cally, you can get by on very little if your comfort needs are minimal (rooms in older motels go for as little as $40 a night). Then again, you could spend $1,000 or more on a room—per night. Most of the nicer rooms fall between $125 and $225 a night.

Restaurant prices offer as wide a range. You could dine on clam rolls, for instance, at less than $10 a head, or blow that much or more on a mere appetizer. With such a great variety of dining styles available everywhere, the choice is yours.

Hotels and inns are listed according to price range, based on midsummer rates for double occupancy: **Very Expensive** refers to rooms that average $200 or more per night; **Expensive,** $150 to $200; **Moderate,** $100 to $150; and **Inexpensive,** under $100.

Restaurants are listed according to price range, based on dinner main-course prices: **Very Expensive** refers to restaurants in which most entrees exceed $30; **Expensive** includes those where main courses generally cost between $20 and $30; **Moderate,** $15 to $25; and **Inexpensive,** most main courses under $15.

TRAVELER'S CHECKS, ATMs & CREDIT CARDS   Traveler's checks are ac-cepted at hotels, motels, restaurants, and most stores, as are credit cards. ATMs are available throughout the area, at banks and supermarkets, so you can get cash as you travel. Call one of the major networks, such as **Cirrus** (☎ 800/424-7787) or **PLUS** (☎ 800/843-7587), to find out the nearest location. (Foreign travelers should check with their banks beforehand to make sure their PINs will work abroad.)

Should you require personal service, the banks with the greatest number of branches include **BankBoston** (☎ 800/788-5000) and **Fleet** (☎ 800/841-4000). The 25-odd branches of **Cape Cod Bank and Trust Company** (☎ 800/458-5100) will exchange all foreign currencies; or stop off at the exchange booths at Logan Air-port in Boston.

2 When to Go: Climate & Events

Once a strictly seasonal destination, opening with a splash on Memorial Day week-end and shuttering up come Labor Day, the Cape and Islands now welcome more and more tourists to witness the tender blossoms of spring and the fiery foliage of autumn. During these "shoulder seasons," lodging tends to cost less, and a fair number of restaurants and attractions remain open. Most important, traffic is manageable. In addition, the natives tend to be far more accommodating in the off-season, and shopping bargains abound. *Insider's tip:* Provincetown's October sales are to die for.

August is by far the most popular month, followed by July (especially the July 4th weekend). You are virtually guaranteed good beach weather in July and August. September and October, though, are splendid, too: The ocean retains enough heat to make for bearable swimming during the sunny days of "Indian summer," and the subtly varied hues of the trees and moors are always changing, always lovely. The Atlantic will be bone-chillingly cold, but May and June are also enticing: Gardening goes way beyond hobby in this gentle climate, and blooms are profuse from May right through the summer. Unless your idea of the perfect vacation requires a swim in the ocean, you'd be better off visiting the Cape slightly off-season: May, June, September, or October.

OFF-SEASON   In the last few years, a number of entertaining town festivals and events have attracted crowds in the spring and fall. Provincetown has the **Arts Festival** in late September and **Women's Week** in October. Truro's town festival, **Truro Treasures,** is also held in September. Of course, the **cranberry festivals** all take place in the fall. Harwich has the largest event, usually spanning 2 weekends in September. Nantucket's Cranberry Weekend in October is also popular. Some say the most crowded time on Nantucket is during the **Christmas Stroll** in early December; the entire month before Christmas is known as **Nantucket Noel,** with lots of holiday events. Martha's Vineyard also rolls out the red carpet in December with events in Edgartown and Vineyard Haven, including Santa arriving on the ferry. Many towns on the Cape, including Sandwich, Osterville, Falmouth, and Chatham, also have big holiday festivals. Spring brings **daffodil festivals** in Brewster, Osterville, and on Nantucket (book your ferry reservations way in advance for this one).

Some establishments persist straight through the truly quiet season—January through March—and it's a rare treat to enjoy these historic towns and pristine landscapes with almost no one but natives stirring about. To avoid disappointment in the off-season, however, always be sure to call ahead to check schedules.

WILDLIFE   The wetlands of the Cape and Islands are part of one of the country's greatest annual wildlife spectacles: the passage of thousands of **migratory sea-, shore-, and songbirds** in spring and fall. Warblers, herons, terns and oystercatchers, shorebirds like avocets and the endangered piping plover, dozens of species of ducks, huge flocks of snow geese, owls, hawks—these are just a few of the birds that take a rest stop on the Cape as they pass along the Atlantic Flyway, which for some birds extends from winter homes in South America to breeding grounds in the vast, marshy tundra within the Arctic Circle. March, April, October, and November are all good months to catch migrating waterfowl. August is the month to catch migrating shorebirds, with thousands stopping to feed at places like Monomoy Island, Nauset Marsh, and Sandwich's Great Marsh. Fewer shorebirds stop on the Cape in spring, but those that do will be decked out in the bird equivalent of a tux—their breeding plumage. And the songbirds pass through in May, in their brightest plumage and in full-throated song (both color and voice are muted in the fall migration). If you're birding on the Cape during the height of the summer season, you'll find plenty of herons, egrets, terns, and osprey wherever you find sand and wetlands.

The other great wildlife-watching opportunity this region is known for is **whale watching.** The humpbacks, huge finbacks, and small minkes all cluster to feed around the Stellwagen Bank north of Provincetown from April all the way through November.

Monomoy Island is worth a special trip in late winter, when thousands of **harbor seals** take their version of holiday in the sun, retreating to Monomoy from Maine and points north. At that time of year, they share the island with many thousands of wintering sea ducks. For info on a tour, call the **Cape Cod Museum of Natural History** (☎ **508/896-3867**).

CLIMATE

The Gulf Stream renders the Cape and Islands generally about 10° warmer in winter than the mainland, and offshore winds keep them about 10° cooler in summer (you'll probably need a sweater most evenings). The only downside of being surrounded by water is a tendency for fog; typically, it's sunny about 2 days out of 3—not bad odds. And the foggy days can be rather romantic. Pack some good books for when it pours.

THE SEASONS

SUMMER   The official beginning of summer on Cape Cod is heralded by the **Figawi sailboat race** from Hyannis to Nantucket on Memorial Day weekend. Traffic all over the Cape is horrendous, and ferries are booked solid. It's a rowdy party weekend, but then, strangely, things slow down for a few weeks until late June. The first few weeks of June can be a perfect time to visit the region, but be forewarned: You may need to request a room with a fireplace. Weather this time of year, particularly in the Outer Cape, can be unpredictable at best. At worst, it's cold and rainy. Don't count on swimming in the ocean unless you're a member of the Polar Bear Club. Late June weather is usually lovely. July 4th is another major mob scene weekend to be avoided. July and August can be perfect—sunny and breezy—or damp, foggy, and humid. Usually it's a combination of the two. Heavily trafficked Labor Day is another weekend you'll probably want to avoid.

AUTUMN   It usually starts feeling like fall around mid-September on Cape Cod. Leaves start to change color, roads start to unclog, and everyone seems happier. Day temperatures are perfect for long hikes along the seashore. By October, you'll need a sweater during the day, and evenings can be downright chilly. But this is a lovely time of year on the Cape and Islands.

WINTER   It's not supposed to snow on Cape Cod, but it does. A few years ago, some towns got close to 100 inches. Another recent winter, the Cape received virtually no snow until a surprise blizzard on April 1st. The holidays are quite popular for family gatherings on the Cape and Islands. January to March are on the bleak side. This is when a lot of locals head south to sunnier climes.

SPRING   April is a cheerful time on the Cape and Islands. Daffodil festivals abound. Folks are gearing up for the summer season. It's a time for last minute fix-up jobs: painting and repairing. In May and June, the entire Cape blossoms, but the weather can be quite rainy this time of year.

Hyannis's Average Monthly Temperatures

	Jan	Feb	Mar	Apr	May	June	July	Aug	Sept	Oct	Nov	Dec
High Temps. (°F)	40	41	42	53	62	71	78	76	70	59	49	40
Low Temps. (°F)	25	26	28	40	48	56	63	61	56	47	37	26

CAPE & ISLANDS CALENDAR OF EVENTS

April

- **Brewster in Bloom,** Brewster. Open houses, a crafts fair and flea market, parade, and hot-air balloons. The Old King's Highway (Route 6A) is lined with thousands of daffodils. Call ☎ **508/896-8088.** Late April.
- ✪ **Daffodil Festival,** Nantucket. Spring's arrival is heralded with masses of yellow blooms adorning everything in sight, including a cavalcade of antique cars. Call ☎ **508/228-1700.** Late April.
- **Daff O'Ville Day,** Osterville. Celebrating the arrival of spring with flower exhibits, children's activities, concerts, and other events. Call ☎ **508/428-9700.** Late April.

May

- **Herb Festival,** Sandwich. Exhibits, talks, and garden walks at the Green Briar Nature Center. Call ☎ **508/888-6870.** Mid-May.
- ✪ **Cape Maritime Week,** Cape-wide. A multitude of cultural organizations mount special events—such as lighthouse tours—highlighting the region's nautical history. Activities include Coast Guard open houses, lectures, walking tours, and more. Sponsored by the Cape Cod Commission. Call ☎ **508/362-3828.** Mid-May.
- **Spring Fling,** Chatham. A family-oriented festival featuring clowns, pets, and a crazy hat parade. Call ☎ **508/945-5199.** Mid-May.
- **Figawi Sailboat Race,** Hyannis to Nantucket. The largest—and wildest—race on the East Coast. Intensive partying in Hyannis and on Nantucket surrounds this popular event. Call ☎ **508/778-1691.** Late May.
- **Dexter Rhododendron Festival,** Sandwich. **Heritage Plantation**—at the peak of bloom—sells offshoots of its incomparable botanical collection. Call ☎ **508/888-3300.** Late May.

June

- **Brewster Historical Society Antiques Fair,** Brewster. An outdoor extravaganza, featuring 80 top dealers. Call ☎ **508/896-7389.** Early June.
- **Hyannis Harbor Festival,** Hyannis. A boat parade and sailboat races, live music, crafts, and maritime exhibits. Call ☎ **800/449-6647** or 508/362-5230. Early June.
- **Heritage Cape Cod,** Cape-wide. Ten days of special tours and events hosted by historic sites and museums. Additional events are spread throughout the year. Call ☎ **508/888-1233.** Mid-June.
- **A Taste of the Vineyard,** Martha's Vineyard. Island restaurateurs offer samplings of their specialties at Edgartown's Whaling Church to benefit the Martha's Vineyard Preservation Trust. Call ☎ **508/627-8017.** Mid-June.
- ✪ **Harborfest Celebration,** Nantucket. A chance to sample competing chowders and board tall ships. Call ☎ **508/228-1700.** Mid-June.
- **Nantucket Film Festival,** Nantucket. New annual event focuses on storytelling through film and includes showings of short and feature length films, documentaries, staged readings, panel discussions, and screenplay competition. Sponsors include *Vanity Fair* magazine, so you may see a celebrity or two. Call ☎ **212/642-6339.** Late June.
- **Strawberry Festival,** Bourne. **The Aptucxet Trading Post Museum,** a replica of the country's first store, hosts crafts demonstrations, accompanied by fresh strawberry shortcake. Call ☎ **508/759-9487.** Late June.
- **Provincetown Portuguese Festival,** Provincetown. This new cultural event celebrates Provincetown's Portuguese heritage with music, dancing, exhibits, food,

parade, fireworks, and the traditional Blessing of the Fleet. Call ☎ **508/487-3424.** Late June.

- **Rock & Roll Ramble,** Sandwich. Vintage cars from the fifties and sixties converge on Heritage Plantation for a concert and mutual admiration. Call ☎ **508/ 888-3300.** Late June.

July
- **Edgartown Regatta,** Martha's Vineyard. A highly social sailing event. Call ☎ **508/627-4361.** Early July.
- **Wampanoag Pow Wow,** Mashpee. Native American tribes from around the country converge to enjoy traditional dances and games. Call ☎ **508/477-0208.** July 4th weekend.
- **Independence Day,** Falmouth. Festivities include a Blessing of the Fleet and fireworks at Falmouth Heights Beach. Your best bet is to park in town earlier in the evening and walk over to the Heights. Call ☎ **508/548-8500.** July 4th weekend.
- **Independence Day,** Provincetown. Festivities include a spirited parade, entertainment, and fireworks over the harbor. Call ☎ **508/487-3424.** July 4th weekend.
- **Independence Day,** Barnstable. A spectacular fireworks display over either Barnstable Harbor or Hyannis Harbor (depending on the nesting of the piping plovers). Call ☎ **800/4-HYNNIS.** July 4th weekend.
- ✪ **Barnstable County Fair,** East Falmouth. An old-fashioned 6-day agricultural extravaganza, complete with prize produce and livestock. Call ☎ **508/563-3200.** Mid-July.

August
- **Beach Plum Music Festival,** Provincetown. Town Hall hosts some top jazz and folk acts. Call ☎ **508/349-6874.** Early August.
- **Jazz by the Sea and Pops by the Sea,** Hyannis. Celebrity "conductors"—such as Julia Child wielding a wooden spoon—enliven these two outdoor concerts. Call ☎ **508/790-2787.** Early August.
- **Possible Dreams Auction,** Martha's Vineyard. Resident celebrities give—and bid—their all to support the endeavors of Martha's Vineyard Community Services. Call ☎ **508/693-7900.** Early August.
- **In the Spirit Arts Festival,** Martha's Vineyard. Oak Bluffs celebrates its cultural diversity, with food, music, and children's fun. Call ☎ **508/693-0085.** Early August.
- **Carnival Week,** Provincetown. The gay community's annual blowout, featuring performers, parties, and an outrageous costume parade. Call ☎ **508/487-2313.** Mid-August.
- ✪ **Agricultural Society Livestock Show and Fair,** Martha's Vineyard. In West Tisbury, a classic country carnival, and a great leveler. Call ☎ **508/693-4343.** Mid-August.
- **Sandcastle and Sculpture Day,** Nantucket. A fairly serious contest, but fun; categorization by age group ups the odds of winning. Call ☎ **508/228-1700.** Mid-August.
- **Falmouth Road Race,** Falmouth. Joggers and world-class runners turn out in droves—9,000 strong—for this annual 7.1-mile sprint. Entry registration is by lottery and ends in May. No unregistered runners are allowed to participate. Call ☎ **508/540-7000.** Mid-August.
- **Festival Days,** Dennis. Fun-for-the-family activities, including a kite-flying contest, canoe race, crafts fair, and more. Call ☎ **800/243-9920** or 508/398-3568. Late August.

- **Illumination Night,** Martha's Vineyard. The Oak Bluffs campground is lit with hundreds of Japanese lanterns. Campground officials keep this event a secret until the last minute, so it's hard to plan ahead for this one. Call ☎ **508/693-0085.** Late August.
- **New England Jazz Festival,** Mashpee. Sponsored by the Boch Center for the Performing Arts. A weekend of big-name performers. Call ☎ **508/477-2580.** Late August.
- **Oak Bluffs Fireworks and Band Concert,** Martha's Vineyard. The summer's last blast. Call ☎ **508/693-5380.** Late August.

September

- **Bourne Scallop Festival,** Bourne. This annual weekend event features food, crafts, rides, musical entertainment, and more. Call ☎ **508/759-6000.** Early September.
- **Windmill Weekend,** Eastham. This jolly community festival includes a sand-art competition, road races, band concerts, an arts and crafts show, a tricycle race, and professional entertainment. The highlight of this weekend is the square dance held under the historic windmill. Call ☎ **508/255-0558.** Early September.
- **Cranberry Festival,** Harwich. A chance to observe and celebrate the colorful harvest, with 9 days of events ranging from pancake breakfasts to fireworks. Call ☎ **800/441-3199** or 508/430-2811. Mid-September.
- **Provincetown Arts Festival,** Provincetown. Building up to the **Provincetown Art Association and Museum Annual Consignment Auction** (☎ 508/487-1750), this festival is an extraordinary opportunity to collect works spanning the past century. Local artists hold open studios, actors stage readings of Eugene O'Neill, and stalwart swimmers participate in the **Harbor Swim for Life** (☎ **508/487-3684**) to raise money for local AIDS organizations. The race is followed by a festive Mermaid Brunch and a sunset "Festival of Happiness" on Herring Cove Beach. This is a relatively new festival for Provincetown, but it looks to be a keeper. Mid-September.

October

- **Bourne Farm Pumpkin Festival,** West Falmouth. A fun-for-the-whole-family day of pumpkin picking, hayrides, and pony rides at a 1775 farmstead. Call ☎ **508/ 548-0711.** Early October.
- **Trash Fish Banquet,** Provincetown. Undersung species are creatively cooked to benefit the Center for Coastal Studies. Call ☎ **508/487-3622.** Mid-October.
- **Women's Week,** Provincetown. A gathering of artists, entertainers, and educators, as well as women who just want to have fun. Call ☎ **800/933-1963** or 508/ 487-2313. Mid-October.
- **Walking Weekend,** Cape-wide. Over 45 guided walks (averaging 2 hours in length) sponsored by the Cape Cod Commission to foster appreciation for the Cape's unique ecology and cultural accomplishments. Call ☎ **508/362-3828.** Mid-October.
- **Cranberry Harvest Festival,** Nantucket. Bog tours, inn tours, and a cranberry cook-off, just when the foliage is at its burnished prime. Call ☎ **508/228-1700.** Mid-October.
- **Nantucket Arts Festival,** Nantucket. This weeklong event includes a wet-paint sale, mini–film festival, writers and their works, gallery exhibitions, artist demonstrations, theater, concerts, photography, and more. Call ☎ **508/228-3424.** Mid-October.
- **Yarmouth Seaside Festival,** Yarmouth. Parade, fireworks, arts and crafts, contests, and sporting events. Call ☎ **508/778-1008.** Mid-October.

- **Happy Haunting Weekend,** Martha's Vineyard. Edgartown hosts Halloween festivities, including a pumpkin-carving contest and trick or treating. Call ☎ **508/627-4711.** Late October.

November

- **Chatham's Christmas By The Sea,** Chatham. Ten days of town-wide events include historic inn tours, carolers, hay rides, open houses, dinner dance, and Santa. Call ☎ **508/945-5199.** Late November.
- **Lighting of the Pilgrim Monument,** Provincetown. The Italianate tower turns into a monumental holiday ornament, as carolers convene below. Call ☎ **508/487-1310.** Thanksgiving Eve (late November).
- **Harbor Lighting,** Hyannis. The boats parade by, atwinkle with lights, and Santa arrives via lobster boat. Call ☎ **508/362-5230.** Late November.
- **Fall Festival,** Edgartown. Family activities at the Felix Neck Wildlife Sanctuary, including a treasure hunt, wildlife walks, and wreath-making. Call ☎ **508/627-4850.** Late November.

December

- **Christmas Stroll,** Nantucket. The island briefly stirs from its winter slumber for one last shopping/feasting spree, attended by costumed carolers, Santa in a horse-drawn carriage, and a "talking" Christmas tree. This event is the pinnacle of ✪ **Nantucket Noel,** a month of festivities starting in late November. Ferries and lodging establishments book up months before this event, so you'll need to plan ahead. Call ☎ **508/228-1700.** Early December.
- **Falmouth Christmas by the Sea,** Falmouth. A weekend of caroling, tree lighting, Santa, entertainment, and a parade that centers on the historic and lavishly decorated Falmouth Village Green. Call ☎ **508/548-8500.** Early December.
- **Christmas in Sandwich,** Sandwich. Seasonal open houses, exhibits, community caroling, and merchant promotions take place throughout the town. Call ☎ **508/759-6000.** Early December.
- **Yarmouth Port Christmas Stroll,** Yarmouth Port. Stroll along the Old King's Highway for open houses, visits with Santa, and caroling. Call ☎ **508/778-1008.** Early December.
- **Christmas Weekend in the Harwiches,** Harwich. This town-wide celebration features entertainment, merchant promotions, hay rides, visits with Santa, and more. Call ☎ **508/432-1600.** Mid-December.
- **First Night,** Chatham. Following Boston's lead, Chatham puts on a festive evening featuring local performers. Call ☎ **508/945-5199.** New Year's Eve.
- **First Night,** Vineyard Haven and Edgartown. The two island towns mount their own Boston-inspired jamborees featuring local artists and performers. Call ☎ **508/693-0085.** New Year's Eve.

3 Health & Insurance

STAYING HEALTHY   Even in this northerly clime, sunburn is a real hazard—as is, increasingly, **sun exposure,** whatever the latitude. For most skin types, it's safest to start with a lotion with a high SPF (Sun Protection Factor) and work your way down. Be sure to reapply often, according to the directions, and no matter how thoroughly you slather up, try to stay in the shade during prime frying time—11am to 2pm. Sunglasses with UVP (Ultra Violet Protection) lenses will help shield your eyes.

The sea breezes keep most **mosquitoes** on the move, but not always (said Thoreau: "I have never been so much troubled by mosquitoes as in such localities"), so pack some bug spray. The most dangerous insect you're likely to encounter may not be so easily dissuaded. Unfortunately, pinhead-sized **deer ticks,** which transmit Lyme disease (named for the Connecticut community where the malady was diagnosed) are quite widespread along the Massachusetts coast, and they're especially active just when you're apt to be there: April through October. Nantucket has the dubious distinction of having the highest concentration of Lyme disease in the country. (A vaccine is being tested there, but is not yet on the market.) If caught in its early stages—symptoms include a ring-shaped rash and flulike achiness—the disease is easily countered with antibiotics; if it's left untreated, however, the effects could eventually be fatal.

The best protection, so far, is prevention. Avoid walking in brush or high grass— it's bad for the dunes anyway. If you insist on bushwhacking, cover up in light-colored clothing (the better to spot any clinging ticks), consisting of a long-sleeved shirt and long pants tucked into high white socks. Camping stores such as EMS sell bush pants that are perfect for this purpose—they're actually comfortable in warm weather. For double protection, spray your clothes and hands (but not face) with a DEET-based insect repellent. Check your clothes before removing them, and then check your body; it helps to use a mirror, or call upon a significant other. Showering after such an outing is a good safeguard. If, despite your best precautions, you find you've brought home a parasite, remove it with tweezers by pulling directly outward, if you can manage to do so without squeezing the body (that would only serve to inject more bacteria into your bloodstream). Dab the bite with alcohol to help disinfect it, and save the tick in a closed jar. If you're within a few minutes of a medical facility, have a doctor deal with the extraction; if you do it yourself, go for testing and treatment as soon as you can and take the tick with you.

The **Lyme Disease Foundation** (☎ **860/525-2000**) distributes brochures to tourist areas, and is also able to field questions. Other good sources of information are the **Centers for Disease Control** (☎ **888/232-3228** or 404/332-4555) and the **Massachusetts Department of Public Health** (☎ **508/947-1231**).

There's one other very good reason not to go in for splendor in the grass: **poison ivy.** The shiny, purplish, three-leafed clusters are ubiquitous and potent: If you so much as brush past a frond, the plant's oil is likely to raise an itchy welt. Clothing that has been in contact with the plant can spread the harmless but irritating toxin to your skin; it's even transmitted by smoke. If you think you've been exposed, your best bet is to wash with soap immediately (otherwise the oil may spread elsewhere on your body). Calamine lotion—available without prescription at all drugstores— should help soothe the itching. You won't spread the rash by scratching, since it's the oil that does the spreading, but scratches could get infected, so resist the temptation.

There's one key health precaution you can take if you're planning to do any bicycling while on the Cape and Islands: a **helmet.** In Massachusetts, children 12 and under are required to wear one. All the good bike shops rent out helmets as well, and those few extra bucks could save your life.

Pack an adequate supply of any **prescription drugs** you'll need in your carry-on luggage, and also bring copies of your prescriptions. If you have a serious condition or allergy, consider wearing a Medic Alert identification bracelet, available from the **Medic Alert Foundation** (☎ **800/432-5378**).

INSURANCE   Before leaving home, check with your credit-card companies to find out whether you're entitled to any free travel coverage as a cardholder. Many companies offer personal accident insurance or rental-car insurance at no extra charge; they may also be able to help you get a refund if there's a problem with an airline ticket or hotel room charged to your card. Also check your homeowner's policy to see if it covers off-premises theft.

If you feel the need to purchase extra travel insurance, contact **Travel Guard International** (☎ **800/826-1300** or 715/345-0505), which offers policies that protect against trip cancellation and include provisions for medical coverage and lost luggage as well. Prices start at $100 for 1 week of coverage. **Travel Insured International** (☎ **800/243-3174** or 860/528-7663) and **Mutual of Omaha** (☎ **800/228-9792**) offer similar protection.

4 Tips for Travelers with Special Needs

FOR TRAVELERS WITH DISABILITIES   The free *Getaway Guide* offered by the **Massachusetts Office of Travel and Tourism** (☎ **800/447-MASS** or 617/727-3201) is keyed for handicapped accessibility. Though the larger, more popular establishments, as well as newer (1990s) construction, are generally up to code, a great many of the Cape's older, historic buildings are difficult to retrofit, and the task is prohibitively expensive for many small-business owners, much as they might like to upgrade. Your best bet is to check accessibility when calling ahead to confirm hours or make reservations. You'll find most places eager to do whatever they can to ease the way, but if you run into problems, you might want to contact the **Cape Organization for Rights of the Disabled** (☎ **800/541-0282** or 508/775-8300). For information on services available in the state, call the **Massachusetts Network of Information Providers** (☎ **800/642-0249** or TTY 642-0200) during business hours. Other informational resources include **Mobility International USA** (☎ **541/343-1284**), **Travel Information Service** (☎ **215/456-9600**), and the **Society for the Advancement of Travel for the Handicapped** (☎ **212/447-7284**).

Among the tour operators that specialize in meeting the needs of differently abled travelers are **Accessible Journeys** (☎ **800/TINGLES** or 610/521-0339), **Flying Wheels Travel** (☎ **800/535-6790** or 507/451-5005), and **The Guided Tour Inc.** (☎ **215/782-1370**).

In addition, both **Amtrak** (☎ **800/USA-RAIL**) and **Greyhound** (☎ **800/752-4841**), which serves Boston, offer special fares and services for travelers with disabilities; call at least a week in advance for details.

FOR SENIORS   With relatively mild winters and splendid summers, Cape Cod and the Islands are popular retirement spots. In fact, as of the 1990 U.S. Census, a third of the population was 55 or older. Businesses from museums to B&Bs cater to this clientele with attractive discounts, and a great many restaurants offer early-bird specials (smaller portions at lower prices, offered before the ordinary dinner hour). Mention that you're a senior when you first call to make your travel reservations, and be sure to carry some form of identification that establishes your birth date, such as a driver's license or passport.

For information on the discounted airfares, car rentals, and accommodations available to members, contact the **American Association of Retired Persons,** 601 E St. NW, Washington, DC 22049 (☎ **202/434-2277**). You might also want to inquire about the resources of **Elder Services of Cape Cod and the Islands** (☎ **800/244-4630** or 508/394-4630).

Elderhostel is a national organization that offers affordably priced educational programs for people over 55. Programs generally last a week, and prices average about $350 per person, including classes, room, and board. For information on programs held on the Cape and Islands, contact the main office at 75 Federal St., Boston, MA 02110-1941 (☎ **617/426-7788**) and request a free catalog.

Both **Amtrak** (☎ **800/USA-RAIL**) and **Greyhound** (☎ **800/752-4841**), which serves Boston, offer discounted senior fares.

FOR GAY & LESBIAN TRAVELERS Gay and lesbian travelers, singly or in pairs, will feel right at home in Provincetown, a world-renowned gay vacation capital. They should also feel comfortable wandering farther afield. This is a sophisticated, semiurban population, and you'll rarely encounter a overtly bigoted innkeeper, shopkeeper, or restaurateur (if you do, report them to the **Massachusetts Commission against Discrimination,** 1 Ashburton Place, Room 601, Boston, MA 02108; ☎ 617/727-3990). To avoid unpleasant situations, read between the lines of promotional literature ("fun for the whole family" may mean rampant bedlam and not much fun for you), or be blunt in stating your expectations (for example, "It will be for myself and my partner [name goes here], and we'd like a queen bed, if possible"). The descriptions of each establishment listed in this book should give some idea of their suitability and compatibility. For a detailed, insider's look at Provincetown beyond the scope of this book, consult *Gay USA* by George Hobica, published by First Books, P.O. Box 578147, Chicago, IL 60657 (☎ 773/276-5911).

FOR FAMILIES Basically a giant sandbox with a fringe of waves, the Cape and Islands are ideal family vacation spots. A number of the larger hotels and motels offer deals whereby kids can share their parents' room for free. But beware the fancier B&Bs: Although it's quite illegal for them to do so, some actively discriminate against children (see "Tips on Accommodations," below). The kind that do are apt to be the kind that children dislike, so it's no great loss. For the most part, the local tourism industry is big on serving family needs, so there's not much you'll need to do by way of advance preparation. For establishments that are extra-welcoming, as well as especially appealing, see the "Family-Friendly Hotels & Restaurants" listings in each chapter.

5 Getting There

BY CAR Visitors from the west (New York, for example) will approach the Cape Cod Canal via Route 25 and the Bourne Bridge; those coming from Boston can either come that way (reaching Route 25 via I-95 or I-93 south, then Route 24 and I-495) or by heading directly south from Boston on I-93 and Route 3, leading to the Sagamore Bridge. The bridges are only 3 miles apart, with connecting roads on both sides of the canal, so either will do. The one you choose will most likely depend on whether you're planning to head farther south on the Cape to Falmouth along Route 28 or its more rural parallel, Route 28A (in that case, take the Bourne Bridge), or further east of the Sagamore along Route 6 and its scenic sidekick, Route 6A, which merges with Route 28 in Orleans. From Orleans, the main road is Route 6 all the way to Provincetown.

The big challenge, actually, is getting over either bridge, especially on summer weekends, when upwards of 100,000 cars are all trying to cross at once. Savvy residents avoid at all costs driving onto the Cape on Friday afternoon or joining the mass exodus on Sunday (or Monday, in the case of a holiday weekend), and you'd be wise to follow suit. Call **SmarTraveler** (☎ 617/374-1234 or cellular *1) for up-to-the-minute news on congestion and alternate routes, as well as parking availability in the pay-per-night parking lots that serve the island ferries.

Traffic can throw a major monkey wrench into these projections, but on average driving time to Hyannis is about 7 hours from New York, and 2 hours from Boston. It'll take about 1 to 1¹/₂ hours more to drive all the way to Provincetown.

Traffic can truly be a nightmare on peak weekends. Cars are enough of a bother on the Cape itself: If you're not planning to cover much ground, forgo the "convenience" and rent a bike instead (some B&Bs even offer "loaners"). On the Islands,

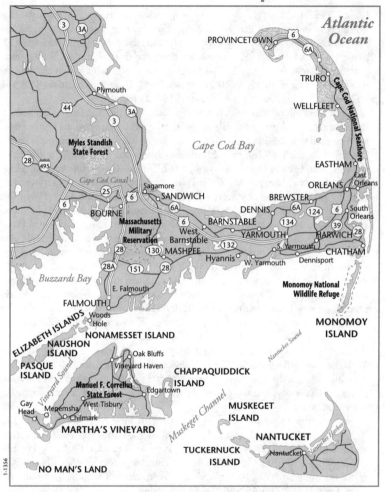

Atlantic Ocean

PROVINCETOWN

TRURO

WELLFLEET

Cape Cod National Seashore

Plymouth

Cape Cod Bay

Myles Standish State Forest

Cape Cod Canal

Sagamore

SANDWICH

BOURNE

Massachusetts Military Reservation

West Barnstable

MASHPEE

Hyannis

W. Yarmouth

E. Falmouth

FALMOUTH

Woods Hole

ELIZABETH ISLANDS

NONAMESSET ISLAND

NAUSHON ISLAND

PASQUE ISLAND

Oak Bluffs

Vineyard Haven

Manuel F. Correllus State Forest

West Tisbury

Gay Head

Menemsha

Chilmark

MARTHA'S VINEYARD

EASTHAM

East Orleans

ORLEANS

BREWSTER

South Orleans

DENNIS

BARNSTABLE

YARMOUTH

S. Yarmouth

HARWICH

CHATHAM

Dennisport

Monomoy National Wildlife Refuge

MONOMOY ISLAND

Nantucket Sound

Vineyard Sound

CHAPPAQUIDDICK ISLAND

Edgartown

Muskeget Channel

MUSKEGET ISLAND

TUCKERNUCK ISLAND

NANTUCKET

Nantucket

Nantucket Harbor

NO MAN'S LAND

1-1356

they're truly superfluous. Quite expensive to ferry back and forth ($101 one-way to Nantucket in season, and that's *if* you manage to make a reservation months, even a year, in advance or are willing to sit in "standby" for many hours), a car will only prove a nuisance in the crowded port towns, where urban-style gridlock is not uncommon. Should you change your mind and want to go motoring once you arrive, you can always rent a car on-island, usually for *less than the cost of bringing your own vehicle over.*

If you do come by car, have a mechanic check it out beforehand. If you're a member of the **American Automobile Association** (☎ **800/222-4357**) or another national auto club, call beforehand to ask about travel insurance, towing services, free trip-planning, and other services that may be available.

BY BOAT   Arriving by water gives you a chance to decompress from city worries, while taking in glorious views both coming and going. All the ferries are equipped to carry bikes, for about one-third the cost of a ticket. **Bay State Cruises**

(☎ **617/457-1428**) runs a daily round-trip passenger ferry to Provincetown from Boston (Commonwealth Pier at the World Trade Center) late June through Labor Day, and on weekends late May to late September; the voyage ($18 one-way or $30 round-trip for adults, $15–$23 for senior citizens and children under 13) takes about 3 hours each way, and there's a 3-hour lunchtime layover. You can also ferry directly to Provincetown from Plymouth, in season, with **Cape Cod Cruises** (☎ **508/747-2400**); it's a bit shorter and cheaper ($14–$24 round-trip).

For detailed information on ferries to the islands, see the "Getting There" sections in chapter 9. The three "down-island" ports of Martha's Vineyard are hooked up to the Cape and mainland in various ways. Oak Bluffs has the busiest harbor in season. It's served by the **Hy-Line** from Hyannis or Nantucket (☎ **508/778-2600**), the **Island Queen** from Falmouth Harbor (☎ **508/548-4800**), and the state-run **Steamship Authority** car ferry from Woods Hole (☎ **508/477-8600**). Edgartown is serviced by the Falmouth Ferry Service, a passengers only ferry called the *Pied Piper*, (☎ **508/548-9400**), which leaves from the Falmouth Heights side of Falmouth Harbor and makes a 1 hour crossing (6 crossings a day in season). Vineyard Haven welcomes Steamship Authority car and passenger ferries from Woods Hole year-round (over 30 crossings a day on weekends in season). If you want to bring your car, you'll need a reservation (☎ **508/477-8600**), although there's limited standby space available for those willing to wait around, except during certain peak-demand stretches in summer. Passengers not planning to bring a car do not need a reservation. The **Cape Island Express** (☎ **508/997-1688**) runs a passenger ferry, called Schamonchi, from New Bedford daily in summer. There are four trips a day on weekends in season. The Island Queen makes the quickest crossing, at about 40 minutes; the Cape Island Express takes about 1¹⁄₂ hours but spares travelers coming from New York the long drive onto the Cape. One-way fares range from about $5 to $14, depending on the distance, and the one-way rate for cars in season is $44. Parking averages $10 per day. Including all of the ferry services, there are dozens of crossings a day in summer.

Nantucket is linked in season to Harwich Port by the **Freedom Cruise Line** (☎ **508/432-8999**), which makes 3 trips a day in season, one trip a day in the spring and the fall. Nantucket is also linked to Hyannis and Oak Bluffs by **Hy-Line** (☎ **508/778-2600**). The Steamship Authority passenger/car ferry from Hyannis operates year-round, making 6 crossings each day in season. The passengers-only **M/V Grey Lady II** (☎ **800/492-8082**), a recent addition to the Hy-Line fleet, is the quickest way to get to Nantucket by boat. Ordinarily, the ferries to Nantucket take over 2 hours, but the Grey Lady II, a high-speed catamaran cuts the time in half, for more than twice the slow-boat price ($29 one-way, versus $11). The best deal may be Hy-Line's passenger ferry, the Great Point, which makes the trip in under 2 hours and offers a first class lounge for $10 extra. Incidentally, transporting a car costs an astronomical $101 one-way in season—pretty silly when you consider that the island is only 3 miles wide and 15 miles end to end. A bike ($5 one-way) will more than suffice.

A certain frenzy usually accompanies the ferry departures, but if you arrive about an hour ahead of time, you should have plenty of time to drop off your luggage at the pier beforehand, so you won't have to lug it around. This may not always work in Woods Hole, which is a cul-de-sac: call SmarTraveler (see "By Car," above) or listen to the radio station 1610 AM to find out what's up and whether traffic is clogged. The Steamship Authority boats offer a luggage trolley, which often fills to capacity a half-hour or more before departure, so it pays to get there early. The Hy-Line staff cheerfully attends to all the loading of luggage and bikes. It's a lot less hassle.

With enough time to spare, you can comparison-shop for a parking space. While the adjacent lots charge as much as $10 a day, you might find one for half that much a few blocks away—and the difference can really add up if you're planning a long sojourn.

Note: See the note on bus-ferry connections under "By Bus," below. The same holds true for return journeys: Ferry arrival times tend to be more reliable, but give yourself plenty of time, and don't take a chance on the last bus of the day.

BY PLANE Most major carriers offer service to Boston's Logan Airport, and from there it's a quick (half-hour) commuter flight to Hyannis (about $100, round-trip), Provincetown (about $160, round-trip), or the Islands (to the Vineyard, about $100 round-trip; to Nantucket, about $125 round-trip). It's also easy to shuttle in from New York (from La Guardia to Hyannis, about $160 round-trip; from La Guardia to Martha's Vineyard, about $210 round-trip; from La Guardia to Nantucket, about $315 round-trip). Connections are also available between these airports and to New Bedford, and private charters are easy to arrange. Comparison-shopping by phone (or computer) can pay off, since preliminary research will help you find the best deal. For example, Continental offers service to Hyannis from La Guardia Airport and a seasonal service from Newark Airport to Martha's Vineyard. US Airways services Hyannis from Logan, La Guardia, and Newark; they also service Martha's Vineyard and Nantucket from both Logan and La Guardia. Cape Air is the only airline currently offering service from Logan Airport to Provincetown.

Among the larger airlines serving Logan are **American** (☎ 800/433-7300), **Continental** (☎ 800/525-0280), **Delta** (☎ 800/221-1212), **Northwest** (☎ 800/225-2525), **TWA** (☎ 800/221-2000), **United** (☎ 800/241-6522), and **US Airways** (☎ 800/428-4322).

Carriers to the Cape and Islands include all of the above except TWA, plus **Cape Air** (☎ 800/352-0714 or 508/771-6944), **Colgan Air** (☎ 800/272-5488 or 508/775-7077), **Island Airlines** (☎ 800/248-7779 or 508/775-6606), and **Nantucket Airlines** (☎ 800/635-8787 or 508/790-0300). Flying over to Nantucket from Hyannis takes only 12 minutes, costs about $65 round-trip, and is a great way to avoid the hectic ferry scene. Island Air and Cape Air make the most frequent trips from Hyannis to Nantucket and between these two air carriers alone, there are over 30 flights per day. Charter flights are offered by Cape Air and Nantucket Airlines (see above), as well as by **Air New England** (☎ 508/693-8899), **Island Air Charter** (☎ 508/778-8360), **King Air Charters** (☎ 800/247-2427), and **Westchester Air** (☎ 800/759-2929). The commuter flights have their own little fare wars, so it's worth calling around. And though flights may lessen in frequency during the off-season, fares descend as well.

From Logan, the Cape is about a 1½- to 2½-hour drive, depending how far along it you intend to go. Hyannis, the Cape's transportation hub, is about a 2-hour drive, or 2½ hours via the **Plymouth & Brockton bus line** (☎ **508/771-6191**); from there you can take a 2-hour ferry ride to either island.

BY BUS Greyhound (☎ **800/231-2222**) connects Boston with the rest of the country, and **Bonanza Bus Lines** (☎ **800/556-3815** or 508/548-7588) covers a good portion of southern New England. Logan Airport to Falmouth costs about $15 each way. Bonanza links Boston's Logan Airport and South Station with Bourne, Falmouth, and Woods Hole; its buses from New York reach the same destinations, plus Hyannis. From New York to Hyannis or Woods Hole, the 6-hour ride costs about $45 each way. **Plymouth & Brockton** (☎ **508/771-6191**) offers service from Logan and South Station to Hyannis by way of Sagamore and Barnstable, and offers connections from there to the towns of Yarmouth, Dennis, Brewster, Orleans, Eastham, Wellfleet, Truro, and Provincetown.

Note: If you're planning to catch a ferry, don't count on the bus arriving on time (there's no telling what the traffic may do). Plan to take the second-to-last ferry of the day, so you have a back-up, and even so, schedule your arrival with an hour to spare.

6 Getting Around

BY CAR   Traveling by car does offer the greatest degree of flexibility, although you'll probably wish everyone else didn't think so, too. While traffic can often be treacly, parking is another problem. In densely packed towns like Provincetown, finding a free, legal space is like winning the lottery. Parking is also problematic at many beaches. Some are closed to all but residents, and visitors will almost always have to pay a day rate of about $5 to $10. Renters staying a week or longer can arrange for a discounted week- or month-long sticker through the local town hall (you'll probably need to show your lease, as well as your car registration). You can usually squeeze into the Cape Cod National Seashore lots if you show up early (by 9am); here the fee is only $5 a day, or $15 per season.

Further complicating the heavy car traffic on the Cape is the seemingly disproportionate number of bad drivers. A few key traffic rules: A right turn is allowed at a red light after stopping, unless otherwise posted. In a rotary (something of a Massachusetts bugaboo), cars within the circle have the right of way until they manage to get out. Four-way stops call for extreme caution or extreme courtesy, sometimes both.

Rental cars are available at the Hyannis Airport and at branch offices of major chains in several towns. The usual maze of rental offers prevails. Almost every rental firm tries to pad its profits by selling Loss-Damage Waiver (LDW) insurance at a cost of $8 to $15 extra per day. Before succumbing to the hard sell, check with your insurance carrier and or credit-card companies; chances are, you're already covered. If not, the LDW may prove a wise investment. Exorbitant charges for gasoline are another ploy to look out for: Be sure to top off the tank just before bringing the car in.

Certain car-rental agencies have also set maximum ages, or may refuse to rent to those with bad driving records. If such restrictions might affect you, ask about requirements when you book, to avoid problems later.

It's worth calling around to the various rental companies to compare prices and to inquire about any discounts available (members of the AAA or AARP, for instance, may be eligible for reduced rates). The national companies represented on the Cape and Islands include **Avis** (☎ 800/331-1212), **Budget** (☎ 800/527-0700), **Hertz** (☎ 800/654-3131), **National** (☎ 800/227-7368), and **Thrifty** (☎ 800/367-2277).

BY BOAT   For ferries linking the Cape and Islands, see "Getting There," above. Other local water-taxi services and cruise opportunities are listed by town in the appropriate chapter.

BY BIKE   The perfect conveyance for the Cape and Islands, for distances great and small. The Cape has some extremely scenic bike paths, including the glorious Cape Cod Rail Trail, which meanders through seven towns for over 25 miles. By bike is the best way to explore Nantucket's flat terrain, and there are scenic bike routes through all six towns on Martha's Vineyard. You'll find a rental shop in just about every town (see the listings under "Bicycling" in subsequent chapters), or better yet, bring your own.

Travel Times to Cape Cod & the Islands

New York to Hyannis	5 to 7 hours, depending on traffic
Boston to Hyannis	1¹/₂ hours with no traffic
Sagamore Bridge to Orleans	1 hour; with high-season traffic, 2 to 3 hours
Sagamore Bridge to Provincetown	1¹/₂ hours with little traffic
Hyannis to the Sagamore Bridge	half an hour; on Sunday afternoons in season, 3 hours
Bourne Bridge to Woods Hole	45 minutes; Friday afternoons in season, 1³/₄ hours
Hyannis to Nantucket by plane	12 minutes
Hyannis to Nantucket by Steamship ferries	2¹/₄ hours
Hyannis to Nantucket by Hy-Line ferries	1³/₄ hours
Hyannis to Nantucket by Hy-Line high speed Catamaran	1 hour and 10 minutes
Woods Hole to Martha's Vineyard aboard the Steamship Authority ferries	45 minutes
Falmouth to Edgartown, Martha's Vineyard, aboard the Pied Piper	1 hour
Falmouth to Oak Bluffs, Martha's Vineyard, aboard the Island Queen	35 minutes

BY MOPED   They're legal on the Islands and can be rented at many bicycle rental shops, but locals loathe them: They're noisy, polluting, traffic-clogging, and a menace both to their riders and to innocent bystanders. In other words, *caveat renter,* and expect some dirty looks.

BY TAXI   You'll find taxi stands at most airports and ferry terminals. The Islands also offer jitney services with set rates, such as **Adam Cab** on Martha's Vineyard (☎ **800/281-4462** or 508/693-3332) and **Aardvark Cab** on Nantucket (☎ **508/ 728-9999**). Several, like Aardvark, offer bike racks or can arrange for bike transportation with advance notice—call around until you find what you need. Some companies offer sightseeing tours. Among the larger taxi fleets on the Cape are **Falmouth Taxi** (☎ **800/618-8294** or 508/548-4100), **Hyannis Taxi Service** (☎ **800/ 773-0600** or 508/775-0400), and Provincetown's **Mercedes Cab** (☎ **508/349-7777** or 508/487-3333), which delivers elegance at no extra charge. Other cab companies are listed in the Yellow Pages, as are limousine liveries.

BY BUS   To discourage congestion and provide a pleasant experience, a growing number of towns offer free or low-cost in-town shuttles in season. You'll find such services in Falmouth, Woods Hole, Mashpee, Hyannis, Dennis, Yarmouth, Harwich, Martha's Vineyard, and Nantucket. Each town's chamber of commerce can fill you in, or call the **Cape Cod Regional Transit Authority** (☎ **800/352-7155** or 508/ 385-8326). For commercial bus service between towns, see "Getting There," above.

TRAVEL TIMES   Please note that traffic is very heavy driving over the bridges onto the Cape on Friday afternoons and going over the bridges off the Cape on Sunday afternoons. Saturdays can also have heavy traffic, because it is the start and end of most rental units. The Bourne Bridge is usually less crowded than the Sagamore Bridge, but unless you are going to Falmouth, you'll have to merge with the Sagamore Bridge traffic on Route 6 traffic anyway. If you are trying to catch a ferry, particularly in Hyannis, always leave plenty of extra time.

7 Tips on Accommodations

The listings in this book feature the range of summer rates for a double room. Keep in mind that this figure does not take into account the sales tax, which can go as high as 9.7%, depending on the town. Prices off-season are typically discounted by about 20% to 30%, sometimes more.

Virtually every town on the Cape has lodgings to suit every taste and budget. The essential trick is to secure reservations months—possibly as much as a year—in advance for the peak season of July through August (June and September are beginning to get crowded, too). You can't count on luck; in fact, unless you're just planning a day trip, you probably shouldn't even visit at the height of summer unless you've prearranged a place to stay.

Accommodations range from sprawling, full-facility resorts to cozy little B&Bs with room for only a handful of guests. The price differential, surprisingly enough, may not be that great. A room at a particularly exquisite inn might run more than a modern hotel room with every imaginable amenity.

Because there are hundreds of lodging establishments of every stripe throughout the Cape and Islands, I've focused only on those with special qualities: superb facilities, for example, or especially friendly and helpful hosts. I've personally visited every place listed here, but worthy new inns—as well as resurrected old ones—are constantly popping up.

RESERVATION SERVICES Several reservations services cover the region, but the only one I can personally vouch for—their standards being as exacting as mine—is **Destinnations** (☎ **800/333-4667** or 508/790-0566). Representing hundreds of top inns throughout New England, Destinnations can also design custom tours that cater to special interests, such as golf or antiquing.

Otherwise, it's buyer beware when it comes to such promotional terms as "water view" or "beachfront" (Provincetown's in-town beach, for instance, is quite scenic for strolls, but a bit too close to an active harbor to make for pleasant swimming). To spare yourself disappointment, always call ahead to request a brochure, if you have time. Some inns and hotels offer special packages, which they may or may not list, so always inquire. Most require a 2-night minimum on weekends, 3 if it's a holiday weekend. All provide free parking, although in a congested area such as Provincetown, you may have to play musical spaces.

FAMILY-FRIENDLY Although all lodgings in the state are prohibited by law from discriminating on the basis of age, a lot of the fancier, fussier B&Bs will be none too happy if you show up with a young child or infant in tow. You might not be too happy either, spending your entire vacation attending to damage control. It can't hurt to inquire—perhaps anonymously, before calling to book—about an establishment's attitude toward children and its suitability for their needs. If you get the impression that your child won't be welcome, there's no point in pushing it: The child, sensing correctly that he/she is not wanted, is likely to exceed your worst expectations. If, on the other hand, you know your child to be a reliable model of "company behavior," you might want to risk an unannounced arrival.

It's probably easier from the outset, though, to seek out places that like having kids around. Motels are always a safe bet (it's what they're designed for), and the descriptions provided here should give some indication of other likely spots. For a sure thing, see the list of "Family-Friendly Hotels & Restaurants" that accompanies each chapter. See also the Appendix, listing toll-free numbers of dozens of hotel and motel chains, a number of which have properties on the Cape.

A popular family option—but again, you must make plans as much as a year in advance—is to **rent a cottage** or house by the week, or even month. Each town's chamber of commerce can put you in touch with local Realtors, or contact the **Cape Cod and the Islands Board of Realtors,** 450 Station Ave., South Yarmouth, MA 02664 (☎ **508/394-2277**). Expect to pay anywhere from about $500 a week (for a small, inland cottage) to several thousand dollars—even tens of thousands!—for a seaside manse.

CAMPING INFORMATION   A number of state parks and recreation areas maintain campgrounds; for a full listing for the state, contact the **Department of Environmental Management,** Division of Forests and Parks (☎ **617/727-3180**).

The largest such area on the Cape is the 2,000-acre **Nickerson State Park** (☎ **508/896-3491**), offering over 400 campsites. The Massachusetts Audubon Society offers limited tenting at its 1,000-acre **Wellfleet Bay Wildlife Sanctuary** (☎ **508/349-2615**).

Note: Camping is expressly forbidden within the Cape Cod National Seashore (with the exception of a few "grandfathered" commercial campgrounds) and on Nantucket Island.

A partial list of private campgrounds that belong to the **Massachusetts Association of Campground Owners** appears in the Massachusetts Office of Travel and Tourism's free *Getaway Guide* (☎ **800/447-6277**), or request a full list (for a nominal charge) from **MOCA** (☎ **617/927-3180**).

FAST FACTS: The Cape & Islands

American Express   The **American Express Travel Service** office is at 1600 Falmouth Rd. in Centerville (☎ **800/221-7282** or 508/778-2310), and is open Monday through Wednesday and Friday from 9am to 5:30pm, Thursday from 9am to 8pm, and Saturday from 9am to 5pm.

Area Code   The telephone area code for the Cape and Islands is **508.** You must always dial this area code first unless you are making a call within the same town.

Business Hours   Business hours in public and private offices are usually Monday through Friday from 8 or 9am to 5pm. Most stores are open Monday through Saturday from 9:30 or 10am to 5:30 or 6pm; many are also open on Sunday from noon to 5pm—or earlier, now that Massachusetts's "blue laws" (intended to curb the sale of alcohol) have been relaxed. Virtually every town has some kind of convenience store carrying food, beverages, newspapers, and some household basics, and the larger communities have supermarkets, which generally stay open as late as 10 or 11pm.

Currency Exchange   See chapter 4.

Dentists   Dentists are listed in the Yellow Pages; among those welcoming emergencies is **Dr. William J. Scheier** of Orleans (☎ **508/255-2511**). Most hospitals will gladly provide referrals, or call ☎ **800/DENTIST.**

Doctors   For a referral, contact **Cape Medsource** at the Falmouth Hospital (☎ **800/243-7963** or 508/457-7963), **Ask-a-Nurse** at Cape Cod Hospital (☎ **800/544-2424**), or the **Physician Referral Service** at Massachusetts General

Hospital in Boston (☎ **617/726-5800**). Physicians and surgeons are also listed by specialty in the Yellow Pages.

Drugstores   All the larger towns have pharmacies that are open daily. The ones with the longest hours are likely to be located within a supermarket. A 24-hour CVS drugstore is scheduled to open soon in Hyannis. At present, there are no 24-hour drugstores, so in an emergency you'll have to contact a hospital.

Emergencies   Phone ☎ **911** for fire, police, emergency, or ambulance; be prepared to give your number, address, name, and a quick report. If you get into desperate straits—if, for example, your money is stolen and you need assistance arranging to get home—contact the **Travelers Aid** office in Boston (☎ **617/542-7286**).

Hospitals   The **Cape Cod Hospital** at 27 Park St., Hyannis (☎ **508/771-1800,** ext. 5235), offers 24-hour emergency medical service and consultation, as does the **Falmouth Hospital** at 100 Ter Heun Dr. (☎ **508/457-3524**). On the Islands, contact the **Martha's Vineyard Hospital** on Linton Lane in Oak Bluffs (☎ **508/693-0410**) or **Nantucket Cottage Hospital** on South Prospect Street (☎ **508/228-1200**).

Hot Lines   The **Poison Hot Line** is ☎ **800/682-9211; the Samaritans Suicide Prevention** line, ☎ **508/548-8900.** For a range of other hot lines related to social and health problems, see the front section of the local NYNEX phone book.

Information   See "Visitor Information" earlier in this chapter, and specific chapters for local information offices.

Liquor Laws   The legal drinking age in Massachusetts is 21. Bars are allowed to stay open until 1am every day, with "last call" at 12:30. Beer and wine are sold at grocery as well as package stores; hard liquor, at package stores only. No liquor can be sold on Sunday, though bars can serve drinks. A few towns on Martha's Vineyard are "dry" by choice or tradition (no alcohol can be sold or served), but at most establishments lacking a liquor license, you're welcome to bring your own wine or beer; if in doubt, call ahead.

Maps   Maps of the Cape and Islands are available from the **Cape Cod Chamber of Commerce,** Routes 6 and 132, Hyannis, MA 02601 (☎ **508/362-3225**); the **Martha's Vineyard Chamber of Commerce,** P.O. Box 1698, Beach Road, Vineyard Haven, MA 02568 (☎ **508/693-0085;** fax 508/696-0433; Web site www.mvy.com); and the **Nantucket Island Chamber of Commerce,** 48 Main St., Nantucket, MA 02554 (☎ **508/228-1700**). For maps of Massachusetts, contact the **Massachusetts Office of Travel and Tourism,** 100 Cambridge St., 13th Floor, Boston, MA 02202 (☎ **617/727-3201;** fax 617/727-6525).

Newspapers/Magazines   The *Cape Cod Times* is published daily, including Sunday, and runs regular supplements on arts and antiques, events and entertainment, and restaurants. Provincetown, Martha's Vineyard, and Nantucket each put out two weekly papers; all six offer insight into regional issues. *Cape Cod Life* is a glossy bimonthly that provides a sophisticated take on the area's cultural and scenic offerings. Each island has its own glossy as well, but they're not quite up to *CCL's* standards. *Provincetown Arts,* published yearly, is a must for those interested in local arts and letters. In addition, a great many summer-guide magazines are available (don't expect much novel information), and free booklets with discount coupons are ubiquitous; the nicest of these, with a friendly tone and a lot of useful information, is the *Cape Cod Guide.*

Overnight Delivery   For the location of the nearest **Federal Express** drop-off box, or to arrange a pickup, call ☎ **800/238-5355.**

Police   For police emergencies, call ☎ **911.**

Radio   Out of about a score of local AM and FM radio stations, two can be counted on for local color (in the "alternative album" mode): WOMR (91.9 FM) out of Provincetown and WMVY (92.7 FM) from Martha's Vineyard. The classical choice is WFCC (107.5 FM), which also features twice-daily birding reports. All three stations come in clearly on the Cape and Islands.

Safety   A great many people on the Cape and Islands still don't even lock their houses, let alone their cars. However, the idyll may not last long: real crime, from petty theft to rape, has made inroads everywhere, even on isolated Nantucket. So all your city smarts should apply. Do lock up, keep a close hold on purses and cameras (especially in restaurants: don't just sling them over a chair), and don't frequent deserted areas alone, even in broad daylight. For the most part, the natives' good faith is warranted.

Taxes   In Massachusetts the state sales tax is 5%. This tax applies to restaurant meals (but not food bought in stores) and all goods with the exception of clothing items priced lower than $175. The hotel tax varies from town to town; the maximum, including state tax, is 9.7%.

Taxis   See "Getting Around" earlier in this chapter.

Telephone   Local pay-phone calls cost a quarter, and "local" typically means a small radius; a call to the next town over could cost a dollar or more. Beware of "slamming" (the usurpation of phone services by a small, overpriced carrier): Whatever the label on the phone, use the 800 number on your calling card. The smaller inns and B&Bs may not have phones in the rooms, but generally provide a communal courtesy phone on which you can make local calls and charge long-distance. If you do have an in-room phone, check if there's a per-call surcharge—they can quickly add up.

Tides   If you have any question about the effect of the tides on beaches you plan to hike (they differ dramatically from town to town and could leave you stranded), check the tide chart in a local newspaper before heading out, or call to inquire (☎ 508/771-5522).

Transit Information   An ever-growing number of towns are providing free or low-cost shuttle services to reduce congestion. To find out if there's one that serves the place where you're planning to stay, contact the **Cape Cod Regional Transit Authority** (☎ 800/352-7155). On the Islands, the phone number for **Martha's Vineyard Transit Authority** is ☎ 508/627-7448 and for **Nantucket Regional Transit Authority** is ☎ 508/228-7025. The respective **chambers of commerce**— for Martha's Vineyard (☎ 508/693-0085) and Nantucket (☎ 508/228-1700)— can also provide maps and schedules for public transportation.

Weather   For the latest reports and forecasts, dial WQRC for the **Weather Line** (☎ 508/771-5522), available around the clock.

4 For Foreign Visitors

Even though American imagery has flooded international media for decades, foreign visitors are still apt to encounter unfamiliar customs and situations. Moreover, the Cape and Islands have their own special ways, distinct from those on the mainland.

In this chapter we'll try to prepare you for any differences you can expect from the way things may be done at home, and illuminate some of the more puzzling aspects of daily life.

1 Preparing for Your Trip

ENTRY REQUIREMENTS

DOCUMENT REGULATIONS **Canadian citizens** may enter the United States without visas; they need only proof of residence.

British subjects and citizens of **New Zealand, Japan, and most Western European countries** traveling on valid passports may not need a visa for fewer than 90 days of holiday or business travel to the United States, providing that they hold a round-trip or return ticket and enter the country on an airline or cruise line participating in the visa-waiver program.

Note: Citizens of these visa-exempt countries who first enter the United States may then visit Mexico, Canada, Bermuda, and/or the Caribbean islands and reenter the United States, by any mode of transportation, without needing a visa. Further information is available from any U.S. embassy or consulate.

Citizens of countries other than those stipulated above, including citizens of Australia, must have two documents: (1) a valid passport, with an expiration date of at least 6 months later than the scheduled end of the visit to the United States; and (2) a tourist visa, available without charge from the nearest U.S. consulate.

To obtain a visa, the traveler must submit a completed application form (either in person or by mail) with a 1¹/₂-inch-square photo and demonstrated binding ties to a residence abroad (which may include bank statements, home ownership/rental documents, and work and family declarations).

Usually you can obtain a visa at once or within 24 hours, but it may take longer during the summer rush from June to August. If you cannot go in person, contact the nearest U.S. embassy or consulate for directions on applying by mail. Your travel agent or airline office may also be able to provide you with visa applications and instructions. The U.S. consulate or embassy that issues your visa will determine whether you will be issued a multiple- or single-entry visa and any restrictions regarding the length of your stay.

MEDICAL REQUIREMENTS   No inoculations are needed to enter the United States unless you're coming from, or have stopped over in, areas known to be suffering from epidemics, especially cholera or yellow fever.

If you have a disease requiring treatment with medications containing narcotics or drugs requiring a syringe, carry a valid signed prescription from your physician to allay any suspicions that you're smuggling drugs.

CUSTOMS REQUIREMENTS   Every adult visitor may bring in free of duty: 1 liter (1.1 qt.) of wine or hard liquor; 200 cigarettes *or* 100 cigars (but no cigars from Cuba) *or* 3 pounds of smoking tobacco; and $100 worth of gifts. These exemptions are offered to travelers who spend at least 72 hours in the United States and who have not claimed them within the preceding 6 months. It's forbidden to bring into the country foodstuffs (particularly cheese, fruit, cooked meats, and canned goods) and plants (vegetables, seeds, tropical plants, and so on). Foreign tourists may bring in or take out up to $10,000 in U.S. or foreign currency with no formalities; larger sums must be declared to customs on entering or leaving the country.

INSURANCE

There is no national health-care system in the United States. Because the cost of medical care is extremely high, we strongly advise every traveler to secure health-insurance coverage before setting out. You may want to take out a comprehensive travel insurance policy that covers (for a relatively low premium) sickness or injury costs (medical, surgical, and hospital); loss or theft of your baggage; trip-cancellation costs; guarantee of bail in case of arrest; and costs associated with accident, repatriation, or death. Such packages (for example, "Europe Assistance" in Europe) are sold by automobile clubs at attractive rates, as well as by insurance companies and travel agencies.

MONEY

CURRENCY & EXCHANGE   The U.S. monetary system has a decimal base: one American **dollar ($1)** = one hundred **cents (100¢)**.

Dollar bills come in denominations of $1 ("a buck"), $2 (these are rare), $5, $10, $20, $50, and $100. However, you'll find few establishments willing to make change for anything over a $20 bill, for fear of counterfeits. If you're carrying larger bills, stop in at any bank to change them.

There are six denominations of coins: 1¢ (one cent, also known as a "penny"), 5¢ (five cents, or a "nickel"), 10¢ (10 cents, or a "dime"), 25¢ (25 cents, or a "quarter"), 50¢ (50 cents, or a "half-dollar"), and $1 (one dollar, sometimes called a "silver dollar"). The last two are rarely circulated, however, so you'll probably be dealing exclusively with the smaller coins.

Opportunities to exchange money used to be confined to Logan Airport and the larger Boston banks. Because of the preponderance of tourists, however, several Cape and Island banks (see "Currency Exchange," in "Fast Facts," below) now offer the service, and some major attractions have followed suit. If you'd rather not fritter away precious vacation time waiting in line at a bank, however, you'd be better off acquiring U.S. currency back home, if possible, or bringing traveler's checks denominated in U.S. dollars (no other kind is likely to be honored).

TRAVELER'S CHECKS   **American Express** traveler's checks are accepted virtually everywhere, but always ask before you sign. The commission, when you purchase them, usually runs about 1%. No commission is charged by **Thomas Cook Currency Services,** which maintains offices in many major cities throughout the world, including Boston (☎ **800/287-7362** or 508/267-5364); smaller establishments may be unwilling to accept these, but you should have no trouble at a bank. Make sure you only carry traveler's checks that are denominated in dollars.

CREDIT CARDS   Credit cards are by far the most popular method of payment among American travelers. The most widely accepted cards are MasterCard (Eurocard in Europe, Access in Great Britain, Chargex in Canada), Visa (Barclaycard in Britain), followed by American Express and Diners Club or Carte Blanche, and, more recently, Discover. Typically, only the most casual of restaurants and smallest of shops operate on a cash-only basis; usually you'll see a credit-card sticker on the door or window, but if in doubt, ask before you order or load up. Under Massachusetts law, vendors are allowed to request and view an additional form of identification (such as a driver's license or passport), but—to prevent credit-card fraud—they are forbidden to request or record any numbers, including your phone number. Again, explaining and insisting on this little-known law may be more trouble than it's worth.

A credit card is a must if you plan to **rent a car** or **boat or sporting equipment:** Rental companies will want to keep a blank imprint as a deposit. The larger hotels may also require an imprint for incidentals such as phone calls.

Credit cards can be used to obtain a "cash advance" (*caution:* fees are steep, since the interest starts compounding instantly), and many are now linked to international networks such as Cirrus and PLUS. If your Personal Identification Number (PIN) is compatible with the system in the United States (ask before you leave), you'll be able to pick up cash at any network ATM (automated teller machine). Accessible 24 hours, ATMs can be found at most banks and some supermarkets in the larger towns.

SAFETY

GENERAL   Tourist areas are generally safe, and the Cape and Islands are safer than most. Although a number of towns, particularly the larger ones, suffer their share of crime (much of it drug- and alcohol-related), there's no such thing as a "bad neighborhood" here, per se. However, with crime on the increase everywhere, you need to stay alert and take the usual precautions. Avoid carrying valuables with you on the street or at the beach, and be discreet with expensive cameras and electronic equipment. When milling in crowds (in Hyannis or Provincetown, for example), place your billfold in an inside pocket, and hang onto your purse; anything kept in a backpack should be buried beyond reach. In closely packed places, such as restaurants, theaters, and ferries, keep your possessions in sight, and never sling a bag over the back of your chair: It's too easy a target. Alas, anything left visible in a car, locked or unlocked, is an open invitation, even in secluded Nantucket.

It would be rare in this region to find security staff screening all those who enter a hotel, especially if there's a restaurant on the premises, so don't relax your guard until your door is securely locked. Many areas are still so countrified that homeowners don't even lock their doors, and you'll find that most B&Bs are fairly laissez-faire; a few lack bedroom door locks altogether. If you're traveling light, it shouldn't matter, but if you're the cautious type, inquire about security measures before setting out.

Women, unfortunately, are no more safe here than anywhere else, so avoid visiting deserted areas alone, even during the day. Despite its reputation for tolerance, Provincetown has experienced sporadic incidents of **gay-bashing;** safety in numbers is probably the watchword here. Hyannis can get a bit rowdy when its dance clubs are in full swing, and even more so when they let out. For the most part, though, this is a peaceful place, more like the 1950s than the 1990s, and as long as you keep your wits about you, you should be able to relax, relatively speaking.

DRIVING Though Massachusetts is quite strict, drunk driving is a definite hazard: The police logs are full of offenses, from foolish to fatal. The best tactic is to avoid the offenders as much as possible, primarily by staying off the roads late at night. It's probably not a good idea to cover long distances at night, in any case, since there are no 24-hour gas stations to help out in case of emergency. In the event of a breakdown, drivers are usually advised to stay in the car with the doors locked until the police arrive. This is a small and friendly enough place, though, that it would probably be all right to take a chance on the kindness of strangers. Use your judgment, and err, if at all, on the side of caution.

Carjacking has yet to make an appearance on the Cape, but car theft runs high in Massachusetts as a whole, so lock your doors faithfully, even if the natives never bother.

2 Getting To & Around the Cape & Islands

Travelers from overseas can take advantage of the APEX (advance-purchase excursion) fares offered by all the major U.S. and European carriers. Aside from these, attractive values are offered by Virgin Atlantic from London to Boston and New York.

A number of U.S. airlines offer service from Europe to the United States. If they do not have direct flights from Europe to Boston's Logan Airport (the closest international airport to the Cape and Islands), they can book you straight through on a connecting flight. You can make reservations by calling one of the following numbers in London: **American** (☎ 0181/572-5555), **Continental** (☎ 4412/9377-6464), **Delta** (☎ 0800/414-767), or **United** (☎ 0181/990-9900).

Logan Airport is served by more than 40 carriers, including **British Airways** (☎ 081/897-4000 in the U.K.) and **Air Canada** (☎ 800/776-3000). Any airline not served by this airport—the 15th-busiest in the world—is likely to fly into New York, only a 30-minute commuter flight away.

The visitor arriving by air, no matter what the port of entry, should cultivate patience and resignation before setting foot on U.S. soil. Getting **through immigration control** may take as long as 2 hours on some days, especially summer weekends, so have this guidebook or something else to read handy. Add the time it takes to clear customs and you will see that you should make a very generous allowance for delay in planning connections between international and domestic flights—figure on 2 to 3 hours at least.

In contrast, for the traveler arriving by car or by rail from Canada, the border-crossing formalities have been streamlined to the vanishing point. And for the traveler by air from Canada, Bermuda, and some places in the Caribbean, you can sometimes go through Customs and Immigration at the point of departure, which is much quicker.

On transatlantic or transpacific flights, some large U.S. airlines offer **special discount tickets** for any of their U.S. destinations (American Airlines' Visit USA program and Delta's Discover America program, for example). The tickets or coupons are not on sale in the United States and must be purchased before you leave your point of departure. This system is the best, easiest, and fastest way to see the United States at low cost. You should obtain information well in advance from your travel agent or the office of the airline concerned, since the conditions attached to these discount tickets can be changed without advance notice.

International visitors can also buy a **USA Railpass,** good for 15 or 30 days of unlimited travel on Amtrak. The pass is available through many foreign travel agents. Prices in 1997 for a 15-day pass were $260 off-peak, $375 peak; a 30-day pass costs $350 off-peak, $480 peak (off-peak is September to December). (With a foreign passport, you can also buy passes at some Amtrak offices in the United States including locations in San Francisco, Los Angeles, Chicago, New York, Miami, Boston, and Washington, D.C.) Reservations are generally required and should be made for each part of your trip as early as possible.

Visitors should also be aware of the limitations of long-distance rail travel in the United States. With a few notable exceptions, service is rarely up to European standards: Delays are common, routes are limited and often infrequently served, and fares are rarely significantly lower than discount airfares. Thus, cross-country train travel should be approached with caution.

The cheapest way to travel the United States is by **bus. Greyhound/Trailways** (☎ **800/231-2222**), the sole nationwide bus line, offers an Ameripass for unlimited travel for 7 days (for $199), 15 days (for $299), 30 days (for $409), and 60 days (for $599). Bus travel in the United States can be both slow and uncomfortable, so this option is not for everyone. In addition, bus stations are often located in undesirable neighborhoods.

See the "Getting There" and "Getting Around" sections of chapter 3 for more information on getting from Logan Airport to the Cape and Islands and other transportation questions.

FAST FACTS: For the Foreign Traveler

Automobile Organizations Auto clubs will supply maps, suggested routes, guidebooks, accident and bail-bond insurance, and emergency road service. The major auto club in the United States, with roughly 1,000 offices nationwide, is the American Automobile Association (AAA). Members of some foreign auto clubs have reciprocal arrangements with the AAA and enjoy its services at no charge. If you belong to an auto club in your home country, inquire about AAA reciprocity before you leave. You may be able to join the AAA even if you're not a member of a reciprocal club; to inquire, call the **AAA** (☎ **800/222-8252**).

In addition, some automobile-rental agencies now provide many of these same services. Inquire about their availability when you rent your car.

Automobile Rentals To rent a car, you need a major credit card and a valid driver's license. Minimum age requirements range from 19 to 25; drivers under 25 may be subject to a daily surcharge. Loss Damage Waiver (LDW) protection is sold separately, but check with your credit-card or insurance company before paying the surcharge; you may already be covered. Be sure to return your car with a full tank, since most rental companies routinely overcharge for gasoline. Most of the major car-rental companies are represented on the Cape and Islands (see "Getting Around" in chapter 3).

Business Hours Banks are typically open weekdays from 9am to 3 or 4pm, and there's 24-hour access to the automated teller machines (ATMs) at most banks and other outlets. Generally, offices are open weekdays from 9am to 5pm. Most stores are open 7 days a week and late into the evening in season. See "Business Hours" in "Fast Facts: The Cape & Islands," in chapter 3.

Climate See "When to Go: Climate & Events," in chapter 3.

Currency Exchange With many extensive banking chains, such as the **BankBoston** (☎ 800/788-5000) and **Cape Cod Bank and Trust** (☎ 800/458-5100), now offering exchange services for virtually all foreign currencies, you can wander without fear of running out of cash. To get started, you might want to get some pocket money at the currency-exchange booths at Logan Airport.

Drinking Laws See "Liquor Laws" in "Fast Facts: The Cape & Islands," in chapter 3.

Electricity The United States uses 110 to 120 volts AC, 60 cycles, compared to 220 to 240 volts AC, 50 cycles, as in most of Europe. In addition to a 100-volt transformer, small appliances of non-American manufacture, such as hair dryers and shavers, will require a plug adapter, with two flat, parallel pins.

Embassies and Consulates All embassies are located in Washington, D.C.; some consulates are located in major U.S. cities, and most nations have a mission to the United Nations in New York City. There are no consulates on the Cape or Islands; however, Boston boasts 3 dozen. There is no consular representation in Massachusetts for **New Zealand,** but there are **British** and **Canadian** consulates in Boston (see below).

The **embassy of Australia** is at 1601 Massachusetts Ave. NW, Washington, DC 20036 (☎ **202/797-3000**). There is a consulate at 20 Beacon St., Boston, MA 02108 (☎ 617/248-8655).

The **embassy of Canada** is at 501 Pennsylvania Ave. NW, Washington, DC 20001 (☎ **202/682-1740**). There's a consulate at Copley Place, Boston, MA 02116 (☎ 617/262-3760).

The **embassy of Ireland** is at 2234 Massachusetts Ave. NW, Washington, DC 20008 (☎ **202/462-3939**). There's a consulate at 535 Boylston St., Boston, MA 02116 (☎ 617/267-9330).

The **embassy of New Zealand** is at 37 Observatory Circle NW, Washington, DC 20008 (☎ **202/328-4800**).

The **embassy of Great Britain** is at 3100 Massachusetts Ave. NW, Washington, DC 20008 (☎ **202/462-1340**). There's a consulate at 600 Atlantic Ave., Boston, MA 02110 (☎ **617/248-9555**).

For information on other consulates, call **information** (☎ 411 within Boston, or 617/555-1212 outside of Boston), or consult the "Blue Pages" of the Boston phone book.

Emergencies Call ☎ 911 to report a fire, contact the police, or get an ambulance. This is a toll-free call (no coins are required at a public telephone).

If you encounter serious problems while traveling, call the **Travelers Aid Society of Boston** (☎ 617/542-7286), part of a nationwide, nonprofit, social-service organization dedicated to helping travelers in difficult straits. Services might include reuniting families inadvertently separated while traveling; providing food and/or shelter to people temporarily stranded without cash; and even emotional counseling. The society maintains offices at terminals A and E at Logan Airport, and an information booth at South Station. Though there are no offices on the Cape, give them a call if you need help.

Gasoline (Petrol) One U.S. gallon equals 3.8 liters or .85 Imperial gallons. There are usually several grades (and price levels) of gasoline available at most gas stations, and the names change from company to company. The unleaded ones with the highest octane rating are among the most expensive and probably unnecessary (most rental cars take the least expensive "regular" unleaded gas). Leaded gas is even less expensive but has been virtually phased out: Make sure you get unleaded, for your car's sake, as well as the environment's. Note that the price is often lower if you pay in cash instead of by credit card. Also, most gas stations now offer lower-priced self-service gas pumps—in fact, some gas stations, particularly at night, are entirely self-service.

Holidays   On the following legal national holidays, banks, government offices, and post offices are closed (stores, restaurants, and museums may be as well): January 1 (New Year's Day), the 3rd Monday in January (Martin Luther King Day), the 3rd Monday in February (Presidents' Day), the last Monday in May (Memorial Day), July 4 (Independence Day), the 1st Monday in September (Labor Day), the 2nd Monday in October (Columbus Day), November 11 (Veterans Day), the 4th Thursday in November (Thanksgiving), and December 25 (Christmas). Massachusetts institutions also observe Patriots' Day on the 3rd Monday in April, and Boston's municipal offices may be closed for Evacuation Day (March 17) and Bunker Hill Day (June 17). Also, in presidential election years (1996, 2000, and so on), the Tuesday following the 1st Monday in November is Election Day, a national legal holiday.

Legal Aid   It is the rare foreign tourist who will have any dealings with the American legal system. If you are stopped for a minor infraction (such as driving over the speed limit), never attempt to negotiate directly with the police officer: You could end up charged with the much more serious offense of attempted bribery. The ticket you receive will include instructions on how to pay the fine by mail or to the local Clerk of the Court. Should you be detained on a more serious matter, it's best to offer no resistance and to say nothing before consulting a lawyer. Under U.S. law, anyone under arrest has specific rights, including the right to remain silent (so as to avert possibly self-incriminating remarks). You also have the right to make one phone call, to whomever you choose: In most instances, your first call should be to your consulate or embassy.

In less urgent situations, you may wish to consult the **Legal Aid hot line** (☎ **800/742-4107**).

Mail   If you'd like your mail to follow you on your vacation but aren't sure what your address will be, arrange to have it sent in your name c/o General Delivery at the post office of a town you expect to stay in or pass through; be sure to include the five-digit zip code after the state abbreviation (MA). You'll have to pick up your mail in person and provide an ID, preferably with a photo (a driver's license or passport, for example). There is no charge for this service.

Mailboxes are not as ubiquitous on the Cape and Islands as they are in the city, so you may have to go to the post office in any case to send your own mail—or give it to your innkeeper for inclusion with theirs. The domestic postage rates are currently 20¢ for a postcard and 32¢ for a letter; again, be sure to include the zip code to speed delivery. Overseas rates vary, so ask your innkeeper or inquire at the post office.

The post office offers express mail, or you might use a commercial service such as **Federal Express** (call ☎ **800/238-5355** to arrange for a pickup, at a slight surcharge, or to find out the location of the nearest drop-off box). Credit cards can be used as payment. To be delivered to you, FedEx packages must be labeled with your full address, including zip code, and telephone number.

Newspapers and Magazines   Distributed throughout New England, the *Boston Globe* (owned by the *New York Times*) does an excellent job of reporting international as well as domestic news. For local periodicals offering events listings and coverage of regional issues, see "Newspapers/Magazines" in "Fast Facts: The Cape & Islands," in chapter 3.

Radio and Television Audiovisual media, with four coast-to-coast networks (ABC, CBS, NBC, and Fox), joined by the Public Broadcasting System (PBS) and local channels on UHF, offer a choice of about a dozen channels, and cable ups the choice to dozens more. Because broadcast reception tends to be poor on the Cape and nonexistent on the Islands, most establishments subscribe to cable, including, quite often, "premium channels" such as HBO. Only the more luxurious smaller inns provide TVs in the rooms; most have a set in the sitting room. Many hotels and motels provide in-room cable, both basic and premium, as well as the option of pay-per-view movies. Most lodgings come with a clock radio. You'll find a wide choice of national and local radio stations offering various kinds of talk shows and music, from classical and "country" to jazz and rock. News and weather updates are usually broadcast on the hour, and all but certain educational stations are punctuated by frequent commercials. For local favorites, see "Radio" in "Fast Facts: The Cape & Islands," in chapter 3.

Safety See "Safety," under "Preparing for Your Trip," above.

Taxes In the United States there is no VAT (value-added tax) or other indirect tax at a national level. Every state, and each city in it, has the right to level its own local tax on all purchases. In Massachusetts, the statewide sales tax, with certain exceptions, is 5%. For further details, see "Taxes" in "Fast Facts: The Cape & Islands," in chapter 3.

Telephone, Telegraph, Telex, Fax, and E-Mail The telephone system in the United States is run by private corporations, so rates, especially for long-distance service and operator-assisted calls, can vary widely—even on calls made from public telephones. Local calls in Massachusetts usually cost 25¢.

Hotel surcharges on long-distance and even local calls can be steep (often $1 per call); they should be posted on the phone, and if not, ask the hotel operator before calling around. You're usually better off using a public pay telephone: There should be one in the lobby, and you'll find them in most restaurants and gas stations as well. Outdoor pay phones usually consist of a glass booth, or a waist-level console.

Most long-distance and **international calls** can be dialed directly from any phone. For calls to Canada and other parts of the United States, dial 1 followed by the area code and the seven-digit number. For international calls, dial 011 followed by the country code, city code, and the telephone number.

Note that all calls to area code 800 or 888 are **toll free.** However, calls to numbers with the area codes 700 and 900—commercial lines that reverse the charges—can be very expensive (several dollars or more per minute), and they may exact a minimum charge of $15 or more.

For **reversed-charge or collect calls,** and for **person-to-person calls,** dial 0 (zero, not the letter O) followed by the area code and number; an operator will come on the line to assist you, and you should specify the particular type(s) of service you want. To make an international call, ask for an overseas operator.

For **local directory assistance** ("Information"), dial **411;** for long-distance information, dial 1, then the appropriate area code and ☎ **555-1212.**

Like the telephone system, **telegraph and telex services** are provided by private corporations, such as ITT, MCI, and, most importantly, **Western Union.** You can dictate your message over the phone (☎ **800/325-6000**) or inquire about local offices where you can both send and receive messages as well as money (note, however, that the service charges for wiring money may run as high as 15% to 20% of the total). There are 15 Western Union offices on the Cape and two on each of the Islands.

Most of the larger hotels offer **fax service,** but the fee is usually quite high. Copy shops often offer fax service, as do packing services such as Mail Boxes, Etc., which has four offices on the Cape.

Of course, if you've got a laptop with a modem and phone jack, you can send and receive your own, or access the Internet to send E-mail. The largest on-line service is **America Online** (☎ 800/827-3338), which now also owns **CompuServe** (☎ 800/848-8990). If you're really in a bind, some of the more obliging innkeepers may even fax or E-mail for you, for free.

Telephone Directory   Telephone directories for the Cape and Islands combine several types of listings. Inside the front cover are emergency numbers, followed by community service listings, dialing instructions, and information on rates. The White Pages, which lists subscribers in alphabetical order, are in some cases divided between private and business users (the latter appear grouped at the end, with a dark border). At the back of the book, the Yellow Pages lists businesses by categories, such as automobile repairs, drugstores (pharmacies), restaurants, bookstores, and places of worship. In addition, the NYNEX directories that cover this region also include a supplement offering useful tourist information and discount coupons.

Time   The United States (with the exception of Alaska and Hawaii) falls into four time zones: eastern standard (EST), central standard (CST), mountain standard (MST), and Pacific standard (PST). All of Massachusetts (like New England as a whole) observes eastern standard time, which runs, for example, 5 hours behind London time, or 3 hours ahead of Los Angeles. Daylight saving time, when clocks are set forward an hour, remains in effect from the 1st Sunday in April to the last Sunday in October.

Tipping   Except in cases of exceptionally neglectful or downright rude service, tipping restaurant servers is not so much an option as an expectation (some would say, obligation). The wait staff, as a rule, receives less than the minimum hourly wage, with the assumption that tips will make up the difference. In a seasonal economy such as that prevailing on the Cape and Islands, workers may need to make enough in 3 or 4 months to get through the winter, when the job market all but disappears. Only a handful of restaurants and hotels apply an across-the-board gratuity of 15% (check your bill to see if the gratuity has already been included). That amount is standard, however, for adequate service, and if you have substantial complaints, it would be far better to take it up with the management than take it out on the servers, who have little control, for example, over the pacing of a meal. For especially friendly or helpful service, go to 20% or more of the pretax total, including beverages. A bartender should be tipped at the same rate. As a rule, maitre d's, hostesses, and sommeliers do not expect a separate tip; they'll usually get a share of the total. A tip of $1 per vehicle for valet parking, or $1 per garment for coat-checking (a rarity here), is appreciated. No tipping is expected in self-service or fast-food restaurants, though college-bound employees may leave a cup beside the cash register to collect contributions.

In hotels tip the bellhops $1 per piece (the same goes for redcaps at airports and railroad stations) and leave the housekeeping staff $1 to $2 per night. Cab drivers typically receive 15% of the fare; hairdressers and barbers, 15% to 20% of the bill. Tipping movie and theater ushers or gas-station attendants is not expected.

The Upper Cape: Sandwich, Bourne, Falmouth & Mashpee

5

Just over an hour from Boston by car, Sandwich and the surrounding Upper Cape towns have become bedroom as well as summer communities. They may not have the let-the-good-times-roll feel of towns farther east, but then again they're spared the transient qualities that come with seasonal flows. Shops and restaurants—many catering to an older, affluent crowd—tend to stay open year-round.

The four upper Cape towns are all quite different. Bourne straddles the canal; a couple of its villages (Bournedale and Buzzards Bay) are on the mainland side, and the others (Cataumet, Pocasset, Monument Beach, and Sagamore) are on the Cape side. The Canal provides this area with most of its recreational opportunities: biking, fishing, canal cruises, and the herring run. Cataumet is perhaps the prettiest village in Bourne, while many of Bourne's businesses, including popular factory outlets, are on the mainland side of the bridge in Buzzards Bay.

Sandwich, the oldest town on the Cape, has a lovely historic village, with lots of unique shops and charming inns, at its core. Still, the town is primarily a pastoral place, with several working farms; in East Sandwich, miles of conservation land lead out to Sandy Neck, a barrier beach extending into Barnstable. The Old King's Highway winds its way through Sandwich past a number of fine gift shops, galleries, and specialty stores.

Falmouth, the site of Cape Cod's first summer colony, is one of the larger towns on the Cape; it has a sizable year-round population. Main Street—with a number of high-end boutiques and galleries, in addition to the usual touristy T-shirt shops—offers prime strolling and shopping. Falmouth's village green is quintessential New England, with two imposing historic churches: St. Barnabas, a sturdy reddish stone with climbing moss, and the First Congregational, a white clapboard, steepled church boasting a Paul Revere bell. Just north of Falmouth center, along Route 28A, lies West Falmouth, perhaps the most attractive of Falmouth's eight villages; it has several good antique stores, a fine general store, and a picture-perfect little harbor.

The college crowd gravitates to the beach at Falmouth Heights, a bluff covered with grand, shingled Victorians built during the first wave of touristic fever in the late 1800s. Visitors bound for Martha's Vineyard tend to blow through the village of Woods Hole without so much as a look around. Actually, Woods Hole may be the most highbrow village on the Cape. Home at any given time to several thousand research scientists, it has a certain neobohemian panache, lively bars, and an air of vigorous intellectual inquiry.

Mashpee is the ancestral home of the Cape's Native American tribe, the Wampanoags. Much of the town's coastline is occupied by a huge resort called New Seabury, while inland, the Mashpee National Wildlife Refuge sponsors frequent walking tours through its thousands of woodland acres.

1 Sandwich

3 miles (5km) E of Sagamore, 16 miles (26km) NW of Hyannis

The oldest town in this corner of the Cape (it was founded in 1637 by a contingent of Puritans who even then considered the environs north of Boston a mite crowded), Sandwich embodies quaintness. A 1640 gristmill stands at the mouth of a quiet pond frequented by swans, geese, ducks, and canoeists, while two early-19th-century churches and the columned Greek Revival Town Hall, in service since 1834, preside over the town square—which is more of a triangle, really.

There's a feeling of stability and solidity to this community, and the natural attractions that drew people here still hold sway. Towering trees have grown back in the century or so since their predecessors fueled Sandwich's boomtown days, when it supported the nation's first glass factories, as well as the production of stagecoaches, prairie schooners, and railroad cars. The salt marsh may no longer be so useful as livestock fodder, but it makes for lovely views.

Sandwich still feels very much like a village. Many early dwellings have been left intact; several are now inns. Sleeping in their beds, retracing their footsteps—it's not so difficult to imagine the town's original denizens going about their industrious daily lives.

On the whole, the pleasures that this region offers tend to be considerably quieter and more refined than the thrills offered elsewhere on the Cape; hence it tends to attract a more sedate, settled crowd. Sandwich is fortunate to have two very well-endowed museums—the **Heritage Plantation** and the **Sandwich Glass Museum**—as well as several quirkier sites and a plethora of historic homesteads. New England antique-lust can be satisfied at the many excellent antique shops in the area. Older visitors, as well as young children, will find plenty to intrigue them. Those in-between, however, may get restless and yearn for livelier climes.

ESSENTIALS

GETTING THERE   If you're driving, turn east on Route 6A toward Sandwich after crossing either the Bourne or Sagamore bridge. You can also fly into Hyannis (see "Getting There," in chapter 3).

VISITOR INFORMATION   Contact the **Cape Cod Chamber of Commerce,** Routes 6 and 132, Hyannis, MA 02601 (☎ 508/362-3225; fax 508/362-3698; Web site www.capecod.com) or stop in at the **Cape Cod Chamber of Commerce Information Center** (seasonal) at the Sagamore Bridge rotary. The **Cape Cod Canal Region Chamber of Commerce,** Main Street, Buzzards Bay (☎ 508/759-6000), can provide literature on both Sandwich and Bourne. A consortium of Sandwich businesses has put together an excellent walking guide (with map). For a copy, contact the **Summer House** inn at ☎ 508/888-4991 (see "Where to Stay," below).

A GET-ACQUAINTED STROLL

This walk starts at the Sandwich Glass Museum, ends at the Dunbar Tea Shop, and takes 2 to 4 hours, depending on stops covered; you'll cover about 1¼ miles. Your

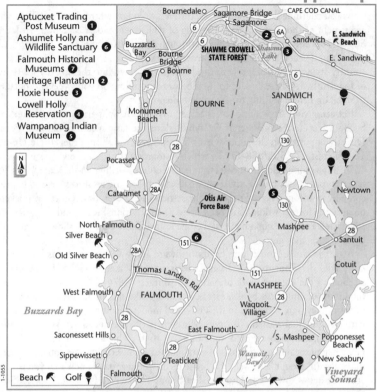

Aptucxet Trading Post Museum ❶
Ashumet Holly and Wildlife Sanctuary ❻
Falmouth Historical Museums ❼
Heritage Plantation ❷
Hoxie House ❸
Lowell Holly Reservation ❹
Wampanoag Indian Museum ❺

Beach 🏖 Golf ⛳

best bet is to set forth on any midsummer day except Sunday, when some spots are closed, between 10am and 4pm.

You may park (free with admission) at the **Sandwich Glass Museum,** 129 Main St. (☎ **508/888-0251**), a repository of the town's 19th-century artisanry and history. When you've had an eyeful, cross the street to **H. Richard Strand Antiques,** 2 Grove St. (☎ **508/888-3230**), where you can find similar artifacts for sale, beautifully arranged in salonlike settings.

Further down Grove Street is **Old Cemetery Point,** overlooking peaceful Shawme Pond, about one-third of a mile down the road. Read the admonitory headstones and keep an eye out for box turtles. Head back through the center of town and observe **Old Town Hall,** on Main Street (☎ **508/888-4910**)—a magnificent Greek Revival edifice, complete with Doric columns. It is still the town hall today. Continue down Main Street, past the **First Church of Christ,** a towering collage of circles and straight edges, topped by an inspiring spire. Built by a colleague of renowned Boston architect Charles Bulfinch in 1847, it was reportedly modeled on Sir Christopher Wren's St. Mary-le-Bow, in London. The next church you'll pass, to your left, is an 1833 meetinghouse, which has been converted into the **Yesteryears Doll Museum** (☎ **508/888-1711;** closed November to mid-May), a nonpareil collection of poppets dating as far back as the 17th century. Depending on your degree of interest, and the memories the creatures may inspire, give yourself about an hour to take it all in. Though the presentation—display cases propped atop church pews—is not exactly state-of-the-art, somehow it contributes to the evocative atmosphere.

As you continue down Main Street, turn left onto Jarves Street, and you'll pass an assortment of shops, the most interesting of which is **Madden & Co.,** at 16 Jarves St. (☎ **508/888-3663;** closed January through April), an upscale emporium of decorative and delectable delights. The interior-design stock is a mix of sophisticated country-style accessories and whimsical antiques; thrown into the mix is a scattering of foodstuffs. It's a great place to shop before descending on your weekend host, or to stock up before heading to your own hideaway.

Retracing your steps along Jarves Street, make a left-right zigzag along Main and School streets to reach Water Street, which skirts the eastern edge of Shawme Pond. Directly opposite, on the shore side of Water Street, you'll spot the **Hoxie House,** 18 Water St. (☎ **508/888-1173**), which restoration specialists now date at around 1675 (it was long held, erroneously, to be the oldest dwelling on the Cape). The interior is spare—not out of any aesthetic ideal, but because resources were so hard to come by in colonial New England. The settlers didn't even have closets or pockets, because the former would have been taxed as an additional room and the latter was considered a waste of good material. Let the knowledgeable docents show you around, explaining as they go.

After the Hoxie House tour, head northward along Water Street, passing (on the same side) the **Thornton W. Burgess Museum,** 4 Water St. (☎ **508/888-4668**), celebrating the life and work of native son Burgess (1874–1965), a highly successful author of children's books. His books may strike the modern ear as rather fustian, but they were a big deal in their day, and modern children tend to react to them with delight. Just past the Burgess Museum is the **Dexter Grist Mill** (☎ **508/888-1173**), a lovingly restored water mill (ca. 1640). The millstones still grind corn; buy a bag of meal to go, but only if you'll have a chance to whip up something later in the day (it doesn't keep well). Or pause to allay hunger pangs, now that you're back at the center of town. The **Dunbar Tea Shop,** 1 Water St. (☎ **508/833-2485**), is the genuine article, operated by a couple of British expats. Mary Bell oversees the kitchen and Victoriana-heavy shop; Mike attends to the antiques, including vintage books. It's a wonderful place to while away a good portion of the afternoon, and if you're so inclined, you could even sleep over: The adjoining Dunbar House operates as a B&B.

SANDWICH HISTORICAL SIGHTS

Dexter Grist Mill. Water St. (on Shawme Pond, near Main St.). ☎ **508/888-1173.** Admission $1.50 adults, 75¢ children 6–12; $2.50 combination ticket available from the Hoxie House (see below). Mid-June to mid-Sept daily 10am–4:45pm. Closed mid-Sept to mid-June.

This charmingly weathered building has survived some $3^1/2$ centuries and at least as many lives. At present it's serving its original purpose, grinding corn with turbine power; you can watch the wooden gears in action and buy a bag to take home and cook up into colonial "jonnycakes" (short for "cakes for the journey") or trendy polenta. During the glassmaking boom of the 1800s, this venerable mill was but one of many pressed into service to keep the factory workers well fed. When the laborers dispersed, the mill sat useless, until a local entrepreneur thought to convert it into a tearoom to serve the new tide of tourists arriving by motorcar. The mill was fully restored in 1961 and will probably be good for a few more centuries of stalwart service.

✪ **Heritage Plantation of Sandwich.** Grove and Pine sts. (about $1/2$ SW of town center). ☎ **508/888-3300.** Admission $8 adults, $7 senior citizens, $4 children 6–18. Mid-May to mid-Oct daily 10am–5pm; no tickets sold after 4:15pm. Closed Nov to mid-May.

This is one of those rare museums equally appealing to adults and the children they drag along: The latter will leave clamoring for another visit. All ages have the run of

76 beautifully landscaped acres, crisscrossed with walking paths and riotous with color in late spring, when the towering rhododendrons burst forth in blooms that range from soft pink to gaudy orange. Scattered buildings house a wide variety of collections, from Native American artifacts to Early American weapons. The art holdings, especially the primitive portraits, are outstanding. The high point for most children will be a ride on the 1912 carousel (safely preserved indoors), where the mounts are not horses but a menagerie of fancifully carved animals. Also sure to dazzle is the replica Shaker round barn packed with gleaming antique automobiles, including some once owned by celebrities (don't miss Gary Cooper's gleaming Duesenberg). These motorcars were massive and a thing of enduring beauty. Next-door is the Carousel Cafe, good for a restorative snack (try a cranberry cookie); the gift shop at the gatehouse is also worth checking out. Call ahead for a schedule of outdoor summer concerts, free with admission.

Hoxie House. 18 Water St. (on Shawme Pond, about ¹/₄ mile S of town center). ☎ **508/ 888-1173.** Admission $1.50 adults, 75¢ children 12–16, free for children under 12. Mid-June to mid-Oct Mon–Sat 10am–5pm, Sun 1–5pm. Closed mid-Oct to mid-June.

A lapsed contender for the title of the Cape's oldest house (a couple of privately owned Provincetown houses appear to have a stronger claim), this saltbox (ca. 1675) is nonetheless a noteworthy beauty, with its diamond-pane windows and broad interior planking—made of "king's wood," so-called because England's king had, under pain of severe penalty, reserved the larger trees for his warships. The house was occupied, pretty much as is, with neither electricity nor plumbing, into the 1950s, which explains how it remained so remarkably intact. Even so, it had to be taken apart and reassembled to serve as the model colonial home you see today. Fortunately, restorers opted not for the cluttered "colonial revival" look but a stark austerity that's much more historically accurate and shows off to advantage a handful of antiques on semipermanent loan from Boston's Museum of Fine Arts.

✪ **Sandwich Glass Museum.** 129 Main St. (in the center of town). ☎ **508/888-0251.** Admission $3.50 adults, $1 children 6–12. Apr–Oct daily 9:30am–4:30pm; Feb–Mar and Nov–Dec Wed–Sun 9:30am–4pm. Closed Jan.

Even if you don't consider yourself a glass fan, make an exception for this fascinating museum, which captures the history of the town above and beyond its legendary industry. A brief video introduces Deming Jarves's brilliant endeavor, which flourished from 1828 to 1888, bringing glassware—a hitherto rare commodity available only to the rich—within reach of the middle classes. Jarves picked the perfect spot, surrounded by old-growth forest, to fuel the furnaces (the greenery has only recently recovered), with a harbor handy for shipping in fine sand from farther up the coast and salt-marsh hay with which to pack outgoing orders. Demand was such that Jarves imported hordes of immigrant workers, housing them in the rather shameful shanties of "Jarvestown." All went well (for him) until Midwestern factories started using coal; unable to keep up with their level of mass production, he switched back to handblown techniques just as his workforce was ready to revolt.

Impressions

Except for Ranch houses, Garrison houses and other obvious productions of the 1900s, all houses on Cape Cod are at least two hundred and fifty years old, and about one third of them are the oldest house in town.

—Clair Baisley, *Cape Cod Architecture*

None of this turmoil is evident in the dainty artifacts displayed in a series of sunny rooms, and, of course, the fact that the factory's output was finite makes surviving examples all the more valuable. Since the museum is run by the Sandwich Historical Society, one room is given over to changing exhibits highlighting other eras in the town's history, such as its stellar seafaring days. Anyone who goes in expecting not to be impressed is liable to leave dazzled. An excellent little gift shop stocks Sandwich glass replicas, as well as original glassworks by area artisans.

1641 Wing Fort House. 69 Spring Hill Rd. (off Rte. 6A, about 1¹/₂ miles E of town). ☎ **508/833-1540.** Admission $2 adults, $1 children 12 and under. Mid-June to mid-Sept Tues–Sat 10am–4pm.

Still owned by descendants of Reverend John Wing, this "peak house" (so named for its steep roof) has undergone continual changes over the generations—here a lean-to turned permanent "keeping room" (or kitchen), there a "wart" (the colonial term for an attached outbuilding). Among the noteworthy architectural features are "gunstock" corner posts in the front parlor, thought by early builders to be capable of handling a heavier load. Each room is arranged to suggest a different era, all the way through the Victorian age. The true beauty, dim as it is without a roaring fire, is the long, low-ceilinged keeping room, which still seems to hum with several centuries' worth of domestic endeavor.

Thornton W. Burgess Museum. 4 Water St. (on Shawme Pond, near the center of town). ☎ **508/888-4668.** Suggested donation $2 adults; $1 children. Apr–Oct Mon–Sat 10am–4pm, Sun 1–4pm; call for off-season hrs. Closed Jan–Mar.

Prominent in the early half of the century, this prolific and locally bred children's book author racked up 170 tomes to his credit, as well as 15,000 stories. His somewhat simple texts, featuring anthropomorphic animals prone to preaching, may seem a bit dated, but they still go over big with little listeners, especially at the summer-afternoon story hours (call for details), which usually include a chance to pet the character in question. The gift shop carries reissues of his work, should they desire a memento. It's also worth a peek inside to see Harrison Cady's spirited illustrations and exhibits attesting to Burgess's other life work, conservation. He may have inherited this interest from his aunt (the original inhabitant of this 1756 cottage), who gained a certain notoriety for claiming that she could communicate directly with the animal and plant worlds.

Yesteryears Doll Museum. Main and River sts. (in the center of town). ☎ **508/888-1711.** Admission $3.50 adults, $3 senior citizens and children 12–17, $1.50 children under 12. Mid-May to Oct Mon–Sat 10am–4pm (last tour 3pm). Closed Nov to mid-May.

Barely funded by the "doll hospital" that occupies the basement, this musty museum is nonetheless a gem. The holdings are extraordinary, from a 17th-century Queen Anne doll to several "Nuremberg kitchens," complete with tiny crockery, and right on up to the recent past—embodied in a passel of Barbies. The collection is housed in a recently restored Gothic Revival meetinghouse; glass cases are set athwart wooden church benches, and there's a certain mazelike quality that could send shivers down the spines of the easily spooked. Women of a certain age will suffer frisson after frisson of recognition and loss; those accompanying them may wonder at the fuss but eventually get caught up in the scaled-down drama of it all.

BEACHES & RECREATIONAL PURSUITS

BEACHES   For the Sandwich beaches listed below, nonresident parking stickers—$20 for the length of your stay—are available at **Sandwich Town Hall,** 130 Rte. 130

(☎ **508/833-8012**). Note that there's no swimming allowe[...] Canal: The currents are much too swift and dangerous.

- ✪ **Sandy Neck Beach,** off Sandy Neck Road in East Sanc[...] stretch of silken barrier beach with hummocky dunes is p[...] gered piping plovers—and, unfortunately, their nemesis, on-road vehicles. Although ORV permits ($80 per season for nonresidents) can be purchased at the gatehouse (☎ **508/362-8300**) as long as it's not nesting season, do this fragile environment and everyone who enjoys it a favor: walk. Parking costs $8 to $10 per day in season, and up to 3 days of camping is permitted at $10 per night.
- **Town Neck Beach,** off Town Neck Road in Sandwich. A bit rocky but ruggedly pretty, this narrow beach offers a busy view of passing ships, plus rest rooms and a snack bar. Parking costs $4 to $8 per day, or you could hike from town (about 1 1/2 miles) via the community-built boardwalk spanning the salt marsh.
- **Wakeby Pond,** Ryder Conservation Area, John Ewer Road (off South Sandwich Road on the Mashpee border). The beach, on the Cape's largest freshwater pond, has lifeguards, rest rooms, and parking ($4 per day).

BICYCLING   The **Army Corps of Engineers** (☎ **508/759-5991**) maintains a flat 14-mile loop along the ✪ **Cape Cod Canal** equally suited to bicyclists and skaters, runners and strollers. The most convenient place to park (free) is at the Buzzards Bay Recreation Area, west of the Bourne Bridge, on the Cape side. The closest bike rental shop is **P&B Cycles** at 29 Main St. in Buzzards Bay (☎ **508/759-2830**), opposite the railroad station; the shop also offers free parking.

BOATING   **Cape Cod Coastal Canoe & Kayak** (☎ **888/226-6393** or 508/ 564-4051; Web site www.capecod.net/canoe/; E-mail cccanoe@capecod.net) runs naturalist-guided trips throughout the Cape, sponsored by the Cape Cod Museum of Natural History. In Sandwich, they paddle around Old Sandwich Harbor and Sandy Neck. Trips (3 1/2 to 4 hr.)—daily April through August, weekends through October—cost $25 per paddler or $50 per family. All equipment is supplied. Call for schedule.

FISHING   Sandwich has eight fishable ponds; for details and a license, inquire at **Town Hall** in the center of town (☎ **508/888-0340**). No permit is required for fishing from the banks of the Cape Cod Canal. Here your catch might include striped bass, bluefish, cod, pollock, flounder, or fluke. Local deep-water charters include the *Tigger Two,* docked in the Sandwich Marina (☎ **508/888-8372**).

FITNESS   The local fitness center is the **Sportsite Health Club** at 315 Cotuit Rd. in Sandwich (☎ **508/888-7900**); it offers 15,000 square feet of Nautilus and other fitness equipment, along with steam baths, saunas, classes, and free child care.

GOLF   The **Round Hill Country Club** on Service Road in East Sandwich (☎ **508/ 888-3384**) does, in fact, have some hills along its 6,200-yard, par-71 course. The **Holly Ridge Golf Course** on Country Club Road (☎ **508/428-5577**) is shorter and easier.

NATURE & WILDLIFE AREAS   The **Shawme-Crowell State Forest,** off Route 130 in Sandwich (☎ **508/888-0351**), offers 285 campsites and 742 acres to roam. Entrance is free; parking costs $2. The Sandwich Boardwalk, which the community rebuilt in 1991 after Hurricane Bob blew away the 1874 original, links the town and Town Neck Beach by way of salt marshes that attract a great many birds, including olue herons. The 76-acre grounds of the **Heritage Museum of Sandwich** ✆ **508/888-3300;** seasonal, admission charged) afford a pleasant stroll, especially when the rhododendrons burst forth in multicolored bloom in May and June. The 57-acre **Green Briar Nature Center** (☎ **508/888-6870;** admission free) in East Sandwich has a mile-long path crossing marsh and stands of white pine. To obtain a map of other conservation areas in Sandwich (some 16 sites encompassing nearly 1,300 acres), stop by the **Sandwich Conservation Commission** at 16 Jan Sebastian Dr. (off Route 130; ☎ **508/888-4200**).

As if to signify how oddly enchanted this little corner of the world is, there's a sweet little (57-acre) nature center here—and within it is an even sweeter kitchen, where local ladies have been cooking up jams and jellies since 1903. The **Green Briar Nature Center & Jam Kitchen** is at 6 Discovery Hill (off Route 6A, about 1 1/2 miles east of town center; ☎ **508/888-6870**); once you've caught a whiff of the jam, you'll want to take some home. (Try the local delicacy, beach-plum jelly.) Children will be intrigued by the expansive kitchen, as well as some old-fashioned nature exhibits, including a resident rabbit.

TENNIS   Sandwich has public courts at three of its public schools; call the **Sandwich Recreation Department** (☎ **508/888-4361**) for details, or the **Cape Cod Chamber of Commerce** (☎ **508/362-3225;** fax 508/362-3698; Web site www.capecod.com) for a Cape-wide listing of tennis facilities open to the public.

KID STUFF

The venerable 18-hole **Sandwich Minigolf** (☎ **508/833-1905**), at the corner of Main Street and Route 6A, is a grassy 1950s classic that encapsulates Cape Cod history. Built on a former cranberry bog, it boasts an unusual floating green. Cool!

SHOPPING

Small as it is, Sandwich has a handful of appealing shops, all personally stocked—some with items you're unlikely to find anywhere else. Most of the shops are concentrated in the center of town. Several of the museums listed (see "Sandwich Historical Sights," above) also have worthwhile gift shops.

ANTIQUES & COLLECTIBLES   **The Brown Jug Antiques,** 155 Main St., in the center of town (☎ **508/833-1088**), is the place to go if you'd like to take home Sandwich glass—the real thing, not a reproduction. Other specialties are cameos and china. Closed January and February. **H. Richard Strand Antiques,** 2 Grove St., at Main Street (in the center of town; ☎ **508/888-3230**), is a treasure-packed federal manse—it's so museumlike, you may be moved to whisper. The prices may stun you into silence, but so will the quality. **Hannah's,** 169 Rte. 6A, at Main Street (☎ **508/ 888-1487**), sells vintage Victorian finery, from wedding gowns to nightgowns, plus romantic hats and accessories. **Madden & Co.,** 16 Jarves St., in the center of town (☎ **508/888-3663**), has some quirky antiques mixed in among the country-chic home accoutrements. Like a newfangled country store, this fun shop even stocks food—condiments and the like. They're closed January through April. Set up like an ongoing garage sale, **Maypop Lane,** 161 Rte. 6A, at Main Street (☎ **508/ 888-1230**), offers all sorts of addictive collectibles, such as china, glass, copper, furniture, and costume jewelry. The shop is small but selectively stocked.

The **Sandwich Antiques Center,** 131 Rte. 6A, at Jarves Street (☎ **508/833-3600**), is a clean, well-lighted place showcasing scores of consignors; it's a new venture headed by a congenial auctioneer and offers virtual one-stop shopping for the likes of paperweights, fishing creels, beaded bags—you name it. The center is open daily year-round.

ARTS & CRAFTS The **Giving Tree Gallery,** 550 Rte. 6A (☎ **508/888-5446**), is an art and fine-craft gallery with something extra: a nature walk through the woods. Intriguing sculptures are placed strategically around the property. There's even a path through a bamboo forest for those who appreciate a Far Eastern aesthetic. In fact, there's something very Zen about the whole Giving Tree experience. There's even a cafe serving cappuccino and sweets.

BOOKS **Titcomb's Book Shop,** 432 Rte. 6A, about ¹/₂ mile east of town center (☎ **508/888-2331**), has the best possible selection of books (both new and used) relating to Cape Cod. Look for the life-size statue of Ben Franklin.

FOOD & WINE In continuous operation since 1903, **Green Briar Jam Kitchen,** 6 Discover Hill Rd., south of Route 6A, 1 mile west of town center (☎ **508/888-6870**), is its own cottage industry. It produces dozens of varieties of delectable homemade jams, jellies, and preserves. The gift shop also offers a nice, affordable selection of nature-related items of interest to children.

  Quail Hollow Farm, Route 130 and Beale Avenue, ¹/₂ mile south of town center (☎ **508/888-0438**), is a picture-perfect farm stand harboring superb, if pricey, produce and kicky accompaniments, most of them locally produced. Pick up a moist and flavorful "tea cake," available in lemon or blueberry, to take home, or—you may not make it that far—for snacking on the road. They're closed Tuesdays and Wednesdays and mid-October through late May.

GIFTS/HOME DECOR At **Home for the Holidays Ltd.,** 154 Main St. (☎ **508/888-4388**), one room of the 1850 house is permanently decorated for Christmas; others are restocked seasonally to reflect relevant holidays. Always on hand are delightful gifts for youngsters and many treats, mostly home-related, for adults. Open daily through Christmas and winter weekends; call for off-season hours. **The Weather Store,** 146 Main St. (☎ **508/888-1200**), has a fascinating collection of meteorological paraphernalia old and new, ranging from antique instruments to coffee-table books. From January through April, it's open by chance or appointment.

SEAFOOD **Joe's Lobster & Fish Market,** off Coast Guard Road, near Sandwich Marina (☎ **800/491-2971** or 508/888-2971), is where to go for the freshest fish and shellfish to prepare at your cottage rental.

WHERE TO STAY

EXPENSIVE

✪ **Bay Beach.** 1-3 Bay Beach Rd. (on Town Beach), Sandwich, MA 02563. ☎ **800/475-6398** or 508/888-8813. Fax 508/888-5416. 6 rms. A/C TV TEL. Summer (including full breakfast) $160–$225 double. MC, V. Closed Nov–Apr.

The quarters of these two homes, overlooking Town Neck Beach with a view of the Sagamore Bridge and the boat traffic along the canal, have been fitted out with every luxury, from CD players to double Jacuzzis. They're clearly geared to romantic interludes. For the fitness-minded, there's even an exercise room on the premises.

The Dan'l Webster Inn. 149 Main St. (in the center of town), Sandwich, MA 02563. ☎ **800/444-3566** or 508/888-3622. Fax 508/888-5156. Web site www.danlwebsterinn.com. 37 rms, 9 suites. A/C TV TEL. Summer $129–$199 double. AE, CB, DISC, MC, V.

On this site once stood a colonial tavern favored by the famous orator, who came to these parts to go fishing. The tavern burned to the ground in 1971, but the modern replacement, operated by the Catania family (owners of the Hearth 'N Kettle restaurants dotted about the Cape), suits modern travelers to a T. All the rooms are ample and nicely furnished with reproductions. The eight suites located in nearby historic houses are especially appealing; they feature fireplaces and canopy beds.

👪 Family-Friendly Hotels & Restaurants

Betsy's Diner in Falmouth *(see p. 88)*   This classic 1950s diner offers all the old faves, plus home-baked pastries.

Cape Cod Chicken in Falmouth *(see p. 88)*   The combo plates are cheap, cheap, cheap, and the booths promote ease of sharing.

The Clam Shack in Falmouth *(see p. 88)*   Children will love the size of this place (it's Lilliputian), the plain fare, and all the activity on the harbor.

Pine Grove Cottages in East Sandwich *(see p. 65)*   Instant communities spring up among the weeklong guests who have free run of this shady grove and its aboveground pool.

Wingscorton Farm Inn in East Sandwich *(see p. 64)*   What could beat a working farm—with a beach within walking distance—for both education and fun?

The Silver Lounge in North Falmouth *(see p. 90)*   The favorite restaurant for generations of kids—there are nine booths in the caboose, so you'll need to get there early if you want to snag one.

Shucker's World Famous Raw Bar & Cafe in Woods Hole *(see p. 90)*   Casual outdoor seating on Eel Pond is perfect for fidgety little ones. The kids menu and toys will keep them busy while you enjoy the view.

A small but prettily landscaped pool suffices for a quick dip, and those seeking a real workout can repair to a local health club, where admission is gratis for guests. The inn's common spaces are convivial, if bustling. This is a very popular place, among locals as well as travelers. The big draw is the restaurant, which turns out surprisingly sophisticated fare, especially considering the high volume (see "Where to Dine," below).

MODERATE

✪ **The Belfry Inne.** 8 Jarves St. (in the center of town), Sandwich, MA 02563. ☎ **800/ 844-4542** or 508/888-8550. Fax 508/888-3922. 9 rms. Summer (including full breakfast) $95–$165 double. MAP plan available. AE, MC, V.

You can't miss it: It's the gaudiest "painted lady" in town, recently restored to its original flamboyant glory after skulking for decades under three layers of siding. Newly liberated, this turreted 1879 rectory has turned its fancy to romance, with queen-size retrofitted antique beds, a claw-foot tub (or Jacuzzi) for every room, and a scattering of fireplaces and private balconies.

Isaiah Jones Homestead. 165 Main St. (in the center of town), Sandwich, MA 02563. ☎ **800/ 526-1625** or 508/888-9115. Fax 508/888-9648. 5 rms. Summer (including full breakfast and afternoon tea) $75–$155 double. AE, DISC, MC, V.

This courtly 1849 Victorian is carefully appointed throughout with fine antiques. Some rooms have romantic touches like fireplaces and whirlpool baths. The room named for industrial magnate Deming Jarves, for instance, boasts an inviting plum-curtained half-canopy bed and an oversize whirlpool tub. The gentility that prevails at the candlelight breakfast completes the picture.

✪ **Wingscorton Farm Inn.** 11 Wing Blvd. (off Rte. 6A, about 2 miles E of town center), E. Sandwich, MA 02537. ☎ **508/888-0534.** 2 suites, 1 carriage house. Summer (including full breakfast) $115–$150 double. AE, MC, V.

A working farm since 1758, this bucolic retreat will transport you back centuries to a simpler, more peaceful, if arduous, time. Sheep, goats, dogs, cats, chickens, and a pet turkey and pot-bellied pig share the 7 acres of tree-shaded grounds; you're welcome to bring along your own "well-trained" animal companion. The main house—whose "keeping room" boasts a 9-foot-long colonial hearth bedecked with vintage pewter—offers two paneled bedrooms with canopy beds, working fireplaces, braided rugs, and enviable antiques. Modernists might prefer the carriage house, with its skylight-suffused loft bedroom, kitchen (with woodstove), and private deck and patio; it doesn't cost appreciably more. Guests enjoy a hearty, five-course farm breakfast, even if they've done no hard labor to earn it. Instead of tending to chores, they can skip off to the private bay beach that's within a short walk.

INEXPENSIVE

Captain Ezra Nye House. 152 Main St. (in the center of town), Sandwich, MA 02563. ☎ **800/388-2778** or 508/888-6142. Fax 508/833-1897. Web site www.sunsol.com/ccvd/lodging/ezranye. 6 rms, 1 suite. Summer (including full breakfast) $85–$110 double. AE, DISC, MC, V.

A handsome federal manse, graced by a fanlight and twin chimneys, this B&B is not so forbidding that you can't kick off your shoes to enjoy a board game in the den. Rooms, if not ultraluxurious, are nicely appointed with eclectic antiques, and breakfast tends to be quite substantial, along the lines of soufflé-of-the-day or apple-cinnamon quiche.

The Dunbar House. 1 Water St. (in the center of town), Sandwich, MA 02563. ☎ **508/833-2485.** Fax 508/833-4713. E-mail dunbar@capecod.net. 3 rms. Summer (including full breakfast and a voucher for the tearoom) $85–$95 double. MC, V.

A scenic, central location—overlooking Shawme Pond—and congenial British innkeepers are the main draws of this renovated 1741 colonial B&B, but you can't discount the complimentary tea, a full meal in itself, served in the adjoining carriage house (see "Where to Dine," below). Of course, the fact that many of the same home-baked pastries turn up at breakfast doesn't hurt either. The simple yet cheerful rooms are named after English lakes: Ennerdale, Loweswater, and Buttermere. Ennerdale is a bit more elaborate, with a four-poster bed and fireplace. All have pastoral pond views.

The Inn at Sandwich Center. 118 Tupper Rd. (in the center of town), Sandwich, MA 02563. ☎ **800/249-6949** or 508/888-6958. Fax 508/833-2770. Web site www.bfbooks.com/innsan.html. E-mail innsan@aol.com. 5 rms. Summer (including continental breakfast) $85–$110. AE, DISC, MC, V.

This historic B&B started out as a plain 1750s saltbox and got a fancy Federal makeover a century later. Happily, the interior decor has been similarly updated. Some rooms have four-poster beds and fireplaces. All rooms are tastefully decorated with antiques and works of art collected from around the world. An extensive continental breakfast, featuring homemade goodies, is served in the Keeping Room, with its original fireplace and beehive oven. It's no coincidence that the inn has European flair; the French hostess is fluent in several languages. The Sandwich Glass Museum is directly across the street.

Pine Grove Cottages. 358 Rte. 6A (near the center of town), E. Sandwich, MA 02537. ☎ **508/888-8179.** 10 cottages. TV. Summer $240–$545 weekly double. AE, DISC, MC, V. Closed Nov–Apr.

Cute as buttons, some of these one-room cottages are barely big enough to squeeze in a double bed. White walls make them seem a bit roomier, while stenciling adds a touch of romance—not that cottage-fanciers would need any added inducement. With lots of families in residence, and a new in-ground pool to splash in, children enjoy good odds of finding a friend.

Seth Pope House. 110 Tupper Rd. (in the center of town), Sandwich, MA 02563. ☎ **888/996-7384** or 508/888-5916. 3 rms. A/C. Summer (including full breakfast) $85 double. MC, V. Closed Nov–Mar.

Each room in this lovingly maintained 1699 saltbox has a distinctive decor. Traditionalists might favor the Colonial Room, with its exposed beams, pencil-post bed, and cherry bonnet chest; romantics, the Victorian—which is pink-accented with plenty of marble. Also pleasant is the "Pineapple" Room, with twin pineapple-post beds and a salt-marsh view. In its settled sedateness, this is a prototypical Sandwich home, and most welcoming.

Spring Garden Motel. 578 Rte. 6A (about 2 miles E of town center), E. Sandwich, MA 02537. ☎ **800/303-1751** or 508/888-0710. Fax 508/833-2849. 11 units. A/C TV TEL. Summer $79–$89 double. AE, DISC, MC, V. Closed mid-Nov to Mar.

Looking like an elongated rose-covered cottage, this pretty double-decker motel overlooks the Great Sandwich Salt Marsh, and every room comes with a southern-oriented patio or porch that takes in the lush green landscape. With its spacious, tree-shaded backyard, the motel is understandably popular with families. Regular summerers also appreciate the complimentary homemade continental breakfasts.

Spring Hill Motor Lodge. 351 Rte. 6A (about 2^1/$_2$ miles E of town center), E. Sandwich, MA 02537. ☎ **800/647-2514** or 508/888-1456. Fax 508/833-1556. 24 units. A/C TV TEL. Summer $83–$95 double; $125 efficiency. AE, CB, DC, DISC, MC, V.

This motel boasts all sorts of stylish touches that make it seem more like a good country inn that just happens to be horizontal. The interiors are cheerfully contemporary, the grounds verdant; they encompass an oversize tennis court, with plenty of room for spectators, and a large, elegantly landscaped heated pool surrounded by a sufficiency of comfortable lounge chairs.

Summer House. 158 Main St. (in the center of town), Sandwich, MA 02563. ☎ **800/241-3609** or 508/888-4991. 5 rms. Summer (including full breakfast and afternoon tea) $75–$95 double. AE, DISC, MC, V.

This elegant Greek Revival house, built around 1835, offers extremely reasonable rates for its exceptionally charming accommodations. The bedrooms are all large corner rooms, brightened up with colorful home-stitched quilts and painted hardwood floors; four have working fireplaces, and a few overlook the English garden in back, which is in riotous bloom throughout the summer. It's here you'll find a hammock to hide away in, stirring only to be called in to breakfast (elaborate) or a bountiful tea.

✪ **The Village Inn at Sandwich.** 4 Jarves St. (in the center of town), Sandwich, MA 02563. ☎ **800/922-9989** or 508/833-0363. Fax 508/833-2063. E-mail capecodinn@aol.com. 8 rms. Summer (including full breakfast) $80–$95 double. AE, DISC, MC, V.

Why envy the guests relaxing in rockers on the wraparound porch of this gracious 1837 Federal house when you could be among them? Better yet, you'll have recourse to surprisingly light and airy sleeping quarters, with gleaming bleached floors, California-ish splashes of colorful fabric, and enveloping duvets. From the French country-style dining room to the cozy dormered attic, the mood is one of carefree comfort. The new innkeeper, an artist, runs a program called Sandwich Artworks with workshops by well-known Cape Cod artists like Karen Wells, Joyce Zavorkas, Rosalie Nadeau, and Lois Griffel. Workshops and B&B packages are available.

WHERE TO DINE
MODERATE

The Belfry Bistro. 8 Jarves St. (in the center of town). ☎ **508/888-8550.** Main courses $15–$20. AE, MC, V. Late May to mid-Oct Wed to Sun 5–11pm; call for off-season schedule. NEW AMERICAN.

Though these are not "white tablecloth" prices, the linens are snowy and dense, the mood luxurious, the menu ingratiating and geared to grazers. Selections change with the seasons, but among the trio of entrees, you might find a superlative spring roll served in a pool of ginger tamari, or seared scallops in their shells, cloaked in chardonnay cream sauce and served with herbed polenta. Desserts (offered independently as well, with specialty coffees) are designed to satisfy in and of themselves, as will the white-chocolate cheesecake with morsels of meringue, in a pool of raspberry coulis.

The Dan'l Webster Inn. 149 Main St. (in the center of town). ☎ **508/888-3623.** Reservations recommended. Main courses $14–$20. AE, CB, DC, DISC, MC, V. Daily 8am–9pm. INTERNATIONAL.

You have a choice of four main dining rooms—from a casual, colonial-motif tavern to a skylight-topped conservatory fronting a splendid garden. The latest dining room, the atmospheric Tavern at the Inn, with its own pub-style menu, is fast becoming the most popular option. All of the dining rooms are served by the same kitchen, under the masterful hand of chef/co-owner Richard Catania. A devotee of fresh local fruit and fish, he has gone so far as to build a model aquaculture farm from which he can tap into at will. The culinary results attest to his good taste. A restaurant on this scale could probably get away with ho-hum, middle-of-the-road food, but his output is on a par with that of the Cape's best boutique restaurants. Try a classic dish like the *fruits de mer* (seafood) in white wine, or entrust your palate to a seasonal highlight (the specials menu changes monthly). The desserts are as superb as all that precedes them.

INEXPENSIVE

The Bee-Hive Tavern. 406 Rte. 6A (about ¹/₂ mile E of town center), E. Sandwich. ☎ **508/833-1184.** Main courses $5–$14. MC, V. Mon–Fri 11:30am–9pm, Sat–Sun 8am–9pm. INTERNATIONAL.

A cut above the rather characterless restaurants clustered along this stretch of road, this modern-day tavern employs some atmospheric old-timey touches without going overboard. Green-shaded banker's lamps, for example, illuminate the dark wooden booths, and vintage prints and paintings convey a clubby feel. The food is good, if not spectacular, and well priced for what it is. Straightforward steaks, chops, and fresh-caught fish are among the pricier choices, while burgers, sandwiches, and salads cater to lighter appetites (and wallets).

✪ The Dunbar Tea Shop. 1 Water St. (in the center of town). ☎ **508/833-2485.** Main courses under $10. MC, V. Summer daily 11am–5:30pm; off-season daily 11am–4:30pm. Closed Tues–Wed Jan–Mar. BRITISH.

Choose the cozy confines of the tearoom or, in summer, a shady grove outside. Either way, you'll get to partake of hearty, authentic English classics, such as savories, before moving on to sweets: fresh-baked shortbread and seasonal pies. The Tea Room also serves tea, of course, with all the traditional fixings and accompaniments.

Horizons on Cape Cod Bay. 98 Town Neck Rd. ☎ **508/888-6166.** Reservations not accepted. Main courses $9–$15. AE, DISC, MC, V. Sun–Thurs 11:30am–9pm, Fri–Sat 11:30am–10pm. Closed Nov–Mar. SEAFOOD.

The location, right on the beach, gives this place its cache. The second-floor deck has the best views of the beach (there's even a telescope!), and inside there is lots of window seating plus a large, lively bar area with a pool table and a large screen TV. Downstairs is usually a bit less rowdy. In season, the place is packed despite the sometimes iffy food and service. Fried seafood platters washed down with chunky clam chowder are the mainstays here.

Marshland Restaurant. 109 Rte. 6A. ☎ **508/888-9824.** Most items under $10. No credit cards. Tues–Sat 6am–9pm, Sun 7am–1pm, Mon 6am–2pm. Open year-round. DINER.

Locals have been digging this diner for 2 decades. This is home-cooked grub, slung fast and cheap. You'll gobble up the hearty breakfast and be back in time for dinner.

SWEETS

Ice cream Sandwich. 66 Rte. 6A (across from the Stop & Shop). ☎ **508/888-7237.** Closed Oct–Mar.

Make a visit here for a couple of scoops of the best local ice cream.

SANDWICH AFTER DARK

The Belfry Bistro. 8 Jarves St. ☎ **508/888-8550.** No cover.

Elegant surroundings, liqueur-spiked coffees, and live-for-the-moment desserts make for a soothing, if sinful, night on the town. Soft jazz sets the mood nightly in season. (See "Where to Dine," above).

Sandwich Auction House. 15 Tupper Rd. (at Rte. 6A). ☎ **508/888-1926.** Free admission. June–Aug Wed at 6:30pm; Sept–May Sat at 6:30pm; previews start at 2pm the same day.

Do you have the guts—not to mention the funds—to be a player? You'll find out soon enough as the bidding grows heated over an ever-changing parade of antique goods, from chests to portraits to spinning wheels. Antique-rug auctions are once a month. The record set here so far was for an antique toy pedal car that fetched $77,000. Sit on your hands if you must.

2 Bourne

4 miles (7km) W of Sagamore, 16 miles (26km) NW of Hyannis

Take a right turn toward Bourne, as you cross either the Sagamore or Bourne bridge, and you'll wonder where the tourists went. Can this really be the Cape? In some ways, this primarily residential community is quintessential Cape Cod. Hugging Buzzards Bay, Bourne doesn't exactly go out of its way to attract thrill-seekers—with the possible exception of the Bourne Kart Track, a family amusement complex right on Route 28. But for the madding traffic, and sundry other evidence of encroaching modernization, the rest of this bucolic community is probably not all that different than what President Grover Cleveland encountered when, evidently attracted by the trout, he decided to set up his summer White House here in the 1890s. That house is long gone, but one vestige—his personal train station, a great way to maintain crowd control—is on view at the Aptucxet Trading Post Museum, a reconstructed version of this country's first place of commerce, where Pilgrims traded with Native Americans and the Dutch. Also visible from here—and from the Cape Cod Canal bike path, which runs right past the post—is the intriguing Vertical Lift Railroad Bridge (built in 1935), whose whole track moves up or down to permit the passage, respectively, of ships or trains.

Somewhat introverted and intent on its own old-fashioned pleasures, Bourne is best savored by those seeking the very, very quiet life.

ESSENTIALS

GETTING THERE   After crossing either the Bourne or Sagamore bridge, turn west on Route 6A toward Bourne. You can also fly into Hyannis (see "Getting There," in chapter 3).

VISITOR INFORMATION   Contact the **Cape Cod Chamber of Commerce,** Routes 6 and 132, Hyannis, MA 02601 (☎ **508/362-3225;** fax 508/362-3698; Web site www.capecod.com) or stop in at the Cape Cod Chamber of Commerce Information Center (seasonal) at the Sagamore Bridge rotary. The **Cape Cod Canal Region Chamber of Commerce,** 70 Main St., Buzzards Bay (☎ **508/759-6000**), can provide literature on both Sandwich and Bourne.

BEACHES & OUTDOOR PURSUITS

BEACHES   Bourne has only one public beach, but at least the parking—when you can find it—is free.

Monument Beach, off Shore Road, is small and pebbly, but picturesque. Full public-beach facilities accompany the relatively warm waters of Buzzards Bay.

BICYCLING   See "Bicycling," under Sandwich, above.

BOATING   Cape Cod Coastal Canoe & Kayak (☎ **888/226-6393** or 508/564-4051; Web site www.capecod.net/canoe/; E-mail cccanoe@capecod.net) runs naturalist-guided trips throughout the Cape, sponsored by the Cape Cod Museum of Natural History. In Bourne, they paddle around Back River and Phinney's Harbor in Monument Beach. Trips ($3^{1}/_{2}$ to 4 hr.) are daily April through August, weekends through October, and cost $25 per paddler or $50 per family. All equipment is supplied. Call for schedule.

FISHING   So plentiful are the herring making their spring migration up the **Bournedale Herring Run** (Route 6 in Bournedale, about 1 mile southwest of the Sagamore Bridge rotary; ☎ **508/759-4431**) that you can net them once they've reached their destination, Great Herring Pond; also plentiful here are pickerel, white perch, walleye, and bass. For freshwater fishing at Flax Pond and Red Brook Pond in Pocasset, you'll need to obtain a license from the **Bourne Town Hall** at 24 Perry Ave. (☎ **508/759-0613**). Surf casting along the Cape Cod Canal requires no permit.

ICE-SKATING   The **John Gallo Ice Arena** at 231 Sandwich Rd. in Bourne (☎ **508/759-8904**) is open to the public daily from September to March; call for hours.

NATURE & WILDLIFE AREAS   The Bourne Conservation Trust has also managed to get hold of a handful of small plots; for information, contact the town **Conservation Commission** (☎ **508/759-0625**). The largest tract, the 40-acre **Nivling-Alexander Reserve** (off Shore Road at Thaxter Road), flanks Red Brook Pond, where fishing is permitted (see above); it offers a half-mile wooded walk passing several cranberry bogs.

TENNIS   In the Bourne area, public courts are located near the old schoolhouse on County Road in Cataumet, and in Chester Park, opposite the railroad station in Monument Beach; for information, call the **Bourne Memorial Community Building** on Main Street in Buzzards Bay (☎ **508/759-0650**), which also has courts.

WATER SPORTS   The **Aquarius Dive Center** at 3239 Cranberry Hwy., Buzzards Bay (☎ **508/759-3483**), offers rentals, instruction, and charters to Sandwich Town Beach, the Plymouth coast, and a wreck site off Provincetown. The salt-marsh maze of Scorton Creek is a lovely spot for canoeing or kayaking; you can head out to Talbot Point, a wooded spit of conservation land. Bring your own boat, or rent one in Falmouth or Hyannis.

A MUSEUM & A CRUISE

Aptucxet Trading Post Museum. 24 Aptucxet Rd., off Perry Ave. (about $^{1}/_{2}$ mile W of town center), Bourne Village. ☎ **508/759-9487.** Admission $2.50 adults, $1 children 6–18. May to mid-Oct Mon–Sat 10am–5pm, Sun 2–5pm. Closed mid-Oct to Apr.

Long before the canal was a twinkle in Myles Standish's (and later, George Washington's and Augustus Belmont's) eye, Native Americans had been portaging goods between two rivers, the Manomet and Scusset, that once almost met at this site; its name, in Algonquian, means "little trap in the river." The Pilgrims were quick to notice that Aptucxet made an ideal trading spot, especially since, as Governor William Bradford pointed out, it would allow them to trade with the Dutch to the south without "the compassing of Cape-Codd and those dangerous shoulds [shoals]." In 1627, as soon as the Pilgrims had essentially declared their independence by assuming the debts of the Merchant Adventurers, they built an outpost here, hoping to cash in as conduits for native-caught pelts. The present building is a replica, built after a pair of local archaeologists, using ancient maps, uncovered the original foundation in 1926. The other detritus they dug up (arrowheads, pottery shards, and more) is displayed in a roomful of rather dim, crowded display cases. Also be sure to have a look at the Bournedale Stone, which was discovered serving as a threshold for a Native American church built in the late 17th century. Overturned, it revealed strange, runelike inscriptions—fueling the legend (unsubstantiated as yet) that Vikings roamed the Cape around A.D. 1000.

Even though the building is not authentic, the curator does a very good job of conjuring the hard, lonely life led by the pair of sentinels assigned here. Several other odd artifacts are scattered about the grounds, such as President Grover Cleveland's personal train station from his estate at Gray Gables, and a windmill used as an art studio by his good friend and fishing companion, the hugely successful actor Joseph Jefferson. Redlined out of Sandwich for his scandalous profession (he was a Democrat to boot!), Jefferson got his revenge by being buried there, with a tart epitaph: "We are but tenants; let us assure ourselves of this, and then it will not be so hard to make room for the new administration, for shortly the Great Landlord will give us notice that our lease has expired."

The Cape Cod Canal path runs right behind the museum. This is a good spot from which to observe the Vertical Lift Railroad Bridge, which represented state-of-the-art technology for its time (1935, when it cost $1.5 million) but is now obsolescent, so scanty is the train traffic. Rush hour, between 5 and 6pm, is your best chance to catch the bridge lowering its trestle (for the garbage cars headed off-Cape); in the off-season, you might get a colorful sunset thrown in for good measure.

Cape Cod Canal Cruises. Onset Bay Town Pier (on the northern side of the canal, about 2 miles W of the Bourne Bridge), Onset. ☎ **508/295-3883.** Fee $7–$12 adults, fee $6 children 6–12. Mid-June to Aug departures daily 10am and 1:30pm; Mon–Sat 4pm; Tues–Thurs 7pm; Fri–Sat 8pm; call for off-season schedule. Closed mid-Oct to Apr.

Get an underbelly view of the Cape's two swooping car bridges and its unusual railroad bridge as you wend your way among a wide array of interesting craft, and a narrator fills you in on the canal's history. Basically, it was the brainchild of New York financial wizard Augustus Perry Belmont, who completed it in 1914 at a cost of $16 million and never saw a penny of profit. Found to be too narrow and perilous (the current reverses with the tides, roughly every 6 hours), the overambitious waterway was handed over to the U.S. Army Corps of Engineers for expansion in 1928, at the discount price of $11.5 million. It continues to serve as a vital shortcut, sparing some 30,000 boats yearly the long, dangerous circuit of the Outer Cape.

The 4pm family cruise, offered Monday through Saturday, is a real bargain, at $7 per adult, with children under 12 free. The Sunday afternoon trip is accompanied by New Orleans–style jazz, and the sunset "Moonlight 'n Music" cruise on Saturday (adults only) features live bands.

An Insiders' Guide to the Cape Cod Baseball League

Many consider the Cape Cod Baseball League the premier NCAA summer baseball league in the country. For those of us enjoying the sun and surf on Cape Cod from June through August every year, the baseball games are just another diversion, something different to do on a Saturday night. But once you start attending the games, it can be hard to break away. Of the 10 hometown teams in the league, one of them is bound to capture your fancy. The diehard fans plan vacations around league playoff games (early August) and all-star games. The teams attract top college talent and serious professional prospects; coaches start scouting colleges from Labor Day to October 15.

Every team has its own home town field, and several of the diamonds are definitely a cut above. Aesthetes may prefer Veterans Field in Chatham, charming and quintessentially Cape-y like the town itself, with the bleachers tucked neatly into a hillside. Orleans's Eldredge Field is the most impressive: It has terraced seating along the first-base line.

The league has been going for most of this century, and longtime fans and rivalries can be intense. Some say the loudest, most enthusiastic fans are for the Cotuit Kettleers, but that could be a result of the tightly packed seats in those stands. Rivalries bring out the crowds, particularly when the Wareham Gatemen come to town; the last couple of years, they've won it all. Other intense rivalries include the Harwich Mariners vs. the Chatham Athletics; the Orleans Cardinals vs. the Brewster White Caps; and the Cotuit Kettleers vs. the Falmouth Commodores.

Crowd size varies over the course of the season, from early games, when a couple hundred locals turn out, to playoff games, when attendance might hit 4,500 to 5,000 at a large venue like Orleans's Eldredge Field. Saturday night games usually play to a full house. The race went down to the wire in 1997, with all 10 teams contenders. Teams to watch closely in 1998 are Wareham (again), Bourne, and Falmouth in the western league, Harwich (no. 2 in 1997), Chatham, and Brewster in the eastern league.

Each team plays 44 games (22 at home). Game times are usually evenings between 7 to 9:30pm or afternoons starting around 4 or 4:30pm. All games are free; when they pass the hat, throw in a few bucks to help defer costs for equipment and uniforms. Concession stands sell steamed hot dogs, popcorn, cookies, candy, and soda pop at reasonable prices. For schedule information, call the league at ☎ **508/ 432-6909** or check out their Web site at **www.capecodbaseball.com.**

BASEBALL

Sports fans of all ages will enjoy taking in nine innings of the Grand Old Game. Part of the elite-amateur **Cape Cod Baseball League** (☎ **508/432-6909**), the Braves play at Coady School Field, in Buzzards Bay, in July and August. Call the **Cape Cod Canal Region Chamber of Commerce** (☎ **508/759-6000**) to check the schedule.

KID STUFF

Stuck with a gray day? Pack the family off to the **Bourne Kart Track** on Route 28, about 2 miles south of the Bourne Bridge (☎ **800/535-2787** or 508/759-2636). Older kids can tackle the go-carts, batting cages, and video games, among other juvenile delights; little kids have their own little amusement park, complete with mini–Ferris wheel and a train with clanging bell. Prices are reasonable—though they're sure to add up rapidly. The Thunder Mine Adventure miniature golf course, at the intersection of County Road and Route 28A in Cataumet (no phone), offers 18 holes of Astroturf with a gold-rush theme. Be forewarned: There's an Emack & Bolio's (a branch of the primo Boston ice-cream parlor) next door, and you can't expect to escape without a lick.

SHOPPING

Instead of the usual cutesy Cape Cod shops, Bourne is known for its factory outlets. **Tanger Outlet Center,** located at the Bourne Rotary on the mainland side of the Bourne Bridge (☎ 800/482-6437), has the following outlets: Liz Claiborne, Levi's, Nine West, Izod, and Adolfo II. **Cape Cod Factory Outlet Mall,** just off Route 6, exit 1, Sagamore (☎ 508/888-8417), has Van Heusen, London Fog, L'Eggs/Hanes/ Bali, Home Decor, Bass Shoe, and American Tourister. Here are a few other notable stops:

GIFTS　You can observe artisans continuing the tradition of the Boston & Sandwich Glass Company at **Pairpoint Glass Works,** 851 Sandwich Rd. (Route 6A, at the foot of the Sagamore Bridge), Sagamore (☎ 800/899-0953 or 508/888-2344). Thomas J. Pairpoint was a leading designer in the 1880s. The output is on the conservative side, and includes skillful replicas. Bargain-lovers flock to the **Christmas Tree Shops** at the Sagamore Bridge, Sagamore (☎ 508/888-7010). The stock here is not just holiday-related. Housed in an oversized thatch-roofed Tudor cottage, complete with spinning windmill (you can't miss it), the array is Woolworthian in scope, but of much higher quality. There are six more outlets elsewhere on the Cape.

SEAFOOD　Skunked again? Not to fret. You couldn't hope for a fresher catch than you'll find at **Cataumet Fish,** Cataumet Square (Route 28A and County Road), Cataumet (☎ 508/564-5956). Buy a whole fish and fib a little (they'll even gut it), or cart home a couple of lobsters—who's going to care?

WHERE TO STAY

The Beachmore. 11 Buttermilk Way, Buzzards Bay, MA 02532. ☎ 508/759-7522. 6 rms. Summer (including continental breakfast) $75–$95 double. AE, MC, V.

New owners have awakened this sleepy property located right at the mouth of the Cape Cod Canal next to the Massachusetts Military Academy. Views (particularly sunsets) from one of the bedrooms, the commons room, and from the superb casual restaurant on the first floor (see "Where to Dine," below) are memorable. Rooms are decorated individually and with flair, and there's a loving attention to detail throughout. For instance, iron bedsteads are romantically draped with gauzy fabric, and curtains are handmade with lacy netting. Out front is a private beach perfect for sunning.

WHERE TO DINE

The Beachmore. 11 Buttermilk Way, Buzzards Bay. ☎ 508/759-7522. Reservations recommended. Main courses $12–$19. AE, MC, V. Apr–Sept daily 11:30am–10pm. Call for off-season hrs. NEW AMERICAN.

If you happen to be anywhere near the Bourne Bridge and in need of sustenance (lunch or dinner), you'll want to head over to the Beachmore in Buzzards Bay. They're serving up terrific food along with a wonderful view of the Cape Cod Canal. Specialties at dinner include Beachmore Stew (shrimp, clams, scallops, lobster, and fish in a saffron broth) and the daily trilogy which might include poached salmon with béarnaise sauce, grilled swordfish with basil butter, and broiled scallops in lemon butter. Save room for dessert, and if baked pear is on the menu, don't hesitate. It's a heavenly concoction with crisp-on-the-outside, doughy-on-the-inside squares surrounding the delicate baked pears, served with vanilla ice cream with raspberry sauce. Yumm.

The Bridge. 21 Rte. 6A (at the Cape end of the Sagamore Bridge), Sagamore. ☎ **508/ 888-8144.** Main courses $9–$17. CB, DC, DISC, MC, V. Daily 11:30am–9:30pm. ITALIAN/THAI.

The location isn't too promising (right next to the often gridlocked Sagamore bridge), and neither is the boxy exterior. Venture in, though, to encounter pleasant decor and a warm welcome from the Prete family, who has been serving up a wide array of well-priced Italian specialties like homemade tortellini and minestrone soup since 1953. The biggest surprise is the authentic Thai food prepared by present chef and daughter-in-law Pon Prete, the likes of which you won't find anywhere else on the Cape.

The Chart Room. 1 Shipyard Lane (in the Cataumet Marina, off Shore Rd.), Cataumet. ☎ **508/ 563-5350.** Main courses $10–$18. AE, MC, V. Mid-June to mid-Sept daily 11:30am–10pm; mid-May to mid-June and mid-Sept to mid-Oct Thurs–Sun 8am–1am. Closed mid-Oct to mid-May. SEAFOOD.

Great sunset views and fresh fish are reason enough to visit this dockside restaurant, housed in a former railroad barge in a busy marina. A piano bar lends a bit of elegance, as does the well-heeled clientele.

The Courtyard Restaurant and Bar. Cataumet Sq. (Rte. 28A and County Rd.), Cataumet. ☎ **508/563-1818.** Main courses $9–$15. AE, MC, V. Apr–Oct Sun–Thurs 11:30am–9:30pm, Fri–Sat 11:30am–10pm. Closed Mon Nov–Mar. INTERNATIONAL.

In summer, the trellised patio is packed with locals, young and old, enjoying a night on the town—or village, to be more precise. There's not a lot of competition in this neck of the woods, but the Courtyard—owned by former Boston Bruin Jay Miller—holds up its end admirably, with well-prepared grazing food such as designer pizzas. In inclement weather, the indoor dining room is agreeable, too, and on weekends there's the bonus of live bands.

The Parrot. 1356 Rte. 28A, Cataumet. ☎ **508/563-6464.** Reservations not accepted. Main courses $10–$15. AE, DISC, MC, V. Tues–Sun 11:30am–10pm, Mon 4:30–10pm. NEW AMERICAN.

For years the Blue Parrot, a gritty bar with a sour reputation, occupied this crossroads in Cataumet. New owner Eddie Hannon has cleaned the place up and resuscitated it as an up-beat Caribbean-themed restaurant specializing in seafood and pasta. Try the lobster pie or the blackened swordfish with Southwestern salsa. Weekends feature live piano music.

Sagamore Inn. 1131 Rte. 6A (about a $^{1}/_{4}$ mile E of the Sagamore Bridge), Sagamore. ☎ **508/888-9707.** Main courses $8–$17. AE, MC, V. Wed–Mon 11am–9pm. Closed Dec–Mar. AMERICAN/ITALIAN.

It's a chunk out of the past, a classic roadhouse preserved virtually intact since the 1920s, with the original wooden booths and tin ceiling. The menu—a mix of seafood staples and Italian specialties—is nostalgic, too, offering such all-but-extinct treats as Grapenut pudding.

BOURNE AFTER DARK

On weekends, local bands draw young adults to the intimate, tasteful **Courtyard Restaurant and Bar,** Cataumet Square (see "Where to Dine," above), Cataumet (☎ **508/563-1818**). There's no cover charge.

You'll find some surprisingly challenging work presented at **Theater on the Bay,** Trading Post Corner, Bourne (☎ **508/759-0977**). This tiny black box of a theater has premiered, for instance, new works by Arthur Miller and Yarmouth Port's glee-fully macabre fantasist, Edward Gorey. Open year-round; call for schedule. Tickets are $10.

3 Falmouth

18 miles (30km) S of Sagamore, 20 miles (33km) SW of Hyannis

Often overlooked in the rush to catch the island ferries, Falmouth is a classic New England town, complete with white steeples encircling the town green. Founded in 1660 by Quaker sympathizers from Sandwich (where Congregationalists considered theirs the only one true path), Falmouth proved remarkably arable territory: By the 19th century, it reigned as the strawberry capital of the world.

Today, after more than a century of catering to summertime guests (it was the first "fashionable" Cape resort, served by trains from Boston starting in the 1870s), residents have hospitality down to an art—a business, too, but people are so genuinely welcoming, you'll tend to forget that. The area around the historic Village Green (given over to military exercises in the pre-Revolutionary days) is a veritable hotbed of B&Bs, with each vying to provide the most elaborate breakfasts and solicitous advice. Put yourself in the hands of your hosts, and you'll soon feel like a native.

Officially a village within Falmouth (one of nine), tiny Woods Hole has been a world-renowned oceanic research center since 1871, when the U.S. Commission of Fish and Fisheries set up a primitive seasonal collection station. Today the various scientific institutes crowded around the harbor—principally, the National Marine Fisheries Service, the Marine Biological Laboratory (founded in 1888), and the Woods Hole Oceanographic Institute (a newcomer as of 1930)—have research budgets in the tens of millions of dollars and employ thousands of scientists. Woods Hole's scientific institutions offer a unique opportunity to get in-depth—and often hands-on—exposure to marine biology.

Belying stereotype, the community is far from uptight and nerdy; in fact, it's one of the hipper communities on the Cape. In the past few decades, a number of agreeable restaurants and shops have cropped up, making the small, crowded gauntlet of Water Street (don't even fantasize about parking here in summer) a very pleasant place to stroll.

West Falmouth (which is really more north of town, stretched alongside Buzzards Bay) has held on to its bucolic character and makes a lovely drive, with perhaps an occasional stop for the more alluring antique stores. Falmouth Heights, a cluster of shingled Victorian summerhouses on a bluff east of Falmouth's harbor, is as popular as it is picturesque; its narrow ribbon of beach is a magnet for all, especially the younger crowd. The Waquoit Bay area, a few miles east of town, has thus far eluded the overcommercialization that blights most of Route 28, and with luck and foresight will continue to do so. Several thousand acres of this vital estuarine ecosystem are now under federal custody, primarily at the instigation of the region's original residents, the Mashpee Wampanoags.

ESSENTIALS

GETTING THERE   After crossing either the Bourne or Sagamore bridge, take Route 28 or 28A south. Or fly into Hyannis (see "Getting There," in chapter 3).

To get around Falmouth and Woods Hole (where parking in summer is a mathematical impossibility due to ferry traffic to the Islands), use the Whoosh Trolley, which makes an hourly circuit from 9:30am to 6:30pm daily from late May to late September. You can pick up the trolley at the Falmouth Mall on Route 28, where there is plenty of parking. The fare is only $1 for adults, or 50¢ for seniors; children under 5 ride free. The **Sea Line shuttle** (☎ 800/352-7155) connects Woods Hole, Falmouth, and Mashpee with Hyannis year-round (except Sundays and holidays); the fare ranges from $1 to $3.50, depending on distance, and children under 5 ride free.

VISITOR INFORMATION   Contact the **Falmouth Chamber of Commerce,** Academy Lane, Falmouth, MA 02541 (☎ 800/526-8532 or 508/548-8500; fax 508/540-4724), or the **Cape Cod Chamber of Commerce,** Routes 6 and 132, Hyannis, MA 02601 (☎ 508/362-3225; fax 508/362-3698; Web site www.capecod.com).

A STROLL AROUND FALMOUTH

You can start this walk at the Chamber of Commerce, and it'll take you 1 to 3 hours to do the circuit; a museum tour or long walk in the woods will add to your time. The distance is about 1 mile; more if you decide to take a hike. The Falmouth Historical Society Museums are only open Wednesday to Sunday from 2 to 5pm from mid-June to mid-September, if you want to fit them in. Otherwise, any time of day (or year) is fine.

From Main Street in the center of town, head to the **Chamber of Commerce** on Academy Lane (☎ 508/548-8500), a columned Greek Revival building that was once a temple of learning (it was built to house a boys' academy). You can school yourself in Falmouth's sights with the help of the chamber staff, having first taken advantage of the free parking out back (the meters on Main Street tend to fill up fast), as well as the phones and rest rooms. Firm up your plans while enjoying a park-bench view of Shiverick Pond, then, brochures in hand, go back to Main Street and turn right.

In $\frac{1}{8}$ mile, you'll near the triangular point of the **Village Green,** laid out in 1749, where the all-volunteer Falmouth Militia readied itself for the War of Independence. So well trained were they that they succeeded in repelling a British would-be invasion in 1779. Seventeen years later, patriot hero Paul Revere cast the bell that tops the First Congregational Church on the Green's northern side. Its inscription reads: "The living to the church I call, and to the grave I summon all." The Green is encircled by a catalog of architectural styles, including colonial, Federal, Georgian, Greek Revival, and Italian Villa Victorian; several houses are now B&Bs.

Continuing beyond the church, you'll encounter the **Falmouth Historical Society Museums** (☎ 508/548-4857; summer only), two buildings' and a barn's worth of fascinating artifacts. Docents will gladly relate the many intriguing stories they entail. Rest and smell the roses at the historically accurate colonial garden. Then continue down Palmer and turn left on North Main to visit **Enseki Antiques** (☎ 508/548-7744), which offers a small but astute sampling of local treasures dating as far back as the colonial days.

Cross Route 28 onto Depot Avenue, where on your right you'll come across the **Market Bookshop** (☎ 508/540-5636) and **Market Barn Gallery** (☎ 508/540-0480). A family operation since the 1960s, this former butcher's shop offers superb service and a great selection of Cape and Island books. Summertime readings and art shows are mounted in the adjoining barn; ask for a schedule if you plan to stick around.

Keep walking about $\frac{1}{8}$ mile west, bearing right on Depot Avenue Extension, where you'll spot **Highfield Hall,** one of a pair of twin mansions (the other was razed) built by two summering brothers in the 1870s. It's thoroughly derelict (locals are mobilizing to have it restored) but lovely nonetheless. Farther to the right, in the mansion's former stable, is the **Highfield Theatre** (☎ 508/548-0668), where the

College Light Opera Company, with talent drawn from colleges all over the country, mounts musicals throughout the summer. They're often sold out, but see if there's a ticket to spare.

If you still have energy to spare, wander **Beebe Woods,** a 650-acre preserve bought for the town by local philanthropist Josiah K. Lilly. Or go back to Palmer Avenue (Route 28), zigzag briefly right, then left on West Main Street, and you'll be headed back toward the Village Green. On your left, look for plaques commemorating the Falmouth-raised luminary **Katharine Lee Bates,** author of the poem-turned-anthem "America the Beautiful"; she spent her formative years (1859–71) in this modest house. (A statue of Bates stands in the green in front of the library in Falmouth center.) Across the street is **Mostly Hall,** a grand Southern-style mansion built by a New England captain in 1849 to please his New Orleans–born wife. It's now a superb B&B, and the owners are more than happy to greet curiosity-seekers, most of whom will want to come back someday and spend the night.

☕ **WINDING DOWN**   For a well-earned pick-me-up, take a biscotti break at **The Coffee Obsession,** a hip yet friendly coffee bar back at the corner of North Main and Palmer Avenue (☎ **508/540-2233**).

BEACHES & RECREATION

BEACHES   Renters can obtain temporary beach parking stickers for Falmouth—$40 per week, $75 per month—at **Falmouth Town Hall,** 59 Town Hall Sq. (☎ **508/548-8623**), or at the Surf Drive Beach bathhouse in season. The town beaches for which a parking fee is charged all have rest rooms and a concession stand. Here is a list of Falmouth's public shores:

- **Old Silver Beach,** off Route 28A in West Falmouth. Western-facing (great for sunsets) and relatively calm, this is a popular, often crowded choice (parking costs $10 per day). Young mothers and their charges cluster on the opposite side of the street where a shallow pool formed by a sandbar is perfect for toddlers.
- **Nobska Beach,** by the Nobska Lighthouse in Woods Hole. Accessible by bike, via the Shining Sea Bicycle Path, this beach boasts a magnificent view.
- **Surf Drive Beach,** off Shore Street in Falmouth. About a mile from downtown, and appealing to families, this is a serviceable choice with limited parking ($5 per day, $8 on weekends and holidays).
- ✪ **Falmouth Heights Beach,** off Grand Avenue in Falmouth Heights. Acknowledged college-kid turf, this is where teens and twentysomethings tend to congregate. Parking is sticker-only. This neighborhood supported the Cape's first summer colony; the grand Victorian mansions still overlook the beach, though now they are joined by a bevy of motels. Folks have been staggering into the Casino, a bar/restaurant right on the beach, for generations.
- **Menauhant Beach,** off Central Avenue in East Falmouth. A bit off the beaten track, Menauhant is a little less mobbed than Surf Drive Beach, and better protected from the winds. Parking is $5 per day, $8 on weekends and holidays.

BICYCLING   The ✪ **Shining Sea Bicycle Path** (☎ **508/548-8500**) is a 3.6-mile beauty skirting the sound from Falmouth to Woods Hole, by way of the scenic Nobska Lighthouse; it also connects with a 23-mile scenic-road loop through pretty Sippewissett. You can park at the trailhead on Locust Street in Falmouth, or any spot in town (parking in Woods Hole is scarce). The closest bike shop—convenient to the main cluster of B&Bs, some of which offer "loaners"—is **Corner Cycle** at Palmer Avenue and North Main Street (☎ **508/540-4195**). For a broad selection of vehicles—

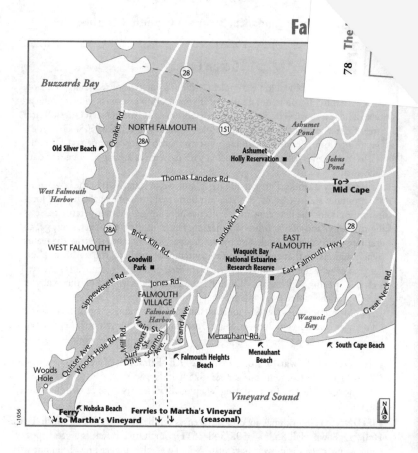

Within the map:

from six-speed cruisers to six-passenger "surreys"—and good advice on routes, visit **Holiday Cycles** at 465 Grand Ave. in Falmouth Heights (☎ **508/540-3549**).

BOATING   Patriot Party Boats, 227 Clinton Ave. (at Scranton Avenue on the harbor), Falmouth (☎ **800/734-0088** or 508/548-2626), offers one-stop shopping for would-be boaters. The Patriot fleet includes a high-speed fishing boat, the *Minuteman;* a poky fishing/sightseeing vessel, the *Patriot Too;* and a sleek replica 1750s Pinky schooner, the *Liberte* (2-hr. sails; $20 adults, $14 children 12 and under). Scenic cruises are offered on the last two, sometimes with company founder Bud Tietje on board. While wending among the Elizabeth Islands, some privately owned by the Forbes family, he can give you the scoop on local gossip and lore. Even if the scenery weren't so lovely, his stories would make the time fly. The Patriot crew also offers ferry service directly to Oak Bluffs on Martha's Vineyard ($5 per person). Boats operate off-season, Monday to Saturday, four times a day; call for schedule and hours.

Cape Cod Coastal Canoe & Kayak (☎ **888/226-6393** or 508/564-4051; Web site www.capecod.net/canoe/; E-mail cccanoe@capecod.net) runs naturalist-guided trips throughout the Cape, sponsored by the Cape Cod Museum of Natural History. In Falmouth, they paddle around West Falmouth Harbor, Waquoit Bay, and over to Washburn Island. Trips (3½ to 4 hr.) are daily April through August, weekends through October, and cost $25 per paddler or $50 per family. All equipment is supplied. Call for schedule.

Ocean Quest

No visit to the Cape would be complete without some type of seafaring excursion on the Atlantic. If you're not a sailor or if you just don't have the time or budget for an all-day boat trip, consider a unique, hands-on cruise with **Ocean Quest,** Water Street (in the center of town), Woods Hole (☎ **800/376-2326** or 508/457-0508). Departing from Woods Hole, these $1^{1}/_{2}$-hour harbor cruises are perfect for families, as real marine research is conducted with passengers serving as bona fide data collectors.

Here's how it works. Participants are split into two teams. Up in the bow, company founder Kathy Mullin, or a scientist borrowed from one of the revered local institutes, trains the new crew in the niceties of reading water temperature, assessing turbidity, and taking other key measurements; in the stern, passengers get to examine the specimens hauled up by the dredger. Midway into the trip, the teams switch stations, so that everyone gets to contemplate, perhaps, the sex life of a spider crab or why the water looks a particular shade of blue or green. Kids get a real kick out of being addressed as "Doctor," and even adults who think they know it all will probably come away much better informed.

The 90-minute rides cost $14 for adults and $10 for children 3 to 12; boats shove off daily at 10am, noon, 2pm, and 4pm from mid-June through early September.

In addition, **Edward's Boat Yard,** 1209 E. Falmouth Hwy., East Falmouth (☎ **408/548-2216**), rents out canoes ($25 half day, $35 full day) and kayaks ($20 half day, $30 full day) for exploring Waquoit Bay (see "Nature & Wildlife Areas," below).

FISHING Falmouth has six ponds: Licenses can be obtained at **Falmouth Town Hall,** 59 Town Hall Sq. (☎ **508/548-7611**). Surf Drive Beach is a great spot for surf casting, once the crowds have dispersed. To go after bigger prey, head out with a group on one of the **Patriot Party Boats** based in Falmouth's Inner Harbor (☎ **800/734-0088** or 508/548-2626). The clunky *Patriot Too,* with an enclosed deck, is ideal for family-style "bottom fishing," (half-day sails $20 adults, $14 children; equipment provided) and the zippy *Minuteman* ($60 per person) is geared to pros. Serious aficionados will want to go gunkholing with 30-year veteran Capt. John Christian on his **Aquasport** *Susan Jean* (☎ **508/548-6901**), moored in Woods Hole's Eel Pond, to hunt for trophy bass among the neighboring Elizabeth Islands.

FITNESS If you're jonesing for some time in the gym, the **Falmouth Sports Club** at 33 Highfield Dr. (☎ **508/548-7433**) offers racquet sports and weight-training facilities for $6 per day.

GOLF As befits its conservative image, Falmouth abounds in golf courses—six public ones at last count, more than any other Cape town. Among the more notable is the challenging 18-hole championship course at **Ballymeade Country Club,** 125 Falmouth Woods Rd. (☎ **508/540-4005**). Greens fees are $58 to $75 and include carts.

HORSEBACK RIDING Experienced English-style riders can head out on wooded trail rides at **Haland Stables,** 878 Rte. 28A in West Falmouth (☎ **508/540-2552**); those lacking experience can stay in the ring and learn.

ICE-SKATING Public skating is offered mid-September to mid-March at the **Falmouth Ice Arena,** 9 Skating Lane off Palmer Avenue (☎ **508/548-9083**); call for information.

NATURE & WILDLIFE AREAS   Though hardly in its natural state, the
❂ **Ashumet Holly and Wildlife Sanctuary,** operated by the Massachusetts
Audubon Society at 186 Ashumet Rd., off Route 151 (☎ **508/563-6390**), is an
intriguing 49-acre collection of more than 1,000 holly trees—spanning 65 species,
culled worldwide—preserved by the state's first commissioner of agriculture, who was
concerned that commercial harvesting might wipe out native species; they're flour-
ishing here, along with over 130 species of birds and a carpet of Oriental lotus blossoms, which covers a kettle pond come summer. The trail fee is $3 for adults, $2 for
seniors and children under 13.

Right in the town of Falmouth (just follow Depot Road to the end) is the 650-acre
Beebe Woods, equally appealing to hikers and mountain-bikers. Though small (the
standard 40 acres), the former farmland surrounding the 1775 **Bourne Farm** off
Route 28 in North Falmouth (☎ **508/438-0711**) makes for very pleasant walks, but
beware of poison ivy and ticks. Quite tiny but dazzling, the privately owned **Spohr's
Garden** on Fells Road, off Oyster Pond Road in Woods Hole, invites visitors to explore 3 acres in continuous bloom from spring to fall.

The 2,250-acre **Waquoit Bay National Estuarine Research Reserve,** at 149
Waquoit Hwy. in East Falmouth (☎ **508/457-0495**), maintains a 1-mile, self-
guiding nature trail. Also inquire about WBNERR's ferry over to Washburn Island
on Saturday in season by reservation (it's about a half-hour paddle via canoe) and its
11 primitive campsites—permits cost a mere $4 a night. The reserve offers a num-
ber of interpretive programs, including the popular "Evenings on the Bluff," geared
to families.

Call of the Wild (☎ **508/548-0521**), a new shop at 47 N. Main St. (in the
Queens Buyway), Falmouth, runs nature tours all over the Cape. Cost is $60 for the
day, including box lunch. Call for schedule.

TENNIS   Among the courts open to the public are those at the **Falmouth High
School,** 874 Gifford Rd. (Falmouth Recreation Dept. ☎ **508/457-2567**). It's
come first served; if they're filled up, ask about the half-dozen other sites open to all
comers. Among the commercial enterprises offering outdoor courts—clay, Har-Tru,
and hard—are the **Falmouth Tennis Club,** Dillingham Avenue Extension (☎ **508/
548-4370**) and the **Ballymeade Country Club** (see "Golf," above). The **Falmouth Sports Club** (see "Fitness," above) has six indoor courts in addition to three
outside.

WATER SPORTS   Falmouth is something of a sailboarding mecca, prized for its
unflagging southwesterly winds. Both boards and boats can be rented at **Cape Cod
Windsurfing Academy & Watersports Rentals** (☎ **508/495-0008**), located at the
Surfside Resort in Falmouth Heights; they also offer windsurfing lessons by appointment. Windsurfers can be rented for $15 an hour, $40 for a half day, or $50 for a
full day. Kayaks rent for $15 an hour, $25 for a half day, or $35 for a full day. Sun-
fish sailboats rent for $30 an hour, $50 for a half day, and $90 for a full day. Among
the best boarding sites is Old Silver Beach in North Falmouth, where tyros can take
lessons—again, by appointment—at the **New England Windsurfing Academy**
(☎ **508/540-8106**) located alongside the Sea Crest resort and the Trunk River area
on the west end of Falmouth's Surf Drive Beach—the only public beach where
Windsurfers are allowed during the day.

SEA SCIENCE

Marine Biological Laboratory. Water St. (at MBL St., in the center of town), Woods Hole.
☎ **508/289-7623.** Free admission. Tours June–Aug Mon–Fri at 1, 2, and 3pm. Closed to the
public Sept–May.

A visit to this cutting-edge think tank, housed in an 1836 candle factory, requires a little forethought—the MBL prefers that reservations be made a week in advance—but will definitely reward the curious. After a slide presentation, a retired scientist leads a guided tour through the holding tanks, and then to the lab to observe actual research in progress. The MBL's area of inquiry is not limited to the aquatic, but encompasses the "biological process common to all life forms"; some of what you see may have an immediate bearing on your own life, or that of your descendants.

National Marine Fisheries Service Aquarium. Albatross St. (off the western end of Water St.), Woods Hole. ☎ **508/495-2000.** Free admission. Mid-June to mid-Sept daily 10am–4pm; mid-Sept to mid-June Mon–Fri 10am–4pm.

A little beat up after 1¼ centuries of service and endless streams of eager school-children, this aquarium—the first such institution in the country—is no longer what you'd call state of the art, but is a treasure nonetheless. The displays, focusing on local waters, might make you think twice before taking a dip. Children show no hesitation, though, in getting up to their elbows in the "touch tanks"; adults are also welcome to dabble. A key exhibit that everyone should see concerns the effect of plastic trash on the marine environment. You might time your visit to coincide with the feeding of two seals who summer here: The fish fly at 11am and 3pm.

Woods Hole Oceanographic Institution Exhibit Center and Gift Shop. 15 School St. (off Water St.), Woods Hole. ☎ **508/289-2663.** Donations encouraged. May–Oct Tues–Sat 10am–4:30pm, Sun noon–4:30pm; call for off-season hrs. Closed Jan–Mar.

Unlike its older neighbor, the Marine Biological Laboratory, this world-class research organization—locally referred to by its acronym, pronounced "Hooey"—does not cotton to the idea of curious onlookers peering over their scientists' shoulders. With some $80 million in annual funding at stake, it's easy to see why. Instead, would-be visitors are steered to a visitor center where they can watch revolving videos covering, among other topics, WHOI's discovery of the Titanic in 1985.

FALMOUTH HISTORICAL SIGHTS

The Falmouth Historical Society runs air-conditioned trolley tours of Falmouth's historic sites on select dates in summer and fall. In 1997, the trolley ran every other Saturday from late June to mid-November and tickets were $10 for adults and $8 for children. Stop by the Historical Society, 55-56 Palmer Ave. or the Chamber of Commerce, Academy Lane, for this year's schedule.

Falmouth Historical Society Museums. 55-65 Palmer Ave. (at the Village Green). ☎ **508/548-4857.** Admission $3 adults, 50¢ children under 12. Mid-June to mid-Sept Wed–Sun 2–5pm. Closed mid-Sept to mid-June.

Knowledgeable volunteers will lead you through three buildings that contain fascinating vestiges of Falmouth's colorful history. Tours begin at the 1790 Julia Woods House, built in 1790 by Revolutionary physician Dr. Francis Wicks; a simulacrum of his office, complete with terrifying tools, is not for the faint of heart. Next door, past an authentic colonial garden, is the mid-18th-century Conant House, which evolved from a half-Cape built to accommodate the town's minister; it now houses nautical collections, including intricate "sailor's valentines" made of shells, alongside some South Seas booty. One room is dedicated to native daughter Katharine Lee Bates, who in 1893 wrote the poem that would become the popular anthem "America the Beautiful." Also on the grounds is the Dudley Hallett Barn, which contains vintage farm tools and the sleigh that Dr. Wicks used for house calls.

Woods Hole Historical and Maritime Museum. 573 Woods Hole Rd. (on the eastern edge of town), Woods Hole. ☎ **508/548-7270.** Suggested donation, $1. Tues and Thurs 10am–2pm.

Exhibits change and can be just a touch amateur—this is, after all, a local labor of love. However, the permanent 1895 diorama of town should give you the former flavor of this combination seaport/scientific community and tourist destination, and the neighboring barn shelters a fine example of a "spritsail" boat. To delve into town lore in more detail, reserve a place on one of the free walking tours offered Tuesdays at 4pm in July and August.

BASEBALL

Part of the elite-amateur **Cape Cod Baseball League** (☎ 508/432-6909), the Commodores play at Fuller Field, off Main Street, in July and August. Call the **Falmouth Chamber of Commerce** (☎ 508/548-8500) to check the schedule, or pick one up at the **Falmouth Recreation Center,** 790 E. Main St. (☎ 508/457-2567).

KID STUFF

If the rain is driving you all up the wall, head to the Falmouth Mall on Route 28, where you'll find the **Cape Cod Children's Museum** (☎ 508/457-4667; call for hours). Here, children can blow off steam—educationally—in the bubble room or on the pirate ship for a mere $3 (only $2 for youngsters 1 to 4).

SHOPPING

Conservative sorts will like the sturdy bourgeois stock of Falmouth's better stores. More adventurous types might prefer the offerings in West Falmouth and Woods Hole.

ANTIQUES/COLLECTIBLES   Somewhat musty and mysterious, in the manner of traditional antique shops, **Aurora Borealis,** 104 Palmer Ave. (1 block west of the Village Green), Falmouth (☎ 508/540-3385), specializes in vintage china, Japanese prints, and local memorabilia. **Chrisalis Country Home,** 550 Rte. 28A (in the center of town), West Falmouth (☎ 508/540-5884), a pleasantly packed shop, is owned by Dorothy Donlan. She operates an interior-design business from these digs—it ought to be booming, judging from her astute antique selection and inspired pairings of old and new.

On her way to the Martha's Vineyard ferry in Woods Hole, Jackie O. often stopped into the **Antiquarium** at 204 Palmer Ave. (located next to the Steamship Parking lots; ☎ 508/548-1755), the exquisite red clapboard Greek Revival house with the intriguing geometric fence. This is a quirky place, open only when the flag is out, but inside are treasures. Mr. O. D. Garland carries a general mixture of American and European antiques, as well as decorative arts. Though I've yet to find any true treasures at **Village Barn,** 606 Rte. 28A (in the center of town), West Falmouth (☎ 508/540-3215), housed in a beautiful old barn, that doesn't mean I've given up—I'm willing to bet that next time, a windfall awaits.

ARTS & CRAFTS   The **Falmouth Artists Guild,** 744 Main St. (at Scranton Avenue), Falmouth (☎ 508/540-3304), is a definite cut above comparable community enterprises. This coalition shows keen aesthetic judgment in its juried group shows. A sideline of the beloved Market Bookshop (see "Books," below), the roomy **Market Barn Gallery,** 15 Depot Ave. (west of North Main Street), Falmouth (☎ 508/540-0480), is host to shows by promising local artists, as well as readings by accomplished local authors.

Owner/artist Marcia Szent-Gyorgyi's own vibrant abstract paintings line the stairway as you make your way up to **Gallery Szent-Gyorgyi** (☎ 508/540-8164) on Main Street. Szent-Gyorgyi started this gallery to bring "contemporary work not of a seasonal nature" to the area. She has succeeded with shows featuring

Cuban art and other international fare. Don't miss the work of one of Cape Cod's premier artists, Wellfleet's John Grillo, who paints dynamic and colorful figures.

The **Woods Hole Gallery,** 14 School St. (north of Water Street), Woods Hole (☎ 508/548-7594), is far enough off the beaten path so you won't stumble onto it by accident, but collectors will want to call on Edith Bruce, an art restorer who operates a distinguished gallery out of her home. Landscapes—dunescapes, specifically—are a specialty; closed mid-September to late June.

The compact but focused **Woods Hole Handworks,** 68 Water St. (by the Eel Pond drawbridge), Woods Hole (☎ 508/540-5291), features the handiwork of a dozen or so local artisans—including weaver Gunjan Laborde, known for her rainbow-hued chenilles.

BOOKS   Market Bookshop, 15 Depot Ave. (off North Main Street), Falmouth (☎ 508/540-5636), has been a well-loved institution for over 2 decades. This select bookstore welcomes browsers: In fact, a massive reading table surrounded by comfortable armchairs awaits before a brick hearth that blazes in winter. The subject groupings are sensible, the staff sets out their favorites with firsthand reviews, and the Cape Cod collection is comprehensive.

FASHION   The clothing at **Caline For Kids,** 149 Main St. (in the center of town), Falmouth (☎ 508/548-2533), ranges from practical to elegant, and sometimes manages to be both. Sizes from newborn to 14 are available.

Europa Imports Outlet, 628 Rte. 28A (in the center of town), West Falmouth (☎ 508/540-7814), features imports from all over the world—including straw bags from Africa and handmade fashions from Central America. It adds up to a sophisticated look, liberated from cookie-cutter predictability. There's also a small but adorable selection of clothes for very young children.

Liberty House, 89 Water St. (in the center of town), Woods Hole (☎ 508/548-7568), specializes in the kind of women's clothes that are de rigueur on the Cape and Islands—floaty dresses, nonchalant knits, and fanciful hats. At **Maxwell & Co.,** 200 Main St. (in the center of town), Falmouth (☎ 508/540-8752), men and women alike will find a stylish alternative to all-purpose preppy in this shop featuring neo-Italian designs in laid-back cotton, linen, and cashmere.

FOOD & WINE   People drive from all over the region for the wine selection (and prices) at **Kappy's,** 21 Spring Bars Rd., off Route 28 (☎ 508/548-2600), the Cape's largest liquor, beer, and wine store. "Pick your own" is the password at the long-established **Tony Andrews Farm and Produce Stand,** 398 Old Meeting House Rd. (about 1¹/₂ miles north of Route 28), East Falmouth (☎ 508/548-5257), where it's strawberries early in the summer, tomatoes and more as the season progresses. Of course, you could just buy them here, too, though the Puritans wouldn't have approved.

GIFTS   Bojangles, 239 Main St. (☎ 508/548-9888), a high-end gift shop/boutique, is a significant new addition to Falmouth's Main Street shopping. Stop here for funky gifts and fine crafts including exceptional hand-painted glassware.

MALLS & SHOPPING CENTERS   Falmouth Mall, Route 28 (about 1¹/₂ miles east of town center), Falmouth (☎ 508/540-8329), is pretty generic, but worth seeking out for the Cape Cod Children's Museum if you have little ones in need of amusement (see "Kid Stuff," above).

WHERE TO STAY
EXPENSIVE

Coonamessett Inn. Jones Rd. and Gifford St. (about ¹/₂ mile N of Main St.), Falmouth, MA 02540. ☎ **508/438-2300.** Fax 508/540-9831. 25 suites, 1 cottage. A/C TV TEL. Summer (including continental breakfast) $150–$225 double. AE, MC, V.

A gracious, traditional inn built around the core of a transplanted 1796 homestead (the river it originally flanked was named "place of the big fish"), the Coonamessett has been the social center of town since the century's teens. Its future was in question until the late Josiah K. Lilly, a local resident, funded it with a trust designed to keep its body and soul intact. Set on 7 lushly landscaped acres overlooking a pond, it has the feel of a country club where all comers are welcome. Some of the rooms, decorated in reproduction antiques, can be a bit somber, so try to get one with good light.

The Coonamessett Inn Dining Room is unabashedly formal, and surprisingly good (see "Where to Dine," below). In the adjoining Eli's, a clubbily decorated tavern, a mellow jazz combo holds forth on weekends.

✪ Inn at West Falmouth. 66 Frazar Rd. (off Rte. 28A, in the center of town), West Falmouth, MA 02574. ☎ **508/540-7696.** 6 rms. TEL. Summer (including continental breakfast) $150–$185 double. AE, MC, V.

So thoroughly perfect is this opulent B&B that it has garnered national attention; in 1994 *Country Inns Magazine* voted it one of the top 12 inns in the country. The turn-of-the-century shingle-style mansion, set high on a wooded hill with views to Buzzards Bay, had suffered some hard knocks in its day, serving at one point as a children's camp. New innkeepers have purged it of the last trace of institutionalism: Welcoming your gaze at every turn are tableaux of rare, seemingly serendipitous beauty, from the spacious rooms lavished with custom linens and accented by a few judicious, unusual antiques, to the large living room set about with fresh flowers and heaps of best-sellers begging to be borrowed. Most recently, owner Karen Calvacca has concentrated on the exterior, with glorious landscaping planted around the house. After a leisurely continental breakfast highlighted by fresh-baked pastries, you might carry off a tome to the small, sparkling heated pool set in the deck or wander the beautifully landscaped grounds, seeking the optimal bower. There's a clay tennis court right at hand, and the beach is about a 10-minute walk down a country lane. On blustery days, you might take refuge in the tiny conservatory perfumed by lemon trees, sink into one of the voluminous couches by the fireplace, or retreat to your own private marble whirlpool bath. Whatever the weather, and whatever you do (or don't do), you're sure to come away refreshed.

MODERATE

Bed and Breakfast of Waquoit Bay. 176 Waquoit Hwy. (Rte. 28, about 3 miles SW of the Mashpee rotary), Waquoit, MA 02536. ☎ **508/457-0084.** Fax 508/457-0084. 4 rms. Summer (including full breakfast) $100–$125 double. MC, V.

Tom and Janet Durkin developed an avid following during their years at the Longwood Inn in Marlboro, Vermont, and many devoted guests have sought them out in this remote corner of the Cape. Take a walk around the grounds—3 acres—before settling in: Behind the house, built around 1920, is the unspoiled bank of Child's River, purview of gliding geese and swans. The bedrooms are comfort incarnate, and very private: Two on the second floor adjoin and have their own secluded deck. You may find yourself gravitating to the great room, though—a high-ceilinged, informal salon awash in the Caribbean-influenced paintings by the Durkins' daughter,

Patti. The piano here has been played by such distinguished visitors as Tony Bennett—the Durkins are major jazz fans.

Grafton Inn. 261 Grand Ave. S., Falmouth Heights, MA 02540. ☎ **800/642-4069** or 508/540-8688. Fax 508/540-1861. 10 rms. A/C TV. Summer (including full breakfast) $129–$169 double. AE, MC, V. Closed mid-Dec to mid-Feb.

Reminiscent of a more leisurely age, this turreted Victorian grande dame has a front-row seat on Falmouth Heights's lively beach. View-seekers will be delighted with the vista beyond: Martha's Vineyard, glimmering across the sound. All rooms have extra touches like hair dryers, extra pillows, homemade chocolates, and fresh flowers—as well as coveted ocean views. Breakfast is served at individual tables on the screen porch overlooking the beach. The alternating breakfast menu might include Belgian waffles, Hawaiian toast, or herb omelets. In the afternoon, wine and cheese is served. The ferry to Martha's Vineyard, leaving from Falmouth Harbor, is only an 8-minute walk away.

✪ **Inn on the Sound.** 313 Grand Ave., Falmouth Heights, MA 02540. ☎ **800/564-9668** or 508/457-9666. Fax 508/457-9631. Web site www.falmouth-capecod/fww/inn.on.the.sound. 10 rms. Summer (including full breakfast) $95–$155 double. AE, DISC, MC, V.

The ambiance here is as breezy as the setting, high on a bluff beside Falmouth's premier sunning beach, with a sweeping view of Nantucket Sound. Innkeeper Renee Ross is an interior decorator, and it shows: none of the usual frilly/cutesy stuff in these well-appointed guest rooms, most of which have ocean views. The focal point of the living room is a handsome boulder hearth (nice for those nippy nights). The breakfasts served, especially the surprise French toast (baked and stuffed with cream cheese and berries) or egg-and-cheddar soufflé, offer incentive to dawdle, but the outdoors exerts an even stronger attraction.

The Marlborough. 320 Woods Hole Rd. (about 1 mile SW of Falmouth), Woods Hole, MA 02543. ☎ **800/320-2322** or 508/548-6218. Fax 508/457-7519. 5 rms, 1 cottage. A/C. Summer (including full breakfast) $85–$125. AE, MC, V.

You might mistake it for a private home, this imposing Cape set back from the road atop a terraced garden. The illusion continues in the cozy parlor, and especially in the back yard, where there's a personal-size pool accompanied by a cabana for two that's the ultimate in playhouse romance: It's virtually all bed, with a tiny brick-floor sitting room/foyer. The rooms within the house are quite nice, too, with thoughtful touches such as handmade quilts and lavender-scented sheets.

✪ **Mostly Hall.** 27 W. Main St. (W of the Village Green), Falmouth, MA 02540. ☎ **800/682-0565** or 508/548-3786. Fax 508/457-1572. 6 rms. A/C. Summer (including full breakfast) $115–$125 double. AE, DISC, MC, V. Closed Jan to mid-Feb.

Built by a sea captain to please his New Orleans–born bride, this plantation-style house (unique on the Cape) exudes Southern graciousness and style. Longtime innkeepers Caroline and Jim Lloyd have pretty much mastered the art, providing memorable breakfasts (for example, eggs Benedict soufflé), loaner bikes for exploring the Shining Sea Bikeway to Woods Hole, and plenty of valuable advice for making the most of your stay. The six stately corner bedrooms each boast a canopied four-poster, cheery floral wallpaper, and a lazily whirring ceiling fan (more for effect than function, since the inn is centrally air-conditioned). The gardens are lovely, and the gazebo makes a pleasant retreat—as does the house's cupola, a combo library/videotheque.

Nautilus Motor Inn. 533 Woods Hole Rd. (about $1/2$ mile W of town), Woods Hole, MA 02543. ☎ **800/654-2333** or 508/548-1525. Fax 508/457-9674. Web site www.nautilusinn.com. E-mail JPNautilus@aol.com. 54 rms. A/C TV TEL. Summer $98–$150 double. AE, DC, DISC, MC, V. Closed mid-Oct to mid-Apr.

A crescent-shaped complex poised above Woods Hole's picturesque Little Harbor, the Nautilus doesn't have to do much to make itself attractive: nature has already seen to that. The two tiers of rooms are standard motel-ish, but each comes with a private balcony for taking in the view and/or sunning, and a very spacious wooden deck flanks the fair-sized pool. A rather curious restaurant, The Dome, is right on the premises. An architectural landmark, this very sturdy geodesic dome was R. Buckminster Fuller's first and must have seemed grandly futuristic in 1953. The Martha's Vineyard ferry is a very short stroll away. Not so much a destination in and of itself, the Nautilus makes an ideal launching pad for day trips.

The Palmer House Inn. 81 Palmer Ave. (^{1}/$_2$ block NW of the Village Green), Falmouth, MA 02540. ☎ **800/472-2632** or 508/548-1230. Fax 508/540-1878. 12 rms, 1 cottage. A/C. Summer (including full breakfast) $105–$165 double; $185 cottage. AE, CB, DC, DISC, MC, V.

Full of period details, such as darkly gleaming woodwork and stained-glass windows, this 1901 inn will delight Victoriana-philes. An elegant 19th-century sculptural fountain greets guests, and bold wallpaper enlivens all the rooms. Each has its own brand of romance—especially Tower Room, with its brass bed practically perched in the treetops. Several of the rooms are equipped with Jacuzzis. There is also a handicap accessible first-floor room. And innkeeper Joanne Baker's breakfasts are geared to gourmet/gourmands. How about chocolate stuffed French toast slathered with vanilla cream first thing in the day? Or an afternoon pick-me-up of mulled cider and oven-warm cookies? Here, self-indulgence is the order of the day.

Sands of Time Motor Inn & Harbor House. 549 Woods Hole Rd. (about ^{1}/$_2$ mile W of town), Woods Hole, MA 02543. ☎ **800/841-0114** or 508/548-6300. Fax 408/457-0160. 33 rms (2 with shared bath), suites, and efficiencies. A/C TV TEL. Summer (including continental breakfast) $95–$140 double. AE, CB, DC, DISC, MC, V. Closed Nov–Mar.

It's really two facilities in one: a two-story block of motel rooms (with crisp, above-average decor, plus private porches) and, next door, a shingled 1879 Victorian manse, where the quarters tend to be more lavish and romantic—some with four-posters, working fireplaces, wicker furnishings, the works. Both types of accommodation, though, afford the same charming harbor views and share the well-kept grounds and small pool. A pair of couples traveling together—one B&B-crazy, the other not—could both get their needs met here.

Village Green Inn. 40 W. Main St. (at the Village Green), Falmouth, MA 02540. ☎ **800/ 237-1119** or 508/548-5621. Fax 508/457-5051. E-mail VGI40@aol.com. 4 rms, 1 suite. A/C TV. Summer (including full breakfast) $115–$130 double; $150 suite. Closed Jan–Feb. AE, MC, V.

An 1804 Federal house decked out with Victorian trim toward the turn of the century, this B&B proudly presides over the historic Village Green. The ambiance is comfy rather than stuffy. For room to really stretch out, opt for the sunny suite, complete with desk and daybed for (respectively) tackling the homework you imprudently lugged along or, alternately, ditching it in favor of a novel and bonbons—provided you're still peckish after a breakfast of, say, caramelized French toast, plus a sweet afternoon snack on the geranium-bedecked porch.

Wildflower Inn. 167 Palmer Ave. (2 blocks N of Main St.), Falmouth, MA 02540. ☎ **800/ 294-5459** or 508/548-9524. Fax 508/548-9524. 5 rms, 1 cottage. A/C. Summer (including full breakfast) $115–$165 double; cottage $750 weekly. AE, MC, V.

Converted in the summer of 1994, this B&B appears to be doing everything right. Decor in the main-house rooms ranges from mostly countrified (innkeeper Donna

Stone also teaches quilting) to one "safari-style" aberration, featuring an iron canopy bed draped with purely decorative mosquito netting, and accents of burlap, bamboo, and rattan. Two dormered rooms on the top floor come with whirlpool baths, and the attached "town house" (a former stable) features a loft bedroom served by a spiral staircase. Breakfast, enjoyed on the wraparound porch in summer, starts with a fruit compote and might culminate in such treats as apple-pie French toast. The inn was recently featured on a TV show about country-inn cooking, which aired on PBS.

Woods Hole Passage. 186 Woods Hole Rd. (about 2 miles N of town center), Woods Hole, MA 02540. ☎ **800/790-8976** or 508/548-9575. Fax 508/540-4771. Web site www.ccsnet.com/whpassage. E-mail woods.hole.inn@usa.net. 5 rms. A/C. Summer (including full breakfast) $105–$115 double. AE, CB, DC, DISC, MC, V.

The decorative approach here is ultratasteful, yet anything but quaint. In the main building, a former carriage house, the walls have been painted a somewhat shocking pink—which actually works quite well to frame the greenery of the extensive garden out back. Guests rave over delicious breakfasts served at individual tables by new innkeeper Deb Pruitt. In season, you can dine outside on the slate porch overlooking the grounds. The two cathedral-ceiling loft rooms in the adjoining 18th-century barn are definitely the most covetable, and seem custom-made for honeymooning (or otherwise cocooning) couples.

INEXPENSIVE

Inn at One Main. 1 W. Main St. (at N. Main St., 1 block SW of the Village Green), Falmouth, MA 02540. ☎ **508/540-7469.** 6 rms. A/C. Summer (including full breakfast) $95–$115 double. AE, MC, V.

Though a centenarian (built in 1892), this shingled house with Queen Anne flourishes has a youthful air—imparted by the innkeepers, Mari Zylinski and Karen H. Peirson. The bedrooms embody barefoot romance, rather than the Victorian brand. Lace, chintz, and wicker have been laid on lightly, leaving plenty of room to kick about. The Turret Room, with its big brass bed, is perhaps the most irresistible, and breakfasts would instantly convert a "just coffee, please" morning-grouch. Gingerbread pancakes, cranberry-pecan waffles, homemade scones—it's a good thing the Shining Sea Bikeway is right at hand.

WHERE TO DINE
EXPENSIVE

✪ **The Regatta at Falmouth-by-the-Sea.** 217 Clinton Ave. (off Scranton Ave., about 1 mile S of Main St.). ☎ **508/548-5400.** Reservations recommended. Dress: "Attractively formal or informal." Main courses $20–$30. AE, MC, V. May–Sept daily 4:30–10pm. Closed Oct–Apr. INTERNATIONAL.

A dazzler since its very debut in 1970, this exemplary restaurant has it all: views (it's right on the harbor), polished yet innovative cuisine, and superb service. You're likely to find owner Brantz Bryan affably circulating: He's the one who seems to have wandered in off a golf course, vigorous and "attractively informal" in tastefully lurid preppy attire. His wife and partner, Wendy Bryan, designed the decor, from the rose-petal pale walls to the custom Limoges china on which two roses entwine. New chef Gilbert Pepin continues the excellence and innovation in the kitchen. Customers would rightfully squawk if certain menu offerings were to vanish. These include a celestial crab-and-corn chowder, and the lamb *en chemise*—stuffed with chèvre, spinach, and pine nuts, baked in puff pastry, and cloaked in a cabernet-sauvignon sauce. If the dessert decision throws you into a tizzy, abandon all caution and order the "trilogy"—or several, with sufficient spoons.

For those who would dine here every summer night but for the prices, note that the Regatta serves a lighter-fare menu nightly (excluding Saturdays and holidays) from 4:30 on; there is also a seven-course "early dinner" from 4:30 to 5:45pm—an elegant meal deal.

The Waterfront. 77 Water St. (W of the Eel Pond drawbridge), Woods Hole. ☎ **508/ 548-9206.** Reservations recommended. Main courses $15–$29. AE, CB, MC, V. Early June to early Sept daily 6–11pm. Closed late Sept to early June. INTERNATIONAL.

Surprising culinary sophistication lurks within this dark-timbered, sail-loft–like space, camouflaged behind the most popular bar in town (Cap'n Kidd). Sticker shock quickly subsides as you contemplate such well-wrought dishes as seafood en croute, or simply broiled swordfish, splashed with champagne beurre blanc. Provided the sky permits, you'll want to request one of the tables on the pier that juts out into Eel Pond.

MODERATE

✪ **Coonamessett Inn Dining Room.** Jones Rd. and Gifford St. (see "Where to Stay," above). ☎ **508/548-2300.** Reservations recommended. Main courses $9–$24. AE, MC, V. Daily 8– 10am and 5–9:30pm; Mon–Sat 11:30am–4:30pm, Sun 11:30am–2pm. NEW AMERICAN.

If the somewhat stuffy ambiance has led you to expect bland country-club fare, you're in for a very pleasant surprise indeed. New owners Bill and Linda Zammer have brought back chef Rich Cole, who regales diners with fresh fish dishes, like pecan-encrusted halibut, in addition to the usual fare. Whimsical mermaid paintings, the work of local legend Ralph Cahoon, plus chandeliers shaped like hot-air balloons, render the middle dining room (the largest of three, capable of accommodating 300 in total) a semiplayful power spot. If you arrive early, you may be able to snag one of the comfy leather armchairs in pubby Eli's, a great place to settle in for an evening of dining and entertainment.

✪ **Fishmonger's Cafe.** 56 Water St. (at the Eel Pond drawbridge), Woods Hole. ☎ **508/ 540-5376.** Main courses $10–$19. AE, MC, V. Mid-June to mid-Oct Mon–Thurs 7–11am, 11:30am–4pm, and 5–10pm; Fri 7–11am, 11:30am–4pm, and 5–10:30pm; Sat 7–11:30am, noon–4:30pm, and 5:30–10:30pm; Sun 7am–noon, 12:30–4:30pm, and 5:30–10:30pm. Call for off-season hrs. Closed mid-Dec to mid-Feb. NATURAL.

A cherished carryover from the early 1970s, this sunny cafe attracts local young people and execs as well as Bermuda-shorted tourists, with an ever-changing array of imaginatively prepared dishes. Regulars might grab a bite at the counter while schmoozing with staff bustling about the open kitchen. Newcomers usually go for the tables by the window, where you can watch the Eel Pond boats come and go. The menu ranges widely (lunch could be a tempeh burger, made with fermented soybeans, or ordinary beef), and longtime customers look to the blackboard for the latest innovations, which invariably include some delectable albeit politically correct desserts, such as pumpkin-pecan pie. Many visitors, one suspects, must miss the Martha's Vineyard ferry on purpose, as an excuse to stop in for a bite.

Landfall. Luscombe Ave. (half a block S of Water St.), Woods Hole. ☎ **508/548-1758.** Fax 508/549-6477. Web site www.ccsnet.com/landfall. Reservations recommended. Main courses $15–$21. MC, V. Mid-Apr to Oct daily 11am–11pm. Closed Nov to mid-Apr. AMERICAN.

A terrific setting overshadows the middling cuisine and ho-hum entertainment. Come for a drink, at least, to enjoy this massive wooden building constructed of salvage, both marine and terrestrial. The weighty beams once supported a Cape Ann pier; the stained-glass panels were purloined from a jettisoned Harvard Square trolley. A large bank of windows looks out onto the harbor, and the Martha's Vineyard ferry, when docking, appears to be making a beeline straight for your table.

INEXPENSIVE

Betsy's Diner. 457 Main St. (in the center of town). ☎ **508/540-0060.** Main courses $4–$10. AE, MC, V. May–Aug Sun–Thurs 5am–10pm, Fri–Sat 5am–11pm; call for off-season hrs. AMERICAN.

Nothing could be finer than a resurrected diner—especially one offering time-travel food. Turkey dinner, breakfast all day, homemade pies—now, these are traditions worth maintaining. The original aluminum features dazzle as they surely did back then, and the jukebox is primed for retro-rock.

Cape Cod Chicken. 235 Main St. (in the center of town). ☎ **508/457-1302.** Main courses under $7. Daily 11am–9pm. No credit cards. AMERICAN.

For a quick, cheap, delicious meal, duck into this tiny storefront restaurant, where you can custom-compose a platter of succulent rotisserie chicken plus such enticing sides as tarragon carrots and garlic-roasted bliss potatoes. While awaiting your order, check out the evocative flea-market artifacts decorating the walls.

✪ **Cap'n Kidd.** 77 Water St. (W of the Eel Pond drawbridge), Woods Hole. ☎ **508/548-9206.** Main courses $8–$15. AE, MC, V. Daily 11am–3pm and 5–9pm. SEAFOOD.

The semiofficial heart of town, this well-worn bistro really comes into its own once the tourist hordes subside. It's then that the year-round scientists and fishing crews can again belly up to the hand-carved mahogany bar (thought to date from the early 1800s), or huddle around the woodstove in the glassed-porch back, beside the pond, and order up reasonably priced seafood, or drink to their heart's content—mostly the latter, judging from the degree of general bonhomie. The notorious 17th-century pirate, who is rumored to have debarked in Woods Hole on his way back to England to be hung, would probably get a warm reception were he to wander in today. The Kidd shares a kitchen with The Waterfront (see above) though the fare here is mainly pub grub and some seafood. Individual pizzas, burgers, and sandwiches are the mainstays. Homemade clam chowder is thick as paste with large chunks of potato and clam.

Chapaquoit Grill. 410 Rte. 28A, W. Falmouth. ☎ **508/540-7794.** Main courses $8–$16. MC, V. Daily 5–10pm. NEW AMERICAN.

One of the few worthwhile dining spots in this sleepy neck of the woods, this little roadside bistro has Californian aspirations—and attains them, with wood-grilled slabs of fish accompanied by trendy salsas, and crispy personal pizzas delivered straight from the brick oven.

The Chickadee at Peach Tree Circle Farm: 818 Old Palmer Ave. (between Rtes. 28 and 28A). ☎ **508/548-2354.** Lunch main courses $5–$10. No credit cards. July–Aug Mon–Sat 8am–6pm, Sun 10am–4pm; Sept–June daily 10am–4pm. AMERICAN.

You'd have to pick your own produce and race to the kitchen to get meals any fresher. This charming farm stand fronts vast fields of flowers and fine produce, which you're welcome to roam; some of the bounty ends up in the little cafe attached. You may never encounter a crisper, healthier salad. Vegetables also star in the improvised soups and home-baked quiches; fruits in the jellies and jams and in the fiendish pastry bars. Whether you pack a picnic or choose to settle in, definitely stock up before departing.

✪ **The Clam Shack.** 227 Clinton Ave. (off Scranton Ave., about 1 mile S of Main St.). ☎ **508/540-7758.** Main courses $5–$11. No credit cards. Daily 11:30am–7:45pm. Closed mid-Sept to late May. SEAFOOD.

"Shack" is the appropriate name for this place, a tumble-down shanty that clings to its pier like a barnacle, having weathered 3 decades of nor'easters, not to mention the occasional hurricane. The fare has withstood the test of time, too: your basic fried clams (with belly intact, the sign of a joint that knows clams) and whatever else the nets have tossed up. Sitting at a postage-stamp table hinged to the wall, you can soak up a truly magnificent view.

The Flying Bridge. 220 Scranton Ave. (about $^1/_2$ mile S of Main St.). ☎ **508/548-2700.** Main courses $8–$16. AE, MC, V. Late May to early Sept daily 11:30am–9:30pm; call for off-season hrs. AMERICAN/CONTINENTAL.

Seafood, appropriately enough, predominates at this shipshape harborside mega-restaurant (capacity: some 600). With three bars tossed into the mix and live music on weekends, things can get a bit vociferous; you'll find comparative peace and quiet—as well as tiptop nautical views—out on the deck. In addition to basic bar food (Buffalo chicken wings and the like), you'll find hefty hunks of protein and fish in many guises, from fish-and-chips—with optional malt vinegar—to appealing blackboard specials.

Moonakis Cafe. 460 Waquoit Hwy. (about 2$^1/_2$ miles SW of the Mashpee rotary). ☎ **508/457-9630.** Lunch main courses $4–$9. No credit cards. Mar–Nov Mon–Sat 7am–2pm, Sun 7am–1pm; call for off-season hrs. AMERICAN.

This cheery little country-style cafe could put the most dedicated of B&B chefs to shame. Breakfast is their main stock in trade, and they're going for the gold, with such omelet combos as lobster, asparagus, and Swiss. The pancakes of the day could be pumpkin-nut; the Belgian waffles might come topped with sliced kiwi. Lunch choices may be less outré, though the caloric largesse returns with dessert.

Oysters Too. 876 Rte. 28 (midway between Falmouth and the Mashpee rotary). ☎ **508/548-9191.** Reservations not accepted. Main courses $12–$15. AE, DISC, MC, V. May–Oct Mon–Thurs 4:30–9pm, Fri–Sat 4:30–10pm, Sun 4–9pm. Closed Mon Nov–Apr. NEW AMERICAN/CONTINENTAL.

From the roadside, this looks like the kind of interchangeable modern restaurant that scarcely warrants a second look. Give it one, though, because the spotless interior is actually quite pleasant, with retro-looking wooden booths where a quartet could order a meal easily worth twice the price. Swordfish, for instance, might come stuffed with crabmeat and sun-dried tomatoes, and the scampi *amoureuse* arrive basking on a bed of tomato concasse and angel-hair pasta, sprinkled with almonds and anisette. Everything available has "good value" written all over it. *One caveat:* during the summer, the no reservations policy means long waits—an hour is not uncommon.

Peking Palace. 452 Main St. (in the center of town). ☎ **508/540-8204.** Fax 508/540-8382. Main courses $8–$12. AE, DC, MC, V. June–Aug daily 11:30am–2am; Sept–May Sun–Thurs 11:30am–midnight, Fri–Sat 11:30am–1:30am. CHINESE.

Incontrovertibly the best Chinese restaurant on the Cape, and among the top contenders in the state, this smallish restaurant has been infused with TLC at every turn. From the fringes of bamboo gracing the parking lot to the gleaming rosewood tables, no detail has been overlooked to create a cosseting, exotic environment. It's a wonder the staff finds the time, what with 300-plus items on the menu, spanning three regional cuisines (Cantonese, Mandarin, and Szechuan), as well as Polynesian. Sip a fanciful drink to give yourself time to take in the menu, and be sure to solicit your server's opinion: That's how we encountered some heavenly spicy chilled squid.

The Quarterdeck Restaurant. 164 Main St. (opposite Town Hall Sq.). ☎ **508/548-9900.** Main courses $10–$16. AE, CB, DC, DISC, MC, V. June–Sept daily 11:30am–10:30pm; call for off-season hrs. INTERNATIONAL.

Chef Keith Pacheco is amazingly versatile. He'll turn out Portuguese pork chops, Cajun-spiced barbecue, and veal meunière all in the course of an ordinary evening.

Despite the standard-issue nautical trappings, this civilized spot is a definite cut above other look-alikes.

Shucker's World Famous Raw Bar & Cafe. 91A Water St. ($^{1}/_{2}$ block W of the Eel Pond drawbridge), Woods Hole. ☎ **508/540-3850.** Main courses $9–$15. AE, MC, V. Mid-May to mid-Oct daily 11am–11pm. Closed mid-Oct to mid-May. INTERNATIONAL.

A tight cluster of cafe tables hugging the edge of Eel Pond, this outdoor cafe has a loyal following, drawn by the well-priced, excellent seafood. The chowder is so thick with seafood (including the odd shrimp and crab) that it's truly a meal. Kids get star treatment here with their own menu and a little surprise (like a pig nose or a toy car). In season, jaunty calypso performers may be performing. Owner Kevin Murphy is also the force behind Falmouth's beloved local brew, Nobska Light, named for the resident lighthouse.

The Silver Lounge. 412 Rte. 28A, N. Falmouth ☎ **508/563-2410.** Main courses $10–$17. AE, DISC, MC, V. Daily 11:30am–1am. REGIONAL.

In the middle of winter, when many Cape restaurants are struggling to survive, this place has an hour wait and a line out the door. It's long been a favorite with locals, and visitors often "discover" it while driving scenic Route 28A. Overall, it's a publike place with a large stone hearth, but families come in droves because kids love to sit in the caboose where there are just nine booths (come early if you want one). This is a meat-and-potatoes crowd and the most popular menu item is the Black Diamond steak. Weekends in summer, you might find the talented kids from the College Light Opera Company at the piano, entertaining the late-night dinner crowd with show tunes.

The Wharf Restaurant. 281 Grand Ave. S. (off Main St., on the Falmouth Heights Beach), Falmouth Heights. ☎ **508/548-0777.** Main courses $9–$15. AE, MC, V. Mid-May to mid-Sept daily 11:30am–1am; call for off-season hrs. Closed Jan–Apr. AMERICAN.

Set atop a bluff overlooking Nantucket Sound, this grand old restaurant has served sea-seekers since the turn of the century; you can admire their bathing attire in the vintage photos lining the entry. The walls are decorated with the usual intriguing mishmash of weathered signs and wreckage, and the view across to Martha's Vineyard is pretty transporting. The seafood offerings may be run-of-the-mill, but all of it is as fresh as can be; Captain Bill, the owner, even catches some of it himself.

TAKE-OUT & PICNIC FARE

Cape Cod Bagel Co., 419 Palmer Ave. (☎ **508/548-8485**), carries the usual bagel sandwiches, soups, coffee, and other beverages, but the bagels here, made on the premises, are definitely the best in town. **Box Lunch,** 781 Main St. (☎ **508/457-7657**), is one of a number of franchises on the Cape that carry the pita "rollwiches." These are excellent sandwiches (over 50 selections) made fast, and they're perfect for picnics.

COFFEEHOUSES

Laureen's, at 170 Main St. in the center of town (☎ **508/540-9104**), is a sophisticated coffee bar/deli, ideal for a quick bite or sip. In addition to the usual fare, they have a selection of Middle Eastern food. You can also take some of this good stuff home. Kitchen gear, and gifts in general, including some great stuff for kids, round out the stock. Another spot is **The Coffee Obsession** (☎ **508/540-2233**), a hip yet friendly coffee bar back at the corner of North Main and Palmer Avenue.

SWEETS

Falmouth residents are the beneficiaries of a three-way struggle for ice-cream bragging rights: **Ben & Bill's Chocolate Emporium,** at 209 Main St., in the center of town (☎ **508/548-7878**), draws crowds even in winter, late into the evening. They come for the homemade ice cream, not to mention the hand-dipped candies showcased in a wraparound display—a chocoholic's nightmare or dream come true, depending. Those who can trust themselves not to go hog-wild might enjoy watching the confections being made. **Dutchland Farms Ice Cream,** at 809 E. Main St., about 1 mile east of town center (☎ **508/548-9032**), is a mecca as well: This seemingly undistinguished shop, the descendant of a Brockton concern established in 1897, has flavors that would give those two guys in Vermont a run for their money. Honolulu Crunch, for instance, comes fortified with crushed macadamias, coconut, and chocolate chips; the "zundap" consists of coffee ice cream laced with fudge and studded with cookies. And **Whistlestop Ice Cream,** at 854 Rte. 28A in West Falmouth (☎ **508/540-7585**), is a tiny shack, packing vintage railroad memorabilia, stopworthy mainly for its locally cranked ice cream, the most noteworthy of which is a concoction called Death by Chocolate.

FALMOUTH AFTER DARK

DRINKS   God knows whom you'll meet in the rough-and-tumble old **Cap'n Kidd,** 77 Water St., in Woods Hole (☎ **508/548-9206**): maybe a lobsterwoman, maybe a Nobel Prize winner. Good grub, too—see "Where to Dine," above.

   ✪ **Casino by the Sea** (a.k.a. the Dry Dock Lounge), at 281 Grand Ave., beneath the Wharf Restaurant (☎ **508/548-0777**), is essentially a dance hall catering to twentysomethings. The fun spills over from the sand; locally bred bands provide the beat. There's a $5 cover. Closed October through April.

   Everyone heads to **Liam McGuire's Irish Pub** on 273 Main St. in Falmouth (☎ **508/548-0285**) for a taste of the Emerald Isle. Liam's the jolly, back-slapping guy with a touch of the blarney.

   An alternative to rowdy bars is **The Coffee Obsession,** 110 Palmer Ave., near Route 28 (☎ **508/540-2233**), a *Friends*-style coffeehouse—something like a communal living room. Occasionally, someone may be moved to play some music or recite some poetry, but mostly the entertainment engenders itself. Props include various games, books, and dictionaries, but talking is what it's really all about. In summer (May through September) the salon tends to wind down at about 10pm on weeknights, an hour later on weekends; off-season hours vary, so call ahead. No cover.

PERFORMANCE   The **Woods Hole Folk Music Society** (☎ **508/540-0320**) mounts biweekly concerts October through May, attracting a real grassroots crowd to Community Hall on Water Street, by the Eel Pond drawbridge.

   The **Cape Cod Theatre Project** (☎ **508/362-7575**), a playwrights workshop open to the public, is now 4 years old and going strong. These staged play readings are performed for just a couple weeks in July, usually at the Woods Hole Community Hall. The rest of the year the talent behind these productions are most likely strutting the boards in New York City. Call for schedule. Ticket prices vary.

   Starting at about 7:30pm on Thursday evenings in July and August, the spirited volunteers of the **Falmouth Town Band** swing through big-band numbers as small fries (and some oldsters) dance about. Concerts are held at the Harbor Band Shell, on Scranton Avenue at the harbor in Falmouth, and are free.

   The crème de la crème of college drama departments across the country form the **College Light Opera Company** (☎ **508/548-0668**), which puts on a fast-paced summer repertory—a musical a week, from late June through August. So winning is the work of these 32 young actors and 17 musicians (many of them ultimately Broadway-bound) that the house is usually booked solid, so call well ahead or keep your fingers crossed for a scattering of singles. Its venue, the Highfield Theatre, on the Depot Avenue Extension off North Main Street in Falmouth, is a former horse barn, and for the past half century has been a terrific strawhat theater. Performances are held Tuesdays to Saturdays at 8:30pm; there's also a Thursday matinee at 2:30pm. Tickets are $20.

4 Mashpee

11 miles (18km) SE of Sagamore, 12 miles (20km) W of Hyannis

Mashpee is a study in contrasts and awash in controversy. A sizable chunk of it is occupied by the Otis Air Force Base (a source, it turns out, of troublesome ground-water pollution), and the major portion of its shoreline has been claimed by the New Seabury Resort development. Further housing developments are rapidly carving up the inland woods, leaving less and less room for the region's original residents, the Mashpee Wampanoags, whose nomadic ancestors began convening in summer camps by these shores millennia ago. In 1660, concerned by the natives' rapid disenfranchisement and heartened by their willingness to convert, missionary Richard Bourne got the Plymouth General Court to grant his "praying Indians" a 10,500-acre "plantation" in perpetuity. The provision proved far from perpetual, as settlers—and much later, developers—began chipping away at their holdings.

After lengthy litigation in the 1970s and early 1980s, the Mashpee Wampanoags—whose tribal roster now numbers about 1,000—were denied tribal status (unlike the Gay Head Wampanoags of Martha's Vineyard) and stymied in their efforts to preserve the land. It was only in 1995, with the backing of senators Edward Kennedy and John Kerry (both of whom summer on the Cape), that the sizable—5,871 acres—Mashpee National Wildlife Refuge was carved out of the disputed territory. Influential supporter Gerry Studds hailed the move as "a harbinger of things to come . . . Creation of this refuge ranks in significance with the Cape Cod National Seashore."

ESSENTIALS

GETTING THERE   After crossing the Sagamore bridge, take Route 6 to Exit 2, and Route 130 south. Or fly into Hyannis (see "Getting There," in chapter 3).

VISITOR INFORMATION   Contact the **Mashpee Chamber of Commerce** at the Cape Cod Five Cent Savings Bank, Mashpee Commons, P.O. Box 1245, Mashpee, MA 02649 (☎ **800/423-6274** or 508/477-0792), or the **Cape Cod Chamber of Commerce,** Routes 6 and 132, Hyannis, MA 02601 (☎ **508/362-3225;** fax 508/362-3698; Web site www.capecod.com).

MASHPEE HISTORICAL SIGHTS

Visitors who know a bit about the troubled history of this region have an opportunity to learn more; those who don't will be rewarded with greater insight if they do.

Old Indian Meetinghouse. Meetinghouse Rd. (at Rte. 28). ☎ **508/477-1536.** Free admission. Services open to public on Powwow Sunday (July 4th weekend) and the 2nd Sun in Aug, 11am; call for additional visiting hrs.

The oldest meetinghouse on the Cape, this small chapel was built for the "praying Indians" in 1684 and moved to this site, beside what was then a native burying ground, in 1717; intriguing headstones survive. Considerably more modest than the churches erected for colonial Congregationalists, the chapel is worth a visit, if only to see the graffiti of clipper ships up in the gallery, most likely carved by restless children more than a century ago.

Wampanoag Indian Museum. Rte. 130 (opposite The Flume, on Lake Ave.). ☎ **508/ 477-1536.** Donation requested. Mon–Fri 10am–2pm or Sat by appointment.

Centuries of heartbreaking history are encapsulated in this unprepossessing museum, housed in a 1793 half-Cape built by a great-grandson of pioneer missionary Richard Bourne. Though the native population embraced the colonists' religion wholeheartedly, they never fully grasped the ethos of private property; thus over the years the land vouchsafed to them by the Plymouth court in 1660 was steadily whittled away—most egregiously, starting in the 1960s, when the ratio of undeveloped to developed land in Mashpee was roughly 80% to 20%. The percentages have since been reversed, despite a long legal wrangle.

The museum sells copies of Russell M. Peters's tribal history, *The Wampanoags of Mashpee*—must reading for anyone who hopes to understand the divided nature of this semirural/semisuburban region, much less the role that indigenous peoples played in ensuring the colonists' foothold in the wilderness. The story is far from over, and tourists who take the time to look beneath the surface will gain a deeper appreciation of an area still in flux.

BEACHES & OUTDOOR PURSUITS

BEACHES   The small part of the shoreline not reserved for the New Seabury Resort is an undersung sleeper—and a bargain, too: ۞ **South Cape Beach,** off Great Oak Road (5 miles south of the Mashpee rotary). Mashpee is set amid the 450-acre **South Cape Beach State Park** (☎ **508/457-0495**); this lengthy stretch of beach fronts miles of hiking trails; parking costs $2 per day for nonresidents.

BOATING   Cape Cod Coastal Canoe & Kayak (☎ **888/226-6393** or 508/ 564-4051; Web site www.capecod.net/canoe/; E-mail cccanoe@capecod.net) runs naturalist-guided trips throughout the Cape, sponsored by the Cape Cod Museum of Natural History. In Mashpee, they paddle around the Mashpee River, Popponesset Bay, and Mashpee/Wakeby Pond. Trips ($3^1/_2$ to 4 hr.) are daily April through August, weekends through October, and cost $25 per paddler or $50 per family. All equipment is supplied. Call for schedule.

FISHING   Mashpee has two fishing ponds. **Mashpee/Wakeby** Pond (boat landing off Route 130, Fisherman's Drive) is considered one of the top 10 bass-fishing lakes in the country. Saltwater fishing licenses can be obtained at Sandwich, Falmouth, or Barnstable town halls. **South Cape Beach** in Mashpee (see "Beaches," above) is a primo spot for surf casting.

GOLF   Though one has to question the wisdom of its placement amid delicate wetlands, the **New Seabury Resort** at 155 Rock Landing Rd. (☎ **508/477-9110**) is, from all reports, tops. In fact, the championship-level Blue Course has consistently ranked among the top 100 courses in the country. Relative slackers have recourse to an Executive Course.

NATURE TRAILS   A shady peninsula jutting into the Cape's largest body of freshwater (the adjoining Wakeby and Mashpee ponds), the 135-acre **Lowell Holly Reservation** off South Sandwich Road in the northern corner of the township harbors some 500 holly trees and a number of magnificent centennial beeches. The stewards of this enchanted place, the **Trustees of the Reservation** (☎ 617/740-7233), charge $6 per day for the 2-mile trail loop on summer weekends; weekday admission is free. **South Cape Beach State Park** (see "Beaches," above) also offers a network of sandy trails.

WATER SPORTS   The town of Mashpee offers swimming lessons at **Attaquin Park** at Mashpee/Wakeby Pond, off Route 151; call the **town recreation department** (☎ **508/539-1446**) for details.

SHOPPING

Shopping in Mashpee is pretty much limited to the **Popponesset Marketplace,** a small cluster of gift shops within the New Seabury Resort, and **Mashpee Commons,** at the Mashpee Rotary, Routes 151 and 28 (☎ **508/477-5400**). The latter, designed to resemble an ideal New England village (right down to the sidewalk measurements, modeled on Woodstock, Vermont), is a gussied-up shopping complex with a facadelike feel to it: The been-here-forever look to which it aspires has never quite materialized, despite massive influxes of capital. There's also the matter of the ongoing land dispute between the complex's developers—the Fields Point Limited Partnership, which also owns New Seabury—and local Native Americans. Many of the shops—such as **M. Brann** for retro accessories, and the **Signature Gallery** for superb American crafts—are quite appealing, but I can never quite shake the sense that I've blundered onto the set of the cult TV series "The Prisoner."

WHERE TO STAY

New Seabury Resort. Great Oak Rd. (about 4 miles S of the Mashpee rotary), New Seabury, MA 02649. ☎ **800/999-9033** or 508/477-9111. Fax 508/477-9790. About 170 units (depending on rental pool). TV TEL. Summer $210–$260 1-bedroom villa; $280–$380 2-bedroom villa. AE, DC, MC, V.

One of the few full-bore "destination resorts" on the Cape, this 2,300-acre complex, packing some 1,600 condos, occupies more than half the town's shoreline—land formally granted to the Mashpee Wampanoags in 1660. That fact might make some uncomfortable being the beneficiary of such a troubled legacy, and one would also have to question the wisdom of siting and maintaining golf courses in the midst of fragile wetlands. Still, the damage is mostly done, and vacationers not saddled with such concerns are sure to enjoy themselves here. The tastefully decorated condos are clustered into "villages" of varying personalities: Maushop, for instance, with its crushed-shell walkways and clambering roses, is meant to mimic Nantucket. Relatively speaking, the rates are a real "steal"—provided you don't factor in the long-term impact of such intensive development on the environment.

   Dining/Entertainment: Five restaurants can be found within the development, the most notable of which is the Popponesset Inn (see "Where to Dine," below), the upscale venue of choice in this region for a good half-century. The Popponesset Marketplace harbors several casual eateries, such as the congenial Raw Bar, and mounts concerts and other family-fun events.

   Services: Scheduled children's activities.

   Facilities: In addition to its two 18-hole golf courses, the complex encompasses 16 all-weather tennis courts, a health club, two outdoor pools, a 3¹/₂-mile stretch of private beach, bike trails (with rentals), plus a minimall offering miniature golf.

WHERE TO DINE

The Flume. Lake Ave. (off Rte. 130, about 2¹/₂ miles N of the Mashpee rotary). ☎ **508/ 477-1456.** Main courses $9–$26. MC, V. Apr–Nov Mon–Sat noon–2:30 and 5–9pm, Sun noon–8pm. Closed Dec–Mar. AMERICAN.

At this small, friendly restaurant set above a herring run, chef Earl Mills, who is also Chief Flying Eagle of the Wampanoag tribe, dishes up solid Yankee fare, from a classic clam chowder to fried smelts, pot roast, lobster Newburg, and a colonial-era Indian pudding spiced with molasses and ginger. Seasonal specialties include, in the spring, herring roe plucked right from the flume (a stream that fish climb to spawn), which runs right beside its namesake.

Gone Tomatoes. Mashpee Commons, Mashpee Rotary (Rtes. 151 and 28). ☎ **508/477-8100.** Main courses $8–$15. MC, V. Mon–Thurs 11:45am–10:30pm, Fri–Sat 11:45am–11pm, Sun 11am–10:30pm. ITALIAN.

A shopping mall is about the last place I'd go hunting for a good Italian restaurant, but at this very stylish cafe, both the Sicilian and Tuscan repertoires are expertly rendered, in preparations such as wild-mushroom scampi served atop an angel-hair pasta pancake or a piquant veal piccata. It's not exactly the Old Country, but the food itself travels well.

Popponesset Inn. Mall Way (off Shore Dr., within the New Seabury resort, about 4 miles S of the Mashpee rotary), New Seabury. ☎ **508/477-1100.** Fax 508/477-8893. Reservations recommended. Jacket preferred. Main courses $18–$23. AE, DC, MC, V. Late May to mid-Oct daily noon–10pm; call for off-season hrs. Closed mid-Oct to Mar. NEW AMERICAN.

A favored haunt of the rich and famous in its 1940s heyday, this charming seaside spot now attracts movers and shakers of a less flamboyant sort. The sun-washed color scheme, mostly white with walls of palest blue, reflects the backdrop of the sea. The menu abounds in rarefied delights, such as a delicately sauced lobster Newburg or seafood steamed in parchment. The adjoining cafe, Poppy's, serves lighter fare geared to grazers.

MASHPEE AFTER DARK

Some pleasures never grow old—traditionalists get their kicks the old-fashioned way at New Seabury's **Popponesset Inn** (☎ 508/477-1100), dinner-dancing to a big-band sound against the background beat of lapping surf.

Though still on the drawing board, the **Boch Center for the Performing Arts,** to be built near Mashpee Commons at the Mashpee Rotary (☎ 508/477-2580), is already the beneficiary of some interesting fund-raisers, staged here and there and attracting some big-name talent. It's been designed by renowned Cambridge architect Graham Gund and backed by automobile mogul Ernie Boch, and at this point is slated to debut in 1999. Sporadic performances; call for schedule. Ticket prices vary.

6

The Mid Cape: Barnstable, Hyannis, Yarmouth & Dennis

If the Cape could be said to have a capital, Hyannis would have to be it. It's a big, sprawling, mall-monstrosity (let's be blunt), where the Kennedy mystique of the 1960s had the unfortunate side effect of spurring heedless development over the next several decades—a period during which, not so incidentally, the Cape's year-round population nearly doubled to approximately 200,000. The summer population is about three times that, and you'd swear every single person had daily errands to run in Hyannis. And yet even this over-run town still has pockets of charm. The waterfront area in particular, where the Island ferries dock, has benefited greatly from an influx of civic pride and attention, and Main Street, long eclipsed by the megastores along Route 132, is once again a pleasant place to stroll.

The town of Barnstable, the seat of Cape Cod's Barnstable County government, is made up of eight villages: Hyannis, Hyannisport, Barnstable Village, West Barnstable, Osterville, Centerville, Cotuit, and Marstons Mills. Along the north side of the Cape along Route 6A, the Old King's Highway, are Barnstable Village, with a compact Main Street anchored by an imposing granite county courthouse, and West Barnstable, containing a handful of delightful specialty stores and views of acres of salt marsh leading out to Cape Cod Bay. Along the south coast (off Route 28) are Cotuit, Marstons Mills, Osterville, and Centerville, all with gracious residential sections. Osterville has the best strolling Main Street in these parts, and Centerville has the hippest public beach, at Craigville.

While Barnstable is an ideal location for exploring the rest of the Cape and the Islands, there's also fun to be had nearby. If you are staying in the vicinity of Hyannis, you'll certainly want to head over to the north side of the Cape for a drive along the Old King's Highway, but you'll also want to stroll around the Hyannis Harbor, stopping for lunch at Tugboat's or Baxter's, where the seagulls compete for a bite of your lobster roll. Main Street Hyannis has had its good and bad years; currently, it's a good year, and you'll find a number of interesting shops and galleries (see "Shopping," below), as well as cafes and bars (see "Hyannis & Environs After Dark," below).

Some of the finest seaside mansions on the Cape are in the old-money villages of Cotuit, Osterville, Centerville, and Hyannisport. To explore this "Gold Coast" by car, take some detours off Route 28, driving south towards Nantucket Sound. These winding country roads are also good for biking (see below).

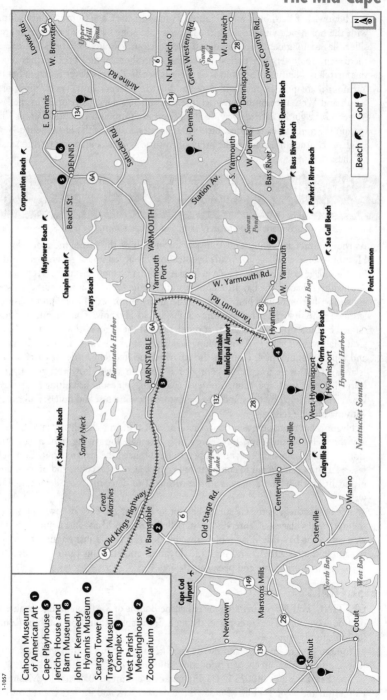

N

Cahoon Museum
of American Art 1
Cape Playhouse 5
Jericho House and
Barn Museum 8
John F. Kennedy
Hyannis Museum 4
Scargo Tower 6
Trayser Museum
Complex 3
West Parish
Meetinghouse 2
Zooquarium 7

Beach ← Golf ●

1-1057

The towns of Yarmouth and Dennis also straddle the Cape from north to south, with the north-side villages along the historic Old King's Highway and the south-side villages along commercialized and overdeveloped Route 28. That's not to say there aren't some very nice enclaves along the south shore. Some of the beaches along this stretch of Nantucket Sound (West Dennis Beach, Parker's River Beach in South Yarmouth) are quite popular with families, but the villages themselves (Dennisport, South and West Yarmouth) have definitely seen better days. Developers in the last 30 years have gotten carried away. In stark contrast, Yarmouth Port and Dennis Village on the north side are perfect little time capsules, loaded with old-fashioned New England charm, an encyclopedic array of historic homes, and many terrific small businesses.

1 Barnstable, Hyannis, Neighboring Villages & Environs

15 miles (25km) E of Sagamore, 44 miles (71km) S of Provincetown

As the commercial center and transportation hub of the Cape, hyperdeveloped Hyannis—a mere "village"—grossly overshadows the actual seat of government in the bucolic village of Barnstable. The two locales couldn't be more dissimilar. As peaceful as Hyannis is hectic, the bay area along historic Route 6A unfolds in a blur of greenery and well-kept colonial houses. No wonder many visitors experience "post-Camelot letdown" the first time they venture southward to Hyannis. The downtown area, sapped by the strip development that proliferated at the edges of town after the Cape Cod Mall was built in 1970, is making a valiant comeback, with attractive banners and a pretty public park flanking the wharf where frequent ferries depart for the Islands. If you were to confine your visit to this one town, however, you'd get a warped view of the Cape. Along Routes 132 and 28, you could be visiting Anywhere, USA: They're lined by the standard chain stores, restaurants, and hotels, and mired with maddening traffic.

Hyannis has more beds and better "rack rates" (in the travel-industry jargon) than anywhere else on the Cape, but there's little rationale for staying right in town or along the highways—unless you happen to have missed the last ferry out. Even full resort facilities can't begin to compensate for the lack of local color, and propinquity means little when the scenery is so dispiriting as to deter the most determined of walkers.

The best strategy is to stay somewhere peaceful near the edge of town, in one of the moneyed villages—Centerville, Osterville, Marstons Mills, and Cotuit—to the west, or in the bay-side villages of Barnstable due north, and just go into the "city" to sample the restaurants and nightlife. Hyannis and environs can offer plenty of both, to suit every palate and personality.

ESSENTIALS

GETTING THERE   After crossing either the Bourne or Sagamore bridge, head east on Route 6 or 6A. The latter passes through Barnstable; Route 132 south of Route 6A leads to Hyannis.

You can fly into Hyannis, and there's good bus service from Boston and New York (see "Getting There" in chapter 3 for more information).

The **Sea Line** (☎ 800/352-7155) makes a circuit of Barnstable, Mashpee, Falmouth, and Woods Hole Monday through Saturday, and the fare is a reasonable $1 to $4 (depending on the distance); children under 6 ride free. The **Hyannis Area Trolley** (☎ 800/352-7155 or 508/385-8326) covers two loops—the Route 132 malls and the Main Street/waterfront area—every 45 minutes from 10am to 9pm from late June to early September. Rates are 50¢ for adults, 25¢ for senior citizens, and gratis for children under 6.

VISITOR INFORMATION   For information, contact the **Hyannis Area Chamber of Commerce,** 1481 Rte. 132, Hyannis, MA 02601 (☎ **800/449-6647** or 508/ 362-5230; E-mail chamber@capecod.net; Web site www.hyannischamber.com), or the **Cape Cod Chamber of Commerce,** Routes 6 and 132, Hyannis, MA 02601 (☎ **508/362-3225;** fax 508/362-3698; Web site www.capecod.com).

BEACHES & OUTDOOR PURSUITS

BEACHES   Barnstable's primary Bay beach is **Sandy Neck,** accessed through East Sandwich (see "Beaches" under Sandwich in chapter 5). Most of the sound beaches are fairly protected and thus not big in terms of surf. Beach parking costs $8 a day, usually payable at the lot; for a weeklong parking sticker ($35), visit the **Recreation Department** at 141 Basset Lane, behind the Kennedy Memorial Skating Rink (☎ **508/790-6346**).

* **Craigville Beach,** off Craigville Beach Road in Centerville. Once a magnet for Methodist "camp" meetings (conference centers still line the shore), this broad expanse of sand boasts lifeguards and rest rooms. A magnet for the bronzed and buffed, it's known as "Muscle Beach."
* **Orrin Keyes Beach** (a.k.a. Sea Beach), at the end of Sea Street in Hyannis. This little beach at the end of a residential road is popular with families.
* **Kalmus Beach,** off Gosnold Street in Hyannisport. This 800-foot spit of sand stretching toward the mouth of the harbor makes an ideal launching site for windsurfers, who sometimes seem to play chicken with the steady parade of ferries. The surf is tame, the slope shallow—the conditions are ideal for little kids, too, and lifeguards, a snack bar, and rest rooms facilitate family outings.
* **Veterans Beach,** off Ocean Street in Hyannis. A small stretch of harborside sand adjoining the John F. Kennedy Memorial (a moving tribute from the town), this spot is not tops for swimming, unless you're very young and easily wowed. Parking is usually easy, though, and it's walkable from town. The snack bar, rest rooms, and playground will see to a family's needs.

BICYCLING   While there are no paved bike paths in Barnstable (the Rail Trail in Dennis is the closest), the winding roads in Marstons Mills and Osterville make for a pleasant scenic ride. There's free public parking at the Marstons Mills millpond at the intersection of Routes 28 and 149 or behind the stores in Osterville Center. From the intersection of Routes 28 and 149, bear right on Route 149 where it turns into Main Street, cross Route 28 (carefully), and then cruise down South County Road into Osterville. There are several roads here that afford wonderful bay views, not to mention views of some of the finest homes on Cape Cod. For the best views, bike to the end of Bay Street, West Bay Road, and Eel River Road to Sea View Avenue. You can rent bikes at **One World Bike Rental** at the corner of Main and Sea streets, in Hyannis (☎ **508/771-4242**). They charge $12 for 3 hours; $20 for 24 hours; and only $5 per day after the first 24 hours. They also provide a map and directions for a lovely 3-hour ride (about 8$^1\!/_2$ miles) through Craigville and Hyannisport with lots of ocean views. A leisurely bike ride through this area, a veritable "Gold Coast," is perhaps the best way to see some of the most impressive seaside mansions of the Cape.

BOATING   Cape Cod Coastal Canoe & Kayak (☎ **888/226-6393** or 508/ 564-4051; Web site www.capecod.net/canoe/; E-mail cccanoe@capecod.net) runs naturalist-guided trips (sponsored by the Cape Cod Museum of Natural

History) throughout the Cape. In West Barnstable and Barnstable Village, they paddle around Scorton Creek, Great Marsh, Sandy Neck, and Barnstable Harbor. In Osterville, they paddle around Great Island. In Centerville, they paddle around the Centerville River. Trips (3¹/₂ to 4 hr.) are daily April through August, weekends through October, and cost $25 per paddler or $50 per family. All equipment is supplied. Call for schedule.

For experienced paddlers, Barnstable's Great Marsh—one of the largest in New England—offers beautiful waterways out to Sandy Neck.

FISHING   The township of Barnstable has 11 ponds for freshwater fishing; for information and permits, visit **Town Hall** at 367 Main St., Hyannis (☎ 508/790-6240). Shellfishing permits are available from the **Department of Natural Resources** at 1189 Phinneys Lane (☎ 508/790-6272). Surf casting, sans license, is permitted on Sandy Neck (see "Beaches" under "Sandwich," in chapter 5). Among the charter boats berthed in Barnstable Harbor is the *Drifter* (☎ 508/398-2061), a 35-foot boat offering half- and full-day trips. The **Tightlines Sport Fishing Service** at 65 Camp St., Hyannis (☎ 508/790-8600), conducts saltwater fly-fishing expeditions. **Hy-Line Cruises** offers seasonal sonar-aided "bottom" or blues fishing from its Ocean Street dock in Hyannis (☎ 508/790-0696). **Helen H Deep-Sea Fishing** at 137 Pleasant St., Hyannis (☎ 508/790-0660), offers year-round expeditions aboard a 100-foot boat with a heated cabin and full galley. For a smaller, more personalized expedition, get in touch with Capt. Ron Murphy of **Stray Cat Charters** (☎ 508/428-8628).

FITNESS   The Cape at its most urban incarnation, Hyannis abounds in health clubs, including the reasonably priced **Galaxy Fitness Center** at 45 Plant Rd., off Airport Road (☎ 508/790-1931); a state-of-the-art **Gold's Gym** at the Radisson Inn, 287 Iyanough Rd. (Route 28; ☎ 580/790-4477), which offers access to an indoor pool; and the single sex **Woman's Body Shop** at 155 Attucks Lane (off Route 132; ☎ 508/771-1600).

GOLF   Open year-round, the **Hyannis Golf Club,** Route 132 (☎ 508/362-2606), offers a 46-station driving range, as well as an 18-hole championship course. Smaller, but scenic, is the 9-hole **Cotuit High Ground Country Club,** 31 Crockers Neck Rd., Cotuit (☎ 508/428-9863).

ICE-SKATING   The **Kennedy Memorial Skating Rink,** Bearses Way, Hyannis (☎ 508/790-6346), is open to the public mid-November to late April; call for details.

NATURE & WILDLIFE AREAS   **Sandy Neck,** accessed through East Sandwich (see "Beaches" under "Sandwich," in chapter 5), is great for hiking; take care to avoid the endangered piping plovers.

SOARING   **Cape Cod Soaring Adventures,** Cape Cod Airport, Race Lane (at Route 149), Marstons Mills (☎ 800/660-4563 or 508/540-8081), allows you to see the curve of the Cape (as well as Boston and the New Hampshire mountains beyond) as an eagle might, coasting—motorless—on thermal currents 6,000 feet up. Once the glider has been towed aloft and released, owner/pilot Randy Charlton is in charge of steering and, perhaps more important, landing. All you have to do is sit back in supreme silence and enjoy the ride—which could include some "aerobatics" if you so choose. Timid types can take heart in the fact that Charlton has wafted onto this rural field hundreds of times without incident since 1984 and trained many an instant aficionado. Prices start at $60 for 20 minutes; reservations recommended.

TENNIS   Seven local schools open their courts to the public; all are first-come, first-served. For information, call the **Barnstable Recreation Department** (☎ 508/790-6345). In addition, **King's Grant Racquet Club** on Main Street in Cotuit (☎ 508/428-5744) has seven courts (three hard, four clay).

WATER SPORTS   The **Goose Hummock Shop** at 2 Iyanough Rd./Route 28 (☎ 508/778-0877) rents the usual craft; **Eastern Mountain Sports,** 1513 Iyanough Rd./Route 132 (☎ 508/362-8690), offers rental kayaks—tents and sleeping bags, too—and sponsors occasional overnights to Washburn Island in Waquoit Bay, as well as free clinics.

For those who prefer to do their sightseeing underwater, **East Coast Divers** at 237 Rte. 28 (☎ 508/775-1185) attends to all snorkeling and scuba needs, including instruction and charters; for the super-hardy, they're open year-round.

WHALE WATCHING   Although Provincetown is about an hour closer to the whales' preferred feeding grounds, it would take you at least an hour (possibly hours on a summer weekend) to drive all the way down-Cape. If your time and itinerary are limited, hop aboard at **Hyannis Whale-Watch Cruises,** Barnstable Harbor (about ¹/₂ mile north of Route 6A on Mill Way), Barnstable (☎ 888/942-5392 or 508/362-6088; fax 508/362-9739), for a 4-hour voyage on a 100-foot high-speed cruiser. Naturalists provide the narration, and should you fail to spot a whale, your next trek is free. Tickets $23 adults, $19 seniors, $15 children 4 to 12 from April through October; call for schedule and off-season rates. Closed November through March.

TOURING BY RAIL, STEAMER & SLOOP

Cape Cod Scenic Railroad. 252 Main St., Hyannis. ☎ 800/872-4508 or 508/771-3788. Rates $11.50 adults, $7.50 children 3–12. AE, DISC, MC, V. Departures daily at 10am, 12:30pm, and 3pm June to late Oct; call for off-season hrs. Closed Jan.

Offering a chance to get off the gridlocked roads and actually see the countryside, three vintage cars make a leisurely trip to Buzzards Bay, with a stop in Sandwich; round-trip, the 42 miles take a little under 2 hours. Occasionally, special "ecology" tours are scheduled, led by a local naturalist from the Cape Cod Museum of Natural History and including a half-hour stop for a guided marsh walk in Sandwich's Talbots Point Conservation Preserve. The dinner trains (see "Where to Dine," below) are also very popular.

The *Hesperus*. Pier 16, Ocean St. Dock, Hyannis. ☎ 508/790-0077. Rates $22 adults, $15 senior citizens and children 12 and under. Late May to early Sept daily 12:30, 3, and 5:30pm; call for off-season schedule. Closed Nov–Apr.

Offering an elegant means of exploring the harbor (while sneaking a peak at the Kennedy compound), the 50-foot John Alden sloop accommodates only 22 passengers, who are welcome to help trim the sails or even steer. Most opt to luxuriate in the sparkling sun and cooling breezes. The sporadic moonlight sails are especially romantic.

Hyannisport Harbor Cruises. Ocean St. Dock, Hyannis. ☎ 508/778-2600. Tickets $8 adults, free–$3.50 children 12 and under. Late June to Aug, 16 departures daily; call for schedule. Closed Nov to early Apr.

For a fun and informative introduction to the harbor and its residents, take a leisurely—1- to 2-hour—narrated tour aboard the Hy-Line's 1911 steamer replicas *Patience* and *Prudence*. Five family trips a day in season offer free passage for children under 12, but for a real treat take them on the Sunday 3:30pm "Ice Cream Float,"

Camelot on Cape Cod: The Kennedys in Hyannisport

Images of Jack Kennedy sailing his jaunty *Wianno Senior,* on Nantucket Sound off Hyannisport, form part of this nation's collective memory. The vacationing JFK was all tousled hair, toothy grin, earthy charisma, and attractive *joie de vivre.* Remember Jackie sitting beside him, wearing a patterned silk scarf around her head and looking like she'd rather be in Newport, where no one had ever heard of touch football?

The Kennedys always knew how to have fun, and they had it in Hyannisport. And ever since the early 1960s, when JFK was president and Hyannisport became the Summer White House, Cape Cod has been inextricably linked to the Kennedy clan. While the Kennedys spend time elsewhere—working in Washington, wintering in Palm Beach—when they go home, they go to Cape Cod. Generations of Kennedys have sailed these waters, sunned on these beaches, patronized local businesses, and generally had a high old time.

Meanwhile, much has changed since the early 1960s on Cape Cod, especially in the Mid Cape area. In those 30-plus years, the mall was built in Hyannis, and urban sprawl infested Routes 132 and 28. Yet much, thankfully, remains the same. The Kennedy compound, with its large gabled Dutch Colonial houses, still commands the end of Scudder Avenue in Hyannisport. Nearby is the private **Hyannisport Golf Club,** where Rose loved to play a short round on the foggy oceanfront course. The beaches here are still pristine.

To bask in the Kennedy's Cape Cod experience, visit the **John F. Kennedy Hyannis Museum,** 397 Main St., Hyannis (☎ **508/790-3077**). Admission is $3, (children under 17 free) and hours are Monday to Saturday from 10am to 4pm and Sunday from 1 to 4pm. The museum shows a documentary on Kennedy narrated by Walter Cronkite and contains several rooms worth of photos of the

which includes a design-your-own Ben & Jerry's sundae, or the Thursday 9pm "Jazz Boat," accompanied by a Dixieland band.

John F. Kennedy Hyannis Museum. 397 Main St. (in the center of town), Hyannis. ☎ **508/790-3077.** Admission $3 adults, children under 17 free. Mid-April to mid-Oct Mon–Sat 10am–4pm, Sun 1–4pm; call for off-season hrs.

This primarily photographic display—supplemented by a brief video program narrated by Walter Cronkite—captures the Kennedys during the glory days of 1934 to 1963. Most of us have seen some of these photos before, but here they are all blown up, mounted, and neatly labeled; if you get confused about lineage, consult the family tree on the wall at the end of the exhibit.

MUSEUMS & HISTORIC BUILDINGS

Barnstable Superior Courthouse. 3195 Rte. 6A (in the center of town), Barnstable. ☎ **508/362-2511.** Free admission. Open during business hrs.

This grand public edifice, built between 1831 and 1832, still serves its original purpose vis-à-vis Barnstable County, which is to say the entire Cape. Attributed to Alexander Parris, this Greek Revival temple of justice indeed resembles his previous granite masterpieces, Boston's Quincy Market and Plymouth's Pilgrim Hall Museum, down to the grand Doric colonnade. Anyone is free to listen in on the arguments and deliberations. It's an educational pastime that the Puritans would no doubt have approved.

Kennedys on Cape Cod. The candid shots included in this permanent display capture some of the quieter moments, as well as JFK's legendary charm. Most of us have seen some of these photos before, but here they are all blown up, mounted, and neatly labeled; if you get confused about lineage, consult the family tree on the wall at the end of the exhibit. The last 3 years of JFK's life were a bit chaotic (some 25,000 well-wishers thronged the roads when the senator and president-to-be returned from the 1960 Democratic Convention), but he continued to treasure the Cape as "the one place I can think and be alone."

Busloads of tourists visit the **Kennedy Memorial** just above Veterans Beach on Ocean Avenue; it's a moving tribute, beautifully maintained by the town, but crowds in season can be distracting. Finally, you may want to drive by the simple white clapboard church, **St. Francis Xavier,** on South Street; Rose attended mass daily, and Caroline Kennedy, and several other cousins, got married here.

Spend your day in the Mid Cape recreating like a privileged Kennedy scion. Rent a Windsurfer at Kalmus Beach. Sail on the 50-foot John Alden sloop, the *Hesperus,* which cruises past the compound. The boat leaves from Pier 16 at the Ocean Street Dock, Hyannis (☎ **508/790-0077**). Play a round of golf at **Hyannis Golf Club,** a public course on Route 132. Stop for picnic supplies at **Lambert's Rainbow Fruit** on West Main Street in Centerville—where you may see Joe Kennedy behind the deli counter making his own sandwich. **Four Seas Ice Cream,** at 360 S. Main St. in Centerville, apparently a favorite of secret-service agents, is a must. For lodging right in Hyannisport, stay at **The Simmons Homestead Inn,** 288 Scudder Ave., Hyannisport (☎ **508/778-4999**).

Rose Kennedy once told a reporter, "Our family would rather be in Hyannisport in the summer than any place else in the world." And yours?

Cahoon Museum of American Art. 4676 Falmouth Rd. (Rte. 28, near Rte. 130), Cotuit. ☎ **508/428-7581.** Free admission. Tues–Sat 10am–4pm.

For some 4 decades, post–World War II, this 1775 Georgian colonial house served as an atelier for two popular primitivists, Ralph and Martha Calhoun. Their playful, decorative works, featuring such Cape staples as cavorting mermaids and swaggering tars, is on permanent display, along with other American works spanning early portraiture to impressionism. Local contemporary artists are often shown as well. The interior itself is worth a look: it still boasts its 1810 stenciling, and the upstairs "ballroom"—a makeshift affair typical of Early American taverns—remains intact. Friday gallery talks at 11am are free and open to the public.

Osterville Historical Society Museum at the Captain John Parker House. 155 W. Bay Rd. (at Parker Rd., about ⅛ of a mile S of town center), Osterville. ☎ **508/428-5861.** Admission $2. Mid-June to mid-Oct Thurs to Sun 1:30–4:30pm. Closed mid-Oct to mid-June.

This 1824 house displays the Osterville Historical Society's cache of China Trade treasures, as well as other valuable antiques of local interest; don't miss the toys and dolls. The rustic 1790 Cammett House, next door, is a one-room "narrow house," notable mainly for its clear exposition of the colonists' building techniques. Also on the grounds (beautifully and historically landscaped by the Osterville Garden Club) is the original Herbert F. Crosby Boat Shop, progenitor of such worthy craft as the trusty Catboat and the Wianno Senior, President Kennedy's preferred pleasure boat. Some venerable examples can be viewed, and research is encouraged. The museum's annual antique show (call for details) is held the fourth Thursday in August every year.

Centerville Historical Society Museum. 513 Main St. (about ¹/₃ of a mile S of Rte. 28), Centerville. ☎ **508/775-0331.** Admission $2.50 adults, $2 seniors, $1 students 6–17. Mid-June to mid-Sept Wed–Sun 1:30–4:30pm (last admission at 4pm). By appointment only mid-Sept to mid-June.

Downright palatial compared to its peers, this local-history museum boasts 14 rooms filled with varied collections covering 2 centuries or more, from perfume bottles to early currency (including lottery tickets used to finance the Revolution), ball gowns to bird carvings. The toy collection is especially strong, and among the eerier tableaux is a complete "colonial" kitchen as envisioned by clutter-inclined Victorians; it's chockablock with handsome antiques and intriguing artifacts. Planned for 1998 is a special exhibit of wedding gowns from the museum's collection of historic clothing.

Sturgis Library. 3090 Rte. 6A (about ¹/₂ mile W of Hyannis Rd.), Barnstable. ☎ **508/ 362-6636.** Free admission. Mon 10am–2pm, Tues and Wed 1–9pm, Thurs 10am–2pm, Fri 1–5pm, Sat 10am–4pm.

In 1863 William Sturgis, a cabin boy turned megamerchant who was an eighth-generation descendent of the town founder, willed Congregational minister John Lothrop's 1646 "half-house" to the town as the nucleus of a public library. Surrounded by subsequent additions containing extraordinary genealogical and maritime collections, the one-room home still holds the rarest book of all, Lothrop's 1609 Bible, charred by tallow drippings during the tumultuous ocean journey, then diligently patched and restored from memory.

Trayser Museum Complex. 3353 Rte. 6A (at Hyannis Rd.), Barnstable. ☎ **508/362-2092.** Donations requested. Mid-June to mid-Oct Tues–Sun 1:30–4:30pm. Closed mid-Oct to mid-June.

Named for local historian Donald G. Trayser, this former customhouse, built in 1856, showcases the collections of the Barnstable Historical Commission. The painted-brick Italian Renaissance building is quite a beauty itself, both outside and in; the interior's grandly scaled rooms, elaborate balustrades, and massive pillars attest to the harbor's prosperous past. Artifacts have been gathered to illustrate every era, from Native American tools sculpted from stone to nautical art (paintings, models) and the spoils of the China Trade. A Children's Corner filled with dolls and toys is intriguing—though not intended for touching. Behind the museum proper is a carriage house containing a horse-drawn hearse, a couple of early-prototype bicycles, and antique fishing gear. Adjoining it is a wooden "gaol" built in the last decade of the 17th century, the oldest surviving structure of its sort on the continent. Perhaps it lasted so long because, as Henry David Thoreau noted during his 1850s peregrinations, "Sometimes, when the court comes together at Barnstable, they have not a single criminal to try, and the jail is shut up"—or offered for rent.

West Parish Meetinghouse. 2049 Meetinghouse Way (at Rte. 149), W. Barnstable. ☎ **508/ 362-4445.** Free admission. Usually open during business hrs.; call ahead to confirm.

Up until the mid-1800s, in most New England towns there was literally no separation between church and state: Typically, the Congregational church, supported by local taxes, doubled as town hall. Such was the case with this meetinghouse, built between 1717 and 1723. Once it had lost its civic function, it was subjected to disastrous neoclassical, then Victorian, renovations, both of which were finally reversed in the 1950s, unveiling the building's original glorious oak and pine woodwork. The half-ton Paul Revere bell, forged in 1806, still summons parishioners to worship, and visitors are welcome to enter at will to admire the handsome, honey-toned interior of the oldest public building on the Cape.

BASEBALL

The two locally based Cape Cod Baseball League elite amateur teams are the Hyannis Mets (who play at McKeon Field on Old Colony Boulevard) and the Cotuit Kettleers (Lowell Park). For a schedule, contact the **Hyannis Area Chamber of Commerce** (☎ 800/449-6647 or 508/362-5230), or the **Barnstable Recreation Department** (☎ 508/790-6345).

KID STUFF

The **Cape Cod Storyland minigolf course,** in the middle of town at 70 Center St. (☎ 508/778-4339), actually provides a bit of a local history lesson, with traps that replicate notable sites on the Cape and Islands; adjoining the course is a little lagoon set up for refreshing bumper-boat rides. Right next door is the Cape Cod Scenic Railroad (see "Touring by Rail, Steamer & Sloop," earlier in this chapter). About a mile north, off Route 132, the **Cape Cod Potato Chips factory** at Independence Way (☎ 508/775-7253) offers free quickie tours that end in a tasting. Tours are held in July and August, Monday to Friday from 9am to 5pm and Saturday from 10am to 4pm. On Wednesday mornings in summer, the **Cape Cod Melody Tent** at the West End Rotary (☎ 508/775-9100) offers children's theater productions.

SHOPPING

Although Hyannis is undoubtedly the commercial center of the Cape, the stores you'll find there are fairly standard for the most part; you could probably find their ilk anywhere else in the country. It's in the wealthy enclaves west of Hyannis, and along the antiquated King's Highway (Route 6A) to the north, that you're likely to find the real gems.

ANTIQUES/COLLECTIBLES ✪ **The Farmhouse,** 1340 Main St. (about 1 mile south of Route 28), Osterville (☎ 508/420-2400), Carolyn and Barry Crawford's 1742 farmhouse, is set up like an adult-scale dollhouse, and the "lifelike" settings should lend decorative inspiration. Self-confident sorts will go wild in the barn; it's packed with intriguing architectural salvage.

Of the hundreds of antique shops scattered through the region, perhaps a dozen qualify as destinations for well-schooled collectors. ✪ **Harden Studios,** 3264 Rte. 6A (in the center of town), Barnstable (☎ 508/362-7711), is one. Owner Charles M. Harden, ASID, used to supply to-the-trade-only dealers in the Boston Design Center. An architect by training, he renovated this deaconage, built around 1720, to display his finds. Some items, such as the primitive portraits and mourning embroidery, are all but extinct outside of museums. Other sturdy, serviceable pieces, such as colonial corner cabinets and slant-top desks, are competitively priced, as are the antique Oriental carpets underfoot. An adjoining barn gallery features nature-centered works by area artists, including Harden's son, an accomplished etcher.

Devoted primarily to collectibles, **Hyannis Antique Co-op,** 500 Main St. (in the center of town), Hyannis (☎ 508/778-0512), is a huge group-shop that yields few real valuables, but tons of nostalgic trinkets.

Prince Jenkins Antiques, 975 Rte. 6A (at the intersection of Route 149), West Barnstable (no phone), is one spooky shop, the piled-high kind that captivates scavengers. Wend your way (carefully) around the narrow path still discernible amid the heaped-up inventory, and you'll come across case upon case of vintage jewelry and watches, paintings, tapestries, urns and jade carvings, musty 18th-century garb, a Pilgrim chair or two, and all sorts of oddments, including—on my last visit—a glass-topped coffin complete with skeleton. The aged proprietor, Dr. Alfred King, DFA, claims that the admittedly ancient-looking house next door belonged to Governor William Bradford in 1626—a dubious boast, given that the town wasn't settled until 1639, and Bradford was awfully busy in Plymouth. But what would you expect from a man whose card reads "In Business since 1773"? Closed mid-November to March.

A. Stanley Wheelock Antiques, 870 Main St. (in the center of town), Osterville (☎ **508/420-3170**), features all sorts of decorative pieces. The Orientalia is outstanding, and everything is shoehorned, gracefully, into a couple of rather crowded rooms. The owner, an interior designer, is a source not only of great goods, but good advice.

ARTS & CRAFTS   The intricate, infinitely variable patterns of Jacquard weaving not only prompted the Industrial Revolution but prefigured the computer chip. Today there's only one weaver in the United States creating Jacquard designs by hand, and that's Bob Black, who began his trade at age 14 and refined it at the Rhode Island School of Design. He works out of **The Blacks' Handweaving Shop,** 597 Rte. 6A (about 1 mile west of Route 149), West Barnstable (☎ **508/362-3955**), and specializes in custom coverlets on commission; the double-sided designs can be used as blankets, throws, even tapestries. Customers often ask for special motifs to be worked in, with the ultimate goal a one-of-a-kind, commemorative artifact. Bob's wife, Gabrielle, contributes colorful fashion accessories—hats, scarves, shawls, even ties.

The caliber of the shows at the **Cape Cod Art Association,** 3480 Rte. 6A (about $^1/_3$ mile west of Hyannis Road), Barnstable (☎ **508/362-2909**), may vary—this is, after all, a nonprofit community venture—but it's worth visiting just to see the skylit studios, designed by CCAA member Richard Sears Gallagher in 1972. Everyone raves about "Cape light," and here you'll see it used to optimal advantage. If the setting fires up artistic yearnings, inquire about classes, which are held year-round.

Ex-Nantucketer Bob Marks fashions the only authentic Nantucket lightship baskets, crafted off-island, and as aficionados know, they don't come cheap (a mere handbag typically runs in the thousands). The other handmade furnishings found at **Oak and Ivory,** 1112 Main St. (about 1 mile south of Route 28), Osterville (☎ **508/428-9425**), from woven throw rugs to pared-down neo-Shaker furniture, fit the country-chic mode at more approachable prices.

It takes a certain amount of chutzpah to name an art center for yourself, but Barre Pinske took his cue from idol—and fellow self-promoter—Andy Warhol: "People who have their names on a building become famous." Just so no one could miss the point, he constructed a giant mailbox right on historically correct Route 6A to signal his presence to passersby. Town pooh-bahs fussed and fumed, but he'd found a legal loophole: There are no local laws (as yet) that dictate mailbox size. So you can't miss it, and it can't hurt to stop in. All his stuff has a sense of humor, from the couch he carved out of paper bags to his "Post-Industrial Expressionist" chain-saw art. It can all be seen at the **Pinske Art Center,** 1989 Rte. 6A (about $^1/_4$ mile east of Route 132), West Barnstable (☎ **508/362-5311**).

At 374 Main St. in Hyannis, **Red Fish, Blue Fish** (☎ **508/775-8700**) wins the funky gallery award, hands down. Owner Jane Walsh makes jewelry in the front window, but inside every inch of this closetlike space is covered with something unusual and handmade. There is usually a teen or two hanging out here.

Believe it or not, theft of weather vanes is a real threat on the Cape, so valuable are some of these copper toppers. Some of Marilyn Strauss's prize specimens, displayed in an informal museum adjoining her shop, **Salt & Chestnut Weathervanes,**

Hyannis

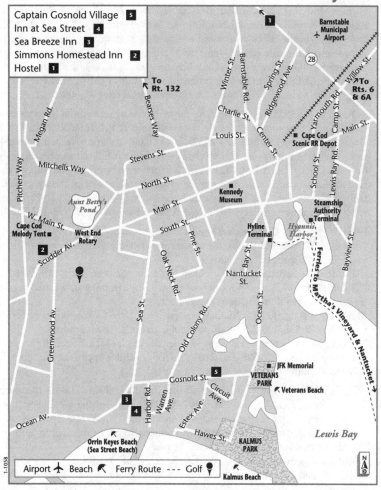

Captain Gosnold Village **5**
Inn at Sea Street **4**
Sea Breeze Inn **3**
Simmons Homestead Inn **2**
Hostel **1**

Airport ✈ Beach 🏖 Ferry Route --- Golf ⛳

651 Rte. 6A (about ¹/₃ mile west of Route 149), West Barnstable (☎ **508/ 362-6085**), would fetch as much as $30,000, were she willing to part with them. Mostly she's in the business of creating replicas and custom orders, with the help of 2 dozen local artisans. Prices range from about $200 to $2,000.

Albert Barbour practices a craft familiar to the furniture makers of colonial times: turning. But instead of elaborate chairs and table legs, he makes modernist bowls, vases, and candlesticks of native woods, varnished to a gemlike shine. Each wood— from oak and elm to apple and cherry—has its own distinctive characteristics, and "flaws" lend the kind of accidental beauty that occurs only in nature. These unique pieces, each signed and dated, range from about $30 to $500, and browsers are welcome: You can watch a work of art in the making. **Tern Studio,** 2454 Meetinghouse Way (off Route 149 near the intersection of Route 6A), West Barnstable (☎ **508/ 362-6077**).

Richard Kiusalas and Steven Whittlesey salvage antique lumber and turn it into cupboards, tables, and chairs, among other things; old windows are retrofitted as mirrors. Most of the stock at **West Barnstable Tables,** 2454 Meetinghouse Way (off Route 149 near the intersection of Route 6A), West Barnstable (☎ 508/362-2676), looks freshly made, albeit with wood of unusually high quality. Pieces are priced accordingly: A dining room set—pine trestle table with six bow-back chairs—would run over $4,000. When the wood still bears interesting traces of its former life, it's turned into folk-art furniture. A cupboard made out of old painted red boards, secured with Model T Ford hinges, for example, might fetch $3,600.

BOOKS & EPHEMERA   Named for the revolutionary printer who helped foment the War of Independence, ✪ **Isaiah Thomas Books & Prints,** 4632 Rte. 28 (near Route 130), Cotuit (☎ 508/428-2752), has a 60,000-volume collection, housed—sometimes precariously—in an 1850 home. The shop is full of treasures, clustered by topic. Owner/expert James S. Visbeck is happy to show off his first editions and rare miniatures and maps; you get the sense that sales are secondary to sheer bibliophilic pleasure. You can buy a 200-year-old map of your favorite Cape Cod village at **Maps of Antiquity,** 1022 Rte. 6A, West Barnstable (☎ 508/362-7169).

FASHION   The Children's Shop, 27 Wianno Ave. (in the center of town), Osterville (☎ 508/428-9458), features incomparable clothes for kids (see "Shopping" under "Chatham," in chapter 7).

Europa, 37 Barnstable Rd. (at North Street, in the center of town), Hyannis (☎ 508/790-0877), is a boutique where women can bone up on that world-traveler look, even if they've never been abroad.

Mark, Fore & Strike, 21 Wianno Ave. (at Main Street, in the center of town), Osterville (☎ 508/428-2270), stocks preppie classics for both genders.

The ladies' wear carried at **Talbot's,** 32 Wianno Ave. (at Main Street, in the center of town), Osterville (☎ 508/428-2204), is reliably capable of crossing over from the office to a country-club lunch.

FOOD/WINE   Cape Cod Potato Chips, Breed's Hill Road (at Independence Way, off Route 132), Hyannis (☎ 508/775-7253), really are the world's best. Long a local favorite—they're chunkier than the norm—these snacks actually do originate here. Free factory tours are offered Monday through Friday from 9am to 5pm and Saturday from 10am to 4pm in July and August.

At **Country Store,** 877 Main St. (in the center of town), Osterville (☎ 508/428-2097), no elaborate retrofitting was required to capture the essence of an old-fashioned general store: This 1890 honey, scarcely touched by time, is the real thing. Proprietor Charlie Kalas, who grew up here, is now the grown-up dispensing penny candy and ice-cream pops.

GIFTS/HOME DECOR   As a Nantucket innkeeper whiling away the winter, Claire Murray took up hooking rugs and turned her knack into an international business. At **Claire Murray,** 867 Main St. (in the center of town), Osterville (☎ 508/428-3562), hobbyists can find all the fixings for various needle-crafts here, as well as kits and advice as needed. The time-pressed can just buy the finished goods, from sweaters and quilts to the signature folk-motif rugs.

The country's premier source of reproduction 18th-century (pre–Machine Age) furniture, **Eldred Wheeler,** 864 Main St. (in the center of town), Osterville (☎ 508/428-9049), turns out such lovely pieces, an appraiser would be hard put to distinguish them from originals at a glance. These simulacra cost only a fraction as much as the museum pieces they imitate, and they'll hold up better as well.

Flowery pastels are the hallmark of **Joan Peters,** 885 Main St. (in the center of town), Osterville (☎ 508/428-3418), favored by the Town & Country set. She designs a wide array of compatible fabrics and ceramics—right down to the bathroom sink, if need be—so that it's easy to achieve a pervasive light-splashed look that doesn't look too overtly matched and mixed.

Multiculturalism rules at **Tibetan Mandala International Imports,** 584 Main St. (in the center of town), Hyannis (☎ **508/778-4134**), the summer outpost of a Greenwich Village boutique. The clothes and accessories come from the four corners of the earth: trade beads from Africa, jewelry and tapestries from the Himalayas, handwoven clothes from Guatemala. Closed January through March.

On Main Street in Hyannis, you'll find a world of wonderful kitchen products at **Nantucket Trading Company,** 354 Main St. (☎ **508/790-3933**).

MALLS/SHOPPING CENTERS With nearly 100 shops and 2 cineplexes, the **Cape Cod Mall,** Route 132 (about 1 mile northwest of the airport), Hyannis (☎ **508/771-0200**), is the mother mall of all, the largest shopping center on the whole Cape. At least one chain store warrants a visit: **Filene's Basement** (☎ **508/790-6931**), located across the street from the mall at the K-Mart Plaza on Route 132, for current, albeit cut-rate, fashion.

SEAFOOD Besides Mill Way at Barnstable Harbor (see "Take-Out & Take-Home Food," below), the best place to buy fresh seafood in the vicinity of Hyannis is **Cape Fish & Lobster** at 406 W. Main St. in Centerville (☎ **508/771-1122**). This is where the top restaurateurs in Hyannis get their seafood. The prices are reasonable, and the catch is the freshest in town.

SPORTING GOODS **Eastern Mountain Sports,** 1513 Iyanough Rd. (Route 132), Hyannis (☎ **508/362-8690**), an outdoor outfitter known for its commitment to service, offers more than mere sales and rentals (of everything from sleeping bags and tents to sea kayaks). Advice flows freely; they also organize free clinics and occasional outings.

Why pay top dollar for sports equipment you're bound to batter—if not tire of or outgrow—sooner or later? Visitors who forgot to pack their in-line skates, tennis racquet, golf clubs, or other sports equipment, can pick up a bargain substitute at **Play It Again Sports,** 25 Iyanough Rd. (Route 28), Hyannis (☎ **508/771-6979**), for little more than the cost of a daily rental.

WHERE TO STAY
IN HYANNIS AND HYANNISPORT
Expensive
✪ **Simmons Homestead Inn.** 288 Scudder Ave. (at W. Main St., about ¹/₄ mile W of the W. End Rotary), Hyannisport, MA 02647. ☎ **800/637-1649** or 508/778-4999. Fax 508/790-1342. Web site www.capecod.com/simmonsinn. 11 rms, 1 suite. Summer (including full breakfast) $150–$200 double; $280 suite. AE, DISC, MC, V.

A former ad exec and race-car driver, innkeeper Bill Putman has a silly side and isn't afraid to show it. He started collecting animal artifacts—stuffed toys, sculptures, even needlepoint and wallpaper—to differentiate the rather traditional rooms in this rambling 1820s captain's manse and kind of got carried away. The animal kingdom, plus his general friendliness, serve as an icebreaker, though: This is an inn where you'll find everyone mulling around the hearth sipping complementary wine (served at "6-ish") while they compare notes and nail down dinner plans. Guests who prefer privacy may book the spiffily updated "servants' quarters," a spacious, airy wing with its own private deck. Well-known athletes (such as O.J., in sunnier days, and Bruce Jenner) and performers from the nearby Cape Cod Melody Tent (Carly Simon, for example) have sought refuge here over the years, and Putman promises every guest a special spot that's "10 million miles from anywhere, and 2 minutes from everything."

Moderate

Captain Gosnold Village. 230 Gosnold St. (off Ocean St., about 1 mile S of town center), Hyannis, MA 02601. ☎ 508/775-9111. 33 rms, 8 cottages. A/C TV TEL. Summer $75 double; $250 efficiency. MC, V. Closed Dec–Mar.

A cluster of grizzled cottages with gay pink shutters, this little compound would make a pleasant family retreat. Far enough from the bustle of downtown, and a short walk from placid Kalmus Beach, the cottages—which can be rented by the room and day, as well as by the week—are remarkably cheery within, with fresh, modern decor. A lifeguard watches over the small outdoor pool, and lawn games and a play area keep kids happily occupied. For the inevitable rainy day, the office rents out videos.

Sea Breeze Inn. 397 Sea St. (about 1 mile S of the West End Rotary), Hyannis, MA 02601. ☎ 508/771-7213. Fax 508/862-0663. E-mail seabreeze@capecod.net. Web site www.capecod.net/seabreeze. 14 rms, 1 cottage. A/C TV TEL. Summer (including continental breakfast) $69–$130 double; cottages $690–$1,600 weekly. AE, DISC, MC, V.

Within whistling distance of the beach, this classic shingled beach house has been decked out with the totems of small-town America: a picket fence, exuberant plantings, and even a wooden rocker built for two couples—or better yet, one. All this attention to the exterior is mirrored in the neat and cheerful interior. The coast used to be lined with superior guest houses of this sort, and to find one still in its prime is a real treat. Also on the intensively gardened grounds are three cottages that rent by the week, including one with a "honeymooners'" double Jacuzzi.

Inexpensive

HyLand American Youth Hostel. 465 Rte. 28 (about 1 mile W of the Rte. 132 intersection), Hyannis, MA 02601. ☎ 508/775-2970. 42 beds. $12 for members, $15 for nonmembers. No credit cards. Closed Dec–Feb.

It's a bit out of the way (no problem if you're traveling by car or bike), and there are much prettier hostels awaiting in North Truro and on the Islands (see "Where to Stay" in chapters 8 through 10), but if you're just looking for a no-frills stopover while you check out the Mid Cape, the rates here are rock-bottom. *One caveat:* Don't count on catching much nightlife, what with a strict 11pm curfew.

Inn at Sea Street. 358 Sea St., Hyannis, MA 02601. ☎ 508/775-8030. 9 rms, 1 cottage. Summer (including full breakfast) $78–$110 double; $125 cottage. AE, MC, V.

Just a short walk from Sea Street beach, this establishment comprises two well-maintained historic houses across the street from each other, with a tiny cottage nestled behind one. The main house, more formally decorated in a Victorian style, has high ceilings throughout. Some of the rooms have four-poster or canopy beds and claw-foot tubs. The house across the street, mansard-roofed with a wraparound porch, has larger rooms decorated with a lighter touch. All rooms in this house have TVs and air-conditioning. The cute little cottage in back, with kitchen and sitting room, is a white-on-white delight. All guests get a complimentary package of inn recipes, like rhubarb coffee cake and Aubrey's maple-syrup poppy-seed loaf.

IN BARNSTABLE, WEST BARNSTABLE & MARSTONS MILLS

Moderate

✪ **Ashley Manor Inn.** 3660 Rte. 6A (about 1 mile E of Hyannis Rd.), Barnstable, MA 02630. ☎ 888/535-2246 or 508/362-8044. Fax 508/362-9927. 2 rms, 4 suites. A/C. Summer (including full breakfast) $120–$140 double; $165–$180 suite. DISC, JCB, MC, V.

Nearly everyone has a vision of the perfect country inn; this one could well fulfill it. The house is a much-modified 1699 colonial mansion that still retains many of its original features, including a hearth with beehive oven (the perfect place to sip port on a blustery evening), built-in corner cupboards in the wainscoted dining room, and wide-board floors, many of them brightened with Nantucket-style splatter-paint. The rooms, all but one of which boast a fireplace, are spacious and inviting: a true retreat. The 2-acre property itself is shielded from the road by an enormous privet hedge, and fragrant boxwood camouflages a Har-Tru tennis court. (You'll find loaner bikes beside it, ready to roll.) Romantics can sequester themselves in the flower-fringed gazebo. Breakfast on the brick patio is worth waking up for: You wouldn't want to miss the homemade granola, much less the main event—quiche, perhaps, or crepes.

✪ **Beechwood Inn.** 2839 Rte. 6A (about 1¹/₂ miles E of Rte. 132), Barnstable, MA 02630. ☎ **800/609-6618** or 508/362-6618. Fax 508/362-0298. E-mail bwdinn@virtualcapecod.com. Web site www.virtualcapecod.com/market/beechwood. 6 rms. Summer (including full breakfast) $125–$160 double. AE, MC, V.

Look for a butterscotch-colored 1853 Queen Anne Victorian all but enshrouded in weeping beeches. Admirers of late-19th-century decor are in for a treat: The interior remains dark and rich, with a red-velvet parlor and tin-ceilinged dining room where innkeeper Debbie Traugot serves a three-course breakfast that features home-baked delights such as applesauce pancakes and raspberry bread. Two of the upstairs bedrooms embody distinctive period styles: The Cottage Room contains furniture painted in an 1860s mode, and Eastlake Room is modeled on the aesthetic precepts of William Morris that flourished in the 1880s. Each affords a distant view of the sparkling bay.

Charles Hinckley House. 8 Scudder Lane (at Rte. 6A, about 1¹/₂ miles E of Rte. 132), Barnstable, MA 02630. ☎ **508/362-9924.** 4 rms. Summer (including full breakfast), $119–$149 double. AE, MC, V.

Set atop a riotous wildflower garden, this hip-roofed 1809 Federal manse hints at tasteful pleasures within—a promise on which it fully delivers. The period decor is almost stark, and deeply pleasing to those who prefer authenticity to misguided colonial clichés. Yet it's all very comfortable. Fireplaces are a given in each room, and some have special features, such as a conservatory/sitting room with bay views (that's part of the Plum Suite) or a window seat flanked by walls of well-stocked bookshelves (the Library Room). Innkeeper Miya Patrick is a caterer of local renown, and her breakfasts are delightful eye-openers. They might begin with a fresh-fruit plate (mangos, raspberries, and bananas, for instance) adorned with edible flowers, and culminate in a crab-cake variation on eggs Benedict. A 5-minute walk down a historic lane lined with stone walls will bring you to the bay.

Honeysuckle Hill. 591 Rte. 6A (about 1 mile W of Rte. 149), W. Barnstable, MA 02668. ☎ **800/441-8418** or 508/362-8418. Fax 508/362-4854. 3 rms, 1 suite. A/C. Summer (including full breakfast) $115 double; $175 suite. AE, DISC, MC, V.

This 1810 farmhouse is full of cozy touches, from featherbeds topped with handmade quilts to homemade cookies atop bedside tables. New owners Judith and Richard Field have freshened up the property with renovations and new decor. They pamper guests in every way possible, without hovering. The suite, joined by a dramatically curved hallway, includes two bedrooms and a kitchenette. For guests planning activities, area events are posted on a bulletin board.

Lamb and Lion Inn. 2504 Main St. (Rte. 6A), Barnstable, MA 02630. ☎ **508/362-6823.** Fax 508/362-0227. Web site www.capecod.com/lamb-lion. 4 rms, 6 suites. Summer (including continental breakfast) $115 double; $140–$175 suite. MC, V.

This is an unusual property: part B&B, part motel. From the roadside, it's one of the most charming old Cape Cod cottages—circa 1740—along the Old King's Highway (where charming "capes" are ubiquitous) set up on a knoll with a sloping lawn full of colorful flowers. Inside, it's a motel-like space with units encircling a heated pool. The rooms are all individually decorated, and many contain kitchenettes. The multilevel barn suite, with three loft-type bedrooms, is a funky space, filled with rustic nooks and crannies. Innkeeper Don McKeag is known as something of a character around these parts; in the evenings he's likely to instigate a sing-along around the keeping room's piano.

Inexpensive

✪ **The Acworth Inn.** 4352 Rte. 6A (near the Yarmouth Port border), Cummaquid, MA 02637. ☎ **800/362-6363** or 508/362-3330. Fax 508/375-0304. 6 rms. Summer (including full breakfast) $90–$115 double. AE, DISC, MC, V.

Cheryl Ferrell knows that it's the small touches that make a stay memorable, and anyone lucky enough to land in this sunnily rehabbed house is sure to remember every last one, from the cranberry spritzer offered on arrival to the handmade chocolates that take the place of pillow mints. She even grinds the whole grains that go into her home-baked breakfasts, in the form of cinnamon rolls or fruit-topped waffles. The inn is close to charming Barnstable Village and popular Cape Cod Bay beaches, so the complimentary bikes may be all you need in the way of wheels.

Crocker Tavern Bed and Breakfast. 3095 Rte. 6A (opposite the Sturgis Library, about 1/2 mile W of Hyannis Rd.), Barnstable, MA 02630. ☎ **508/362-5115.** 5 rms. A/C. Summer (including continental breakfast) $80–$115 double. MC, V. No children under 12.

A hotbed of Whig intrigue, this stagecoach inn, built around 1750, has remained remarkably true to its original appearance. The tavern room, with welcoming hearth and paneled woodwork, would seem right at home in a historic preserve like Old Deerfield. The owners, Sue and Jeff Carlson, have taken care to decorate in keeping with the no-frills austerity of the era, but they did take liberties with the buttery: It's still basically intact, but now it's a bathroom.

✪ **Inn at the Mills.** 71 Rte. 149 (at the intersection of Rte. 28), Marstons Mills, MA 02648. ☎ **508/428-2967.** Fax 508/420-0075. 6 rms. A/C. Summer (including continental breakfast) $75–$110 double. No credit cards.

Unheralded by so much as a sign, this 1780 inn looks more like someone's enviable private estate—an illusion maintained once one ventures indoors, right into a rustic beamed kitchen. Beyond are further common rooms: a proper parlor with wingback chairs, and a sunporch harboring a white baby grand and comfy wicker couches. The view from here is of a small pool and below, beyond a sloping lawn, a good-sized pond occupied by gliding waterfowl and flanked by an inviting gazebo. The rooms are the picture of tasteful primness, too—except for the cathedral-ceilinged "hayloft" room, with dimensions fit for a medieval dining hall. This is where the honeymooners usually end up after a picture-perfect gazebo wedding.

WHERE TO DINE
IN HYANNIS AND HYANNISPORT

Moderate

✪ **Alberto's Ristorante.** 360 Main St., Hyannis. ☎ **508/778-1770.** Reservations recommended. Main courses $13–$25. AE, CB, DC, DISC, MC, V. Daily 11:30am–10pm. ITALIAN.

Alberto's explores the full range of Italian cuisine, with a classicist's attention to components and composition. Owner/chef Felisberto Barreiro's sole Florentine, for instance, consists of gray sole fresh from Chatham, topped with lobster, spinach, and fontina and enhanced with sun-dried tomatoes and beurre blanc sauce. Hand-cut pasta is a specialty, including the ultrarich seafood ravioli cloaked in saffron cream

> ### 👥 Family-Friendly Hotels & Restaurants
>
> **Baxter's Boat House** in Hyannis *(see p. 115)*   Set not just on but over the harbor, this self-service eatery is the perfect spot to stage a messy seafood feast alfresco.
>
> **The Beach House Inn** in West Dennis *(see p. 133)*   Equipped with its own playground, guest kitchen, and cookout deck, this B&B right on the beach is the answer to every parent's prayers.
>
> **The Lighthouse Inn** in West Dennis *(see p. 132)*   It's the 1950s again at this classic family resort right on the beach. If the sun is shining, the kids will want to romp in the surf all day; otherwise there are children's programs. Families often know each other here, because they've been coming back for generations.
>
> **Captain Gosnold Village** in Hyannis *(see p. 110)*   With a small pool, play area, and plenty of age-mates to play with, kids soon feel at home in this charming little cluster of weathered cottages.
>
> **Craigville Pizza & Mexican** in West Hyannisport *(see p. 115)*   The price and ambiance are right for meals that are quick, cheap, filling, and fun.
>
> **Jack's Outback** in Yarmouth Port *(see p. 126)*   Kids get a kick out of all the funny "stern" signs and the silly communal menu at this rambunctious neighborhood diner.

sauce. Though the atmosphere is elegant, with sconces shedding a warm glow over well-spaced, linen-draped tables, the atmosphere is not one of hushed reverence: People clearly come here to have a good time, and the absolute assurance of friendly service and fabulous food ensures that they do. Indicative of the all-out approach is the fact that the restaurant offers limo service off-season from within a nearby radius. Locals who appreciate a bargain know to come between 4 and 6pm, when a full dinner, with soup, salad, and dessert, costs as little as $11.

The Black Cat. 165 Ocean St. (opposite the Ocean St. dock), Hyannis. ☎ **508/778-1233.** Main courses $11–$24. AE, DC, DISC, MC, V. Apr–Oct daily 11:30am–10pm; call for off-season hrs. NEW AMERICAN.

Conveniently located less than a block from the Hy-Line ferries, this is a fine place to catch a quick bite or full meal while you wait for your boat to come in. The menu is pretty basic—steak, pasta, and, of course, fish—but attention is paid to the details; the onion rings, for instance, are made fresh. The dining room, with its bar of gleaming mahogany and brass, will appeal to chilled travelers on a blustery day; in fine weather, you might prefer the porch.

The Paddock. W. End Rotary (at the intersection of W. Main St. and Main St.), Hyannis. ☎ **508/775-7677.** Reservations recommended. Main courses $14–$25. AE, DC, MC, V. Apr to mid-Nov Mon–Sat 11:45am–2:30pm and 5–10pm, Sun noon–10pm. Closed mid-Nov to Mar. CONTINENTAL.

In 1970, when it opened, this Victorian-motif restaurant was right in style, with a saucy continental menu (you can still order extra béarnaise sauce on the side) and such cosmopolitan touches as valet parking and a pianist to lend sparkle to the evening. The place is still going strong—it doesn't hurt that the Cape Cod Melody Tent, which often caters to retro musical tastes, is right next door—but the whole experience might strike you as the kind of "fancy" restaurant place your parents may have favored: When's the last time you encountered a relish tray? There's nary a nouvelle touch in sight, though you could patch together a relatively light, healthy meal by trying such specialties as Mussels à la Grecque, steamed with white wine and shallots, or Scallops Bangkok, sautéed with garlic, ginger, and lime. Opt for the plant- and wicker-filled summer porch rooms if you're not in the mood for pseudo-Tudor.

✪ **Penguin SeaGrill.** 331 Main St. (in the center of town), Hyannis. ☎ **508/775-2023.** Reservations recommended. Main courses $15–$24. AE, CB, DC, DISC, MC, V. Sun–Thurs 5–10pm, Fri–Sat 5–11pm; call for off-season hrs. INTERNATIONAL.

Chef/owner Bob Gold is one of those restless types who, having mastered one style of cuisine (Italian), can't wait to take on another. Hence the versatile menu, which bounces from "Thai Jumpin' Squid," to codfish Portuguese (in a red sauce, with spicy chourico sausage). The specialty here is definitely seafood; pay attention to the specials and you can't go wrong. The setting is handsome and contemporary, with brick walls, mirrored accents, and mammoth carved fish. For years, this has been considered one of the top restaurants on the Cape.

✪ **Ristorante Barolo.** 1 Financial Place (297 North St., just off the W. End Rotary), Hyannis. ☎ **508/778-2878.** Main courses $8–$22. AE, DC, MC, V. June–Sept Sun–Thurs 4–11pm, Fri– Sat 4pm–midnight; call for off-season hrs. ITALIAN.

Part of a smart-looking brick office complex, this thoroughly up-to-date Italian restaurant does everything right, from offering extra-virgin olive oil for dunking its crusty bread to getting those pastas perfectly al dente. Patrons favor the fillet Barolo, an Angus steak served with a reduction sauce of Barolo wine, with sun-dried tomatoes and wild mushrooms.

✪ **Roadhouse Cafe.** 488 South St. (off Main St., near the W. End Rotary), Hyannis. ☎ **508/775-2386.** Main courses $11–$22. AE, CB, DC, DISC, MC, V. Daily 4pm–1am. AMERICAN/NORTHERN ITALIAN.

The humble name belies the culinary caliber of this intimate but ambitious restaurant. This is not the hybrid "Italian-American" fare that so poorly represents both. Instead, the extensive menu is pretty much split between American standards such as steak (not to mention oysters Rockefeller or casino) and real Italian cooking, unstinting on the garlic. There's also a less expensive lighter-fare menu, including what some have called "the best burger in the world," served in the snazzy bistro in back. Among the appetizers are such delicacies as carpaccio with fresh-shaved Parmesan, and vine-ripened tomatoes and buffalo mozzarella drizzled with balsamic vinaigrette. The latter also makes a tasty marinade for native swordfish headed for the grill. The signature dessert, a distinctly non-Italian cheesecake infused with Bailey's Irish Creme, is itself an excuse to come check out the live jazz in the bistro (see "Hyannis & Environs After Dark," below).

Roo Bar. 586 Main St., Hyannis. ☎ **508/778-6515.** Main courses $4–$25. AE, DC, MC, V. Daily 5–10pm. BISTRO.

This moody and stylish bistro is the new kid on the block. You may want to sit at the bar and have a few appetizers like the chicken pot sticker (pan-seared wonton wrappers filled with an Asian chicken and vegetable stuffing with an orange marmalade dipping sauce) or even a plate of oysters on the half shell. The most popular entree may be the seafood Provençal (jumbo shrimp and sea scallops sautéed with fresh tomatoes and basil in a white-wine garlic sauce over fresh angel-hair pasta), but there are a number of other lobster, fish, and steak dishes. If you're a cigar aficionado, you may want to show up after 10pm, when cigar smoking is allowed and encouraged (see "Hyannis & Environs After Dark," below).

Steamers Grill & Bar. 235 Ocean St. (opposite the Hy-Line dock), Hyannis. ☎ **508/ 778-0818.** Main courses $10–$19. AE, DC, MC, V. Late May to early Sept daily 11:30am–10pm; call for off-season hrs. Closed mid-Nov to Mar. AMERICAN.

Around sunset, the deck starts to fill to overflowing. While most patrons are imbibing and revving up for the night, a few will dally over the food: mesquite-grilled swordfish or steak, or maybe stuffed shrimp. Night owls need plenty of protein, after all.

Inexpensive

☸ Baxter's Boat House. 177 Pleasant St. (near Steamship Authority ferry), Hyannis. ☎ **508/775-7040.** Main courses $8–$14. AE, MC, V. Late May to early Sept Mon–Sat 11:30am–10pm, Sun 11:30am–9pm; call for off-season hrs. Closed mid-Oct to Mar. SEAFOOD.

A shingled shack on a jetty jutting out into the harbor, Baxter's has catered to the boating crowd since the mid-1950s, with Cape classics such as fried clams and fish virtually any way you like it, from baked to blackened.

Craigville Pizza & Mexican. 618 Craigville Beach Rd. (midway between Centerville and Hyannisport), W. Hyannisport. ☎ **508/775-2267.** Main courses $5–$9. DISC, MC, V. Late May to early Sept daily 11am–11pm; call for off-season hrs. ITALIAN/MEXICAN.

Hearty appetites will appreciate the cross-pollination of cuisines—as embodied, for example, in a chicken fajita pizza—but above all, the budget-conscious prices. No wonder families and the young and impecunious start crowding into this casual locale straight from the beach. The Italian fast-food side of the menu includes the option of Sicilian, whole-wheat, or "Kelly" (garlic) crust, and the Mexican standards (nachos, burritos, enchiladas, and more) are supplemented by a "piñata pie" for two: three tortillas piled high with taco fixings. The children's menu is a real boon, too, with such ever-popular entrees as spaghetti and meatballs for under $2, milk or soda included.

The Egg & I. 521 Main St. (in the center of town), Hyannis. ☎ **508/771-1596.** All items under $10. AE, CB, DC, DISC, MC, V. Daily 11pm–1pm. Mar and Nov, weekends only. Closed Dec–Feb. AMERICAN.

Yes, those are the correct hours. This Tudor-storefront diner opens at 11 at night, then serves past noon. A town with this many bars needs a place where patrons and staff alike can unwind and/or sober up after last call; a wholesome meal wouldn't hurt either. Breakfast is usually the meal of choice, especially the "create an omelet" option, but the pancakes—from chocolate-chip to fruit-loaded Swedish—are strong contenders. Children go gaga over the Mickey Mouse waffle (only $2, with bacon or sausage), and those who feel silly having breakfast before bed can order sandwiches or one of a dozen or so daily specials that change with the season.

Harry's. 700 Main St. (near the W. End Rotary), Hyannis. ☎ **508/778-4188.** Main courses $9–$17. AE, DISC, MC, V. Daily 11:30am–1am. INTERNATIONAL.

Seemingly transported from the French Quarter, this small restaurant/bar—park benches serve as booths—has added some Italian and French options to its menu, but it's the authentic Southern cooking that keeps customers coming back: ribs, jambalaya, hoppin' John, red beans and rice. On the weekends get set for a heaping serving of R&B (see "Hyannis & Environs After Dark," below).

Sam Diego's. 950 Rte. 132 (about 1 mile W of the airport), Hyannis. ☎ **508/771-8816.** Main courses $6–$13. AE, DISC, MC, V. Daily 11:30am–1am. MEXICAN.

Margaritas lure the singles to this popular restaurant/bar; fun, affordable dinners bring in the family crowd. Serapes and gaudy paper toucans provide a splash of color, and the kitchen does well by all the standard dishes, from enchiladas to chimichangas and that luscious oxymoron, fried ice cream.

Sophie's Bar & Grill. 334 Main St. (in the center of town), Hyannis. ☎ **508/775-1111.** Main courses $6–$10. AE, MC, DISC, V. Daily 11:30am–10pm. AMERICAN.

There's nothing fancy about this good old bar, but on summer days you'll find the booths stuffed with families taking advantage of the "home-style cooking"—made-from-scratch soups, wood-grilled pizzas—at approachable prices. In the evening the young crowd comes in to do the same.

Spiritus. 500 Main St. (in the center of town), Hyannis. ☎ **508/775-2955.** Most items under $10. DISC. June–Aug Sun–Thurs 11:30am–midnight, Fri–Sat 11:30am–1am; call for off-season hrs. ITALIAN/ECLECTIC.

A branch of the Provincetown pizza palace, this one sports a ceiling mural of demented cherubs and tends to attract local young folks and artistes. Most everything's homemade, from the soup to the carrot juice, even the biscotti, and the whole scene is very low-key.

Starbucks. 645 Rte. 132 (near the airport), Hyannis. ☎ **508/778-6767.** Main courses $7–$12. AE, DC, DISC, MC, V. Daily 11:30am–midnight. INTERNATIONAL.

This hangarlike space actually contains an airplane, a decommissioned Fokker D-7, suspended from the ceiling, along with a lot of other odd conversation pieces conducive to the singles-mingling going on below. The bar tends to attract a slightly older (postcollege) crowd, and it's a fun place for families as well. Kids can order scaled-down desserts as well as entrees—provided you can talk them out of the Oreo-cookie pie. Or you can slap together a multicultural meal spanning baked Brie and Philly cheese steak, jambalaya and Thai scallops, or go traditional with their chunky clam chowder.

Sweetwaters Grille. 644 Main St. (about ¹/₄ mile E of the W. End Rotary), Hyannis. ☎ **508/775-3323.** Main courses $7–$15. AE, MC, V. Mid-June to early Sept Mon–Thurs 4–10pm, Fri–Sat 11:30am–11pm, Sun noon–10pm; early Sept to mid-June Mon–Thurs 11:30am–10pm, Fri–Sat 11:30am–11pm, Sun noon–10pm. SOUTHWESTERN.

The Cape is no more immune to Tex-Mex fever than any other halfway-hip community—or to fusion influences, which explains the seafood spring roll (wrapped in a tortilla with green chili sauce) and the Thai grilled beef with lemongrass salsa. Chili-heads can test themselves on the chicken Diablo, flambéed with brandy, with a red-chili garlic sauce chaser, and any masochist begging for more can slather on a side of "rattlesnake venom." There are plenty of less-incendiary choices, and the setting itself is soothing and understated, done in shades of sage green.

Tugboats. 21 Arlington St. (at the Hyannis Marina, off Willow St.), Hyannis. ☎ **508/775-6433.** Main courses $11–$15. AE, DC, DISC, MC, V. July–Aug daily 11:30am–10:30pm; call for off-season hrs. Closed Nov–Mar. AMERICAN.

Yet another harborside perch for munching and ogling, this one's especially appealing: The two spacious outdoor decks are angled just right to catch the sunset, with cocktail/frappes to match—or perhaps a bottle of Moët et Chandon. Forget fancy dining and chow down on blackened-swordfish bites (topping a Caesar salad, perhaps) or lobster fritters, or the double-duty Steak Neptune, topped with scallops and shrimp. Among the "decadent desserts" (must we constantly be reminded?) are a shortbread-crusted Bourbon Pecan Pie, and a Key Lime Pie purportedly lifted straight from Papa's.

Up the Creek. 36 Old Colony Blvd. (about 1 mile S of Main St.), Hyannis. ☎ **508/771-7866.** Reservations recommended. Main courses $9–$13. AE, CB, DC, DISC, MC, V. June–Aug daily 11:30am–10pm; call for off-season hrs. INTERNATIONAL.

Good luck finding it (tucked away in a residential area) and better luck getting in! Locals know a good deal when they see one, and dinner prices in the single digits draw an avid crowd. House specialties include a seafood strudel cloaked with hollandaise, and a broiled seafood platter comprising half a lobster, clams casino, scallops, scrod, and baked stuffed shrimp (that's the priciest entree at all of $13). Decorated like an Ivy League boathouse, the restaurant has grace and style, even when the occupancy maxes out.

Coffee & Dessert

Offering indisputable proof that Hyannis has its hip side, **Caffe e Dolci,** 430 Main St. (in the center of town; ☎ **508/790-6900**), is a chic coffeehouse that serves up a mean cappuccino, as well as addictive Italian desserts: Try a coffee granita for the ultimate in summertime refreshment.

Vermont's favorite sons, **Ben & Jerry,** have one of their playful ice-cream parlors at 352 Main St., Hyannis (☎ **508/790-0910**).

This modest luncheonette may make an unlikely shrine, but since 1934 several generations of summerers—including enthusiastic Kennedys—have fed their ice-cream cravings at **Four Seas,** 360 S. Main St. (at Main Street, in center of Centerville; ☎ **508/775-1394**). Founder Richard Warren was into exotic flavors long before they became the norm. His specialties include rum butter toffee, cantaloupe, and—at the height of the season—Cape Cod beach plum. Closed early September to late May.

Take-Out and Picnic Fare

Another branch of the popular **Box Lunch** (☎ **508/790-5855**), serving pita "rollwiches," is right on Main Street (no. 357) in Hyannis. These are the best—and fastest—sandwiches in town.

For the freshest produce, deli items, and specialty foods, stop in **Lambert's Rainbow Fruit** at 1000 W. Main St., Centerville (☎ **508/778-4066**). Family-owned and -managed for decades, this is the place to pick up summer's bounty.

Boston foodies are gaga over the earthy European breads at **Pain d'Avignon,** 192 Airport Rd. (in the center of Hyannis; ☎ **508/771-9771**), prepared by a quartet of East European buddies: They're shipped in at dawn to the city's finest shops and restaurants. Here, you can get the likes of chewy pecan-and-raisin loaf and hard-crusted European-style baguettes straight from the oven.

IN BARNSTABLE VILLAGE, OSTERVILLE & COTUIT

Expensive

✪ **The Regatta of Cotuit at the Crocker House.** 4613 Falmouth Rd. (Rte. 28, near the Mashpee border), Cotuit. ☎ **508/428-5715.** Reservations recommended. Main courses $18–$26. AE, MC, V. Daily 5–10pm. NEW AMERICAN.

The year-round cousin of the Regatta at Falmouth-by-the-Sea (see "Where to Dine" under "Falmouth," in chapter 5) serves many of the same signature dishes—such as the stellar lamb *en chemise*—in a suite of charmingly decorated Federal-era rooms: this 1790 Cape was once a stagecoach inn. The wayfarers of old couldn't possibly have fared as well. The cuisine is at once exquisite and hearty, fortified by herbs and vegetables plucked fresh from the kitchen garden, and the mood is invariably festive. You're likely to experience the best service on Cape Cod at this enchanting locale.

Moderate

Barnstable Tavern & Grille. 3176 Main St., Barnstable. ☎ **508/362-2355.** Main courses $11–$22. AE, DISC, MC, V. Sun–Thurs 11:30am–10pm, Fri–Sat 11:30am–11pm. REGIONAL.

From the outside, this restaurant—a former stagecoach stop smack dab in the middle of Barnstable Village—feels like it's been here forever. Inside has been cheerfully revamped. The new tavern area, serving 30 wines by the glass, is separate from the dining room and serves food till midnight. Specialties here include Black Angus sirloin and fresh grilled swordfish. Off-season there's a large brunch buffet on Sundays.

Dolphin Restaurant. 3250 Rte. 6A (in the center of town), Barnstable. ☎ **508/362-6610.** Main courses $14–$19. AE, CB, DC, MC, V. Daily 11:30am–3pm and 5–9:30pm. NEW AMERICAN.

It looks like just another run-of-the-mill roadside eatery, so don't blame yourself if you passed at first glance. Never mind the corny decor (pine paneling and clunky captain's chairs), a carryover from the restaurant's 1953 debut. The finesse is to be found in the menu, where amid the more typical fried fish you'll find such delicacies as scallops sautéed with lobster and saffron, or lightly breaded veal cloaked in a sauce of crushed hazelnuts. It's a painless segue from there to the signature dessert: amaretto bread pudding.

Mattakeese Wharf. 271 Mill Way (about ¹/₂ mile N of Rte. 6A), Barnstable. ☎ **508/362-4511.** Reservations recommended. Main courses $11–$25. AE, MC, V. June–Oct daily 11:30am–10pm; call for off-season hrs. Closed Nov–Apr. SEAFOOD.

Jutting out into the harbor, this classic fish house has broad decks with blue-and-white awnings. The outdoor seating fills up fast on summer evenings, and no wonder, with Sandy Neck sunsets to marvel over and fish so fresh it could have flopped on deck. There's a Mediterranean subtext to the extensive menu. The bouillabaisse is worthy of the name, and the varied combinations of pasta, seafood, and sauce—from Alfredo to fra diavolo—invite return visits.

Inexpensive

Wimpy's Seafood Cafe & Market. 752 Main St. (in the center of town), Osterville. ☎ **508/428-6300.** Reservations recommended. Main courses $7–$19. AE, MC, V. June–Oct daily 11:30am–10pm; call for off-season hrs. AMERICAN.

In 1938, Osterville had to come up with some means of feeding the laborers brought in to set up the town's water mains. That six-stool luncheonette evolved into this 300-seat restaurant, still pretty reasonably priced with early-bird specials daily. In the cold months, a fire in the massive stone fireplace takes the edge off; in summer the greenhouse section in back is especially inviting. The menu tends to favor the tried and true, with fresh native seafoods a specialty. The attached market offers a full take-out service of fish and specialty foods.

Take-Out & Take-Home Food

Area residents like to think of ✪ **Mill Way,** Millway Road (on Barnstable Harbor, about ¹/₃ mile north of Route 6A; ☎ 508/362-2760), a highfalutin fish shack, as their own little secret. Certainly there are no outward signs to suggest that chef/co-owner Ralph Binder is a product of the prestigious Culinary Institute of America. You can order the usual Cape specialties, from chowder to lobster, from the take-out window, but be sure to step inside to see what else is available: perhaps a pungent calamari salad, or seafood sausage, a delicately seasoned melange of lobster, shrimp, and scallops. Closed mid-October through April.

HYANNIS & ENVIRONS AFTER DARK
LOW-KEY EVENINGS

Baxter's Boat House. 177 Pleasant St. (see "Where to Dine," above), Hyannis. ☎ **508/755-4490.** No cover.

This congenial little lounge, with map-topped tables and low-key blues piano, draws an attractive crowd, including the occasional vacationing celebrity.

✪ **Roadhouse Cafe.** 488 South St. (see "Where to Dine," above), Hyannis. ☎ **508/775-2386.** No cover.

In case you want to see the world.

At American Express, we're here to make your journey a
smooth one. So we have over 1,700 travel service locations in
over 120 countries ready to help. What else would you expect
from the world's largest travel agency?

do more

Travel

http://www.americanexpress.com/travel

In case you want to be welcomed there.

We're here to see that you're always welcomed at establishments everywhere. That's why millions of people carry the American Express® Card – for peace of mind, confidence, and security, around the world or just around the corner.

do more®

In case you're running low.

We're here to help with more than 118,000 Express Cash

locations around the world. In order to enroll, just call

American Express before you start your vacation.

do more

Express Cash

And just in case.

We're here with American Express® Travelers Cheques and Cheques *for Two*.® They're the safest way to carry money on your vacation and the surest way to get a refund, practically anywhere, anytime.

Another way we help you...

do more

**Travelers
Cheques**

If raucous rock is the last thing you seek in after-dinner entertainment, duck into this dark-paneled bar, decorated in burgundy leather like an English gentlemen's club. The bar stocks 48 boutique beers, in addition to all the usual hard, soft, and sweet liquors, and you won't go hoarse trying to converse over the soft jazz. The new bistro area next to the bar has live jazz piano nightly. Insiders know to show up Monday nights to hear local jazz great Dave McKenna.

Roo Bar. 586 Main St. (see "Where to Dine," above), Hyannis. ☎ **508/778-6515.** No cover.

The newest bistro to hit Main Street feels very Manhattan, with ultracool servers, a long sleek bar area, and lots of attitude. Bistro food is good too (see "Where to Dine," above). Trendy cigar smoking commences after 10pm.

Windjammer Lounge. Airport Shopping Plaza, Hyannis. ☎ **508/771-2020.** No cover.

How did this classic 1950s gin joint end up in a strip mall next to T. J. Maxx? Best not to think about it too hard; just enjoy the live acoustic performers, weekends in season.

LIVE & LOUD

Duval Street Station. 477 Yarmouth Rd. (about 1 mile NE of Main St.), Hyannis. ☎ **508/771-7511.** Nominal cover charge Fri–Sat in season.

Hyannis's first and so far only gay bar (Provincetown is not far off, of course) occupies an old train station. The lower level is a comfortable lounge, and upstairs there's a dance bar complete with light show and DJ mixes that spin from Latin rhythms to New Wave to "gay disco classics" of the seventies and eighties.

Harry's. 700 Main St. (see "Where to Dine," above), Hyannis. ☎ **508/778-4188.** Cover Fri–Sat $1–$2.

There's hardly room to eat here, let alone rock out, but the cramped dance floor makes for instant camaraderie. The music heard here—blues, jazz, rock, and blends thereof—really demands to be absorbed in such an intimate space.

Hyannisport Brewing Company. 720 Main St. (about 1/4 mile E of the W. End Rotary), Hyannis. ☎ **508/775-4110.** No cover.

Though it lacks the atmosphere of other New England brew pubs (built in 1993, it looks like any other mall restaurant), this is the only place on the Cape where you can get traditionally made suds straight from the spigot. The crowd is young and rambunctious.

Sophie's Bar & Grill. 334 Main St. (see "Where to Dine," above), Hyannis. ☎ **508/775-1111.** Cover $3–$5 in season.

The dance bar in back is where buttoned-down prepsters convene to cut loose. The live rock leans to such freaky extremes as the Strangemen out of Martha's Vineyard, a quintet of platinum-pompadoured alien-dandies who describe their sound as "sci-fi rockabilly surf rock." Yee haw!

Starbuck's. 645 Rte. 132 (see "Where to Dine," above), Hyannis. ☎ **508/778-6767.** No cover.

The fact that there's occasional karaoke—interspersed amid acoustic acts and soft-rock bands—should give you some idea of what kind of crowd to expect: not exactly cutting-edge. But the drinks range from silly (for example, Grape Crush) to serious (27-oz. margaritas), and both setting and staff contrive to ensure a good time.

Steamers Grill & Bar. 235 Ocean St. (see "Where to Dine," above), Hyannis. ☎ **508/778-0818.** No cover.

Everyone's glowing with the day's exertions as they cram onto the deck to enjoy a lingering sunset with liberal libations. It's a young, sporty crowd for the most part (despite the fuddy-duddy duffers' motif in the downstairs Putter's Pub), drawn by the live bands on weekends.

PERFORMANCE, READINGS, LECTURES

The Barnstable Comedy Club. 3171 Rte. 6A (in the center of town), Barnstable. ☎ **508/362-6333.** Tickets $10–$12; call for schedule.

A local favorite since 1922, the oldest amateur theater group in the country (Kurt Vonnegut is an admiring ex-member) offers shows by and for kids in the summer; off-season, grown-up thespians take over, in a mix of old chestnuts and original farces.

✪ The Cape Cod Melody Tent. W. End Rotary, Hyannis. ☎ **508/775-9100.** Curtain 8pm nightly July to early Sept. Tickets $13–$37. Most performances 8pm; call for schedule.

Built as a summer theater in 1950, this billowy blue big-top proved even better suited to variety shows. A nonprofit venture since 1990 (proceeds fund other cultural initiatives Cape-wide), the Melody Tent hosted the major performers of the past half century, from jazz greats to comedians, crooners to rockers. Every seat is a winner in this grand oval, only 20 banked aisles deep. There's also a children's theater program Wednesday mornings at 11am.

Tales of Cape Cod. Olde Colonial Courthouse, 3018 Rte. 6A (about ¹/₂ mile W of Hyannis Rd.), Barnstable. ☎ **508/362-8927.** Tickets $3. Early July to Aug, Tues at 8pm.

Housed in the 1772 courthouse that was superseded by the Barnstable Superior Courthouse, this nonprofit research organization dedicated to preserving Cape folk-lore opens its doors for lively lectures on topics of local interest.

2 Yarmouth

19 miles (31km) E of Sandwich, 38 miles (61km) S of Provincetown

This cross-section represents the Cape at its best—and worst. Yarmouth Port, on Cape Cod Bay, is an enchanting town, clustered with interesting shops and architectural pearls, whereas the sound-side "villages" of West to South Yarmouth are an object lesson in unbridled development run amuck. This section of Route 28 is a nightmar-ish gauntlet of ticky-tacky accommodations and "attractions." Yet even here you'll find a few spots worthy of the name.

Legend has it that Leif Eriksson found the region very attractive indeed, and set up what was meant to be a permanent camp by the Bass River around A.D. 1000. No trace has as yet been found—other than the puzzling "Bournedale stone," with its vaguely runic inscriptions, now housed at the Aptucxet Trading Post Museum in Bourne. Why Eriksson left—and whether, in fact, he came to Cape Cod at all, and not some similar spot—are mysteries still unanswered. We do know that Yarmouth, most likely named for an English port, was the second Cape town to incorporate, following closely on the heels of Sandwich, and that at the height of the shipping boom, Yarmouth Port boasted a "Captain's Row" of 50 fine houses, most of which remain showpieces to this day.

You've got the north shore for culture and refinement, the south shore for kitsch. Take your pick, or ricochet schizophrenically, enjoying the best of both worlds.

ESSENTIALS

GETTING THERE After crossing either the Bourne or Sagamore bridge, head east on Route 6 or 6A. Route 6A (north of Route 6's Exit 7) passes through the village of Yarmouth Port. The villages of West Yarmouth, Bass River, and South Yarmouth are located along Route 28, east of Hyannis; to reach them from Route 6, take Exit 7 south (Yarmouth Road), or Exit 8 south (Station Street), or fly into Hyannis (see "Getting There" in chapter 3).

If you need to get around the area without a car, the Yarmouth Easy Shuttle circles Route 28 from Hyannis's bus terminal; for details, contact the **Yarmouth Area Chamber of Commerce** (☎ **508/778-1008**).

VISITOR INFORMATION   Contact the **Yarmouth Area Chamber of Commerce,** 657 Rte. 28, West Yarmouth, MA 02673 (☎ **508/778-1008**), or the **Cape Cod Chamber of Commerce,** Routes 6 and 132, Hyannis, MA 02601 (☎ **508/ 362-3225;** fax 508/362-3698; Web site www.capecod.com).

BEACHES & OUTDOOR PURSUITS

BEACHES   Yarmouth boasts 11 saltwater and 2 pond beaches open to the public. The body-per-square-yard ratio can be pretty intense along the sound, but so's the social scene, so no one seems to mind. The beachside parking lots charge $8 a day and sell weeklong stickers ($30).

- **Bass River Beach,** off South Shore Drive in Bass River (South Yarmouth). Located at the mouth of the largest tidal river on the eastern seaboard, this sound beach offers bathroom facilities and a snack bar, plus a bonus—a wheelchair-accessible fishing pier. The beaches along the south shore (Nantucket Sound) tend to be clean and sandy with comfortable water temps (kids will want to stay in all day), but they can also be quite crowded during peak times. You'll need a beach sticker to park here.
- **Grays Beach,** off Center Street in Yarmouth Port. Tame waters excellent for children; adjoins the Callery-Darling Conservation Area (see "Nature & Wildlife Areas," below). The Bass Hole boardwalk offers one of the most scenic walks in the Mid Cape. Parking is free here, and there's a picnic area with grills.
- **Parker's River Beach,** off South Shore Drive in Bass River. The usual amenities like rest rooms and a snack bar, plus a 20-foot gazebo for the sun-shy.
- **Seagull Beach,** off South Sea Avenue in West Yarmouth. Rolling dunes, a boardwalk, and all the necessary facilities, like rest rooms and a snack bar, attract a young crowd. Bring bug spray, though: Greenhead flies get the munchies in July.

BICYCLING   The **Cape Cod Rail Trail** is just a few miles away on Route 134 in South Dennis. Rent a bike at the trailhead, and if you are feeling Olympian, bike all the way to Wellfleet (25 miles).

BOATING   **Cape Cod Coastal Canoe & Kayak** (☎ **888/226-6393** or 508/ 564-4051; Web site www.capecod.net/canoe/; E-mail cccanoe@capecod.net) runs naturalist-guided trips throughout the Cape, sponsored by the Cape Cod Museum of Natural History. In Yarmouth, they paddle along the Bass River. Trips (3^1/2 to 4 hr.) are daily April through August, weekends through October, and cost $25 per paddler or $50 per family. All equipment is supplied. Call for schedule.

FISHING   Of the five fishing ponds in the Yarmouth area, **Long Pond** near South Yarmouth is known for its largemouth bass and pickerel; for details and a license (shellfishing is another option), visit **Town Hall** at 1146 Rte. 28 in South Yarmouth (☎ **508/398-2231**). Full-season licenses for Massachusetts residents cost $28.50; for out-of-staters, $38.50. You can cast for striped bass and bluefish off the pier at Bass River Beach (see "Beaches," above).

FITNESS   The **Mid-Cape Racquet Club** (see "Tennis," below) doubles as a fitness center.

GOLF   The township maintains two 18-hole courses: the seasonal **Bayberry Hills,** off West Yarmouth Road in South Yarmouth (☎ **508/394-5597**), and the **Bass River Golf Course,** off High Bank Road in South Yarmouth (☎ **508/398-9079**), founded in 1900 and open year-round. Two more 18-holers are open to the public: the par-54 **Blue Rock Golf Course** off High Bank Road in South Yarmouth (☎ **508/398-9295**), open year-round, and the seasonal **Kings Way Golf Club,** off Route 6A in Yarmouth Port (☎ **508/362-8870**).

NATURE & WILDLIFE AREAS   For a pleasant stroll, follow the 2 miles of trails maintained by the Historical Society of Old Yarmouth on 53 acres behind the **Captain Bangs Hallet House** (see "Museums," below). Park behind the post office, and check in at the gatehouse, whose herb garden displays a "Wheel of Thyme." The in-season trail fee (50¢ adults, 25¢ children) includes a keyed trail guide: look for—but do not pick—the endangered pink lady's slipper, a local orchid. Your path will cross a former seamen's bethel, the transplanted 1873 Kelley Chapel, which is said to have been built by a Quaker grandfather to comfort his daughter after the death of her child.

In Yarmouth Port, follow Center Street about a mile north and bear northeast on Homers Dock Road; from here a 2^1/$_2$-mile trail through the **Callery-Darling Conservation Area** leads to Grays Beach, where you can continue across the Bass Hole Boardwalk for a lovely view of the marsh.

TENNIS   There are four public courts at Flax Pond, off North Main Street in South Yarmouth; four more at Sandy Pond, on Buck Island Road off Higgins Crowell Road; plus 10 at Dennis-Yarmouth High School at Station Avenue in South Yarmouth; for details, contact the **Yarmouth Recreation Department** (☎ **508/ 398-2231,** ext. 284). The **Mid-Cape Racquet Club,** 193 Whites Path, South Yarmouth (☎ **508/394-3511**), has nine indoor courts, plus racquetball and squash courts (two each) and health-club facilities.

MUSEUMS

Captain Bangs Hallet House. 11 Strawberry Lane (off Rte. 6A about ^{1}/$_2$ mile E of town center; park behind the post office at 231 Rte. 6A), Yarmouth Port. ☎ **508/362-3021.** Admission $3 adults, 50¢ children 12 and under. June–Oct Sun 1–3:30pm; July–Aug Thurs and Sun 1–3:30pm. Closed Nov–May.

Typical of the sumptuous tastes of the time, this 1840 Greek Revival house is named for the China Trade seafarer who lived here from 1863 to 1893. The Historical Society of Old Yarmouth, which oversees the property, has filled its beautifully proportioned rooms with the finest furnishings of the day, from Hitchcock chairs to a Hepplewhite sofa. The rustic kitchen in back belongs to the 1740 core around which this showy edifice was erected. Note the nearly 2-century-old weeping beech and the herb garden beyond, which lead to a scenic 2-mile walking trail (see "Nature & Wildlife Areas," above).

✪ **Winslow Crocker House.** 250 Rte. 6A (about ^{1}/$_2$ mile E of town center), Yarmouth Port. ☎ **508/362-4385.** Admission $4 adults, $3.50 senior citizens, $2 children 5–12. June to mid-Oct hourly tours Sat–Sun 11am–5pm (last tour at 4pm). Closed mid-Oct to May.

The only property on the Cape currently preserved by the prestigious Society for the Preservation of New England Antiquities, this house, built around 1780, deserves every honor. Not only is it a lovely example of the shingled Georgian style, it's packed with outstanding antiques—Jacobean to Chippendale—collected in the 1930s by Mary Thacher, a descendant of the town's first land grantee. Anthony Thacher and his family had a rougher crossing than most: Their ship foundered off Cape Ann in 1635 (near an island that now bears their name), and though their four children drowned, Thacher and his wife were able to make it to shore, clinging to the family cradle. You'll come across a 1690 replica in the parlor. Thacher's son, John, a colonel, built the house next door in around 1680, and—with the help of two successive wives—raised a total of 21 children. All the museum-worthy objects in the Winslow Crocker House would seem to have similar stories to tell. For antique lovers, as well as anyone interested in local lore, this is a valuable cache and a very worthwhile stop.

BASEBALL AND SOCCER

The Dennis-Yarmouth Red Sox, part of the Cape Cod Baseball League, play at Dennis-Yarmouth High School's Red Wilson Field off Station Avenue in South Yarmouth. For a schedule, contact the **Yarmouth Chamber of Commerce,** 657 Rte. 28, West Yarmouth, MA 02673 (☎ **508/778-1008**), the **Yarmouth Recreation Department** (☎ **508/398-2231,** ext. 284), or the **League** (☎ **508/432-6909**).

The Cape Cod Crusaders take on a dozen other Atlantic-coast soccer teams mid-May to early August, also at the Dennis-Yarmouth Regional High School. For details, contact the **Yarmouth Chamber of Commerce,** 657 Rte. 28, West Yarmouth, MA 02673 (☎ **508/778-1008**).

KID STUFF

Children tend to crave the "junk" we adults condemn, so they're likely to be enthralled by the rainy-day enticements of Route 28. Among the more enduringly appealing miniature-golf courses clamoring for attention is **Pirate's Cove,** at 728 Rte. 28, South Yarmouth (☎ **508/394-6200;** open daily 9am to 11pm in season), where the trap decor is strong on macabre humor. For something a little more wholesome, treat the kids to an ice-cream soda at **Hallet's,** an 1889 drugstore on Route 6A in Yarmouth Port (see "A Soda Fountain" under "Where to Dine," below), or spend an afternoon at **Taylor Bray Farm,** a working 1800s farmstead maintained by the town of Yarmouth (☎ **508/385-6499,** or Town Hall 508/398-2231, ext. 270).

ZooQuarium. 674 Rte. 28 (midway between W. Yarmouth and Bass River), W. Yarmouth. ☎ **508/775-8883.** Admission $7.50 adults, $4.50 children 2–9. July–Aug daily 9:30am–8pm; off-season 9:30am–5pm. Closed late Nov to mid-Feb.

This slightly scruffy wildlife museum has made great strides in recent years toward blending entertainment with education. It's a little easier to enjoy the sea-lion show once you've been assured that the stars like performing, have been trained with positive reinforcement only, and, furthermore, arrived with injuries that precluded their survival in the wild. The aquarium is arranged in realistic habitats, and the "zoo" consists primarily of indigenous fauna, both domesticated and wild (the pacing bobcat is liable to give you pause). Children will be entranced by the zoorific theater (a live animal education program) and the children's discovery center with hands-on activities. In addition, a very creditable effort is made to convey the need for ecological preservation. A special agriculture exhibit is planned for 1998.

SHOPPING

Route 6A through Yarmouth Port remains a rich vein of antique shops. Check them all out, if you're so inclined and have the time, and be sure to visit the two noted below. Unless you have children in tow, you may want to bypass Route 28 entirely. If you do find yourself down that way, though, you might stock up on tried-and-true sundries at Nineteenth Century Mercantile.

ANTIQUES/COLLECTIBLES   Most Cape antique stores offer plenty of "smalls" (decorative items such as glass, china, and silver) but scant the big stuff—major pieces of centuries-old furniture. There's plenty of the latter at **Nickerson Antiques,** 162 Rte. 6A (in the center of town), Yarmouth Port (☎ **508/362-6426**), mostly imported from Great Britain and much of it skillfully refinished in situ.

Check out **Town Crier Antiques,** 153 Rte. 6A (in the center of town), Yarmouth Port (☎ **508/362-3138**), for fun stuff, from well-priced (if not museum-quality) quilts to dolls and attendant paraphernalia. Closed mid-October to mid-May.

ARTS & CRAFTS   Ron Kusins's designs range from the traditional (for example, a burnished porringer) to the contemporary (for example, sleek and shiny asymmetrical candlesticks). There's a style to suit every look, and you can watch this nearly extinct art in action at **Pewter Crafters of Cape Cod,** 933 Rte. 6A (near the Dennis border), Yarmouth (☎ **508/362-3407**).

BOOKS   The most colorful bookshop on the Cape (if not the whole East Coast) is ✪ **Parnassus Books,** 220 Rte. 6A (about ¼ mile east of town center), Yarmouth Port (☎ **508/362-6420**). This jam-packed repository—housed in an 1858 Swedenborgian church—is the creation of Ben Muse, who has been collecting and selling vintage tomes since the 1960s. Relevant new stock, including the Cape-related reissues published by Parnassus Imprints, is offered alongside the older treasures, and don't expect much hand-holding on the part of the gruff proprietor. You'll earn his respect by knowing what you're looking for or, better yet, being willing to browse until it finds you. The outdoor racks, maintained on an honor system, are open 24 hours a day, for those who suffer from anbibliophobia—fear of lacking for reading material.

GIFTS/HOME DECOR   To emulate that Cape look—breezy chic—study the key ingredients artfully assembled at **Design Works,** 159 Rte. 6A (in the center of town), Yarmouth Port (☎ **508/362-9698**): stripped-pine antiques, crisp linens, colorful majolica.

Nineteenth Century Mercantile, 2 N. Main St. (about ¼ mile west of the Bass River Bridge), South Yarmouth (☎ **508/398-1888**), a resuscitated general store, is like a crash course in the customs of an earlier age—one that was more labor-intensive, to be sure, but had its own sensory pleasures. The stock is what you'd see in a historical collection, only it's all freshly manufactured for a nostalgia market. Some treats, such as refreshing rosewater cologne, have never gone completely out of style. Many of the home furnishings and fixtures not only blend well in period houses, but are as enduringly practical as they are quaint. Thursday through Saturday evenings, the Mercantile is the site for folk tales and ghost stories for the entire family. Call for the schedule.

The design approach at **Peach Tree Designs,** 173 Rte. 6A (in the center of town), Yarmouth Port (☎ **508/362-8317**), is much more adventurous and eclectic. A bold hand is evident in the juxtaposition of disparate elements, from hunting prints to beribboned hats, model ships to handwoven throws. The gift pickings are superlative as well—especially if you're shopping for yourself.

WHERE TO STAY
EXPENSIVE

Red Jacket. S. Shore Dr. (Box 88), S. Yarmouth, MA 02664. ☎ **800/672-0500** or 508/398-6941. Fax 508/398-1214. 150 rms, 13 cottages. A/C TV TEL. Summer $158–$240 double; $235–$325 cottages. AE, DC, DISC, MC, V.

Of the huge resort motels lining Nantucket Sound in Yarmouth, Red Jacket has the best location. It is the last hotel at the end of the road and borders Parker's River on the west, so sunsets are particularly fine. Families who want all the fixings will find them here, though the atmosphere may be a bit impersonal. All rooms have a balcony or private porch; you'll want one overlooking the private beach on Nantucket Sound or looking out towards Parker's River. Also, all rooms have fridges and some have Jacuzzis. Off-season, rooms can be as cheap as $80 a night.

Dining/Entertainment: The dining room, serving breakfast and dinner, may come in handy in the morning, though you'll probably want to try something more inspiring for dinner. There's a lounge/bar area open for cocktails nightly.

Services: Full concierge service. Daily summertime children's program of sports and activities supervised by "Coach Tom," which may take advantage of the playground and minigolf.

Facilities: Tennis, basketball and volleyball courts (one of each), as well as a putting green. Indoor and outdoor heated pools, plus whirlpool, sauna, and exercise rooms. Water sports include parasailing, sailboat rentals, and catamaran cruises.

MODERATE

✪ **Captain Farris House.** 308 Old Main St. (about ¹/₄ mile W of the Bass River Bridge), S. Yarmouth, MA 02664-4530. ☎ **800/350-9477** or 508/760-2818. Fax 508/398-1262. Web site www.captainfarriscapecod.com. 10 rms and suites. A/C TV TEL. Summer (including full breakfast) $95–$140 double; $155–$185 suite. AE, MC, V.

"Sumptuous" is the only way to describe this small inn, improbably set amid a peaceful garden, a block off bustling Route 28. Lavished with a blend of fine antiques and striking contemporary touches, this 1845 manse has been carved into lovely spaces designed for relaxing. Some suites are apartment-size with fireplaced sitting rooms and whirlpool-tubbed bathrooms bigger than the average bedroom. Next door, the 1825 Elisha Jenkins House contains an additional large suite with its own sundeck. Breakfast consists of three courses served in the formal dining room, the courtyard, or the wraparound veranda. The central location puts the entire Cape, from Woods Hole to Provincetown, within a 45-minute drive, assuming you can bestir yourself from this pampering environment.

The Inn at Cape Cod. 4 Summer St. (Box 96), Yarmouth Port, MA 02675. ☎ **800/850-7301** or 508/375-0590. Web site www.capecod.com/inn-at-capecod. 8 rms. A/C TV TEL. Summer (including continental breakfast and afternoon tea) $110–$175 double. AE, MC, V.

Innkeepers Diana and Lee Malloy have taken a formerly grand, but recently down on its luck, captain's manse and refurbished it as a stylish new inn. You can't miss the building; it's the one that looks like an elongated Southern plantation with four towering ionic columns. Upon entering, the elegant foyer with its grandly curving staircase leads you into a comfortable common seating-and-breakfast area. Ceilings in the guest rooms are probably the highest you'll find in the area, and the rooms are furnished with well-chosen antiques and period reproductions. Some rooms have canopy beds and/or fireplaces.

✪ **Wedgewood Inn.** 83 Rte. 6A (in the center of town), Yarmouth Port, MA 02675. ☎ **508/362-5157.** Fax 508/362-5851. Web site www.virtualcapecod.com/market/wedgewoodinn. 9 rms. A/C. Summer (including full breakfast) $125–$175 double. AE, DC, MC, V.

This elegant 1812 Federal house sits atop its undulating lawn with unabashed pride. The first house in town to be designed by an architect, it still reigns supreme as the loveliest home—one that happens to welcome strangers, though you won't feel like one for long. Innkeeper Gerrie Graham provides a warm welcome, complete with tea delivered to your room: one of the four formal front rooms (all with cherry-wood pencil-post beds, Oriental rugs, antique quilts, and wood-burning fireplaces; some with private porches), the two romantic hideaways under the eaves, or the three spacious suites, with canopy beds, fireplaces, and decks, wedged into the picturesque barn in back.

INEXPENSIVE

Windjammer. 192 S. Shore Dr., S. Yarmouth, MA 02664. ☎ **508/398-2370.** 47 rms, 2 suites. A/C TV TEL. Summer $89–$105 double; $135–$150 suite. AE, DISC, MC, V.

This is for dog lovers looking for a good motel on the beach. The limited number of rooms where pets are allowed are slightly more expensive than the regular rooms. The location couldn't be better: right across the street from Parker's River Beach. Rooms are standard motel fare, but all have a minifridge, and there's a good-sized pool in the courtyard.

WHERE TO DINE
MODERATE

✪ **abbicci.** 43 Main St. (Rte. 6A, near the Cummaquid border), Yarmouth Port. ☎ **508/362-3501.** Reservations recommended. Main courses $15–$25. AE, DC, DISC, MC, V. Daily 11:30am–2:30pm and 5–10pm. NORTHERN ITALIAN.

Many consider this sophisticated venue *the* place to eat on Cape Cod these days, comparable to the type of stylish establishments found on the islands or even in the big city. While the exterior is a modest mustard-colored 18th-century Cape, the interior features mosaic floors and muralled walls in several cozy dining rooms. The knowledgeable and efficient wait staff deliver delicious and artfully prepared, innovative dishes. In fact, the whole setup seems almost out of place in folksy Yarmouth Port. A taste of the veal *nocciole* (with toasted hazelnuts and a splash of balsamic vinegar) and you'll be transported straight to Tuscany.

✪ **Inaho.** 157 Main St. (Rte. 6A, in the center of town), Yarmouth Port. ☎ **508/362-5522.** Reservations recommended. Main courses $12–$20. MC, V. Tues–Sun 5–11pm; call for off-season hrs. JAPANESE.

What better application of the Cape's oceanic bounty than fresh-off-the-boat sushi? You can sit in communal awe at the sushi bar to watch chef/owner Yuji Watanabe perform his legerdemain or enjoy the privacy afforded by a gleaming wooden booth. An ordinary house on the outside, Inaho is a shibui sanctuary within, with minimalist decor (the traditional shoji screens and crisp navy-and-white banners) softened by tranquil music and service. On chilly days, opt for the tempura or a steaming bowl of shabu-shabu.

INEXPENSIVE

✪ **Jack's Outback.** 161 Main St. (in the center of town), Yarmouth Port. ☎ **508/362-6690.** Most items under $5. No credit cards. Daily 6:30am–2pm. AMERICAN.

This is a neighborhood cafe as Dr. Seuss might have imagined it: hyperactive (okay, semicrazed) and full of fun. Chef/owner Jack Braginton-Smith makes a point of dishing out good-natured insults along with the home-style grub, which you bus yourself from the open kitchen, thereby saving big bucks as well as time. This is a perfect place for impatient children, who'll find lots of familiar, approachable dishes on the hand-scrawled posters that serve as a communal menu.

Lobster Boat. 681 Rte. 28 (midway between W. Yarmouth and Bass River), W. Yarmouth. ☎ **508/775-0486.** Main courses $10–$18. AE, MC, V. May–Oct daily 4–10pm. SEAFOOD.

Just about every town seems to have one of these barnlike restaurants plastered with flotsam and serving the usual array of seafood in the usual manner, from deep-fried to boiled or broiled. True to its sound-side setting, this tourist magnet advertises itself rather flamboyantly with a facade that features the hull of a ship grafted onto a shingled shack.

A SODA FOUNTAIN

Unsuspecting passersby invariably do a double-take when they happen upon **Hallet's,** 139 Rte. 6A, Yarmouth Port (☎ **508/362-3362**), an 1889 drugstore where the sun-faded window displays seem to have been left untouched for decades. Not much has changed over the past 100-plus years: The biggest difference is that it is Mary Hallet Clark, the granddaughter of town pharmacist (and postmaster and justice-of-the-peace) Thacher Taylor Hallet, who is now the one dishing out frappés and floats from the original marble soda fountain. Rumor has it that some years ago a couple of honchos from Walt Disney offered to buy the entire interior for their "Main Street USA" at Disney Land; fortunately, the generous offer was declined. Visit the display area upstairs for a look at old apothecary knickknacks and historic photos.

EVENING FUN IN YARMOUTH

Yarmouth Summer Band Concerts (call ☎ **508/778-1008**) are held Monday evenings in July and August from 7:30 to 9pm at the Mattacheese Middle School on Higgins Crowell Road in West Yarmouth. Bands featured include traditional brass, jazz, and blues. Get there early and bring a picnic.

3 Dennis

20 miles (32km) E of Sandwich, 36 miles (58km) S of Provincetown

If Dennis looks like a jigsaw puzzle piece snapped around Yarmouth, that's because it didn't break away until 1793, when the community adopted the name of Rev. Josiah Dennis, who'd ministered to Yarmouth's "East Parish" for close to 4 decades. His 1736 home has been restored and now serves as a local-history museum.

In Dennis, as in Yarmouth, virtually all the good stuff—pretty drives, inviting shops, restaurants with real personality—are in the north, along Route 6A. Route 28 is chockablock with more typical tourist attractions, RV parks, and family-oriented motels—some with fairly sophisticated facilities, but nonetheless undistinguished enough to warrant even a drive by (the few exceptions are noted below). In budgeting your time, be sure to allocate the lion's share to Dennis itself and not its southern offshoots. It's as stimulating and unspoiled today as it was when it welcomed the Cape Playhouse, the country's oldest surviving strawhat theater, in the anything-goes 1920s.

ESSENTIALS

GETTING THERE   After crossing either the Bourne or Sagamore bridge, head east on Route 6 or 6A. Route 6A passes through the villages of Dennis and East Dennis (which can also be reached via northbound Route 134 from Route 6's Exit 9). Route 134 south leads to the village of South Dennis; if you follow Route 134 all the way to Route 28, the village of West Dennis will be a couple of miles to your west, and Dennisport a couple of miles east. Or fly into Hyannis (see "Getting There" in chapter 3).

VISITOR INFORMATION   Contact the **Dennis Chamber of Commerce,** 242 Swan River Rd., West Dennis, MA 02670 (☎ **800/243-9920** or 508/398-3568)

or the **Cape Cod Chamber of Commerce,** Routes 6 and 132, Hyannis, MA 02601 (☎ **508/362-3225;** fax 508/362-3698; Web site www.capecod.com).

BEACHES & OUTDOOR PURSUITS

BEACHES   Dennis harbors more than a dozen saltwater and two freshwater beaches open to nonresidents. The bay beaches are charming and a big hit with families, who prize the easygoing surf, so soft it won't bring toddlers to their knees. The beaches on the sound tend to attract wall-to-wall families, but the parking lots are usually not too crowded, since so many beachgoers are billeted within walking distance. The lots charge $8 per day; for a weeklong permit ($25), visit **Town Hall** on Main Street in South Dennis (☎ **508/394-8300**).

- **Chapin Beach,** off Route 6A in Dennis. A nice, long bay beach pocked with occasional boulders and surrounded by dunes. No lifeguard, but there are rest rooms.
- **Corporation Beach,** off Route 6A in Dennis. Before it filled in with sand, this bay beach—with wheelchair-accessible boardwalk, lifeguards, snack bar, rest rooms, and a children's play area—was once a packet landing owned by a shipbuilding corporation comprised of area residents. It was donated to the town by Mary Thacher, owner of Yarmouth Port's Winslow Crocker House (see "Museums" in Section 2 of this chapter).
- **Mayflower Beach,** off Route 6A in Dennis. This 1,200-foot bay beach has the necessary amenities, plus an accessible boardwalk. The tidal pools attract lots of children.
- **Scargo Lake** in Dennis. This large kettle-hole pond (formed by a melting fragment of a glacier) has two pleasant beaches: Scargo Beach, accessible right off Route 6A, and Princess Beach, off Scargo Hill Road, where there are rest rooms and a picnic area.
- **West Dennis Beach,** off Route 28 in West Dennis. This long (1¹/₂-mile) but narrow beach along the sound has lifeguards, a playground, a snack bar, rest rooms, and a special kite-flying area. The eastern end is reserved for residents; the western end tends, in any case, to be less packed.

BICYCLING   The 25-mile ✪ **Cape Cod Rail Trail** (☎ **508/896-3491**) starts— or, depending on your perspective, ends—here, on Route 134, ¹/₂ mile south of Route 6's Exit 9. Once a Penn-Central track, this 8-foot-wide paved bikeway extends all the way to Wellfleet (with a few on-road lapses), passing through woods, marshes, and dunes. Sustenance is never too far off-trail, and plenty of bike shops dot the course. At the trailhead is **Barbara's Bike and Sports Equipment,** 430 Rte. 134, South Dennis (☎ **508/760-4723**), which rents bikes and in-line skates and does repairs. Another paved bike path runs along Old Bass Road, 3¹/₂ miles north to Route 6A.

BOATING   Cape Cod Coastal Canoe & Kayak (☎ **888/226-6393** or 508/ 564-4051; E-mail cccanoe@capecod.net; Web site www.capecod.net/canoe/) runs naturalist-guided trips throughout the Cape, sponsored by the Cape Cod Museum of Natural History. In West Dennis, they paddle along the Bass River. Trips (3¹/₂ to 4 hr.) are daily April through August, weekends through October, and cost $25 per paddler or $50 per family. All equipment is supplied. Call for a schedule.

Cape Cod Bay Cruises. Northside Marina, Sesuit Harbor, E. Dennis. ☎ **508/385-3244.** Tickets $12 adults, $8 children under 12. Late June to early Sept daily 10:30am and 2pm; Thurs and Fri, 6pm; call for off-season hrs. Closed Oct to late June.

The *Blue Heron* is a standard sightseeing vessel—lots of windows, flat bottom, slow but steady speed—but the highlight of the tour may be the history lesson as the boat passes such old Cape Cod points of interest like the site of the Shiverick Shipyard, where clipper ships were built; the site of the East Dennis saltworks; and the wreck sites of several sailing ships. Kids will like it when lobster traps are hauled aboard. Daytime trips last 1 hour 45 minutes; evening trips last 1 hour 20 minutes.

Freya. Northside Marina, Sesuit Harbor, E. Dennis. ☎ **508/385-4399.** Tickets $12–$16 adults, $6–$10 children 2–12. Call for schedule.

This 63-foot schooner offers 2-hours sails around Cape Cod Bay, morning through sunset (higher rates prevail as the day progresses).

Water Safaris. Bass River Bridge (at Rte. 28), W. Dennis. ☎ **508/362-5555.** Tickets $10 adults, $5 children under 12. Mid-June to mid-Oct daily at 11am, 1, 4, and 6pm; call for off-season hrs. Closed mid-Oct to late May.

Explore the Bass River the way Leif Eriksson might have—by boat. This one, a poky but stable custom minibarge, is motorized, of course, so the whole circuit only takes $1^{1}/_{2}$ hours. If some of the tales strike you as rather tall, there's still plenty of wildlife and prime real estate to ogle.

FISHING   Fishing is allowed in **Fresh Pond** and **Scargo Lake,** where the catch includes trout and smallmouth bass; for a license (shellfishing is also permitted), visit **Town Hall** on Main Street in South Dennis (☎ **508/394-8300**). Plenty of people drop a line off the **Bass River Bridge** along Route 28 in West Dennis. Several charter boats operate out of the Northside Marina in East Dennis's Sesuit Harbor, including the *Bluefin* (☎ **800/244-6464** or 508/697-2093).

FITNESS/JOGGING   David's Gym at 50 Rte. 134 in South Dennis (☎ **508/ 394-7199**) offers aerobics, weight training, cardio equipment, plus Cybex equipment, nautilus, boxing and karate training, and whirlpool, steam, and sauna.

For joggers, and fitness freaks in general, the $1^{1}/_{2}$-mile **Lifecourse trail,** located at Old Bass River and Access roads in South Dennis, features 20 exercise stations along its tree-shaded path.

GOLF   The public is welcome to use two 18-hole championship courses: the hilly, par-71 **Dennis Highlands** on Old Bass River Road in Dennis (☎ **508/385-8347**) and the even more challenging par-72 **Dennis Pines** on Golf Course Road in East Dennis (☎ **508/385-8347**). Both are open year-round.

ICE-SKATING   During the drama that permeated the 1994 Olympics, regular Nancy Kerrigan rendered the **Tony Kent Arena** at 8 Gages Way in South Dennis (☎ **508/760-2415**) world-famous. This nonprofit, donation-supported facility is open for public skating most afternoons year-round; call for a current schedule.

NATURE & WILDLIFE AREAS   Behind the Town Hall parking lot on Main Street in South Dennis, a half-mile walk along the **Indian Lands Conservation Trail** leads to the Bass River, where blue herons and kingfishers often take shelter. Dirt roads off South Street in East Dennis, beyond the Quivet Cemetery, lead to Crow's Pasture, a patchwork of marshes and dunes bordering the bay; this circular trail is about a $2^{1}/_{2}$-mile round-trip. **Crow's Pasture,** accessible from South Street in the northeasterly corner of East Dennis, offers $1^{1}/_{2}$ miles of dirt roads leading through evergreen groves to marsh and beach.

TENNIS   Public courts are located at the Dennis-Yarmouth Regional High School in South Yarmouth and Wixon Middle School, Route 134 in South Dennis; for details, contact the **Dennis Recreation Department** (☎ **508/398-7600**). Or you may be able to book time at the **Dennis Racquet Club** off Oxbow Way in Dennis (☎ **508/385-2221**) or the **Sesuit Tennis Centre** at 1389 Rte. 6A in East Dennis (☎ **508/385-2200**).

WATER SPORTS   Located on the small and placid Swan River, **Cape Cod Waterways,** 16 Rte. 28, Dennisport (☎ **508/398-0080**), rents canoes, kayaks, and paddleboats for exploring 200-acre Swan Pond (less than a mile north) or Nantucket Sound (2 miles south).

MUSEUMS

Cape Museum of Fine Arts. 60 Hope Lane (on Rte. 6A in the center of town). ☎ **508/385-4477.** Admission $3 adults, free for children under 16; free admission Thurs evening in summer. June–Sept Mon–Wed and Fri–Sat 10am–5pm, Thurs 10am–7:30pm, Sun 1–5pm; call for off-season hrs.

In 1997—a good year for this modest institution—pop artist Red Grooms was the first summer blockbuster show for the relatively new (1985) museum. Part of the prettily landscaped Cape Playhouse complex, the museum has done a great job of acquiring hundreds of works by representative area artists dating back to the turn of the century. Unfortunately, only a small portion are on view at any given time (expansion plans are underway), and these are not always optimally displayed. Still, it's worth prowling the rather dim halls to unearth an evocative little landscape by early-20th-century "speed painter" Arthur Diehl, who dashed off canvases in a matter of minutes to keep one step ahead of his bills; an evocative portrait by Henry Hensche; or perhaps a more recent work by Provincetown colorist Paul Resika. Call ahead for a schedule of special shows, lectures, concerts, and classes.

Jericho House and Barn Museum. Trotting Park Rd. (at Old Main St., off Rte. 28 about 1/2 mile E of the Bass River Bridge), W. Dennis. ☎ **508/398-6736.** Donations accepted. July–Aug Wed and Fri 2–4pm. Closed Sept–June.

For a century and a half, this classic 1801 Cape house remained in the family of its builder, Capt. Theophilus Baker, the model for Richard Henry Dana's *Two Years Before the Mast.* Its mostly Federal furnishings embody the understated elegance of the era. Out back is an 1810 barn housing assorted displays, from a miniature saltworks (the clearest possible depiction of one of the Cape's earliest and most lucrative industries) to an ingenious "driftwood zoo" improvised several decades ago by a playful summerer.

Josiah Dennis Manse and Old West Schoolhouse. 77 Nobscusset Rd. (N of Rte. 6A, about 1/2 mile W of town center). ☎ **508/385-2232.** Donations accepted. July–Aug Tues and Thurs 2–4pm. Closed Sept–June.

This compact 1736 saltbox housed Rev. Josiah Dennis, the town's first minister. Though not necessarily original, the furnishings are fascinating, as is a diorama of the Shiverick Shipyard, the source, in the mid-1800s, of the world's swiftest ships. Don't miss the 1770 schoolhouse, where a comprehensive (if strict) approach to learning is beautifully preserved.

Scargo Tower. Scargo Hill Rd. (off Old Bass River Rd., S of Rte. 6A in the center of town). No phone. Free admission. Daily 6am–10pm.

All that remains of the grand Nobscusset Hotel, this 28-foot stone observatory looks out from its 160-foot perch over the entire Outer Cape, including the tightly furled tip that is Provincetown. In the foreground is Scargo Lake—the legacy, native legends have it, of either the giant god Maushop or perhaps a princess who bid her handmaidens to scoop it out with clamshells.

BASEBALL

The Dennis-Yarmouth Red Sox, part of the Cape Cod Baseball League, play at Dennis-Yarmouth High School's Red Wilson Field off Station Avenue in South Yarmouth. For a schedule, contact the **Yarmouth Area Chamber of Commerce,** 657 Rte. 28, West Yarmouth, MA 02673 (☎ **508/778-1008**), the **Yarmouth Recreation Department** (☎ **508/398-2231,** ext. 284), or the **League** (☎ **508/432-6909**).

KID STUFF

Dennisport boasts the best rainy-day—or any-day—destination for little kids on the entire Cape, the nonprofit **Cape Cod Discovery Museum & Toy Shop,** at 444 Rte. 28 (☎ **508/398-1600**). Hours are 9:30am to 7:30pm daily (except Thanksgiving, Christmas, and Easter) in season; 9:30am to 5:30pm off-season. For a nominal admission fee ($2.50 adults, $4.50 children 1 to 15, $2 senior citizens), whole families can amuse themselves amid a vast educational play space equipped with a frozen-shadow wall, a transparent piano, a pretend diner, a dress-up puppet theater, reptile room, and all sorts of other fun stuff. Special workshops are offered daily.

On Friday mornings in season, at 9:30 and 11:30, the **Cape Playhouse** at 36 Hope Lane in Dennis (☎ **508/385-3911**) hosts various visiting companies that mount musicals geared to children 4 and up; at only $6, tickets go fast.

SHOPPING

You can pretty much ignore Route 28. There's a growing cluster of antique shops in Dennisport, but the stock is flea-market level and requires more patience than most mere browsers—as opposed to avid collectors—may be able to muster. Save your time, and money, for the better shops along Route 6A, where you'll also find fine contemporary crafts.

ANTIQUES/COLLECTIBLES More than 136 dealers stock the co-op **Antiques Center of Cape Cod,** 243 Rte. 6A (about 1 mile south of Dennis Village center), Dennis (☎ **508/385-6400**); it's the largest such enterprise on the Cape. You'll find all the usual "smalls" on the first floor; the big stuff—from blanket chests to copper bathtubs—beckons above.

Eldred's, 1483 Rte. 6A (about ¼ mile west of Dennis Village center), East Dennis (☎ **508/385-3116**), where the gavel has been wielded for more than 40 years, is the Cape's most prestigious auction house. Specialties include Oriental art, marine art, and Americana. Call for a schedule.

Fiesta-ware freaks (you know who you are) will have a field day at **Ellipse,** 427 Rte. 6A (about ½ mile west of Dennis Village center), Dennis (☎ **508/385-8626**), devoted primarily to 20th-century design.

The premier place for antique wicker furniture on the Cape is **Leslie Curtis Antiques** at two locations in Dennis Village, 776 Main St. and 838 Main St. (Route 6A) (☎ **508/385-2921**). Her wicker selection includes Victorian pieces and Bar Harbor wicker of the 1920s. She also specializes in French Quimper pottery, as well as an eclectic stock of other antiques.

With auctions at Eldred's (see above) so close, **Webfoot Farm Antiques,** 1475 Rte. 6A (about ¼ mile west of town center), East Dennis (☎ **508/385-2334**)—occupying most of an 1854 captain's house—gets the cream of the crop. A fine array of Orientalia jockeys for space amid American and continental furniture; the garden statuary is outstanding.

ARTS & CRAFTS The creations of **Ross Coppelman,** 1439 Rte. 6A (about ¼ mile west of town center), East Dennis (☎ **508/385-7900**)—mostly fashioned of lustrous 22-karat gold—have an iconic drama to them: They seem to draw on the aesthetics of some grand, lost civilization.

At **Grose Gallery,** 524 Rte. 6A (about ¹/₄ mile south of town center), Dennis Village (☎ **508/385-3434**), discover David Grose's intricate wood engravings, which have graced such classics as John Hay's *The Great Beach.* In this handsomely renovated outbuilding (a former slaughterhouse), you can not only acquire original prints, but you can watch the prints being pulled.

Scargo Stoneware Pottery and Art Gallery, 30 Dr. Lord's Rd. S. (off Route 6A, about 1 mile east of town center), Dennis (☎ **508/385-3894**), is a magical place. Harry Holl set up his glass-ceilinged studio here in 1952; today his work, and the output of his four grown daughters, fills a sylvan glade overlooking Scargo Lake. Much of it—such as the signature birdhouses shaped like fanciful castles—is meant to reside outside. The other wares deserve a place of honor on the dining-room table or perhaps over a mantle. Hand-painted tiles by Sarah Holl are particularly enchanting.

Relocated from its prestigious Newbury Street location, **Wilson Gallery,** 800 Main St. (Route 6A) in Dennis Village (☎ **508/385-0856**), has recently opened on Cape Cod. Here you'll find some of the finest representational artwork in the region.

FASHION   Specializing in the kind of women's clothing that's essentially classic with a bit of a kick, **Bougainvillea of Cape Cod,** 744 Rte. 6A (in the center of town), Dennis (☎ **508/385-3535**), features such contemporary lines as Adrienne Vittadini and that grande dame from Palm Beach, Lilly Pulitzer.

Cape regulars know to put off the annual hunt for a flattering bathing suit until they've arrived at **Emily's** Beach Barn, 710 Rte. 6A (about ¹/₄ mile west of town center), Dennis (☎ **508/385-8328**), where the range of choices is nonpareil. Stylish cover-ups and preppie sportswear complete the ensemble. Closed November through March.

GIFTS/HOME DECOR   A far cry from the same-old, same-old country-schlock stock that crowds most Cape Cod gift shops, the stuff at **B. Mango and Bird,** 780 Rte. 6A (Mercantile Place, in the center of town), Dennis (☎ **508/385-6700**), is stylish and cutting-edge. Among the tamer (though tasteful) items are stripped European armoires. It's the small stuff that dazzles, especially the imaginative handcrafted housewares.

Seeking just the right antique fixture to illumine a vintage dwelling? You're liable to find it at **Boston Brassworks,** 804 Rte. 6A (Theatre Marketplace, in the center of town), Dennis (☎ **508/385-7188**), either restored or made to order. Ranging from electrified "colonial" to contemporary styles, these lamps, sconces, and chandeliers should suit virtually any decor.

If you've ever longed to commission a colonial-look wool braided rug, custom-made to match a specific color scheme or to fit an odd-sized floor, here's your chance. Small samples go for as little as $25 at **Cape Cod Braided Rug Co.,** 259 Great Western Rd. (near the Harwich border), South Dennis (☎ **508/398-0089**).

WHERE TO STAY
VERY EXPENSIVE

✪ **Lighthouse Inn.** 4 Lighthouse Rd. (off Lower County Rd., ¹/₂ mile S of Rte. 28). W. Dennis, MA 02670. ☎ **508/398-2244.** Fax 508/398-5658. Web site www.lighthouseinn.com. 34 rms, 27 cottages. TV TEL. Summer (including full breakfast and all gratuities) $190–$230 double. MC, V. Closed mid-Oct to mid-May.

In 1938 Everett Stone acquired a decommissioned 1885 lighthouse and built a 9-acre cottage colony around it. Today his grandsons run the show, pretty much as he envisioned it; the light has even been resuscitated. As they have for at least two generations, families still gather at group tables in the summer-camp–scale dining room to plot their day over breakfast and recap over dinner. With a private beach, heated outdoor pool, tennis courts, and motley amusements such as miniature golf and shuffleboard right on the premises, there's plenty to do. Most families pay a small daily surcharge to enroll their kids in "InnKids," the supervised play program, and many coordinate their vacations so that they can catch up with the same group of friends year after year. The rooms aren't what you'd call fancy, but they're adequate (some have great Nantucket Sound views), and you'll probably be too busy to spend much time there anyway.

Dining/Entertainment: Serving three meals, the sail-loftlike dining room—decorated with state flags rippling from the rafters—is open to the general public. The prices are quite reasonable (entrees, for example, rarely exceed $16), and the menu isn't half as stuffy as you might expect: in fact, it's enlivened by reverberations of the New American revolution. Down the road, at the entrance to the complex, The Sand Bar serves as on-site nightspot (see "The Dennises After Dark," below).

MODERATE

Corsair & Cross Rip Resort Motels. 41 Chase Ave. (off Depot St., 1 mile SE of Rte. 28), Dennisport, MA 02639. ☎ **800/345-5140** or 508/398-2279. Fax 508/760-6681. 7 rms, 40 efficiencies. A/C TV TEL. Summer $89–$185 double. Special packages available. AE, DISC, MC, V.

Of the many family-oriented motels lining this part of the sound, these two neighbors are among the nicest, with fresh contemporary decor, two heated beach-view pools, and their own chunk of sand. As rainy-day backup, there's an indoor pool plus a game room, and even a toddler playroom equipped with toys.

INEXPENSIVE

The Beach House Inn. 61 Uncle Stephen's Rd. (about $^1/_2$ mile S of town center), W. Dennis, MA 02670. ☎ **508/398-4575.** 7 rms. TV. Summer (including continental breakfast) $65–$75 double. No credit cards.

Families will feel right at home in this breezy B&B, set right on the beach in a residential—i.e., motel-free—community. Whereas much of Dennis's southern shore is lined with big modern resorts, this untouched area, with a smattering of weather-silvered cottages, looks and feels like a carryover from the predevelopment decades. Some rooms feature private ocean-view decks, and all guests have access to a communal kitchen with two microwaves, a barbecue deck complete with grill, and a state-of-the-art climbing structure that should keep kids happily occupied should they ever tire of the beach (not likely).

The Four Chimneys Inn. 946 Rte. 6A (about $^1/_2$ mile E of town center), Dennis, MA 02638. ☎ **800/874-5502** or 508/385-6317. Fax 508/385-6285. 7 rms, 1 suite. TV. Summer (including continental breakfast) $80–$125 double; $125 suite. AE, DISC, MC, V. Closed Nov to late April.

Scargo Lake is directly across the street and the village is a brief walk away from this imposing 1880 Victorian, former home to the town doctor. Opulent tastes are evident in the high ceilings and marble fireplace of the front parlor. Rooms vary in size, but innkeeper Kathy Tomasetti has rendered them all quite appealing, with hand-painted stenciling and summery wicker furnishings. The breakfasts are knockouts, featuring such inspirations as blueberry blintz soufflé. The only element that doesn't seem to fit the overall aura of elegance is the surprisingly reasonable rates.

✪ **Isaiah Hall B&B Inn.** 152 Whig St. (1 block NW of the Cape Playhouse), Dennis, MA 02638. ☎ **800/736-0160** or 508/385-9928. Fax 508/385-5879. 9 rms, 1 suite. A/C. Summer (including continental breakfast) $85–$117 double; $142 suite. AE, MC, V. Closed mid-Oct to mid-Apr.

So keyed-in is this Greek Revival farmhouse to the doings at the nearby Cape Playhouse that you might as well be backstage. Many stars have stayed here over the past half century, and if you're lucky, you'll find a few sharing the space. The "great room" in the carriage-house annex is a virtual green room: It seems to foment late-night discussions, to be continued over home-baked breakfasts at the long plank table that dominates the 1857 country kitchen. Rooms range from retro-touristy (pine paneling . . .) to spacious and spiffy.

WHERE TO DINE
MODERATE

✪ **Gina's by the Sea.** 134 Taunton Ave. (about 1¹/₂ miles NW of Rte. 6A, off New Boston and Beach sts.). ☎ **508/385-3213.** Main courses $12–$21. AE, MC, V. June–Sept Mon–Fri 11:30am–3pm; daily 5–10pm; call for off-season hrs. Closed mid-Dec to Mar. ITALIAN.

A landmark amid Dennis's "Little Italy" beach community since 1938, this intimate little restaurant has a few nuovo tricks up its sleeve, such as homemade ravioli stuffed with smoked mozzarella. Fare is mostly fairly traditional, but nonetheless tasty: The ultragarlicky shrimp scampi, for instance, needs no updating. This popular place fills up fast; if you want to eat before 8:30, arrive before 5:30. Take a sunset or moonlight walk on the beach (just over the dune) to round off the evening.

✪ **The Red Pheasant Inn.** 905 Main St. (about ¹/₂ mile E of town center), Dennis. ☎ **508/385-2133.** Reservations recommended. Main courses $13–$21. DISC, MC, V. Late May to early Sept daily 5–10pm; call for off-season hrs. NEW AMERICAN.

An enduring Cape favorite since 1977, this handsome space—an 18th-century barn turned chandlery—has managed not only to keep pace with contemporary trends, but to remain a front-runner. Chef/owner Bill Atwood has a way with local victuals. He transforms the ubiquitous zucchini of late summer, for instance, into homemade ravioli enfolding tasty chèvre, and his signature cherrystone-and-scallop chowder gets its zip from fresh-plucked thyme. Two massive brick fireplaces tend to be the focal point in the off-season, drawing in the weary—and delighted—wanderer. In fine weather the garden room exerts its own green draw.

Scargo Cafe. 799 Main St. (opposite the Cape Playhouse). ☎ **508/385-8200.** Main courses $13–$19. AE, DISC, MC, V. Mid-June to mid-Sept 11am–11pm; call for off-season hrs. INTERNATIONAL.

A richly paneled captain's house given a modernist reworking, this lively bistro—named for Dennis's scenic lake—deftly spans old and new with a menu neatly split into "traditional" and "adventurous" categories. In the former you'll find surf and turf, and other such straightforward preparations; the latter features the likes of " wildcat chicken" (a sauté with sausage, mushrooms, and raisins, flambéed with apricot brandy) or "Scargo skillets," a pan of pasta tossed with your choice of chicken or seafood and a trio of international sauces. Lighter nibbles, such as burgers or "Scallop Harpoon"—a bacon-wrapped skewerful, served over rice—are available throughout the day, a boon for beachgoers who tend to return ravenous. Serving food till 11pm makes this the perfect (and only) place in the neighborhood to go after a show at the Cape Playhouse across the street. The owners of Scargo are proud to have the only smoke-free bar and cocktail lounge on Cape Cod.

Swan River Seafood. 5 Lower County Rd. (at Swan Pond River, about ²/₃ mile SE of town center), Dennisport. ☎ **508/394-4466.** Main courses $11–$18. AE, MC, V. Late May to Sept daily noon–3:30pm and 5–9:30pm. Closed Oct to late May. SEAFOOD.

Every town has its own version of the fish place with the fantastic view. Here the scenic vista is relatively low-key: a marsh punctuated by an old windmill. The fish—from the adjoining market—is snapping fresh and available deep-fried, as it is everywhere, but also smartly broiled or sautéed. Go for the assertive shark steak *au poivre* (with black pepper) and such specialties as scrod San Sebastian, fresh fillets poached in a garlic-infused broth.

INEXPENSIVE

✪ **Bob Briggs' Wee Packet.** 79 Depot St. (at Lower County Rd., about $^1/_3$ mile S of town center), Dennisport. ☎ **508/398-2181.** Main courses $6–$12. MC, V. July and Aug 8am–9pm, May, June, and Sept 11:30am–8:30pm. Closed Oct–Apr. SEAFOOD.

It's been Bob Briggs's place since 1949; otherwise, the name that might leap to mind would be "Mom's." This tiny joint serves exemplary diner fare, plus all the requisite seafood staples, fried and broiled. Five generations have been known to commandeer a couple of Formica tables for a traditional summer feast topped off by a timeless dessert such as blueberry shortcake.

Captain Frosty's. 219 Rte. 6A (about 1 mile S of town center). ☎ **508/385-8548.** Entrees $3–$13. No credit cards. July–Aug daily 11am–9pm; call for off-season hrs. Closed late Sept to early Apr. SEAFOOD.

Here you won't find the typical, tasteless deep-fried seafood seemingly dipped in greasy cement. The breading is light (thanks to healthy canola oil), and the fish itself is the finest available—fresh off the local day boats, and hooked rather than netted (the maritime equivalent of clear-cutting a forest). You won't find a more luscious lobster roll anywhere, and the clam-cake fritters seem to fly out the door.

Marathon Seafood. 231 Rte. 28, W. Dennis. ☎ **508/394-3379.** Main courses $7–$15. No credit cards. Daily 11:30am–9:30pm. Call for off-season hrs. Closed Dec–Feb. SEAFOOD.

Family-owned and -operated for 15 years, this place holds its own among the Route 28 fast-food/clam-shack competition. You should order a heaping, steaming platter of fried fish, clams, scallops, shrimp, or a combo served with french fries, and onion rings. Wash it down with a chocolate milkshake. Hard on the heart, but easy on the wallet.

A DELICATESSEN & A FARM STAND

The Dennis Mercantile. 766 Rte. 6A (in the center of town), Dennis Village. ☎ **508/385-3877.**

Every town ought to have a deli/bakery like this, where you can peruse a wide array of trendy magazines while awaiting the culinary equivalent: a shrimp salad sparked with fresh mango, perhaps, or a silky chocolate cake. In fact, the huge central table is so inviting, you might want to do your picnicking right on the spot, trading pleasantries with whomever else happens to be gathered round.

Tobey Farm. 352 Rte. 6A (about $^1/_2$ mile W of town center). ☎ **508/385-2930.**

The remarkable thing about this farm stand is that it has been in the same family since 1681. The fresh-picked corn should go straight into the pot; a dried flower arrangement might make a nice memento. In October, Tobey Farm comes alive with Halloween treats like Hobgoblin hayrides at night and not-so-scary hayrides during the day on weekends. Call for schedule.

ICE-CREAM SHOPS & BAKERIES

Ice Cream Smuggler. 716 Rte. 6A (about $^1/_4$ mile W of town center). ☎ **508/385-5307.** Closed Oct–Mar.

A noteworthy stop on any Cape-wide ice-cream crusade, this cheerful parlor dispenses terrific custom flavors, as well as seductive sundae concoctions and "fudge-bottom pies."

✪ **Sundae School.** 387 Lower County Rd. (at Sea St., about $^1/_3$ mile S of Rte. 28), Dennisport. ☎ **508/394-9122.** Summer daily 11am–11pm. Closed mid-Oct to mid-Apr.

For a time-travel treat, visit this spacious barn retrofitted with a turn-of-the-century marble soda fountain and other artifacts from the golden age of ice cream. Local berries make for especially tasty toppings.

Woolfie's Home Baking. 279 Lower County Rd. (about $^1/_2$ mile SW of town center), Dennisport. ☎ **508/394-3717.** Closed Oct–Apr.

The families clustered along the southern shore have a friend in Terri Moretti, who gets up before dawn to bake fabulous megamuffins as well as strudel, Danish, and other tasty eye-openers

THE DENNISES AFTER DARK
PERFORMANCE

✪ **The Cape Playhouse.** 36 Hope Lane (on Rte. 6A, in the center of town). ☎ **508/385-3911.** Fax 508/385-8162. Performances late June to early Sept Mon–Tues and Fri–Sat at 8pm, Wed–Thurs at 2 and 8pm. Tickets $13–$27.

The oldest continuously active strawhat theater in the country and still one of the best, this way-off-Broadway enterprise was the 1927 brainstorm of Raymond Moore, who'd spent a few summers as a playwright in Provincetown and quickly tired of the strictures of "little theater." Salvaging an 1838 meetinghouse, he plunked it amid a meadow, and got his New York buddy, designer Cleon Throckmorton, to turn it into a proper theater. Even with a roof that leaked, it was an immediate success, and a parade of stars—both established and budding—trod the boards in the coming decades, from Ginger Rogers to Jane Fonda (her dad spent his salad days there, too, playing opposite Bette Davis in her stage debut), Humphrey Bogart to Tab Hunter. Not all of today's headliners are quite as impressive (many hail from the netherworld of TV reruns), but the theater—the only Equity enterprise on the Cape—can be counted on for a varied season of polished work. On Friday mornings, performances of children's theater are at 9:30 and 11:30am. Admission is $6.

DANCING & LIVE MUSIC

Christine's Restaurant. 581 Rte. 28 (about $^1/_4$ mile E of town center). ☎ **508/394-7333.** Cover varies.

The 300-seat show room of this Lebanese/Italian restaurant draws some big acts nightly in season, and weekends off-season, including local jazz great pianist Dave McKenna and all sorts of oldies bands; also on the roster are comedy acts and a Sunday-night cabaret-cum-buffet.

The Sand Bar. At the Lighthouse Inn (see "Where to Stay," above), W. Dennis. ☎ **508/398-2244.** Cover varies. Admission is free for guests of the Lighthouse Inn.

This homey cabana was built in 1949, the very year Dennis went "wet." Rock King, a combination boogie-woogie pianist and comedian, still rules the evening and wows the crowd.

A MOVIE THEATER

✪ **Cape Cinema.** 36 Hope Lane (off Rte. 6A, in the center of town). ☎ **508/385-2503** (recording) or 508/385-5644. Early Apr to mid-Nov daily 4:30, 7, and 9pm. Closed mid-Nov to early Apr.

In 1930, Raymond Moore—perceiving motion pictures as a complement rather than a threat to live theater—added a movie house modeled on Centerville's Congregational Church to the Cape Playhouse complex. The interior decoration is an art-deco surprise, with a Prometheus-themed ceiling mural and folding curtain designed by artist Rockwell Kent and Broadway set designer Jo Mielziner. Independent-film maven George Mansour, curator of the Harvard Film Archive, sees to the art-house programming. That, plus the setting and seating—black leather armchairs—may spoil you forever for what passes for cinemas today.

7

The Lower Cape: Brewster, the Harwiches, Chatham & Orleans

Although the Cape's elbow makes a logical jumping-off point for those arriving by way of the Atlantic, by land it requires an intentional detour, which has helped to preserve Harwich and Chatham from the commercial depredations evident elsewhere along the Nantucket Sound. The quaint village of Harwich Port was all set for an upscale overhaul when the recession struck; faltering funds have left it in an agreeable limbo. Here, the beach is a mere block off Main Street, so the eternal summertime verities of a barefoot stroll capped off by an ice-cream cone can still be easily observed. Chatham, a larger, more prosperous community, is being touted by local Realtors as "the Nantucket of the Cape," an apt sobriquet. Its Main Street, a gamut of appealing shops and eateries, approaches an all-American, small-town ideal—complemented nicely by a scenic lighthouse and plentiful beaches nearby.

Occupying the easternmost portion of historic Route 6A, Brewster still enjoys much the same cachet that it boasted as a high roller in the maritime trade. But for a relatively recent incursion of condos and, of course, the cars, it looks much as it might have in the late 19th century, its general store still serving as a social center point. For some reason—perhaps because excellence breeds competition—Brewster has spawned several fine restaurants in recent years and has become something of a magnet for gourmets.

As the gateway to the Outer Cape, where all roads merge (most annoyingly), Orleans is a bit too frantic to offer the respite most travelers seek. Its nearby cousin, East Orleans, is on the upswing as a destination, though, offering a couple of fun restaurants and—best of all—a goodly chunk of magnificent, unspoiled Cape Cod National Seashore.

1 Brewster

25 miles (40km) E of Sandwich, 31 miles (50km) S of Provincetown

The "youngest" of the Cape towns, Brewster—named for the Pilgrim leader William Brewster—dissociated itself from Harwich in 1803, the better to enjoy its newfound riches as a hotbed of the shipping industry. All along the winding curves of the King's Highway (now Route 6A), successful captains erected scores of proud houses—99 in all, according to the local lore. When Henry David

The Lower Cape

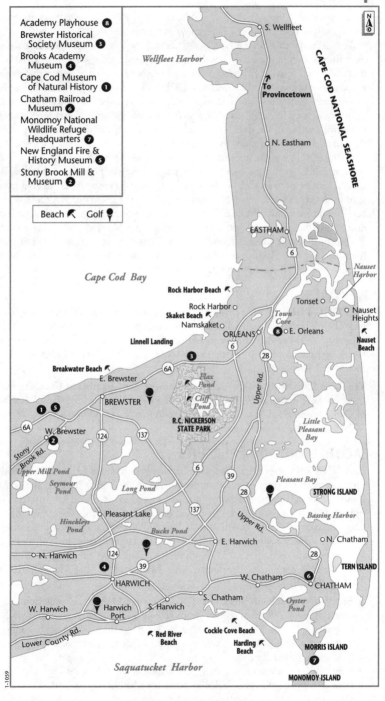

Academy Playhouse ⑧
Brewster Historical Society Museum ③
Brooks Academy Museum ④
Cape Cod Museum of Natural History ①
Chatham Railroad Museum ⑥
Monomoy National Wildlife Refuge Headquarters ⑦
New England Fire & History Museum ⑤
Stony Brook Mill & Museum ②

Beach ⬈   Golf ⚑

N

S. Wellfleet

Wellfleet Harbor

CAPE COD NATIONAL SEASHORE

To Provincetown

N. Eastham

EASTHAM

6

Nauset Harbor

Cape Cod Bay

Rock Harbor Beach ⬈

Rock Harbor

Tonset

Nauset Heights

Skaket Beach ⬈
Namskaket

Town Cove

Nauset Beach

Linnell Landing

ORLEANS

⑧ E. Orleans

6

28

Breakwater Beach ⬈

③

6A

E. Brewster

Flax Pond

Upper Rd.

① ⑤

BREWSTER ⚑

Cliff Pond

Little Pleasant Bay

6A

W. Brewster

R.C. NICKERSON STATE PARK

Stony Brook Rd.

②

124

137

Upper Mill Pond

6

Seymour Pond

Long Pond

39

Pleasant Bay

28

STRONG ISLAND

Bassing Harbor

Hinckleys Pond

Pleasant Lake

137

Bucks Pond

Upper Rd.

N. Chatham

N. Harwich

124

E. Harwich

28

④

39

W. Chatham

⑥ CHATHAM

TERN ISLAND

HARWICH

Oyster Pond

W. Harwich

Harwich Port

S. Harwich

S. Chatham

Cockle Cove Beach

MORRIS ISLAND

Lower County Rd.

Red River Beach ⬈

Harding Beach ⬈

⑦

Saquatucket Harbor

MONOMOY ISLAND

1-1059

139

Thoreau passed through in the mid-1850s, he remarked: "This town has more mates and masters of vessels than any other town in the country."

The Greek/Gothic Revival First Parish Church, built in 1834, embodies many of their stories. Among the more dramatic tales conjured by the gravestones in back is that of Captain David Nickerson, who is said to have rescued an infant during the French Revolution—possibly the son of Louis XVI and Marie Antoinette. Whatever his origins, "Rene Rousseau" followed in his adoptive father's footsteps, ultimately drowning at sea. His name was incised on the back of Nickerson's headstone, according to the custom of the day. Nickerson's name also appears on a pew in the white clapboard church, surrounded by those of his peers.

Brewster still gives the impression of somehow setting itself apart. Mostly free of the commercial encroachments that have plagued the southern shore, this thriving community seems to go about its business as if nothing were amiss. It has even managed to absorb an intrusively huge development within its own borders, the 380-acre condo complex known as Ocean Edge, on what was once a huge private estate. The dust settled, the trees grew back, the buildings started to blend in, and it's life as usual, if a bit more closely packed. Brewster also welcomes the tens of thousands of transient campers and day-trippers who arrive each summer to enjoy the nearly 2,000 wooded acres of Nickerson State Park.

ESSENTIALS

GETTING THERE   After crossing either the Bourne or Sagamore bridge (see "Getting There" in chapter 3), head east on Route 6 or 6A. Route 6A passes through the villages of West Brewster, Brewster, and East Brewster. You can also reach Brewster by taking Route 6's Exit 10 north, along Route 124. Or fly into Hyannis (see "Getting There" in chapter 3).

VISITOR INFORMATION   Contact the **Brewster Chamber of Commerce,** 74 Locust Lane, Brewster, MA 02631 (☎ **508/255-7045**) or the **Cape Cod Chamber of Commerce,** Routes 6 and 132, Hyannis, MA 02601 (☎ **508/362-3225;** fax 508/362-3698; Web site www.capecod.com).

BEACHES & OUTDOOR PURSUITS

BEACHES   Brewster's eight lovely bay beaches have minimal facilities, which make for a more natural experience. When the tide is out, the "beach" extends as much as 2 miles, leaving behind tide pools to splash in and explore, and vast stretches of rippled, reddish "garnet" sand. On a good day, you can see the whole curve of the Cape, from Sandwich to Provincetown. That hulking wreck midway, incidentally, is the USS *James Longstreet,* pressed into service for target practice in 1943 and used for that purpose right up until 1970; it's now a popular dive site. For a beach parking sticker ($8 per day, $25 per week), visit **Town Hall** at 2198 Main St., (Route 6A; ☎ **508/896-3701**).

- **Breakwater Beach,** off Breakwater Road, Brewster. Only a brief walk from the center of town, this calm, shallow beach (the only one with rest rooms) is ideal for young children. This was once a packet landing, where packet boats would unload tourists and load up produce—a system that saved a lot of travel time until the railroads came along.

- **Flax Pond** in Nickerson State Park (see "Nature & Wildlife Areas," below). This large freshwater pond, surrounded by pines, has a bathhouse and offers watersports rentals. The park contains two more ponds with beaches—Cliff and Little Cliff. Access and parking are free.

Biking the Cape Cod Rail Trail

The 25-mile Cape Cod Rail Trail is one of New England's longest and most popular bike paths. Once a bed of the Penn Central Railroad, the trail is relatively flat and straight. On weekends in summer months, you'll have to contend with dogs, in-line skaters, young families, and bikers who whip by you on their way to becoming the next Greg LeMond. Yet, if you want to venture away from the coast and see some of the Cape's countryside without having to deal with motorized traffic, this is one of the few ways to do it.

The trail starts in South Wellfleet on Lecount Hollow Road or in South Dennis on Mass. 134, depending on which way you want to ride. Beginning in South Wellfleet, the path cruises by purple wildflowers, flowering dogwood, and small maples, where red-winged blackbirds and goldfinches nest. In Orleans, you have to ride on Rock Harbor and West Roads until the City Council decides to complete the trail. At least you get a good view of the boats lining Rock Harbor. Clearly marked signs lead back to the Rail Trail, on which you'll soon enter Nickerson State Park bike trails, or continue straight through Brewster to a series of swimming holes—Seymour, Long, and Hinckleys ponds. A favorite picnic spot is the Pleasant Lake General Store in Harwich. Shortly afterwards, you cross over U.S. 6 on Mass. 124 before veering right through farmland, soon ending in South Dennis.

—by Stephen Jermanok

- **Linnells Landing Beach,** on Linnell Road in East Brewster. This is a half-mile, wheelchair-accessible bay beach.
- **Paines Creek Beach,** off Paines Creek Road, West Brewster. With 1 1/2 miles to stretch out in, this bay beach has something to offer sun-lovers and nature-lovers alike. Your kids will love it if you arrive when the tide's coming in—the current will give an air mattress a nice little ride.

BICYCLING The ✪ **Cape Cod Rail Trail** intersects with the 8-mile **Nickerson State Park** trail system at the park entrance, where there's plenty of free parking: You could follow the Rail Trail back to Dennis (about 12 miles) or onward toward Wellfleet (13 miles). **Idle Times** (☎ **508/255-8281**) provides rentals within the park, in season. Another good place to jump in is on Underpass Road about 1/2 mile south of Route 6A. Here you'll find **Brewster Bicycle Rental,** 442 Underpass Rd. (☎ **508/896-8149**), and Brewster Express, which makes sandwiches to go. Just up the hill is the well-equipped **Rail Trail Bike & Blade,** 302 Underpass Rd. (☎ **508/896-8200**), next door to **Pizza & More** (☎ **508/896-8600**), serving terrific Italian and Greek fare, loaded with carbos. Both shops offer free parking.

BOATING Cape Cod Coastal Canoe & Kayak (☎ **888/226-6393** or 508/564-4051; E-mail cccanoe@capecod.net; Web site www.capecod.net/canoe/) runs naturalist-guided trips throughout the Cape, sponsored by the Cape Cod Museum of Natural History. In Brewster, they paddle around Paine's Creek and Quivett Creek, as well as Upper and Lower Mill Ponds. Trips (3 1/2 to 4 hr.) are daily April through August, weekends through October, and cost $25 per paddler or $50 per family. All equipment is supplied. Call for schedule.

FISHING Brewster offers more ponds for fishing than any other town: 14 in all. Among the most popular are Cliff and Higgins ponds within Nickerson State Park, which are regularly stocked. For a license, visit **Town Hall** at 2198 Rte. 6A

(☎ **508/896-3701**). Brewster lacks a deep harbor, so would-be deep-sea fishers will have to head to Barnstable or, better yet, Orleans.

GOLF Part of a large resort, the 18-hole championship **Ocean Edge Golf Course** at 832 Villages Dr. (☎ **508/896-5911**) is the most challenging in Brewster, followed closely by **Captain's Golf Course** at 1000 Freemans Way (☎ **508/896-5100**).

HORSEBACK RIDING Head over to **Moby Dick Farm** (☎ **508/896-3544**) at 179 Great Field Road in Brewster for scenic rides over 200 acres of conservation land where you'll see kettle ponds, cranberry bogs, and inevitably some wildlife. All levels and all ages are invited to participate for $35, and the ride lasts a couple of hours. Owner Nick Rodday, 76 years young, is a real character and has been riding these woods for a couple of decades. This is a great way to experience the Cape's terrain, particularly in shoulder seasons.

NATURE & WILDLIFE AREAS Admission is free to the two trails maintained by the Cape Cod Museum of Natural History (see below). The **South Trail,** covering a ³/₄ mile round-trip south of Route 6A, crosses a natural cranberry bog beside Paines Creek to reach a hardwood forest of beeches and tupelos; toward the end of the loop, you'll come upon a "glacial erratic," a huge boulder dropped by a receding glacier. Before heading out on the ¹/₄ mile **North Trail,** stop in at the museum for a free guide describing the local flora, including wild roses, cattails, and sumacs. Also accessible from the CCMNH parking lot is the **John Wing Trail,** a 1¹/₂-mile network traversing 140 acres of preservation land, including upland, salt marsh, and beach. (*Note:* This can be a soggy trip. Be sure to heed the posted warnings about high tides, especially in spring, or you might very well find yourself stranded.) Keep an eye out for marsh hawks and blue herons.

As it crosses Route 6A, Paines Creek Road becomes Run Hill Road. Follow it to the end to reach **Punkhorn Park Lands,** an undeveloped 800-acre tract popular with mountain bikers; it features several kettle ponds, a "quaking bog," and 45 miles of dirt paths comprising three marked trails (you'll find trail guides at the trailheads).

Though short, the ¹/₄ mile jaunt around the **Stony Brook Grist Mill** (see below) is especially scenic. In spring you can watch the alewives (freshwater herring) vaulting upstream to spawn, and in the summer the millpond is surrounded and scented by honeysuckle. Also relatively small, at only 25 acres, the **Spruce Hill Conservation Area** behind the Brewster Historical Society Museum (see below) includes a 600-foot stretch of beach, reached by a former carriage road reportedly favored by Prohibition bootleggers.

Just east of the museum is the 1,955-acre **Nickerson State Park** at Route 6 and Crosby Lane (☎ **508/896-3491**), the legacy of a vast, self-sustaining private estate that once generated its own electricity (with a horse-powered plant) and attracted notable guests, such as President Grover Cleveland, with its own golf course and game preserve. Today it's a back-to-nature preserve encompassing 418 campsites (reservations pour in a year in advance, but some are held open for new arrivals willing to wait a day or 2), eight kettle ponds, and 8 miles of bicycle paths. The rest is trees—some 88,000 evergreens, planted by the Civilian Conservation Corps. This is land that has been through a lot but, thanks to careful management, is bouncing back.

TENNIS Public courts are located behind the police station; for details, contact the **Brewster Recreation Department** (☎ **508/896-9430**). You may also be able to book one at the **Bambergh House Tennis Club** (☎ **508/896-5023**).

WATER SPORTS Various small sailboats, kayaks, canoes, and even aqua bikes (a.k.a. sea cycles) are available seasonally at **Jack's Boat Rentals** (☎ **508/896-8556**), located on Flax Pond within Nickerson State Park.

BREWSTER HISTORIC SIGHTS & MUSEUMS

Brewster Historical Society Museum. 3341 Rte. 6A (about 1 mile E of town center).
☎ **508/896-9521.** Donation requested. July–Aug Tues–Fri 1–4pm; call for off-season hrs.
Closed early Sept to Apr.

This somewhat scattershot collection offers glimpses of Brewster's past. It includes
a model of the town's first house (built in 1660), vestiges of an old post office and
barber shop, and various relics of the China Trade—the import business that made
the town's fortune.

Brewster Ladies' Library. 1822 Rte. 6A (about ⅛ mile SW of town center). ☎ **508/
896-9372.** Fax 508/896-2297. Free admission. Call for schedule; hrs. vary.

So inviting is the buttercup-yellow facade of this Victorian library, built in 1868, that
curiosity will draw you inside. A major new addition has doubled the space and added
meeting rooms, an auditorium, and a Brewster history room. The original pair of
reading rooms remain, however, with facing fireplaces and comfy armchairs. The two
young ladies who started up this enterprise in 1852 with a shelf full of books had the
right idea.

✪ Cape Cod Museum of Natural History. 869 Rte. 6A (about 2 miles W of town center).
☎ **800/479-3867** or 508/896-3867. Admission $5 adults, $2 children 5–12. Mid-Apr to mid-
Oct Mon–Sat 9:30am–4:30pm, Sun 11am–4:30pm.

Long before "ecology" had become a buzzword, noted naturalist writer John Hay
helped to found a museum that celebrates—and helps to preserve—Cape Cod's
unique landscape. Open since 1954, the CCMNH was also prescient in presenting
interactive exhibits. The display on whales, for instance, invites the viewer to press
a button to hear eerie whale songs; the children's exhibits include an animal-puppet
theater. All ages are invariably intrigued by the "live hive"—like an ant farm, only
with busy bees. The bulk of the museum, naturally, is outdoors, where 85 acres invite exploration (see "Nature & Wildlife Areas," above). Visitors are encouraged to
log their bird and animal sightings upon their return. The museum features an on-
site archaeology lab on Wing Island, thought to have sheltered one of Brewster's first
settlers—the Quaker John Wing, driven from Sandwich in the mid-17th century by
religious persecution—and before him, summering native tribes dating back 10 millennia or more, when the Cape and Islands were still all of a piece. A true force in
fostering environmental appreciation, the museum sponsors all sorts of activities to
engage the public, from lectures and concerts to marsh cruises and "eco-treks"—
including a sleep-over on uninhabited Monomoy Island off Chatham.

Harris-Black House and Higgins Farm Windmill. 785 Rte. 6A (about 2 miles W of town
center). ☎ **508/896-9521.** Free admission. July–Aug Tues–Sun 1–4pm; May–June and Sept–
Oct Sat–Sun 1–4pm. Closed Nov–Apr.

Most Cape towns can still boast a windmill or two, a few of them even still function-
ing, but this no-longer-working model is especially handsome. Built in 1795 in the
"smock" style that can be traced back to colonial days, it boasts an unusual cap shaped
like a boat's hull. A few steps away is a classic half-Cape house, built that same year,
consisting of one square room, 16 feet to a side. Here, one of the poorer members
of the community—a blacksmith who doubled as barber—lived simply yet apparently happily with his wife and 10 children.

New England Fire & History Museum. 1429 Rte. 6A (about 1 mile W of town center).
☎ **508/896-5711.** Admission $5 adults, $4.25 seniors, $2.50 children 5–12. Late May to mid-
Sept Mon–Fri 10am–4pm, Sat–Sun noon–4pm; mid-Sept to mid-Oct Sat–Sun noon–4pm.
Closed mid-Oct to late May.

The gaslit displays may come across a little hokey (as well as murky), but little kids as well as grown-up fire-fighting aficionados will probably find the array of equipment pretty enthralling. More than 30 antique fire engines have found a home here, including an extraordinarily decorative 1837 French Provincial rig from Philadelphia and a unique 1929 Mercedes Benz worth a cool million. Also on the grounds, and included with admission, is a smithy offering frequent demos and an old-fashioned Apothecary Shop.

Stony Brook Grist Mill and Museum. 830 Stony Brook Rd. (at the intersection of Satucket Rd. in the town center). ☎ **508/896-6745.** Free admission. July–Aug Thurs–Sat 2–5pm; May–June Fri 2–5pm. Closed Sept–Apr.

It may be hard to believe, but this rustic mill beside a stream was once one of the most active manufacturing communities in New England, cranking out cloth, boots, and ironwork for over a century, starting with the American Revolution. The one remaining structure was built in 1873, toward the end of West Brewster's commercial run, near the site of a 1663 water-powered mill, America's first. After decades of producing overalls and, later, ice cream (with ice dredged from the adjoining pond), the factory was bought by the town and fitted out as a corn mill, with period millstones. Volunteers now demonstrate, and urge onlookers to get in on the action. The second story serves as a repository for all sorts of Brewster memorabilia, including some ancient arrowheads. Recent archaeological excavations in this vicinity, sponsored by the Cape Cod Museum of Natural History, have unearthed artifacts dating back some 10,000 years. As you stroll about the millpond (see "Nature & Wildlife Areas," above), be on the lookout—who knows what you'll stumble across?

BASEBALL

The Brewster Whitecaps of the Cape Cod Baseball League play at the Cape Cod Tech field off Route 6's Exit 11. For a schedule, contact the **Brewster Chamber of Commerce** (☎ 508/255-7045), the **Brewster Recreation Department** (☎ 508/896-9430), or the **League** (☎ 508/432-6909).

KID STUFF

If you've got very little kids in tow who have never been to a "real" zoo, they might enjoy the **Bassett Wild Animal Farm** at 620 Tubman Rd. off Route 124 (☎ 508/896-3224). Open only in season, this facility is a bit bedraggled (not to mention cruel: The lion and cougar deserve more room to roam), but young children will probably go for the pony rides and a chance to feed the goats. For a much more educational experience that's every bit as much fun, take them to the **Cape Cod Museum of Natural History,** as well as to the **Stony Brook Grist Mill** (see above).

SHOPPING

ANTIQUES/COLLECTIBLES　Brewster's stretch of Route 6A offers the best antiquing on the entire Cape. Diehards would do well to stop at every intriguing-looking shop; you never know what you might find. There are several consistent stand-outs.

Serious collectors with bankrolls to match will want to make a beeline to ✪ **William M. Baxter Antiques,** 3439 Main St. (Route 6A), about 1 mile east of the town center (☎ 508/896-3998). Mr. Baxter has been in the business for decades, first on Charles Street (Boston's antique mecca), then here in the boondocks, where fans gladly followed. There aren't too many colonial highboys still bobbing about, but he's got several, along with a dazzling array of mirrors and much distinguished Orientalia. Closed late November to late May.

The artifacts gathered at **Kingsland Manor Antiques,** 440 Rte. 6A, about 1 mile east of the Dennis border (☎ **800/486-2305** or 508/385-9741), tend to be on the flamboyant side, accent pieces rather than serviceable, retiring classics—which makes browsing all the more fun.

There's always an interesting variety of items at **Monomoy Antiques,** 3425 Rte. 6A (☎ **508/896-6570**) including many fascinating finds from local estate sales. Specialties include rare books, English china, and decoys.

Imagine a town dump full of treasures all meticulously arranged, and you'll get an idea of what's in store at **Diane Vetromile's Antiques** at 3884 Rte. 6A in Brewster (no phone). If the sign that reads ANTIQUES is out, it's open; if not, it's closed. This place is a tad kooky, but any junk aficionado will be thrilled by the pickings: hubcaps, wooden nails, iron rakes, wood shudders—the more peeled paint the better. Owner Diane Vetromile is herself a sculptor, who works with (surprise) found objects, and you'll find her work on view at Jacob Fanning Gallery and Farmhouse Antiques, both in Wellfleet.

ARTS & CRAFTS   Clayton Calderwood's **Clayworks,** 3820 Main St. (Route 6A), Brewster (☎ **508/255-9315**), is always worth a stop, if only to marvel at the famous mammoth urns. There's also a world of functional ware here like bowls, pots, and lamps, in porcelain, stoneware, and terra-cotta.

At **The Spectrum,** 369 Rte. 6A, about 1 mile east of the Dennis border (☎ **800/221-2472** or 508/385-3322), you'll find the kind of crafts that gave crafts a good name: fun stuff, with a certain irony to it, but unmistakably chic. In 1966 two young RISD (Rhode Island School of Design) grads opened shop in a rural schoolhouse. Bob Libby and Addison Pratt now oversee five stores: three on the Cape (the other branches are in Hyannis and Nantucket), and one each in Newport and Palm Beach. Their taste is top-of-the-line, as you'll see in a quick tour of this split-level, country-modern shop.

Every community deserves an endearing eccentric, and Malcolm Wells is a peach. He also happens to be a highly regarded authority in the field of subterranean architecture: His 1977 tome, *Underground Designs,* has sold some 100,000 copies to date and remains a source of inspiration. Wells himself experienced an epiphany in the early 1960s when, as a corporate architect, he came to the conclusion that "green plants and not buildings are intended to cover the earth." His fresh and light-filled passive-solar studio, known as **Underground Art Gallery,** 673 Satucket Rd., at Newcomb Road, about ²/₃ mile south of Route 6A (☎ **508/896-3757**), peeks out from under 200 tons of grassy soil dotted with wildflowers. Here he and his wife, Karen North Wells, an accomplished watercolorist, sell their paintings and spread the word.

BOOKS   David L. Luebke is a neat-freak—a desirable trait in an antiquarian book-seller. Visit his **Punkhorn Bookshop,** 672 Rte. 6A, about ¹/₂ mile east of the Dennis border (☎ **508/896-2114**), and you'll notice that each volume logged in his carefully selected stock—strong on regional and natural history—is shelved according to the Dewey decimal system and protectively coddled in a see-through wrapper to keep fingerprints and "foxing" (stains) to a minimum. If you're in the market for a vintage print, you'll find some beauties here. Closed Monday year-round; open by appointment only off-season.

GIFTS/HOME DECOR   Though quite a bit spiffier than a "real" general store, **The Brewster Store,** 1935 Rte. 6A, in the center of town (☎ **508/896-3744**), an 1866 survivor—fashioned from an 1852 Universalist church—is a fun place to shop for sundries and catch up on local gossip. The wares are mostly tourist-oriented these days, but include some handy kitchen gear (cobalt glassware, for example) and beach paraphernalia. Give the kids a couple of dimes to feed the Nickelodeon piano machine, and relax on a sunny church pew out front as you pore over the local paper.

The volunteer-staffed gift shop at the **Cape Cod Museum of Natural History,** 869 Rte. 6A, about 2 miles west of town center (☎ **800/479-3867** or 508/896-3867), has a terrific selection of nature-related toys and gifts suitable for all ages, from stuffed animals to science kits, kites, and books, to polished stones (starting at an allowance-preserving $1 apiece).

You don't have to be a foodie—though it helps—to go gaga over the exhaustive collection of culinary paraphernalia, from esoteric instruments to foodstuffs, at **The Cook Shop,** 1091 Rte. 6A, about 1¹/₂ miles west of town center (☎ **508/896-7698**). If you're stuck cooking up a practical yet unusual house gift, look no further.

It seems fitting that the area of the Cape thought to have sheltered the earliest indigenous inhabitants—the Saugautucket people—should have attracted a New Age entrepreneur dedicated to reviving natural, traditional approaches to healing. **Great Cape Cod Herb, Spice & Tea Company,** 2628 Main St. (Route 6A), about 1 mile east of the town center (☎ **800/427-7144** or 508/896-5900; fax 508/896-1972), stocks over 170 herbs, many in the form of tasty blended teas, such as Bee Happy and Monomoy Morning.

SEAFOOD **Breakwater Fish and Lobster** on Underpass Road in Brewster (☎ **508/896-7080**) stocks the freshest fish in town, and they also sell smoked fish.

WHERE TO STAY
VERY EXPENSIVE

Ocean Edge Resort. 2907 Main St. (about 2¹/₃ miles E of town center), Brewster, MA 02631. ☎ **800/343-6074** or 508/896-9000. Fax 508/896-9123. 90 rms, about 180 condos. A/C TV TEL. Summer $225–$295 double; $225–$275 condo. Golf, tennis, and holiday weekend packages available. AE, DISC, MC, V.

If the price of admission strikes you as high, consider the built-ins: two fitness rooms and six pools (two indoor, four outdoor) scattered around an intensively landscaped 380-acre property, part of which fronts a private 1,000-foot stretch of bay beach. The entire tract, plus the nearby Nickerson State Forest, once belonged to a single family, whose prosperity appears to have been dogged by tragedy. Samuel Mayo Nickerson, a Chatham boy who made good as a Chicago banker, built the original mansion, Fieldstone Hall, in 1890 as a gift for his only son, Roland, who died 2 weeks after it burned down in 1906. His widow, Addie, built a 400-foot-long Renaissance Revival replacement—now a conference center and hotel—with an eye to meeting fire codes; it's rather homely, grandiose, and not exactly enhanced by the accretion of dense condo accommodations begun in the building boom of the early 1980s. Rooms are spacious and comfortable with views of gardens, fairways, or Cape Cod Bay. Villa condos have two or three bedrooms with living and dining rooms, full kitchens, and washers/dryers. Some rooms are equipped with computer lines. If you're up for the kind of stay-put vacation where every need is met right on the premises (for a price), this might make a good choice, but you're liable to miss out on the quirks that constitute a good portion of the Cape's charms.

Dining/Entertainment: There are four restaurants on the grounds: the refined Ocean Grille and British-style Bayzo's Pub within the mansion, and Mulligan's (New American) and the Reef Cafe (casual Caribbean) overlooking the golf course.

Services: "Kidstart," a supervised program for children 4 to 12.

Facilities: There are six pools (four outdoor, two indoor), and two fitness rooms. The 18-hole golf course features Scottish pot bunkers. There are 11 tennis courts on the grounds: five clay and six Plexipave. Instruction and clinic packages are offered in both sports.

EXPENSIVE

✪ **Captain Freeman Inn.** 15 Breakwater Rd. (off Rte. 6A, in town center), Brewster, MA 02631. ☎ **800/843-4664** or 508/896-7481. Fax 508/896-5618. 11 rms (3 with shared bath). A/C TV TEL. Summer (including full breakfast and afternoon tea) $95–$225 double. AE, DC, MC, V.

The creation of an exemplary country inn is part business, part art, and Carol Covitz Edmondson—the ex–marketing director behind this beauty—poured plenty of both into her mint-green 1866 Victorian. The "luxury suites"—each complete with fire-place and a private porch with cloverleaf hot tub—incorporate every extra you could hope to encounter: a canopied, four-poster queen-size bed, a love seat facing the cable TV/VCR (she has a store's worth of tapes available for loan), even a little fridge prestocked with cold soda, juices, and mineral water. The plainer rooms are just as pretty—one nice feature of the porch-encircled house is that the second-story win-dows reach almost to the floor. The three dormered third-floor rooms, though small-ish, have enviable water views and are nicely priced; families often claim the whole floor. Delectable yet healthy breakfasts—Edmondson, a culinary maven, hosts week-end cooking courses off-season—are served in bed (indulge yourself!), in the elegant parlor, or on a screened porch overlooking the heated pool and a lush lawn set up for badminton and croquet. Breakwater Landing is a bucolic 10-minute walk, or just moments away, if you avail yourself of a loaner bike. Bliss.

MODERATE

Beechcroft Inn. 1360 Rte. 6A (about 1^1/4 miles W of town center), Brewster, MA 02631. ☎ **508/896-9534.** Fax 508/896-8812. 10 rms. Summer (including full breakfast), $75–$155. AE, DC, DISC, MC, V.

Though it looks every inch the gracious summer home, this 1828 building, an inn since 1852, began as a meetinghouse. Subtract one steeple, relocate atop a little hillock crowned with magnificent beeches (people seem to have moved houses in those days the way we change jobs), and presto—a made-to-order country retreat. The rooms, none terribly grand, are nevertheless sweet as can be, with fresh country accents. The in-house bistro (see "Where to Dine," below), though up against some stiff local com-petition (Brewster is saturated with excellent restaurants), can hold its own and is certainly convenient.

The Bramble Inn. 2019 Rte. 6A (about ^{1}/3 mile E of town center), Brewster, MA 02631. ☎ **508/896-7644.** Fax 508/896-9332. 8 rms. A/C. Summer (including full breakfast) $98–$128 double. AE, DISC, MC, V. Closed Jan to mid-May.

Cliff and Ruth Manchester oversee two rambling mid-19th-century homes, decorated in a breezy, country-casual manner. The main inn building, built in 1861, houses one of the Cape's best restaurants on the first floor. The 1849 Greek Revival house next door has additional rooms, all very quaint with antique touches like crocheted bed spreads. Ruth is a phenomenal chef (see "Where to Dine," below), so you know you'll be in good hands come breakfast time.

Brewster Farmhouse Inn. 716 Rte. 6A (about 2 miles W of town center), Brewster, MA 02631. ☎ **800/892-3910** or 508/896-3910. Fax 508/896-4232. 5 rms (2 with shared bath). A/C TV. Summer (including full breakfast and afternoon tea) $110–$175. AE, CB, DC, DISC, MC, V.

A perfect truffle of a B&B, this sedate 1846 Greek Revival house is a softie inside. The decor is more California than Cape, starting with a cathedral-ceilinged living room lightly dressed with Oriental rugs and down-filled sofas. Glass doors lead to a spacious wooden deck where you'll find a heated pool and hot tub and a roomy lawn ringed with fruit trees (their bounty is likely to turn up on the dining-room table). The bedrooms, like the gathering room, are done up in subtle, muted hues, and the beds tend to make a simple statement—"Relax." Extras include hair dryers and turn-down service, in which an imported chocolate may be plunked on your pillow. Bikes are available for exploring Brewster. New innkeepers Carol and Gary Concors are focused on hospitality. Gary is an award-winning pastry chef, and that talent is reflected at both the full breakfast and the afternoon tea.

Candleberry Inn. 1882 Main St. (Rte. 6A), Brewster, MA 02631. ☎ **800/573-4769** or 508/896-3300. 6 rms. A/C. Summer (including full breakfast) $95–$125 double. AE, MC, V.

New owners Gini and David Donnelly graciously welcome guests to their restored 18th-century home. These spacious accommodations feature wide-board floors, wainscoting, and windows with original glass. In addition, some have fireplaces and canopy beds. Extras include hair dryers and robes in every room. In season, the three-course full breakfast is frequently served on the sunny porch, which overlooks the $1^1/_2$ acres of landscaped grounds—which have colorful flower beds throughout. Guests love the view of Main Street from the "glider" rocking bench on the lawn.

✪ **High Brewster Inn.** 964 Satucket Rd. (off Rte. 6A, about 2 miles SW of town center), Brewster, MA 02631. ☎ **800/203-2634** or 508/896-3636. 3 rms, 3 cottages. Summer (including continental breakfast) $90–$110 double; $150–$210 cottage. AE, MC, V. Closed Dec–Mar.

There are just a few bedrooms topping the exquisite restaurant that occupies most of this 1738 farmhouse. An ancient stairway with mismatched high steps leads the way up, where rooms are appropriately furnished in the classic "Ye Olde" style. The boldly decorated cottages, on the other hand, are like having your own $3^1/_2$-acre place in the country, prettily situated on a hill overlooking a millpond. Your hosts Catherine and Tim Mundy are most hospitable. If you are staying in one of the cottages, you may bring your well-behaved dog, who may enjoy frolicking with the frisky resident cocker spaniel.

Isaiah Clark House. 1187 Rte. 6A, Brewster, MA 02631. ☎ **800/822-4001** or 508/896-2223. Fax 508/896-7054. 7 rms. A/C TV. Summer (including full breakfast and afternoon tea) $98–$120 double. AE, DISC, MC, V.

Many mementos of bygone days are found throughout this expanded 1780 Cape cottage, owned for many years by the prominent Clark family of Brewster. Antique hardware and wide-board floors are original to the house, and innkeeper Richard Griffin can show you the 1836 newspaper the Clarks used to line the wall of a closet. Many beds are canopied, but the most spectacular is the suspended canopy bed in the front room with its plaid curtains. For breakfast, keep your fingers crossed for the Belgian waffles with fresh-fruit (the strawberries, blueberries, and raspberries are all picked locally) and whipped-cream toppings.

✪ **Ruddy Turnstone Inn.** 463 Main St. (Rte. 6A), Brewster, MA 02631. ☎ **800/654-1995** or 508/385-9871. 4 rms, 1 suite. Summer (including full breakfast) $95–$150. MC, V. Closed Jan–Feb.

Bird lovers will be particularly entranced by this cozy B&B: The acres of salt marsh make for frequent sightings. In addition, the lovely 1880 home offers Cape Cod Bay views (from the suite or the common sitting room), for about the same price as other inns along this stretch without water views. The house is beautifully situated up on a knoll and is furnished with antiques, Oriental rugs, and some canopy beds. The

200-year-old barn, moved here from Nantucket, houses the spacious suite. Innkeepers "Swanee" and Sally Swanson are the kind you look forward to seeing year after year.

INEXPENSIVE

✪ **Old Sea Pines Inn.** 2553 Main St. (about 1 mile E of town center), Brewster, MA 02631. ☎ **508/896-6114.** Fax 508/896-7387. 19 rms (5 with shared bath), 3 suites. A/C TV. Summer (including full breakfast and afternoon tea) $55–$115 double; $110–$150 suite. AE, CB, DC, DISC, MC, V. Closed Jan–Mar.

In the early part of the century, this grand 1907 shingle-style mansion was the site of the Sea Pines School of Charm and Personality for Young Women. A great deal of that charm is still evident. In fact, the hosts, Michele and Steve Rowan, have done their best to recreate the gracious ambiance of days gone by. The parlor and expansive porch lined with rockers are just as the young ladies might have found them, as are a handful of rather minuscule boarding-school–scale rooms on the second floor. This is one of the few places on the Cape where solo travelers can find a single room and pay no surcharge. The Rowans like to be able to offer a few lower-priced rooms, says Michele, because "It means we can get a real mix of people." Their inclusiveness is also evident in an added annex that's fully wheelchair-accessible (another rarity among historic inns). Whereas the main house has an air of exuberance muted by gentility, the annex rooms are outright playful, with colorful accoutrements, including pink TVs. Steve does double duty as the breakfast chef—dinner, too, in July and August—and prepares good old-fashioned food. You won't find any kiwis staring you down first thing in the morning. In season, Old Sea Pines is the site of the Cape Cod Repertory Theatre (see "Brewster After Dark," below).

WHERE TO DINE
VERY EXPENSIVE

✪ **The Bramble Inn Restaurant.** 2019 Main St. (about ¹/₃ mile E of Rte. 124). ☎ **508/ 896-7644.** Reservations recommended. Fixed-price $42–$52. AE, DISC, MC, V. June to mid-Oct Tues–Sun 6–9pm; call for off-season hrs. Closed Jan–Apr. NEW AMERICAN.

There's an impromptu feel to this intimate restaurant, an enfilade of five small rooms each imbued with its own personality, from sporting (the Tack Room) to best-Sunday-behavior (the Elegant Parlor). One-of-a-kind antique table settings add to the charm. Such niceties fade to mere backdrop, though, beside Ruth Manchester's extraordinary cuisine. A four-course (six- to eight-option) menu that evolves every few weeks gives her free rein to follow fresh enthusiasms, as well as seasonal delicacies, and it's a thrill to be able to follow along. Any specifics are quickly history, but she has a solid grounding in Mediterranean cuisines and a gift for improvisatory cross-pollination.

Chillingsworth. 2449 Main St. (about 1 mile E of town center). ☎ **508/896-3640.** Reservations required. Jacket requested. Fixed-price $40–$56. AE, DC, MC, V. July–Aug daily 11:30am–2:30pm and 6–9:30pm; call for off-season hrs. Closed late Nov to mid-May. FRENCH.

A longtime contender for the title of best restaurant on the Cape, Chillingsworth is certainly the fanciest, what with antique appointments reaching back several centuries and a seven-course Francophiliac table d'hôte menu that will challenge the most shameless gourmands. There's a rote quality to the ritual, however, which can undercut what might otherwise amount to a transcendental culinary experience. See if you can ignore all the rigmarole and just focus on the taste sensations, which are indeed sensational. Or, for a sampling, lunch or dine (sans reservations) in the à la carte Bistro.

☺ High Brewster. 964 Satucket Rd. (off Rte. 6A, about 2 miles SW of town center). ☎ **508/ 896-3636.** Reservations required. Fixed-price $35–$55. AE, MC, V. Late May to mid-Sept daily 5:30–9pm; call for off-season hrs. Closed Dec–Mar. CLASSIC AMERICAN.

By candlelight, the close yet cozy keeping rooms and paneled parlors of this 1738 colonial are irresistibly romantic. It's difficult to decide between the Rooster Room, with its whimsical wallpaper, or the Front Room, with its clever hand-painted murals. Stephen Arden and Robert Hickey's sensual, sophisticated cuisine only serves to intensify the mood. Dishes tend to be bold in the modern manner—mushroom-filled ravioli, for instance, with fresh tomato salsa, or pan-seared salmon with sun-dried tomato vinaigrette—yet they're good at adapting local ingredients and traditional preparations to treats our ancestors could have imagined only in their dreams. What they would have given, heaven only knows, to be able to celebrate the harvest with apple crisp topped with homemade apple rum ice cream.

MODERATE

Beechcroft Bistro. At the Beechcroft Inn (see "Where to Stay," above). ☎ **508/896-9534.** Reservations recommended. Main courses $12–$24. AE, DC, DISC, MC, V. Mid-May to mid-Sept Wed–Sun 5–9:30pm; call for off-season hrs. INTERNATIONAL.

Generosity and warmth are the key ingredients of bistro fare, and you'll get plenty of both in the cozy fireplaced pub and more formal dining room. The fresh-seafood "bisque du jour" is just the ticket at the end of a blustery day. Lighter options include creatively sauced pastas and Boboli pizzas such as the "Mykonos" (eggplant and feta and olives, oh my), and there's usually a choice of at least five entrees, including sole Tivoli—wrapped around a core of seafood stuffing and artichoke heart, and topped with lemon butter. You're welcome, too, to stop in just for dessert, subject to the chef's whim, but usually some fiendish delight: Beware the Chocolate Oblivion!

☺ The Brewster Fish House. 2208 Main St. (about ¹/₂ mile E of town center). ☎ **508/ 896-7867.** Reservations not accepted. Main courses $13–$22. MC, V. June to early Sept Tues– Sat 11:30am–3pm and 5–10pm, Sun noon–3pm and 5–9:30pm; call for off-season hrs. Closed mid-Dec to mid-Apr. NEW AMERICAN.

Spare and handsome as a Shaker refectory, this small restaurant bills itself as "nonconforming" and delivers on the promise. The approach to seafood borders on genius: Consider, just for instance, squid delectably tenderized in a marinade of soy and ginger, or silky-tender walnut-crusted ocean catfish accompanied by kale sautéed in marsala. These are but two examples of the daily specials devised to take advantage of the latest haul. No wonder the place is packed. Better get there early if you want to get in.

The Old Manse Inn. 1861 Main St. (about a ¹/₃ mile W of town center). ☎ **508/ 896-3149.** Reservations recommended. Main courses $15–$21. AE, DISC, MC, V. Late June to early Sept daily 6–9pm. Closed early Sept to late June. NEW AMERICAN.

The setting bespeaks a calm gentility—the parlors and porch given over to dining bask in the relaxed glow of candlelight—but the cuisine is downright jazzy, almost startlingly so. Young chefs David and Suzanne Plum (she's the granddaughter of the previous owners) are both graduates of the acclaimed Culinary School of America and have revamped the menu extensively. Your meal might begin with Cuban-style grilled shrimp with black-bean salad; move on to a salad of marinated pear and cherry tomatoes served on a *chiffonade* of spinach, Boston lettuce, and radicchio; and as the main course, Nauset striped bass, grilled and served with fresh vegetable succotash, stewed plum tomatoes, and thyme. In a town of superior dining, this is very good, reasonably priced, creative food.

⊕ Family-Friendly Hotels & Restaurants

Barley Neck Inn in East Orleans *(see p. 177)*   Tastefully rehabbed, this former motel offers low-priced, country-inn–style rooms, a small pool, and a pair of superb, unstodgy restaurants.

Binnacle Tavern in Orleans *(see p. 178)*   Design-your-own pizzas are the draw at this often raucous eatery decorated with nautical salvage.

Chatham Bars Inn in Chatham *(see p. 164)*   This luxury beachside resort offers well-heeled tots the best of everything, including organized play programs morning, noon, and night.

Kadee's Gray Elephant in East Orleans *(see p. 176)*   This cute little compound comprises a colorful, all-kitchenette inn, a lively open-air clam bar, and even a minigolf course.

Old Sea Pines Inn in Brewster *(see p. 149)*   Children will appreciate the traditional (i.e., recognizable) food and friendly, informal atmosphere of this former finishing school.

INEXPENSIVE

Brewster Inn & Chowder House. 1993 Rte. 6A (in the center of town). ☎ **508/896-7771.** Main courses $12–$16. AE, DISC, MC, V. Late May to mid-Oct daily 11:30am–4pm; Sun–Thurs 5–9:30pm, Fri–Sat 5–10pm; call for off-season hrs. ECLECTIC.

To really get the gist of the expression "chow down," just observe the early-evening crowd happily doing so at this plainish century-old restaurant known mostly by word of mouth. The draw is hearty, predictable staples—the homemade chowder, various fried, broiled, or baked fish—at prices geared to ordinary people rather than splurging tourists. Check the blackboard for some interesting variations—maybe mussels steamed in cream and curry. If you like to indulge in a martini before your meal, this place makes the best ones in town. There's also a good old bar, The Woodshed (see "Brewster After Dark," below), out back.

Cobie's. 3260 Rte. 6A (about 2 miles E of Brewster center). ☎ **508/896-7021.** Most items under $10. No credit cards. Late May to mid-Sept daily 11am–9pm. Closed mid-Sept to late May. AMERICAN.

Equally accessible to cars whizzing along Route 6A and cyclists exploring the Rail Trail (it's within collapsing distance), this picture-perfect clam shack has been dishing out exemplary fried clams, lobster rolls, foot-long hot dogs, black-and-white frappés, and all the other beloved staples of summer since 1948.

Pizza & More. 302 Underpass Rd. (about $^1/_2$ mile S of Rte. 6A). ☎ **508/896-8600.** Most items under $10. No credit cards. Open daily late May to early Sept 11am–10pm, early Sept to late May 11am–9pm. MEDITERRANEAN.

You don't have to be Rail Trail–bound to appreciate this pizzeria, though summer brings swarms of cyclists. It's worth a visit any time of year just for the Greek extras, such as gyros and a sunny baklava.

The Tower House Restaurant. 2671 Rte. 6A (about 1 mile E of town center). ☎ **508/896-2671.** Main courses $8–$18. MC, V. Late May to mid-Oct daily 8am–9pm; call for off-season hrs. INTERNATIONAL.

Every beach town needs a good cafe where the hours are as you like them (so you can sun at will). This one is unusually good-looking, with a contemporary/colonial look—lofty ceilings, wooden beams, rugged wrought-iron chandeliers. There's also a pretty outdoor patio, often packed. The food is reliable and competently done, if not exactly radical; the "fish-market specials" are apt to be your best bet. Off-season, this is one of the only good places to get breakfast in Brewster.

BREWSTER AFTER DARK

Performances at the **Cape Cod Repertory Theatre Company,** 3379 Rte. 6A, about 2¹/₂ miles east of Brewster center (☎ **508/896-1888**), are given Tuesday through Saturday at 8:30pm from early July to early September. In summer, this shoestring troupe tackles the Bard, as well as serious contemporary fare, at a 200-seat outdoor theater on the old Crosby estate (now state-owned and undergoing restoration). Sunday evenings in season, they also put on a Broadway-musical dinner revue at the Old Sea Pines Inn ($35 prix fixe; see "Where to Stay," above). Off-season they perform here and there; if you're lucky, you might find Chatham resident Julie Harris fronting a benefit. Call for off-season hours. Tickets $15 adults, $8 for those under 22.

Hot local bands take the tiny stage seasonally at **The Woodshed,** at the Brewster Inn & Chowder House, 1993 Rte. 6A (☎ **508/896-7771**), a far cry from the glitzy discos on the southern shore. If your tastes run more to Raitt and Buffett than techno, you'll feel right at home in this dark, friendly dive. Cover charge $3 to $5.

2 The Harwiches

24 miles (39km) E of Sandwich, 32 miles (52km) S of Provincetown

Harwich Port is the quintessential sleepy seaside village, not too mucked up—as yet—by the creeping commercialization of Route 28. The town's main claim to fame was as the birthplace, in 1846, of commercial cranberry cultivation: The "bitter berry," as the Narragansetts called it, is now Massachusetts's leading agricultural product. The curious can find elucidating displays on this and other local distinctions at the Brooks Academy Museum in the inland town of Harwich. The incurious, or merely vacation-minded, can loll on the beach.

ESSENTIALS

GETTING THERE   After crossing either the Bourne or Sagamore bridge (see "Getting There" in chapter 3), head east on Route 6 and take Exit 10 south along Route 124. Harwich is located at the intersection of Route 39, where the two routes converge and head southwest to Harwich Port and West Harwich, both located on Route 28. East Harwich (more easily reached from Route 6's Exit 11) is inland, a few miles northeast. Or fly into Hyannis (see "Getting There" in chapter 3).

VISITOR INFORMATION   Contact the **Harwich Chamber of Commerce,** Route 28, Harwich Port, MA 02646 (☎ **800/441-3199** or 508/432-1600; fax 508/430-2105) or the **Cape Cod Chamber of Commerce,** Routes 6 and 132, Hyannis, MA 02601 (☎ **508/362-3225;** fax 508/362-3698; Web site www.capecod.com).

BEACHES & OUTDOOR PURSUITS

BEACHES   The Harwich coast is basically one continuous beach punctuated by the occasional harbor. Harwich Port is so close to the sound that it's a snap to walk the block or 2 to the water—provided you find a parking place in town (try the lot near the Chamber of Commerce booth in the center of town). Parking right at the beach is pretty much limited to residents and renters, who can obtain a weekly sticker for $25 at the **Highway Garage,** 273 Queen Anne Rd., Harwich (☎ **508/432-7638** or 508/430-7553).

- **Bank Street Beach,** at the end of Bank Street in Harwich Port. This is one of the few sound beaches in Harwich Port that has parking, but you will need a sticker. The sound beaches are generally warm and calm, very good beaches for swimming. This is a pretty (and popular) stretch where you'll see lots of families as well as the self-conscious college crowd.
- **Red River Beach,** off Uncle Venies Road south of Route 28 in South Harwich. This is the only sound beach in town offering parking for day-trippers (they still have to turn up early); the fee is $5 on weekdays or $10 weekends and holidays. Marked off with stone jetties, this narrow, 2,700-foot beach has full facilities.
- **Sand Pond,** off Great Western Road near Depot Street. This beach honors the weekly beach sticker, as do the two parking lots at Long Pond.
- **Hinckleys Pond and Seymour Pond,** west of Route 124 and right off the Rail Trail, and Bucks Pond, off Depot Road at Route 39 northeast of Harwich. They welcome all comers.

BICYCLING Transecting Harwich for about 5 miles, the Cape Cod Rail Trail skirts some pretty ponds in the western part before veering north and zigzagging toward Brewster along Route 124. For rentals and information, contact **Harwich Port Bike Co.,** 431 Rte. 28 (☎ **508/430-0200**); they can also provide in-line skates, kayaks, and canoes.

BOATING **Cape Cod Coastal Canoe & Kayak** (☎ **888/226-6393** or 508/564-4051; E-mail cccanoe@capecod.net; Web site www.capecod.net/canoe/) runs naturalist-guided trips throughout the Cape, sponsored by the Cape Cod Museum of Natural History. In Harwich, they paddle around the Herring River. Trips (3$^{1}/_{2}$ to 4 hr.) are daily April through August, weekends through October, and cost $25 per paddler or $50 per family. All equipment is supplied. Call for schedule.

  Cape Water Sports at 337 Rte. 28 in Harwich Port (☎ **508/432-7079**) offers lessons and rentals on several beaches: available craft include canoes, Sunfish, and sailboats up to 42 feet. Meandering from a reservoir south to the sound, West Harwich's Herring River—a natural herring run framed by a cattail marsh—is ideal for canoeing. The **Harwich Port Bike Co.** at 431 Main St. (☎ **508/430-0200**) offers family tours and rents out canoes and kayaks. **Cape Sail,** out of Saquatucket Harbor (☎ **508/896-2730**), offers sailing lessons as well as private charters.

FISHING There are six ponds available for fishing in the Harwich area, as well as extensive shellfishing in season; for details and a license, visit **Town Hall** at 732 Main St. in Harwich (☎ **508/430-7516**). For supplies and instruction, visit **Fishing the Cape,** at the Harwich Commons, Routes 137 and 39 (☎ **508/432-1200**); it's the official Cape headquarters for the **Orvis Saltwater Fly-Fishing School** (☎ **800/235-9763**). Several deep-sea fishing boats operate out of Saquatucket Harbor (off Route 28, about $^{1}/_{2}$ mile east of Harwich Port), including the 33-footers *Fish Tale* (☎ **508/432-3783**) and *Arlie Ex* (☎ **508/430-2454**), and the 65-foot *Yankee* (☎ **508/432-2520**). The *Golden Eagle* (☎ **508/432-5611**), offering evening bluefish trips several times a week, heads out from Wychmere Harbor.

GOLF Both the championship 18-hole **Cranberry Valley Golf Course** at 183 Oak St. in Harwich (☎ **508/430-7560**), which wends its way among cranberry bogs, and the 9-hole **Harwich Port Golf Club** on Forest and South streets in Harwich Port (☎ **508/432-0250**) are open to the public.

NATURE & WILDLIFE AREAS The largest preserve in Harwich is the 245-acre **Bells Neck Conservation Area** north of Route 28 near the Dennis border. It encompasses the Herring River, ideal for birding and canoeing (see "Boating," above).

TENNIS   Public courts are available on a first-come, first-served basis at the Cape Cod Technical High School on Route 124 and Brooks Park on Oak Street, about ¹/₄ mile east of Harwich center off Route 29; for details, contact the **Harwich Recreation Department** (☎ 508/432-4500). Open late May through September, the **Wychmere Harbor Tennis Club** at 792 Main St. in Harwich Port (☎ 508/430-7012) comprises nine Har-Tru courts and three hard courts; lessons can be scheduled. Court time costs a whopping $30 an hour.

HARWICH HISTORICAL SOCIETY

Brooks Academy Museum. 80 Parallel St. (at the intersection of Sisson Rd. and Main St., about 1 mile N of Harwich Port center). ☎ **508/432-8089.** Free admission. Early June to mid-Oct Wed–Sun 1–4pm. Closed mid-Oct to early June.

Gathered in an 1844 Greek Revival academy that offered the country's first courses in navigation, the collections of the Harwich Historical Society are good for a rainy afternoon's worth of wonderment. On permanent display is an extensive exhibition chronicling the early days of the cranberry industry, when harvesting was a back-breaking chore performed on hands and knees with a wooden scoop, mostly by migrant workers. (It simplified matters enormously once someone figured out that the bogs could be flooded and threshed so that the berries bob to the surface.) Other holdings include Native American tools, nautical items of historical interest, and extensive textiles, imaginatively presented. The complex also includes a Revolutionary powder house and—kids might get a kick of out this—a nicely restored 1872 outhouse.

BASEBALL

The Harwich Mariners, part of the Cape Cod Baseball League, play at Whithouse Field behind the High School in Harwich. For a schedule, contact the **Harwich Chamber of Commerce** (☎ 508/432-1600), the **Harwich Recreation & Youth Commission** (☎ 508/432-7553), or the **League** (☎ 508/432-6909).

KID STUFF

West Harwich gets some spillover from Dennis's overdevelopment, including such junior-tourist attractions as **Harbor Glen Miniature Golf** at 168 Rte. 28 (☎ 508/432-8240), the **Trampoline Center** at 296 Rte. 28 (☎ 508/432-8717), and **Bud's Go-Karts** at the intersection of Routes 28 and 39 (☎ 508/432-4964), which welcomes hot-rodders as young as 8, provided they meet the height requirement. All three are open late into the evening in summer. For free self-entertainment, visit **Castle in the Clouds,** a community-built playground behind the Harwich Elementary School on South Street in Harwich. Young culture mavens might want to take in a performance at the **Harwich Junior Theatre** at 105 Division St. in West Harwich (☎ 508/432-2002), which has been satisfying summer customers since 1952; if you plan to stick around for a while, they could even take classes and maybe work their way on-stage.

SHOPPING

Route 28 harbors lots of minimalls and shops, big on gifts (on the trite side) and unsensational art. With a few exceptions, save your power-shopping for Chatham.

ANTIQUES/COLLECTIBLES   ✪ **The Barn at Windsong,** 245 Bank St., ¹/₂ mile north of Harwich Port center, midway between Routes 28 and 39 (☎ 508/432-8281), is the kind of archetypal shop antiquers crave: a lovely old barn in the country, packed with premium goods. Highlights include needle arts including embroidered linens. Closed November through April.

The Mews at Harwich Port, 517 Rte. 28, in the center of town (☎ **508/ 432-6397**), is a shop run by five specialist dealers. It attracts collectors with certain categories to fill out—such as handwoven baskets. Closed November through April.

ARTS & CRAFTS   Cape Cod Cooperage, 1150 Old Queen Anne Rd., at the intersection of Route 137 (☎ **800/479-0788** or 508/432-0788), is the oldest surviving barrel factory in the state (in fact, the only one), and is packed to the rafters with useful wooden goods, mostly made on-site. You might come away with a naif-painted chest or just a set of Shaker pegs, but you're unlikely to depart empty-handed.

WHERE TO STAY
EXPENSIVE
✪ **The Beach House Inn.** 4 Braddock Lane (off Bank St., S of Rte. 28 in the center of town), Harwich Port, MA 02646. ☎ **800/870-4405** or 508/432-4444. Fax 508/432-9152. 14 rms. A/C TV TEL. Summer (including continental breakfast) $165–$275 double. MC, V.

One of the few waterside hostelries to remain open year-round (a boon for solitary-minded beachcombers), this intensively renovated 1920s honey is a real find. The original rooms still boast their varnished pine paneling, as well as updated whirlpool baths, and the four glorious front rooms, added in 1995, each feature a fireplace or deck as well, plus sweeping views of Nantucket Sound.

Dunscroft by the Sea. 24 Pilgrim Rd. (S of Rte. 28 near the beach), Harwich Port, MA 02646. ☎ **800/432-4345** or 508/432-0810. Fax 508/432-5134. 7 rms, 1 cottage. Summer (including full breakfast) $125–$250 double; $195 cottage. AE, MC, V.

Most people, upon finding such a prime property (a block from town, 500 feet from the beach), would be tempted to keep it all to themselves. But this gracious shingled colonial-revival home had been taking in guests since 1950, so Alyce and Wally Cunningham—who already owned a local motel—decided to make the leap to innkeeping. They've enhanced the house and honeymoon cottage (formerly the chauffeur's quarters) with extensive renovations in a Valentine-ish vein. One room, perfect for honeymooning types, has a king-size bed and a Jacuzzi for two. The cottage includes a kitchenette and TV with VCR.

Sandpiper Beach Inn. 16 Bank St. (S of Rte. 28 on the beach), Harwich Port, MA 02646. ☎ **800/433-2234** or 508/432-0485. 17 rms, 2 suites. A/C TV TEL. Summer (including continental breakfast) $120–$250 double; $225 suite. MC, V. Closed Nov–Apr.

Plunked right on the beach, this motel appears far too tasteful to be a motel. The breezy rooms are further brightened by splashy fabrics and pretty wicker furniture. All rooms have fridges and the suites have kitchenettes and Jacuzzis. For those who appreciate country-inn aesthetics but prefer the freedom of movement afforded by a more impersonal atmosphere, this could be just the ticket.

MODERATE
✪ **The Augustus Snow House.** 528 Main St. (in the center of town), Harwich Port, MA 02646. ☎ **800/320-0528** or 508/430-0528. Fax 508/432-7995, ext. 15. 5 rms. TV TEL. Summer (including full breakfast) $145–$160 double. AE, DISC, MC, V.

A local landmark for almost a century, this Queen Anne Victorian with gabled dormers and wraparound veranda is once again accepting guests. The house was precisely situated so that Captain Snow could look out the front door and see the ocean at the end of Pilgrim Lane. Rooms are spacious, immaculate, and very comfortable, with interesting antique appointments throughout. Several of the bathrooms are particularly unique, some with claw-foot tubs, old sink tables, and restored antique toilets. The full breakfast features such delicacies as peach kuchen, baked pears with raspberry and cream sauce, and cinnamon apple quiche. (Innkeeper Joyce Roth suggests you don't swim after breakfast.) The traditional Victorian high tea served in the Garden Room (open to the public) is becoming a popular tradition among locals.

The Commodore Inn. 30 Earle Rd. (about ^{1}/2 mile S of town center, off Rte. 28), W. Harwich, MA 02671. ☎ **800/368-1180** or 508/432-1180. Fax 508/432-4643. 27 rms. A/C TV TEL. Summer (including full breakfast) $119–$175 double. AE, MC, V. Closed Jan–Feb.

From the outside, it looks like an especially nice motel encircling a heated pool; from the inside, the rooms resemble upscale condos, with cathedral ceilings and handsome, functional furniture. Guests are treated to a buffet breakfast, and special dinners (a barbecue or clambake, for example) are offered regularly. Your lovely Scottish hostess, Flora MacFarlane-Jones, is exceptionally organized and gracious. This is one of the few small properties on the Cape that can accommodate meetings and provide business amenities.

WHERE TO DINE
MODERATE

Bishop's Terrace. 108 Rte. 28 (about ^{1}/2 mile E of Dennis border), W. Harwich. ☎ **508/432-0253.** Reservations recommended. Main courses $10–$25. MC, V. July–Aug daily 11:30am–2:30pm and 5–9pm; call for off-season hrs. Closed Jan–Feb. AMERICAN.

For decades this captain's manse was the place to dine. Generations have done so, since 1942, and will probably continue to, perceiving the rather retro menu a plus to be preserved. If your taste buds grow bored, peruse the top-quality scrimshaw in the parlor-turned-dining-room.

✪ **The Cape SeaGrille.** 31 Sea St. (S of Rte. 28 in the center of town), Harwich Port. ☎ **508/432-4745.** Reservations recommended. Main courses $11–$20. AE, MC, V. July–Aug daily 5–10pm; call for off-season hrs. Closed Nov–Mar. NEW AMERICAN.

A pair of ambitious chef/owners are the power behind the stove of this relatively recent (1994) upscale enterprise occupying the pared-down, peach-toned shell of an ordinary beach house. The menu is under constant revision, the better to springboard off market finds, but among the keepers are a refreshing appetizer platter of marinated seafoods (from ceviche to salmon carpaccio), and a grilled medley starring lobster, shrimp, and bacon-wrapped swordfish. City sophisticates who insist on creativity and innovation will find this the most consistently rewarding source in town.

L'Alouette. 787 Rte. 28 (about ^{1}/2 mile E of town center), Harwich Port. ☎ **508/430-0405.** Reservations recommended. Main courses $15–$23. AE, DC, DISC, MC, V. Tues–Sun 5–9pm; Sun noon–2:30pm. CLASSIC FRENCH.

Just as nothing can quite duplicate the delicate scent of a freshly washed Paris sidewalk, there's no way to fake the seductive aromas of an authentic French restaurant. The secrets are all in the stock, and chef Jean Louis Bastres, formerly of Biarritz, of course makes his from scratch. He's a strict classicist (none of this nouvelle nonsense): Specialties at this *auberge*-style restaurant include such time-honored tests of prowess as bouillabaisse and chateaubriand.

INEXPENSIVE

Seafood Sam's. 302 Rte. 28 (about ^{1}/2 mile E of town center), W. Harwich. ☎ **508/432-1422.** Most items under $12. Late May to early Sept daily 11am–8pm; call for off-season hrs. Closed Nov to mid-March. SEAFOOD.

Strategically located within a big bounce of the Trampoline Center, this McDonald's-style clam shack—part of a Cape-wide chain—dishes out deep-fried seafood, fast.

PICNIC FARE

The Cafe at Thompson's Farm Market. 761 Rte. 28 (about ¹/2 ｜
Harwich Port. ☎ **508/432-5415.**

Don't be dissuaded by the size: Yes, it's a full-size grocery store, but seek out the ᵈ…
bakery to throw together a beach lunch, or shop for some trendy comestibles.

SWEETS

Nick and Dick's. 606 Main St. (in the center of town), Harwich Port. ☎ **508/430-2444.**
Closed mid-Oct to late May. ICE CREAM.

Offering inspired sundaes like the "gooey grasshopper" and "pie in a dish," this ice-
cream stand is understandably a family favorite.

HIGH TEA

The Augustus Snow House. 528 Main St. (Rte. 28), Harwich Port. ☎ **508/432-7995.** Fixed-
price $12 regular tea, $20 tea plus special event. Thurs–Sat 1–5pm.

Elegant high tea at the prominent Augustus Snow House, a restored painted lady,
features three courses including delicate sandwiches (cucumber with mint butter for
instance), quiche, scones, and sweets. On selected dates, there are events like folk stories, ballads, and appropriately-themed lectures (Romance of the Rose, Victorian
Wedding Traditions).

THE HARWICHES AFTER DARK

Bishop's Terrace. 108 Rte. 28 (see "Where to Dine," above), W. Harwich. ☎ **508/432-0253.**
Cover varies.

There's usually a pops-oriented pianist playing in the barn-turned-bar, and on weekends you might encounter a jazz ensemble.

The Irish Pub. 126 Main St. (Rte. 28), W. Harwich. ☎ **508/432-8808.** No cover.

For years, this has been the premier Irish bar on the Cape. It feels authentic because
it is. Live entertainment on weekends is usually rollicking good fun.

3 Chatham

32 miles (52km) E of Sandwich, 24 miles (39km) S of Provincetown

Sticking out like a sore elbow (and out of the way of much of the Cape's tourist flow),
Chatham was one of the first spots to attract early explorers. Samuel de Champlain
stopped by in 1606 but got into a tussle with the prior occupants over some copper
cooking pots; he ended up leaving in a hurry. The first colonist to stick around was
William Nickerson, from Yarmouth, who befriended a local sachem (tribal leader)
and built a house beside his wigwam in 1656. One prospered; the other—for obvious reasons—didn't. To this day, listings for Nickersons still occupy a half-page in
the Cape Cod phone book.

Chatham, along with Provincetown, is the only area on the Cape to support a
commercial fishing fleet—against increasing odds. Overfishing has resulted in
closely monitored limits, to give the stock time to bounce back. Boats must now
go out as far as 100 miles to catch their fill. Despite the difficulties, it's a way of
life few locals would willingly relinquish. As in Provincetown, there's surprisingly
little animosity between the hard-working residents and summerers at play, perhaps
because it's clear that discerning tourist dollars are helping to preserve this lovely
town for all.

ESSENTIALS

GETTING THERE   After crossing either the Bourne or Sagamore bridge (see "Getting There" in chapter 3), head east on Route 6 and take Exit 11 south (Route 137) to Route 28. From this intersection, the village of South Chatham is about 1/2 mile west, and West Chatham is about 1 1/2 miles east. Chatham itself is about 2 miles farther east on Route 28.

To fly to Chatham, take a commercial flight into Hyannis (see "Getting There" in chapter 3), or contact **Chatham Air Charter** at the Chatham Municipal Airport (☎ **508/945-9000**).

VISITOR INFORMATION   Contact the **Chatham Chamber of Commerce,** 533 Main St., Chatham, MA 02633 (☎ **800/715-5567** or 508/945-5199) or the **Cape Cod Chamber of Commerce,** Routes 6 and 132, Hyannis, MA 02601 (☎ **508/ 362-3225;** fax 508/362-3698; Web site www.capecod.com).

A STROLL AROUND CHATHAM

Parking on Main Street can be a challenge at the height of summer, so pretend you're a turn-of-the-century traveler and start out at the **Chatham Railroad Museum** on 153 Depot St. (closed mid-September to mid-June), 1 block north of Main Street at the western end of town. You can't miss it: It's a gaudy 1887 Victorian station in the "Railroad Gothic" style, painted yellow with fanciful russet ornamentation. The building itself is full of railroading memorabilia, and the big exhibits—antique passenger cars—are out back.

If you've got children along, they'll surely want to stretch their legs (and imaginations) at the **Play-a-round park,** opposite. Dreamed up by prominent playground designer Robert Leathers, it's a marvelous maze of tubes and rope ladders, slides, and swings. The only way you'll get going again is to promise to come back.

Head west to the end of Depot Street and right on Old Harbor Road, which, followed past Main Street, becomes State Harbor Road. About 2/3 of a mile farther along, past Oyster Pond, you'll encounter the **Old Atwood House and Museums** at 347 Stage Harbor Rd. (☎ **508/945-2493;** closed October to mid-June). The 1752 house itself shelters the odds and ends collected by the Chatham Historical Society over the past 7 decades; piece by piece, they tell the story of the town. The Society even managed to save an entire 1947 "fishing camp," a run-down cottage that looks as if the occupant just stepped out to check a line.

Heading back toward Main Street, bear right on Cross Street and look for Chase Park and Bowling Green, presided over by the Old Grist Mill, built in the late 18th century. You might actually try some lawn bowling along the lovingly tended greens, before returning to Main Street, where the shops are too prolific and special to pass up. Then head eastward toward the shore, but be sure to duck into the **Mayo House** at 540 Main St. (☎ **508/945-4084**), a sweet little three-quarter Cape built in 1818. Entrance is free, and—if you've studiously avoided lengthy historical house tours so far—it can give you, in just a couple of minutes, a good sense of what life might have been like here in centuries past.

Main Street veers right when it reaches the shore. Continue along for about 1/4 mile to view the **Chatham Light,** an 1876 beacon not open to the public, but still in operation: its light shines 15 miles out to sea. This is a good vantage point from which to marvel over the "break" that burst through Chatham's barrier beach in 1987. In the years since, the newly created island, South Beach, has already glommed onto the coastline, becoming a peninsula. This is one landscape that rarely stays put for long.

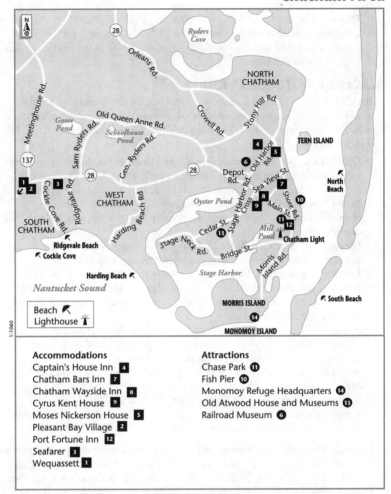

Accommodations
Captain's House Inn **4**
Chatham Bars Inn **7**
Chatham Wayside Inn **8**
Cyrus Kent House **9**
Moses Nickerson House **5**
Pleasant Bay Village **2**
Port Fortune Inn **12**
Seafarer **3**
Wequassett **1**

Attractions
Chase Park **11**
Fish Pier **10**
Monomoy Refuge Headquarters **14**
Old Atwood House and Museums **13**
Railroad Museum **6**

Retrace your steps northward along the shore. In about ³/₄ of a mile, you'll pass the grand **Chatham Bars Inn** at Shore Road and Seaview Street (☎ **800/527-4884** or 508/945-0096), which started out life as a private hunting lodge in 1914. Passersby are welcome to look around the lobby, recently restored to reflect its original Victorian splendor. Linger on the porch over coffee or a drink, if you like, before pressing on to the **Chatham Fish Pier,** about ¹/₈ mile farther along Shore Road (☎ **508/945-5186**). If you've timed your visit right (from noon on), the trawlers should just now be bringing in the catch of the day: you can observe the haul from an observation deck. Also have a look at *The Provider,* an intriguing outdoor sculpture by Woods Hole artist Sig Pursin.

☕ **WINDING DOWN** When you've had enough, or the insects seem to be insisting that you head on home, go back to Main Street down Seaview Street, past the Chatham Seaside Links golf course. One long block later (about ¹/₂ mile), you're back in the center of town. You can relax and unwind at the **Chatham**

Wayside Inn at 512 Main St. (☎ **800/391-5734** or 508/945-5550), which underwent a much-needed renovation in 1995. Secure a table on the greenery-curtained patio and watch the world go by, as you fortify yourself with regionally inspired snacks and sweets.

BEACHES & OUTDOOR PURSUITS

BEACHES   Chatham has an unusual array of beach styles, from the peaceful shores of the Nantucket Sound to the treacherous, shifting shoals along the Atlantic. For information on beach stickers ($7 per day, $35 per week), call **Town Hall** (☎ **508/945-5180**).

- **Cockle Cove Beach, Ridgevale Beach, and Hardings Beach.** Lined up along the sound, each at the end of its namesake road south of Route 28, these family-pleasing beaches offer gentle surf suitable for all ages, as well as full facilities.

- **Forest Beach.** No longer an officially recognized town beach (there's no lifeguard), this sound landing near the Harwich border is still popular, especially among surfboarders.

- **Oyster Pond Beach,** off Route 28. Only a block from Chatham's Main Street, this sheltered saltwater pond (with rest rooms) swarms with children.

- **Chatham Light Beach.** Located directly below the lighthouse parking lot (where stopovers are limited to 30 min.), this narrow stretch of sand is easy to get to: Just walk down the stairs. Currents here can be tricky and swift, though, so swimming is discouraged.

- **South Beach.** A former island jutting out slightly to the south of the Chatham Light, this glorified sandbar can be equally dangerous, so heed posted warnings and content yourself with strolling or, at most, wading.

- **North Beach.** Extending all the way south from Orleans, this 5-mile barrier beach is accessible from Chatham only by boat; for a fee, you can hop a water taxi from the **Chatham Fish Pier** on Shore Rd. (☎ **508/430-2346**). The round-trip cost is $12 adults, $5 children. Inquire about other possible drop-off points if you'd like to beach around.

BICYCLING   Though Chatham has no separate recreational paths per se, a demar-cated bike/blading lane makes a scenic, 8-mile circuit of town, heading south onto "The Neck," east to the Chatham Light, up Shore Road all the way to North Chatham, and back to the center of town. A descriptive brochure prepared by the **Chatham Chamber of Commerce** (☎ **800/715-5567** or 508/945-5199) shows the suggested route, and there are lots of lightly trafficked detours worth taking. Rent-als are available at **Bikes & Blades,** 195 Crowell Rd., Chatham (☎ **508/945-7600**).

BIRD WATCHING   In summer both the Cape Cod Museum of Natural History (see above) and the Wellfleet Bay Wildlife chapter of the **Audubon Society** (☎ **508/896-3867**) offer bird-watching trips to the **Monomoy National Wildlife Refuge** on North Monomoy Island. After a 10-minute boat ride from Chatham, you'll embark on a 4^1/$_2$-hour guided tour of the island, where you'll encounter a variety of species—from herring gulls and sandpipers to black-bellied plovers and willets. Tours cost around $40 and are recommended not just for avid bird-watchers, but for anyone who enjoys the outdoors.

BOATING   **Cape Cod Coastal Canoe & Kayak** (☎ **888/226-6393** or 508/564-4051; E-mail cccanoe@capecod.net; Web site www.capecod.net/canoe/) runs naturalist-guided trips throughout the Cape, sponsored by the Cape Cod Museum of Natural History. In Chatham, they paddle down the Oyster River, past Hardings

Beach, and over to Morris Island. There is also a special all-day trip through Pleasant Bay to the inside shore of the Outer Beach. Trips (3½ to 4 hr.) are daily April through August, weekends through October, and cost $25 per paddler or $50 per family. All equipment is supplied. Call for schedule.

Seaworthy vessels, from surf- and sailboards to paddle craft and Sunfish, can be rented from **Monomoy Sail and Cycle** at 275 Rte. 28 in North Chatham (☎ 508/945-0811). Pleasant Bay, the Cape's largest embayment, is the best place to play, for those with sufficient experience; if the winds don't seem to be going your way, try Forest Beach on the South Chatham shore.

FISHING   Chatham has five ponds and lakes that permit fishing; Goose Pond off Fisherman's Landing is among the top spots. For saltwater fishing sans boat, try the fishing bridge on Bridge Street at the southern end of Mill Pond. First, though, get a license at **Town Hall** at 549 Main St. in Chatham (☎ **508/945-5101**). If you hear the deep sea calling, sign on with the *Booby Hatch* (☎ 508/430-2312), a 33-foot sportfisherman out of Chatham, or the *Banshee* (☎ 508/945-0403) or *Tiger Too* (☎ 508/945-9215), both berthed in Stage Harbor. Shellfishing licenses are available at the **Town Hall Annex** on George Ryder Road in West Chatham (☎ **508/945-5180**).

FITNESS   The **Chatham Health & Swim Club** at 251 Crowell Rd. in Chatham (☎ 508/945-3555) offers bicycles and treadmills, weights and aerobics, steam rooms and whirlpool, a five-lane indoor lap pool, and more.

GOLF   Once part of the Chatham Bars Inn property and now owned by the town, the scenic 9-hole, par-34 **Chatham Seaside Links** at 209 Seaview St. in Chatham (☎ 508/945-4774) isn't very challenging, but fun for neophytes; inquire about instruction.

NATURE & WILDLIFE AREAS   Heading southeast from the Harding's Beach parking lot, the 2-mile, round-trip **Seaside Trail** offers beautiful parallel panoramas of Nantucket Sound and Oyster Pond River; keep an eye out for nesting pairs of horned lark. Access to 40-acre Morris Island, southwest of the Chatham Light, is easy: You can walk or drive across and start right in on a marked ¾ mile trail. Heed the high tides, as advised, though—they can come in surprisingly quickly, leaving you stranded.

Chatham's natural bonanza lies southward: The uninhabited ✪ **Monomoy Islands,** 2,750 acres of brush-covered sand favored by some 285 species of migrating birds, is the perfect pit stop along the Atlantic Flyway. Harbor and gray seals are catching on, too: Hundreds now carpet the coastline from late November through May. If you go out during that time, you won't have any trouble seeing them— they're practically unavoidable. Shuttle service to South Island is available aboard the **Rip Ryder** out of the Stage Harbor Marina (☎ 508/945-5450), but you'll get a lot more out of the trip—and probably leave this unspoiled landscape in better shape— if you let a naturalist lead the way. Both the **Wellfleet Bay Wildlife Sanctuary** operated by the Audubon Society (☎ 508/349-2615) and Brewster's **Cape Cod Museum of Natural History** (☎ 508/896-3867) offer guided trips. The Audubon's 3-hour or 7-hour trips take place April through November, and they cost $25 to $55 per person. The boat to Monomoy leaves from Chatham and the trip includes a naturalist-guided nature hike. About a dozen times each summer, the museum even organizes sleep-overs in the island's only surviving structure, a clapboard "keeper's house" flanked by an 1849 lighthouse. The cost is $130 per person, (dinner and breakfast provided), and the trip lasts from 10am until returning the next day at 1pm. Reservations should be made at least a month prior, as there is only space for six people in the three rooms. It's just you and the birds and seals and lots of deer, plus various other species that are harder to spot.

TENNIS   Public courts are located near the Railroad Museum on Depot Street and at Chatham High School on Crowell Road; for details, contact the **Chatham Recreation Department** (☎ **508/945-5100**). In addition, you may be able to rent a court at the **Chatham Bars Inn** on Shore Road (☎ **508/945-6759**), or the **Chatham Beach and Tennis Club** at 12 Main St. (☎ **508/945-0464**).

A FLIGHTSEEING TOUR

✪ **Cape Cod Flying Circus.** Chatham Municipal Airport, off George Ryder Rd. (about ¹/₄ mile N of Rte. 28). ☎ **508/945-9000.** Flights $50 and up. By appointment, May to mid-Sept 8:30am–8:30pm; mid-Sept to Apr 8:30am–7pm.

The best way to get a feel for the dramatic changes affecting Chatham's shoreline is a fly-by. Pilot Jim McDevitt has three planes at the ready: two tiny (three-passenger) Cessna Skyhawks and a 1978 replica of a 1927 open-cockpit biplane, in which he'll gladly treat thrill-seeking sorts to loops, rolls, and other inversionary maneuvers.

CHATHAM HISTORICAL SIGHTS

Chatham Railroad Museum. 153 Depot St. (off Main St., 1 block N of the rotary). No phone. Free admission. Mid-June to mid-Sept Tues–Sat 10am–4pm. Closed mid-Sept to mid-June.

Even if you're not a railroad fanatic, it's worth visiting this beautiful 1887 depot to imagine the sights that would greet a Victorian visitor. To begin, the building itself is a "Railroad Gothic" work of wooden art, topped by a tapering turret. Inside you'll find vintage-uniformed volunteers dispensing lore and explaining the many displays. The museum's major holdings are lined up in back: an assortment of vintage train cars, including a "walk-through" 1918 New York caboose.

Mayo House. 540 Main St. (in the center of town). ☎ **508/945-4084.** Free admission. Mid-June to Sept Tues–Thurs 11am–4pm. Closed Oct to mid-June.

For a speedy version of the historical house tour (these can get awfully drawn out), duck into this cheerful little yellow cottage, a three-quarter Cape that has stood its ground on Main Street since 1818. Ask all the questions you like—or just zip through, admiring the needlepoint handiwork of local lasses long gone, or the economy of movement required to subsist in one of the tiny dormered bedrooms.

The Old Atwood House Museum. 347 Stage Harbor Rd. (about ²/₃ of a mile S of Main St.). ☎ **508/945-2493.** Admission $3 adults, $1 students under 12. Mid-June to Sept Tues–Fri 1–4pm. Closed Oct to mid-June.

For further glimpses of Chatham's past, visit this gambrel-roofed 1752 homestead, chopped up (rather awkwardly) into assorted wings celebrating different phases and products of the local culture. The house harbors all sorts of odd collections, from seashells to the complete works of early-20th-century author Joseph C. Lincoln, a renowned Cape writer who now goes all but unread. One room definitely worth a visit is the New Gallery, featuring admirably direct portraits of crusty sea-goers by local artist Frederick Stallknecht. His work, unfortunately, was always overshadowed by the oeuvre of his mother, Alice Stallknecht Wight, who executed pretend-primitive murals of villagers enacting religious scenes (a contemporary Christ-as-fisherman, for instance, celebrating the Last Supper). Her work occupies an adjoining barn; see if you think she deserves it. By far the most enchanting exhibit on hand is an entire 1947 fishing "camp"—a one-room old boy's club salvaged, complete with shabby furnishings, from the onslaught of the winter storms that brought about the "break" of 1987.

BASEBALL

The Chatham Athletics (or "A's"), part of the Cape Cod Baseball League, play at Veterans Field off Depot Street. For a schedule, contact the **Chatham Chamber of Commerce** (☎ 800/715-5567 or 508/945-5199), the **Chatham Recreation Center** (☎ 508/945-5175), or the **League** (☎ 508/432-6909).

KID STUFF

The **Play-a-round park** on Depot Street (see "A Stroll Around Chatham," above) will suffice to keep kids entertained for hours on end. Treat them to lunch at the quirkily casual Breakaway Cafe at the Chatham airport (perhaps followed by a sightseeing flight?). The weekly **band concerts** at Kate Gould Park, held Friday nights in summer, are perfectly gauged for underage enjoyment: There's usually a bunny-hop at some point in the evening. Junior connoisseurs get a chance, once a year in late July, to enjoy some really fine music, when the Monomoy Chamber Ensemble puts on a free morning children's performance at the **Monomoy Theatre** (☎ 508/945-1589), and musicals there are always fun.

SHOPPING

Chatham, its tree-shaded Main Street lined with specialty stores, offers a terrific opportunity to shop and stroll. The goods tend to be on the conservative side, but every so often you'll happen upon a hedonistic delight.

ANTIQUES/COLLECTIBLES Mildred Georges Antiques, 447 Main St., in the center of town (☎ 508/945-1939), is a fun jumble of a shop. If you're the kind of antiques-seeker who is keen on clutter, you'll find the jewelry cases are especially rewarding. You can also paw through sheet music, beyond-vintage clothing, and all sorts of odd collectibles. Closed November through April.

The Spyglass, 618 Main St., is located in the center of town (☎ 508/945-9686). Ancient nautical instruments are the raison d'être of this intriguing shop: antique telescopes, sextants, barometers, captains' desks, and maps and charts.

1736 House Antiques, 1731 Rte. 28, is located about ¹/₂ mile east of Route 137 (☎ 508/945-5690). This rambling old full Cape is loaded with real finds, including such rarities as primitive painted furniture.

ARTS & CRAFTS The Artful Hand Gallery, 459 Main St., in the center of town (☎ 508/945-4933), Boston's premier purveyor of superlative contemporary crafts, has two Cape outposts, here and in Orleans (see "Shopping" under "Orleans," below).

Headed for such prestigious outlets as Neiman Marcus, the handblown glassworks of husband-and-wife team James Holmes and Deborah Doane originate at **Chatham Glass,** 758 Main St., just west of the Chatham rotary (☎ 508/945-5547), where you can literally look over their shoulders as the pieces take shape. Luscious colors are their hallmark; the intense hues, combined with a purity of form at once traditional and cutting-edge contemporary, add up to objects that demand to be coveted. Closed Sunday.

At **Chatham Pottery,** 2058 Rte. 28, east of intersection with Route 137 (☎ 508/430-2191), striking graphics characterize the collaborative work of Gill Wilson (potter) and Margaret Wilson-Grey (glazer). Their work consists primarily of blue block-print–style designs set against off-white stoneware: it's a look that's somewhat addictive. Luckily, it's available in everything from platters and bowls to lamps and tiles.

One of Chatham's oldest and most respected galleries is **Falconer's** (492 Main St., Chatham; ☎ 508/945-2867), which started by showing just the work of Marguerite

Falconer: oil paintings of Cape Cod scenes. Since 1991, her daughter Susan has managed the gallery and expanded the work on display to include some of the more interesting fine crafts available in town. This is a good place to look for that one-of-a-kind gift.

Installed in a 1920s horse barn (the rough-hewn stalls make handsome niches), **Munson Gallery,** 880 Rte. 28, about ¹/₈ mile northwest of the rotary, Chatham (☎ **508/945-2888**), has maintained a stellar track record since 1955. Most of the artists represented at this primarily contemporary gallery are still active; then again, you might come across such venerable work as magazine engravings by Winslow Homer. Closed mid-October to mid-June.

BOOKS   Yellow Umbrella Bookstore, 501 Main St., in the center of town (☎ **508/945-0144**), offers both new and used books (from rare volumes to paperbacks perfect for a disposable beach read), this full-service, all-ages bookstore invites protracted browsing.

FASHION   **Catering to fashionable parents and their kids, ages newborn well into the teens, **The Children's Shop, 515 Main St., in the center of town (☎ **508/945-0234**), is the best children's clothing store in a 100-mile radius. While according a nod to doting grannies with such classics as hand-smocked party dresses, Ginny Nickerson Carter also stays up-to-speed on what kids themselves prefer.

The flagship store of **Puritan Clothing Company** is located at 573 Main St., Chatham (☎ **508/945-0326**). This venerable institution, with stores all over the Cape, has updated its clothing considerably in the last 10 years. You'll find a wide range of quality men's and women's wear, including Polo, Nautica, Eileen Fisher, and Teva, at good prices.

Another Cape Cod institution, the elite **Mark, Fore & Strike** at 482 Main St., Chatham (☎ **508/945-0568**), offers upscale and classic men's and women's sportswear. There's also a branch in Osterville.

GIFTS/HOME DECOR   **Consider it a test of self-esteem: If you allow yourself to indulge in the luxurious personal-care products and boudoir accessories at **Midsummer Nights, 471 Main St., in the center of town (☎ **508/945-5562**)—including some very stylish, understated lingerie—your self-image couldn't be healthier.

For quintessentially Cape-y gifts, stop in the **Regatta Shop,** 582 Main St., Chatham (☎ **800/432-1365** or 508/945-4999). It's a colorful shop with items like a brass clipper-ship lamp, a lighthouse table (hand-painted with a glass top), and the intriguing weather glass that supposedly predicts the weather.

Pentimento, 584 Main St., in the center of town (☎ **508/945-0178**), is one of those great stores for browsing, even on a sunny day. Pentimento is packed with perfect summery clothing, ranging in style from neo-Victorian to minimalist contemporary. It also stocks some fun baby stuff, tasteful home accents, and not-too-tacky tourist gewgaws.

WHERE TO STAY
VERY EXPENSIVE

✪ **Chatham Bars Inn.** Shore Rd. (off Seaview St., about ¹/₂ mile NW of town center), Chatham, MA 02633. ☎ **800/527-4884** or 508/945-0096. Fax 508/945-5491. 132 rms, 20 suites. A/C TV TEL. Summer $170–$365 double; $385–$675 1-bedrm suite; $540–$1,000 2-bedrm suite. MAP and off-season packages available. AE, DC, MC, V.

A private hunting lodge built for a Boston family in 1914, this curved and colonnaded brick building—surrounded by 26 shingled cottages on 20 acres—has regained its glory days with recent renovations. The latest undertaking is a Victorian makeover, meant to lend the lovely behemoth a more imposing air. It still lends itself well to relaxing, though, with private balconies pitched off most of the rooms, and a large and cushy lobby that clearly invites lingering. The best spot to take in the grandeur—as well as the sweeping sea views—is the breezy veranda.

Dining/Entertainment: Options include the formal Main Dining Room (see "Where to Dine," below); the adjoining North Beach Tavern & Grille, which serves much the same menu, with many more choices and extended hours (open daily 11am to 10pm); and the seasonal Beach House Grill, which, in addition to offering a breakfast buffet and lunch (7am to 3pm) and light fare into the evening (3 to 8pm), puts on a prix-fixe theme feast with live bands (see "Chatham After Dark," below) 3 evenings a week.

Services: "Beach Buddies," a complimentary children's program for ages 3¹/₂ and up, is available morning through night in summer; baby-sitters are on call for younger guests. Room service is available from 7am to 10am in season, and the concierge can offer advice on local excursions.

Facilities: The property encompasses four all-weather tennis courts and a putting green (Seaside Links, a town-owned 9-hole course open to the public, adjoins the resort), plus shuffleboard, croquet, and volleyball. There is a basic fitness room, and a heated outdoor pool beside ¹/₄ mile private beach, where you can also catch a complimentary launch to Nauset Beach. The inn can accommodate conferences large and small.

✪ **Pleasant Bay Village.** 1191 Rte. 28 (about 3 miles N of Chatham center), Chathamport, MA 02633. ☎ **800/547-1011** or 508/945-1133. Fax 508/945-9701. 48 rms, 10 suites. A/C TV TEL. Summer $195–$245 double; $395–$455 1- or 2-bedrm suite (for 4 occupants). AE, MC, V. Closed Nov–Apr.

Owner Howard Gamsey is a prodigious gardener: Over the past quarter-century, he has transformed what was an ordinary motel into a playful Zen paradise, where a waterfall cascades through a colorful rock garden into a stone-edged pool dotted with lily pads and flashing koi. Actually, he has poured that kind of attention into the entire 6-acre complex. The rooms and cottages, done up in restful pastels, are unusually pleasant. Many bathrooms feature marble countertops and stone floors. Howard is an art collector, and all rooms display wonderful pieces he has picked up at Wellfleet's finest galleries. The rooms have hair dryers and refrigerators. The breakfast room features antique kilims, crewel curtains, and antique tables. In summer, you can order lunch from the grill without having to leave your place at the heated pool. In season, dinner is also served here.

✪ **Wequassett Inn.** 178 Rte. 28 (about 5 miles NW of town center, on Pleasant Bay), Chatham, MA 02633. ☎ **800/225-7125** or 508/432-5400. Fax 508/432-1915. 104 rms. A/C MINIBAR TV TEL. Summer $270–$500 double. AE, DC, DISC, MC, V. Closed late Nov to Mar.

A virtual village occupying its own little "crescent on the water" (the Algonquian name for Round Cove on Pleasant Bay), this low-key, 22-acre complex should quash any preconceived notions of what constitutes a cottage colony. Tucked amid the woods along the shore, 15 modest dwellings, built in the 1940s, harbor roomy quarters done up in an opulent country style: They cost a bit more than the 56 more modern "villa" rooms but, with their picturesque settings, are definitely worth the surcharge. This is one of those places where—well housed, well fed, and pleasantly occupied indeed—you're assured of a temporary respite from the "real" world. And that has its price.

Dining/Entertainment: The 18th-century Eben Ryder House is home to an excellent restaurant (see "Where to Dine," below); lighter fare is served at the Pool Bar & Grille from 10am to 6pm for guests only.

Services: Instruction is available in tennis (there are three pros on-site), sailing (coordinated by Cape Water Sports), and saltwater fly-fishing (a branch of the Orvis School); inquire about clinic packages. Complimentary van service is offered to two public golf courses, Cranberry Valley in Harwich and Captain's Course in Brewster, and to Chatham and Orleans villages for shopping; box lunches are available on request. A concierge is on hand to recommend activities; a recreation manager, to facilitate them.

Facilities: Guests have access (for a fee) to four all-weather Plexipave tennis courts, plus a pro shop. Bikes and water crafts—sailboards, Sunfish, Daysailers, and Hobie Cats—may be rented on-site. Croquet and volleyball equipment may be borrowed gratis. A fitness room (with weights and aerobics videotapes) adjoins the heated pear-shaped pool set at the neck of Clam Point, a calm beach. Nauset Beach is a 15-minute ride via the inn's Power Skiff; bay tours and fishing charters can also be arranged. A total of 11 meeting rooms can accommodate up to 220 conference participants.

EXPENSIVE

✪ **Captain's House Inn.** 369-377 Old Harbor Rd. (about $1/2$ mile N of the rotary), Chatham, MA 02633. ☎ **800/315-0728** or 508/945-0127. Fax 508/945-0866. 16 rms, 3 suites. A/C TEL. Summer (including full breakfast and afternoon tea) $135–$325 double. AE, MC, V.

This 1839 Greek Revival house set—along with a cottage and carriage house—on 2 meticulously maintained acres is a shining example of its era and style. The rooms, named for Capt. Hiram Harding's ships, are richly furnished, with a preponderance of canopied four-posters, beamed ceilings, and, in some cases, brick hearths. All rooms have hair dryers, and some are equipped with Jacuzzis and televisions with VCRs. Bikes are available for guests intent on exploring. One of the few B&Bs to serve the morning repast at noncommunal tables (a thoughtful touch for those of us slow to rev up, sociability-wise), the window-walled breakfast room is also the site of a traditional tea—presided over by innkeeper Jan McMasters, formerly of Bournemouth in Great Britain, who knows how to pour a proper cuppa.

Chatham Wayside Inn. 512 Main St. (in the center of town), Chatham, MA 02633. ☎ **800/391-5734** or 508/945-5550. Fax 508/945-3407. 48 rms, 8 suites. A/C TV TEL. Summer $145–$255 double; $285–$310 suite. Off-season packages available. AE, DISC, MC, V.

Resurrected from the brink of dereliction, this former stagecoach stop dating from 1860 has reassumed its rightful stature. Don't expect any musty antique trappings: This is a thoroughly modern reno, with lush carpeting, a warehouse worth of Waverly fabrics, and polished reproduction furnishings, including four-posters. Most rooms have VCRs. There's an outdoor heated pool in the back. The restaurant serves sophisticated New American fare, indoors and out, and the prize rooms—for old-fashioned heavy-metal fans, at least—boast patios or balconies overlooking the town bandstand.

The Cyrus Kent House Inn. 63 Cross St. (1 block S of Main St. in the center of town), Chatham, MA 02633. ☎ **800/338-5368** or 508/945-9104. 8 rms, 3 suites. A/C TV TEL. Summer (including continental breakfast) $135–$165 double; $185–$250 suite. AE, MC, V.

Built in 1877, when sea captains lived like modern-day software moguls, this tall Victorian beauty was lavished with the latest in fancy fixings, including marble fireplaces (in both the butterscotch-yellow parlor and the wainscoted dining room) and a heavy helping of decorative plasterwork. Rooms, with very high ceilings, have canopy beds and are decorated with antiques. There are more fireplaces scattered about: an open hearth in the lovely country kitchen where innkeeper Sharon Mitchell Swan bakes the day's complement of muffins and breads, and one each in the slightly more modern carriage-house suites, rendered light and airy by a lofty Palladian window on the top floor and, below, French doors that give onto the garden.

Port Fortune Inn. 201 Main St. (on the shore, near Chatham Light), Chatham, MA 02633. ☎ **800/750-0792** or 508/945-0792. Fax 508/945-0792. 13 rms. A/C TEL. Summer (including continental breakfast) $130–$190 double; call for off-season rates. AE, MC, V. Closed Jan.

This classic shingled cottage (formerly named Inn Among Friends), newly restored and redecorated, is just a short stroll from the beach. The cheerful name comes from explorer Samuel de Champlain, who named this area Port Fortune when he landed in Chatham in 1606. A couple of the cozy rooms have water views, and all have queen-size beds. One room is also handicapped accessible. Breakfast with an ocean view is served in the front building, which also has a few rooms upstairs that share the view.

MODERATE

Moses Nickerson House. 364 Old Harbor Rd. (about $^1/_2$ mile N of Main St.), Chatham, MA 02633. ☎ **800/628-6972** or 508/945-5859. Fax 508/945-7087. Web site www.virtualcapecod.com/market/mnickerson/. 7 rms. A/C. TV on request. Summer (including full breakfast and tea or wine) $129–$179 double. AE, DISC, MC, V.

There's that last name again. A grand captain's home in the classicist style, this 1839 manse is every inch devoted to stylish comfort. Whether you opt for a canopied featherbed with hand-ironed linens or a ruggedly handsome, hunt-club–style room, rest assured you'll be pampered—with a home-baked breakfast in the garden-view solarium, and later a late-afternoon pick-me-up in the dazzling parlor, which is mostly white, with glints of vintage cranberry glass.

The Seafarer of Chatham. 2079 Rte. 28 (about $^1/_2$ mile E of Rte. 137), W. Chatham, MA 02633. ☎ **800/786-2772** or 508/432-1739. Fax 508/432-1739. 20 rms. A/C TV TEL. Summer $98–$145 double. AE, MC, V. Closed Dec–Mar.

Convenient to Chatham's sound-side beaches (Ridgevale Beach is about $^1/_2$ mile due south), this personable Cape-style motel is shielded from the road by stately trees. Innkeeper Cathleen Houhoulis has decorated the spotless rooms with Early American–style stenciling, and both she and her husband, John, take pains to familiarize neophytes with the area. Behind the low-slung building you'll find a sheltered garden—sans pool, the better to celebrate the peace and quiet.

WHERE TO DINE
EXPENSIVE

☼ **Eben Ryder House.** Wequassett Inn on Pleasant Bay, 178 Rte. 28 (about 5 miles NW of town center). ☎ **800/225-7125** or 508/432-5400. Fax 508/432-1915. Reservations suggested. Jacket requested. Main courses $18–$34. AE, DC, DISC, MC, V. Apr to late Nov 7am–10pm. Closed late Nov to Mar. REGIONAL AMERICAN.

Reliably, season after season, Frank McMullen has proved himself to be a deft and often dazzling chef. Guests would surely squawk if some of his cherished dishes were ever supplanted. The sautéed lobster and crab cakes, for instance, are a definite keeper, as are the grilled Nantucket scallops with cracked black pepper, parsnip puree, and creamy Chatham lobster sauce. But it's always fun to see him kick up his heels with some world-beat concoction like banana-chip encrusted striped bass served with guava and coconut nectars, or an incendiary Jamaican mixed grill of salmon, shrimp, and swordfish. All this, and dreamy cove views.

MODERATE

Chatham Wayside Inn. 512 Main St. (in the center of town). ☎ **508/945-5550.** Main courses $13–$22. AE, DISC, MC, V. Daily 7am–10pm. NEW AMERICAN.

Refreshingly spare and airy, this dining room makes not the slightest nod to its tavernal past (unless you count the small, sleek bar). Napery is minimal, the better to show off the gleaming wood tables, and seating takes the form of comfy Windsor chairs. More important, perhaps, is what's on the plate. New chef Shane Coughlin brings his own flair to basic Wayside specialties like crab cakes, or entrees like rack of lamb and pesto cod. For something a little different, try the chowder; it's prepared Portuguese style with double-smoked bacon, fresh quahogs, and red bliss potatoes. Whether summer or winter, you'll want to end your meal with the apple-and-cranberry crisp; the secret is the oatmeal and brown-sugar crust.

Christian's. 443 Main St. (in the center of town). ☎ **508/945-3362.** Reservations recommended. Main courses $10–$20. AE, DISC, MC, V. Apr–Dec 11:30am–3pm and 5–10pm; call for off-season hrs. NEW AMERICAN.

This popular boîte is now owned by the Chatham Wayside Inn, but they are keeping the atmosphere, particularly the fab bar upstairs, the same. Specifically, the summer-only downstairs dining rooms enjoy an *auberge*-like French country decor, whereas Upstairs at Christian's (open year-round) is British clubby, with leather couches, mahogany paneling, and a smattering of classic movie posters. The same cinematic-motif menu applies to both venues: famous movie titles are accorded to such specialties as escargots in marsala sauce—a.k.a. Casablanca.

The Impudent Oyster. 15 Chatham Bars Ave. (off Main St., in the center of town). ☎ **508/945-3545.** Reservations suggested. Main courses $8–$20. AE, MC, V. Mon–Sat 11:30am–3pm, Sun noon–3pm; daily 5–10pm. INTERNATIONAL.

All but hidden off the main drag, this perennially popular 1970s-era eatery—complete with decorative stained glass—continues to cook up fabulous fish in exotic guises, ranging from Mexican to Szechuan, but mostly continental.

✪ **The Main Dining Room.** Chatham Bars Inn, Shore Rd. (about ¹⁄₃ mile NW of town center). ☎ **800/527-4884** or 508/945-0096. Fax 508/945-5491. Reservations and jacket required. Main courses $13–$20. AE, DC, MC, V. Mid-May to mid-Nov daily 8–11am; Sun–Fri 6–9pm, Sat 6:30–9pm; call for off-season hrs. NEW AMERICAN.

If it's grandeur you're after, the setting supplies a surplus. This water-view dining room is vast, of the ballroom dimensions all but lost in the modern age. In assuming the reins in the kitchen, Al Hynes, formerly of Harwich Port's HarborWatch Room (now a private club), has reined in the prices as well, while upping the portions. His roast rack of lamb Provençal—seasoned with three mustards, coated with herbed bread crumbs, and cloaked in a *vert pré* sauce—would set you back considerably more just about anywhere else, without presenting so interesting a twist.

✪ **Vining's Bistro.** 595 Main St. (in the center of town). ☎ **508/945-5033.** Reservations not accepted. Main courses $12–$17. AE, DC, MC, V. Apr to early Sept daily 5:30–10pm; call for off-season hrs. FUSION.

If you're looking for cutting-edge cuisine in a sophisticated setting, venture upstairs at Chatham's innocuous-looking minimall and into this ineffably cool cafe. The film-noirish wall murals suggest a certain bohemian abandon, but the menu is up-to-the-minute and priced to suit young people. Warm lobster taco with salsa fresca and crème fraîche, a spit-roasted chicken suffused with achiote-lime marinade and sided with a salad of oranges and jicama—these are very intelligent juxtapositions, and reason enough to keep returning.

INEXPENSIVE

The Breakaway Cafe. Chatham Municipal Airport, off George Ryders Rd. (about a ¹⁄₄ mile N of Rte. 28). ☎ **508/945-3637.** All items under $10. DISC, MC, V. July–Aug daily 7am–2pm; call for off-season hrs. AMERICAN.

Basically the attic of Chatham's tiny airport, this playful cafe is smaller than a Cessna. Kids will enjoy watching the private planes take off and land. Breakfast items include a number of special waffle dishes with fresh fruits. For lunch, the homemade soups, including the clam chowder, are standouts. There's always locally caught seafood on the menu, too.

Carmine's Pizza. 595 Main St. (in the center of town). ☎ **508/945-5300.** Most items under $15. No credit cards. July to mid-Sept Sun–Thurs 11am–8pm, Fri–Sat 11am–11pm; mid-Sept to June Sun–Thurs 11:30am–9pm, Fri–Sat 10am–9pm. ITALIAN.

A New Wave pizzeria that pays homage to the old ways with checkered tablecloths and soda-parlor chairs, this little eatery takes a bold approach to toppings—e.g., pineapple, jalapenos, and hot cherry pepper rings, in addition to the traditional garlic and crushed red pepper. Actually, that's the lineup of special ingredients for the "Pizza from Hell," sure to be a hit with hotheads. Cool down with creamy gelato.

TAKE-OUT & PICNIC FARE

Chatham Cookware. 524 Main St. (in the center of town). ☎ **508/945-1550.**

Stop in to get a lemon-grater or latte-maker, and you're bound to walk out with some of Vera Champlain's edible goods: a stunning soup du jour accompanied by some tasty hors-d'oeuvres-to-go, or perhaps some knockout pastries, as pretty as they are delectable. You might even end up lunching, soup and sandwich, in the tiny dining room so thoughtfully provided.

The Cornfield. 1291 Rte. 28 (about 3/4 of a mile W of the Chatham rotary).

A minimall catering to discriminating tastes, this cheerful roadside complex encompasses a branch of **Fancy's Farm Market,** an excellent greengrocer based in Orleans (☎ **508/945-1949**); an inviting deli/bakery, the **Pampered Palate** (☎ **800/724-5354** or 508/945-3663); and the retail outlet of local wholesaler **Chatham Fish & Lobster Co.** (☎ **508/945-1178**). The main tourist attraction, though, is the somewhat deceptively named **Chatham Winery** (☎ **508/945-0300**), whose products are blended, rather than made, here. If you like sweetish wines, you're in luck. Otherwise, the lobster-shaped bottles make a nice gift presentation (preferably for someone who doesn't drink, though the cranberry vinegar's not bad).

Marion's Pie Shop. 2022 Rte. 28 (about 1/2 mile E of Rte. 137). ☎ **508/432-9439.**

Nearly a half-century's worth of summerers have come to depend on this bakery for dinner and dessert pies, from sea clam to lemon meringue. Load up on the fruit breads and sweet rolls, and you can pretend you're having a four-course B&B breakfast—on the beach.

FRESH SEAFOOD

Nickerson Fish & Lobster. Chatham Fish Pier, Shore Rd. ☎ **508/945-0145.** Closed mid-Oct to late May.

The fish have to travel all of 50 yards from the boat, so you can imagine how fresh they are. And you don't need a kitchen to partake: They sell homemade quahog (giant clam) chowder and precooked frozen entrees to go.

SWEETS

Chatham Candy Manor. 484 Main St. (in the center of town). ☎ **800/221-6497** or 508/945-0825.

Normally, I cross the street to avoid this type of temptation, but Naomi Turner's hand-dipped chocolates (her mother opened the shop in the 1940s) are just too good to pass up. Surely there can't be anything too terribly harmful in an occasional "cranberry cordial" or chocolate-tipped strawberry, right? But once you start perusing the old-fashioned oak cases, it can be very hard to stop.

CHATHAM AFTER DARK

While most towns boast some comparable event, Chatham's **free band concerts**—40 players strong—are arguably the best on the Cape and attract crowds in the thousands. This is small-town America at its most nostalgic, as the band, made up mostly of local folks, plays those standards of yesteryear that never go out of style. Held in Kate Gould Park (off Chatham Bars Avenue, in the center of town) from July through early September, it kicks off at 8pm every Friday. Better come early to claim your square of lawn, and be prepared to sing—or dance—along. Call ☎ **508/945-5199** for information.

PERFORMANCE ARTS

Monomoy Theatre. 776 Rte. 28 (about $^1/_4$ mile W of the rotary). ☎ **508/945-1589.** Performances mid-June to Aug Tues–Wed and Fri–Sat at 8:30pm, Thurs 2 and 8:30pm. Closed Sept to mid-June. Tickets $12–$23.

Every summer since 1958, the Ohio University Players have commuted to this jewel box of a 1930s theater to put on a challenging play a week, from musicals to Shakespeare. In late July they take a well-earned week off to cede the stage to the highly accomplished Monomoy Chamber Ensemble.

BARS & LIVE MUSIC

The Beach House Grill. At Chatham Bars Inn (see "Where to Stay," above). ☎ **508/945-0096.** Closed early Sept to mid-June. Cover varies.

Live bands accompany the three weekly feasts held at this casual beachside restaurant: Beach party music to go with the Monday-night barbecue, Dixieland to accompany Wednesday's clambake, and Calypso for Thursday's Caribbean blowout.

✪ **The Chatham Squire.** 487 Main St. (in the center of town). ☎ **508/945-0945.** Cover varies.

A great leveler, this local institution attracts patrons from all the social strata in town. CEOs, seafarers, and collegiates alike convene to kibitz over the roar of a jukebox or band, and the din of their own hubbub.

Upstairs at Christian's. 443 Main St. (in the center of town). ☎ **508/945-3362.** No cover.

Beloved of moneyed locals, this sporting piano bar has the air of a vintage frat house—it summons up young scions gracefully slumming it among scuffed leather couches and purloined movie posters. Cinematically themed nibbles are always available to offset the generous movie-motif drinks.

4 Orleans

31 miles (50km) E of Sandwich, 25 miles (40km) S of Provincetown

Orleans is where the "Narrow Land" (the early Algonquian name for the Cape) starts to get very narrow indeed: From here on up—or "down," in paradoxical local parlance—it's never more than a few miles wide from coast to coast, and in some spots as little as one. All three main roads (Routes 6, 6A, and 28) converge here, too, so on summer weekends it acts as a rather frustrating funnel.

But this is also where the ocean-side beaches open up into a glorious expanse some 40 miles long, framed by dramatic dunes and blessed—from a swimmer's or boarder's perspective—with serious surf. The thousands of ship crews who crashed on these shoals over the past 4 centuries could hardly be expected to assume so sanguine a view. Shipwrecks may sound like the stuff of romance, but in these frigid waters, hitting a sandbar usually spelled a death sentence for all involved. So enamored were local inhabitants of the opportunity to salvage that some improved their odds by becoming "mooncussers"—praying for cloudy skies and, lacking them, luring ships toward shore by tying a lantern to the tale of a donkey, so as to simulate the listing of a ship at sea.

Such dark deeds seem very far removed from the Orleans of today, a sedate town that shadows Hyannis as a year-round center of commerce. Lacking the cohesiveness of smaller towns and somewhat chopped up by the roadways coursing through, it's not the most ideal town to hang out in, despite some appealing restaurants and shops. The village of East Orleans, however, is fast emerging as a sweet little off-beach town with both family and singles allure. About 2 miles east is seemingly endless (nearly 10-mile-long) Nauset Beach, the southernmost stretch of the Cape Cod National Seashore preserve, and a magnet for the young and the buff.

ESSENTIALS

GETTING THERE   After crossing either the Bourne or Sagamore bridge, head east on Route 6 or 6A; both converge with Route 28 in Orleans. Or fly into Hyannis (see "Getting There" in chapter 3).

VISITOR INFORMATION   Contact the **Orleans Chamber of Commerce,** 44 Main St. (Box 153), Orleans, MA 02653 (☎ **800/865-1386** or 508/255-1386) or the **Cape Cod Chamber of Commerce,** Routes 6 and 132, Hyannis, MA 02601 (☎ **508/362-3225;** fax 508/362-3698; Web site www.capecod.com). There's an **information booth** at the corner of Route 6A and Eldredge Parkway (☎ **508/ 240-2484**).

BEACHES & OUTDOOR PURSUITS

BEACHES   From here on up, on the eastern side you're dealing with the wild and whimsical Atlantic, which can be kittenish one day and tigerish the next. While storms may whip up surf you can actually take a board to, less confident swimmers should definitely wait a few days until the turmoil and riptides subside. In any case, current conditions are clearly posted at the entrance. Weeklong parking permits ($25 for renters, $30 for transients) may be obtained from **Town Hall** on School Road (☎ 508/240-3775). Day-trippers who arrive early enough—better make that before 9am—can pay at the gate (☎ **508/240-3780**).

- ✪ **Nauset Beach,** in East Orleans (☎ **508/240-3780**). Stretching southward all the way past Chatham, this 10-mile-long barrier beach—part of the Cape Cod National Seashore, but managed by the town—has long been one of the Cape's more gonzo beach scenes—good surf, big crowds, lots of young people. Full facilities can be found within the 1,000-car parking lot; the in-season fee is $8 per car, which is also good for same-day parking at Skaket Beach (see below). Substantial waves make for good surfing in the special section reserved for that purpose, and boogie boards are ubiquitous. In July and August, there are concerts from 7 to 9pm in the gazebo.
- **Skaket Beach,** off Skaket Beach Road to the west of town (☎ **508/255-0572**). This peaceful bay beach is a better choice for families with young children. When the tide recedes (as much as a mile), little kids will enjoy splashing about in the tide pools left behind. Parking costs $8, and you'd better turn up early.
- **Pilgrim Lake,** off Monument Road about 1 mile south of Main Street. Because it's covered by a lifeguard in season, this small freshwater beach charges an $8 parking fee.

- **Crystal Lake,** off Monument Road about ³/₄ mile south of Main Street. Parking—if you can find a space—is free, but there are no facilities.

BICYCLING   Orleans presents the one slight gap in the 25-mile off-road **Cape Cod Rail Trail** (☎ **508/896-3491**): Just east of the Brewster border, the trail merges with town roads for about 1¹/₂ miles. The best way to avoid vehicular aggravation and breathing fumes is to zigzag west to scenic Rock Harbor. Bike rentals are available at **Orleans Cycle** at 26 Main St. in the center of town (☎ **508/255-9115**), and there are several good places (see "Take-Out & Picnic Fare," below) to grab some comestibles.

BOATING   **Cape Cod Coastal Canoe & Kayak** (☎ **888/226-6393** or 508/564-4051; E-mail cccanoe@capecod.net; Web site www.capecod.net/canoe/) runs naturalist-guided trips throughout the Cape, sponsored by the Cape Cod Museum of Natural History. In Orleans, they have several routes around Little Pleasant Bay (to Sampson Island, to Hog Island, and to Pochet Island), and they paddle the body of water called simply, The River. There is also a special all-day trip through Pleasant Bay to the inside shore of the Outer Beach. Trips (3¹/₂ to 4 hr.) are daily April through August, weekends through October, and cost $25 per paddler or $50 per family. All equipment is supplied. Call for schedule.

   Arey's Pond Boat Yard, off Route 28 in South Orleans (☎ **508/255-0994**), offers sailing lessons. The **Goose Hummock Outdoor Center** at 15 Rte. 6A, south of the rotary (☎ **508/255-0455;** Web site www.goose.com), rents out canoes, kayaks, and more, and the northern half of Pleasant Bay is the perfect place to use them; inquire about guided excursions.

FISHING   Fishing is allowed in Baker Pond, Pilgrim Lake, and Crystal Lake; the third is a likely spot to reel in trout and perch. For details and a license, visit **Town Hall** at Post Office Square in the center of town (☎ **508/240-3700,** ext. 305). Surf casting—no license needed—is permitted on Nauset Beach South, off Beach Road. Rock Harbor, a former packet landing on the bay (about 1¹/₄ miles northwest of the town center) shelters New England's largest sportfishing fleet: some 18 boats at last count. One call (☎ **800/287-1771** or 508/255-9757) will get you information on them all. Or go look them over; the sunsets are sublime.

   You can rent fishing rods and other gear from **Goose Hummock** at 15 Rte. 6A, just south of the rotary (☎ **508/255-0455**).

FITNESS   If you're here for a while and need a place to stay in shape on rainy days, check out **Willy's Gym and Fitness Center** at 21 Old Colony Way at Orleans Marketplace (☎ **508/255-6826**). It takes the title as the Cape's biggest (21,000 sq. ft.) exercise facility; it's air-conditioned and open year-round. Dozens of classes are offered weekly, from basic aerobics to t'ai chi and Indonesian martial arts.

ICE-SKATING   Orleans boasts a massive municipal rink, the Charles Moore Arena on O'Connor Way, off Eldredge Park Way, about 1 mile southwest of town center (☎ **508/255-2971;** call for schedule and fees). From September through March, it's usually open to the public Tuesday, Wednesday, and Friday from 11am to 1pm, Thursday from 3:30 to 5pm, and Sunday from 2 to 4pm. Friday night is "Rock-Nite," for party animals aged 9 through 14.

NATURE & WILDLIFE AREAS   Inland there's not much, but on the Atlantic shore is a biggie: **Nauset Beach.** Once you get past the swarms of people near the parking lot, you'll have about 9 miles of beach mostly to yourself. You'll see lots of birds (take a field guide) and perhaps some harbor seals off-season.

TENNIS   Hard-surface public courts are located at the Nauset Middle School in Eldredge Park on a first-come, first-served basis; for details, contact the **Orleans Recreation Department** (☎ 508/240-3700).

WATER SPORTS   The ✪ **Pump House Surf Co.** at 9 Rte. 6A (☎ 508/240-2226) will meet all your sailboarding and surfing needs, while providing up-to-date reports on where to find the best waves. **Nauset Sports** at Jeremiah Square (Route 6A at the rotary; ☎ 508/255-4742) also rents surfing and other water-sports equipment.

HISTORICAL MUSEUMS

French Transatlantic Cable Station Museum. 41 S. Orleans Rd. (corner of Cove Rd. and Rte. 28, N of Main St.). ☎ **508/240-1735.** Free admission. July–Aug Mon–Sat 2–4pm. Closed Sept–June.

This ordinary-looking house was, from 1890 to 1940, a nexus of intercontinental communications. Connected to France via a huge cable laid across the ocean floor, local operators bore the responsibility of relaying stock-market data, keeping tabs on World War I troops, and receiving the joyous news of Lindbergh's 1927 crossing. Service was discontinued with the German invasion of France in 1940, and resumed briefly between 1952 and 1959, when newer, automated technologies rendered the facility obsolete. The exhibits, prepared with the assistance of the Smithsonian, are a bit technical for the nonscientifically inclined, but there are docents on hand who will patiently fill in the blanks.

The Meeting House Museum. 3 River Rd. (at Main St., about 1 mile E of town center). ☎ **508/240-1329.** Free admission. July–Aug Mon–Fri 1–4pm; call for off-season hrs.

Other towns may have fancier facilities to house their historical societies, but few have quite so colorful a history as Orleans—the only town on the Cape with a non-English, non-native name. Upon separating from Eastham in 1797, Orleans assumed the name of an honored guest: future king Louis-Philippe de Bourbon, Duke of Orleans, who safely sat out the Revolution abroad, earning his living as a French tutor. Not that all remained quiet on these shores either: Orleans suffered British naval attacks during the War of 1812, and German submarine fire in 1918. You'll find a great many mementos in the basement of this 1833 Greek Revival church, along with assorted artifacts—from arrowheads to hand-hewn farm tools—and a thinly veiled terrorist threat, dated 1814, from a British captain offering to spare the town's saltworks in Rock Harbor for a paltry $1,000. The townspeople balked, a warship struck, and the home team triumphed in the Battle of Orleans. Though the displays are far from jazzy, a great many have interesting stories attached and could spark an urge to learn more.

A WATER TOUR

Cape Cod Bay Cruises. On Town Cove (behind the Orleans Inn, S of the rotary). ☎ **508/385-3244.** Tickets $10 adults, $7 children. July–Aug departures at 10:30am, 1 and 3pm; call for off-season hrs., and departures. Closed mid-Oct to May.

You don't need much in the way of sea legs to survive a placid sightseeing trip aboard this bus-size barge. Bring your binoculars, though, to observe some fascinating seabirds.

BASEBALL

The Orleans Cardinals, the easternmost team in the Cape Cod Baseball League, play at Eldredge Park (off Eldredge Park Way between Routes 6A and 28). For a schedule, call the **Orleans Chamber of Commerce** (☎ **800/865-1386** or 508/ 255-1386), the **Orleans Recreation Department** (☎ **508/240-3785**), or the **League** (☎ **508/432-6909**).

KID STUFF

The **Charles Moore Arena** (see "Ice-Skating," above) offers respite from a rainy day. Young skater dudes—and anxious parents—might be interested to know that the Nauset Regional Middle School in Eldredge Park has its own **skateboard park,** with four ramps and a "fun box"; helmets are required.

SHOPPING

Though shops are somewhat scattered, Orleans is full of great finds for browsers and grazers.

ANTIQUES/COLLECTIBLES   Got an old house in need of illumination, or just a new one in want of some style? You'll find some 400 vintage light fixtures at **Continuum Antiques,** 7 S. Orleans Rd. (Route 28, south of the junction of Route 6A; ☎ **508/255-8513**), from Victorian on down, along with a smattering of old advertising signs and venerable duck decoys.

Deborah Rita, proprietor of **Countryside Antiques,** 6 Lewis Rd. (south of Main Street in the center of East Orleans; ☎ **508/240-0525**), roams the world in search of stylish furnishings, mostly old, though age—and price—are evidently no object. She could give lessons on how to juxtapose objects of different eras and origins for maximum effect.

East Orleans Art & Antiques, 204 Main St. (in the center of East Orleans; ☎ **508/255-7799**), houses Katherine Fox's finds, which are refreshingly priced, whether the object in question is a sumptuous antique kilim or a modest watercolor freshly executed by some talented local artist. Closed January through May.

You'd have to head south to Sotheby's to find a finer collection of Early American antiques than the collection at **Pleasant Bay Antiques,** 540 S. Orleans Rd. (Route 28, about $^1/_2$ mile south of town center in South Orleans; ☎ **508/ 255-0930**). These are big pieces, mostly, of museum quality and priced for serious, well-schooled collectors.

Yellow House, 21 S. Orleans Rd. (Route 28, north of Main Street; ☎ **508/ 255-9686**), is stocked by a decorator—Lucille Danneman—and it shows. You get the added bonus of seeing how beautiful, disparate objects can be played against one another.

ARTS & CRAFTS   As a publicist, Helen Addison has forged friendships with some of the most interesting artists now working on the Cape. Her gallery, **Addison Holmes Gallery,** 43 Rte. 28 (north of Main Street; ☎ **508/255-6200;** E-mail addison@capecod.net), run with partner Herb Holmes, represents such diverse artists as Peter Quidley, a realist painter of romantic subject matter, and Gary Gilmartin of Truro, a realist working in egg tempera and watercolor, who paints Cape-inspired subjects.

The Artful Hand Gallery, 47 Main St. (between Routes 6A and 28; ☎ **508/ 255-2969**), is a branch of a top crafts gallery based in Boston's *haute* Copley Place; the selections tend to be fun, but smart, too. Jewelry and glass are among what you'll find.

Stop by **Kemp Pottery,** 9 Rte. 6A (about $^1/_8$ mile south of the rotary; ☎ **508/ 255-5853**), and check out Steve Kemp's turned and slab-built creations—from soup tureens to fanciful sculptures; they're remarkably colorful and one of a kind.

In 1998, ✪ **Tree's Place** (Route 6A at the intersection of Route 28, Orleans; ☎ **888/255-1330** or 508/255-1330), considered the premier gallery for contemporary realist work in the region, is debuting the work of the New American Luminists, a locally based art movement. There is also an extensive fine craft, gift, and tile shop here.

BOOKS   **Compass Rose Book Shop,** 43-45 Main St. (in the center of town; ☎ **508/255-1545**), is well laid-out and offers strong showings in the areas of local lore, nature, and nautical know-how; inquire about the bargain basement.

FASHION   **Head & Foot Shop,** 42 Main St. (at the center of town; ☎ **508/ 255-1281**), is a dream come true for the teenager—female, male, or stubbornly androgynous—who complains of having "nothing to wear." This friendly shop stocks all the latest styles and trendy labels (Woolrich and Esprit, for example) at relatively reasonable prices. Larger children and youthful adults will also find plenty that pleases. The store has branches in Chatham and Provincetown, but you'll find the broadest selection right here.

With her main headquarters in trendy Northampton, Massachusetts, designer/ buyer Susan Hannah displays her casual yet elegant chic at **Hannah,** 47 Main St. (in the center of town; ☎ **508/255-8324**). Look for her larger shop when in Wellfleet.

✪ **Karol Richardson,** 47 Main St. (in the center of town; ☎ **508/255-3944**), is a preview of Richardson's main showroom in Wellfleet; stop in to see the latest from this gifted ex-Londoner.

GIFTS/HOME DECOR   Birders will go batty over **Bird Watcher's General Store,** 36 Rte. 6A (south of the rotary; ☎ **800/562-1512** or 508/255-6974). The brainchild of local aficionado Mike O'Connor, who'd like everyone to share his passion, it stocks virtually every bird-watching accessory under the sun, from basic binoculars to costly telescopes, modest birdhouses to birdbaths fit for a tiny Roman emperor. Recorded birdsong trills through the rafters, and in addition to CDs and field guides to take home, the store offers hundreds of bird-motif gifts, from mobiles to mugs.

The tasteful selections—tapes, books, jewelry, clothing, and more—to be found in **Oceana,** 1 Main St. Sq. (north of Main Street, in the center of town; ☎ **508/ 240-1414**), celebrate the myriad gifts of nature.

MUSIC   **Instant Karma,** 121 Rte. 6A (south of Main Street; ☎ **508/240-7166**), has a handpicked selection of CDs, tapes, and even vinyl.

SEAFOOD   **Nauset Fish & Lobster Pool,** just south of the rotary on Route 6A in Orleans (☎ **508/255-1019**), is the area's premier place to buy fresh seafood; the selection is extensive and bountiful.

WHERE TO STAY
MODERATE

The Barley Neck Inn Lodge. 5 Beach Rd. (in the center of town), E. Orleans, MA 02643. ☎ **800/281-7505** or 508/255-8484. Fax 508/255-3626. 18 rms. A/C TV TEL. Summer (including continental breakfast in season) $95–$115. Off-season MAP packages available. AE, DC, MC, V.

Having radically transformed the Barley Neck Inn restaurant (see "Where to Dine," below), new owners Kathi and Joe Lewis treated the adjoining motel to an equally intensive makeover. Every room is a little different, but all boast fluffy designer comforters, minifridges, and stylish appointments. There's a little pool within the complex, and Nauset Beach is less than a mile down the road.

The Cove. 13 S. Orleans Rd. (Rte. 28, N of Main St.), Orleans, MA 02653. ☎ **800/343-2233** or 508/255-1203. Fax 508/255-7736. 39 rms, 7 suites, 1 efficiency. A/C TV TEL. Summer $99–$169 double; $145–$169 suite or efficiency. AE, CB, DC, DISC, MC, V.

Sensibly turning its back on busy Route 28, this well-camouflaged motel complex focuses instead on placid Town Cove, where guests are offered a free minicruise in season. The interiors are adequate, if not dazzling, and a small heated pool and a restful gazebo overlook the waterfront. All rooms have hair dryers and minifridges. Some have kitchenettes, VCRs, and balconies with cove views. Meeting facilities are available for those whose business needs don't go on vacation.

✪ **Kadee's Gray Elephant.** 216 Main St. (in the center of town), E. Orleans, MA 02643. ☎ **508/255-7608.** Fax 508/240-2976. 10 studio apts. A/C TV TEL. Summer $110–$120. Weekly rates available. MC, V.

Available short- or long-term, these exuberantly decorated units are extremely cheery and ideal for families. Nauset Beach is a few miles down the road; meanwhile, everything you'll need is right in town—or right on the grounds. There's a friendly restaurant/snack bar right next door (see "Where to Dine," below), and the little minigolf course out back is geared just right for minigolfers.

Morgan's Way. 9 Morgan's Way (off Rte. 28, about 1 mile S of Main St.), Orleans, MA 02653. ☎ **508/255-0831.** E-mail morgnway@capecod.net; Web site www.capecodaccess.com/morgansway. 2 bedrms, 1 cottage. A/C. Summer (including full breakfast) $115 double; cottages $805 weekly. No credit cards.

It's a privilege to stay at this contemporary country house, set on 5 secluded acres with a 40-foot heated pool. Yet Page McMahan acts as if it's her privilege to have you. While serving up a superb breakfast on heirloom china, she'll gladly brief you on local highlights. The loftlike upstairs living room is outfitted with an office (complete with computer) and TV/VCR, warmed by a woodstove, and offers a lovely woodland view.

Nauset Knoll Motor Lodge. 237 Beach Rd. (at Nauset Beach, about 2 miles E of town center), E. Orleans, MA 02643. ☎ **508/255-2364.** 12 rms. TV. Summer $130 double. MC, V. Closed late Oct to mid-Apr.

If you're the type who's determined to keep the sea within sight at all times—past a very busy beach, in this case—this nothing-fancy motel with picture windows should suit you to a T.

INEXPENSIVE

Hillbourne House. 654 Orleans Rd. (Rte. 28, near the Harwich border), S. Orleans, MA 02662. ☎ **508/255-0780.** 8 rms. Summer (including continental breakfast) $70–$95 double. No credit cards. Closed Nov to late Apr.

Overlooking a pocket of Pleasant Bay once popular with pirates, this 1798 homestead has seen a lot of history: Innkeeper Barbara Hayes can show you the trap door that conceals a stone pit pressed into service for the Underground Railroad. The three carriage-house rooms are beautiful examples of their era, and can be booked en masse, with their own kitchen and living room. Three more modern units, carved out of the erstwhile paddocks, are nearly as charming, with high ceilings countrified by wooden beams. All guests are offered a lavish breakfast and have access to the inn's little private beach and dock; in fact, some regulars arrive by sea.

✪ **Nauset House Inn.** 143 Beach Rd. (about 1¹/₂ miles E of town center), E. Orleans, MA 02653. ☎ **508/255-2195.** 14 rms (6 with shared bath). Summer (including full breakfast) $55–$128 double. DISC, MC, V. Closed Nov–Mar.

Heathcliff would have loved this place, or at least the surrounding moors. Modern nature-lovers with a taste for creature comforts will, too. Several of the rooms in greenery-draped outbuildings feature such romantic extras as a sunken bath or private deck. The most romantic hideaway here, though, is a 1907 conservatory appended to the 1810 farmhouse inn. It's the perfect place to lounge with a novel or lover (or both) as the rain pounds down, prompting the camellias to waft their heady perfume. Breakfast would seem relatively workaday, were it not for the setting—a pared-down, rustic refectory—and innkeeper Diane Johnson's memorable muffins and pastries.

The Parsonage Inn. 202 Main St., Box 1501, (in the center of town), E. Orleans, MA 02653. ☎ **888/422-8217** or 508/255-8217. Fax 508/255-8216. E-mail lizian@capecod.net. 8 rms. A/C. Summer (including full breakfast) $85–$125. AE, MC, V.

Blessed with charming British innkeepers, this 1770 full Cape—whose name describes its original function—offers the kind of unique, personalized experience especially prized by "innies" (the country-inn counterpart to foodies). Elizabeth Browne is an accomplished pianist who might, if the evening mood is right, take flight in a Chopin mazurka or Mozart sonata, as her husband, Ian, treats guests to a glass of wine.

WHERE TO DINE
MODERATE

The Arbor. 20 S. Orleans Rd. (Rte. 28, N of Main St.). ☎ **508/255-4847.** Reservations recommended. Main courses $13–$18. AE, MC, V. Mid-May to mid-Oct daily 5–10pm; mid-Oct to mid-May Fri–Sun 5–10pm. ECLECTIC.

With every spare inch crammed with junk—including intentionally mismatched crockery—this place is a visual maelstrom, but all the more fun for it. The cuisine tends toward the saucy continental. If you'd like to just take a look around and dine more simply—not to mention cheaply—try the adjoining and equally interesting Binnacle (see below).

✪ **The Barley Neck Inn.** 5 Beach Rd. (about ¹/₂ mile E of town center). ☎ **800/281-7505** or 508/255-0212. Reservations recommended. Main courses $14–$24. AE, DC, MC, V. June to early Sept daily 5–10pm; call for off-season hrs. FRENCH.

Recently rescued from dereliction and tastefully restored, complete with fanlight door and mullioned windows, this 1857 captain's house immediately ascended into the first rank. The owners, enterprising ex–New Yorkers Joe and Kathi Lewis, have recruited a superb chef in Franck Champely, who came from Taillevent and Maxim's by way of New York's Four Seasons. His classical background shines in straightforward yet subtle dishes such as grilled Atlantic salmon fillet with a red-pepper coulis and basil vinaigrette, or sautéed shrimp in a sauce of sweet garlic and Chablis atop lemon angel-hair pasta and shiitake mushrooms. The cuisine may be worshipworthy, the wine list a connoisseur's delight, but the ambiance is populist and festive, verging on boisterous. It's a very good mix.

Captain Linnell House. 137 Skaket Beach Rd. (about 1 mile NW of Rte. 6A). ☎ **508/255-3400.** Reservations recommended. Main courses $15–$26. AE, MC, V. Daily 5–10pm. NEW AMERICAN.

The plantationlike facade of this colonnaded 1854 mansion, modeled on a Marseilles villa, is so impressive that the interior can't help but suffer by comparison. Certain shortcomings—e.g., wall-to-wall carpeting in the foyer, ungainly metal chairs—undercut the decor and overall ambiance, but chef/owner William Conway's cuisine more than compensates. His lobster bisque, bolstered with bourbon, is the kind that lingers in memory as a standard to aspire to. Ask to be seated in the garden room, where the pleasing view will enable you to accord the food the undivided focus it deserves. Better yet, be really smart and come early (before 6:15pm) to score a free soup and dessert.

Off the Bay Cafe. 28 Main St. (at Rte. 6A, in the center of town). ☎ **508/255-5505.** Reservations recommended. Main courses $18–$24. AE, CB, DC, DISC, MC, V. Daily July–Aug 11:30am–4pm and 5:30–10pm; call for off-season hrs. NEW AMERICAN.

Admirably ambitious since its inception in the early 1980s, this snappy 19th-century storefront keeps delivering the goods. In light of the neonautical decor (lots of varnished wood and polished brass), one might expect passable seafood; instead, it's superlative, with such brilliant accompaniments as pineapple salsa or papaya hollandaise. The rotisseried game birds are every bit as well dressed, and superb.

Old Jailhouse Tavern. 28 W. Rd. (N of Rte. 6A, about 1 mile SW of town center). ☎ **508/255-5245.** Main courses $13–$17. AE, DISC, MC, V. Daily 11:30am–1am. INTERNATIONAL.

Lackluster food doesn't seem to dissuade the faithful patrons of this restaurant retrofitted into a century-old stone house that once belonged to the town constable. He may have held some prisoners here, and that tenuous scenario has been worked into a prison motif, complete with a wrought-iron gate to fence off the popular bar.

INEXPENSIVE

Binnacle Tavern. 20 S. Orleans Rd. (Rte. 28, N of Main St.). ☎ **508/255-4847.** Most items under $12. AE, MC, V. Mid-May to mid-Oct daily 5–11:30pm; mid-Oct to mid-May Thurs–Sun 5–11:30pm. ITALIAN.

All sorts of strange nautical salvage adorns the barn-board walls of this popular pizzeria, where the pies—reputed to be the Cape's best—come with some very peculiar toppings, for those so inclined. More conservative combos are available, along with traditional Italian fare.

✪ **Cap't Cass Rock Harbor Seafood.** 117 Rock Harbor Rd. (on the harbor, about 1¹/₂ miles NW of town center). No phone. Most main courses under $12. No credit cards. Late May to mid-Oct daily 11am–2pm and 5–9pm. Closed mid-Oct to late May. SEAFOOD.

Most tourists figure that a silvered shack sporting this many salvaged lobster buoys has an inside track on the freshest of seafoods. The supposition makes sense, but the stuff here is about par for the area and the preparations plain, but it's fun to eat in a joint left untouched for decades as time—and dining fads—marched on.

✪ **Joe's Beach Road Bar & Grille.** The Barley Neck Inn, 5 Beach Rd. (about ¹/₂ mile E of town center). ☎ **800/281-7505** or 508/255-0212. Fax 508/255-3226. Reservations not accepted. Main courses $7–$16. AE, DC, MC, V. Early July to early Sept daily 5–10pm; call for off-season hrs. NEW AMERICAN.

Joe Lewis's self-imposed mandate for his namesake bar is "good food, large drinks, and big fun." That's exactly what you'll find in this spacious tavern, built with rugged beams salvaged from a local saltworks. World War II posters (found in the inn's attic) and snazzy Roaring Twenties menswear ads (Joe's own collection, reflecting his previous occupation) adorn the barn-board walls. Off-season a fire blazes in the huge fieldstone fireplace. Inviting navy-blue armchairs are in the quieter nonsmoking section dining room, around the corner from the bar. Most everyone crowds around the 28-foot mahogany bar, though, where it's mingling room only. Once you've secured your own table—the tablecloths are denim, the napkins bandannas—you have the run of a terrifically varied menu, which includes the exquisite dishes served in the more formal restaurant next door (see above). If you just want to nosh, consider Joe's pizza (with goat cheese, roasted peppers, and spinach) or highfalutin fish-and-chips—beer-battered, with watercress aioli. There's a kid's menu too, which is available in both dining rooms.

Kadee's Lobster & Clam Bar. 212 Main St. (in the center of town). ☎ **508/255-6184.** Fax 508/240-2926. Reservations not accepted. Main courses $7–$17. MC, V. Late June to Aug daily 11:30am–9:30pm; late May to late June Sat–Sun 11:30am–9:30pm. Closed early Sept to late May. AMERICAN.

Achieving an air of effortless authenticity, this atmospheric sea shanty has been rigged to improve on the climate. When the sun's out, the flower-print umbrellas pop up in the patio; as soon as the chilly sea-borne fog moves in, a curtained awning drops down. The menu is equally adaptable: There's nothing like the classic chowders and stews or a platter of sautéed "seafood simmer" to take the chill off; fine weather, on the other hand, calls for a lobster roll, or perhaps the obligatory (at least once a summer) shore-dinner splurge.

Land Ho! 38 Main St. (at Rte. 6A, in the center of town). ☎ **508/255-5165.** Reservations not accepted. Main courses $7–$15. AE, DISC, MC, V. Daily 11:30am–1am. AMERICAN.

A longtime hit with the locals (who call it, affectionately, "the Ho"), this rough-and-tumble pub attracts its share of knowledgeable tourists as well, drawn by the reasonable prices and relaxed feeling. The food may be nothing to write home about, but it's satisfying and easy on the budget. Just being there (provided you can find the door: it's around back) will make you feel like an insider.

The Lobster Claw Restaurant. Rte. 6A (just S of the rotary), Orleans. ☎ **508/255-1800.** Main courses $10–$19. AE, MC, V. Daily 11:30am–9pm. Closed Nov–Apr. SEAFOOD.

This family-owned and -operated business has been serving up quality seafood for almost 30 years. There's plenty of room for everyone in this sprawling restaurant, where booths spill over with boisterous families, and the usual flotsam and jetsam hang artfully from the ceiling. Get the baked stuffed lobster here with all the fixings. There's a children's menu, as well as early-bird specials served daily from 4 to 5:30pm.

Nauset Beach Club. 222 Main St. (about $^1/_2$ mile E of town center). ☎ **508/255-8547.** Reservations not accepted. Main courses $12–$18. AE, DC, DISC, MC, V. Late May to mid-Oct Sun–Thurs 5:30–9pm, Fri–Sat 5:30–9:30pm; mid-Oct to May Tues–Sat 5:30–9pm. NORTHERN ITALIAN.

The first thing you may notice about this peachy roadside trattoria (once a duck-hunter's cottage) is the tantalizing aromas. Unfortunately, the next impression is apt to be a surfeit of attitude, when, for example, the maitre d' informs you, unbidden, that each person in your party must order an entree—no exceptions made for young diners or small appetites. If you're willing to play by the rules (reliable rumor tells of a multimillionaire turned away who was willing to pay—but not eat—up), the reward is apt to be worth it: lusciously sauced, perfectly al dente pastas and other Italian-accented regional fare.

TAKE-OUT & PICNIC FARE

Clambake Celebrations. 9 W. Rd. (at Skaket Corners., about 1 mile W of town center). ☎ **800/423-4038** or 508/255-3289.

Pick your spot anywhere on the Cape—or within the continental United States, for that matter—and this firm will provide you with a coastal feast to go: lobsters, steamers, mussels, sausage, corn, potatoes, all packed in a steamer pot and ready to go. If you're in the vicinity, they'll even lend you a charcoal grill.

Fancy's Farm. 199 Main St. (in the center of town). ☎ **508/255-1949.**

Rarely are vegetables rendered so appealing. They're especially prime, to begin with, whether domestic or imported from halfway across the world. The charming barnlike setting helps, as do the extras—fresh breads, pastries, juices, and exotic salads and soups to go.

New York Bagels. 125 Rte. 6A (S of Main St.). ☎ **508/255-0255.**

Longing for the real thing, a real mouth-wrestler? These chewy rounds are authentic and tasty; add the customary accompaniments for a satisfying sandwich. Among the other "Noo Yawk" mainstays are knishes and potato pancakes—and, of course, chicken soup. While awaiting your order, you can study the decorative pastiche of nostalgic tchotchkes.

Orleans Whole Food. 46 Main St. (in the center of town). ☎ **508/255-6540.**

One of the nicest health-food stores on the entire Cape, this bright and cheerful porch-fronted grocery offers all sorts of freshly made snacks and sandwiches to take out—or to tear into during an impromptu picnic in the adjoining garden.

SWEETS

The Hot Chocolate Sparrow. 85 Rte. 6A (N of Main St.). ☎ **508/240-2230.**

It's more Schraft's-style than Seattle, but this coffeehouse-cum-bakery makes the most of its chocolatier connections (the candy is hand-dipped at a sister shop in North Eastham). Real fudge, for instance, flavors the hot chocolate and all mocha derivatives thereof. It's a good place to stop in, casually check the posters announcing local happenings, then dive in for a remorseless pig-out.

Sundae School. 201 Main St. (in the center of town). ☎ **508/255-5473.**

A smaller branch of the Dennisport institution, this little ice-cream shop offers some mighty sophisticated flavors, drawing on fruits in season and even the liqueur cabinet.

ORLEANS AFTER DARK

Joe's Beach Road Bar & Grille (☎ **508/255-0212;** see "Where to Dine," above) is a big old barn of a bar that might as well be town hall: It's where you'll find all the locals exchanging juicy gossip and jokes. On Sunday evenings in season, the weekend warriors who survived in style can enjoy live "Jazz at Joe's." Other nights there's Jim Turner, a blind piano player, who entertains with show tunes and boogie-woogie. There's never a cover charge.

There's live music on weekends off-season at the **Land Ho** (☎ **508/255-5165;** see "Where to Dine," above), the best pub in town. No cover charge.

The Academy Playhouse, 120 Main St. (about ³/₄ mile southeast of town center; ☎ **508/255-1963**), makes a fine platform for local talent in the form of musicals and drama, recitals and poetry readings. The 162-seat arena-style stage is housed in the town's old town hall (built in 1873). Tickets $10 to $16. Shows July through August Monday through Saturday at 8:30pm; call for off-season hours.

8

The Outer Cape: Eastham, Wellfleet, Truro & Provincetown

The rest of the Cape may have its civilized enticements, but it's only on the Outer Cape that the landscape and even the air feel really beachy. You can smell the seashore just over the horizon—in fact, everywhere you go, because you're never more than a mile or two away from sand and surf.

You won't find any high-rise hotels here. No tacky amusement arcades or T-shirt shops. Not a whole lot of anything, in fact, other than dune grass rippling in the wind. That and the occasional cottage inhabited by some lucky soul who managed to get his or her hands on it (inevitably through some grandfather clause) before the coastline became the federally-protected Cape Cod National Seashore in the early 1960s.

Henry David Thoreau witnessed virtually the same peaceful panorama when he roamed here in the 1850s. With luck and determination on the part of current inhabitants and visitors, the landscape will remain untouched. The Outer Cape, after all, is a place to play—in the sand, and in the delightful, nonconformist towns that sprouted up here, far from the censures of civilization.

While they share the majestic National Seashore, Outer Cape towns are quite diverse. Eastham, as the official gateway to the National Seashore, certainly gets its share of visitors, yet there is also a sleepy quality to this town, which used to have the distinction of being the turnip capital of the country. Grab a stool at a locals' joint like Flemings Donut Shop on Route 6 for a taste of old Cape Cod before there was ever any talk of a National Seashore.

Wellfleet, called the art-gallery town, is in my view one of the nicest towns on Cape Cod. Perfectly strollable Main Street is lined with intriguing shops in historic buildings. Many streets house art galleries, filled with work by mainly local artists inspired by this region. Wellfleet was for years one of the premier fishing villages on Cape Cod, and it still has the bustling and picturesque harbor to prove it. There are also freshwater ponds and National Seashore beaches; some of Cape Cod's finest swimming holes and most spectacular beaches line the coast of Wellfleet.

Tiny Truro is the least developed of the Cape's towns; it has the smallest population and the highest percentage of acres reserved for the National Seashore. The center of town is one of those blink-and-you-missed-it affairs, though the fact that Truro has three libraries should tell you something about the property owners here.

Provincetown is a former Portuguese fishing village turned into an internationally famous art and gay colony with a flamboyant nightlife. The main drag (so to speak) is Commercial Street, with the best shopping on Cape Cod. Families come for the strolling, museums, and whale watching; sophisticates for the restaurants, cafes, and entertainment; and gays come for the camaraderie. And the beaches? On a clear day they say you can see Europe.

1 Eastham

35 miles (56km) E of Sandwich, 21 miles (34km) S of Provincetown

Despite its optimal location (the distance from bay to ocean is as little as 1 mile in spots), Eastham is one of the least pretentious locales on the Cape—and yet highly popular as the gateway to the magnificent Cape Cod National Seashore.

The downside—or upside, depending on how you look at it—is that there aren't many shops or attractions worth checking out. Even Eastham's colorful history, as the site of the Pilgrims' "First Encounter" with hostile natives, has faded with time. One prominent vestige remains as a reminder of the days when, according to Cape historian Arthur Wilson Tarbell, Eastham served as "the granary of eastern Massachusetts": the smock-style 1680s windmill in the center of town. Also, those who take the trouble to track them down will find the graves of three "First Comers" in the Old Cove Burying Ground, near a condo complex across from Arnold's clam shack.

Most visitors won't bother though—this is a place to kick back and let the sun, surf, and sand dictate your day.

ESSENTIALS

GETTING THERE   After crossing either the Bourne or Sagamore bridge, head east on Route 6 or 6A to Orleans, and north on Route 6. Or fly into Hyannis or Provincetown (see "Getting There" in chapter 3).

VISITOR INFORMATION   Contact the **Eastham Chamber of Commerce,** Box 1329, Eastham, MA 02642 (☎ **508/240-7211**) or the **Cape Cod Chamber of Commerce,** Routes 6 and 132, Hyannis, MA 02601 (☎ **508/362-3225;** fax 508/ 362-3698; Web site www.capecod.com). An information booth run by the town is located on Route 6 at Fort Hill Road (☎ **508/255-3444**) and is open Memorial Day to Columbus Day.

BEACHES AND OUTDOOR PURSUITS

BEACHES   From here on up, the Atlantic beaches are best reserved for strong swimmers: Waves are *big* (often taller than you) and the undertow can be treacherous. The flat, nearly placid bay beaches, on the other hand, are just right for families with young children. The sand slopes so gradually that you won't have to worry about them slipping in over their heads. When the tide recedes (twice daily), it leaves a mile-wide playground of rippled sand full of fascinating creatures, including horseshoe and hermit crabs.

- **Coast Guard** and **Nauset Light,** off Ocean View Drive. Connected to outlying parking lots by a free shuttle, these pristine National Seashore beaches have lifeguards and rest rooms. Parking is $5 per day, $15 per season.
- **First Encounter, Thumpertown, Campground,** and **Sunken Meadow.** These town-operated bay beaches generally charge $5 a day; permits ($20 per week) can be obtained from the Highway Department on Old Orchard Road in North Eastham (☎ **508/255-1965**).

- **Great Pond** and **Wiley Park** beaches. These two town-run freshwater beaches are also open to the public, on the same terms as the bay beaches.

BICYCLING With plenty of free parking available at the Cape Cod National Seashore's **Salt Pond Visitor Center** (☎ 508/255-3421), Eastham makes a convenient access point for the ✪ **Cape Cod Rail Trail** (☎ 508/896-3491). Northward, it's about 5 wildflower-lined miles to Wellfleet, where the trail currently ends (further expansion is planned); Dennis is about 20 miles southwest. A 1.6-mile spur trail, winding through locust and apple groves, links the Visitor Center with glorious Coast Guard Beach: It's for bikes only (no blades). Rentals are available at the **Little Capistrano Bike Shop** (☎ 508/255-6515), on Salt Pond Road just west of Route 6, or at **Idle Times** at 4550 Rte. 6 in the center of North Eastham (☎ 800/924-8281 on the Cape or 508/255-8281). The best trail-side eatery—fried clams, lobster, and the like—is **Arnold's** (☎ 508/255-2575), located on Route 6 about 1 mile north of the Visitor Center.

BOATING The best way to experience Nauset Marsh is by kayak or canoe. Rentals are available in neighboring towns: The closest source would be the **Goose Hummock Outdoor Center** at 15 Rte. 6A in Orleans (☎ 508/255-0455). **Jack's Boat Rentals** (☎ 508/349-9808) is located on Route 6 next to the Cumberland Farms in Wellfleet. They also have a seasonal outlet on Wellfleet's Gull Pond, which connects to Higgins Pond by way of a placid, narrow channel lined with red maples and choked with yellow water lilies. In addition to watercraft to go, Jack's is also the place for info about **Eric Gustavson's guided kayak tours** (☎ **508/349-1429**), which include tours of Eastham's Herring River and also Nauset Marsh. For information about other excellent naturalist-guided tours, inquire about trips sponsored by the **Cape Cod Museum of Natural History** (☎ **800/479-3867** or 508/896-3867) and the **Wellfleet Bay Wildlife Sanctuary** (☎ **508/349-2615**).

Cape Cod Coastal Canoe & Kayak (☎ **888/226-6393** or 508/564-4051; E-mail cccanoe@capecod.net; Web site www.capecod.net/canoe/) runs naturalist-guided trips throughout the Cape, sponsored by the Cape Cod Museum of Natural History. In Eastham, they paddle through Nauset Marsh. Trips ($3^1/_2$ to 4 hr.) are daily April through August, weekends through October, and cost $25 per paddler or $50 per family. All equipment is supplied. Call for schedule.

FISHING Eastham has four ponds open to fishing: **Herring Pond** is stocked. Freshwater fishing licenses (starting at $16 for residents of Massachusetts) can be purchased at **Goose Hummock,** Route 6A, Orleans (☎ **508/255-0455**). For a shellfishing license, visit the **Department of Public Works** at 555 Old Orchard Rd. (☎ **508/255-5972**). Surf casting is permitted at **Nauset Beach North** (off Doane Road) and **Nauset Light Beach** (off Cable Road).

FITNESS The **Norseman Athletic Club,** 4730 Rte. 6, North Eastham (☎ **508/ 255-6370**), offers racquet sports, plus Nautilus and free weights, various classes, an Olympic pool, saunas, steam rooms, and whirlpools.

NATURE TRAILS There are five "self-guiding nature trails" with descriptive markers—for walkers only—within this portion of the Cape Cod National Seashore (CCNS). The $1^1/_2$-mile **Fort Hill Trail** off Fort Hill Road (off Route 6, about 1 mile south of town center) takes off from a free parking lot just past the **Captain Edward Penniman House,** a fancy multicolored 1868 Second Empire manse maintained by the CCNS. The house is open daily from 1 to 4pm in season (or call the Visitor Center at ☎ **508/255-3421**), but the exterior far outshines the interior, and more interesting sights await outside. Following the trail markers, you'll pass "Indian Rock" (bearing the marks of untold generations who used it to sharpen their tools) and enjoy scenic vantage points overlooking the channel-carved marsh—keep an eye out for egrets and great blue herons—and out to sea. The Fort Hill Trail hooks up with the $^1/_2$-mile Red Cedar Swamp Trail, offering boardwalk views of an ecology otherwise inaccessible.

Three relatively short trails fan out from the Salt Pond Visitor Center. The most unusual is the $^1/_4$-mile **Buttonbush Trail,** specially adapted for the sight-impaired, with a guide rope and descriptive plaques in both oversize type and Braille. The **Doane Loop Trail,** a $^1/_2$-mile woodland circuit about 1 mile east of the Visitor Center, is graded to allow access to wheelchairs and strollers. The 1-mile **Nauset Marsh Trail** skirts Salt Pond to cross the marsh (via boardwalk) and open fields before returning by way of a recovering forest. Look both ways for bike crossings!

TENNIS Five public courts are located at the Nauset Regional High School in North Eastham and can be used on a first-come, first-served basis; for details, contact the **Nauset High School** (☎ **508/255-1505**). The **Norseman Athletic Club,** 4730 Rte. 6, North Eastham (☎ **508/255-6370**), offers six indoor courts, for a fee.

TWO MUSEUMS

The 1869 Schoolhouse Museum. Nauset Rd. (off Rte. 6, opposite the Salt Pond Visitor Center). ☎ **508/255-8725.** Free admission. July–Aug Mon–Fri 1–4pm; Sat in Sept 1–4pm.

Run by the volunteers of the Eastham Historical Society, this former one-room schoolhouse—with separate entrances for boys and girls—encapsulates the town's

Impressions

Late in the afternoon, there descends upon the beach and the bordering sea a delicate overtone of faintest violet. There is no harshness here in the landscape line, no hard Northern brightness or brusque revelation; there is always reserve and mystery, always something beyond. . . .

—Henry Beston, *The Outermost House*

accomplishments. Exhibits range from early Native American tools to mementos of author Henry Beston's year-long stay on Coast Guard Beach, which resulted in *The Outermost House,* as compelling a read today as it was back in 1928. And in case you were wondering—yes, that strange garden gate is in fact the washed-up jawbones of a rather large whale.

✪ **Salt Pond Visitor Center.** Salt Pond Rd. (E of Rte. 6). ☎ **508/255-3421.** Free admission. June–Aug daily 9am–5pm; call for off-season hrs.

Since you're undoubtedly going to spend a fair amount of time on the beach, you might as well find out how it came to be, what other creatures you'll be sharing it with, and how not to harm it or them.

Occupying more than half the land mass north of Orleans and covering the entire 30-mile oceanfront, the 44,000-acre Cape Cod National Seashore is a free gift from legislators who had the foresight to set it aside as a sanctuary in 1961. Actually, it's not entirely free: If you're an American citizen, you own it and contribute to its upkeep. Get your money's worth, and more, by taking advantage of the excellent educational exhibits and continuous film loops offered here. Particularly fascinating is a video about the accidental discovery, in 1990, of an 11,000-year-old campsite amid the storm-ravaged dunes of Coast Guard Beach—which was about 5 miles inland when these early settlers spent their summers here. After absorbing some of the local history, be sure to take time to venture out—on your own or with a ranger guide—on some of the surrounding trails (see "Nature Trails," above).

KID STUFF

No one will look askance if you let your kids try the Buttonbush Trail (see "Nature Trails," above) in a blindfold: In fact, it's encouraged, not only as a good way to foster empathy for the blind, but to heighten "multisensory awareness." You'll find more predictable pastimes, such as miniature golf, along Route 6, and, of course, the beaches are the big draw.

SHOPPING

Eastham is certainly less commercial than its southern neighbors, and there are fewer businesses; but poking around in unexpected places can pay off.

ANTIQUES   It would be easy to pass by **Collectors' World,** on Route 6 in Eastham (1 mile north of the Salt Pond Visitor Center; ☎ **508/255-3616**), without ever realizing the prime pickings inside. Interesting items line every square inch of the shop, from nautical antiques and weathervanes to lamps, toys, and furniture.

ARTS & CRAFTS   **Sunken Meadows Basketworks and Pottery,** Sunken Meadow Road (off Aspinet Road), North Eastham (☎ **508/255-8962**) is a hidden gem tucked into the pines of North Eastham. Paulette Penney and her husband Hugh make stoneware pinched pots, begging bowls, and wall pieces, as well as woven baskets and sculptures.

BOOKS   Eastern National Park Bookstore, Salt Pond Visitor Center, Salt Pond Road, Eastham (☎ **508/255-6220**), offers a small but astute sampling of books dealing with local history (both natural and human). This Park Services–run store is great for speed-shopping. There's a good selection of related children's books, and if you're planning to do some bushwhacking, stock up on topo maps.

WHERE TO STAY
EXPENSIVE

✪ **The Whalewalk Inn.** 220 Bridge Rd. (about ³/₄ mile W of Orleans rotary), Eastham, MA 02642. ☎ **508/255-0617.** Fax 508/240-0017. 11 rms, 5 suites. A/C. Summer (including full breakfast) $135–$210 double; $175–$190 suite. AE, DISC, MC, V. Closed Dec–Mar.

Regularly hailed as one of the Cape's prettiest inns, this 1830s Greek Revival manse—sequestered in a quiet residential area just a few blocks off the Rail Trail—fully deserves its reputation. Innkeeper Carolyn Smith has dressed up every last space in a tasteful, mostly pastel palette with sunny Waverly fabrics; eclectic furnishings (many of them culled from Countryside Antiques in Orleans) cohabit harmoniously in the common rooms, where complimentary evening hors d'oeuvres are served. A new six-room carriage house sports deluxe rooms with air-conditioning, fireplaces, and some with whirlpool baths for two. The suites all have kitchenettes. Both Carolyn and Dick, who is responsible for the indulgent gourmet breakfasts, can knowledgeably steer you to the best the area has to offer and will lend you a bike if you like.

MODERATE

Over Look Inn. 3085 Rte. 6 (about ¹/₄ mile N of town center, opposite Salt Pond Visitor Center), Eastham, MA 02642. ☎ **508/255-1886.** Fax 508/240-0345. 10 rms, 3 suites. Summer (including full breakfast and afternoon tea) $125–$145 double; $165 suite. AE, CB, DC, DISC, MC, V.

Henry Beston slept in this multicolored 1869 Queen Anne Victorian while planning his legendary sojourn at the Outermost House. You can bet it was a lot less cushy—and enchanting—before Scottish innkeepers Nan and Ian Aitchison took over in 1983. The house now reflects their many enthusiasms: The library, for instance, is dedicated to Winston Churchill, and the Ernest Hemingway Billiard Room is lined with trophies that would have done Papa proud. Their son Clive's colorful canvases adorn many of the common spaces and rooms, some of which come enhanced with brass beds and claw-foot tubs. All of the rooms have either ceiling fans or air-conditioning. Pilgrims hiking along the Rail Trail will appreciate the hearty breakfasts, including an authentic "kedgeree," whose contents are best left unlisted until you've had a taste.

The Penny House. 4885 Rte. 6, N. Eastham, MA 02651. ☎ **800/554-1751** or 508/255-6632. Fax 508/255-4893. 11 rms. Summer (including full breakfast) $110–$175 double. AE, DISC, MC, V.

Whizzing past on Route 6, you'd scarcely suspect there's a peaceful inn tucked away behind a massive hedge. This neat, comfortable B&B, graced with the warmth of Australian innkeeper Margaret Keith, is clustered around a 1751 saltbox, now the setting for rather rich homemade breakfasts. The rooms vary widely in terms of space and price, but all are nicely appointed and meticulously maintained. All but one room have air-conditioning. A communal phone and TV in the cathedral-ceilinged "gathering room" encourage socializing while leaving the rooms as distraction-free oases.

INEXPENSIVE

Beach Plum Motor Lodge. 2555 Rte. 6 (about $^1/_4$-mile N of town center), Eastham, MA 02642. ☎ **508/255-7668.** 5 rms. Summer (including continental breakfast) $50 double. MC, V. Closed mid-Oct to mid-May.

Look for the riot of flowers that Gloria Moll tenderly cultivates each year around her tiny front-yard pool, just big enough for a cool dip and some fragrant sunning. The rooms—in classic little cabins out back—are also smallish, but more than adequate for most people's needs and very generously priced, especially when you take into account the home-baked breakfast treats. After 20 years in business, Beach Plum's regulars may outnumber new guests, so make your reservations early.

Mid-Cape American Youth Hostel. 75 Goody Hallet Dr. (off Bridge Rd., about $^1/_2$ mile W of Orleans rotary), Eastham, MA 02642. ☎ **508/255-2785.** 50 beds. $12 for members, $15 for nonmembers. No credit cards. Closed mid-Sept to mid-May.

Though nowhere near as picturesque as the Little America hostel 14 miles north (see "Where to Stay" in Section 3 of this chapter), this inland cluster of cabins makes a good stopover along the almost adjacent Rail Trail, and the bay is a quick glide away.

WHERE TO DINE
MODERATE

Eastham Lobster Pool. 4380 Rte. 6 (in the center of town). ☎ **508/255-9706.** Reservations not accepted. Main courses $11–$25. AE, DC, DISC, MC, V. Early July to early Sept daily 11:30am–10pm; April to early July and early Sept through Oct daily 11:30am–9:30pm. Closed Nov–Mar. AMERICAN.

For 3 decades, the scrape of metal chairs against the cement floor of this no-frills dining hall has been synonymous with seafood feasts. You can eye your potential entree—scrabbling among a tankful of feisty lobsters—as you wait in line to gain admittance. (The locals, along with smarter tourists, know to show up in the early, early evening—i.e., late afternoon.) Beyond the lobsters, which come in some monster proportions, there are all sorts of fish, all available grilled, broiled, baked, fried, stuffed, or simply poached. As far back as the early 1980s, the specials were exhibiting harbingers of New American panache, and they still pack some sophisticated surprises: champagne-shallot butter, perhaps, to top a halibut steak. The bluefish, always affordable, is always fabulous. Some rather nice wines are available by the glass.

Mitchel's Bistro. At Lori's Family Restaurant, Main St. Mercantile (about $^1/_4$-mile S of town center). ☎ **508/255-4803.** Main courses $10–$22. AE, MC, V. July–Aug daily 6–10pm; call for off-season hrs. NEW AMERICAN/INDIAN.

Mitch Rosenbaum is a gifted chef (he used to run Wellfleet's Cielo), and Laxmi Venkateshwaran prepares some lovely and authentic Indian fare. However, it's hard to imagine how they'll ever make a go of this operation, which "moonlights" as a mall restaurant, the kind indifferently decorated with pseudo captain's chairs: The culture gap is just too glaring. But one wishes them luck. Anyone who can whip up grilled butterflied leg of lamb, much less grilled duck with fresh mango-pineapple glaze, at these prices deserves a round of applause—and steady patronage.

INEXPENSIVE

Arnold's. 3580 Rte. 6 (about $1^1/_4$ mile N of town center). ☎ **508/255-2575.** Main courses $7–$16. No credit cards. Mid-May to mid-Sept daily 11am–10pm. Closed mid-Sept to mid-May. AMERICAN.

Offering a take-out window on the Rail Trail and a picnic grove for those who hate to waste vacation hours sitting indoors, this popular eatery dishes out all the usual

---

🏧 Family-Friendly Hotels & Restaurants

Bayside Lobster Hutt in Wellfleet *(see p. 195)*   A quaint old shack serving seafood "in the rough."

Even'Tide Motel in South Wellfleet *(see p. 194)*   Shaded by towering pines, this roomy complex has its own huge heated indoor pool and a wooded path leading straight to the seashore.

Kalmar Village in North Truro *(see p. 203)*   A spiffy standout among the motels and cottage colonies lined up along the bay, this one—a family enterprise since the early 1940s—has its own personality; wholesome and fun.

The Lobster Pot in Provincetown *(see p. 226)*   Even the self-styled sophisticates in town willingly line up for the straightforward seafood and fabulous views.

The Best Western Tides Beachfront in Provincetown *(see p. 219)*   Well removed from the road, this manicured beachfront motel offers everything a child could want: sun, sand, salt water, and a freshwater pool for variation.

Watermark Inn in Provincetown *(see p. 218)*   Perched atop its own little beach in the quiet West End, this small all-suite hotel offers colorful, light-washed quarters variously endowed with private decks, fireplaces, galley kitchens, and sleeping lofts.

---

seashore standards, from rich and crunchy fried clams (cognoscenti know to order whole clams, not strips) to foot-long chili dogs.

BREAKFAST GOODIES

Hole-in-One Donut Shop. 4295 Rte. 6 (about $^1/_4$ mile S of town center). ☎ **508/255-9446.**

Old-timers convene at the counter of this tiny shop (open 5am to noon daily) to ponder the state of the world. You can join in—or scurry home with your haul of hand-cut donuts and fresh-baked muffins and bagels.

TAKE-OUT & PICNIC FARE

Box Lunch. 4205 Rte. 6, N. Eastham. ☎ **508/255-0799.**

And yet another source of the popular, Cape-invented pita "rollwiches."

SWEETS

Ben & Jerry's Scoop Shop. 50 Brackett Rd. (at Rte. 6 in the center of town). ☎ **508/255-2817.**

This premium ice-cream parlor is just about all most Eastham residents need in the way of evening entertainment.

The Chocolate Sparrow. 4205 Rte. 6, N. Eastham. ☎ **508/240-0606.**

Let the seductive aroma of simmering chocolate lead you to this source of hand-dipped delights.

EASTHAM AFTER DARK

Most Saturday nights in season (the schedule is somewhat erratic), the **First Encounter Coffee House,** Chapel in the Pines, 220 Samoset Rd. (off Route 6, $^1/_4$-mile west of town center), Eastham (☎ **508/255-5438**), a tiny 1899 church, hosts some very big names on the folk/rock circuit, such as local faves—and national acts—Livingston Taylor and Patty Larkin. Tickets $10; call for schedule. Closed May and September.

The Salt Pond Visitor Center, on Salt Pond Road in Eastham (east of Route 6; ☎ 508/255-3421), puts on a varying schedule of entertainment (including concerts, sing-alongs, and storytelling) in season. Admission is free. Call for schedule.

2 Wellfleet

42 miles (68km) NE of Sandwich, 14 miles (23km) S of Provincetown

Wedged between tame Eastham and wild Truro, Wellfleet—with the well-tended look of a classic New England town—is the golden mean, the perfect destination for artists, writers, off-duty psychiatrists, and other contemplative types who hope to find more in the landscape than mere quaintness or rusticity. Distinguished literati such as Edna St. Vincent Millay and Edmund Wilson put this rural village on the map in the 1920s, in the wake of Provincetown's bohemian heyday. In her brief and tumultuous tenure as Wilson's wife, Mary McCarthy pilloried the pretensions of the summer population in her novel *A Charmed Life,* but had to concede that the region boasts a certain natural beauty: "steel-blue fresh-water ponds and pine forests and mushrooms and white bluffs dropping to a strangely pebbled beach."

To this day, Wellfleet remains remarkably unspoiled. Once one departs from Route 6, commercialism is kept to a minimum, though the town boasts plenty of appealing shops—including a score of distinguished galleries—and a couple of excellent New American restaurants. It's hard to imagine any other community on the Cape supporting so sophisticated an undertaking as the Wellfleet Harbor Actors' Theatre, or hosting such a wholesome event as public square-dancing on the adjacent Town Pier. And where else could you find, right next door to an outstanding nature preserve (the Wellfleet Bay Wildlife Sanctuary), a thriving drive-in movie theater?

ESSENTIALS

GETTING THERE   After crossing either the Bourne or Sagamore bridge, head east on Route 6 or 6A to Orleans, and north on Route 6. Or fly into Provincetown or Hyannis (see "Getting There" in chapter 3).

VISITOR INFORMATION   Contact the **Wellfleet Chamber of Commerce,** off Route 6, Wellfleet, MA 02663 (☎ 508/349-2510) or the **Cape Cod Chamber of Commerce,** Routes 6 and 132, Hyannis, MA 02601 (☎ 508/362-3225; fax 508/362-3698; Web site www.capecod.com).

BEACHES & OUTDOOR PURSUITS

BEACHES   Though the distinctions are far from hard and fast, Wellfleet's fabulous ocean beaches tend to sort themselves demographically: LeCount Hollow is popular with families, Newcomb Hollow with high-schoolers, White Crest with the college crowd (including surfers and off-hour hang-gliders), and Cahoon with thirtysomethings. Alas, only the latter two beaches permit parking by nonresidents. To enjoy the other two, as well as Burton Baker Beach on the harbor and Duck Harbor on the bay, plus three freshwater ponds, you'll have to walk or bike in, or see if you qualify for a sticker ($25 per week). Bring proof of residency to the seasonal Beach Sticker Booth on the Town Pier, or call the **Wellfleet Recreation Department** (☎ 508/349-9818).

- **Marconi Beach,** off Marconi Beach Road in South Wellfleet. A National Seashore property, this cliff-lined beach (with rest rooms) charges an entry fee of $5 per day, or only $15 for the season. *Note:* The bluffs are so high that the beach lies in shadow by late afternoon.

- **White Crest and ✪ Cahoon Hollow beaches,** off Ocean View Drive in Wellfleet. These two town-run ocean beaches—big with surfers—are open to all. Both have snack bars and rest rooms. Parking costs $10 per day.
- **Mayo Beach,** Kendrick Avenue (near the Town Pier). Right by the harbor, facing south, this beach (with rest rooms) is hardly secluded but will please young waders and splashers. And the price is right; parking is free. You could grab a tasty, cheap bite at Painter's Lunch next to the Wellfleet Harbor Actors' Theatre; it's a neo-bohemian ramshackle, keeps odd hours, and has no phone, but it's fun.

BICYCLING The terminus (to date) of the 25-mile (and growing) **Cape Cod Rail Trail** (☎ 508/896-3491), Wellfleet is also among its more desirable destinations: A country road off the bike path leads right to LeCount Hollow Beach. Located at the current terminus, the **Black Duck Sports Shop** at 1446 Rte. 6 in Wellfleet (at the corner of LeCount's Hollow Road; ☎ 508/349-9801) stocks everything from rental bikes to "belly boards" and inflatable boats; the deli at the adjoining **South Wellfleet General Store** (☎ 508/349-2335) can see to your snacking needs.

BOATING **Jack's Boat Rentals,** located on Gull Pond off Gull Pond Road, about ¹/₂ mile south of the Truro border (☎ 508/349-9808), rents out canoes, kayaks, sailboards, Windsurfers, Sunfish, as well as sea cycles and surf bikes, on Gull Pond. Renting a kayak at Gull Pond for a couple of hours costs $20; a canoe costs $30. If you'd like a canoe for a few days, you'll need to go to Jack's Boat Rentals location on Route 6 in Wellfleet (next to the Cumberland Farms). There, a canoe rents for about $35 for 24 hours, but only $70 for 3 days. Rentals come with a roof rack if you need it. There are many wonderful places to canoe in Wellfleet. A trip from Wellfleet's Town Pier across the harbor to Great Island, for instance, will get you nowhere fast, beautifully.

In addition to watercraft to go, Jack's is also the place for information about **Eric Gustavson's guided kayak tours** (☎ 508/349-1429) of nearby kettle ponds and tidal rivers. For information about other excellent naturalist-guided tours, inquire about trips sponsored by the **Cape Cod Museum of Natural History** (☎ 800/479-3867 or 508/896-3867) and the **Wellfleet Bay Wildlife Sanctuary** (☎ 508/349-2615).

The **Chequessett Yacht & Country Club** on Chequessett Neck Road in Wellfleet (☎ 508/349-3704) offers sailing lessons for approximately $30 an hour. For those who already know how, **Wellfleet Marine Corp.** on the Town Pier (☎ 508/349-2233) rents 14- to 20-foot sailboats in season.

FISHING For a license to fish at Long Pond, Great Pond, or Gull Pond (all stocked with trout and full of native perch, pickerel, and sunfish), visit **Town Hall** at 300 Main St. (☎ 508/349-0301). Costs vary, but in general, Massachusetts residents pay $28.50 for a season pass and nonresidents pay $38.50 for a season pass or $24.50 for a 3-day pass. Surf casting, which doesn't require a license, is permitted at the town beaches. Shellfishing licenses—Wellfleet's oysters are world-famous—can be obtained from the **Shellfish Department** on the Town Pier off Kendrick Avenue (☎ 508/349-0325). Also heading out from here, in season, is the 60-foot party fishing boat *Navigator* (☎ 508/349-6003), and three smaller sports-fishermen: the *Erin-H* (☎ 508/349-9663), *Jac's Mate* (☎ 508/255-2978), and *Snooper* (☎ 508/349-6113).

GOLF Hugging a pretty cove, the **Chequessett Yacht & Country Club** on Chequessett Neck Road (☎ 508/349-3704) has one of the loveliest 9-hole courses on the Cape; nonmembers need to reserve at least 5 days ahead.

NATURE & WILDLIFE AREAS   You'll find 6 miles of very scenic trails lined with lupines and bayberries—Goose Pond, Silver Spring, and Bay View—within the **Wellfleet Bay Wildlife Sanctuary** in South Wellfleet (see below). Right in town, the short, picturesque boardwalk known as **Uncle Tim's Bridge,** off East Commercial Street, crosses Duck Creek to access a tiny island crisscrossed by paths. The Cape Cod National Seashore maintains two spectacular self-guided trails. The 1¼-mile **Atlantic White Cedar Swamp Trail,** off the parking area for the Marconi Wireless Station (see below), shelters a rare stand of the light-weight species prized by Native Americans as wood for canoes; red maples are slowly crowding out the cedars, but meanwhile the tea-tinted, moss-choked swamp is a magical place, refreshingly cool even at the height of summer. A boardwalk will see you over the muck (these peat bogs are 7 feet deep in places), but the return trip does entail a calf-testing ½-mile trek through deep sand. Consider it a warm-up for magnificent **Great Island,** jutting 4 miles into the bay (off the western end of Chequessett Neck Road) to cup Wellfleet Harbor. Before attaching itself to the mainland in 1831, Great Island harbored a busy whaling post; a 1970 dig turned up the foundations of an early-18th-century tavern. These days the "island" is quite uninhabited and a true refuge for those strong enough to go the distance. Just be sure to cover up, wear sturdy shoes, bring water, and venture to **Jeremy Point**—the very tip—only if you're sure the tide is going out.

A spiffy new eco-friendly visitor center serves as both introduction and gateway to the ✪ **Wellfleet Bay Wildlife Sanctuary,** a 1,000-acre refuge maintained by the Massachusetts Audubon Society. Passive solar heat and composting toilets are just a few of the waste-cutting elements incorporated in the seemingly simple $1.6 million building, which nestles into its wooded site like well-camouflaged wildlife. You'll see plenty of the latter—especially lyrical redwing blackbirds and circling osprey—as you follow 5 miles of looping trails through pine forests, salt marsh, and moors. To hone your observation skills, avail yourself of the naturalist-guided walks scheduled throughout the day, and sometimes into the night (see "Wellfleet After Dark," below): You'll see and learn so much more. Also inquire about special workshops for children (some, like the Japanese "fish-printing" session, are truly ingenious) and about canoeing, snorkeling, birding, and off-season seal-watching excursions.

Note: It's worth joining the **Massachusetts Audubon Society** just for the chance—afforded only to members—to camp out here. The center is located off West Road (off Route 6, a couple hundred yards north of the Eastham border), in South Wellfleet (☎ **508/349-2615;** fax 508/349-2632). Trail use is free for Massachusetts Audubon Society members; the trail fee for nonmembers is $3 adults, $2 seniors and children. Trails are open July through August from 8am to 8pm, and September through June from 8am to dusk. The visitor center is open Memorial Day to Columbus Day daily from 8:30am to 5pm; during the off-season it's closed Mondays.

TENNIS   Public courts are located at Mayo Beach on Kendrick Avenue near the harbor; for details (a small fee is charged), contact the **Wellfleet Recreation Department** (☎ **508/349-0330**). For a fee, book one of the five clay courts at the **Chequessett Yacht & Country Club** on Chequessett Neck Road (☎ **508/349-3704**) or the eight at **Oliver's Clay Courts** at 2183 Rte. 6, about 1 mile south of town (☎ **508/349-3330**). At Chequessett, 1 hour of singles play costs $9, doubles $12. Both settings are beautiful.

WATER SPORTS   Surfing is restricted to White Crest Beach, and sailboarding to Burton Baker Beach at Indian Neck during certain tide conditions; ask for a copy of the regulations at the Beach Sticker Booth on the Town Pier.

WELLFLEET HISTORICAL SIGHTS

Marconi Wireless Station. Marconi Park Site Rd. (off Rte. 6, about ³/₄ S of town center). ☎ **508/349-3785.** Open dawn–dusk. Free parking and admission.

It's from this bleak spot that Italian inventor Guglielmo Marconi broadcast, via a complex of 210-foot cable towers, the world's first wireless communiqué: "cordial greetings from President Theadore [*sic*] Roosevelt to King Edward VII in Poldhu, Wales." It was also here that news of the troubled *Titanic* first reached these shores. There's scarcely a trace left of this extraordinary feat of technology (the station was dismantled in 1920); still, the displays convey the leap of imagination that was required.

Wellfleet Historical Society Museum. 266 Main St. (in the center of town). ☎ **508/349-9157.** Admission $1 adults, free for children under 12. Late June to early Sept Tues–Sat 2–5pm. Closed early Sept to late June.

Every last bit of spare Wellfleet memorabilia seems to have been crammed into this old storefront. The volunteer curators have taken pains to arrange the surfeit of artifacts so that visitors can follow up on a particular interest—the United Fruit Co., say, which got its start here in 1870 when one of Lorenzo Dow Baker's swift clipper ships delivered a cargo of exotic bananas, or Marconi's mysterious transoceanic experiments. Even restless children are likely to find something of interest, particularly among the antique toys in the attic. Inquire about the lecture schedule: The museum hosts some fascinating speakers and sponsors a chowder supper once a summer.

KID STUFF

No conceivable nocturnal treat beats an outing to the Wellfleet Drive-In Theater— unless it's a double-feature prefaced by a game of on-site minigolf while you're waiting for the sky to darken and for Tang Dynasty (see "Where to Dine," below) to pack up your custom pupu platter. During the day, check out what's up at the Wellfleet Bay Wildlife Sanctuary (see "Beaches & Outdoor Pursuits," above).

SHOPPING

Boasting over a dozen arts emporia, Wellfleet has begun hailing itself as "the art-gallery town." Though it may lag behind Provincetown in terms of quantity, the quality does achieve comparable heights. Crafts make a strong showing, too, as do contemporary women's clothing and eclectic home furnishings. Just one drawback: Unlike Provincetown, which has something to offer virtually year-round, Wellfleet pretty much closes up come Columbus Day, so buy while the getting's good.

ANTIQUES/COLLECTIBLES   Wheeler-dealers should head for the **Wellfleet Flea Market,** 51 Rte. 6 (north of the Eastham-Wellfleet border; ☎ **800/696-3532** or 508/349-2520). A few days a week in summer and during the shoulder seasons, the parking lot of the Wellfleet Drive-In Theater "daylights" as an outdoor bazaar featuring as many as 300 booths. Though a great many vendors stock discount surplus, there are usually enough collectible-dealers on hand to warrant a browse-through. An added bonus: Kids can kick loose in the little playground or grab a quick bite at the snack bar. Lookers are charged $1 to $2 per carload. Open weekends and Monday holidays, from mid-April through June, September, and October, from 8am to 4pm; Wednesdays, Thursdays, weekends, and Monday holidays, in July and August, from 8am to 4pm.

Farmhouse Antiques, Route 6 at Village Lane, South Wellfleet (☎ **508/349-1708**), is a large storehouse filled with an enormous variety of good stuff, including a wide array of furniture, stacks of books and ephemera, and the antique chandeliers that didn't fit in the Orleans shop, Continuum (Farmhouse is a dealer for Continuum's wares).

ARTS & CRAFTS ✪ **Cherry Stone Gallery,** 70 E. Commercial St. (about ¹/₈ mile south of East Main Street; ☎ **508/349-3026**), is slightly off the main arts drag and intentionally out of step (it holds its openings on Tuesday evenings, shunning the Saturday consensus), but this tiny gallery is probably more influential than all the others put together. It got a head start, opening in 1972 and showing such luminaries as Rauschenberg, Motherwell, and, more recently, Wellfleet resident Helen Miranda Wilson. Closed late September through May.

One of the more distinguished galleries in town, the smallish ✪ **Cove Gallery,** 15 Commercial St. (by Duck Creek; ☎ **508/349-2530**)—with a waterside sculpture garden—carries the paintings and prints of many well-known artists, including Barry Moser and Leonard Baskin. John Grillo's work astounds every summer during his annual show, which recently featured boldly painted opera-themed paintings, watercolors, and prints. Alan Nyiri, whose dazzling color photographs are collected in the coffee-table book *Cape Cod,* shows regularly, as does Carla Golembe, whose lively Caribbean-influenced tableaux have graced several children's books. Closed mid-October through April.

Crafts make a stronger stand than art at ✪ **Left Bank Gallery,** 25 Commercial St. (by Duck Creek; ☎ **508/349-9451**). A 1933 American Legion Hall, it's an optimal display space. Whereas the paintings occupying the former auditorium sometimes verge on hackneyed, the "Potter's Room" overlooking the cove is packed with sturdy, handsome, useful vessels, along with compatible textiles. Also definitely worth hunting out are the curious collages of Kim Victoria Kettler, whose work also graces Aesop's Tables (see "Where to Dine," below). The **Left Bank Print Gallery,** 3 W. Main St. (in the center of town; ☎ **508/439-7939**) features the spillover from the Left Bank Gallery, and in some ways it is superior. The prints, to begin with, are striking, and represent some of the best work being done in the region. In addition, there's an irresistible sampling of new-wave jewelry designs, collected from over 100 noted artisans across the nation and arrayed in clever thematic displays.

Swansborough Gallery, 230 Main St. (in the center of town; ☎ **508/349-1883**), is itself a work of art: an 1830 barn transformed by gallery owner and architect Dick Hall into a roomy caracole of exhibition space, five levels in all. The guiding aesthetic is "eclectic," and with some 2 dozen artists to call upon, there's always something interesting on hand. Among the premier artists are Arthur Cohen, who paints oils of Provincetown scenes, and Miriam Freed, whose abstract works are in acrylic and also fabric collages. Closed mid-October to late May.

FASHION A half-century ago, Mary McCarthy complained that Wellfleet's "gay, smart wives, mottled and bedizened, fantastically got up with shawls and peasant bangles . . . made the First National check-out look like a fortune-tellers' convention." The style hasn't changed all that much, except to grow universally popular. At **Hannah,** 234 Main St. (☎ **508/349-9884**), Susan Hannah, whose main store is in ultrahip Northampton, Massachusetts, shows her own private label in this nicely rehabbed house, along with other designers' works. The emphasis is on flowing lines and relaxed fabrics—slinky rayons, soft cotton jersey, nubby linen. Closed mid-September through late May.

Slightly more mainstream—which is to say, citified—is **Off Center,** 354 Main St. (☎ **508/349-3634**), is neither traditional nor trendy, but right on the money for that look of effortless, go-anywhere chic. Closed January through March.

Somewhat to the left of—and across the street from—its parent shop, Off Center, is **Eccentricity,** 361 Main St. (in the center of town; ☎ **508/349-7554**), which lives up to its name with dramatic antique kimonos and artifacts from Japan, India, and Africa. Closed January through March.

✪ **Karol Richardson,** 3 W. Main St. (☎ **508/349-6378**) is owned and operated by its namesake, Karol Richardson, an alumna of the London College of Fashion and a refugee from the New York rag trade. She has a feel for sensuous fabrics and a knack for fashions that, in her own words, are "wonderfully comfortable but sophisticated at the same time and very flattering to the less than perfect body." The lovely clothes that are seasonally displayed in this barn showroom, and slavered over by several generations, bear out the claim. Closed mid-October through April.

GIFTS **Jules Besch Stationers,** 275 Main St. (☎ **508/349-1231**), specializes in stationery products, including papers, ribbon, gift cards, handmade journals, desktop pen sets, and unusual gift items. This is an exquisite store and certainly worth a quick browse.

WHERE TO STAY
VERY EXPENSIVE
The Colony of Wellfleet. 640 Chequessett Neck Rd. (about 1¹/₂ miles W of the Town Pier), Wellfleet, MA 02667. ☎ **508/349-3761.** Fax 508/349-1182. 10 cottages. TEL. Summer $138–$275. No credit cards. Closed late Sept to late May.

No cookie-cutter colony, this 10-acre retreat is really a living-history museum, preserving the postwar Bauhaus style (Marcel Breuer summered in Wellfleet and built a handful of private houses here). These modernist blocks, most with the original, museum-worthy artwork and furnishings, usually rent by the week ($825 to $1,700) to the same coterie year after year, but you might catch one between occupants.

MODERATE
✪ **Surfside Cottages.** Ocean View Dr. (at LeCount Hollow Rd.), Box 937, S. Wellfleet, MA 02663. ☎ **508/349-3959.** E-mail surfside@capecod.net. 18 cottages. TV. Summer $700–$1,275 weekly; off-season $70–$125 per day. MC, V.

This is where you want to be: smack dab on a spectacular beach with 50-foot dunes, biking distance to Wellfleet Center, a short drive to Provincetown for dinner. These cottages, fun and modern in a 1960s way, have one, two, or three bedrooms. All cottages have kitchens, fireplaces, barbecues, and screened porches. Reserve early.

INEXPENSIVE
Cahoon Hollow Bed & Breakfast. 56 Cahoon Hollow Rd. (E of Rte. 6), Wellfleet, MA 02667. ☎ **508/349-6372.** 2 suites. Summer (including full breakfast) $100 double. MC, V.

Those fortunate enough to stay at Bailey Ruckert's pretty 1842 house—midway between the ocean and "downtown" Wellfleet—have a definite leg up on mere tourists. Guests get a real sense of what it would be like to be lucky enough to live here—and have a gourmet breakfast chef on call, willing to dish up a French-toast custard, perhaps, sparked with homemade beach-plum jam. The quarters are private and elegant, and bikes are provided so you can go exploring.

✪ **Even'tide.** 650 Rte. 6 (about 1 mile N of Eastham border), S. Wellfleet, MA 02663. ☎ **800/368-0007** in MA only, or 508/349-3410. Fax 508/349-7804. 28 rms, 3 apts. A/C TV TEL. Summer $75–$106 double; $105 efficiency. AE, CB, DC, DISC, MC, V.

Set back from the road in its own roomy compound complete with playground, this motel feels more like a friendly village centered around a large, heated indoor pool—

a godsend in inclement weather. The Rail Trail goes right by it, and a ³/₄-mile foot-path through the woods leads to Marconi Beach.

The Inn at Duck Creeke. 70 Main St., Box 364, Wellfleet, MA 02667. ☎ **508/349-9333.** Fax 508/349-0234. E-mail duckinn@capecod.net. 25 rms (8 with shared bath). Summer (including continental breakfast) $65–$90 double. MC, V.

This historic complex consists of four buildings set on 5 woodsy acres overlooking a tidal creek and salt marsh. Three lodging buildings include the main building, an 1880s captains house. Rooms are a bit worn at the seams, but at these prices, who cares? There are two good restaurants (see "Where to Dine," below) on site: Sweet Seasons, the more expensive, and the Tavern Room, with a publike atmosphere and live entertainment in season.

WHERE TO DINE
MODERATE

✪ **Aesop's Tables.** 316 Main St. (in the center of town). ☎ **508/349-6450.** Reservations recommended. Main courses $16–$23. AE, CB, DISC, MC, V. July–Aug Wed–Sun noon–3pm; daily 5:30–9:30pm. Call for off-season hrs. Closed mid-Oct to mid-May. NEW AMERICAN.

This delightful restaurant—offbeat and avant-garde enough to stay interesting year after year, since 1965—has it all: a handsome, historic setting (this was a 19th-century governor's summer house, the pride of a proud town), a relaxed and festive atmosphere, and utterly delectable food, reliably and artistically turned out by executive chef Peter Rennert. Brian Dunne is at once owner and host; it's he who sets the mood and oversees the sourcing of the superb local provender—even growing some of the edible flowers and delicate greens that go into the "Monet's Garden" salad. The scallops (served whole) and oysters come straight from the bay to be imaginatively treated. While some entrees have begun to show evidence of Southwestern savvy and other welcome world-beat influences, the desserts are sacrosanct. Many followers simply could not get through the summer without enjoying at least one encounter with "Clementine's Citrus Tart," a rich *pâte sablée* (sablé pastry) offset by a piquant mousse blending fruit and white chocolate.

Bayside Lobster Hutt. 91 Commercial St. (about ¹/₄ mile N of the Town Pier), Wellfleet. ☎ **508/349-6333.** Reservations not accepted. Main courses $8–$20. DISC, MC, V. Late May to mid-Sept daily 4:30–9pm. Closed mid-Sept to late May. AMERICAN.

For your "dress-down" night (or several in a row), you couldn't do better than this classic, locally owned lobster joint, housed in a grizzled 1857 oyster shack—look for the life-size lobsterman on the roof. David Francis, the son of an oysterman, started the business in 1974 and has had no reason so far to mess with success—even if it means streams of customers willing to wait an hour or more to crowd into the communal mess hall at the height of summer. "Feeding frenzy" is the only way to describe the claw-cracking hordes at the long oilcloth-covered plank tables. Afterwards, if you have an ounce of appetite—or a micron of room—left, check out the Just Dessert annex (see below) out back.

Flying Fish Cafe. 29 Briar Lane (off Main St.). ☎ **508/349-3100.** Reservations not accepted. Main courses $12–$18. MC, V. Late June to early Sept daily 7am–10pm; call for off-season hrs. Closed Nov–Mar. NEW AMERICAN.

Just the thing: a cafe catering to esoteric cravings (for example, Jamaican jerk chicken, tabbouleh, Brie omelets) during the day, and loftier expectations (such as "lobster romantique" atop black pepper fettuccine with ginger-cinnamon beurre blanc) at night. Better yet, the on-site bakery means immediate access to such devilish confections as chocolate Chambord cake—plus, the tourists who clog Main Street haven't yet caught on.

Sweet Seasons Restaurant. At the Inn at Duck Creeke, 70 Main St. (about ⅛ mile W of Rte. 6). ☎ **508/349-6535.** Reservations recommended. Main courses $15–$22. AE, DC, MC, V. Late June to mid-Sept daily 6–10pm. Closed mid-Sept to late June. NEW AMERICAN.

The competition has grown heated of late, but chef-owner Judith Pihl's Mediterranean-influenced fare is still appealing after 20-plus years, as is this mullion-windowed dining room's peaceful pond view. Some of the dishes can be a bit heavy by contemporary standards, but there's usually a healthy alternative: Wellfleet littlenecks and mussels in a golden, aromatic tomato-and-cumin broth, for instance, as opposed to Russian oysters with smoked salmon, vodka, and sour cream. Lighter fare is served in the adjoining Duck Creeke Tavern (see below).

INEXPENSIVE

Duck Creeke Tavern. At the Inn at Duck Creeke, 70 Main St. (about ⅛ mile W of Rte. 6). ☎ **508/349-7369.** Main courses $10–$17. AE, MC, V. Late May to mid-Oct daily 5–11pm. Closed mid-Oct to late May. NEW AMERICAN.

Issuing from the Sweet Seasons's kitchen (see above), the food served in this rustic, early 1800s tavern is on the lighter side—in terms of your budget, if not your calorie intake. Late into the evening, you can snack on baby cakes (dense, local cod cakes), or the house specialty, Beef and Ale, a beef sirloin and chunky onion stew topped with a puff pastry cap (Guinness being the not-so-secret ingredient).

Finely JP's. 19 Freedjum Rd. (on Rte. 6, about 1 mile N of Eastham border). ☎ **508/349-7500.** Reservations not accepted. Main courses $12–$15. DISC, MC, V. July–Aug Sat–Sun 8am–noon; daily 5–10pm. Call for off-season hrs. Closed mid-Dec to mid-Jan. NEW AMERICAN.

The passing motorist who happens upon this roadside eatery will feel like a clever explorer indeed, even if locals have long been in on the secret. Were it not for the venue—a rather nondescript wood-paneled box right by the busy roadway—chef-owner John Pontius could charge a lot more for his polished cuisine. As it is, you could feast on baked oysters Bienville (doused with wine and cream and topped with a mushroom-onion duxelle and grated Parmesan) and an improvisatory "Wellfleet paella," having barely broken a 20-note. Pass it on.

The Lighthouse. 317 Main St. (in the center of town). ☎ **508/349-3681.** Main courses $9–$13. DISC, MC, V. Daily 6:30am–10pm. AMERICAN.

Nothing special in and of itself, this bustling year-round institution is an off-season haven for locals and a beacon to passing tourists year-round. Except on Thursday's "Mexican Night," the menu is all-American normal, from the steak-and-eggs breakfast to the native seafood dinners. Appreciative patrons usually keep up a dull roar throughout the day, revving up to a deafening roar as the Bass and Guinness flow from the tap.

✪ **Moby Dick's Restaurant.** Rte. 6, Wellfleet. ☎ **508/349-9795.** Reservations not accepted. Main courses $6–$16. No credit cards. June–Sept 11:30am–10pm; call for off-season hrs. SEAFOOD.

This is your typical clam shack, with requisite netting and buoys hanging from the ceiling. Order your meal at the register, sit at a picnic table, and a cheerful college student brings it to you. Fried fish, clams, scallops, and shrimp are all good here; get the Moby's Seafood Special, a heaping platter of all of the above plus coleslaw and fries. Then there's the clambake special with lobster, steamers, and corn on the cob. Portions are huge; bring the family and chow down.

⊙ **Painter's.** 50 Main St. (near Rte. 6). ☎ **508/349-3003.** Reservations recommended. Main courses $10–$18. AE, MC, V. May–Oct Wed–Mon 5–11pm. Closed Nov–Apr. NEW AMERICAN.

The offspring of local literati, Kate Painter trained at some pretty fancy establishments: San Francisco's world-famous Stars, Boston top spot Biba, and Cape Cod's own Chillingsworth. Still, if she had her druthers—and now she does, having set up her own restaurant in a rambling 1750 tavern—she'd still prefer, in the words of her motto and mission statement, "simple food in a funky place." The modesty is misplaced because, although the setting is pretty low-key (a wood-beamed bistro dressed up with friends' artwork), her culinary skills are top-notch. Consider a warm duck-breast salad with plum-balsamic vinaigrette or Thai soup with pan-seared scallops and sunflower sprouts—that's just for starters. The hearty entrees include such robust dishes as clams Cataplana (like a sunnily spiced Portuguese bouillabaisse), flounder rubbed with roasted garlic, and an always-affordable linguine *aglio e olio*. Painter's sense of humor shows up in the desserts: "Something Chocolate" and "Something Lemon" are just that, an intriguing cross between cake and soufflé. Or you could just order a straight pint of Ben & Jerry's, served just like at home—in the carton, with bowls and a scoop.

Tang Dynasty. 49 Rte. 6 (N of Eastham border). ☎ **508/349-7521.** Most items under $8. AE, MC, V. Apr–Nov daily 11:30am–1am; call for off-season hrs. CHINESE.

It's an inspired pairing, the presence of this competent Chinese restaurant at the very doorstep of the drive-in means that you can import a world-class supper, of the sort that would drive indoor cineastes insane with hunger and envy. We usually load up on finger-food appetizers—and then hit the drive-in's snack bar for dessert.

PICNIC & TAKE-OUT FARE

Box Lunch, 20 Briar Lane (north of Main Street in the town center; ☎ **508/349-2178**)—its porch usually hemmed in by bicycles—is the original source of the Cape's signature "rollwiches": rolled pita sandwiches with unusual fillings.

A former fishing shack, **Hatch's Fish & Produce Market,** 310 Main St. (behind Town Hall; ☎ **508/349-2810**), is the unofficial heart of Wellfleet. You'll find the best of local bounty from fresh-picked corn and fruit-juice Popsicles to steaming lobsters and home-smoked local mussels and pâté. Virtually no one passes through without picking up a little something, along with the latest talk of the town. Closed late September to late May.

SWEETS

The closet-sized outlet of a local chocolatier, **The Chocolate Sparrow,** 326 Main St. (in the center of town; ☎ **508/349-1333**), is hard to pass by once you've happened upon it. Closed mid-September to late May. **Just Dessert,** 91 Commercial St. (behind the Bayside Lobster Hutt; ☎ **508/349-6333**), is a cove-side cottage with a breezy deck and a deli case full of sweet finales—from sophisticated cheesecakes to "mile-high apple pie." Closed early September to late June. **A Nice Cream Stop,** 326 Main St. (in the center of town; ☎ **508/349-2210**), is Wellfleet's premier premium ice-cream parlor, scooping Emack & Bolio's, a luscious Boston boutique brand. Closed mid-September to mid-June.

WELLFLEET AFTER DARK
CLUBS & WATERING HOLES

⊙ **The Beachcomber.** 1220 Old Cahoon Hollow Rd. (off Ocean View Dr. at Cahoon Hollow Beach). ☎ **508/349-6055.** Fax 508/349-1953. Late June to mid-Sept Mon–Fri 8pm–1am, Sat–Sun 4pm–1am; call for off-season hrs. Closed mid-Sept to late May. Cover $5–$10.

Arguably the best dance club on Cape Cod, the 'Comber—housed in a 1897 life-saving station—is definitely the most scenic, and not just in terms of the barely legal-age clientele. It's right on Cahoon Hollow Beach—so close, in fact, that late beachgoers on summer weekends can count on a free concert: reggae, perhaps, or the homegrown "Incredible Casuals." Other nights, you might run into jazz, blues, hip-hop, or comedy, and often some very big names playing mostly for the fun of it. For victims of late-night munchies, the Beachcomber serves food till midnight.

Duck Creeke Tavern. At the Inn at Duck Creeke, 70 Main St. (about $^1/_8$ mile W of Rte. 6). ☎ **508/349-7369.** Closed mid-Oct to late May. No cover.

Local talent—jazz, pop, folk, and various hybrids—also accompany the light fare here. Check out the bar itself, fashioned from old doors.

Painter's Upstairs. 50 Main St. (near Rte. 6). ☎ **508/349-3003.** Closed Tues and Nov–Apr. No cover.

Local jazz acts regale the nondining drinkers and noshers in this popular restaurant, where the bar food is way better than average (see "Where to Dine," above).

Upstairs Bar at Aesop's Tables. 316 Main St. (in the center of town). ☎ **508/349-6450.** July–Aug daily 5:30pm–closing; call for off-season hrs. Closed mid-Oct to mid-May. No cover.

Locally spawned blues and jazz usually inhabit this cozy attic, where revelers can recline in comfy armchairs and velvet settees. A cafe menu from the superb restaurant downstairs (see "Where to Dine," above) can be enjoyed, along with the signature desserts and some seductive "special finales," blending coffee or tea and select liqueurs.

PERFORMANCE, ETC.

The First Congregational Church of the United Church of Christ, 200 Main St. (about $^1/_8$ mile west of Route 6; ☎ **508/349-6877**), hosts organ concerts Sundays at 8pm during July and August on its elaborate 1873 instrument. They're a good excuse to stop in and take a look around—the soaring 1850 Greek Revival church has the world's only bell tower ringing ship's time (an innovation introduced in 1952). Admission is free.

Wednesday nights in summer, Wellfleet's workaday fishing pier (off Kendricks Avenue) resounds to the footfalls of avid amateur **square dancers** of every age. Call ☎ **508/349-0330** for more information.

How about a night hike or bat walk? Both are offered at the **Wellfleet Bay Wildlife Sanctuary** (☎ **508/349-2615;** see "Beaches & Outdoor Pursuits," above). Rates vary; call for schedule and reservations. Just don't take in any vampire movies at the drive-in beforehand.

The **Wellfleet Drive-In Theater,** 51 Rte. 6 (just north of the Eastham border; ☎ **800/696-3532** or 508/349-2520), clearly deserves National Landmark status: Built in 1957, it's the only drive-in left on Cape Cod and one of a scant half-dozen surviving in the state. The rituals are unbending and every bit as endearing as ever: the playtime preceding the cartoons, the countdown plugging the allures of the snack bar, and finally, two full first-run features. The drive-in is open daily from late May through mid-September; show time is at dusk. Call for off-season hours. Admission is $6 adults, $3.50 seniors and children 5 to 11.

The principals behind the ✪ **Wellfleet Harbor Actors' Theatre,** 1 Kendrick Ave. (near the Town Pier; ☎ **508/349-6835**), aim to provoke—and usually succeed, even amid this very sophisticated, seen-it-all summer colony. Co-artistic directors Jeff Zinn and Gip Hoppe go to great lengths to secure original work, some local and some by playwrights of considerable renown, with the result that the repertory rarely suffers a dull moment. Tickets are $14. Performances are given daily at 8pm from late May through October; call for schedule.

3 Truro

46 miles (74km) E of Sandwich, 10 miles (16km) S of Provincetown

Truro is one of those blink-and-you'll-miss-it towns. With only 1,600 year-round residents (fewer than it boasted in 1840, when Pamet Harbor was a whaling and ship-building port), the town amounts to little more than a smattering of stores and public buildings, and lots of low-profile houses hidden away in the woods and dunes. Again, as in Wellfleet, writers, artists, and vacationing therapists are drawn to the quiet and calm. Edward Hopper lived in contented isolation in a South Truro cottage for nearly 4 decades.

If you find yourself craving cultural stimulation or other kinds of excitement, Provincetown is only a 10-minute drive away (you'll know you're getting close when you spot the wall-to-wall tourist cabins lining the bay in North Truro). Here, the natives manage to entertain themselves pretty well with get-togethers at the Truro Center for the Arts or, more simply, among themselves. However much money may be circulating in this rusticated community (the answer is: a lot), inconspicuous consumption is the rule of the day. The culmination of the social season, tellingly enough, is the late-September "dump dance" held at Truro's recycling center.

ESSENTIALS

GETTING THERE   After crossing either the Bourne or Sagamore bridge, head east on Route 6 or 6A to Orleans and north on Route 6. Or fly into Provincetown (see "Getting There" in chapter 3).

The **North Truro Shuttle System** (☎ **508/487-6870**) connects the town with Provincetown in season, for only $2 one-way.

VISITOR INFORMATION   Contact the **Truro Chamber of Commerce,** Route 6A at Head of the Meadow Road, Truro, MA 02666 (☎ **508/487-1288**) or the **Cape Cod Chamber of Commerce,** Routes 6 and 132, Hyannis, MA 02601 (☎ **508/362-3225;** fax 508/362-3698; Web site www.capecod.com).

BEACHES & OUTDOOR PURSUITS

BEACHES   Parking at all of Truro's exquisite Atlantic beaches, except for one Cape Cod National Seashore access point, is reserved for residents and renters. To obtain a sticker ($30 for 2 weeks), inquire at the **beach-sticker office** at 14 Truro Center Rd. (☎ **508/349-3939**) or **Town Hall** on Town Hall Road (☎ **508/349-3635**). Walkers and bikers are welcome, however, to visit such natural wonders as Ballston Beach, where all you'll see is silky sand and grass-etched dunes.

- ✪ **Head of the Meadow,** off Head of the Meadow Road. Among the more remote National Seashore beaches, this spot (equipped with rest rooms) is known for its excellent surf. Parking costs $5 per day, or $15 per season.
- **Corn Hill Beach,** off Corn Hill Road. Offering lifeguard supervision and rest rooms, this bay beach—near the hill where the Pilgrims found the seed corn that ensured their survival—is open to nonresidents for a parking fee of $5 per day.

BICYCLING   Although it has yet to be linked up to the Cape Cod Rail Trail, Truro does have a stunning 2-mile bike path of its own: the Head of the Meadow Trail, off the road of the same name (look for a right-hand turn about $^1/_2$ mile north of where Routes 6 and 6A intersect). Part of the old 1850 road toward

Cape Cod National Seashore

No trip to Cape Cod would be complete without a visit to the Cape Cod National Seashore on the Outer Cape. Take a late-afternoon barefoot stroll along **"The Great Beach"** and see why the Cape is filled with artists and poets. On August 7, 1961, President John F. Kennedy signed a bill designating 27,000 acres in the 40 miles from Chatham to Provincetown as The Cape Cod National Seashore, a new national park. However, as early as the 1930s, the National Park Service had been interested in Cape Cod's Great Beach; back then, the land would have cost taxpayers about $10 an acre! Unusual in a national park, the Seashore includes 500 private residences, the owners of which "lease" land from the park service. Convincing residents that a National Seashore would be a good thing for Cape Cod was an arduous task back then, and Provincetown still grapples with Seashore officials over town land issues.

The Seashore's claim to fame is its spectacular beaches—in reality, one long beach—with dunes 50 to 150 feet high. This is the Atlantic Ocean, so the surf is rough (and cold), but a number of the beaches have lifeguards. Seashore beaches include: Coast Guard and Nauset Light beaches in Eastham, Marconi Beach in Wellfleet, Head of the Meadow Beach in Truro, and Provincetown's Race Point and Herring Cove beaches. A $15 pass will get you into all of them for the season, or you can pay a daily rate of $5.

The Seashore also has a number of walking trails—all free, all picturesque, and all worth a trip. In Eastham, ✪ **Fort Hill** (off Route 6) has one of the best scenic views on Cape Cod, and a popular boardwalked trail through a red maple swamp. The **Nauset Marsh Trail** is accessed from the Salt Pond Visitor Center on Route 6 in Eastham. **Great Island** on the bay side in Wellfleet is surely one of the finest places to have a picnic; you could spend the day hiking the trails. On **Pamet Cranberry Bog Trail** off North Pamet Road in Truro, hikers pass the decrepit old cranberry-bog building (restoration is in the works) after a boardwalked romp over the bog itself. **Atlantic White Cedar Swamp Trail** is located at the Marconi Station site. **Small Swamp** and **Pilgrim Spring** trails are found at

Provincetown—Thoreau traveled this same route—it skirts the bluffs, passing Pilgrim Heights (where the Pilgrims found their first drinking water) and ending at High Head Road. Being fairly flat as well as short, this stretch should suit youngsters and beginners. Rentals can be arranged at **Bayside Bikes,** 102 Shore Rd. (Route 6A), North Truro (☎ **508/487-5735**).

BOATING The inlets of the Pamet Harbor are great for canoeing and kayaking; when planning an excursion, study the tides so you won't be working against them. The closest rentals are in Wellfleet at **Jack's Boat Rentals** (☎ **508/349-9808**) on Route 6, next to the Cumberland Farms. **Eric Gustavson** (☎ **508/349-1429**) leads naturalist kayak tours along the Pamet River and other locations on the Outer Cape. You can find out the schedule from Jack's Boat Rentals.

FISHING Great Pond, Horseleech Pond, and Pilgrim Lake—flanked by parabolic dunes carved by the wind—are all fishable; for a license (inquire about shellfishing, too), visit **Town Hall** on Town Hall Road (☎ **508/349-3860**). Surf casting is permitted at Highland Light Beach, off Highland Road.

Pilgrim Heights Beach, and **Beech Forest Trail** is located at Race Point in Provincetown. The best bike path on Cape Cod is the **Province Lands Trail,** 5 swooping and invigorating miles, at Race Point Beach. If that's not enough in the way of sports, surf fishing is allowed from the ocean beaches—Race Point is a popular spot.

The Seashore also includes several historic buildings that tell their part of the region's history. At Race Point Beach in Provincetown, the **Old Harbor Lifesaving Station** serves as a museum of early lifesaving techniques. **Captain Edward Penniman's 1868 house** at Fort Hill in Eastham is a grandly ornate Second Empire home, and the 1730 **Atwood-Higgins House** in Wellfleet is a typical Cape-style home; both are open for tours. Five lighthouses dot the Seashore, including Highland Light in Truro and Nauset Light in Eastham, both recently moved back from precarious positions on the edge of the dunes.

Most of the Seashore beaches have large parking lots, but you'll need to get there early (before 10am) on busy summer weekends. If the beach you want to go to is full, try the one next door—most of the beaches are 5 to 10 miles apart. Don't forget your beach umbrella; the sun exposure here can get intense.

Getting There: Take Route 6, the Mid-Cape Highway to Eastham (about 45 miles). Pick up a map at the Salt Pond Visitor Center in Eastham. There is another visitor center at Race Point. Both centers have ranger activities, maps, gift shops, and bathrooms. Seashore beaches are all off Route 6 and are clearly marked. Additional beaches along this stretch are run by individual towns, and you must have a sticker or pay a fee.

Recommended Reading: Henry David Thoreau's *Cape Cod,* an entertaining account of Thoreau's journeys on the Cape in the late 19th-century—the writer/naturalist walked along the beach from Eastham to Provincetown. You can follow in his footsteps. Henry Beston's *The Outermost House* describes a year of living on the beach in Eastham in a simple one-room dune shack. The shack washed out to sea about 20 years ago, but "The Great Beach" remains.

GOLF North Truro boasts the most scenic—and historic—9-hole course on the Cape. Created in 1892, the minimally groomed, Scottish-style **Highland Links** at 10 Lighthouse Rd. (off South Highland Road; ☎ 508/487-9201), shares a lofty bluff with the 1853 Highland Light, where Thoreau used to crash during his Outer Cape expeditions. Visible (but not visitable) to the south is the granite "Jenny Lind Tower," part of a Boston railroad depot where the celebrated Swedish nightingale sang to compensate her fans for an overbooked concert. Greens fees at the federally owned, town-run Highland Links are reasonable, especially considering the spectacular setting.

NATURE TRAILS The Cape Cod National Seashore—comprising 70% of Truro's land—offers three informative self-guided nature trails. The $1/2$-mile **Cranberry Bog Trail** leads from the Little America youth hostel parking lot (see "Where to Stay," below) past a number of previously cultivated bogs reverting to their natural state. The **Pilgrim Spring Trail** and **Small Swamp Trail** (each a $3/4$ mile-loop) head out from the CCNS parking lot just east of Pilgrim Lake. Pilgrim Spring is where the parched colonists sipped their first freshwater in months—with "much delight," according to a contemporary account. Small Swamp is named for Thomas Small, a rather overly optimistic 19th-century farmer who tried to cultivate fruit trees in a soil more suited to salt hay. Both paths overlook Salt Meadow, a freshwater marsh favored by hawks and osprey.

TENNIS   Courts are available for rent at the **Pamet Harbor Yacht and Tennis Club** on Depot Road (☎ **508/349-3772**).

AN ARTS CENTER & A MUSEUM

✪ **Truro Center for the Arts at Castle Hill.** 10 Meetinghouse Rd. (at Castle Rd., about 3/4 mile NW of town center). ☎ **508/349-7511.** Admission varies; call for schedule. Closed Sept–June.

Send ahead for a brochure, and you could work some learning into your vacation. A great many celebrated writers and artists—from poet Alan Dugan to painter Edith Vonnegut—emerge from their summer hideaways to offer courses, lectures, and exhibits at this bustling little complex, an 1880s horse barn with windmill (now home to the administrative offices). The roster changes slightly from year to year, but you can rest assured that the stellar instructors will be at the top of their form in this stimulating environment. The center also offers lots of children's workshops for artists age 7 and up.

✪ **Truro Historical Museum.** 6 Lighthouse Rd. (off S. Highland Rd., 2 miles N of town center on Rte. 6). ☎ **508/487-3397.** Admission $3 adults, free for children under 12. Late May to mid-Sept daily 10am–5pm. Closed mid-Sept to mid-June.

Built as a hotel in 1907, the Highland House is a perfect repository for the odds and ends collected by the Truro Historical Society: ship's models, harpoons, primitive toys, a pirate's chest. . . . Be sure to visit the second floor, set up as if still occupied by 19th-century tourists.

SHOPPING

There's not a whole lot, but what there is, is good.

ANTIQUES/COLLECTIBLES   Want to stay one step ahead of the antique dealers, while enjoying pre-markup prices? Make regular visits to **Estate Furniture Sales,** 346 Rte. 6 (behind Seamen's Savings Bank; ☎ **508/487-2705**), where Jack Albacker stores entire households of vintage furnishings and goods. His goal is to keep the stuff moving, at modest prices. Collectors could be in luck.

Trifles and Treasures, 11 Truro Center Rd. (☎ **508/349-1708**), is a darling little shop right in the center of town. Antique buffs will enjoy browsing through the furniture, mainly American country pine. There's also authentic iron work and other kitchen items.

ARTS & CRAFTS   ✪ **The Susan Baker Memorial Museum,** 46 Shore Rd. (Route 6A, 1/4-mile northwest of Route 6; ☎ **508/487-2557**), showcases Ms. Baker's creative output, from fanciful/functional papier-mâché *objets* to primitivist landscapes. Despite the place's name, Baker has not passed on; it seems that she herself has exaggerated rumors of her death so as to rate her own museum without actually croaking. You might guess that she is definitely a character, as original as her work. Her main stock in trade—here, and at her Provincetown outlet—is humor displayed in various media, from artist's books to very atypical T-shirts (among the more popular of slogans in Provincetown: "too mean to marry"). Picture Nicole Hollander with a bit more bite. Call ahead October through May.

WHERE TO STAY

Kalmar Village. 674 Shore Rd. (Rte. 6A, about $^3/_4$ mile S of the Provincetown border), N. Truro, 02652. ☎ **508/487-0585.** Fax 508/487-5827. 9 rms, 7 efficiency suites, 40 cottages. TV. Summer $80 double; $115 suite; cottages $895–$1,595 weekly. DISC, MC, V. Closed mid-Oct to mid-May.

Spiffier than many of the motels and cottages along this spit of sand between Pilgrim Lake and Pilgrim Beach, this 1940s complex resembles a miniaturized Edgartown, with little white cottages shuttered in black. The clientele—largely families—can splash the day away in the 60-foot freshwater pool or on the 400-foot private beach.

Little America AYH-Hostel. 111 N. Pamet Rd. ($1^1/4$ miles E of Rte. 6), Truro, MA 02666. ☎ **508/349-3889.** 42 beds. $13 for members, $16 for nonmembers. JCB, MC, V. Closed mid-Sept to mid-June.

By far the most scenic of the youth hostels on the Cape (Nantucket's former life-saving station would be the closest contender), this Hopperesque house on a lonely bluff a short stroll from Ballston Beach was once a Coast Guard station; these days, it winters as an environmental-studies center. During the all-too-short summer, it's a magnet for hikers, cyclists, and surfers.

Outer Reach Motel. 535 Rte. 6 (midway between N. Truro center and Provincetown border), N. Truro, MA 02652. ☎ **800/942-5388** or 508/487-9090. Fax 508/487-2911. 58 rms. TV. Summer $79–$124 double. MC, V. Closed mid-Oct to mid-May.

The only tradeoff worth forfeiting a spot right on the beach is a fabulous view of the beach. This sprawling motel—the last development to sneak under the wire, pre–National Seashore—offers glorious vistas of Provincetown, where guests have privileges at another big (and equally unsightly) motel, the Provincetown Inn, on a narrow bay beach at the very western end of town. On-site here in North Truro, you'll find an outdoor pool and tennis court; the ocean is 1 mile east. The rooms are standard-issue, but there's a terrific independent restaurant, Adrian's, within the complex (see "Where to Dine," below).

✪ South Hollow Vineyards Bed-and-Breakfast Inn. 11 Shore Rd. (Rte. 6A, off Rte. 6, $^1/2$ mile S of town center), N. Truro, MA 02652. ☎ **508/487-6200.** Fax 508/487-4248. 4 rms, 1 suite. Summer (including full breakfast) $89–$99 double; $129 suite. MC, V.

You don't have to be a wine-lover to appreciate this beautiful 1836 B&B set amid 5 vine-covered acres. If you are, though, you'll be in your element. Each of the five bedrooms—including the Vintage Suite, with its double Jacuzzi—comes with a four-poster bed draped in particular wine tones, ranging (imperceptibly, for all but the trained eye) from claret to burgundy. Horticulturist/innkeepers Kathy Gregrow and Judy Wimer uncorked their first homegrown chardonnay and cabernet Franc in the fall of 1996, and the muscadet is well on its way. The slate-floored living room, with its exposed beams, looks more French than Federal, and is decorated with interesting oenological artifacts. For the nonconnoisseur, the draw is likely to be the bucolic setting (this is one of the last working farms on the Outer Cape), only 6 miles from the center of Provincetown.

WHERE TO DINE

✪ Adrian's. 535 Rte. 6 (midway between N. Truro center and Provincetown border). ☎ **508/487-4360.** Fax 508/487-6510. Main courses $7–$17. AE, MC, V. Mid-June to early Sept Mon–Fri 8am–noon, Sat–Sun 8am–1pm; daily 5:30–10pm. Call for off-season hrs. Closed mid-Oct to mid-May. NORTHERN ITALIAN.

Sharing a bluff with the Outer Reach Motel, Adrian Salcedo Cyr's stylish restaurant is greatly prized—not just for its knockout wood-fired pizzette and other creative fare, but for the superb breakfasts. Try for a table on the sunny deck overlooking all of Provincetown Harbor, and sample such eye-openers as orange-cinnamon French toast or huevos rancheros. Come back for the sunset and the Tuscan bread-and-tomato soup, the grilled eggplant salad, a thin-crusted "Quattro Stagioni" pizza, some masterful pasta—oh, and don't forget the tiramisu, heady with espresso brandy.

The Blacksmith Shop Restaurant. 17 Truro Center Rd. (in the center of town). ☎ **508/ 349-6554.** Main courses $9–$20. MC, V. Late May to early Sept Sat–Sun 8am–1pm; daily 4:30– 10pm. Call for off-season hrs. INTERNATIONAL.

Don't be dissuaded by the boxy exterior. Inside, this village institution (est. 1946) is charmingly decorated with smithy tools and folk art, including a rocking horse and seven dollhouses of varying provenance. The homemade cuisine is a form of contemporary folk art, too, from the baked goods that pack in a continental breakfast crowd on summer weekends to the enticing entrees—from fish of the day to rich pasta combos—that are even more affordably priced during the "early bird" period pre-6pm.

Terra Luna. 104 Shore Rd. (Rte. 6A), N. Truro. ☎ **508/487-1019.** Reservations accepted. Main courses $10–$19. AE, MC, V. Late May to mid-Oct daily 8am–1pm and 5:30–10pm. Closed mid-Oct to late May. FUSION.

People come from miles around to sample the outstanding breakfasts at this modest restaurant. The muffins and scones emerge fresh from the oven, and "entrees" such as the breakfast burrito or raisin French toast stuffed with cream cheese and walnuts call for a hearty appetite. You can start in again in the evening, on well-priced Pacific Rim and/or neo-Italian fare, such as penne in a fresh tomato-and-cream sauce splashed with vodka. Main courses include many local seafood and lobster dishes. The two-for-one pizzas, served nightly from 5 to 6:30, are a super deal and really hit the spot après-beach. There's even a creative children's menu here.

SWEETS & TAKE-OUT

Seeing as this deli/bakery/grocery is basically the whole enchilada in terms of downtown Truro, and seasonal to boot, it's a good thing ❂ **Jams,** 14 Truro Center Rd. (off Route 6, in the center of town; ☎ **508/349-1616**), is so delightful. It's full of tantalizing aromas: fresh creative pizzas (from pesto to pupu), rotisseried fowl sizzling on the spit, or cookies straight from the oven. The pastry and deli selections deserve their own four-star restaurant, but are all the more savory as part of a picnic. Closed early September to late May.

Hot, thirsty travelers will think they've died and gone to Hawaii when they happen upon **ParadIce,** 1 Depot Rd. (at Old County Road, about 1/2 mile west of Route 6; ☎ **508/349-2499**), dispensing "shave ice," a Pacific treat available here in 38 flavors, from Kahlua to apple pie à la mode. Closed early September through June.

4 Provincetown

56 miles (90km) NE of Sandwich, 42 miles (68km) NE of Hyannis

You made it, all the way to the end of the Lower Cape: one of the most interesting, rewarding spots on the eastern seaboard. Explorer Bartholomew Gosnold must have felt much the same thrill in 1602 when he and his crew happened upon a "great stoare of codfysshes" here (it wasn't quite the gold they were seeking, but valuable enough to warrant changing the peninsula's name). The Pilgrims, of course, were overjoyed when they slogged into the harbor 18 years later: Never mind that they'd landed several hundred miles off course—it was a miracle they'd made it 'round the treacherous Outer Cape at all. And Charles Hawthorne, the painter who "discovered" this near-derelict fishing town in the late 1890s and introduced it to the Greenwich Village intelligentsia, was besotted by this "jumble of color in the intense sunlight accentuated by the brilliant blue of the harbor."

He'd probably be aghast at the commercial circus his enthusiasm has wrought—though proud, perhaps, to find the Provincetown Art Association & Museum, which he helped found in 1914, still going strong. Although it's bound to experience the occasional off year or dull stretch (as does the art world in general), the town is wholeheartedly dedicated to creative expression, both visual and verbal, and right now it's on a roll. Some would ascribe the inspiration to the quality of the light (and it is particularly lovely, soft and diffuse) or the solitude afforded by long, lonely winters. But the general atmosphere of open-mindedness plays at least as pivotal a role, allowing a very varied assortment of individuals to pull together in pushing the cultural envelope.

That same warm embrace of different lifestyles accounts for Provincetown's ascendancy as a gay and lesbian resort. During peak season, Provincetown's streets are a celebration of the individual's freedom to be as "out" as imagination allows. This isolated outpost has always been a magnet for the adventurous-minded. In fact, the tightly knit Portuguese community mostly descends from fishermen and whaling crews who set out from the Azores in centuries past. One might think that a culture so bound by tradition and religion would look askance at a way of life so antithetical to their own, but "family values" enjoy a very broad definition here. "Family" is understood in terms of diversity. Those who've settled here know they've found a very special place, and in that they have something precious in common.

ESSENTIALS

GETTING THERE   After crossing either the Bourne or Sagamore bridge (see "Getting There" in chapter 3), head east on Route 6 or 6A to Orleans, then north on Route 6.

Bay State Cruises (☎ **617/457-1428**) makes round-trips from Boston, daily from late June to early September and weekends in the shoulder seasons. The boat leaves Boston's Commonwealth Pier at 9am and arrives in Provincetown at noon. At 3:30pm the boat leaves Provincetown, arriving in Boston at 6:30pm. The round-trip fare is $30 per person.

Cape Cod Cruises (☎ **508/747-2400**) connects Plymouth and Provincetown in summer. The 1^1/$_2$-hour boat ride leaves Plymouth at 10am; it leaves Provincetown at 4:15pm. The adult round-trip fare is $25; $15 for children 12 and under. You can also fly into Provincetown (see "Getting There" in chapter 3).

As far as getting around once you're settled, you can enjoy the vintage fleet of the **Mercedes Cab Company** (☎ **508/487-3333**).

VISITOR INFORMATION   Contact the **Provincetown Chamber of Commerce,** 307 Commercial St., Provincetown, MA 02657 (☎ **508/487-3424;** fax 508/487-8966; Web site www.capcodaccess.com/provincetownchamber); the gay-oriented **Provincetown Business Guild,** 115 Bradford St., Box 421, Provincetown, MA 02657 (☎ **800/637-8696** or 508/487-2313); or the **Cape Cod Chamber of Commerce,** Routes 6 and 132, Hyannis, MA 02601 (☎ **508/362-3225;** fax 508/362-3698; Web site www.capecod.com).

A STROLL AROUND PROVINCETOWN

Park wherever you can—at the edge of town or in the big public lot on MacMillan Wharf. From there, it's just 1 block inland to **Provincetown Town Hall** at 260 Commercial St. (☎ **508/487-7000**). The "meet rack"—a row of facing benches out front—is a good place to get acclimated while planning your assault. The 1878 building itself is worth poking around in for its cache of historic artworks by Charles Hawthorne and others; gay and lesbian couples might even want to consider registering as "domestic partners."

One block west is the **Unitarian-Universalist Meetinghouse,** at 236 Commercial St. (☎ **508/487-9344**), an 1851 Greek Revival beauty with trompe-l'oeil interiors by 19th-century architectural muralist Carl Wendte and pews adorned with whale-tooth scrimshaw emblems. These days, the congregation is dedicating most of its resources not to decorative finery but to caring for the needs of people with AIDS (Provincetown, tragically, has the second-highest per capita concentration of cases in the country).

Take your next right, on Masonic Place, to pass **The Atlantic House,** 6 Masonic Place (☎ **508/487-3821**). Built around a 1798 core, this has been the nation's foremost gay bar for several decades now. The owner once recounted how, in 1918, the town's only police officer here arrested Eugene O'Neill as a suspected German spy, having seen the fledgling playwright distractedly pacing the dunes.

Continuing on up a short flight of stone stairs, take a right on Bradford Street. On the northern side, you'll see several colonial-era houses (some transformed into B&Bs) and the bas-relief, a plaque by Cyrus Dalin commemorating the Pilgrims' landing on November 21, 1620. To quell a potential rebellion among the indentured servants (who could not be held to the laws of the Virginia colony), the founding fathers composed the Mayflower Compact, the text of which is reproduced here. In formulating the colonists' intent to "covenant & combine our selves togeather into a civill body politick," the document presaged the quest for self-government that would give rise to the Constitution.

Directly above the Town Green, off Winslow Street, is the **Pilgrim Monument & Provincetown Museum** on High Pole Hill Road (☎ **800/247-1620** or 508/487-1310). Modeled on Sienna's Torre del Mangia, Provincetown's not-so-little (252-ft.) "Freudian joke"—the highest granite structure in the country—was erected between 1907 and 1910 by civic-minded locals ticked off that Plymouth was getting all the attention as the birthplace of the nation. It makes a fabulous vantage point from which to gaze down on the entire Cape, and the museum of local history at its foot deserves a close look (see "Provincetown Museums," below).

Returning to Bradford Street, follow it eastward a little over $^1/_4$-mile and turn left on Pearl Street to visit the **Fine Arts Work Center** at 24 Pearl St. (☎ **508/487-9960**), formerly Day's Lumber Yard, where in 1911 the softhearted owner built studios to accommodate impecunious artists. At the munificent rate of $50 a season, many a painter—such as Hawthorne protégé Edwin Dickinson, who wrapped himself in canvas to survive the iciest nights—contrived to winter over. The 20 FAWC fellows who now spend the off-season here—plus the summer visitors who come to take advantage of weekend and weeklong workshops with outstanding instructors—have it much softer, and townspeople and tourists alike get the benefit of students' and mentors' shows, talks, and readings.

The works of Provincetown's most accomplished artists reside back on Commercial Street, another $^1/_4$ mile east, through a zone thick with galleries, at the ❂ **Provincetown Art Association & Museum,** 460 Commercial St. (☎ **508/487-1750**). Founded by Hawthorne and cohorts in 1914, this prescient organization

Provincetown

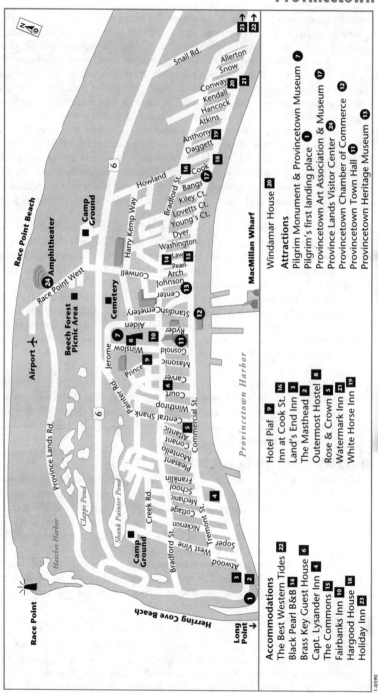

Accommodations
The Best Western Tides 22
Black Pearl B&B 14
Brass Key Guest House 6
Capt. Lysander Inn 4
The Commons 15
Fairbanks Inn 10
Hargood House 18
Holiday Inn 23
Hotel Piaf 9
Inn at Cook St. 16
Land's End Inn 3
The Masthead 2
Outermost Hostel 8
Rose & Crown 5
Watermark Inn 21
White Horse Inn 19

Attractions
Pilgrim Monument & Provincetown Museum 7
Pilgrim's first landing place 1
Provincetown Art Association & Museum 17
Province Lands Visitor Center 24
Provincetown Chamber of Commerce 12
Provincetown Town Hall 11
Provincetown Heritage Museum 13
Windamar House 20

1-0590

207

was on hand to scoop up some of the seminal American works of the 20th century—some 1,700 items so far. Only a small number can make it onto the walls of this expanded colonial homestead at any given time, but the selections are usually astute, and there's always some brand-new work displayed that gives hope for the future. (Incidentally, a former fish house across the street, at no. 463, still serves as headquarters for another Hawthorne institution: the Beachcombers, an invitational clubhouse for male artists, going strong since 1918.) In the sculpture garden on the museum grounds, look for Chaim Gross's *Dance Rhythms.* Another spirited work by this longtime summerer, *Tourists,* can be found about ¹/₂ mile west, signaling the **Provincetown Heritage Museum** at 356 Commercial St. (☎ **508/487-7098**). A community enterprise, this local-history museum—housed in an Italianate 1860 Methodist church—is a bit rough around the edges, but nonetheless fascinating for the insights it offers on Provincetown's multiple personalities as fishing port and arts colony. The former chapel shelters a half-scale schooner, and some fascinating paintings are hung somewhat haphazardly.

From this point westward, you'll be entering the epicenter of Provincetown's tourist zone. Take in whatever shops appeal (see "Shopping," below) before seeking refuge on **MacMillan Wharf,** named for the town's illustrious native son, who made a name for himself exploring the North Pole in 1909. One of the few survivors among the 50-odd piers that once lined the shore, MacMillan Wharf is home to Provincetown's whale-watching fleet and other charter boats, as well as the new **Expedition** *Whydah* **Sea Lab & Learning Center** (☎ **508/487-7955**), where relics from the 1717 shipwreck—discovered off Wellfleet in 1984—are undergoing painstaking reclamation. You can watch marine archaeologists at work while learning more about this pirate ship and its place in Cape Cod history.

🌀 **WINDING DOWN**   **The Lobster Pot,** 321 Commercial St., (☎ **508/ 487-0842**), is a longtime favorite of locals and visitors alike. They may also have the most extensive appetizer (read: midday munchies) selection in town. Stop here for a steaming cup of their award-winning clam chowder, a bucket of steamers, or even blackened tuna sashimi.

BEACHES & OUTDOOR PURSUITS

BEACHES   With nine-tenths of its territory (basically, all but the "downtown" area) protected by the Cape Cod National Seashore, Provincetown has miles of beaches. The 3-mile bay beach that lines the harbor, though certainly swimmable, is not all that inviting compared to the magnificent ocean beaches overseen by the CCNS. The two official access areas (see below) tend to be crowded; however, you can always find a less densely populated stretch if you're willing to hike.

Note: Local beachgoer activists have been lobbying for "clothing-optional" beaches for years, but the rangers—fearful of voyeurs trampling the dune grass—are firmly opposed and routinely issue tickets, so stand forewarned (and fully clothed).

- **Herring Cove** and ✪ **Race Point.** Both CCNS beaches are known for their spectacular sunsets; observers often applaud. Race Point, on the ocean side, is rougher, and you might actually spot whales en route to Stellwagen Bank. Calmer Herring Cove is a haven for same-sex couples, who tend to sort themselves by gender. Parking costs $7 per day, $20 per season.
- **Long Point.** Trek out over the breakwater and beyond, or catch a water shuttle—$7 one-way, $10 round-trip—from Flyer's Boat Rental (see "Water Sports," below) to visit this very last spit of land, capped by an 1827 lighthouse. Locals call it "the end of the Earth."

BICYCLING North of town, nestled amid the Cape Cod National Seashore preserve, is one of the more spectacular bike paths in New England, the 7-mile ✪ **Province Lands Trail,** a heady swirl of steep dunes (watch out for sand drifts on the path) anchored by wind-stunted scrub pines. With its free parking, the **Province Lands Visitor Center** (☎ **508/487-1256**) is a good place to start: You can survey the landscape from the observation tower to try to get your bearings before setting off amid the dizzying maze. With any luck, you'll find a spur path leading to one of the beaches—Race Point or Herring Cove—lining the shore. Bike rentals are offered seasonally, practically on-site, by **Nelson's Bike Shop** at 43 Race Point Rd. (☎ **508/487-8849**). It's also an easy jaunt from town, where you'll find plenty of good bike shops—such as the centrally located **Ptown Bikes** at 42 Bradford St. and 306 Commercial St. (☎ **508/487-TREK;** reserve several days in advance)—as well as all the picnic fixings you could possibly desire. Bike rentals cost a few dollars an hour or $10 to $14 a day.

BOATING In addition to operating a Long Point shuttle from its own dock (see "Beaches," above), **Flyer's Boat Rental** at 131 Commercial St. in the West End (☎ **508/487-0898**)—established in 1945—offers all sorts of craft, from canoes and dinghies to sailboats of varying sizes; they also give sailing lessons and organize fishing trips.

FISHING Surf casting is permitted at **New Beach** (off Route 6) and **Race Point Beach** (near the Race Point Coast Guard Station); also, many people drop a handline or light tackle right off the West End breakwater. For low-cost deep-sea fishing via party boat, board the *Cee Jay* (☎ **800/675-6723** or 508/487-4330). For serious fishing, sign on for the *Shady Lady II* (☎ **508/487-0182**). Both depart from MacMillan Wharf.

FITNESS For days when the weather's forcing your workouts indoors, the **Provincetown Gym** at 170 Commercial St. (☎ **508/487-2776**) has the usual equipment and promises a "nonintimidating" atmosphere; the **Mussel Beach Health Club,** located at 35 Bradford St. (☎ **508/487-0001**), attracts a rather buff clientele. For postworkout pampering, book a massage or herbal wrap at the **West End Salon & Spa,** 155 Commercial St. (☎ **508/487-1872**).

HORSEBACK RIDING **Nelson's Riding Stable** on Race Point Road (☎ **508/487-1112**) offers slow, guided, 1-hour trail rides through the dunes daily at 10am, noon, 2, 4, and 6pm from April through October ($30 per person); equestrians can make a reservation for a sunset sprint along the beach ($60). **Bayberry Hollow Farm,** 72 W. Vine St. Extension (☎ **508/487-6584**), offers pony rides for children—$6 a spin—in a paddock surrounded by flower gardens. There's also a pony-care camp and riding lessons.

IN-LINE SKATING   In-line skates are banned on the CCNS paths, and unless you're a pro, you'll have a tough time wending through the pedestrian crush along Commercial Street. Nevertheless, you can rent them for $20 a day at **Cape Tip Sports** at 224 Commercial St. (☎ 508/487-3736).

NATURE TRAILS   Within the Province Lands (off Race Point Road, ¹/₂ mile north of Route 6), the CCNS maintains the 1-mile, self-guided **Beech Forest Trail,** a shaded path that circles a shallow freshwater pond blanketed with water lilies (also look for sunning turtles) before heading into the woods. You can see the shifting dunes (much of this terrain is soft sand) gradually encroaching on the forest.

   Another wonderful walk (though only half "natural") is along the **West End breakwater** out to the end of Long Point, about 3 miles round-trip. The breakwater is located at the end of Commercial Street, next to the Provincetown Inn. It's about a 20-minute walk across the wide breakwater; then it's soft sand for the remainder of the hike. **Wood End Lighthouse** is directly across the spit of sand near the breakwater. It will take about another 40 minutes to reach **Long Point Light** at the very tip of Cape Cod. Hikers determined to reach the end of Long Point will want to bring a hat, water, and sunscreen for this intense trek along the beach. The outside of the arm tends to be the more scenic route for contemplative hikers; the inside coast can be crowded with picnicking families and surf casters. Long Point Shuttle runs from MacMillan Wharf across to Long Point for about $10 round-trip. Service is continuous in season.

TENNIS   Three public courts are located at Motta Memorial Field at the top of Winslow Street (near the Provincetown Monument); for details, contact the **Provincetown Recreation Department** (☎ 508/487-7097). Open mid-May to mid-October, the **Provincetown Tennis Club** at 186 Bradford St. (☎ 508/ 487-9574) has seven courts—two asphalt, five clay—tucked away amid tall trees.

WATER SPORTS   In 1998, **Flyer's Boat Rental** at 131 Commercial St. in the West End (☎ 508/487-0898)—established in 1945—plans to start leading scuba-diving trips locally. Dives may explore early-20th-century wrecks in Provincetown Harbor or on the "backside," off Race Point. Call for details and pricing information.

ORGANIZED TOURS

✪ **Art's Dune Tours.** At the corner of Commercial and Standish sts. (in the center of town). ☎ 800/894-1951 or 508/487-1950. Fee $10 adults, $7 children under 12. Call for schedule and reservations.

In 1946 Art Costa started driving sightseers out to ogle the decrepit "dune shacks" where such transient luminaries as Eugene O'Neill, Jack Kerouac, and Jackson Pollock found their respective muses; in one such hovel, Tennessee Williams cooked up the steamy *Streetcar Named Desire.* The Park Service wanted to raze these eyesores, but luckily saner heads prevailed: They're now National Historic Landmarks, and they are even available for rent through a lottery held among the members of the Peaked Hill Trust (P.O. Box 1705, Provincetown 02657). Art's tours, via Chevy Suburban, typically take about 1¹/₄ hours, and though he "narrates" straight through, his stories never seem scripted; one suspects (rightly) that he has scores more up his sleeve. Don't forget your cameras for the views of this totally unique landscape.

Bay Lady II. MacMillan Wharf (in the center of town). ☎ 508/487-9308. Fee $10–15 adults, $6 children under 12. Mid-May to mid-Oct 4 2-hr. sails daily; call for schedule and reservations. Closed mid-Oct to mid-May.

In sightseeing aboard this 73-foot reproduction gaff-rigged Grand Banks schooner, you'll actually be adding to the scenery for those onlookers onshore. The sunset trip is especially spectacular.

Whale Watching

In 1975, 4 years after the U.S. government—fearing the species' extinction—called an official halt to whaling, fisherman Al Avellar noticed that they seemed to be making a comeback in the Stellwagen Bank feeding area, 8 miles off Provincetown. Together with marine biologist Charles "Stormy" Mayo of the Center for Coastal Studies, he came up with the notion of a new kind of hunt, spearheaded by tourists bearing cameras. An immediate success, their ✪ *Dolphin* **Fleet,** on MacMillan Wharf (☎ **800/826-9300** or 508/349-1900), was widely copied up and down the coast. These are still the prime feeding grounds, however, which is why all the whale-watching fleets can confidently "guarantee" sightings—they offer a free rain check should the cetaceans fail to surface.

Most cruises carry a naturalist (a very vague term) to provide running commentary; the difference on the *Dolphin* is that the CCS scientists are out there doing research crucial to the whales' survival, and part of the proceeds goes to further their worthwhile efforts. Serious whale aficionados will want to try one of the daylong trips to the Great South Channel, where humpbacks and finbacks are likely to be found by the dozen.

Some tips for first-timers: Dress very warmly, in layers (it's cold out on the water), and definitely take along a windbreaker—waterproof, if you've got one, or maybe your innkeeper can offer a spare. The weather's capricious, and if you stand in the bow of the boat—the best viewing point—you can count on getting drenched. Veteran whale watchers know to bring a spare set of dry clothes, as well as binoculars—although if the whales seem to be feeling friendly and frisky, as they often are, they'll play practically within reach. And last but not least, if you're prone to seasickness, you'd better bring along some motion-sickness pills—it can get pretty rough out there.

Tickets are $17 to $18 for adults, $16 senior for citizens, $15 for children 7 to 12, and free for children under 7. From April through October there are three $3^1/2$-hour trips daily; in July and August there's also one 8-hour trip each week. Call for a schedule and reservations (required). Closed November through March.

Provincetown Trolley. In front of Town Hall, 260 Commercial St. (in the center of town). ☎ **508/487-9483.** Tickets $8 adults, $7 seniors, $6 children 12 and under. Departures May–Oct daily every half-hr. 10am–4pm and hourly 5–8pm. Closed Nov–Apr.

For a quick high-points tour, this 40-minute narrated circuit covers all the bases: West End, Province Lands, East End, and "home." Don't expect to learn a whole lot if you already have some sense of town history. On the other hand, with the ability to dismount and reboard at will, you can pretty much create your own tour, with stopovers for taking in the sights and/or shopping.

Rambling Rose Carriage Co. In front of Town Hall, 260 Commercial St. (in the center of town). ☎ **508/487-4246.** Fee $15 and up per couple. June–Aug daily 11am–11pm; May and Sept–Oct 10am–4pm. Closed Nov–Apr. No credit cards.

Christine Lorenz cuts a dashing figure driving her well-groomed draft horse and beflowered carriage through town. In fact, she looks so cool, you're unlikely to feel the least bit embarrassed as a passenger; if people are staring, it's only with envy. Families with children will want to visit the "horsies" at home at the Bayberry Hollow Farm (see "Horseback Riding" under "Beaches & Outdoor Pursuits," above).

○ **Willie Air Tours.** Provincetown Municipal Airport, Race Point Rd. (2 miles NW of town center). ☎ **508/487-0240.** Late May to late Oct, 15-min. flights $25 for 1–4 people; call for schedule. Closed late Oct to late May.

Board a cheery yellow 1931 Stinson Detroiter for a quick look around: It's a great way to fathom the forces still shaping the land. It's hard to believe from the tiny exterior, but you can cram four slim friends (or parents and a couple of lucky kids) into this adorable biplane. Back-seat riders get to luxuriate on a red leather banquette, but the passenger next to the pilot gets the best view. If it weren't for the slim windshield, you could reach out and touch the propeller. The flight is smooth and gentle, an intoxicating way to experience the tip of the Cape.

PROVINCETOWN MUSEUMS

○ **The Expedition** *Whydah* **Sea Lab & Learning Center.** MacMillan Wharf (in the center of town). ☎ and fax **508/487-7955.** Admission $5 adults, $3.50 children 3–12. June–Aug daily 9am–7pm; Sept–Dec and April–May 10am–5pm. Closed Jan–Mar.

Cape Cod native Barry Clifford made headlines in 1984 when he tracked down the wreck of the 17th-century pirate ship *Whydah* (pronounced "*Wid*-dah," like Yankee for "widow") 1,500 feet off the coast of Wellfleet, where it had lain undisturbed since 1717. Only 10% excavated to date, it has already yielded over 100,000 artifacts, including 10,000 gold and silver coins, plus its namesake bell, proving its authenticity. In this museum/lab, visitors can observe the reclamation work—involving electrolytic reduction—as it's done and discuss the ship, its discovery, and its significance with the scientists and scholars on hand, while studying the many interpretive exhibits. You may never approach the beach in quite the same way again: Thousands more wrecks are out there, awaiting the patient and clever.

Province Lands Visitor Center. Race Point Rd. (about 1¹⁄₂ miles NW of town center). ☎ **508/487-1256.** Free admission. July–Aug daily 9am–5pm; call for off-season hrs. Closed Dec–Mar.

Though much smaller than the Salt Pond Visitor Center, this satellite also does a good job of explicating this special environment, where plant life must fight a fierce battle to maintain its toehold amid shifting sands buffeted by salty winds. After perusing the exhibits, be sure to circle the observation deck for great views of the "parabolic" dunes. Also inquire about any special events scheduled, such as guided walks and family campfires.

Old Harbor Life-Saving Museum. Race Point Beach (off Race Point Rd., about 2 miles NW of town center). ☎ **508/487-1256.** Free admission; parking fee for Race Point (see "Beaches," above). July–Aug daily 3–5pm; call for off-season hrs. Closed Nov–Apr.

One of 13 life-saving stations mandated by Congress in the late 19th century, this shingled shelter with a lookout tower—barged to this site from Chatham a few decades ago—was part of a network responsible for saving some 100,000 lives. Before the U.S. Life-Saving Service was founded in 1872 (it became part of the Coast Guard in 1915, once the Cape Cod Canal was in place), shipwreck victims lucky enough to be washed ashore were still doomed unless they could find a "charity shed"—a hut supplied with firewood—maintained by the Massachusetts Humane Society. The six valiant "Surfmen" manning each life-saving station took a more active approach, patrolling the beach at all hours, sending up flares at the first sign of a ship in distress and rowing out into the surf to save all they could. When the breakers were too high to breach, they'd use a Lyle gun to shoot a line to be secured to the ship's mast, and over this, one by one, the crew would be pulled to shore astride a "breeches buoy"—like a life-saving ring fitted out with canvas BVDs. All the old equipment is on view at this museum, and Thursday mornings at 10am, rangers reenact a breeches-buoy rescue.

✪ **Pilgrim Monument & Provincetown Museum.** High Pole Hill Rd. (off Winslow St., N of Bradford St.). ☎ **800/247-1620** or 508/487-1310. Admission $5 adults, $3 children 4–12 (includes 2-hr. free parking). July–Aug daily 9am–7pm; off-season daily 9am–5pm. Last admission 45 min. before closing. Closed Dec–Mar.

You can't miss it: Anywhere you go in town, this granite tower looms, ever ready to restore your bearings. Climb up the 60 gradual ramps interspersed with 116 steps—a surprisingly easy lope—and you'll get a gargoyle's-eye view of the spiraling coast and, in the distance, Boston against a backdrop of New Hampshire mountains. Definitely devote some time to the curious exhibits in the museum at the monument's foot, chronicling Provincetown's checkered past as both fishing port and arts nexus. Among the memorabilia you'll find polar bears brought back from MacMillan's expeditions and early programs for the Provincetown Players.

✪ **Provincetown Art Association & Museum.** 460 Commercial St. (in the E. End). ☎ **508/487-1750.** Suggested donation $3 adults, $1 seniors and children under 12. Late May to early Sept daily noon–5pm and 8–10pm; call for off-season hrs.

This extraordinary cache of 20th-century American art began with five paintings donated by local artists, including Charles Hawthorne, the charismatic teacher who first "discovered" this picturesque outpost. Founded in 1914, only a year after New York's revolutionary Armory Show, the museum was the site of innumerable "space wars," as classicists and modernists vied for square footage; an uneasy truce was finally struck in 1927, when each camp was accorded its own show. In today's less competitive atmosphere, it's not unusual to see a tame still life hanging alongside a statement of twentysomething angst or an acknowledged master sharing space with a less-skilled upstart. Juried members' shows usually accompany the in-depth retrospectives, so there are always new discoveries to be made. Nor is there a hard and firm wall between creators and onlookers. Fulfilling its charter to promote "social intercourse between artists and laymen," the museum sponsors a full schedule of concerts, lectures, readings, and classes, in such disciplines as dance, yoga, and life-drawing.

Provincetown Heritage Museum. 356 Commercial St. (in the center of town), Provincetown. ☎ **508/487-7098.** Admission $3 adults, free for children under 12. Late May to mid-Oct daily 10am–6pm. Closed mid-Oct to late May.

Headquartered in an 1860 Methodist church, this curious collection has a bit of everything town-related. A half-scale Grand Banks fishing schooner (62 ft. long) occupies the former sanctuary (practically poking through the steeple), and some impressive artworks are rather nonchalantly displayed. Wax dummies give the downstairs exhibits an amateurish mien and detract somewhat from the actual stuff: a reproduction dune shack similar to one occupied for decades by Harry Kemp, self-professed "Poet of the Dunes," and a sampling of the Peter Hunt folk-art decor that was all the rage in the 1950s (a vacationing Helena Rubenstein scooped some up and soon it was all the mode). You won't get a comprehensive history here; consider it an elective.

KID STUFF

Kids will love getting on a horse (see "Horseback Riding," above) and going down to the shore to see whales. Little kids will also enjoy the weekly story hour held Wednesdays at 10:30am at the homey and historic (1873) Provincetown Public Library.

SHOPPING

If you want to stay one step ahead of the fashion victims' pack, you have come to the right place. Many mavens visit off-season just to stock up on markdowns that are still well ahead of the curve. Of the several dozen art galleries in town, only a handful (noted below) are reliably worthwhile. (For in-depth coverage of the local arts scene, look to *Provincetown Arts,* a glossy annual sold at the Provincetown Art Association & Museum shop.) In season, most of the galleries and even some of the shops take a supper-time siesta, reopening later and greeting visitors up to as late as 10 or 11pm. Shows usually open Friday evening, prompting a "stroll" tradition spanning the many receptions.

ANTIQUES/COLLECTIBLES   One of the few shops in town to rise above the collectibles level, the second-story **Clifford-Williams Antiques,** 225 Commercial St. (in the center of town; ☎ 508/487-4174), is packed to the gills with substantial English furniture, as well as select works by Provincetown artists.

Part bookstore, part antique shop, **The Ironmongers,** 419 Commercial St. (in the East End; ☎ 508/487-3365), offers a pleasantly dusty trove reflecting the interests of author/owner Leona Rust Egan, whose most recent work is the revelatory *Provincetown as a Stage.* She has most of her resources right at hand, in the form of a nonpareil collection of first-edition Cape Coddiana. Closed January through March.

You'd have to go to Boston—or abroad—to view estate jewelry as fine as that at **Small Pleasures,** 359 Commercial St. (in the center of town; ☎ 508/487-3712). Virginia McKenna's hand-selected stock ranges from romantic Victorian settings to sleek silver for the 1920s-era male.

Remembrances of Things Past, 376 Commercial St. (in the center of town; ☎ 508/487-9443), is a fun kitsch-fest: a jumble of 20th-century nostalgia, ranging from Bakelite bangles to neon advertising art and vintage True Confessions.

"Ephemera" is all that stuff—old advertisements and nostrums, children's toys and books—that you could get rich off today if only you'd had the sense to hang on to it. For those hoping to fill a nostalgic void, **West End Antiques,** 146 Commercial St. (in the West End; ☎ 508/487-6723), would be a good place to start. Closed late December through March.

ARTS & CRAFTS   Founded in 1994 by artist and publishing scion Nick Lawrence, ✪ **DNA (Definitive New Art) Gallery,** 288 Bradford St. (in the East End; ☎ 508/487-7700), an airy loft over the Provincetown Tennis Club, quickly rose to the top tier. It has attracted such talents as photographer Joel Meyerowitz (Provincetown's favorite portraitist, known for such tomes as *Cape Light*); sculptor Conrad Malicoat, whose free-form brick chimneys and hearths can be seen and admired about town; and painter Tabitha Vevers, who devises woman-centered shrines and "shields" out of goatskin vellum and gold leaf. Another contributor is local conceptualist/provocateur Jay Critchley, whose latest enterprise involves condoms adorned with an image of the Virgin Mary and whose ongoing *cause celebre* is to see the town declared a "cultural sanctuary." It's a very lively bunch, appropriately grouped under the rubric "definitive new art," and readings by cutting-edge authors add to the buzz. Closed mid-October to late May.

Julie Heller started collecting early Provincetown paintings as a child—and a tourist at that. She chose so incredibly well, her roster, shown at the **Julie Heller Gallery,** 2 Gosnold St. (☎ 508/487-2169), now reads like a who's who of local art. Hawthorne, Avery, Hofmann, Lazzell, Hensche—all the big names are here, as well as some contemporary artists who, in her view, "continue to carry on the tradition." Closed weekdays December through April.

Cortland Jessup Gallery, 432 Commercial St. (in the East End; ☎ **508/ 487-4479**), features the work of its namesake. A natural-born salonist, Jessup has a knack for mixing media and genres, and initiating interesting cross-pollinations. Ask to see *The Class of Forbidden Dreams* by photographer/performance artist Pat Delzell. Closed January.

Artists invited to show at the venerable ✪ **Long Point Gallery,** 241 Bradford St. (in the East End; ☎ **508/487-1795**)—self-described as "an artists' place"—are indisputably among the elect. Paul Resika's Provincetown landscapes, for example, perfectly capture the intensity of color, the sense of suspension in time. Closed mid-September to mid-June.

Splashy both in selection and in presentation, the **Albert Merola Gallery,** 424 Commercial St. (in the East End; ☎ **508/487-4424**), is not afraid to delve into the decorative and functional. Boston fauve Todd McKie, for instance, contributes colorful platters painted like tribal masks. The art for its own sake can be quite distinguished, with such respected figures as Michael Mazur (*Dante's Inferno*) and Helen Miranda Wilson delivering their latest musings. Closed mid-October through March.

It's all in the family at **The Packard Gallery,** 418 Commercial St. (☎ **508/ 487-4690**), where the work of Anne Packard and her daughter Cynthia are displayed in a majestic former church. Anne Packard's large canvases tend to depict emotive land and seascapes, whereas Cynthia's colorful figurative work has fauvist elements.

Bunny Pearlman, an artist herself, is the gallery director at **East End Gallery,** 349 Commercial St. (in the center of town; ☎ **508/487-4745**). She has an eye for iconic art, such as the para-archaeological signage devised by the team of Nicholas Kahn and Richard Selesnick (you may remember their striking portrait of the Pope as *Time*'s "Man of the Year"). Closed late November through mid-April.

The art shown at **Rice/Polak Gallery,** 430 Commercial St. (in the East End; ☎ **508/487-1052**), has a decorative bent, which is not to say that it will match anyone's sofa, only that it has a certain stylish snap to it. Several gallery artists have fun with dimensions—such as painter Tom Seghi with his mammoth pears, and sculptor Larry Culkins with his assemblages of undersized, antique-look dresses. Photographer Karin Rosenthal's sculptural female nudes blend humor with utmost beauty. Closed December through April.

Sharing a building with the Long Point Gallery, ✪ **Rising Tide Gallery,** 241 Bradford St. (in the East End; ☎ **508/487-4037**), cultivates midcareer artists in a lively co-op atmosphere. An investment in the colorist landscapes of Don Beal or Noa Hall could prove a wise move in the long run. Closed mid-September through mid-June.

Berta Walker is a force to be reckoned with, having nurtured many top artists in this neighborhood—through her association with the Fine Arts Work Center—before opening her own gallery in 1990. Her historic holdings, displayed at the ✪ **Berta Walker Gallery,** 208 Bradford St. (in the East End; ☎ **508/487-6411**), span Charles Hawthorne, Milton Avery, and Robert Motherwell. Whoever has her current attention—such as figurative sculptor Romolo Del Deo—warrants watching. Closed late October to late May.

Not content to have cornered some of the best fine art around, Berta has now opened a small storefront satellite, **Walker's Wonders,** at 153 Commercial St. (in the West End; ☎ **508/487-8794**), to showcase folk and functional art, including furniture, jewelry, and sundry "imaginative objects and special delights."

The **William-Scott Gallery,** 439 Commercial St. (in the East End; ☎ **508/ 487-4040**), is so tiny that it may look, on the surface, like one of those roadside galleries geared to impulsive tourists. But take a closer look. John Dowd's straightforward house portraits are not as simple as they might seem. Still quite young, he's shaping up as Hopper's heir apparent (patrons include the Schiffenhaus brothers, who inherited the Hoppers' Truro house). Other selections, such as John DiMestico's Cape landscapes on paper, Dan Rupe's bold portraits in oil, and Will Klemm's lush and mysterious pastel landscapes, augur well for an influential future. Closed November through late May.

BOOKS   Offering both new and collectible gay and lesbian books, **Now Voyager,** 357 Commercial St. (in the East End; ☎ **508/487-0848**), also serves as an informal social center.

Whatever it is you're trying to kick (a particular substance or person, or just a bad habit), there's sure to be a self-help book for you at **Recovering Hearts Bookstore & Gift Gallery,** 2–4 Standish St. (off Commercial Street at the center of town; ☎ **508/487-4875**), along with plenty of general-interest titles.

DISCOUNT SHOPPING   Adams' Pharmacy, 254 Commercial St. (in the center of town; ☎ **508/487-0069**), is Provincetown's oldest business (est. 1868), complete with an old-fashioned soda fountain. I—and apparently, a great many drag queens—like it for the cheapo makeup (two-for-$1 lipsticks) in outrageous colors.

Want to make a fast buck? Dare someone to go into the jam-packed **Marine Specialties** at 235 Commercial St. (in the center of town; ☎ **508/487-1730**), and come out empty-handed. There's just too much useful stuff, from discounted Doc Martens to cut-rate Swiss Army knives and all sorts of odd nautical surplus whose uses will suggest themselves to you eventually. Be sure to look up: Hung among the rafters are some real antiques, including several carillon's worth of ship's bells.

Veteran scavengers won't be put off by the musty backstage aroma at the **Provincetown Second Hand Store,** 389 Commercial St. (in the center of town; ☎ **508/487-9153**). There are prime pickings to be had here, including some extremely glam outfits and shoes in petite to he-man sizes, and an assortment of first-hand vintage lingerie culled from the owner's family business. Closed January through February.

FASHION   Perfect examples of the art of understatement, Jerry Giardelli's unstructured clothing elements—shells, shifts, palazzo pants—come in vibrant colors and inviting textures; they demand to be mixed and matched and perhaps offset by Diana Antonelli's statement jewelry. You'll find it all at **Giardelli/Antonelli Studio Showroom,** 417 Commercial St. (in the East End; ☎ **508/487-3016**).

A gallery of "art to wear," **Halcyon Gallery,** 371 Commercial St. (in the center of town; ☎ **508/487-9415**), features playful fashions that are as distinctive as they are relaxed. Some items are handwoven or painted, and all are handmade. An unpredictable assortment of handblown glass and exceptional accessories—you'll find some great gifts here—round out the mix.

Want to try on new identities like Princess Ozma of Oz, who had a cabinet full of alternative heads? **Mad Hatter,** 360 Commercial St. (in the center of town; ☎ **508/487-5063**), may be the next best thing, with hats to suit every style and inclination, from folksy to downright diva-esque. Closed January through mid-February.

In terms of breezy women's clothing, the selection at **Moda Fina,** 349 Commercial St. (in the center of town; ☎ **508/487-0311**), is so appropriate and of-the-moment that you'll want to walk off wearing whatever you try on. To complete the look, there's a good range of casual shoes—and, perhaps more important, cool shades. Closed March to mid-April.

Check out **No. 5,** 199 Commercial St. (in the West End; ☎ **508/487-1594**), an ultrastylish men's shop, for a glimpse of what tomorrow's best-dressed males will be wearing.

The seasonal styles at **Silk & Feathers,** 377 Commercial St. (in the center of town; ☎ 508/487-2057), are what every woman wants, and the lingerie is almost too pretty to cover up. Other indulgences include seaweed soaps and statement jewelry.

Turning Point, 379 Commercial St. (in the center of town; ☎ **508/487-0642**), is a tasteful boutique specializing in the Eileen Fisher line—an array of delicate-hued cottons in classic shapes.

GIFTS/HOME DECOR A cache of authentic and exquisite international artifacts, from Oriental rugs to African carvings, **Llama,** 382 Commercial St. (in the center of town; ☎ **508/487-2921**), is a real jewel set amid the more typical tourist gewgaws. Closed January through April.

A tiny shop in the foyer of the ✪ **Provincetown Art Association & Museum,** 460 Commercial St. (in the East End; ☎ **508/487-1750**), stocks a fabulous selection of related art books (some small-press and hard to find), as well as a smattering of local crafts.

Another tongue-in-chic enterprise by North Truro's alive-and-kicking artist/author/artisan/rumor-monger, the tiny **Susan Baker Memorial Museum Franchise,** 379 Commercial St. (in the center of town; ☎ **508/487-1063**), is bursting with primitivist papier-mâché home accessories and other vehicles for her wonderfully sardonic wit.

At **Tiffany Lamp Studio,** 432 Commercial St. (in the East End; ☎ **508/487-1101**), Louis Comfort himself would have smiled upon the handiwork of Stephen Donnelly, who not only repairs originals but makes his own updated versions in delicious hues.

A breath of fresh contemporary design, **Utilities,** 393 Commercial St. (in the center of town; ☎ and fax **508/487-6800**), is a kitchenware/tabletop shop featuring sleek and colorful essentials.

A study in beiges and blacks, **WA,** 184 Commercial St. (in the West End; ☎ **508/487-6355**) is a minimalist shop—its name means "harmony" in Japanese—specializing in decorative home accessories that embrace a Zen aesthetic. This might mean a trickling stone fountain or Chinese calligraphy stones.

Profits on the gifts and books you buy at **The Whale and Dolphin Information Center & Shop,** 2 Ryder St. Extension (off Commercial Street, in the center of town; ☎ **508/487-6115;** Web site provincetown.com/coastalstudies/), all help to support the cetacean research-and-rescue work carried out by the Center for Coastal Studies, a local nonprofit organization founded in 1976 by Dr. Charles "Stormy" Mayo, a Provincetown native and a pioneer in the field. Identifying individuals by their distinctive markings, CCS staffers have managed to compile the world's largest whale population database to date and have participated in many a dramatic disentanglement. To appreciate the depth of their dedication, go whale watching with a CCS scientist aboard a *Dolphin* Fleet cruise (see "Whale Watching," above); you might also inquire about CCS-sponsored lectures, walks, and Elderhostel programs. Closed November through mid-April.

MUSIC At **Calliope Music,** 244 Commercial St. (in the center of town; ☎ **508/487-6339**), music by and for women is a specialty.

TOYS Take advantage of strong winds and wide open beaches to try your hand at kiting, with supplies from **Outer Cape Kites,** 277A Commercial St. (at Ryder Street Extension, near MacMillan Wharf; ☎ **508/487-6133**). Closed November through March.

Puzzle Me This, 336 Commercial St. (in the center of town; ☎ **508/487-1059**) carries everything from fiendish jigsaw puzzles to *New York Times* crossword collections and ever-popular puzzle rings. Closed January through March.

Toys of Eros, in the Aquarium Park Mall at 205 Commercial St. (in the center of town; ☎ 508/487-0056), owned by a Harvard MBA–toting mother of four, is a cheerfully brazen shop carrying every conceivable gizmo you were ever curious about but too embarrassed to track down.

WHERE TO STAY
VERY EXPENSIVE

✪ **The Brass Key Guesthouse.** 12 Carver St. (in the center of town), Provincetown, MA 02657. ☎ **800/842-9858** or 508/487-9005. Fax 508/487-9029. 33 rms, 4 cottages. A/C TV TEL. Summer (including continental breakfast) $185–$325 double; $245–$325 cottage. AE, DISC, MC, V. Closed Jan–Mar.

After a multimillion-dollar expansion, the Brass Key Guesthouse, now a compound consisting of three buildings, has been transformed into *the* place to stay in Provincetown. With Ritz-Carlton–style amenities and service in mind, Michael MacIntyre and Bob Anderson have created a paean to luxury. These are the kind of innkeepers who think of everything: pillows are goose down, showers have wall jets, and gratis iced tea is delivered poolside. While all rooms share top-notch amenities like Boze radios, minifridges, and VCRs, there is a range of decorative styles according to building. The original 1860s Victorian is decorated in a more playful country style—a loft is filled with teddy bears, for instance—while rooms in the colonial-era building are classically elegant. In the center is the extensively landscaped multileveled patio area with outdoor heated pool and large (17 ft.) whirlpool. All deluxe guest rooms have gas fireplaces, operated with a handy remote control, and oversized whirlpool tubs. Fortunately those bathrooms also include telephones and televisions, so that you can be entertained while soaking. There are also two wheelchair-accessible rooms.

EXPENSIVE

Land's End Inn. 22 Commercial St. (in the W. End), Provincetown, MA 02657. ☎ **800/276-7088** or 508/487-0706. 17 rms (1 with separate bath), 2 apts, 1 suite. Summer (including continental breakfast) $120–$190 double; $140–$150 apt; $285 suite. MC, V.

Enjoying a prime 2-acre perch atop Gull Hill, this 1907 bungalow is stuffed to bursting with rare and often outlandish antiques. Some rooms would suit a 19th-century sheik, others your everyday hedonist. In the dark-paneled living room, it's always Christmas: The ornate decorations never come down. The place is quite unique, in other words, in a way that will delight some guests and overwhelm others. There's no denying that the octagonal loft suite, a virtual goldfish bowl poised to take in views in every direction, is a spectacular setting for romance (shy types need not apply). Though the inn is predominantly gay, cosmopolitan visitors will be made to feel welcome, regardless of gender or orientation.

✪ **Watermark Inn.** 603 Commercial St. (in the E. End), Provincetown, MA 02657. ☎ **800/734-0165** or 508/487-0165. Fax 508/487-2383. 10 suites. TV TEL. Summer $135–$290 suite. AE, MC, V.

If you'd like to experience Provincetown without being stuck in the thick of it (the carnival atmosphere can get tiring at times), this contemporary inn at the peaceful edge of town is the perfect choice. Resident innkeeper/architect Kevin Shea carved this beachfront manor into 10 dazzling suites: The prize ones, on the top floor, have peaked picture windows and sweeping views from their own decks. Innkeeper/designer Judy Richland, his wife, saw to the interior decoration—bold Marimekko quilts and plenty of primary colors. Even the lack of breakfast is a plus in its own way: you have an excuse to brunch about town.

MODERATE

Best Western Tides Beachfront. 837 Commercial St. (near the Truro border), Provincetown, MA 02657. ☎ **800/528-1234** or 508/487-1045. Fax 508/487-3557. Web site bwprovincetown.com. 62 rms, 2 suites. A/C TV TEL. Summer $132–$166 double; $221 suite. AE, CB, DC, DISC, MC, V. Closed Nov–Apr.

Located on a peaceful 6-acre parcel well removed both from Provincetown's bustle and North Truro's ticky-tacky congestion, this surprise oasis—part of the Best Western chain—boasts every feature one might require of a beachfront retreat, including a nice wide beach you can literally flop onto from the ground-level units. Most of the rooms overlook Provincetown's quirky skyline, as does the generously proportioned outdoor pool. Every inch of this complex has been groomed to the max, including the ultragreen grounds, the Wedgwood-blue breakfast room which seems to have been lifted whole from an elegant country inn, and the spotless rooms decorated in a soothing palette of ivory and pale pastels. And the only sound you'll hear at night is the mournful refrain of a foghorn.

✪ **Captain Jack's Wharf.** 73A Commercial St., Provincetown, MA 02657. ☎ **508/487-1450.** Web site www.ptown.com/ptown/captjacks. 14 studio/apts. Summer $675–$1,000 weekly. No credit cards.

These apartments, located on one of the last remaining wharves in Provincetown, are quintessential Provincetown beach kitsch. Each space is individually and artistically decorated with exuberant splashes of color, funky artwork, and general panache. If you want the ultimate bohemian Provincetown lodging experience, you simply can't do any better than this. From late June through early September, 1-week rentals are required. Off-season, the nightly rate (3-night minimum) is around $100.

The Commons. 386 Commercial St. (in the center of town), Provincetown, MA 02657. ☎ **800/487-0784** or 508/487-7800. 12 rms, 2 suites. TV TEL. Summer (including continental breakfast) $85–$125 double; $140 suite. AE, MC, V.

Right in the thick of town, but removed from the hurly-burly by a street-side bistro (see "Where to Dine," below) and peaceful brick patio, this venerable old guest house has received a stylish renovation at the hands of co-owners Carl Draper and Chuck Rigg, an erstwhile Washington, D.C., interior designer whose colorful landscapes decorate the rooms. The parlor is formal and opulent, the bedrooms only slightly less so, with their marble-look baths and (in most cases) bay views. At the pinnacle is a beamed attic studio with its own deck overlooking MacMillan Wharf. All the delights of Provincetown are easily within reach, including—on-site—one of Provincetown's best up-and-coming restaurants.

✪ **The Fairbanks Inn.** 90 Bradford St. (near the center of town), Provincetown, MA 02657. ☎ **800/324-7265** or 508/487-0386. 13 rms (2 with shared bath), 1 efficiency, 1 apt. Summer (including continental breakfast) $95–$149 double; $169 efficiency; $175 apt. AE, MC, V.

This colonial mansion (built in 1776) looks its era without looking its age. Beautifully maintained, it boasts gleaming wooden floors softened by rich Orientals and romantic bedding—sleigh beds and four-posters. Most of the rooms have fireplaces. A patio, porch, and rooftop sundeck lend themselves to pleasant socializing. The attention to detail throughout the inn makes this one of the top places to stay in town.

Hargood House at Bayshore. 493 Commercial St. (in the E. End), Provincetown, MA 02657. ☎ and fax **508/487-9133.** 2 studios, 17 efficiencies. TV TEL. Summer $99–$103 studio; $132–$194 efficiency. AE, MC, V.

Recently taken over and "cheerified" by a trio of owners, including Louise Walker Davy (whose twin sister is the eminent gallery director Berta Walker), this cherished beachfront complex is enjoying a new lease on life. While retaining some of their improvisatory charm, such as a few select antiques and salvaged architectural details, the rooms have been lightened up, the better to reflect the waterside setting. The prize rooms surround a flower-lined lawn, with pride of place going to a cathedral-ceiling loft right over the water; several more apartments, including a freestanding little house, can be found across the street. The decor is still not quite designer-level, but the big plus is the opportunity to live among artworks on loan from the Walker Gallery, many of which would rightly hang on a museum wall. From late June to early September, rooms are available on a weekly basis only.

Holiday Inn. 6 Snail Rd. (at Rte. 6A, in the E. End), Provincetown, MA 02657. ☎ **800/ 422-4224** or 508/487-1711. Fax 508/487-3929. 78 rms. A/C TV TEL. Summer $140 double. AE, CB, DC, DISC, MC, V. Closed Nov–Apr.

A good choice for first-timers not quite sure what they're getting into, this no-surprises motel-with-pool at the eastern edge of town is a bit far from the action but congenial enough. Guests get a nice view of town, along with cable TV and free movies in the restaurant/lounge.

✪ **Hotel Piaf.** 3 Prince St. ($^1/_2$ block NW of Bradford St. in the center of town), Provincetown, MA 02657. ☎ **800/340-7423** or 508/487-7458. Fax 508/487-8646. E-mail reserve@piaf.com. Web site www.piaf.com. 2 rms, 1 suite, 1 cottage. TV TEL. Summer (including continental breakfast and afternoon tea) $110–$135 double; $165–$185 suite; $135 cottage. AE, MC, V.

Cute enough for the "Little Sparrow" herself, this tiny Federal three-quarter Cape, built around 1800 and located in a shady locust grove, has been casually lavished with family heirlooms and pedigreed antiques, such as a painted bed fit for a Vanderbilt (which it was). This comfy bower is the centerpiece of the master bedroom, "La Vie en Rose." The duplex apartment suite, called "Hymne a l'Amour," is, if anything, more inviting, with a cathedral-ceilinged sitting room/library, striking artwork, private deck, full kitchen, marble bath—the works. A stay in the rustic-beamed "Milord" cottage, done up in Provençal prints, is as relaxing as a *séjour* in the south of France. All the Gallic charm mirrors that of co-innkeeper Vincent Coll, who with partner Christopher Sands will see to your every need, providing down comforters and terry robes, complimentary laundry and shoe-shine services, bikes for tooling about town, a challenging course for boules, a home-baked breakfast, plus insiders' advice on the best that Provincetown has to offer.

The Masthead. 31-41 Commercial St. (in the W. End), Provincetown, MA 02657. ☎ **800/ 395-5095** or 508/487-0523. Fax 508/487-9251. Web site www.capecod.com/masthead. 8 rms (2 with shared bath), 3 efficiencies, 6 apts, 4 cottages. A/C TV TEL. Summer $79–$179 double; $128–$150 efficiency; $128–$260 apt; cottages $893–$1,725 weekly. Off-season $57–$85 double; $68–$92 efficiency; $94 apt; $92–$110 cottage. AE, CB, DC, DISC, MC, V.

One person's "quaint" is another person's dingy. There's no disguising the fact that this beachside complex has grown a bit shabby since its late-1950s heyday, when glam types like Helena Rubenstein came here to rough it. On the plus side, it's one of the few places in town, other than the impersonal motels, that actively welcomes families, and the placid beach will delight young splashers. The cottages are fun, decorated with net stair railings and hand-painted antique furniture by Peter Hunt. Rates here off-season are a steal, considering the waterfront locale. The yachting crowd can take advantage of free deep-water moorings and launch service.

INEXPENSIVE

✪ **The Black Pearl Bed & Breakfast.** 11 Pearl St. (off Commercial St., near the center of town), Provincetown, MA 02657. ☎ **508/487-6405.** Fax 508/487-7412. E-mail ptown11@aol.com. 6 rms, 1 cottage. Summer (including continental breakfast) $80–$95 double; $150 cottage. MC, V. Closed Jan to mid-Mar.

Every room in this cheerily updated captain's house has a look all its own, from bold Southwestern to fanciful Micronesian, and several boast skylights and private decks. The Connemara Cottage takes the cake, with an antique bedstead, wood-burning fireplace, and double Jacuzzi, plus such niceties as air-conditioning and a cable TV with VCR. One room is wheelchair accessible.

Captain Lysander Inn. 96 Commercial St. (in the W. End), Provincetown, MA 02657. ☎ **508/487-2253.** Fax 508/487-7579. 14 rms (6 with shared bath), 1 apt, 1 cottage. Summer (including continental breakfast) $95–$105 double; $120 apt; $155 cottage. MC, V.

This 1852 captain's house has definite curb appeal: Set back a bit from the street, it's fronted by a flower-lined path leading to a sunny patio. The conservatively furnished rooms are quite nice for the price, and some have lovely water views. The whole gang can fit in either the apartment or the cottage, both of which sleep six.

✪ **The Inn at Cook St.** 7 Cook St. (at Bradford St., in the E. End), Provincetown, MA 02657. ☎ **888/COOK-655** or 508/487-3894. E-mail cookst@tiac.net. Web site www. capecodaccess.com/cook. 3 rms, 2 suites, 1 cottage. TV. Summer (including continental breakfast) $95 double; $125 suite; $100 cottage. MC, V.

A welcome addition to the B&B scene, this 1836 Greek Revival beauty, tucked away in a quiet neighborhood, positively exudes tasteful warmth, from its pale-yellow exterior trimmed with black shutters to its hidden garden, complete with goldfish pool. All the handsomely appointed rooms are oriented to this oasis, with an assortment of private and shared decks, and the tiny rose-trellised cottage, with sleeping loft, is an integral part of its charm. Innkeepers Paul Church and Dana Mitton arrived at their dream house by way of the elegant Cambridge House near Boston, and their enthusiasm is evident in every welcoming touch.

The Outermost Hostel. 28 Winslow St. (off Bradford St., 1/8 mile NW of Provincetown Museum entrance), Provincetown, MA 02657. ☎ **508/487-4378.** 30 beds. Summer $14 per bed. No credit cards. Reservations not accepted. Registration daily 8–9am and 6–9:30pm at 30A Winslow St. Closed Oct to late May.

So what if these "European-style" dorms look more like an outtake from *The Grapes of Wrath?* Fourteen bucks a night! And, unlike the straitlaced American Youth Hostels, they're curfew-free! For grungers (or misers) basically looking for a place to crash should the urge arise, these bunks will fill the bill.

The Rose & Crown. 158 Commercial St. (in the W. End), Provincetown, MA 02657. ☎ **508/487-3332.** Web site ptown.com/ptown/rosecrown/. 6 rms (3 with shared bath), 1 apt, 1 cottage. TV. Summer (including continental breakfast) $50 single; $75–$95 double; $110 apt; $135 cottage. MC, V.

Follow the yellow brick road, over a tiny footbridge spanning a minilagoon full of disporting Barbies and Kens, to enter a tchotchke-rich world where, as the brochure brags, "Anything worth doing is worth overdoing!" That maxim is borne out at every turn, in the lace-draped lamps and movie-star dolls. The kitschy front yard of this 1780s Georgian "square rigger" has secured the inn's title as Provincetown's most photographed, and any pennies you care to toss in Barbie's Dream Pool go toward the fight against AIDS and a local organization called Helping Our Women.

✪ **White Horse Inn.** 500 Commercial St. (in the E. End), Provincetown, MA 02657. ☎ **508/487-1790.** 12 rms (9 with shared bath), 6 efficiencies. Summer $60–$70 double; $125 efficiency. No credit cards.

The rates are a literal steal, especially given the fact that this inn is the very embodiment of Provincetown's bohemian mystique. Frank Schaefer has been tinkering with this late–18th-century house since 1963; the rooms may be a bit austere, but each is enlivened by some of the artwork he has collected over the decades. A number of his fellow artists helped him out in cobbling together the studio apartments out of salvage: There's an aura of Beatnik improv about them still. This is where cult filmmaker John Waters stays every summer when he comes to town.

Windamar House. 568 Commercial St. (in the E. End), Provincetown, MA 02657. ☎ **508/487-0599.** Fax 508/487-7505. Web site www.provincetown.com/windamar. 6 rms (4 with shared bath), 2 apts. Summer (including continental breakfast) $60–$110 double; apts $750–$850 weekly. No credit cards.

Pretty furnishings and a peaceful atmosphere characterize this B&B (ca. 1840), which appeals mostly to women, though men are welcome. Rooms range from relatively small and restrained to large and dramatic. The cathedral-ceilinged Studio, for example, has a fourth wall that's all glass and overlooks the inn's spacious backyard garden. The Penthouse apartment also ascends to the peaked rooftop and is illumined by a large skylight with a view of the wharf.

WHERE TO DINE
EXPENSIVE

✪ **Martin House.** 157 Commercial St. ☎ **508/487-1327.** Reservations recommended. Main courses $14–$30. AE, CB, DC, DISC, MC, V. June–Oct daily 6–11pm; call for off-season hrs. FUSION.

Easily one of the most charming restaurants on the Cape—it occupies a house built around 1750 that's turned away from Commercial Street for the simple reason that this thoroughfare didn't yet exist—this snuggery of rustic rooms also just happens to contain one of the Cape's most forward-thinking kitchens. Co-owners Glen and Gary Martin are the conceptualizers behind the inspired regional menu, and chef Alex Mazzocca the gifted creator. The team favors regional delicacies, such as the Thai crab-and-shrimp soup with green curry and crispy rice noodles, or the local littlenecks that appear in a kafir lime-tamarind broth with Asian noodles. Main courses might include local lobster–stuffed squash blossoms with a warm porcini-saffron vinaigrette, or grilled rack of pork with mango salsa and cactus-pear demiglace on spicy masa. The dinners, pleasantly delivered, exceed every expectation: They're like nothing you've ever had before, and the peaceful, softly lit rooms make an optimal setting for exploring new tastes. In season, there's also seating in the rose-choked garden terrace beside the small fountain.

MODERATE

The Boatslip Restaurant. 161 Commercial St. ☎ **508/487-4200.** Reservations recommended. Main courses $13–$22. AE, MC, V. Mid-Apr to late Oct daily 9am–1pm and 6–11pm; call for off-season hrs. Closed Nov to early Apr. NEW AMERICAN.

Formerly at the Flagship Restaurant, chef Polly Hemstock and her partner/manager Susan Leven have moved across town to this lively location in one of Provincetown's premier party-scene hotels (the Boatslip Beach Club). While the outside of the hotel is a rather uninspiring rectangular block, the interior decor is cool and modern, with lots of glass. All tables have a view of the pool and the ocean beyond. Hemstock does marvelous things with seafood, splashing oysters with tequila, lime, and jalapenos; wrapping salmon in rice paper and serving it with Chinese fermented black-bean sauce; and pairing roasted garlic-crusted rack of lamb with a red-wine demiglace and warm tabbouleh.

Bubala's by the Bay. 183 Commercial St. (in the W. End). ☎ **508/487-0773.** Main courses $9–$19. AE, DISC, MC, V. Apr–Oct daily 8am–1am. Closed Nov–Mar. ECLECTIC.

Once a nothing-special seaside restaurant, this trendy bistro—miraculously transformed with a gaudy yellow paint job and Picassoesque wall murals—promises "serious food at sensible prices." That's what it delivers, all day long—from buttermilk waffles with real maple syrup to lobster tarragon salad and creative focaccia sandwiches to fajitas, Cajun calamari, and pad Thai.

✪ Cafe Edwige. 333 Commercial St. ☎ **508/487-2008.** Reservations recommended. Main courses $15–$22. AE, DC, MC, V. July–Aug daily 8am–1pm and 6–11pm; call for off-season hrs. Closed late Oct to Mar. NEW AMERICAN/FUSION.

The tourist throngs generally walk right on by this second-story eatery, little suspecting what they're passing up. To start: superlative breakfasts in a healthful mode, featuring everything from tofu frittatas to broiled flounder with stir-fried vegetables. The cathedral-ceilinged space, with hippie-era wooden booths and deco accents, is a great place to greet the day. At night it's commensurately romantic, with subdued lighting and the cuisine of chef Laura Hopper-Fish. She prepares Edwige specialties like "our" Maine crab cakes, fun, delicious salads, and wild-berry shortcake.

Ciro & Sal's. 4 Kiley Ct. (at Commercial St.). ☎ **508/487-0049.** Reservations recommended. Main courses $9–$21. MC, V. Late May to Sept daily 6–10pm; call for off-season hrs. NORTHERN ITALIAN.

Having evolved from a 1951 cafe, Ciro Cozzi's cozy trattoria is retro in setting only—the usual raffia-wrapped Chianti bottles, an operatic sound track, etc. Preparations, adapted from Italy's regional cuisines, can pack an unexpected punch, as in the horseradish sauce accompanying the fried calamari. Though pasta prevails, local fish and hand-cut veal get equal play, with treatments varying night to night.

✪ The Commons Bistro & Bar. 386 Commercial St. (see "Where to Stay," above). ☎ **508/487-7800.** Reservations recommended. Main courses $9–$19. Late June to early Sept daily 8:30–1am; call for off-season hrs. ECLECTIC.

It's a toss-up: The sidewalk cafe provides an optimal opportunity for studying Provincetown's inimitable street life, whereas the plum-colored dining room inside affords a refuge adorned with the owners' extraordinary collection of original Toulouse-Lautrec prints. Either way, you'll get to partake of Lea Forant's (formerly of the Boatslip) tasty and creative fare. At lunchtime, her overstuffed "lobster club" sandwich on lemon bread is nonpareil, and the grilled duck medaillons served atop soba, Asian greens, and shredded jicama is the ultimate summertime refresher. The Commons boasts the only wood-fired pizza oven in town to date, and the soft-crusted pizzette with various toppings—consider the crisped duck, scallions, chèvre, and wild mushrooms—makes a great snack whatever the hour. Another long-overdue first for this seafaring town is a seasonal sushi bar.

✪ The Dancing Lobster Cafe/Trattoria. 463 Commercial St. (in the E. End). ☎ **508/487-0900.** Main courses $10–$19. MC, V. July–Sept Tues–Sun 6pm–11pm; call for off-season hrs. Closed Dec–Apr. MEDITERRANEAN.

Native son Nils "Pepe" Berg, who virtually grew up at Pepe's Wharf (see below), has moved from his popular Fisherman's Wharf location to a former sail loft at the far end of Commercial Street. This is the site of Provincetown's oldest restaurant, The Flagship, where literati like Gertrude Stein and Anais Nin flocked after its early-1930s debut. Things have changed considerably in the new location; now he accepts credit cards and reservations. This is still a popular place though, and you should expect to wait a half-hour, even with a reservation. The food is still excellent. Start with the grilled-squid bruscetta, the saffrony Venetian fish soup, the crab ravioli, or perhaps the steamed mussels with a basil aioli. Main courses may include steak al "Pepe" with green and black peppercorns, brandy, demiglace and cream; or Basque stew with littleneck clams, chicken, shrimp, linguica, squid and mussels steamed with white beans.

Euro Island Grill. 258 Commercial St. ☎ **508/487-2505.** Reservations not accepted. Main courses $13–$17. AE, DC, MC, V. Late May to mid-Oct daily 11:30am–10:30pm; call for off-season hrs. Closed mid-Oct to mid-May. CARIBBEAN.

The perfect place to acclimate to "Provincetown time" (while critiquing the fashion parade unfurling below), this Caribbean-style cafe with thatched bar features Jamaican beer, killer tropical drinks, and savory munchies—from blackened tuna sashimi to fresh-grilled mahimahi. Check out what's going on in the colorful Club Euro (see "Provincetown After Dark," below).

✪ Front Street. 230 Commercial St. (in the center of town). ☎ **508/487-9715.** Reservations recommended. Main courses $17–$24. AE, DISC, MC, V. June–Oct daily 6–10:30pm; call for off-season hrs. Closed Jan–Apr. NEW AMERICAN/MEDITERRANEAN.

A longtime fave, this bustling little bistro—housed in the brick basement of a Victorian manse—continues to surprise and delight year after year. Chef Donna Aliperti revises her menu weekly, so aficionados know to check the latest posting, even if they've already reserved prime seating—in the high-backed wooden booths—weeks in advance. Among the signature dishes that regularly surface in season are the grilled salmon splashed with raspberry balsamic vinegar, tea-smoked duck, and an unforgettable nectarine *croustade*. Off-season, a less expensive Italian menu is offered in addition to the regular menu.

Gallerani's Cafe. 133 Commercial St. (in the E. End). ☎ **508/487-4433.** Reservations for parties of 5 or more only. Main courses $11–$23. DISC, MC, V. June to mid-Sept Mon–Thurs 6–10:30pm, Fri–Sun 6–11pm; call for off-season hrs. INTERNATIONAL.

Tucked away as it is in the far eastern end of town, this congenial storefront cafe is likely to elude tourists—and it's just as well, for the locals keep it packed year-round. Here the fusion is not so much east-west as comfort-chic, as evidenced in a dish such as zucchini latkes with spicy tomato coulis and a dollop of dilled yogurt; chicken with roasted red peppers, mozzarella, and pear chutney; or a dreamy banana cream pie. Off-season the menu features old-time staples like pizza, lasagna, meat loaf, and chicken pot pie.

Mario's Mediterraneaneo on the Beach. 265–267 Commercial St. ☎ **508/487-0002.** Reservations recommended. Main courses $12–$24. AE, DISC, MC, V. June–Sept daily 7am–2am; call for off-season hrs. Closed mid-Oct to late Apr. MEDITERRANEAN.

Don't let the cafe tables in the storefront portion of this restaurant mislead you into thinking that the place is geared to grazers. There's some serious eating going on out back, in the big water-view dining room bedecked with strange lamps fashioned from sliced agates. Portions are on the large side, so order conservatively—you can always catch up, if need be, when passing by the enticing pastry case on your way out. The bountiful salads—including grilled eggplant with balsamic vinaigrette—make a satisfying light lunch, and you might treat your table to an array of international tapas.

✪ The Mews Restaurant & Cafe Mews. 429 Commercial St. ☎ **508/487-1500.** Reservations recommended. Main courses $15–$22. AE, CB, DC, DISC, MC, V. Mid-June to mid-Sept daily 11am–3pm and 5:30pm–1am; call for off-season hrs. Closed late Dec (except New Year's Eve) to mid-Feb. NEW AMERICAN.

An enduring favorite since 1961, the Mews moved to its current location in 1992, carting along its century-old carved mahogany bar. You can still bank on fine food and suave service. The formal dining room downstairs is right on the beach—and practically of the beach, with its sand-toned walls warmed by toffee-colored Tiffany table lamps. Perennial pleasures include the marsala-marinated portobello mushrooms and a mixed seafood carpaccio. Among the showier entrees is "captured scallops": prime Wellfleet specimens enclosed with a shrimp-and-crab mousse in a crisp wonton pouch and served atop a petite filet mignon with chipotle aioli. Desserts and coffees—you might take them upstairs in the cafe to the accompaniment of improvisatory soft-jazz piano—are delectable. Awash in sea blues that blend with the view, Cafe Mews offers a lighter menu and serves as an elegantly informal community clubhouse almost year-round.

Napi's. 7 Freeman St. (at Bradford St.). ☎ **800/571-6274** or 508/487-1145. Reservations recommended. Main courses $11–$20. AE, CB, DC, DISC, MC, V. May–Oct daily 5–10pm; Nov–Apr daily 11am–4:30pm and 5–10pm. INTERNATIONAL.

Restaurateur Napi Van Dereck can be credited with bringing Provincetown's restaurant scene up to speed—back in the early 1970s. His namesake restaurant still reflects that zeitgeist, with its rococo hippie carpentry, select outtakes from his sideline in antiques, and some rather outstanding native art, including a crazy quilt of a brick wall by local sculptor Conrad Malicoat. The cuisine is a lot less granola than it was when it started out, or maybe we've just caught up—hearty peasant fare never really goes out of style. And these peasants really get around, culling dumplings from China, falafel from Syria, and, from Greece, shrimp feta flambéed with ouzo and Metaxa.

Pepe's Wharf. 371 Commercial St. (in the center of town). ☎ **508/487-0670.** Reservations recommended. Main courses $13–$29. MC, V. July–Aug daily 11:30am–10pm; call for off-season hrs. Closed mid-Oct to mid-May. CONTINENTAL.

Rather sedate by Provincetown standards, this local institution evolved from a humble 1967 sandwich shop. Chef Astrid Berg, who trained at the Culinary Institute of America, emphasizes the "class" in such classical peasant fare as *bouillabaisse au Pernod* and its Italian counterpart, *zuppa di pesce.* The wait staff sports nautical whites, and the view from the glass-walled dining room is the equal of any yacht's. The Top Deck, a casual grill with more modest prices, makes a fine place to survey the harbor while slurping back bivalves and frozen fruit drinks.

The Red Inn. 15 Commercial St. ☎ **508/487-0050.** Reservations recommended. Main courses $21–$26. AE, MC, V. Late May to mid-Oct Sun 11am–3pm; daily 6–10pm. Call for off-season hrs. NEW ENGLAND.

Co-owners Mike Clifford and Bob Kulesza (the resident chef) have done everything in their power to restore this Federal inn to its turn-of-the-century graciousness. They've even replicated the original look by studying vintage photographs. The location couldn't be improved upon: By all accounts, it's the very spot the Pilgrims picked to come ashore. A long bank of windows makes the most of the view, and oil lamps illumine a fine collection of Provincetown paintings. The cuisine—standards such as baked stuffed lobster, roast duckling, rack of lamb—tends to be soothing rather than exciting, but such meals have their uses, too. The Sunday brunch offers a fine opportunity to celebrate one's luck in having found so pretty a place.

INEXPENSIVE

Café Blasé. 328 Commercial St. (in the center of town). ☎ **508/487-9465.** Reservations not accepted. Main courses $9–$16. AE, MC, V. Mid-June to early Sept daily 9am–midnight; call for off-season hrs. Closed late Sept to late May. ECLECTIC.

The turnover beneath these tasseled pink-and-navy umbrellas tends to be constant; everyone wants to see and be seen here. The menu has been expanded to include pastas and dinner specials like hearty bourbon steak. You can also find some excellent salads, or subsist on sodas made from an assortment of esoteric European syrups (Richard Gere is said to have favored the *orzata*). The beers are pretty rarefied, too— everything from a microbrewed Vermont amber, courtesy of Catamount, to a pricey Belgian *framboise*.

Café Crudité. 336 Commercial St. (in the center of town). ☎ **508/487-6237.** Most items under $8. No credit cards. June–Sept 11am–10pm; call for off-season hrs. Closed Dec–Mar. NATURAL.

With its tiny deck overlooking Provincetown's main drag, this health-conscious vegetarian hideaway is a great place to sit out the hype and its empty-caloric enticements. In addition to the basic macrobiotic breakfast (a bowl of miso-and-rice soup), the many morning options include an unusual "Egg Saag"—two eggs poached and served atop seven-grain bread spread with Indian spiced spinach. Cold sesame noodles are available throughout the day, as are double-bean burritos (featuring pinto and black beans). Coffees—including a wicked frozen cappuccino—represent the only departure from the straight and narrow.

Cafe Heaven. 199 Commercial St. (in the center of town). ☎ **508/487-9639.** Reservations not accepted. Most items under $10. No credit cards. Late May to early Sept daily 8am–3pm and 6:30–10pm; call for off-season hrs. Closed Nov–Apr. AMERICAN.

Prized for its leisurely country breakfasts (served till midafternoon, for you reluctant risers), this modernist storefront—adorned with big, bold paintings by acclaimed Wellfleet artist John Grillo—also turns out substantive sandwiches, such as avocado and goat cheese on a French baguette. The salads are appealing as well—especially the "special shrimp," lightly doused with dilled sour cream and tossed with tomatoes and grapes. Innumerable pasta options, plus "heavenly" burgers with a choice of internationally inspired toppings, are the main event come evening.

Dodie's Diner. 401 Commercial St. (in the E. End). ☎ **508/487-3868.** Most items under $10. MC, V. June–Sept daily 8am–10pm; call for off-season hrs. Closed Dec–Mar. AMERICAN.

With a sign heralding her modest joint as JUSTLY FAMOUS SINCE 1993, Dodie Silano has the kind of Provincetown chutzpah for which out-of-towners are willing to pay a premium. The grub at this water-view cottage, plastered with 1950s kitsch (including license plates, advertising art, and vintage toys), is far from cheap: You'd be hardpressed to find a bacon-cheeseburger stacking up at $9 elsewhere. But once people venture in for a breakfast featuring mammoth blueberry muffins and homemade corned-beef hash, they tend to keep coming back.

The Lobster Pot. 321 Commercial St. (in the center of town). ☎ **508/487-0842.** Reservations not accepted. Main courses $8–$19. AE, CB, DC, DISC, MC, V. Mid-June to mid-Sept daily 11:30am–10:30pm; call for off-season hrs. Closed Jan. SEAFOOD.

Snobbish foodies might turn their noses up at a venue so flagrantly Olde Cape Coddish, but for Provincetown regulars, no season seems complete without at least one pilgrimage. You may feel like a long-suffering pilgrim waiting to get in: The line, which starts near the aromatic albeit frantic kitchen, often snakes into the street. While waiting, check out the hand-painted bar stools which provide an architectural history of Provincetown. A lucky few will make it all the way to the outdoor deck; however, most tables, indoors and out, afford nice views of MacMillan Wharf. Spring for a jumbo lobster, by all means—boiled or broiled, sauced or simple. And definitely start off with the chowder, a perennial award-winner.

Lorraine's. 237 Commercial St. (in the center of town). ☎ **508/487-8600.** Main courses $11–$16. MC, V. Late June to Aug daily 11:30am–10pm; call for off-season hrs. Closed Jan–Mar. MEXICAN/NEW AMERICAN.

There's a bit of a decadent twilight-of-Havana look to this deco-accented cafe, and chef/owner Lorraine Najar brings a certain daring to bear on the cuisine she learned at her grandmother's knee. Consider duckling *taquitos,* chunks of marinated breast enrobed in corn tortillas, then deep-fried, or a dish like *viere verde*—sea scallops sautéed with tomatillos, flambéed in tequila, and cloaked in a green-chili sauce. For samplings of other great hits in the making, stop in for late-night tapas, served till 1am.

The Moors. 5 Bradford St. Ext. (at Province Lands Rd.). ☎ **800/843-0840** or 508/487-0840. Reservations recommended. Main courses $9–$18. AE, CB, DC, DISC, MC, V. May to mid-Oct daily 5:30–10pm; call for off-season hrs. Closed late Nov to Mar. PORTUGUESE.

A salty classic since 1939, this ramshackle restaurant, composed primarily of nautical salvage, serves traditional Azorean fare, such as *espada cozida* (flash-broiled swordfish marinated in lemon juice, olive oil, parsley, and garlic) and *galinha à moda da Madeira* (chicken breast baked Madeira style). The standout is *porco em pau,* a Brazilian casserole of fork-tender pork tenderloin cubes in a spicy marinade.

Pucci's. 539 Commercial St. (in the E. End). ☎ **508/487-1964.** Main courses $10–$17. AE, MC, V. Mid-Apr to mid-Oct daily 11:30am–3pm and 5–10pm; call for off-season hrs. Closed Nov to mid-Apr. ECLECTIC.

Plain and unpretentious, this harborside hideaway attracts an after-work crowd drawn by plentiful portions—even for appetizers—at real-people prices. The owners hail from Buffalo, which explains the exemplary chicken wings with bleu cheese dipping sauce.

Sal's Place. 99 Commercial St. (in the W. End). ☎ **508/487-1279.** Reservations recommended. Main courses $9–$20. MC, V. July–Aug daily 6–10pm; call for off-season hrs. Closed Nov–Apr. SOUTHERN ITALIAN.

Sal spun off from Ciro (see Ciro & Sal's, above) back in 1963, and his place is a little looser. The kitchen's right out in the open, for one thing, so you can see those shrimp Adriatica (with calamari and pesto) jumping in the pan, and see that someone's tending to the *spaghettini alla foriana* (with pine nuts, raisins, and anchovies) so that it will arrive perfectly al dente. The nostalgic dining rooms, festooned with old posters, are great for blustery days, but on a fine evening nothing beats the harborside arbor.

Sebastian's Waterfront Restaurant. 177 Commercial St. (in the E. End). ☎ **508/ 487-3286.** Main courses $9–$16. AE, MC, V. June–Aug 11am–11pm; call for off-season hrs. Closed late Oct to mid-Apr. AMERICAN.

It's refreshing to come across a restaurant with honest goals and modest aspirations. Owners Scott Belding and Larry Wald, the force behind Larry's Bar (see "Provincetown After Dark," below), see little need to embellish upon the enviable water views and a menu promising generous portions of popular dishes—prime rib, for instance, and baked stuffed shrimp. If it's novelty you're after, you'll find the occasional flash—perhaps a dessert of chocolate-Chambord layer cake. Larry, by the way, created that crystal-beaded whale that serenely surveys the dining room.

ICE CREAM

Not only a good spot to satisfy any ice-cream cravings (how about a 20-scoop "Vermonster"?), **Ben & Jerry's,** 258 Commercial St., in the center of town (☎ 508/ 487-3360), is also handy for refueling midstroll with a fresh-fruit drink or espresso.

TAKE-OUT & PICNIC FARE

The rollwiches—pita bread packed with a wide range of fillings—at **Box Lunch,** 353 Commercial St. (in the center of town; ☎ 508/487-6026) are ideal for a strolling lunch.

The aroma at **Clem & Joe's,** 338 Commercial St. (in the center of town; ☎ 508/ 487-8303), will lure you to this barbecue/rotisserie, which also delivers. Ample servings of "homemade comfort food" will fuel that marathon bike jaunt or see you satedly home.

At **Flying Cups & Saucers,** The Aquarium Shops, 205 Commercial St. (in the center of town; ☎ 508/487-3780), the offerings are limited but to the point: "juice, java, pastries." Among the first category is a lovely concoction called the "Ruby Slipper Sipper," a smoothie made from pineapple, strawberries, and apple juice.

One thing you absolutely have to do while in town is peruse the cases of *pasteis* (meat pies) and pastries at ✪ **Provincetown Portuguese Bakery,** 299 Commercial St. (in the center of town; ☎ 508/487-1803). Point to a few and take your surprise package out on the pier for delectation. Though perhaps not the wisest course for the whale watch–bound, it's the best way to sample the scrumptious international output of this beloved institution. Closed November through March.

A local landmark, **Spiritus,** 190 Commercial St. (in the center of town; ☎ 508/ 487-2808), is an extravagant pizza parlor known for post–last-call cruising: It's open until 2am. The pizza's good, as are the fruit drinks, specialty coffees, and four brands of premium ice cream, from Emack & Bolio's to Coconut Joe's. For a peaceful morning repast—and perhaps a relaxed round of bocce—check out the little garden in back. Closed November through March.

PROVINCETOWN AFTER DARK

Note: There's so much going on in season on any given night that you might want to simplify your search by calling or stopping in at the **Provincetown Reservations System** office at 293 Commercial St., in the center of town (☎ 508/487-6400).

THE CLUB SCENE

The Atlantic House. 6 Masonic Place (off Commercial St., 2 blocks W of Town Hall). ☎ **508/487-3821.** Cover for the Big Room: $5.

Open year-round, the "A-house"—the nation's premier gay bar—also welcomes straights of both sexes, except in the leather-oriented Macho Bar upstairs. Late in the evening, there's usually plenty going on in the Big Room dance bar. Check out the Tennessee Williams memorabilia, including a portrait *au naturel;* there's more across the street in a new restaurant called Grand Central.

Boatslip Beach Club. 161 Commercial St. (see "Where to Dine," above). ☎ **508/487-2660.** Cover varies.

Come late afternoon, if you wonder where all the beachgoers went, it's a safe guess that a goodly number are attending the gay-lesbian tea dance held daily in season from 3:30 to 6:30pm on the hotel's pool deck. Later in the evening, after a post-tea dance at Pied Piper (see below), they'll probably be back for some disco or two-stepping.

Club Euro. 258 Commercial St. (at the Euro Island Grill; see "Where to Dine," above). ☎ **508/487-2505.** Closed Nov–Apr. Cover varies; call for schedule.

Weekends bring live jazz, reggae, and blues—usually in that order, Friday through Sunday—to this fanciful, oceanic-themed dance hall carved out of an 1843 Congregational church. On weekday evenings, the space reverts to sports and music videos and an open-mike night. Some big names (Taj Mahal, for example) sometimes spark the lineup, so check to see who's on.

Crown & Anchor. 247 Commercial St. (in the center of town). ☎ **508/487-1430.** Cover varies; call for schedule.

There's something for everyone at this warren of specialty bars, spanning leather (in "The Vault"), disco, comedy, drag shows (including headliner "Musty Chiffon" singing 1960s camp classics), and cabaret (the irresistible trio known simply as Betty, for example). Facilities include a pool bar and game room.

Pied Piper. 193 Commercial St. (in the center of town). ☎ **508/487-1527.** Closed Nov to mid-Apr. Cover varies; call for schedule.

In season, a "parade" of gay revelers descends in early evening from the Boatslip to "the Pied," for its After Tea T-Dance. The late-night wave consists of a fair number of women, or fairly convincing simulacra thereof (Monday and Wednesday nights feature the "female illusionists" of the Drag Factory). For a glimpse of stars-in-the-making, check out "Putting on the Hits," a sampling of local talent held Tuesday nights at 10.

Vixen. Pilgrim House, 336 Commercial St. (in the center of town). ☎ **508/487-6424.** Cover varies; call for schedule.

Provincetown's oldest hotel was overhauled in 1995, yielding this chic new women's bar. On the roster are jazz, blues, and comedy acts—including the unabashedly butch (even in a prom dress) and very funny Lea Delaria, who resembles a punk Bud Costello.

THE BAR SCENE

✪ **Cafe Mews.** At the Mews (see "Where to Dine," above). ☎ **508/487-1500.** Cover $10 for entertainment acts; no cover for cafe/lounge.

This highly civilized venue, with its bay view and vintage mahogany bar, is one of the few nightspots in town to lend itself well to the art of conversation. The jazz piano enhances rather than intrudes, and occasional guest artists—such as the mellow local act, Men in Comfortable Shoes—add a novel edge.

Governor Bradford. 312 Commercial St. (in the center of town). ☎ **508/487-9618.** Cover varies; call for schedule.

It's a good old bar, featuring a summer-long lineup of blues acts, plus the inimitable homegrown, gender-bending rock group known as Space Pussy.

✪ **Larry's Bar.** At Sebastian's Waterfront Restaurant (see "Where to Dine," above). ☎ **508/487-3286.** Closed late Oct to mid-Apr. No cover.

Mrs. Wald did not raise a retiring child. Her irrepressible son Larry—perennial chair and chief cheerleader for Provincetown's campy Carnival Week—is a drink-dispensing one-man entertainment committee. Once he gets going on one of his riffs (usually centered on an assortment of mutant Barbie dolls), you can just sit back and enjoy the show. This tiny bar, wallpapered with classic paint-by-numbers chef-d'oeuvres, is the place to go when you need a good laugh.

The Moors. 5 Bradford St. Ext. (at Province Lands Rd.). ☎ **508/487-0840.** Closed late Nov to Mar. No cover.

Pianist/comedian Lenny Grandchamp provides a grand old time nightly in this piratelike lair, cajoling his audience with corny jokes and instigating show-tune sing-alongs.

PERFORMANCE, ETC.

Meetinghouse Theatre. At the Unitarian-Universalist Meetinghouse, 236 Commercial St. (in the center of town). ☎ **508/487-9344.** Ticket prices vary; call for schedule.

In season, this glorious space (see "A Stroll Around Provincetown," above) is given over to a wide range of performances, from plays to opera to cabaret. The season is usually capped off by a series of concerts by the Flirtations, a gay a cappella ensemble.

Post Office Cabaret. 303 Commercial St. ☎ **508/487-3892.** Cover varies; call for schedule.

This cramped shoe-box space hardly leaves room for laughing in the aisles, but regulars like comedian Suzanne Westenhiffer and female-vocalist impersonator Jimmy James invariably exert that effect. Several shows, spanning drag and folk, are staggered throughout the evening.

✪ **Provincetown Playhouse Muse Series.** Provincetown Town Hall, 260 Commercial St. ☎ **508/487-0955.** Ticket prices vary; call for schedule.

Several times in the course of the summer, this venerable, 600-seat hall goes SRO for such popular acts as comedienne Sandra Bernhard, as well as notable classical-to-contemporary soloists and ensembles.

Provincetown Repertory Theatre. Various locations, Provincetown. ☎ **508/487-0600.** Tickets $15; call for schedule.

Pitching their stage in various venues, this ambitious professional company, founded by Equity actor Ken Hoyt in 1995, shows a fondness for works that touch on town history, including the O'Neill canon.

Town House. 291 Commercial St. (in the center of town). ☎ **508/487-0292.** Cover varies; call for schedule.

In season, the "Backroom Cabaret" hosts comedians attuned to a mixed (gay/straight) audience.

LOW-KEY EVENINGS

Fine Arts Work Center. 24 Pearl St. (off Bradford St. in the center of town). ☎ **508/ 487-9960.** Most events free; call for schedule.

Drawing on its roster of visiting artists and scholars, FAWC offers exceptional readings and talks (some serve as fund-raisers) year-round.

New Art Cinema. 214 Commercial St. (in the center of town). ☎ **508/487-9222.** Tickets $8. Closed mid-Sept to mid-May.

This small duplex theater shows the latest releases: usually a blockbuster pitted against an indie art film.

✪ **Provincetown Art Association & Museum.** 460 Commercial St. (in the E. End). ☎ **508/487-1750.** Cover varies; call for schedule.

Concerts, lectures, and readings attract an intellectually inclined after-hours crowd.

9

Martha's Vineyard

Recently, while eating breakfast at the Black Dog Tavern in Vineyard Haven, a friend of mine eavesdropped on John F. Kennedy, Jr., discussing the repair of his dock with a grizzled local contractor. On Martha's Vineyard, John-John is just-folks, like everybody else. Lately the First Family has made a habit of vacationing on the island, which has long been a Democratic stronghold. President Clinton has many golf buddies to choose from, as well as scenic courses for those all-important photo ops. But don't come to the island of Martha's Vineyard for the celebrities; it's considered impolite to gawk, and, like jaded New Yorkers, the locals barely seem to notice the stars in their midst.

Instead, visit the Vineyard to bicycle the shaded paths hugging the coastline. Admire the regal sea captain's houses in Edgartown, and stop by the Scrimshaw Shop for a memento of the sea. Stroll down Circuit Avenue in Oak Bluffs with a Mad Martha's ice cream cone and then ride The Flying Horses Carousel, said to be the oldest working carousel in the country. Don't miss the cheerful "gingerbread" cottages behind Circuit Avenue, where the echoes of 19th-century revival meetings still ring out from the imposing Tabernacle. Marvel at the red clay cliffs of Gay Head, now known as Aquinnah, a national historic landmark. Travel the country roads of West Tisbury and Chilmark, stopping at Allen Farm for sweaters made from the wool of their flock of over 200 sheep. Buy bread at the Scottish Bakehouse in North Tisbury and a lobster roll in the fishing village of Menemsha. There is no dearth of terrific vacation activities on the island.

Unlike much of New England, Martha's Vineyard has long been a melting pot in which locals, homeowners, and summer people co-exist in an almost effortless comfort, united in their disapproval of traffic, their criticism of The Steamship Authority, and their protective attitude towards the island. The roots of Martha's Vineyard's diversity go back more than a hundred years. In the late 19th century, Oak Bluffs, with its religious roots, was one of the first spots where African-Americans of means went on vacation. Dorothy West, the last surviving writer of the Harlem Renaissance, is—at 90 plus—the reigning doyenne of this community, which includes such notable celebrities as film director Spike Lee and Washington power broker Vernon Jordan. In the tiny town of Aquinnah, the Wampanoags are the only Native American tribe in the region to have official status in Washington. And 12th-generation Vineyarders farm the land in Chilmark and rub shoulders at Cronig's Market with posh Yankees from Edgartown.

There's always a lot of "hurry up and wait" involved in ferry travel, so allowing yourself just a weekend on the Vineyard may be less than you need. If you're traveling from New York, take an extra day off, allowing a minimum of 3 days for this trip. Four days will feel more comfortable. From Boston, a couple days is fine (the drive from Boston to Woods Hole takes $1^{1}/_{2}$ hours with no traffic), but beware summer weekend bottlenecks. (Never aim for the last ferry.) You really don't need to bring a car to get around this small island, but if you absolutely must be accompanied by four wheels, you'll need a car reservation for the ferry (see "Getting There," below, for details).

Try to savor the 45-minute ferry ride to and from this pastoral place. The Vineyard's pace is decidedly laid-back, and your biggest chore should be to try to blend in with the prevalent ultracool attitude. The six towns on Martha's Vineyard have distinct identities, but they can be divided into "down-island," referring to Vineyard Haven (officially called Tisbury), Edgartown, and Oak Bluffs; and "up-island," encompassing the towns of West Tisbury, Chilmark, and Gay Head.

Here are some tips for "going native" on Martha's Vineyard. Down-island: If you must buy a Black Dog T-shirt, wait until you get home to wear it. Don't loiter at the Charlotte Inn. Have cocktails on the porch of the Harborview Hotel. Bike Chappaquiddick Island (don't drive drunk). In Oak Bluffs, don't ask when Illumination Night is (it's a secret). Experience Edgartown on a snowy winter weekend or in spring when the lilacs are in bloom. Up-island: When in doubt, don't wear shoes. Sail a boat to a remote beach for a picnic. Don't view the rolling farmlands from a tour bus. By all means, bike. Canoe. Rent a cottage for a week or two. Don't be a day-tripper.

1 Essentials

GETTING THERE

BY FERRY   Most visitors take the ferry service connecting the Vineyard and the mainland. If you're traveling via car or bus, you will most likely be catching the ferry from Woods Hole on Cape Cod; however, boats do run from Falmouth, Hyannis, New Bedford, and Nantucket. On weekends in season, the Steamship Authority ferries make as many as 30 trips a day to Martha's Vineyard from Woods Hole (two other companies provide an additional 12 passenger ferries a day from Falmouth Harbor). Schedules are available from the **Martha's Vineyard Chamber of Commerce** (☎ **508/693-0085;** fax 508/696-0433; Web site www.mvy.com) or the Steamship Authority (see below).

The state-run **Steamship Authority** runs the show in Woods Hole (☎ **508/ 477-8600** daily 5am to 10pm or 508/693-9130 Monday through Friday 7:30am to 9pm; Saturday, Sunday, and holidays 8am to 5pm) and operates every day, year-round (weather permitting). It also maintains the only car ferries, which make the 45-minute trip to Vineyard Haven throughout the year; some boats go to Oak Bluffs from late May to early September (call for seasonal schedules). The cost of a one-way car passage from mid-May to mid-October is $44; in the off-season it drops to $27. During the summer, you'll need a reservation to bring your car to the island, and you must reserve *months in advance* to secure a spot. If you are planning to bring your car over to the island, I suggest you get to the Woods Hole terminal at least 45 minutes before your scheduled departure.

Martha's Vineyard

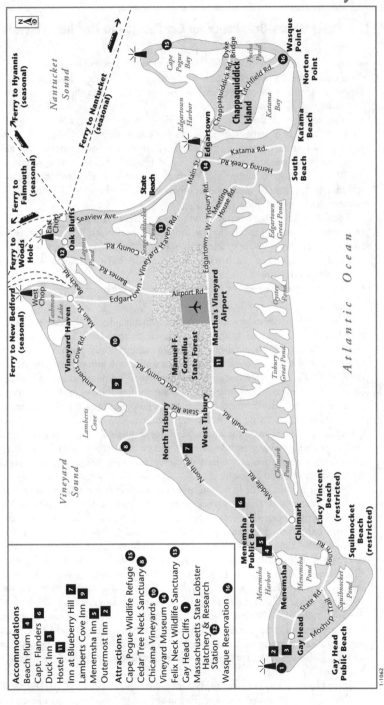

Accommodations
- Beach Plum [4]
- Capt. Flanders [6]
- Duck Inn [3]
- Hostel [11]
- Inn at Blueberry Hill [7]
- Lamberts Cove Inn [9]
- Menemsha Inn [5]
- Outermost Inn [2]

Attractions
- Cape Pogue Wildlife Refuge [15]
- Cedar Tree Neck Sanctuary [8]
- Chicama Vineyards [10]
- Vineyard Museum [14]
- Felix Neck Wildlife Sanctuary [13]
- Gay Head Cliffs [1]
- Massachusetts State Lobster Hatchery & Research Station [12]
- Wasque Reservation [16]

1-1062

New Reservations-Only Policy for Car Passage to Martha's Vineyard

In 1998, vehicle reservations are required to bring your car to Martha's Vineyard on Friday, Saturday, Sunday, and Monday from June 16 to September 10. During these times, standby is in effect only on Tuesdays, Wednesdays, and Thursdays. Vehicle reservations are also required to bring your car to Martha's Vineyard on Memorial Day Weekend (May 22 to 25, 1998). There will be no standby service available during these dates. Although technically, reservations can be made up to 1 hour in advance of ferry departure, ferries in season are almost always full, and you certainly cannot depend on a cancellation during the summer months. Also be aware that your space may be forfeited if you have not checked into the ferry terminal 30 minutes prior to sailing time. Reservations may be changed to another date and time with at least 24 hours notice; otherwise you will have to pay for an additional ticket for your vehicle.

If you arrive without a reservation on a day that allows standby, come early and be prepared to wait in the standby line for hours. The Steamship Authority guarantees your passage if you're in line by 2pm on designated standby days only. For up-to-date **Steamship Authority** information, check out their Web site (**www.islandferry.com**).

Many people prefer to leave their cars on the mainland, take the ferry (often with their bikes), and then rent a car, jeep, or bicycle on the island. You can park your car at the Woods Hole lots (always full in the summer) or at one of the many lots in Falmouth that absorb the overflow of cars during the summer months; parking is $7.50 per day. Plan to arrive at the parking lots in Falmouth at least 45 minutes before sailing time to allow for parking, taking the free shuttle bus to the ferry terminal, and buying your ferry ticket. Free shuttle buses (some equipped for bikes) run regularly from the outlying lots to the ferry terminal. The cost of a one-way passenger ticket on the ferry is $5 for adults, $2.40 for children 5 to 12 (kids under 5 ride free). If you're bringing your bike along, it's an extra $3 each way, year-round. You do not need a reservation on the ferry if you're traveling without a car, and there are no reservations needed for parking.

Once you are aboard the ferry, you have won the right to feel relieved and relaxed. Now your vacation can begin. Ferries are equipped with bathrooms and snack bars. Your fellow passengers will be a gaggle of kids, dogs, and happy-looking travelers.

From Falmouth, you can also board the *Island Queen* at Falmouth Harbor (☎ **508/548-4800**) for a 35-minute cruise to Oak Bluffs (passengers only). The boat runs from late May through mid-October; one-way fare costs $6 for adults, $3 for children under 13, and an extra $3 for bikes. There are seven crossings a day in season, and no reservations are needed. Slightly discounted round-trip tickets are also available, and parking will run you $8 or $10. The **Falmouth Ferry Service** (278 Scranton Ave.; ☎ **508/548-9400**) has a 1-hour passenger ferry, called the *Pied Piper,* from Falmouth Harbor to Edgartown. The boat runs from late May to mid-October, and reservations are recommended. In season, there are six crossings a day. One-way fares are $12.50 for adults, $8 for children under 12. Bicycles are $3 each way. Parking is $10 per day.

From Hyannis, you can take the **Hy-Line** (Ocean Street Dock; ☎ **508/778-2600**) to Oak Bluffs, May through October. Trip time is about 1 hour and 45 minutes; one-way costs $11 for adults, $5.50 for children 5 to 12 ($4.50 extra for bikes). In July and August it's a good idea to reserve a parking spot in Hyannis; the all-day fee is $10. From June through September they also operate a 1-day cruise, called **Around the Sound,** with stops on the Vineyard and Nantucket ($33 adults; $16.50 children 5 to 12).

From New Bedford, Massachusetts, the *Schamonchi* (Billy Woods Wharf; ☎ 508/997-1688; Web site www.mvferry.com) takes island-goers to Vineyard Haven from mid-May through mid-October. Trip time is about 1 1/2 hours. A 1-day/round-trip ticket is $16 for adults, $9 for children under 13, and $2.50 extra for bikes. This is a great way to avoid Cape traffic and to enjoy a scenic ocean cruise.

From Nantucket, you can take the **Hy-Line** (☎ 508/778-2600) to Oak Bluffs, mid-May through mid-September. Trip time is 2 hours and 15 minutes and the one-way fare is $11 for adults, $5.50 for children 5 to 12, and $4.50 extra for bikes. It's the only passenger service (no cars) between the islands.

BY AIR You can fly into **Martha's Vineyard Airport,** also known as Dukes County Airport (☎ 508/693-7022) in West Tisbury, about 5 miles outside Edgartown.

Airlines serving the Vineyard include **Cape Air** (☎ 800/352-0714 or 508/771-6944), which connects the island year-round with Boston (with hourly shuttle service in summer for about $185 to $220 round-trip), Hyannis, Nantucket, and New Bedford; **Continental Express/Colgan Air** (☎ 800/525-0280), which has nonstop flights from Newark (seasonal) for about $180 round-trip; and **US Airways Express** (☎ 800/428-4322), which flies from Boston for about $95 round-trip and also has seasonal weekend service from La Guardia (via Allegheny), which cost approximately $210 round-trip.

Two companies offering year-round charter service are: **Air New England** (☎ 508/693-8899) and **Direct Flight** (☎ 508/693-6688). **Westchester Air** (☎ 800/759-2929) also runs charters from White Plains, New York.

BY BUS **Bonanza Bus Lines** (☎ 800/556-3815) connects the Woods Hole ferry port with Boston (new South Station), New York City, and Providence, Rhode Island.

New Bedford: A Stop En Route

The *Schamonchi* runs only a few trips a day in summer. If you miss the last boat, you may want to take in some of the sights in this historic seaport, depicted in Herman Melville's classic *Moby Dick.* Melville's New Bedford was a rough-and-tumble town, filled with swaggering, worldly sea captains and sailors. There's a lot of historic flavor here still. The neighborhood adjacent to the waterfront has recently been named the **Whaling National Historical Park** and is undergoing revitalization efforts. The streets are cobbled, and there are many finely restored 19th-century buildings. You can pick up a self-guided tour and map at the **Visitors Center,** on the waterfront, Pier #3, or at 33 William St. (☎ 800/508-5353). Visit the excellent **New Bedford Whaling Museum** at 18 Johnny Cake Hill (☎ 508/997-0046), which is filled with interesting whaling artifacts and also has a Moby Dick exhibit. Directly across from the Whaling Museum is the **Seamen's Bethel** (☎ 508/992-3295), made famous as the "Whaleman's Chapel" in Melville's tale. Lunch and dinner is served at **Freestone's City Grill** at 41 William St. (☎ 508/996-7477) and a 5-minute drive—on several expressways—will bring you to the uninspiring but convenient **Day's Inn** at 500 Hathaway Rd. (☎ 800/325-2525 or 508/997-1231). Rooms are $69 to $99 a night.

The trip from Boston takes about 1 hour and 35 minutes and costs $12.50 one way; from New York, it's about a 6-hour trip to Hyannis or Woods Hole and costs approximately $45 each way.

GETTING AROUND

The down-island towns of Vineyard Haven, Oak Bluffs, and Edgartown are fairly compact, and if your inn is located in the heart of one of these small towns, you will be within walking distance of all shopping and attractions in town. Frequent shuttle buses can whisk you to the other down-island towns in 5 to 15 minutes. For up-island exploration, you will need to bike (if so inclined, you could tour the entire island—60 some odd miles—in 1 day), take the shuttle buses, or take a cab (mainly driven by college kids, so you'll be helping with college tuitions).

BY BICYCLE & MOPED   You shouldn't leave without exploring the Vineyard on two wheels, even if only for a couple of hours. There's a little of everything for cyclists, from paved paths to hilly country roads (see "Beaches & Outdoor Pursuits," below for details on where to ride), and you don't have to be an expert rider to enjoy yourself. Plus, biking is a great, relatively hassle-free way to get around the island.

If you have the energy, consider a 1-day, circle-the-island tour. This way you can hit all six towns and some of the unique up-island, off-the-beaten-track businesses on the Vineyard. When biking on the Edgartown–West Tisbury Road out to Gay Head, I always stop at **Campbell and Douglas Harness and Feed** at Rainbow Farm, South Road, Chilmark (☎ **508/645-7800**) (for the horse-y at heart) and **Allen Farm Sheep and Wool Company,** South Road, Chilmark (☎ **508/645-9064**) (for the best handmade wool sweaters). When biking back towards Vineyard Haven on State Road, I love to watch the glassblowing at **Martha's Vineyard Glass Works,** State Road, West Tisbury (☎ **508/693-6026**), and I can't live without the scones from **The Scottish Bake House,** State Road, Vineyard Haven, (☎ **508/693-1873**). There are also a number of terrific galleries along the way.

Mopeds are also a popular way to navigate Vineyard roads, but remember that some roads tend to be narrow and rough—the number of accidents involving mopeds seems to rise every year. You'll need a driver's license to rent a moped.

Bike, scooter, and moped rental shops are clustered throughout all three down-island towns. Bike rentals cost about $10 to $25 a day (the higher prices are for suspension mountain bikes), scooters and mopeds $25 to $70. In Vineyard Haven, try **Martha's Vineyard Scooter & Bikes** (Union Street; ☎ 508/693-0782); **Martha's Bike Rentals** (Lagoon Pond Road; ☎ 508/693-6593); or **Adventure Rentals** (Beach Road; ☎ 508/693-1959), which rents mopeds only. In Oak Bluffs, there's **Anderson's** (Circuit Avenue Extension; ☎ 508/693-9346), which rents bikes only; **DeBettencourt's Bike Shop** (Circuit Avenue Extension; ☎ 508/693-0011); **King's Rental, Inc.** (Circuit Avenue Extension; ☎ 508/693-1887); **Ride-On Mopeds** (Circuit Avenue Extension; ☎ 508/693-2076); **Sun 'n' Fun** (Lake Avenue; ☎ 508/693-5457); and **Vineyard Bike & Moped** (Oak Bluffs Avenue; ☎ 508/693-4498). In Edgartown, you'll find **R. W. Cutler Bike** (1 Main St.; ☎ 508/627-4052); **Edgartown Bicycles** (190 Upper Main St.; ☎ 508/627-9008); and **Wheel Happy** (204 Upper Main St. and 8 S. Water St.; ☎ 508/627-5928), which rents only bikes.

BY CAR   If you're coming to the Vineyard for a few days and you're going to stick to the down-island towns, I think it's best to leave your car at home, since traffic and parking on the island can be brutal in summer. Also, it's easy to take the shuttle buses (see below) from town to town or simply bike your way around. If you're staying for a longer period of time or you want to do some exploring up-island, you should bring your car or rent one on the island—my favorite way to tour the Vineyard is by jeep.

Keep in mind that car-rental rates can soar during peak season, and gas is also much more expensive on the island. Off-road driving on the beaches is a major topic of debate on the Vineyard, and the most popular spots may be closed for nesting piping plovers at the height of the season. If you plan to do some off-road exploration, check with the Chamber of Commerce to see if the trails are open to vehicles before you rent. To drive off-road at Cape Pogue or Cape Wasque on Chappaquiddick, you'll need to purchase a permit from the **Trustees of Reservations** (☎ **508/ 627-7260**); the cost is $70 to $110.

There are representatives of the national car-rental chains at the airport and in Vineyard Haven and Oak Bluffs. Local agencies also operate out of all three port towns and many of them also rent jeeps, mopeds, and bikes. The national chains include: **Alamo** (☎ 800/327-9633); **Avis** (☎ 800/331-1212); **Budget** (☎ 800/ 527-0700); **Hertz** (☎ 800/654-3131); **National** (☎ 800/227-7368); and **Thrifty** (☎ 800/FOR-CARS).

In Vineyard Haven, you'll find **Adventure Rentals** (Beach Road; ☎ 508/ 693-1959) at which a jeep will run you about $130 per day in season; **Atlantic** (15 Beach Rd.; ☎ 508/693-0480); **Bayside** (☎ 508/693-4777), which has no four-wheel–drive vehicles, but does rent midsized cars for about $55 per day in season; and **Holmes Hole Car Rentals** (Five Corners; ☎ 508/693-8838), where a four-wheel–drive vehicle rents for about $120 per day in season. In Oak Bluffs, there's **Vineyard Classic Cars** (☎ 508/693-5551), which rents classic Corvettes and the like. In Edgartown, try **AAA Island Rentals** (141 Main St.; ☎ 508/627-6800). Another recommendable Island company that operates out of the airport is **All Island Rent-a-Car** (☎ 508/693-6868).

BY SHUTTLE BUS & TROLLEY In season, shuttle buses certainly run often enough to make them a practical means of getting around. There are two different types of shuttle buses making the rounds, and they provide the cheapest, quickest, and easiest way to get around the island during the busy summer season. Connecting Vineyard Haven (across from ferry terminal), Oak Bluffs (near Civil War statue in Ocean Park), and Edgartown (Church Street, near the Old Whaling Church), the Island Transport yellow school buses cost about $1.50 to $3, depending on distance, and from late June to early September they run from 7am to midnight. Hours are reduced in spring and fall. From late June through August, buses go out to Gay Head (via the airport, West Tisbury, and Chilmark), leaving every couple of hours from down-island towns and looping about every hour through up-island towns. For information and a schedule call **Island Transport** (☎ **508/693-1589** or 508/693-0058).

The **Martha's Vineyard Transit Authority** (☎ **508/627-9663** or 508/627-7448) also operates several shuttle buses in season (white buses with a purple COME RIDE WITH US logo). The Edgartown Downtown Shuttle and the South Beach Trolley buses circle throughout town or out to South Beach, every 15 minutes in season. They also stop at the free parking lots just north of the town center—this is a great way to avoid circling the streets in search of a vacant spot on busy weekends. A one-way trip in town is just 50¢; a trip to South Beach (leaving from Edgartown's Church Street Visitor Center) is $1.50. The "Tisbury Park and Ride" picks up drivers who park their cars at the State Road parking lot and drops them at the Vineyard Haven ferry terminal.

BY TAXI Upon arrival, you'll find taxis at all ferry terminals and at the airport, and there are permanent taxi stands in Oak Bluffs (at the Flying Horses Carousel) and Edgartown (next to the Town Wharf). Most taxi outfits operate cars as well as vans for larger groups and travelers with bikes. Cab companies on the island include:

Adam Cab (☎ 800/281-4462 or 508/693-3332); **All Island Taxi** (☎ 800/ 693-TAXI or 508/693-2929); **Harbor Taxi** (☎ 508/693-9611); **Marlene's Taxi** (☎ 508/693-0037); and **Martha's Vineyard Taxi/Atlantic Cab** (☎ 508/693-8660). Rates from town to town in summer are generally flat fees based on where you're headed and the number of passengers on board. A trip from Vineyard Haven to Edgartown would probably cost around $10 for two people. Late-night revelers should keep in mind that rates double after midnight.

THE CHAPPAQUIDDICK FERRY   The **On Time ferry** (☎ 508/627-9427) runs the 5-minute trip from Dock Street in Edgartown to Chappaquiddick Island from June to mid-October, 7:30am to midnight. Passengers, bikes, mopeds, dogs, and cars (three at a time) are all welcome. The one-way cost is $1 per person, $4 for one car/one driver, $2.50 for one bike/one person, and $3.50 for one moped or motorcycle/one person.

VISITOR INFORMATION

Contact the **Martha's Vineyard Chamber of Commerce** at Beach Road, Vineyard Haven, MA 02568 (☎ 508/693-0085; fax 508/693-7589) or visit their Web site at www.mvy.com. Their office is just 2 blocks up from the ferry terminal in Vineyard Haven. There are also information booths at the ferry terminal in Vineyard Haven, across from the Flying Horses Carousel in Oak Bluffs, and on Church Street in Edgartown. You'll want to poke your head in these offices to pick up free maps, tourist handbooks, and flyers on tours and events or to get answers to any questions you might have. Most inns also have tourist handbooks and maps available for guests.

Always check the two local newspapers, the *Vineyard Gazette* and the *Martha's Vineyard Times,* for information on current events.

In case of an emergency, call ☎ **911** and/or head for the **Martha's Vineyard Hospital,** Linton Lane, Oak Bluffs (☎ 508/693-0410), which has a 24-hour emergency room.

2 A Stroll Around Edgartown

A good way to get yourself acclimated to the pace and flavor of the Vineyard is to walk the streets of Edgartown. This walk starts at the Dr. Daniel Fisher House and meanders along for about a mile; depending on how long you linger at each stop, it should take about 2 to 3 hours.

If you're driving, park at the free lots at the edge of town (you'll see signs on the roads from Vineyard Haven and West Tisbury) and bike or take the shuttle bus (it only costs 50¢) to the Edgartown Visitor Center on Church Street. Around the corner are three local landmarks: the Dr. Daniel Fisher House, Vincent House Museum, and Old Whaling Church.

The **Dr. Daniel Fisher House,** 99 Main St. (☎ 508/627-8017), is a prime example of Edgartown's trademark Greek Revival opulence. A key player in the 19th-century whaling trade, Dr. Fisher amassed a fortune sufficient to found the **Martha's Vineyard National Bank.** Built in 1840, his prosperous and proud mansion boasts such classical elements as colonnaded porticos, as well as a delicate roof-walk. The only way to view the interior (now headquarters for the Martha's Vineyard Preservation Trust) is with a guided **Vineyard Historic Walking Tour.** This tour originates next door at the **Vincent House Museum,** off Main Street between Planting Field Way and Church Street (☎ 508/627-8619; see "Organized Tours," below), a transplanted 1672 full Cape considered to be the oldest surviving dwelling on the island. Plexiglas-covered cutaways permit a view of traditional building techniques, and three rooms have been refurbished to encapsulate the decorative styles of 3

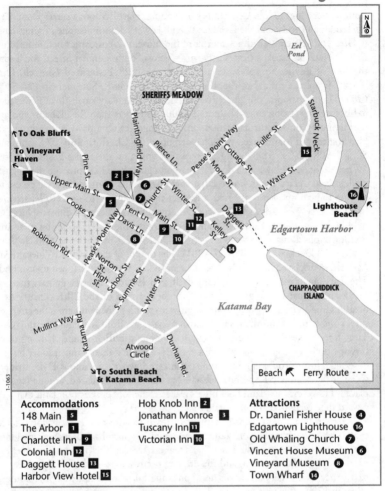

Accommodations

148 Main **5**
The Arbor **1**
Charlotte Inn **9**
Colonial Inn **12**
Daggett House **13**
Harbor View Hotel **15**

Hob Knob Inn **2**
Jonathan Monroe **3**
Tuscany Inn **11**
Victorian Inn **10**

Attractions

Dr. Daniel Fisher House **4**
Edgartown Lighthouse **16**
Old Whaling Church **7**
Vincent House Museum **6**
Vineyard Museum **8**
Town Wharf **14**

centuries, from bare-bones colonial to elegant Federal. The tour also takes in the neighboring **Old Whaling Church,** 89 Main St. (☎ **508/627-4442**), a magnificent 1843 Greek Revival edifice designed by local architect Frederick Baylies, Jr., and built as a whaleboat would have been, out of massive pine beams. With its 27-foot windows and 92-foot tower (a landmark easily spotted from the sea), this is a building that knows its place in the community (central). Maintained by the Preservation Trust and still supporting a Methodist parish, the building is now primarily used as a performance site.

Continuing down Main Street and turning right onto School Street, you'll pass another Baylies monument, the 1839 **Baptist Church,** which, having lost its spire, was converted into a private home with a rather grand, column-fronted facade. Two blocks farther, on your left, is **The Vineyard Museum,** 59 School St. (☎ **508/627-4441**), a fascinating complex assembled by the Dukes County Historical Society. A palimpsest of island history, this cluster of buildings contains exhibits of early Native American crafts; an entire 1765 house; an extraordinary array of maritime art, from whalers' logs to WPA-era studies by Thomas Hart Benton; a carriage house to catch odds and ends; and the Gay Head Light Tower's decommissioned Fresnel lens.

Give yourself enough time to explore the museum's curiosities before heading south 1 block on Cooke Street. Catty-corner across South Summer Street, you'll spot the first of Baylies's impressive endeavors, the 1828 **Federated Church.** One block left are the offices of the *Vineyard Gazette,* 34 S. Summer St. (☎ **508/627-4311**). Operating out of a 1760 house, this exemplary small-town newspaper has been going strong since 1846; its 14,000 subscribers span the globe. If you are wandering by on a Thursday afternoon, you might catch a press run in progress. Heading toward Main Street, you'll happen upon the **Charlotte Inn,** 27 S. Summer St. (☎ **508/627-4751**), among the most charming on the entire East Coast (see "Where to Stay," below). You don't have to be a guest here to appreciate the English gardens, and in fact, the in-house **Edgartown Art Gallery** provides a good excuse to explore the common rooms. Take a look at the restaurant, too—l'étoile, set in a lovely conservatory—or make a reservation if you're considering a dinner splurge.

Now it's time to head down Main Street toward the water, stopping in at any inviting shops along the way. Veer left on Dock Street to reach the **Old Sculpin Gallery,** 58 Dock St. (☎ **508/627-4881**). The output of the Martha's Vineyard Art Association displayed here tends to be amateurish, but you might happen upon a find. The real draw is the stark old building itself, which started out as a granary (part of Dr. Fisher's vast holdings) and spent the better part of the 20th century as a boatbuilding shop. Keep an eye out for vintage beauties when you cross the street to survey the harbor from the deck at Town Wharf. It's from here that the tiny On-Time ferry makes its 5-minute crossing to **Chappaquiddick Island,** hauling three cars at a time and a great many more sightseers—not that there's much to see on the other side. Just so you don't waste time tracking it down, the infamous **Dyke Bridge,** scene of the Kennedy/Kopechne debacle, has been dismantled and, at long last, replaced. However, the island does offer great stretches of conservation land that will reward the hearty hiker or mountain biker.

Mere strollers might want to remain in town to admire the many formidable captain's homes lining **North Water Street,** many of which have been converted into inns. Each has a tale to tell. The 1750 **Daggett House** (no. 59), for instance, expanded upon a 1660 tavern, and the original beehive oven is flanked by a "secret" passageway. Nathaniel Hawthorne holed up at the **Edgartown Inn** (no. 56) for nearly a year in 1789 while writing *Twice Told Tales*—and, it is rumored, romancing a local maiden who inspired *The Scarlet Letter.* On your way back to Main Street, you'll pass the **Gardner-Colby Gallery** (no. 27), filled with beautiful island-inspired paintings.

☕ **WINDING DOWN**   After all that walking, you may need a refreshment. **Espresso Love,** at 2 South Water St. (☎ **508/627-9211**), has legendary muffins and pastries.

3 Beaches & Outdoor Pursuits

BEACHES   Most down-island beaches in Vineyard Haven, Oak Bluffs, and Edgartown are open to the public and just a walk or a short bike ride from town. In season, shuttle buses make stops at **State Beach** between Oak Buffs and Edgartown. Most of the Vineyard's magnificent up-island shoreline, alas, is privately owned or restricted to residents, and thus off-limits to transient visitors. Renters in up-island communities, however, can obtain a beach sticker (around $35 for a season sticker) for those private beaches by applying with a lease at the relevant **town hall:** West

Tisbury, ☎ **508/696-0148;** Chilmark, ☎ **508/645-2113** or 508/645-2100; Gay Head, ☎ **508/645-2300.** Also, many up-island inns offer the perk of temporary passes to a hot spot such as Lucy Vincent beach (see below). In addition to the public beaches listed below, you might also track down a few hidden coves by requesting a map of conservation properties from the **Martha's Vineyard Land Bank** (☎ **508/627-7141**). Below is a list of visitor-friendly beaches:

- **East Beach,** Wasque [pronounced *Way*-squee] Reservation, Chappaquiddick. Relatively few people go to the bother of biking or hiking (or four-wheel driving) this far, so you should be able to find all the privacy you crave. If you're staying in Edgartown, the Chappy ferry is probably minutes by bike from your inn. Biking on Chappaquiddick is one of the great Vineyard experiences, but the roads can be quite sandy here, and you may have to dismount during the 5-mile ride to Wasque. Because of its exposure on the east shore of the island, the surf is rough here. It's one of the Vineyard's best-kept secrets and an ideal spot for bird watching. Pack a picnic, and make this an afternoon adventure. Sorry, no facilities.

- ✪ **Gay Head Beach** (Moshup Beach), Off Moshup Trail. Parking costs $15 a day (in season) at this peaceful $1/2$-mile beach just east (Atlantic side) of the colorful cliffs. Go early, since the lot is small and a bit of a hike from the beach. I suggest that all but one person get off at the wooden boardwalk along the road with towels, toys, lunches, etc., while the remaining one heads back up to park. In season, you can also take the shuttle buses from down-island to the parking lot at the Gay Head cliffs and walk to the beach. Although it is against the law, nudists tend to gravitate towards this beach—perhaps because they enjoy the exhibitionism afforded by the telescope up on the cliff lookout point. Remember that climbing the cliffs or stealing clay for a souvenir here is against the law for environmental reasons: The cliffs are suffering from rapid erosion. Rest rooms are near the parking lot.

- **Joseph A. Sylvia State Beach,** midway between Oak Bluffs and Edgartown. Stretching a mile and flanked by a paved bike path, this placid beach has views of Cape Cod and Nantucket Sound and is prized for its gentle and (relatively) warm waves, which make it perfect for swimming. The wooden drawbridge is a local landmark, and visitors and islanders alike have been jumping off it for years. Be aware that State Beach is one of the Vineyard's most popular; come midsummer it's packed. The shuttle bus stops here, and roadside parking is also available—but it fills up fast, so stake your claim early. Located on the eastern shore of the island, this is a Nantucket Sound beach, so waters are shallow and rarely rough. There are no rest rooms, and only the Edgartown end of the beach, known as Bend-in-the-Road Beach, has lifeguards.

- **Lake Tashmoo Town Beach,** off Herring Creek Road, Vineyard Haven. The only spot on the island where lake meets the ocean, this tiny strip of sand is good for swimming and surf casting, but is somewhat marred by limited parking and often brackish waters. Nonetheless, this is a popular spot, as beachgoers enjoy a choice between the Vineyard Sound beach with mild surf or the placid lake beach. Bikers will have no problem reaching this beach from Vineyard Haven, otherwise you have to have access to a car to get to this beach.

- **Lighthouse Beach,** off North Water Street, Edgartown. Even though tiny, unattended, lacking parking, and often seaweed-strewn, it's terribly scenic and a perfect place to watch the boats drifting in and out of the harbor. Fuller Beach nearby is popular with a college crowd. No lifeguards or rest rooms. Both these beaches are within walking distance from the center of Edgartown.

- **Lobsterville Beach,** at the end of Lobsterville Road in Gay Head. This 2-mile beauty on Menemsha Pond boasts calm, shallow waters, which are ideal for children. It's also a prime spot for birding—just past the dunes are nesting areas for terns and gulls. Surf casters tend to gravitate here, too. The only drawback is that parking is for residents only. This is a great beach for bikers to hit on their way back from Gay Head and before taking the bike ferry over to Menemsha.

- **Lucy Vincent Beach** (restricted), off South Road, Chilmark. It's a shame that the island's most secluded and breathtaking beach is restricted to Chilmark town residents and guests only. Lined with red and brown clay cliffs, this wide stretch of sand and pounding surf is a virtual oasis. If you do manage to get your hands on a pass (don't forget that many up-island inns offer guest passes), wander left down the beach for a voyeuristic glimpse of bathers in the buff.

- **Menemsha Beach,** next to Dutchers Dock in Menemsha Harbor. Despite its rough surface, this small but well-trafficked strand—with lifeguards and rest rooms—is quite popular with families. In season, it's virtually wall-to-wall colorful umbrellas and beach toys. Nearby food vendors in Menemsha—selling everything from ice cream and hot dogs to steamers and shrimp cocktail—are also a plus here. *Tip:* This beach is the ideal place for a sunset. I suggest you get a lobster dinner to go at the famous **Home Port restaurant** in Menemsha (see "The Quintessential Lobster Dinner," below), grab a blanket and a bottle of wine, and picnic here for a spectacular evening. If you are staying at an up-island inn, Menemsha is a fun bike ride downhill. Energetic bikers can make it from down-island towns; plan to make it part of an entire day of scenic biking. Otherwise, you'll need a car to get here.

- **Oak Bluffs Town Beach,** Seaview Avenue. This sandy strip extends from both sides of the ferry wharf, which makes it a convenient place to linger while waiting for the next boat. This is an in-town beach, within walking distance for visitors staying in Oak Bluffs. The surf is consistently calm and the sand smooth, so it's also ideal for families with small children. Public rest rooms are available at the ferry dock, but there are no lifeguards.

- **Owen Park Beach,** off Main Street in Vineyard Haven. A tiny strip of harborside beach adjoining a town green with swings and a bandstand will suffice for young children, who, by the way, get lifeguard supervision. No rest rooms, but this is an in-town beach, which is probably a quick walk from your Vineyard Haven inn.

- **South Beach** (Katama Beach), about 4 miles south of Edgartown on Katama Road. If you only have time for one trip to the beach and you can't get up-island, I'd go with this popular, 3-mile barrier strand that boasts heavy wave action (check with lifeguards for swimming conditions), sweeping dunes, and most importantly, relatively ample parking space. It's also accessible by bike path or shuttle. Lifeguards patrol some sections of the beach, and there are sparsely scattered toilet facilities. The rough surf here is popular with surfers. *Tip:* Families tend to head to the left, college kids to the right.

- **Wasque Beach,** Wasque Reservation, Chappaquiddick. Surprisingly easy to get to (via the On-Time ferry and a bike or car), this $^1/_2$-mile-long beach has all the amenities—lifeguards, parking, rest rooms—without the crowds. Wasque Beach is a Trustees of Reservations property, and if you are not a member of this land preservation organization, you must pay a few dollars at the gatehouse (per car and per person) for access in season.

BICYCLING   What's unique about biking on Martha's Vineyard is that you'll not only find the smooth, well-maintained paths indigenous to the Cape, but also long stretches of virtually untrafficked roads that, while rough in spots, accompany breath-taking country landscapes and sweeping ocean views. Serious cyclists bringing their own bikes will want to do a 1-day ✪ **circle-the-island tour** through the up-island towns and out to Gay Head, stopping in Menemsha before heading back down-island. For much of the trek you'll be traveling country roads, so beware of sandy shoulders and blind curves. You'll avoid tour buses by taking routes outlined below, such as the Moshup Trail to Gay Head or the triangle of bike paths between the down-island towns. The adventurous mountain biker will want to head to the trails at Manuel E. Correllus State Forest (see below). For those seeking an escape from the multitudes in season, the trails are so extensive that during the very height of summer, it is possible to not see another soul for hours. On most of the conservation land on the Vineyard, however, mountain biking is prohibited for environmental reasons.

A triangle of paved bike paths, roughly 8 miles to a side, links the down-island towns of Oak Bluffs, Edgartown, and Vineyard Haven (the sound portion along Beach Road, flanked by water on both sides, is especially enjoyable). From Edgartown, you can also follow the bike path to South Beach. For a more woodsy ride, there are paved paths and mountain biking trails in the **Manuel E. Correllus State Forest** (☎ **508/693-2540**), a vast spread of scrub oak and pine smack dab in the middle of the island that also boasts hiking and horseback-riding trails. The bike paths are accessible off Edgartown–West Tisbury Road in Oak Bluffs, West Tisbury, and Edgartown.

The up-island roads leading to West Tisbury, Chilmark, Menemsha, and Gay Head are a cyclist's paradise, with sprawling, unspoiled pastureland, old farmhouses, and brilliant sea views reminiscent of Ireland's countryside. But keep in mind that the terrain is often hilly, and the roads are narrow and a little rough around the edges. Try **South Road** from the town of West Tisbury to Chilmark Center (about 5 miles). En route, you'll pass stone walls rolling over moors, clumps of pine and wildflowers, verdant marshes and tidal pools, and, every once in awhile, an Old Vineyard farmhouse. About halfway, you'll notice the road becoming hillier as you approach a summit, **Abel's Hill,** home to the **Chilmark Cemetery,** where comedian John Belushi is buried. A mile farther, don't miss the view of **Allen Farm,** a sheep farm still operating amongst picturesque pastureland. **Middle Road** is another lovely ride with a country feel and will also get you from West Tisbury to Chilmark (it's usually less trafficked, too.)

My favorite up-island route is the 6-mile stretch from Chilmark Center out to Gay Head via **State Road** and ✪ **Moshup Trail.** The ocean views along this route are nothing less than spectacular. Don't miss the **Quitsa Pond Lookout,** about 2 miles down **State Road,** which provides a panoramic vista of Nashaquitsa and Menemsha ponds, beyond which you can see Menemsha, the Vineyard Sound, and the Elizabeth Islands—it's an amazing place to watch the sunset on a clear evening. A bit farther, just over the Gay Head town line, is the Gay Head spring, a roadside iron pipe where you can refill your water bottle with the freshest and coldest water on the island. At the fork after the spring, turn left on Moshup Trail—in fact a regular road—and follow the coast, which offers gorgeous views of the water and the sweeping sand dunes. You'll soon wind up in Gay Head, where you can explore the red-clay cliffs and pristine beaches. On the return trip, you can take the handy bike ferry from Gay Head to Menemsha. It runs daily in summer and weekends in May.

A word about Gay Head: Almost every visitor to the Vineyard finds his or her way to the cliffs, and with all the tour buses lined up in the huge parking lot and the rows of tacky concession stands and gift shops, this can seem like a rather outrageous tourist trap. You're right; it's not the Grand Canyon. But the observation deck, with its view of the colorful cliffs, the adorable brick lighthouse, and the Elizabeth Islands beyond will make you glad you bothered. Instead of rushing away, stop for a cool drink and a clam roll at the snack bar with the deck overlooking the ocean.

When tackling the Vineyard by bike, you'll have no trouble finding sustenance in the down-island towns. Up-island pit stops, however, are a bit scattered. The ones I prefer include **Alley's General Store** in the center of West Tisbury (☎ **508/693-0088**), and right behind it, **Back Alley's** (☎ **508/693-7366**), which has sandwiches and specializes in homemade muffins, cookies, and pies. Continuing up-island you'll find the **Chilmark Store** (☎ **508/645-3739**), which has great deli sandwiches and pizzas, and ✪ **The Bite,** on Basin Road in Menemsha (☎ **508/645-9239**), a typical New England seafood shack.

Bike-rental operations are ubiquitous near the ferry landings in Vineyard Haven and Oak Bluffs, and there are also a few outfits in Edgartown. For information on bike rental shops, see "Getting Around," above.

BIRDING   Felix Neck Wildlife Sanctuary, Edgartown–Vineyard Haven Road, Edgartown (☎ **508/627-4850**): Felix Neck is an easy 2-mile bike ride from Edgartown. A Massachusetts Audubon Property, it has a complete visitor center staffed by naturalists who lead bird-watching walks, among other activities. You may see an osprey nest on the way to the center. Pick up a trail map at the center before heading out. Several of the trails pass Sengekontacket Pond, and the orange trail leads to Waterfowl Pond, which has an observation blind with bird sighting information. **Cedar Tree Neck Sanctuary**, (State Road, follow to Indian Hill Road to Obed Daggett Road and follow signs), Tisbury (see "Nature Trails," below): While managed by the conservation group Sheriff's Meadow Foundation, these 300 acres were acquired with the assistance of Massachusetts Audubon. There are several trails here, but you'll eventually arrive out on a picturesque bluff overlooking Vineyard Sound and the Elizabeth Islands. Check out the map posted at the parking lot for an overview of the property. The range of terrain here—ponds, fields, woods, and bog—provides diverse opportunities for sightings. ✪ **Wasque Reservation** on Chappaquiddick, Martha's Vineyard (see "Nature Trails," below): Owned by the Trustees of Reservations, this sanctuary, on the easternmost reaches of the island, can be accessed by bike or four-wheel–drive vehicle (see "Getting Around," above). The hundreds of untouched acres here draw flocks of nesting shorebirds, including egrets, herons, terns, and plovers.

FISHING   For shellfishing, you'll need to get information and a permit from the appropriate town hall (for the telephone numbers, see "Beaches," above). Popular spots for surf casting include **Wasque Point** on Chappaquiddick (see "Nature Trails," below), South Beach, and the jetty at **Menemsha Pond.** The **Trustees of Reservations** (☎ **508/627-3599**) run two fishing safaris a day out to Wasque Point and Cape Pogue on Chappaquiddick. All gear is included. Fees are $65 for adults, $25 for children under 15. The party boat *Skipper* (☎ **508/693-1238**) offers half-day trips out of Oak Bluffs harbor in season. The cost is $25 for adults, $15 for children 12 and under. Bring your own poles and bait. Deep-sea excursions can be arranged aboard the *Slapshot II* (☎ **508/627-8087**) out of Edgartown, which charges $375 for up to six people. Other charter boats include **Big Eye Charters** (☎ **508/627-3649**) out of Edgartown, and **Summer's Lease** (☎ **508/693-2880**) out of Oak Bluffs. Up-island, there are **Conomo Charters** (☎ **508/645-9278**) and *Chantey III* (☎ **508/645-2127**) out of Gay Head; and **North Shore Charters** (☎ **508/645-2993**) and **Flashy Lady Charters** (☎ **508/645-2462**) out of Menemsha, locus of the island's commercial fishing fleet (you may recognize this weathered port from *Jaws*).

Menemsha, A New England Fishing Village

For an authentic slice of the Vineyard, leave the touristy hoards down-island and take the winding roads up-island to the picturesque fishing village of Menemsha. Shuttle buses make the trip a few times daily. Better yet, take the bike ferry from Gay Head. In order to do that, you will have to manage to get yourself and a bike to Gay Head—a spectacularly scenic but exhausting journey. It seems appropriate to approach Menemsha from its colorful harbor, alongside the commercial fishing fleet, the sportfishing vessels, and the pleasure boats. Spend the afternoon strolling the wharves at leisure and experience the pace and industry of a working New England fishing village: there aren't many left. Watch the sun-dappled fishermen unloading their catches—lobsters, tuna, swordfish—on the wharf.

Two family-owned fish markets within yards of each other enjoy a healthy competition. **Larsen's** (☎ 508/645-2680) has picnic tables and is more set up for eating on site. **Poole's Fish Market** (☎ 508/645-2282) is strictly take-out. Everett Poole, an 13th-generation islander, started his business 57 years ago in a doll carriage (gas rationing during World War II), wheeled from house to house. Now Everett has passed the business on to his son and is working as a commercial fisherman. For charter fishing trips operating out of Menemsha, call **North Shore Charters** (☎ 508/645-2993) or **Flashy Lady Charters** (☎ 508/645-2462).

There are several charming clothing, craft, and antique shops in the village, as well as a fried fish shack—✪ **The Bite** (☎ 508/645-9239)—which some have dubbed the best restaurant on Martha's Vineyard. Or, if you prefer, have a celebrity-monikered sandwich (I like the Art Buchwald) at the **Menemsha Deli** (☎ 508/645-9902). Wander over to the town beach, a colorful melange of umbrellas, plastic buckets, and splashing youngsters. The water here can be quite cold, but, after all that biking, you'll appreciate it.

If it's dinnertime, you'll want to eat at the casual **Homeport** (☎ 508/645-2679), perhaps the most famous restaurant on the Vineyard; it has perfect sunset views. Places to stay in Menemsha with ocean views include the **Menemsha Inn and Cottages** (☎ 508/645-2521), a serene compound, and the **Beach Plum Inn** (☎ 800/528-6616 or 508/645-9454), an antique farmhouse with a full-service restaurant.

IGFA world-record holder Capt. Leslie S. Smith operates **Backlash Charters** (☎ 508/627-5894; E-mail backlash@tiac.net), specializing in light tackle and fly-fishing, out of Edgartown. Cooper Gilkes III, proprietor of **Coop's Bait & Tackle** at 147 W. Tisbury Rd. in Edgartown (☎ 508/627-3909), which offers rentals as well as supplies, is another acknowledged authority. He's available as an instructor or charter guide, and even amenable to sharing hard-won pointers on local hot spots.

FITNESS   Gym addicts can get their workout fix at the **Health Club at the Tisbury Inn** on Main Street in Vineyard Haven (☎ 508/693-7400), which accepts visitors for a fee.

GOLF   President Clinton helped to publicize the 9-hole **Mink Meadows Golf Course** off Franklin Street in Vineyard Haven (☎ 508/693-0600), which occupies a top-dollar chunk of real estate but is open to the general public, as well as the semi-private, championship-level 18-hole **Farm Neck Golf Club** off Farm Neck Road in Oak Bluffs (☎ 508/693-3057). The Cafe at Farm Neck serves a wonderful lunch overlooking their manicured greens.

HORSEBACK RIDING   In West Tisbury, both the **South Shore Stables** on Scrubby Neck Farm Road off the Edgartown–West Tisbury Road (☎ 508/693-3770) and the **Misty Meadows Horse Farm** on Old County Road (☎ 508/693-1870) offer family-oriented, quiet trail rides. Prices are around $35 per person.

ICE-SKATING   The **Martha's Vineyard Ice Arena** on Edgartown–Vineyard Haven Road, Oak Bluffs (☎ 508/693-4438), offers public skating mid-July to mid-April; call for details.

IN-LINE SKATING   In-line skaters are everywhere on the island's paved paths. You'll find rentals at **Jamaikan Jam,** 154 Circuit Ave. (☎ 508/693-5003) or **M. V. Blade Runners,** Circuit Avenue Extension (☎ 508/693-8852), both in Oak Bluffs; the latter offers renters complimentary introductory clinics twice daily in season. Other sources include **Sports Haven,** 5 Beach St., Vineyard Haven (☎ 508/696-0456) and the **Vineyard Sports Center** at the Triangle in Edgartown (☎ 508/627-3933).

NATURE TRAILS   About a fifth of the Vineyard's land mass has been set aside for conservation, and all are accessible to the energetic biker. The **West Chop Woods,** off Franklin Street in Vineyard Haven, comprise 85 acres with marked walking trails. Midway between Vineyard Haven and Edgartown, the **Felix Neck Wildlife Sanctuary** (see above) includes a 6-mile network of trails over varying terrain, from woodland to beach. Accessible by ferry from Edgartown, quiet Chappaquiddick is home to two sizable preserves: The **Cape Pogue Wildlife Refuge and Wasque Reservation** (gatehouse ☎ 508/627-7260), covering much of the island's eastern barrier beach, have 709 acres that draw flocks of nesting or resting shorebirds. Also on the island, 3 miles east on Dyke Road, is another Trustees of the Reservations property, the distinctly poetic and alluring **Mytoi,** a 14-acre Japanese garden that is an oasis of textures and flora and fauna.

The 633-acre **Long Point Wildlife Refuge** off Waldron's Bottom Road in West Tisbury (gatehouse ☎ 508/693-7392) offers heath and dunes, freshwater ponds, a popular family-oriented beach, and interpretive nature walks for children. The Trustees of Reservations charge a $7 parking fee in season. The 4,000-acre **Manuel F. Correllus Vineyard State Forest** occupies a sizable, if not especially scenic, chunk midisland; it's riddled with mountain-bike paths and riding trails. This sanctuary was created in 1908 to try to save the endangered heath hen, a species now extinct. (Recently, a longtime vacationer to the island sheepishly admitted that her mother may have run over the last hen on a foggy evening in the 1930s.) In season, there are free interpretive and birding walks.

Up-island, along the sound, the **Menemsha Hills Reservation** off North Road in Chilmark (☎ 508/693-7662) encompasses 210 acres of rocks and bluffs, with steep paths, lovely views, and even a public beach. **The Cedar Tree Neck Sanctuary,** off Indian Hill Road southwest of Vineyard Haven (☎ 508/693-5207), offers some 300 forested acres that end in a stony beach (alas, swimming and sunbathing are prohibited). It's still a refreshing retreat.

TENNIS   Public courts typically charge a small fee and can be reserved in person a day in advance. You'll find clay courts on **Church Street** in Vineyard Haven; nonclay in Oak Bluffs' **Niantic Park,** West Tisbury's **grammar school** on Old County Road, and the **Chilmark Community Center** on South Road. Three public courts—plus a basketball court, roller-hockey rink, softball field, and children's playground—are located at the **Edgartown Recreation Area** on Robinson Road. You can also book a court (1 day in advance only) at two semiprivate clubs in Oak Bluffs: the **Farm Neck Tennis Club** (☎ 508/693-9728) and **the Island Country Club**

on Beach Road (☎ **508/693-6574**). In season, expect to pay around $18 to $22 for court time per hour at these clubs.

WATER SPORTS   Wind's Up at 95 Beach Rd. in Vineyard Haven (☎ **508/ 693-4252**) rents out canoes, kayaks, and various sailing craft, including Windsurfers, and offers instruction on-site, on a placid pond; they also rent surfboards and boogie boards. For scuba equipment, visit **Vineyard Scuba** on South Circuit Avenue in Oak Bluffs (☎ **508/693-0288**). Rank beginners may enjoy towing privileges at **M. V. Parasail** and **M. V. Ski** off Owen Park Pier in Vineyard Haven Harbor (☎ **508/ 693-2838**): For the former you're airborne by parachute, for the latter you straddle water skis, a knee board, a wake board, or an inner tube.

4 Museums & Historic Landmarks

Cottage Museum. 1 Trinity Park (within the Camp Meeting Grounds), Oak Bluffs. ☎ **508/ 693-7784.** Admission $1 (donation). Mid-June to mid-Sept Mon–Sat 10am–4pm. Closed mid-Sept to mid-June.

Oak Bluffs' famous "Camp Ground"—a 34-acre circle with more than 300 multi-colored, elaborately trimmed carpenter's Gothic cottages—looks very much the way it might have more than a hundred years ago. These adorable little houses, loosely modeled on the revivalists' canvas tents that inspired them, have been handed down through the generations. Unless you happen to know a lucky camper, your best chance of getting inside one is to visit this homey little museum, which embodies the late-19th-century zeitgeist even as it displays representative artifacts: bulky black bathing costumes and a melodeon used for informal hymnal sing-alongs.

The compact architecture is at once practical and symbolic. The Gothic-arched French doors off the peak-roofed second-story bedroom, for instance, lead to a tiny balcony used for keeping tabs on community doings. The daily schedule was, in fact, rather hectic. In 1867, when this cottage was built, campers typically attended three lengthy prayer services daily. Today's denizens tend to blend in with the visiting tourists, though opportunities for worship remain: at the 1878 Trinity Methodist Church within the park, or just outside, on Samoset Avenue, at the nonsectarian 1870 Union Chapel, a magnificent octagonal structure with superb acoustics (posted signs give the lineup of guest preachers and musicians).

At the very center of the Camp Grounds is the striking Trinity Park Tabernacle. Built in 1879, the open-sided chapel is the largest wrought-iron structure in the country. Thousands can be accommodated on its long wooden benches, which are usually filled to capacity for the Sunday-morning services in summer, as well as for community sings (Wednesdays in July and August) and occasional concerts (see "Martha's Vineyard After Dark," below). Give yourself plenty of time to wander this peaceful enclave, where spirituality is tempered with a taste for harmless frivolity.

✪ **Flying Horses Carousel.** 33 Circuit Ave. (at Lake Ave.), Oak Bluffs. ☎ **508/693-9481.** Tickets $1 per ride, or $8 for 10. Late May to early Sept daily 9:30am–10pm; call for off-season hrs. Closed mid-Oct to mid-Apr.

You don't have to be a kid to enjoy the colorful mounts adorning what is considered to be the oldest working carousel in the country. Built in 1876 at New York's fabled Coney Island, this National Historic Landmark maintained by the Martha's Vineyard Preservation Trust predates the era of horses that "gallop." Lacking the necessary gears, these merely glide smoothly in place to the joyful strains of a calliope. The challenge lies in going for the gold ring—brass, actually—that entitles the lucky winner to a free ride. Some regulars, adults included, have grown rather adept—you'll see them scoop up several in a single pass. In between rides, take a moment to

Oak Bluffs

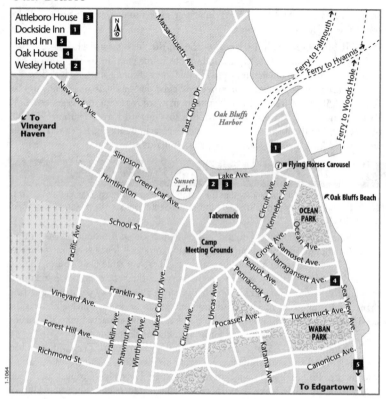

Attleboro House **3**
Dockside Inn **1**
Island Inn **5**
Oak House **4**
Wesley Hotel **2**

New York Ave.

To Vineyard Haven

Massachusetts Ave.

East Chop Dr.

Oak Bluffs Harbor

Ferry to Falmouth
Ferry to Hyannis
Ferry to Woods Hole

Simpson

Green Leaf Ave.

Huntington

Sunset Lake

Lake Ave.

2 **3**

i ■ Flying Horses Carousel

Oak Bluffs Beach

School St.

Tabernacle

Camp Meeting Grounds

Circuit Ave.
Kennebec Ave.
Ocean Ave.

OCEAN PARK

Grove Ave.
Samoset Ave.
Narragansett Ave.
Pequot Ave.
Pennacook Av.

4

Pacific Ave.

Vineyard Ave.

Franklin St.

Dukes County Ave.

Uncas Ave.

Pocasset Ave.

Sea View Ave.

Tuckernuck Ave.

Forest Hill Ave.

Franklin Ave.
Shawmut Ave.
Winthrop Ave.

Circuit Ave.

WABAN PARK

Richmond St.

Katama Ave.

Canonicus Ave.

5

To Edgartown ↓

1-1064

admire the intricate hand-carving and real horsehair manes, and gaze into the horses' glass eyes for a surprise: tiny animal charms glinting within.

✪ **The Martha's Vineyard Historical Society/Vineyard Museum.** 59 School St. (2 blocks SW of Main St.), Edgartown. ☎ **508/627-4441.** Fax 508/627-4436. Admission in season $5 adults, $3 children 6–15. Mid-July to mid-Oct Tues–Sat 10am–5pm; off-season Wed–Fri 1–4pm, Sat 10am–4pm.

All of Martha's Vineyard's colorful history is captured here, in a compound of historic buildings. To acclimate yourself chronologically, start with the precolonial artifacts—from arrowheads to colorful Gay Head clay pottery—displayed in the 1845 Captain Francis Pease House; there's also a gift shop here, and a gallery to showcase the output of local students.

The **Gale Huntington Reference Library** houses rare documentation of the island's history, from genealogical records to whale-ship logs. The recorded history of Martha's Vineyard (the name has been attributed, variously, to a Dutch seaman named Martin Wyngaard, and the daughter and/or mother-in-law of early explorer Bartholomew Gosnold) begins in 1642 with the arrival of missionary Thomas Mayhew, Jr., whose father had bought the whole chain of islands, from Nantucket through the Elizabeths, for 40 pounds as a speculative venture. Mayhew, Jr. had loftier goals in mind, and it is a tribute to his methodology that long after he was lost at sea in 1657, the Wampanoags whom he had converted to Christianity continued to mourn him (a stone monument to his memory still survives by the roadside opposite the airport). In his relatively brief sojourn on-island, Mayhew helped to found what would become, in 1671, Edgartown (named for the British heir apparent). The library's holdings on this epoch are extensive, and some extraordinary memorabilia, including scrimshaw and portraiture, is on view in the adjoining Francis Foster Museum. Outside, there's a reproduction "tryworks" to show the means by which whale blubber was reduced to precious oil.

To get a sense of daily life during the era when the waters of the East Coast were the equivalent of a modern highway, visit the **Thomas Cooke House,** a shipwright-built Colonial, built in 1765, where the customs collector lived and worked (the trees in town having been cut back, he had a clear view of comings and goings in the harbor). A few of the house's 12 rooms are decorated as they might have been at the height of the maritime trade; others are devoted to special exhibits on other fascinating aspects of island history, such as the revivalist fever that enveloped Oak Bluffs. Further curiosities are stored in the nearby Carriage Shed. Among the vintage 19th-century vehicles are a painted peddler's cart, a whaleboat, a hearse, and a fire engine, and the odds and ends include some touching mementos of early tourism.

The latest—and flashiest—addition to the museum's holdings is the Fresnel lens lifted from the Gay Head Lighthouse in 1952, after nearly a century of service. Though it no longer serves to warn ships of dangerous shoals (that light is automated now), it still lights up the night every evening in summer, just for show.

5 Organized Tours

✪ *Arabella.* Menemsha Harbor (at North Rd.), Menemsha. ☎ **508/645-3511.** Rates $40 evening sail; day sail $60 adults, $30 children under 12. Departures mid-June to mid-Sept daily 10am and 6pm. Reservations suggested. Closed mid-Sept to mid-June.

Hugh Taylor (James's equally musical brother) alternates with a couple of other captains in taking the helm of his swift 50-foot catamaran for daily trips to Cuttyhunk and sunset cruises around the Gay Head cliffs; you can book the whole boat if you like, for a private charter. Zipping along at 15 knots, it's a great way to see lovely coves and vistas otherwise denied the ordinary tourist.

Classic Aviators. Edgartown Airfield, Herring Creek Rd. (near South Beach), Edgartown. ☎ **508/627-7677.** Rates start at around $85 per couple. Late May to Sept sunrise to sunset; call for reservations. Closed Nov to mid-May.

Recapture the fun of flying, in a 1941 open-cockpit Waco biplane taking off from the country's largest surviving grass airport; the sightseeing is nonpareil.

Good Fortune. Edgartown Harbor, Edgartown. ☎ **508/627-3445.** Rates $35 per person; call for details and reservations. July–Aug.

Burly Captain Rick Hamilton sails his 1935 classic wooden schooner around Edgartown Harbor three times daily: from 10am to noon, noon to 4pm, and 4pm to sunset. It's a scenic, romantic harbor cruise.

Gosnold Cruises. Pier 44, Vineyard Haven Harbor, Vineyard Haven. ☎ **800/693-8001** or 508/696-0013. Rates $15–$40 adults, $10–$25 children 3–12; call for schedule and reservations. Available for private charter. Closed Oct–May. AE, MC, V.

A 65-foot cruiser, the *Andy Rosse* offers a range of excursions in season, including a brief "Learn about Lobsters" jaunt on a half-day Cuttyhunk trip featuring narration researched by the Dukes County Historical Society. Their new 70-foot luxury vessel, *The Gosnold Spirit,* offers first-class amenities and a unique gift shop. Other options involve food and/or music.

Laissez Faire. Vineyard Haven Harbor, Vineyard Haven. ☎ **508/693-1646.** Rates $65 per person for a half-day sail; call for details and reservations. Closed Oct–May.

A Day Trip: Fishing off Cuttyhunk Island

Like a misplaced Greek Island, tiny Cuttyhunk—just south of Cape Cod—sits at the tip of the mostly private and uninhabited Elizabeth Islands. On the eastern side of the island, homes are tightly clustered on the hill overlooking the popular harbor. Most of the remainder of the island, which measures but $2^1/_2$ by $3/_4$ miles, is conservation land and pristine beaches popular with bird-watchers and solitude-seekers. Accessible from Martha's Vineyard and New Bedford, Cuttyhunk offers an unparalleled off-the-beaten track island experience.

In the late 19th century, an exclusive group of millionaires from New York, Boston, and Philadelphia convened at the Bass Fishing Club, a one-story, shingled bunkhouse on Cuttyhunk, for the ultimate anglers' vacation. The names of several U.S. presidents are scrawled in the guest book alongside railroad and oil magnates. For club members, days were spent perched on the edge of fishing stands jutting out over the rocky shores while hired "chummers" baited the hooks and gaffed the prized catches. Evenings, over sumptuous five-course meals, relaxed industry titans would discuss the stock market, politics, and the best place to catch striped bass. Over cognac and cigars, they'd decide who would be president.

In 1906, William Madison Wood, head of the American Woolen Company and one of the richest men in America at the time, joined the club. Wood, a Horatio Alger poster boy, was born to an impoverished Portuguese family on Martha's Vineyard; by virtue of hard work, good sense, and a timely marriage to the boss's daughter, Wood rose to be head of the American Woolen Company. His passion for Cuttyhunk manifested itself in a keen acquisitive nature. By 1912, he had bought the club and most of the island. Cuttyhunk hasn't changed much in the ensuing 85 years. The Cuttyhunk Club disbanded in 1921, but the building remains as a private home. Wood's descendants are still prominent landowners on the island, and devoted anglers can still ply these waters for striped bass with some of the most skilled fishing guides on the East Coast. The Fishing guides are: **Capt. Roland Coulombe** (☎ 508/971-0923); **Capt. George Isabel** (☎ ☎ 508/991-7352 or off-season 508/679-5675); **Capt. Duane Lynch** (☎ 508/522-4351); **Capt. Jimmy Nunes** (☎ 508/993-7427); and **Capt. Charles Tilton** (☎ 508/992-8181).

A word of warning: Cuttyhunk is a seasonal destination—mid-June to mid-September. Some years, the winter population dips to the single digits. The island has one road and few cars. Those who don't walk use golf carts. Dining and lodging options are quite limited. There are only two shops on the island, and rumor has it that the general store may soon be closing.

How to get there: *By Ferry:* **The M/V Alert II** ferry (☎ 508/992-1432) departs New Bedford Pier #3 at 10am and leaves Cuttyhunk at 3pm. Reservations are highly recommended. Weekdays from mid-June to mid-September. *By Seaplane:* **Bayside air service,** New Bedford (☎ 508/636-3762). To sail on the Catamaran *S/V Arabella* from Menemsha on Martha's Vineyard to Cuttyhunk, call **Hugh Taylor** at ☎ 508/645-3511. **Where to stay: The Avalon House** has weekly rentals available for $600 to $800; **Cuttyhunk Bed and Breakfast** has three rooms at $70 to $100 per night. For information on both, ☎ 508/993-6490. **Where to Eat in Season: Pegleg Seafood Cafe** (☎ 508/992-7530) at Four Corners, open nightly from 5:30 to 8pm. Cuttyhunk Shellfish Farms' **Floating Harbor Raw Bar** (☎ 508/971-1120) offers lunch and dinner to go at the dock. **Small Fry** (☎ 508/984-7167) serves lunch from 11am to 1pm and dinner from 5:30 to 7:30pm.

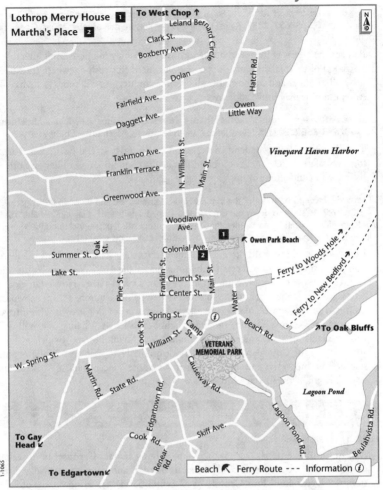

Lothrop Merry House **1**
Martha's Place **2**

To West Chop ↑
Leland Bernard Circle
Clark St.
Boxberry Ave.
Dolan
Fairfield Ave.
Daggett Ave.
Hatch Rd.
Owen Little Way

Vineyard Haven Harbor

Tashmoo Ave.
Franklin Terrace
N. Williams St.
Main St.
Greenwood Ave.

Woodlawn Ave.

1
Colonial Ave.
2

← Owen Park Beach

Summer St.
Oak St.
Lake St.
Pine St.
Franklin St.
Church St.
Center St.
Main St.
Water
Ferry to Woods Hole →
Ferry to New Bedford →

Spring St.
ⓘ
Beach Rd.
↗To Oak Bluffs

Look St.
William St.
Camp St.
VETERANS MEMORIAL PARK

W. Spring St.
Martin Rd.
State Rd.
Causeway Rd.

Lagoon Pond

Edgartown Rd.
Cook Rd.
Skiff Ave.
Lagoon Pond Rd.
Beulahvista Rd.

To Gay Head ↙

Renear Rd.

To Edgartown ↙

Beach ↖ Ferry Route --- Information ⓘ

1-1065

John and Mary Clarke, innkeepers at the Lothrop Merry House (see "Where to Stay," below), offer half-day and daylong sails aboard their 54-foot 1962 Alden ketch. Refreshments—including wine and hors d'oeuvres—are included.

The Shenandoah. Beach St. Ext. (on the harbor), Vineyard Haven. ☎ **508/693-1699.** July–Aug; call for schedule and price information. Reservations required. Closed mid-Sept to mid-June.

Black Dog owner Robert Douglas's prized 108-foot topsail schooner, modeled on an 1849 revenue cutter and fitted out with period furnishings, spends most of the summer doing windjammer duty, transporting some 26 lucky children (ages 9 to 15) wherever the wind happens to take them in the course of a week. With no engine to fall back on, it's very much a matter of the wind's whim—as well as of Douglas's considerable skill. Day sails are offered for 1 week at the height of the season—a great way for adults to experience the cruise. In time for the 1998 season, the *Alabama*—modeled after a Grand Banks fishing schooner—will be available for cruises as well.

Soaring Adventures of America. Edgartown Airfield, Herring Creek Rd. (near South Beach), Edgartown. ☎ **508/627-3833.** Rates start at $59 per person; call for reservations. Open year-round.

Perhaps the best way to view the Vineyard is as an osprey might, circling silently on a cushion of thermal currents. If you've experienced this rush elsewhere (this company offers glider and balloon rides all over the country), you'll know just what's in store; if not, it may prove addictive.

Trustees of Reservations Natural History Tours. Cape Pogue, Chappaquiddick Island. ☎ **508/693-7662.** Call for details, prices, and reservations. Meet at the Chappy ferry.

The Trustees, a statewide land conservation group, offer several fascinating 3-hour tours by safari vehicle or canoe around this idyllic nature preserve. They also offer a fishing safari and a tour of the Cape Pogue lighthouse.

Vineyard History Tours. From the Vincent House Museum, behind 99 Main St., Edgartown. ☎ **508/627-8619.** Also, from the Cottage Museum, 1 Trinity Park, Oak Bluffs. Rates $6–$8 adults, free for children 12 and under; inquire about combination passes including the Vineyard Museum (see above). June–Sept Mon–Sat 11am–3pm; call for off-season hrs.

Laced with local lore, and often led by the entertaining local historian Liz Villard, hour-long tours provide access to the interiors of the 1672 Vincent House (the island's oldest surviving dwelling), the 1840 Dr. Daniel Fisher House (an elegant Greek Revival mansion), and the splendid Old Whaling Church, a town showpiece built in 1843. There are also 75-minute walking tours of Edgartown with intriguing titles like "Ghosts, Gossip, and Downright Scandal"; "A Whaling We Will Go"; and, in Oak Bluffs, "Cottages, Campgrounds, and Flying Horses" (which includes admission to the Cottage Museum and a ride on the Flying Horses). Walking tours start at 3pm most days and meet in Edgartown at the Vincent House Museum and in Oak Bluffs at the Cottage Museum.

6 Activities Away from the Beach

KID STUFF

A must for tots to nearly teens is the unique **Flying Horses Carousel** in the center of Oak Bluffs (see above). Directly across the street is another great rainy-day diversion, the **Dreamland Fun Center** (☎ 508/693-5163), featuring dozens of video games, air hockey, skee-ball, and even a small bumper-car arena. Though rather tame, **Dockside Minigolf,** on the second floor of Dockside Marketplace on Circuit Avenue Extension in Oak Bluffs (☎ 508/693-3392), is half indoors, half out, so a spot of rain doesn't have to spoil your game. For a more atmospheric course, visit **Island Cove Mini Golf,** on State Road outside Vineyard Haven (☎ 508/693-2611), a family-friendly setup with a snack bar serving Mad Martha's ice cream, an Island favorite. On weekdays, from 9am to noon and from 1pm to 3pm, children might also enjoy visiting the **State Lobster Hatchery** off Shirley Avenue on Lagoon Pond in Oak Bluffs (☎ 508/693-0060), where the tasty crustaceans are raised, and the **Felix Neck Wildlife Sanctuary** (see "Beaches & Outdoor Pursuits," above) is always a popular destination. Several paint-your-own-pottery places have opened in the past year; **Vineyard Colors** at 230 Upper Main St., Edgartown (☎ 508/627-7787), has the most impressive set up. Pony-cart rides ($1) and an informal petting zoo are offered summer afternoons at the **Nip 'n' Tuck Farm** on State Road in West Tisbury (☎ 508/693-1449). And cruises for kids can be arranged on *The Shenandoah* (see "Organized Tours," above).

7 Shopping

ANTIQUES/COLLECTIBLES   You don't have to be a bona fide collector to marvel over the museum-quality marine antiques at **C. W. Morgan Marine Antiques,** Beach Road, just east of town center, Vineyard Haven (☎ **508/693-3622**). Frank Rapoza's collection encompasses paintings and prints, intricate ship models, nautical instruments, sea chests, and scrimshaw.

The **Chilmark Flea Market,** Chilmark Community Church, Menemsha Cross Road, Chilmark (☎ **508/645-9216**), convenes Wednesday and Saturday mornings in July and August, from 8:30am to 3pm, attracting a well-heeled crowd that's more accustomed to browsing Neiman Marcus. But, no matter, everybody still loves a bargain.

ARTS & CRAFTS   Stop by **C. B. Stark Jewelers,** 126 Main St., Vineyard Haven (☎ **508/693-2284**) and 27 N. Water St. Edgartown (☎ **508/627-1260**), where proprietor Cheryl Stark started fashioning island-motif charms back in 1966.

In the center of Edgartown, stop in at ✪ **Gardner Colby Gallery** on 27 N. Water St. (☎ **888/969-9500** or 508/627-6002), a soothing and sophisticated art showroom filled with Vineyard-inspired paintings by such popular artists as Robert Cardinal, whose landscapes often feature haunting purple skies, and Ovid Osborn Ward, who paints graphically realistic portrayals of Vineyard motifs.

The **Chilmark Pottery,** off State Road (about 4 miles southwest of Vineyard Haven), West Tisbury (☎ **508/693-6476**), features tableware fashioned to suit its setting. Geoffrey Borr takes his palette from the sea and sky and produces highly serviceable stoneware with clean lines and a long life span. Summer pottery classes are also available.

At the **Edgartown Art Gallery,** in the Charlotte Inn, 27 S. Summer St. (☎ **508/627-8508**), you'll find handsome 19th- and 18th-century paintings and prints, opulently framed, and shown in a setting that does them justice (though the price tags look rather tacky in such an ultradeluxe inn).

✪ **The Field Gallery,** State Road (in the center of town), West Tisbury (☎ **508/693-5595**), set in a rural pasture, is where Marc Chagall meets Henry Moore and where Tom Maley's playful figures have enchanted locals and passersby for decades. You'll also find paintings by Albert Alcalay, and drawings and cartoons by Jules Feiffer. The Sunday-evening openings are high points of the summer social season.

Don't miss the ✪ **Granary Gallery** at the Red Barn, Old County Road (off Edgartown–West Tisbury Road, about ¼ mile north of the intersection), West Tisbury (☎ **800/472-6279** or 508/693-0455), which displays astounding prints by the late longtime summerer Alfred Eisenstaedt, dazzling color photos by local luminary Alison Shaw, and a changing roster of fine artists—some just emerging, some long since discovered. A fine selection of country and provincial antiques are also sold here.

Another rather unique local artisans' venue is **Martha's Vineyard Glass Works,** State Road, North Tisbury (☎ **508/693-6026**). World-renowned master glassblowers sometimes lend a hand at this handsome rural studio/shop just for the fun of it. The three resident artists—Andrew Magdanz, Susan Shapiro, and Mark Weiner— are no slouches themselves, having shown nationwide to considerable acclaim. Their output is decidedly avant-garde and may not suit all tastes, but it's an eye-opening array and all the more fascinating once you've witnessed a work in progress.

Nearby on State Road, **Etherington Fine Art,** housed in an old post office, features estimable work like Vineyard- and Venice-inspired paintings by Rez Williams, nature collages by Lucy Mitchell, pastels and oils by Wolf Kahn, and the colorful, iconographic sculptures by Sam Milstein that grace the front yard. Gallery owner Mary Etherington's selection is a giant step up from the usual seascapes and lighthouses offered by other Vineyard galleries. Big-name museum people like Thomas Hoving and Agnes Gund all stop here when on the island.

BOOKS   Bickerton & Ripley Books, Main Street (in the center of town), Edgartown (☎ 508/627-8463), has a lively presentation of timely titles highlighting local endeavors; inquire about readings and signings.

○ **Bunch of Grapes,** 44 Main St. (in the center of town), Vineyard Haven (☎ 800/ 693-0221 or 508/693-2291), offering the island's broadest selection (some 40,000 tomes), is a year-round institution and a browser's haven.

FASHION   ○ The Great Put On, Dock Street (in the center of town), Edgartown (☎ 508/627-5495), dates back to 1969, but always manages to keep up with the latest styles, including lines by Vivienne Tam, Moschino, and BCBG.

Jamaikan Jam, 154 Circuit Ave. (in the center of town), Oak Bluffs (☎ 508/ 693-5003), is one of the best ethnic shops along Circuit Avenue, carrying colorful and comfortable clothes and Jamaican tchotchkes. You can also buy or rent in-line skates here.

Treading a comfortable middle ground between functional and fashionable, the varied women's and men's labels at **LeRoux,** 89 Main St. (in the center of town), Vineyard Haven (☎ 508/693-6463), include some nationally known names, like Patagonia. They also carry Woodland Waders, an island-made line of sturdy woolen outerwear—everyday clothes for both sexes that are neither staid nor trendy.

GIFTS/HOME DECOR   ** The owners of **Bramhall & Dunn, 19 Main St., Vineyard Haven (☎ 508/693-6437), have a great eye for the kind of chunky, eclectic extras that lend character to country homes. Expect to find the requisite rag rugs, rustic pottery, a smattering of rugged antiques, sensuous linens, and even some personal furnishings to match—from lacy lingerie to bulky knit sweaters. They're also located at 16 Federal St., Nantucket (☎ 508/228-4688). Carly Simon has a new venture in Vineyard Haven. Called **Midnight Farm,** 18 Water-Cromwell Lane, Vineyard Haven (☎ 508/693-1997), after her popular children's book, this home store offers a world of high-end, carefully selected and imaginative gift items starting with soaps and candles and including children's clothes and toys, rugs, furniture, books, and glassware.

A new venture on upper Circuit Avenue (no. 73) is **Argonauta** (☎ 508/696-0097), which carries hand-painted vintage furniture, country pine, wicker, topiary, and artwork. Third World Trading Co., 14 Circuit Ave., **Oak Bluffs** (☎ 508/693-5550), features well-priced clothing, accessories, and home accents gathered from around the globe.

SEAFOOD   ** Feel like whipping up your own lobster feast? For the freshest and biggest crustaceans on the island, head to **The Net Result, 79 Beach Rd., Vineyard Haven (☎ 800/394-6071 or 508/693-6071). Run by the Larsen family, you'll find everything from shrimp, scallops, and swordfish to bluefish and tuna. Their spreadable seafood salad makes a perfect hors d'oeuvre, and if you're feeling sorry for your friends back home, they'll ship fresh lobsters, quahogs, and other aquatic delicacies anywhere in the United States overnight. If you're up-island, stop by **Poole's Fish Market** or **Larsen's Fish Market,** both right on the docks at Menemsha Harbor.

WINE   ** With a name like Martha's Vineyard, you probably expected to find wild grapes, which in fact have always grown on the island. But who knew whether fussy French vinifera would take? California transplants George and Catherine Mathiesen had high hopes when they started cultivating 3 backwoods acres in 1971, and their faith has been borne out in ✪ **Chicama Vineyards, Stoney Hill Road (off State Road, about 3 miles southwest of Vineyard Haven), West Tisbury (☎ **508/693-0309**), a highly successful winery yielding some 100,000 bottles a year. The dozen-plus varieties are not only very palatable drinking wines, but lend themselves beautifully to such gourmet uses as jellies, jams, and flavored oils and vinegars, all prepared and sold on the premises. Visitors are always welcome for a tasting, and in high season they're treated to an entertaining 20-minute tour of the production line.

8 Where to Stay

When deciding where to stay on Martha's Vineyard, you'll need to consider the type of vacation you prefer. The down-island towns of Vineyard Haven, Oak Bluffs, and Edgartown provide shops, restaurants, beaches, and harbors all within walking distance and frequent shuttles to get you all over the island. But all three can be overly crowded on busy summer weekends. Vineyard Haven is the gateway for most of the ferry traffic. Oak Bluffs is a raucous town with most of the Vineyard's bars and nightclubs. And many visitors make a beeline to Edgartown's manicured Main Street. Up-island inns provide more peace and quiet, but you will probably need a car to get around. Also, you may not be within walking distance of the beach (and, after all, isn't that why you came?). Nevertheless, there are some wonderful places to stay on the Vineyard, and all of the following choices have something special to offer. A general guide to price categories: **Very Expensive,** over $200 double; **Expensive,** $150 to $200 double; **Moderate,** $100 to $150 double; and **Inexpensive,** under $100.

EDGARTOWN
VERY EXPENSIVE

✪ **Charlotte Inn.** 27 S. Summer St. (in the center of town), Edgartown, MA 02539. ☎ **508/627-4751.** Fax 508/627-4652. 22 rms, 3 suites. A/C TV TEL. Summer (including continental breakfast and afternoon tea) $260–$450 double; $495–$750 suite. AE, MC, V. Open year-round.

Ask anyone to recommend the best inn on the island, and this is the name you're most likely to hear—not just because it's the most expensive, but because it's easily the most refined. Owners Gery and Paula Conover have been tirelessly fine-tuning this cluster of 18th- and 19th-century houses (five in all, counting the Carriage House, a Gery-built replica) since 1971. Linked by formal gardens, each house has a distinctive look and feel—though the predominant mode is English country house, with hunting prints and quirky decorative accents. In the elegant 1860 Main House, the common rooms double as the Edgartown Art Gallery (see "Shopping," above). This is the only Relais & Chateaux property on the Cape and Islands—a world-class distinction that designates excellence in hospitality.

Dining/Entertainment: However sterling the accommodations at the Charlotte Inn, the restaurant may actually gather more laurels: l'étoile is one of Edgartown's finest. See "Where to Dine," below, for more information.

Services: Turndown service in the evenings; newspapers available at breakfast every morning; in season, afternoon tea for guests.

✪ **Harbor View Hotel.** 131 N. Water St. (about ¹/₂ mile NW of Main St.), Edgartown, MA 02539. ☎ **800/255-6005** or 508/627-7000. Fax 508/627-8417. 124 units. A/C TV TEL. Summer $225–$425 double; $495–$550 suite; $625 cottage. AE, CB, DC, MC, V. Open year-round.

Grander than grand, this shingle-style complex started out as two Gilded Age hotels, ultimately joined by a 300-foot veranda. Treated to a massive centennial makeover in 1991, it now boasts every modern amenity, while retaining its retro charm—and a lobby that's right out of an Adirondack lodge. Front rooms overlook little Lighthouse Beach; in back, there's a large pool surrounded by newer annexes. The hotel is located just far enough from "downtown" to avoid the traffic hassles, but close enough for a pleasant walk past impressive captain's houses.

Dining/Entertainment: The casual Breezes restaurant, stationed in a vintage bar, is open daily for breakfast, lunch, and dinner; you can ask to be served on the veranda or by the pool, if you like. Starbuck's (see "Where to Dine," below) serves more formal meals in an elegant setting.

Services: A concierge is on hand to lend advice and assistance; room service, overnight laundry, and baby-sitting are available.

Facilities: There is a heated outdoor pool with plenty of deck space and two tennis courts. Guests enjoy privileges at the Farm Neck Golf Club (see "Beaches & Outdoor Pursuits," above).

✪ **Hob Knob Inn.** 128 Main St. (on upper Main St., in the center of town), Edgartown, MA 02539. ☎ **800/696-2723** or 508/627-9510. Fax 508/627-4560. E-mail hobknob@vineyard.net. 16 rms. TEL. Summer (including full breakfast and afternoon tea) $185–$375 double. AE, MC, V. Open year-round.

New owner Maggie White has reinvented this 19th-century Gothic Revival inn as an exquisite destination now vying for top honors as one of the Vineyard's best places to stay. Her style is peppy/preppy, with crisp floral fabrics and striped patterns creating a clean and comfortable look. Sure it's meticulously decorated, but nothing is overdone or overstuffed here. Maggie is a Vineyard insider who offers guests a number of extras. The inn has fitness equipment; massages and facials are available on the premises (for an extra charge). Maggie and her attentive staff will pack a splendid picnic basket for a day at the beach or plan a charter fishing trip on Maggie's 27-foot Boston Whaler. The full farm breakfast is a delight and is served at beautifully appointed individual tables in the sunny, brightly painted dining rooms. Bovine lovers will enjoy the agrarian theme, a decorative touch throughout the inn; Maggie keeps a herd of cattle on the island too.

148 Main Bed and Breakfast. 148 Main St., Box 1203, Edgartown, MA 02539. ☎ **508/627-7248.** Fax 508/627-9505. 4 rms. A/C TV TEL. Summer (including full breakfast) $175–$350 double. AE, MC, V. Open year-round.

This is a luxurious B&B, recently saved from demolition and lovingly restored by innkeeper David Drinan. Though built in the 1840s, the home's interior is light and airy. The spacious rooms have been outfitted with every amenity and are positively pristine. The luxurious carriage house suite with its fireplaced sitting area and tiled Jacuzzi tub for two in the bedroom is exceptional. By the way, this is the only small lodging establishment on the Vineyard with an outdoor pool and spa.

✪ **Tuscany Inn.** 22 N. Water St. (in the center of town), Edgartown, MA 02539. ☎ **508/627-5999.** Fax 508/627-6605. 8 rms. A/C. Summer (including full breakfast) $200–$325 double. AE, DC, DISC, MC, V. Closed Feb.

Innkeepers Rusty Scheuer and Laura Sbrana-Scheuer have transformed a derelict captain's house into as winning a little inn as you'll find. The interior decor is straight from sunny Italy, with warm colors and an abundance of fine old paintings—anything but the usual Yankee austerity. Past a little library lined with leather-backed books is Laura's open kitchen, where she gives cooking classes off-season (she's from Florence, and a formidable chef); lavish breakfasts (blueberry buttermilk pancakes or frittata with focaccia) are served here when the weather precludes a patio feast. Each of the eight rooms is a gem, with hand-painted antique armoires and fanciful beds—and, in some cases, skylights, marble whirlpools, and harbor views.

EXPENSIVE

Colonial Inn. 38 N. Water St., Edgartown, MA 02539. ☎ **800/627-4701** or 508/627-4711. Fax 508/627-5904. 39 rms, 2 suites, 1 efficiency. A/C TV TEL. Summer (including continental breakfast) $150–$205 double; $250 suite or efficiency. AE, MC, V. Closed Jan–Mar.

Somewhat big and impersonal, this 1911 inn has been transformed into a fine modern hotel. It's been the unofficial center of town since its doors opened, and its lobby also serves as a conduit to the Nevins Square shops beyond. The lobby has a somewhat transient feel, hardly enhanced by a self-service breakfast cart—but the lack of ceremony is a plus if, like most tourists, you're bursting to get out and about. The 42 rooms, decorated in soothing, contemporary tones (with pine furniture, pastel fabrics, and brass beds), offer all one could want in the way of conveniences. Be sure to visit the roof deck, ideally around sunset or, if you're up for it, sunrise over the water.

✪ **The Daggett House.** 59 N. Water St., Edgartown, MA 02539. ☎ **800/946-3400** or 508/627-4600. 24 rms, 6 suites. TEL. Summer $145–$205 double; $230–$395 suite. AE, MC, V. Open year-round.

What could be more Vineyard-y? Stay in the island's first tavern (the owner was fined for selling strong liquor) that is smack dab on Edgartown Harbor and serves a hearty dinner and the best breakfast in town. Request the secret staircase room, one of many rooms with a harbor view. On your way down to breakfast, check out the photo of the house's resident ghost, a young boy, hovering in the beehive fireplace. This place would be spooky if it weren't so cheerful and elegant.

The Jonathan Monroe House. 100 Main St., Edgartown, MA 02539. ☎ **508/627-5536.** 6 rms, 1 cottage. Summer (including full breakfast) $165–$200 double; $250 cottage. MC, V. Open year-round.

With its lovely wraparound, colonnaded front porch, the Jonathan Monroe House stands out from the other inns and captain's homes on this stretch of upper Main Street. Inside, the formal parlor has been transformed into a comfortable gathering room with a European flair. Guest rooms are immaculate, antique-filled, and dotted with clever details. Many rooms have fireplaces, perfect for curling up with an antiquarian book (provided) or match wits over a game of chess (also provided). At breakfast, don't miss the homemade waffles and pancakes, served on the screened-in porch or in bed. Guests will immediately feel relaxed in the presence of genial host Chip Yerkes, an enthusiastic athlete, who will gladly assist guests with daily excursions that could include a trip around Sengekontacket Pond in one of his three canoes, a game of tennis, a bike ride, or a sail around Edgartown Harbor on his friend's sloop. Request the garden cottage, with its flowering window boxes, if you are in a honeymooning mood.

✪ **Victorian Inn.** 24 S. Water St. (in the center of town), Edgartown, MA 02539. ☎ **508/627-4784.** 14 rms. Summer (including full breakfast and afternoon tea) $125–$265 double. AE, MC, V. Open year-round.

Do you ever long to stay at a quaint, reasonably priced inn that is bigger than a B&B but smaller than a Mariott? In the center of Edgartown, The Victorian Inn is a freshened-up version of those old-style hotels that used to exist in the center of every New England town. There are enough rooms here so you don't feel like you are trespassing in someone's home, yet there's a personal touch. With three floors of long, graceful corridors, the Victorian could serve as a stage set for a 1930s romance. Most rooms have canopied beds and a balcony with a harbor view. Bring your kids (and off-season, your dog) for a perfect family vacation. Each year innkeepers Stephen and Karen Caliri have improved and refined the inn, and they are always quick to dispense helpful advice with good humor.

MODERATE

The Arbor. 222 Upper Main St. (on the western edge of town, about ³/₄ mile from the harbor), Edgartown, MA 02539. ☎ **508/627-8137.** 10 rms (2 with shared bath). A/C. Summer (including continental breakfast) $100–$150. MC, V. Closed Nov–Apr.

This unassuming-looking house, hugging the bike path at the edge of town, packs surprising style: Innkeeper/antiquaire Peggy Hall tacked a lovely cathedral-ceilinged living room onto her 1880 farmhouse to add light and liveliness. That you'll find, as you compare notes with other travelers or peruse a fine collection of coffee-table books from the comfort of an overstuffed chintz couch. The rooms range from tiny to spacious, but all are nicely appointed, largely with antiques, and the rates are singularly gentle, especially considering the fresh-baked breakfast served on fine china.

Edgartown Inn. 56 N. Water St., Edgartown, MA 02539. ☎ **508/627-4794.** 20 rms (5 with shared bath). A/C TV. Summer $85–$185 double. No credit cards. Closed Nov–Mar.

Nathaniel Hawthorne holed up here for nearly a year—secretly courting a Wampanoag maiden, it is rumored, who inspired *The Scarlet Letter.* It's also where a young and feckless Ted Kennedy sweated out that shameful, post-Chappaquiddick night. Questionable karma aside, it's a lovely 1798 Federal manse, a showplace even here on captain's row, and the rooms are traditional but not overdone. Modernists might prefer the two cathedral-ceilinged quarters in the annex out back, which offer lovely light and a sense of seclusion.

OAK BLUFFS

EXPENSIVE

Island Inn. Beach Rd. (about 1 mile S of town center), Oak Bluffs, MA 02557. ☎ **800/462-0269** or 508/693-2002. Fax 508/693-7911. 51 units. A/C TV TEL. Summer $125–$235. AE, CB, DC, DISC, MC, V. Closed Dec–Mar.

Ideally located between Oak Bluffs and Edgartown on a verdant, 7-acre triangle of land (shared with the popular Farm Neck Golf Club; see "Beaches & Outdoor Pursuits," above), this modern complex is ideal for families. It's the kind of place where you'll feel comfortable letting your older kids wander about on their own (they'll head straight for the heated pool), while you hone your golf swing or tennis serve (the three Har-Tru tennis courts have their own resident pro). All the units, from studios to a two-bedroom, two-fireplace cottage that sleeps six, contain all the necessary amenities for an extended stay, including a fully equipped kitchen.

✪ **The Oak House.** Seaview Ave. (on the sound), Oak Bluffs, MA 02557. ☎ **508/693-4187.** Fax 508/696-7385. 8 rms, 2 suites. A/C TV TEL. Summer (including continental breakfast and afternoon tea) $140–$185 double; $250 suite. AE, DISC, MC, V. Closed mid-Oct to mid-May.

An 1872 Queen Anne bay-front beauty, this one-time home of former Massachusetts governor William Claflin has preserved all the luxury and leisure of the Victorian age. Innkeeper Betsi Convery-Luce trained at Johnson & Wales; her pastries (served at breakfast and tea) are sublime. The rooms toward the back are quieter, but those in front have Nantucket Sound views. The common rooms are furnished in an opulent Victorian mode, as are the 10 bedrooms (two are suites). Anyone intent on decompressing is sure to benefit from this immersion into another era—the one that invented the leisure class.

Moderate

The Dockside Inn. Circuit Ave. Ext., Box 1206, Oak Bluffs, MA 02557. ☎ **800/245-5979** or 508/693-2966. Fax 508/696-7293. 17 rms, 3 suites. A/C TV TEL. Summer (including continental breakfast) $125–$175 double; $165–$175 suite. AE, DISC, MC, V. Open year-round.

Set right on the harbor, the Dockside is perfectly located for exploring the town of Oak Bluffs. The welcoming exterior, with its colonnaded porch and balconies, duplicates the inns of yesteryear. Once inside, you'll immediately be transported into the spirit of this rollicking town by all the whimsical Victorian touches in this well-run establishment. Most of the standard-sized rooms have either a garden or harbor view; they're decorated prettily in pinks and greens. Location, charm, and flair mean this is a popular place, so book early.

Wesley Hotel. 1 Lake Ave. (on the harbor), Oak Bluffs, MA 02557. ☎ **800/638-9027** or 508/693-6611. Fax 508/693-5389. 82 rms (20 with shared bath). TV. Summer $135–$175 double. AE, CB, DC, DISC, MC, V. Closed mid-Oct to Apr.

Formerly one of the grand hotels of Martha's Vineyard, this imposing 1879 property, right on the harbor, has certainly seen sunnier times. There are still remnants from its years of grandeur, like the rockers that line the spacious wraparound porch and the lobby with its old photographs, dark-stained oak trim, old-fashioned registration desk, and plenty of Victorian reproductions. The rooms, however, are quite spare and basic, with nary a picture on the wall. One suspects they've seen their share of rowdy guests. The Wesley Arms, behind the main building, is currently undergoing a major face-lift (due to be completed for the 1998 season), which will add a number of air-conditioned rooms with private baths. *Note:* The early bird—reservations-wise—gets the harbor view, sans surcharge.

Inexpensive

Attleboro House. 42 Lake Ave. (on the harbor), Oak Bluffs, MA 02557. ☎ **508/693-4346.** 11 rms (all with shared bath). Summer (including continental breakfast) $65–$105 double. MC, V. Closed Oct–May.

As old-fashioned as the afghans that proprietor Estelle Reagan crochets for every bed, this harborside guest house—serving Camp Meeting visitors since 1874—epitomizes the simple, timeless joys of summer. None of the 11 rooms is graced with a private bath, but the rates are so retro that you may not mind. What was good enough for 19th-century tourists more than suffices today.

VINEYARD HAVEN (TISBURY)
Very Expensive

✪ **Martha's Place.** 114 Main St. (across from Owen Park, in the center of town), Vineyard Haven, MA 02568. ☎ **508/693-0253.** 6 rms. A/C. TV on request. Summer (including continental breakfast and afternoon tea) $175–$275 double. MC, V. Open year-round.

Word travels fast when a terrific new place opens on the Vineyard. Martha's Place is exceptional for its elegance in the heart of this bustling port town. New owners Richard Alcott and Martin Hicks have lovingly restored and refurbished this stately Greek Revival home and surrounded it with rose bushes. Now swags and jabots line the windows; every knob has a tassel, every fabric, a trim. If you enjoy admiring a neoclassical armoire or an antique bed draped in blue velvet, Martha's is the place. The bathrooms here are quite luxurious: Ever seen one with a fireplace? Most rooms have harbor views. There's one handicapped accessible room, too.

EXPENSIVE

The Lothrop Merry House. Owen Park (off Main St.), Vineyard Haven, MA 02568. ☎ **508/ 693-1646.** 7 rms (3 with shared bath). Summer (including continental breakfast) $135–$205 double. MC, V. Open year-round.

You'll get more than the superficial Vineyard experience by opting to stay at this nicely weathered 1790 B&B. It overlooks the harbor, with its own little stretch of beach and a canoe and Sunfish to take out at your leisure. Innkeepers Mary and John Clarke also charter cruises aboard their ketch, the *Laissez Faire* (see "Organized Tours," above). A few of the simply furnished rooms have fireplaces (the island is especially lovely, and exceedingly private, in winter), and the two rooms without water views compensate by having air-conditioning.

CHILMARK (INCLUDING MENEMSHA), WEST TISBURY & GAY HEAD
VERY EXPENSIVE

Beach Plum Inn. Beach Plum Lane (off North Rd., $^1/2$ mile NE of the harbor), Menemsha, MA 02552. ☎ **800/528-6616** or 508/645-9454. Fax 508/645-2801. 5 rms, 4 cottages. A/C TV TEL. Summer (including full breakfast) $225–$325 double or cottage. AE, DC, DISC, MC, V. Closed mid-Oct to mid-May.

It's the ideal hideaway: a prettified farmhouse on 8 verdant acres, with a lawn sloping graciously down to the water. There's a croquet course and Nova Grass tennis court on the grounds, and bikes to take exploring. The decor is predominantly white—all the better to set off a bounty of flowers, outdoors and in. All of the comfortable rooms are equipped with hair dryers, irons, and ironing boards. Some, with canopied beds, are quite romantic. The honeymoon suite has a whirlpool bath. Most rooms have decks, some with views of Menemsha Harbor.

Dining/Entertainment: The inn's restaurant is popular for its continental flair. The full breakfast served daily includes such hearty fare as steak and eggs, as well as a jogger's special (grapefruit, two poached eggs, and dry toast). Dinners are cooked to order and must be ordered several days in advance. The menu changes nightly but may include *Tournedos Rossini* prepared classically with foie gras and served atop a rich demiglace; or salmon *en papillote* with a saffron, mint, and orange butter.

Services: There is a concierge, laundry service, and twice daily maid service. Arrangements can be made for baby-sitting, secretarial services, and in-room massage.

Facilities: On the grounds are two tennis courts, a croquet court, and an exercise room.

✪ **The Inn at Blueberry Hill.** North Rd. (about 4 miles NE of Menemsha), Chilmark, MA 02535. ☎ **800/356-3322** or 508/645-3322. Fax 508/645-3799. 21 rms, 4 suites. TV TEL on request (extra charge). Summer (including continental breakfast) $210–$235 double; $280–$360 suite. AE, MC, V. Closed Dec–Apr.

Energetic young owners Bob and Carolyn Burgess bought this one-time white elephant while on their honeymoon, which may partly explain its runaway romanticism, which is wedded to high ideals. Their goal was to create a spalike retreat of the utmost luxury without in any way compromising the lovely natural setting—56 acres of former farmland, surrounded by vast tracts of conservation forest. They've succeeded splendidly. The 1792 farmhouse has been spruced up to suit a more modern aesthetic—still simple, in the neo-Shaker mode, but suffused with light. The same is true of the scattered cottages (some tucked under towering spruces), where the decor has been kept intentionally minimal, so as to play up the natural beauty all around. Tasteful, handcrafted furnishings and such gentle touches as fluffy comforters bespeak the general dedication to peace and well-being.

Dining/Entertainment: Local victuals are showcased at Theo's (see "Where to Dine," below).

Facilities: The renovated barn contains a full-scale Cybex fitness center overlooking a solar-heated outdoor lap pool and hot tub. Equipment is provided for croquet, boules, horseshoes, and volleyball. Beyond the tennis court, miles of walking paths branch out through the woods. Carolyn Burgess, a personal trainer, can fashion a custom fitness program on request and oversee workouts, or arrange for massages and facials. Inn guests may avail themselves of complimentary passes and shuttles to Lucy Vincent and Squibnocket beaches.

Outermost Inn. Lighthouse Rd. (about $^1/_4$ mile NE of the lighthouse), Gay Head, MA 02535. ☎ 508/645-3511. Fax 508/645-3514. 6 rms, 1 suite. TV TEL. Summer (including full breakfast) $250 double; $285 suite. AE, DISC, MC, V. Closed Nov to mid-Apr.

Location, location, location—you'd have to camp out at Gay Head lighthouse to enjoy a comparable panorama. Commanding a grassy bluff overlooking the Vineyard Sound, with the Elizabeth Islands off in the distance, this comfortable, shingled house was built by Jeanne and Hugh Taylor (JT's sibling) in 1971; it embodies the artisanal ethos of that time. Each bedroom features floors of a distinctive wood, from cherry to ash, and all the furnishings—wool rugs, down comforters—are low-key and upscale natural. The sitting room contains all sorts of musical instruments, ready for an impromptu number ("We encourage guests to play if they know how—and not to, if they don't," says Jean with a laugh).

Dining/Entertainment: Specializing in straightforward seafood, the dining room enjoys a splendid ocean view.

Facilities: The inn is surrounded by some 40 acres of open land with nature trails.

EXPENSIVE

Lambert's Cove Country Inn. Lambert's Cove Rd. (off State Rd., about 3 miles W of Vineyard Haven), W. Tisbury, MA 02568. ☎ 508/693-2298. Fax 508/693-7890. 15 rms. A/C. Summer (including full breakfast) $145–$185 double. AE, MC, V. Open year-round.

A dedicated horticulturist created this haven in the 1920s, expanding on a 1790 farmstead. You can see the old adzed beams in some of the upstairs bedrooms. Among his more prized additions is the Greenhouse Room, a bedroom with its own conservatory. You'll find an all-weather tennis court on the grounds, and the namesake beach nearby. Brunch on the patio is a beloved island tradition, as are the skilled New American dinners (see "Where to Dine," below). Set far off the main road and surrounded by apple trees and lilacs, this secluded estate suggests an age when time was measured in generations. There's no better place to relax.

MODERATE

The Captain R. Flanders House. North Rd. (about 1 mile NE of Menemsha), Chilmark, MA 02535. ☎ 508/645-3123. 5 rms, 2 cottages. Summer (including full breakfast) $130 double; $170 cottage. AE, MC, V. Closed mid-Nov to Apr.

Set amid 60 acres of rolling meadows crisscrossed by stone walls, this late-18th-century farmhouse built by a whaling captain has remained much the same for 2 centuries. The living room, with its broad plank floors, is full of astonishing antiques, but there's none of that "for show" feel that's prevalent in more self-conscious B&Bs. This is a working farm, so there's no time for posing (even if it was featured in Martha Stewart's *Wedding Book*). After fortifying themselves with homemade muffins, honey, and jam at breakfast, guests are free to fritter the day away. The owners will provide you with a coveted pass to nearby Lucy Vincent Beach, or perhaps you'd prefer a long country walk.

Duck Inn. Off State Rd. (about $^1/_2$ mile E of the lighthouse), Gay Head, MA 02535. ☎ **508/ 645-9018.** 5 rms. Summer (including full breakfast) $95–$175 double. MC, V. Closed Feb–Mar.

Elise LeBovit knows that some prospective guests will find her farmhouse B&B "too much," and that's fine with her. Others will find it just right, a place with real personality and glorious ocean views at every turn. Set on a meadow above the Gay Head cliffs, it's like a post-hippie pension, complete with hot tub. The five rooms, including one tucked into the 200-year-old stone foundation, are fancifully decorated (one is arrayed with antique kimonos), and runaway romantic. The pink stucco living room is agreeably cluttered and comfy, and LeBovit dishes out "gourmet organic" breakfasts, such as pear couscous muffins and chocolate-raspberry crepes.

Menemsha Inn and Cottages. Off North Rd. (about $^1/_2$ mile NE of the harbor), Menemsha, MA 02552. ☎ **508/645-2521.** 9 rms, 6 suites, 12 cottages. TV. Summer (including continental breakfast) $115–$170 double; $170 suite; cottages $1,075–$1,475 weekly. No credit cards. Closed Dec–Apr.

There's an almost Quaker-like plainness to this weathered waterside compound, though many of the rooms are quite inviting. Mostly it's a place to revel in the outdoors (on 11 seaside acres) without distractions. The late *Life* photographer Alfred Eisenstaedt summered here for 4 decades, and the interior aesthetics would please any artist. There's no restaurant—just a restful breakfast room with a piano. The most luxurious suites are located in the Carriage House, which has a spacious common room with a fieldstone fireplace and inviting rattan-and-chintz couches. These rooms have private decks: If you just want to sit and gaze out to sea, you're all set.

INEXPENSIVE

Manter Memorial AYH-Hostel. Edgartown–W. Tisbury Rd. (about 1 mile E of town center), W. Tisbury, MA 02568. ☎ **508/693-2665.** Fax 508/693-2699. 78 beds. $12 for members, $15 for nonmembers. MC, V. Closed mid-Nov to Mar.

The first "purpose-built" youth hostel in the United States, this homey cedar shake saltbox set at the edge of a vast state forest is still a front-runner. It hums with wholesome energy, from the huge group kitchen with recycling bins and two communal fridges to the five dorms accommodating 78 beds. The hallways are plastered with notices of local attractions (some stores offer discounts to hostelers), and the check-in desk also serves as a tourist information booth. Outside, there's a volleyball court, a chicken coop, and a sheltered bike rack. By bike, the hostel is a little more than 7 miles from the Vineyard Haven ferry terminal; shuttle buses also make the rounds in summer. You'll have no trouble at all finding enjoyable ways to spend the 10am-to-5pm "lockout"; just don't forget the 11pm curfew.

9　Where to Dine

Restaurants tend to be rather expensive on the Vineyard, but the stiff competition has produced a bevy of places that offer excellent service, evocative settings, and creative cuisine. *A note on spirits:* Outside Oak Bluffs and Edgartown, all of Martha's Vineyard is "dry," including Vineyard Haven, so bring your own bottle; some restaurants charge a small fee for uncorking. **Great Harbour Gourmet & Spirits** at 40 Main St. in Edgartown (☎ **508/627-4390**) has a very good wine selection.

EDGARTOWN
VERY EXPENSIVE

✪ **l'étoile.** Charlotte Inn, 27 S. Summer St. (off Main St.). ☎ **508/627-5187.** Reservations required. Jacket recommended. Fixed-price $62 and up. AE, MC, V. July–Aug daily 6:30–9:45pm; call for off-season hrs. Closed Jan to mid-Feb. FRENCH.

Every signal (starting, perhaps, with the price) tells you that this is going to be one very special meal. Having passed through a pair of ormolu-laden sitting rooms (which double as the Edgartown Art Gallery), one comes upon a conservatory sparkling with the light of antique brass sconces and fresh with the scent of potted citrus trees. Everything is perfection incarnate, from the table settings (gold-rimmed Villeroy & Boch) to a nouvelle-cuisine menu that varies seasonally but is always exquisite. Chef Michael Brisson, who came up through the kitchen of Boston's famed L'Espalier, is determined to dazzle, and he does, with an ever-evolving menu of delicacies flown in from the four corners of the earth. Sevruga usually makes an appearance—perhaps as a garnish for chilled leek soup. An étouffée of lobster with champagne sauce might come with flying-fish-roe ravioli, or warm Mission figs might offset seared pheasant breast in an Armagnac-sage sauce accompanied by sautéed summer greens and quinoa. When dinner with a decent wine runs to $100 or so a head, you expect revelation. You're likely to find it at l'étoile.

EXPENSIVE

✪ **La Cucina Ristorante at the Tuscany Inn.** 22 N. Water St. (in the center of town). ☎ **508/627-8161.** Reservations recommended. Main courses $25–$30. MC, V. May–Sept daily 6–9pm. Closed Feb. NORTHERN ITALIAN.

A few years ago, Laura Sbrana arrived in Edgartown with her husband, opened the Tuscany Inn (see "Where to Stay," above), and brought her signature European panache and sophistication to this sometimes dowdy little town. Soon she opened an acclaimed cooking school, wowing locals and visitors with her culinary skills. Now she runs a new restaurant with her son Marco installed as chef; as expected, it's sensational. Seating is outdoors under a verdant arbor with candles twinkling or indoors in the tiled dining rooms. Specialties of the house are a bit more refined than at most local venues: marinated quail salad; roasted salmon with fennel, red onion and mint salad, ginger-infused fig and port compote; or rosemary- and lavender-marinated lamb chops with cannelini beans, oven-dried tomatoes, sage, and lamb jus. If you are unable to pop over to Tuscany this year, La Cucina will tide you over just fine.

Lattanzi's. 19 Church St. (Old Post Office Sq., off Main St. in the center of town). ☎ **508/627-8854.** Reservations recommended. Main courses $18–$35. AE, DISC, MC, V. June–Sept daily 6–10pm; call for off-season hrs. Open year-round. NORTHERN ITALIAN.

Some say Al does the best veal chops on Martha's Vineyard. He also owns the very good brick-oven pizza joint next door. Lattanzi's would be the ideal place to eat in the dead of winter, by the glow of the paneled living room's handsome fireplace. Service is exceptional here, and the wine list has a wide range of well-priced bottles. Back to the veal chop. You have two choices: Piccolo Fiorentina which is hickory-grilled veal porterhouse chop with black peppercorns and lemon or Lombatina di Vitello al Porcini which serves the chop with porcini mushroom cream. If it's July, get the striped bass special; from local waters, it's luscious.

✪ **Savoir Fare.** 14 Church St. (Old Post Office Sq., off Main St. in the center of town). ☎ **508/627-9864.** Reservations recommended. Main courses $18–$28. AE, MC, V. Late May to mid-Oct Mon–Sat 11:30am–2:30pm; daily 6–10pm; call for off-season hrs. Closed Nov to mid-Apr. NEW AMERICAN.

Scott Caskey initially opened this stylish cathedral-ceiling space as a gourmet deli/catering concern. Spurred by a rumor of impending competition (which never did materialize), he switched to haute restaurateur and has no regrets. He still gets to tend the garde-manger (salad and dessert station) in an open kitchen that enjoys the conviviality of a clubhouse. Some of the prettiest seating is outside, under the graceful pergola (you'd never guess you were surrounded by parking lot), where champagne and shellfish are always on ice. Savor an appetizer of black mission fig and Gorgonzola dolce salad before a main course of house-made tagliatelli and grilled marinated quail. To top it off, Scott has a winning way with unusual desserts.

Starbuck's. At the Harbor View Hotel (see "Where to Stay," above), 131 N. Water St. ☎ **508/627-7000.** Reservations recommended. Main courses $19–$29. AE, MC, V. Mon–Sat 7–11am and noon–2pm, Sun 8am–2pm; daily 6–9pm. NEW AMERICAN.

As befits its setting, Starbuck's—not to be confused with the ever-reproducing chain of coffeehouses from Seattle—is resolutely grand, lushly draped, and formally decorated with lute-back chairs and tasseled curtains. The menu is far less stuffy and includes spicy Thai beef tenderloin, or a seared rare sashimi tuna with wasabi caviar. Most diners in this demographic group favor substantial slabs of fish and beef, and that's what they'll get, however they like it. The elaborate breakfast menu is also a highlight, featuring Yankee red flannel hash and choose-your-own-combo griddle cakes.

MODERATE

Chesca's. At the Colonial Inn, 38 N. Water St. ☎ **508/627-1234.** Main courses $9–$25. AE, MC, V. Reservations not accepted. Late June to early Sept Tues–Sat 9am–2pm, Sun 9am–1pm; daily 5:30–10pm; call for off-season hrs. ITALIAN.

Chesca's is a solid entry, with yummy food at reasonable prices, and you're sure to find favorites like paella (with roasted lobster and other choice seafoods), risotto (with roasted vegetables), and ravioli (with portobello mushrooms and asparagus). Smaller appetites can fill up on homemade soup and salad.

The Newes from America. At The Kelley House, 23 Kelley St. ☎ **508/627-7900.** Main courses $7–$22. AE, DC, MC, V. Daily 11am–11pm. PUB GRUB.

The pub grub is better than average at this subterranean tavern, built in 1742 and only recently resurrected. The decor may be more Edwardian than colonial, but those who come to quaff don't seem to care. Try a "rack" of five esoteric brews, or let your choice of comestibles—from a wood-smoked oyster "Island Poor Boy" sandwich with linguica relish to an 18-ounce porterhouse steak—dictate your draft; the menu comes handily annotated. Other sandwich choices include Brazilian chicken salad and grilled eggplant—reliable and filling, if not especially distinguished. Don't miss their seasoned fries, accompanied by a savory Southwestern dipping sauce.

INEXPENSIVE

Among the Flowers Cafe. Mayhew Lane. ☎ **508/627-3233.** Main courses $8–$15. DC, MC, V. July–Aug daily 8am–11pm; call for off-season hrs. Closed Nov–Apr. AMERICAN.

Everything's fresh and appealing at this outdoor cafe near the dock. Sit under the awning and you'll just catch a glimpse of the harbor. The breakfasts are the best around, and all the crepes, waffles, and eggs are also available at lunch. The comfort-food dinners (lemon chicken, lobster Newburg crepe, and others) are among the most affordable options in this pricey town. There's almost always a wait, not just because it's so picturesque, but because the food is homey, hearty, and kind on the wallet.

Main Street Diner. Old Post Office Sq. (off Main St. in the center of town). ☎ **508/627-9337.** Most items under $10. MC, V. Daily 7am–1am year-round. AMERICAN.

It's a little kitschy-cute, what with cartoon wallpaper decorated with vintage doodads, but tony Edgartown could use a place geared to folks not out to bust the budget. Kids and adults alike will enjoy this ersatz diner, where the food as well as the trimmings hearken back to the 1950s. A one-egg breakfast with home fries and a buttermilk biscuit will set you back only two bucks; the burgers and sandwiches (including a classic open-face hot turkey with gravy, potatoes, and cranberry sauce) less than six. Grab a grilled cheese or BLT, wash it down with a cherry Coke, and head back out into the cool, cold world of the nineties.

SWEETS

Espresso Love. 2 S. Water St., Edgartown. ☎ **508/627-9211.**

Wash down the freshly baked pastries and muffins with strong coffee, and you're on your way for more shopping and sightseeing.

OAK BLUFFS
EXPENSIVE

Brasserie 162. 162 Circuit Ave. (in the center of town). ☎ **508/696-6336.** Reservations suggested. Main courses $20–$35. AE, MC, V. Open May–Oct daily 6pm–10pm. NEW AMERICAN.

New proprietors Larry Johnson and Perry Ambulos, who also own Edgartown's erstwhile cafe (and current catering service) Truly Scrumptious, have reinvented the former, swank Oyster Bar as a dreamy, sophisticated dining spot with a more welcoming spirit. It still sports an open kitchen and a striking 30-foot bar, but the neon is long gone. As Larry puts it, "We're hoping to bring the locals back to the restaurant." Preening celebrities, take note! Still, this is quite a stunning venue, and the beautiful people are sure to come back in droves. Specialties include the delightful Shrimp Martini: spiced, rubbed, seared, and served atop garlic mashed potatoes, garnished with oyster mushrooms and carrot ginger splash; and grilled rack of lamb with a lavender Dijon crust, eggplant and couscous Napoleon, and yellow-bell-pepper coulis. Leave room for the light (relatively) healthful desserts like the lemon chiller: fresh lemon mousse with lemon sorbet.

Sweet Life Cafe. 63 Circuit Ave. ☎ **508/696-0200.** Reservations recommended. Main courses $19–$28. AE, DISC, MC, V. Mid-May to mid-Sept Sun 10am–2pm; daily 6–10pm; call for off-season hrs. NEW AMERICAN.

Locals are crazy about this new restaurant set in a restored Victorian house on upper Circuit Avenue. In season, the most popular seating is outside in the gaily lit garden. Fresh island produce is featured here, and seafood specials are an enticing draw. You can't go wrong with the roasted lobster with potato Parmesan risotto, roasted yellow beets, and smoked-salmon chive fondue.

MODERATE

Jimmy Seas Pan Pasta Restaurant. 32 Kennebec Ave. ☎ **508/696-8550.** Reservations not accepted. Main courses $13–$23. No credit cards. May to mid-Oct daily 5:30–10pm; call for off-season hrs. Closed Jan–Mar. MEDITERRANEAN.

If you're wondering why the luncheonette-level decor at this restaurant, where Frank Sinatra's crooning resounds at all times, doesn't quite match up with menu prices, it's because chef Jimmy Cipolla gives his all to his one-pot pasta dishes, served right in the pan. Pasta comes in such intriguing guises as pumpkin tortellini in a creamy sage sauce, and everything's fair game for toppings, from chicken and shrimp with fresh pesto to swordfish in a balsamic vinaigrette. Portions are enormous. President Clinton ate it up, and you'll probably love it, too.

Lola's Southern Seafood. At the Island Inn, Beach Rd. ☎ **508/693-5007.** Reservations recommended. Main courses $20–$24. DC, MC, V. Mid-May to mid-Sept Sun 10am–2pm; daily 5–9pm; call for off-season hrs. Open year-round. SOUTHERN.

This sultry New Orleans–style restaurant drips with atmosphere: crystal chandeliers, intricate wrought iron, arched doorways, and starched linens in an ochre palette.

Specialties include the chicken and seafood jambalaya and the rib-eye steak spiced either "from heaven or hell." There's live entertainment nightly in season, while brunch features live music, either gospel or jazz. A less-expensive pub menu is served in the bar with its mural of island personalities.

✪ **Zapotec.** 10 Kennebec Ave. (in the center of town). ☎ **508/693-6800.** Reservations not accepted. Main courses $11–$18. AE, MC, V. Apr–Oct daily 11:30am–2pm and 5–10pm. Closed Nov–Mar. MEXICAN/SOUTHWESTERN.

Look for the chili-pepper lights entwining the porch of this clapboard cottage: They're a beacon leading to tasty regional Mexican cuisine, from Mussels Oaxaca (with chipotle peppers, cilantro, lime, and cream) to Crabcakes Tulum (mixed with codfish and grilled peppers, and served with dual salsas), plus the standard chicken and beef burritos. A good mole is hard to find this far north; here you can accompany it with Mexico's unbeatable beers (including several rarely spotted north of the border), refreshing sangria, or perhaps a handpicked, well-priced wine.

INEXPENSIVE

Cafe Luna. Circuit Ave. Ext. (on the harbor). ☎ **508/693-8078.** Main courses $5–$19. MC, V. Late May to mid-Oct daily noon–10pm. Closed mid-Oct to late May. PIZZA.

Check out this gingerbread house for some primo snacking. The pizzas are made with the finest ingredients (some offered for sale), and a focaccia-slathered with roasted vegetables and aged provolone makes an optimal lunch or light dinner. Those still peckish can head upstairs for tapas or desserts at the wine-and-coffee bar.

Dee's Harbor Cafe. 1 Lake Ave. (on the harbor). ☎ **508/693-6506.** Most items under $6. MC, V. May to mid-Oct daily 6:30am–3pm. Closed mid-Oct to Apr. ECLECTIC.

A tiny, cute, bustling restaurant, Dee's gives you gourmet breakfasts on the cheap—how does eggs Florentine for under $5 sound? The sandwiches, quesadillas, and salads are appealing, too, as are refreshing drinks such as the "Southern fruit tea" (iced tea splashed with pineapple juice).

Papa's Pizza. 158 Circuit Ave. ☎ **508/693-1400.** Most items under $8. MC, V. June–Aug 11am–9pm; call for off-season hrs. PIZZA.

The pizza at this vintage-look parlor is on the tame side (so you won't have to pick off the arugula). Nevertheless, some say this is the best pizza on the Vineyard. For families with kids, it's ideal. Stop in if only to see the vintage photos of one-time "campers."

SWEETS

Hilliard's Kitch-in-Vue. 158 Circuit Ave. (in the center of town). ☎ **508/693-2191.**

Not even Candyland could match this pastel-painted cottage, where tantalizing renditions of white, milk, and dark chocolate are whipped up—and snapped up—daily.

✪ **Mad Martha's.** 117 Circuit Ave. (in the center of town). ☎ **508/693-9151.** Branches at 8 Union St., Vineyard Haven (☎ 508/693-9674) and 7 N. Water St., Edgartown (☎ 508/627-8761). Closed mid-Oct to Apr.

Vineyarders are mad for this locally made ice cream, which comes in 2 dozen enticing flavors. President Clinton surprisingly opted for a restrained mango sorbet, which isn't to say you shouldn't go for a hot fudge sundae.

Murdick's Fudge. Circuit Ave. ☎ **888/553-8343** or 508/627-8047.

Since 1887, the Murdick family have been serving up homemade fudge, brittle, clusters, and bark. Bring the kids and watch the candy-makers in progress.

VINEYARD HAVEN (TISBURY)
EXPENSIVE

✪ Dry Town Cafe. 70 Main St. (at the center of town), Vineyard Haven. ☎ **508/693-0033.**
Reservations recommended. Main courses $24–$36. AE, MC, V. June–Oct daily: juice bar
10:30am–2:30pm, dinner 6–10pm; call for off-season hrs. Closed late Feb to late Mar. NEW
AMERICAN.

This black-and-white bistro, transformed from a barber shop, has an uptown snap
(boasting sleek woodwork under an elegant arched ceiling) and jazzy cuisine with a
world-beat bent. Home-style cod cakes, for instance, get a kick with burnt-melon
relish; grilled calamari might come with a fried corn tortilla and soy vinaigrette (that's
got to be at least four countries accounted for). Lunches feature such specialties as
native cod cakes with burnt melon relish, and the "dilla del dia" (quesadilla of the
day). It's the kind of place where the distinguished regulars tend to know one another,
but newcomers won't be made to feel like rubes. Do tuck a bottle of good wine under your arm when coming here.

Le Grenier. 96 Main St. (in the center of town), Vineyard Haven. ☎ **508/693-4906.** Reservations suggested. Main courses $19–$30. AE, DC, MC, V. July–Aug daily 6–10pm; call for off-
season hrs. Closed Jan–Feb. FRENCH.

If Paris is the heart of France, Lyons is the belly—and that's where chef-owner Jean
Dupon grew up on his *Maman's* hearty cuisine (she now helps out here, cooking
lunch). Dupon has the continental moves down, as evidenced in such classics as steak
au poivre, calf's brains Grenobloise with beurre noir and capers or lobster Normande
flambéed with calvados, apples, and cream. Despite the fact that Le Grenier means
(and in fact is housed in) an attic, the restaurant is quite romantic, especially when
aglow with hurricane lamps.

MODERATE

✪ Black Dog Tavern. Beach St. Ext. (on the harbor), Vineyard Haven. ☎ **508/693-9223.**
Reservations not accepted. Main courses $14–$25. AE, MC, V. June to early Sept Mon–Sat
7–11am, 11:30am–2:30pm, and 5–10pm; Sun 7am–1pm and 5–10pm; call for off-season hrs.
NEW AMERICAN.

How does a humble harbor shack come to be a national icon? Location helps. So do
cool T-shirts. Soon after Shenandoah captain Robert Douglas decided, in 1971, that
this hard-working port could use a good restaurant, influential vacationers, stuck
waiting for the ferry, began to wander in to this saltbox to tide themselves over with
a bit of "blackout cake" or peanut-butter pie. The rest is history, as smart marketing moves extrapolated on word of mouth. The smartest of these was the invention
of the signature "Martha's Vineyard whitefoot," a black Lab whose stalwart profile
now adorns everything from baby's overalls to doggy bandannas, golf balls, and
needlepoint kits. Originally the symbol signaled Vineyard ties to fellow insiders; now
it merely bespeaks an acquaintance with mail-order catalogs.

Still, tourists love this rough-hewn tavern, and it's not just hype that keeps them
happy. The food is still home-cooking good—heavy on the seafood, of course (including grilled swordfish with banana, basil, and lime, and bluefish with mustard
soufflé sauce)—and the blackout cake has lost none of its appeal. Though the lines
grow ever longer (there can be a wait to get on the wait list!), nothing much has
changed at this beloved spot. Eggs Galveston for breakfast at the Black Dog Tavern
is still one of the ultimate Vineyard experiences—go early, when it first opens, and
sit on the porch, where the views are perfect.

Louis' Tisbury Cafe & Take-Out. 102 State Rd. ☎ **508/693-3255.** Reservations not accepted. Main courses $12.75–$23. AE, DISC, MC, V. Mon–Sat 11am–9pm, Sun 4–9pm. Open year-round. ITALIAN.

About a mile out of town, toward Gay Head, is this Island pizza house that also whips up fine Italian food at affordable prices in its informal and lively dining room. Pizza and fresh pasta dishes, many of them vegetarian (try the lasagna), highlight the menu, and all entrees come with magnificent, homemade garlic rolls and a trip to Louis' classic Italian salad bar. You can knock $2 off any main dish if you order it as an appetizer, and everything on the menu is available for takeout. Expect a wait after 7pm in the summer—there's a terrific following among the locals here.

TAKE-OUT & PICNIC FARE

Black Dog Bakery. Water St. (near the harbor), Vineyard Haven. ☎ **508/693-4786.**

In need of a snack at 5:30am? That's when the doors to this fabled bakery open; from midmorning on, it's elbow-room only. This selection of freshly baked breads, muffins, and desserts can't be beat. Don't forget some homemade doggie biscuits for your pooch.

WEST TISBURY, CHILMARK (INCLUDING MENEMSHA) & GAY HEAD

VERY EXPENSIVE

✪ **Theo's.** At the Inn at Blueberry Hill, North Rd. (about 4 miles NE of Menemsha), Chilmark. ☎ **508/645-3322.** Reservations required. Fixed-price $38–$55. AE, MC, V. May–Nov daily 6–9:30pm. Closed Dec–Apr. NEW AMERICAN.

It's quite simply the perfect restaurant: sufficiently formal yet soothing and relaxed, satisfying to all the senses, yet still health-conscious. Renowned local chef Robin Ledoux Forte plucks each tender vegetable herself from the inn garden; her husband often hauls in the catch of the day. And while her preparations may be minimalist, all the better to bring out intrinsic flavors, she's awfully good at finding delicious combinations—surrounding noisettes of Menemsha swordfish, for instance, with sesame aioli and a spicy Asian slaw. For dessert, you can choose to be good (individual blueberry plum pot pies) or naughty (ginger mascarpone cheesecake with chocolate cookie crust). The lighting, cast by candles in blue goblets across rag-painted walls, creates an aura of unhurried comfort and a pervasive sense that all is as it should be, here in the unspoiled countryside.

EXPENSIVE

The Feast of Chilmark. State Rd. (in the center of town), Chilmark. ☎ **508/645-3553.** Reservations recommended. Main courses $17–$27. AE, MC, V. July–Aug daily 6–10pm; call for off-season hrs. Closed Nov–Apr. NEW AMERICAN.

Capturing the essence of "up-island," this cored-out clapboard house conceals a sophisticated bilevel restaurant with lots of exposed wood and a menu to make jaded New Yorkers sit up and take notice. Chef Tony Saccocia's specialties include quahog chowder, lobster turnovers with shrimp and lemon cream, and rack of local lamb with a spinach-cognac glaze. On the premises is the Peter Simon Photography Gallery.

Lambert's Cove Country Inn. Lambert's Cove Rd. (off State Rd., about 3 miles W of Vineyard Haven), W. Tisbury. ☎ **508/693-2298.** Reservations recommended. Main courses $22–$27. AE, MC, V. July–Aug daily 6–8pm; Sun 11am–1pm; call for off-season hrs. NEW AMERICAN.

Whether you choose to dine on the outdoor patio, canopied by wisteria, or indoors on candlelit lace tablecloths, the setting here is sheer romance (see "Where to Stay," above). The country-house cuisine shows just enough quirks to tickle the tired

---

The Quintessential Lobster Dinner

When the basics—a huge lobster and a sunset—are what you crave, visitors and locals alike head to **The Home Port** on North Road in Menemsha (☎ **508/ 645-2679;** fax 508/645-3119). At first glance, prices for the lobster dinners may seem a bit high, but note that they include an appetizer of your choice—go with the stuffed quahog—salad, amazing fresh-baked breads, a nonalcoholic beverage (remember, it's BYOB in these parts), and dessert. The decor is on the simple side, but who really cares? It's the scintillating harbor views that have drawn the faithful hordes to this family-friendly place for over 60 years. Locals not keen on summer crowds prefer to order their lobster dinners for pickup (half-price) at the restaurant door, then mosey on down to Menemsha Beach for a private sunset supper. Reservations are highly recommended and the fixed-price platters range from $19 to $30 (MasterCard, Visa, and American Express are all accepted). The Home Port is open June through September, daily from 6 to 10pm; call for off-season hours. Closed mid-October through mid-April.

---

palate. The domestic rack of lamb, for instance, is dressed with raspberry-blackberry mint vinegar, and the cheese-and-walnut ravioli in Gorgonzola cream are bejeweled with asparagus and roasted red peppers. Sunday brunch is a well-regarded feast, with popular standards (eggs Benedict, Belgian waffles, French toast, and more) supplemented by a buffet of fresh-baked pastries.

✪ **Red Cat Restaurant.** 688 State Rd., W. Tisbury. ☎ **508/693-9599.** Reservations recommended. Main courses $24–$30. MC, V. Open through late New Year's Eve. Tues–Sun 6–9:30pm. NEW AMERICAN.

Native son and chef Benjamin deForest may have honed his chops at Boston's formidable and sophisticated Four Seasons, but the laid-back island style comes naturally to him. While the decor has recently been updated, the artistry here is concentrated on the plate: in a tasty "fresca" of tomatoes, corn, and basil, for instance, or a showy dish involving a hefty 14-ounce pork chop sauced with calvados, pears, and blond raisins and topped with crispy sweet-potato curls. Among the more addictive desserts is a home-comfort chocolate bread pudding. For a total treat, try the five-course tasting menu. The place is invariably mobbed: Come early—and midweek, if you can manage it. August is booked here 3 weeks in advance.

INEXPENSIVE

✪ **The Menemsha Bite.** Basin Rd. (off North Rd., about ¹/₄ mile NE of the harbor), Menemsha. ☎ **508/645-9239.** Most items under $9. No credit cards. June to mid-Sept daily 11am–9pm. Closed mid-Sept to June. SEAFOOD.

It's usually places like "The Bite" that we crave when we think of New England. This is your quintessential "chowdah" and clam shack, flanked by picnic tables. Run by two sisters employing their grandmother's recipes, this place makes superlative chowder, potato salad, fried fish, and so forth. The food comes in graduated containers, with a jumbo portion of shrimp topping out at around $25.

TAKE-OUT & PICNIC FARE

Alley's General Store. State Rd. (in the center of town), W. Tisbury. ☎ **508/693-0088.**

That endangered rarity, a true New England general store, Alley's—in business since 1858—nearly foundered in the profit-mad 1980s. Luckily the Martha's Vineyard

Preservation Trust interceded to give it a new lease on life, along with a much-needed structural overhaul. The stock is still the same, though: basically, everything you could possibly need, from scrub brushes to fresh-made salsa (sold, along with other appealing picnic fixings, from Back Alley's Bakery & Deli). Best of all, the no-longer-sagging front porch still supports a popular bank of benches, along with a blizzard of bulletin-board notices. For a local's-eye view of noteworthy activities and events, this is the first place to check.

West Tisbury Farmer's Market. Old Agricultural Hall, W. Tisbury. ☎ **508/696-0100.**

This seasonal outdoor market, open Wednesday 3 to 6pm and Saturday 9am to noon, is among the biggest and best in New England, and certainly the most rarefied, with local celebrities loading up on prize produce and snacking on pesto bread and other international goodies.

SWEETS

✪ **Chilmark Chocolates.** State Rd. (in the town center), Chilmark. ☎ **508/645-3013.** Wed to Sun 11:30am–5:30pm. Closed Jan–Mar.

Should you find a sample plumped on your B&B pillow (a delightful lagniappe), you'll want to hunt down the source. Friendly workers at this cottage industry—many of them coping with mental disabilities—will gladly demonstrate their edible artistry.

10 Martha's Vineyard After Dark

The Vineyard has an active summer social life. TV journalism and pop culture firmament types such as Diane Sawyer, Mike Wallace, Walter Cronkite, Carly Simon, and Art Buchwald may be busy attending private dinner parties, but they are apt to join the rest of us later at a nightspot. While the number-one club on the island is the Hot Tin Roof at the airport, there are plenty of other places within walking distance in the down-island towns. Hit Oak Bluffs for the rowdiest bar scene and best nighttime street life. In Edgartown, you may have to hop around before you find the evening's most happening spot; for instance, you could happen upon an impromptu performance by Vineyard Sound, a grooving all male a cappella group. In addition, there are interesting cultural offerings almost every night in summer, so check local papers for details.

PUBS, BARS, DANCE CLUBS & LIVE MUSIC

Atlantic Connection. 124 Circuit Ave. (in the center of town), Oak Bluffs. ☎ **508/693-7129.** June to early Sept 9pm–1am; call for off-season hrs. Cover varies; call for schedule.

Disco lives! As do—uh-oh—karaoke and comedy, on occasion. Locals such as Spike Lee and Ted Danson seem to love the hodgepodge, and the unofficial house band, Entrain, has begun to attract a wide following (both on the island and on the mainland) with their funky, reggae-laced rock. In fact, President Clinton elicited plenty of national publicity for this up-and-coming band when he played sax with them on one of his recent Vineyard jaunts. Don't miss the Boogies, featuring Sally Taylor (the very hip daughter of Carly Simon and James Taylor) singing vintage disco, on Tuesday nights.

City, Ale & Oyster. 30 Kennebec Ave., Oak Bluffs. ☎ **508/693-2626.** June–Sept daily noon–midnight; call for off-season hrs. No cover.

In 1602, the first barley in the New World was grown on Martha's Vineyard. Last year the Vineyard's first and only brew pub opened, featuring nine locally made beers on tap ($2.75 to $4.95). It's an attractively rustic place, high-ceilinged with oak booths lining the walls and peanut shells strewn on the floor. Late-night munchies are served till midnight, featuring pizza, hamburgers, and Southern fried chicken among other offerings. Local acoustic performers entertain several nights a week in season.

David Ryans. 11 N. Water St., Edgartown. ☎ 508/627-4100. June–Sept daily 11:30am–1am; call for off-season hrs. No cover.

People have been known to dance on the tables at this boisterous bar. You can hear the music blaring from Main Street. The bartender decides the canned tunes, from Sinatra to Smashing Pumpkins. This is where President Clinton went partying the night Hillary was off-island.

✪ Hot Tin Roof. Airport Rd. (at Martha's Vineyard Airport), Edgartown. ☎ 508/693-1137. E-mail theroof@vineyard.net. Web site www.mvhottinroof.com. Cover varies; call for schedule. Closed mid-Sept to Apr.

Carly's back, and the joint is jumping. Simon first opened this nightclub-in-a-hangar in the early 1970s and eventually lost interest (while it lost cachet). Now with multimillion-dollar backing from such high-rollers as hotelier Richard Friedman (who hosted the Clintons' first Vineyard visit), it's on a roll again. Notoriously stage-shy, Carly will sometimes take the mike herself, but she's mostly content to attract an eclectic roster including such notables as Jimmy Cliff, Peter Wolf, Hall & Oates, the "Bacon Brothers" (including Kevin), and Kate Taylor, James's equally talented sister. Comedians command the stage on Tuesday. All in all, it's a family affair, where outsiders in sync with global-family values will feel right at home.

Katy MacDougall's Pub. 14 Kennebec Ave., Oak Bluffs. ☎ 508/693-8887. No cover.

Though it feels like it's been here forever, this place just opened last year. It's an authentic Irish pub, featuring live *seisiún* music on Thursday nights and the perfect pint of Guinness, along with 70 other domestic and imported craft beers.

The Lampost/Rare Duck. 111 Circuit Ave. (in the center of town), Oak Bluffs. ☎ 508/696-9352. Cover varies; call for schedule. Closed Nov–Mar.

Young and loud are the watchwords at this pair of clubs; the larger features live bands and a dance floor, the smaller (down in the basement), acoustic acts.

The Ritz Cafe. 1 Circuit Ave. (in the center of town), Oak Bluffs. ☎ 508/693-9851. Cover varies; call for schedule.

Locals and visitors alike flock to this down-and-dirty blues club that features live music every night in season and on weekends year-round.

LOW-KEY EVENINGS

Old Whaling Church. 89 Main St. (in the center of town), Edgartown. ☎ 508/627-4442. Ticket prices vary; call for schedule.

This magnificent 1843 Greek Revival church functions primarily as a 500-seat performing-arts center offering lectures and symposia, films, plays, and concerts. Such Vineyard luminaries as the actress Patricia Neal and the late *Life* photographer Alfred Eisenstaedt have taken their place at the pulpit.

Wintertide Coffeehouse. Five Corners, Vineyard Haven. ☎ 508/693-8830. Cover varies; call for schedule.

This community-run, alcohol-free folkie haven not only helps keep the natives entertained through the long, lonely winters, it has been hailed by *Billboard* as one of the country's top 10 coffeehouses. The Black Dog Bakery provides the nibbles, while some big names on the folk, blues, and jazz circuits contribute the live soundtrack. You'll also catch an occasional comic, including the homegrown troupe W.I.M.P. (as in Wintertide Improv).

THEATER AND DANCE

✪ **The Vineyard Playhouse.** 10 Church St. (in the center of town), Vineyard Haven. ☎ **508/ 696-6300.** Tickets $15–$25. Late June to early Sept Tues–Sun at 8pm; call for off-season hrs.

In an intimate (112-seat) black-box theater, carved out of an 1833 church-turned-Masonic lodge, Equity professionals put on a rich season of favorites and challenging new work—followed, on summer weekends, by musical or comedic cabaret in the gallery/lounge. Townspeople often get involved in the outdoor Shakespeare production, a 3-week run starting in mid-July at the Tashmoo Overlook Amphitheatre about 1 mile west of town, where tickets for the 5:30pm performances Tuesday through Sunday run only $5 to $10.

The Yard, A Colony for the Performing Arts. Off Middle Rd. near Beetlebung Corner, Chilmark. ☎ **508/645-9662.**

For over 25 years, The Yard has been presenting modern dance performances on Martha's Vineyard. The choreographer residency program here is nationally recognized. There are also classes open to the public. Performances are June to October, and admission is $12 adults, $9 students.

MOVIES

The Vineyard has a brand new movie theater in Edgartown: **Entertainment Cinemas** with two screens on 65 Main St. (☎ **508/627-8008**). Call ☎ **508/627-5900** or check local newspapers or schedules at the three vintage art-deco movie theaters: **Capawok** (Main Street, Vineyard Haven); **Island Theater** (at the bottom of Circuit Avenue, Oak Bluffs); **The Strand** (Oak Bluffs Avenue Extension, Oak Bluffs).

ONLY ON THE VINEYARD

✪ **Der Kunster Drum.** Various beaches. No phone. Free admission. July–Aug Mon at sunset.

A volunteer, but by no means amateur, enterprise, this nine-member ensemble incites onlookers to rhythmic frenzies with its Afro-Caribbean beat. Performance sites are usually posted about the island; check the board at Alley's General Store (see "Where to Dine," above).

Gay Head Lighthouse. Off State Rd., Gay Head. ☎ **508/645-2211.** Admission $2 adults, free for children under 12. Late June to late Sept Fri–Sun 7–9pm.

Though generally closed to the public, this 1856 lighthouse opens its doors on summer-weekend evenings to afford an awe-inspiring view of the sunset over the Devil's Bridge shoals. The light has been automated since 1952 (the original lens lights up the night sky in Edgartown), but the experience continues to be romantic.

Trinity Park Tabernacle. Trinity Park (within the Camp Meeting Grounds), Oak Bluffs. ☎ **508/ 693-0525.** July–Aug Wed at 8pm and occasional weekend evenings. Free admission; call for schedule.

Designed by architect J. W. Hoyt of Springfield, Massachusetts, and built in 1879 for just over $7,000, this open-air church, now on the National Register of Historic Places, is the largest wrought-iron-and-wood structure in America. Its conical crown is ringed with a geometric pattern of amber, carmine, and midnight-blue stained glass. Old-fashioned community sings take place Wednesdays at 8pm, and concerts are scheduled irregularly on weekends. James Taylor and Bonnie Raitt have regaled the faithful here, but usually the acts are more homespun—for example, the Parson's Plunkers, a local banjo band. The Martha's Vineyard Camp Meeting Association publishes a schedule of events open to the public, including interdenominational services and flea markets.

Nantucket 10

n his classic *Moby Dick,* Herman Melville wrote, "Nantucket! Take out your map and look at it. See what a real corner of the world it occupies; how it stands there, away off shore. . . ." More than 100 years later, this tiny island, 30 miles off the coast of Cape Cod, still counts its isolation as a defining characteristic. At only 3¹/₂ by 14 miles in size, Nantucket is smaller and more insular than Martha's Vineyard. But charm-wise, Nantucket stands alone—20th-century luxury and amenities wrapped in an elegant 19th-century package.

The Nantucket we see today is the result of a dramatic boom and bust that took place in the 1800s. Once the whaling capital of the world, the Nantucket of Melville's time was a bustling international port whose wealth and sophistication belied its size. But the discovery of crude oil put an end to Nantucket's livelihood, and the island underwent a severe depression until the tourism industry revived it at the turn of the century. Stringent regulations preserved the 19th-century character of Nantucket town, and today 36% of the island (and counting!) is maintained as conservation land.

Nantucket Island has one town, also called Nantucket, which hugs the yacht-filled harbor. This sophisticated burg features bountiful stores, quaint inns, cobblestoned streets, interesting historic sites, and pristine beaches. Strolling is de rigueur, and you don't want to miss the scores of shops and galleries housed in wharf shacks on the harbor. The rest of the island is mainly residential, but for a couple of notable villages. Siasconset (nicknamed 'Sconset) on the east side of the island is a tranquil community with picturesque, rose-covered cottages and a handful of businesses, including a *très cher* French restaurant. Sunset aficionados head to Madaket, on the west coast of the island, for the evening spectacular.

The lay of the land on Nantucket is rolling moors, heathlands, cranberry bogs, and miles of exquisite public beaches. The vistas are honeymoon-romantic: an operating windmill, three lighthouses, and a skyline dotted with church steeples. Although July and August are still the most popular times to visit the island, Nantucket's tourist season has lengthened considerably by virtue of several popular festivals: Daffodil Festival in April, Cranberry Harvest Weekend in October, and the month-long Nantucket Noel, the granddaddy of all holiday celebrations here. Off-season, visitors enjoy a more tranquil and certainly less expensive vacation. While the "Grey Lady's" infamous fog is liable to swallow you whole, frequent visitors learn to relish this moody, atmospheric touch.

1 Essentials

GETTING THERE

BY FERRY   From Hyannis (South Street Dock), the **Steamship Authority** (☎ **508/477-8600;** from Nantucket, 508/228-3274) operates year-round ferry service (including cars, passengers, and bicycles) to Steamship Wharf in Nantucket. When traveling to the island with your car in summertime, advance reservations are highly recommended, since only six boats make the trip daily. And, unlike car-ferry service to Martha's Vineyard, if you arrive without a reservation and plan to wait in the standby line, there is no guarantee you will get to the island that day. Therefore, your best bet is to reserve months in advance, have several alternatives for departure dates, and arrive at least 30 minutes before departure to avoid your space being released to standbys. Be aware, however, that the penalty for canceling an auto reservation can be as high as 50% of the fare, depending upon when you cancel; check the policy when you make reservations. No advance reservations are required for passengers only.

Total trip time is 2 hours and 15 minutes. A one-way fare with car costs $90 from mid-May to mid-October; $70 mid-March to mid-May and mid-October to November; and $50 from December to mid-March. For passengers, a one-way ticket is $10 for adults, $5 for children 5 to 12, and $5 extra for bikes. Remember that parking at the ferry dock costs $7.50 per day.

From Hyannis, passenger ferries to Nantucket's Straight Wharf are also operated by **Hy-Line Cruises** (Ocean Street Dock; ☎ 508/778-2600). Hy-Line offers year-round service with its new high-speed passenger catamaran, *The Grey Lady II,* which cuts trip time from 2 hours to 1. The cost of a one-way fare is $29 for adults ($52 round-trip), $23 for children 4 to 12 ($39 round-trip), and $4.50 extra for bicycles. This state-of-the-art vessel seats 70 and makes six round-trips daily to Nantucket in season—it's best to make a reservation in advance. From mid-May through October, Hy-Line's standard, 2-hour ferry service is also offered. A one-way ticket is $11 for adults, $5.50 for children ages 4 to 12, and $4.50 extra for bikes. On busy holiday weekends, you may want to order tickets in advance; otherwise, be sure to buy your tickets at least half an hour before your boat leaves the dock. For all Hy-Line ferry service, it's also a good idea to reserve a parking spot in Hyannis in July and August; the all-day fee is $10.

Hy-Line's *MV Great Point* (less than a 2-hr. trip) has a first-class section with a private lounge, bathrooms, bar, and snack bar; a continental breakfast or afternoon cheese and crackers is also served on board. One-way fare is $21 for adults and children. And don't forget about their "Around the Sound" cruise, a 1-day, round-trip excursion from Hyannis with stops in Nantucket and Martha's Vineyard that runs from June through mid-September. The price is $33 for adults, $16.50 for children 4 to 12, and $13.50 extra for bikes.

From Martha's Vineyard, Hy-Line runs passenger-only ferries to Nantucket from June through mid-September (there is no car-ferry service between the islands). The trip time from Oak Bluffs is 2 hours and 15 minutes. The one-way fare is $11 for adults, $5.50 for children 4 to 12, and $4.50 extra for bikes.

From Harwich Port, you can avoid the summer crowds in Hyannis and board one of **Freedom Cruise Line's** (☎ 508/432-8999) passenger-only ferries to Nantucket. From mid-May through mid-October, boats leave from Saquatucket Harbor in Harwich Port; the trip is 1¹/₂ hours. A round-trip ticket is $32 for adults, $25 for children 3 to 10, and $10 extra for bikes. Parking is free for the first 24 hours; $8 each day thereafter. Advance reservations are recommended.

Nantucket

Accommodations

Hostel **3**

Summer House **6**

Wauwinet Inn **4**

Attractions

Brant Point Lighthouse **2**

Great Point Lighthouse **1**

Sankaty Head Lighthouse **5**

BY AIR You can also fly into **Nantucket Memorial Airport** (☎ **508/325-5300**), which is about 3 miles south of Nantucket Road on Old South Road. The flight to Nantucket takes about 30 to 40 minutes from Boston, 15 to 20 minutes from Hyannis, and a little more than an hour from New York City airports.

Airlines providing service to Nantucket include: **Business Express/Delta Connection** (☎ 800/345-3400) from Boston (year-round) and New York (seasonally); **Cape Air** (☎ 800/352-0714) year-round from Boston, Martha's Vineyard, and New Bedford; **Colgan Air** (☎ 800/272-5488) year-round from La Guardia and Hyannis; **Continental Express** (☎ 800/525-0280) from Newark (seasonally); **Island Airlines** (☎ 508/228-7575) year-round from Hyannis; **Nantucket Airlines** (☎ 800/352-0714) year-round from Hyannis; **Northwest Airlink** (☎ 800/225-2525) from Boston (year-round) and Newark (seasonally); and **US Airways Express** (☎ 800/428-4322) year-round from Boston.

Island Airlines and Nantucket Airlines (see above) both offer year-round charter service to the island. Another recommendable charter company is **Ocean Wings** (☎ **800/253-5039**).

GETTING AROUND

Nantucket is easily navigated on bike, moped, or foot, and also by shuttle buses or taxis. If you're staying outside of Nantucket Town, however, or if you simply prefer to explore by car, you might want either to bring your own car or rent one here. Adventure-minded travelers may even want to rent a jeep or other four-wheel–drive vehicle, which you can take out on the sand—a unique Island experience—on

Bumper to Bumper: Nantucket's Four-Wheel Jive

Natives of Nantucket have developed a complex social system to confer status, perhaps comparable only to that of certain tribes on Borneo. Vehicles must be four-wheel drive and either very new—the bigger the better: Hummers have been spotted—or ancient, beat-up army jeeps. And, as you will see, bumper stickers rule. A proper native's vehicle is slathered with at least five Over Sand Vehicle Permits on the back window—lined up side by side to document longevity of association with the island. Other bumper stickers also indicate a Nantucketer in-the-know:

- **ACK.** Usually seen in a square motif with a whale and a flag, this symbol is also prevalent on T-shirts, hats, etc. What's ACK? The three-letter code for Nantucket Airport. Apparently the Navy has the letter "N" all wrapped up, so Nantucket reverted to the name of a previous local airport, Ackerly.
- **FOG HAPPENS.** Nantucketers don't mind the fog; if you do, you'll be marked as an outsider.
- **TWENTY IS PLENTY IN 'SCONSET.** Keep the speed limit down in this village, or you might hit a rose-covered cottage.
- **PIPING PLOVERS TASTE LIKE CHICKEN.** Four-wheel drivers don't like it when the beaches are closed to accommodate nesting endangered piping plovers. It's customary to get into a fist fight with someone over this sticker.
- **WHARF RAT CLUB.** A bunch of old guys have been meeting in this shack on the wharf for about 1,000 years, it seems; during winter, they meet at the Pacific Club.
- **BAG THE MARKET.** Nantucket voters cried an emphatic "No!" to developers wanting to build a new huge supermarket on the island.
- **BOX.** Subtle and enigmatic, unlike the club that spawned the sticker. The Chicken Box, with live bands all summer, is the wildest club scene on the island.
- **UNIVERSITY OF NANTUCKET.** Hint: This is a joke. The highest institute of learning on-island is the Chicken Box (see above).

certain sections of the coast. Keep in mind that if you do opt to travel by car, in-town traffic can reach gridlock in the peak season, and parking can be a nightmare.

BY BIKE & MOPED   When I head to Nantucket for a few days, biking is my preferred mode of transportation. The island itself is relatively flat, and paved bike paths abound—they'll get you from Nantucket Town to Siasconset, Surfside, and Madaket. There are also many unpaved back roads to explore, which make mountain bikes a wise choice when pedaling around Nantucket. *A word of warning for bikers:* One-way street signs apply to you too! This law is enforced in Nantucket Town, and don't be surprised if a tanned but stern island policeman requests that you get off your bike and walk. Mopeds are also prevalent here, but watch out for sand on the roads. Also, be aware that local rules and regulations do exist and are strictly enforced. Mopeds are not allowed on sidewalks or bike paths. You'll need a driver's license to rent a moped, and state law requires that you wear a helmet. Here's a list of shops that rent bikes and scooters (all are within walking distance of the ferries): **Cook's Cycle Shop, Inc.** (6 S. Beach St.; ☎ 508/228-0800); **Holiday Cycle** (4 Chester St.; ☎ 508/228-3644) rents just bikes; **Nantucket Bike Shops** (at Steamboat Wharf and Straight Wharf; ☎ 508/228-1999); and **Young's Bicycle Shop** (at Steamboat Wharf; ☎ 508/228-1151), which also does repairs.

BY SHUTTLE BUS From June through September, free shuttle buses, with bike racks and accessibility for those with disabilities, make a loop through Nantucket Town and to a few outlying spots; for routes and stops, contact the **Nantucket Regional Transit Authority** (☎ 508/228-7025) or pick up a map and schedule at the Visitors Service Center on Federal Street or the Chamber Office on Main Street (see "Visitor Information," below). The shuttle permits you to bring your clean, dry dog along too.

Shuttle routes and fares are pretty simple. Downtown shuttle stops are located on the corner of Salem and Washington streets (for South and Miacomet loops), Broad Street in front of the Foulger Museum (for Madaket loop); Washington Street at the corner of Main Street (for 'Sconset loops).

- **South Loop** services Surfside Beach, Hooper Farm Road, and Pleasant Street area; every 10 minutes from 7am to 11:30pm; 50¢.
- **Miacomet Loop** services Fairgrounds Road, Bartlett Road, and Hummock Pond area; every 20 minutes from 7am to 11:20pm; 50¢.
- **Madaket Route** services Madaket (Broad Street) via Cliff Road and New Lane; every 30 minutes from 7am to 11:15pm; $1 each way.
- **'Sconset Route 1** services 'Sconset via Polpis Road; every 30 minutes from 7:30am to 11pm; $1 each way.
- **'Sconset Route 2** services 'Sconset via Old South Road/Nobadeer Farm Road; every 30 minutes from 7am to 10:30pm; $1 each way.

For a reasonable fee ($2 to $5 round-trip), **Barrett's Tours** (☎ 508/228-0174) runs beach shuttles to Jetties, Madaket, 'Sconset, and Surfside beaches from June through Labor Day; buses leave every 15 minutes across from the Nantucket Visitors Service and Information Bureau at 25 Federal St. (see "Visitor Information," below).

BY CAR & JEEP I'd recommend a car if you'll be here for more than a week, or if you're staying outside Nantucket Town, or if you're just not into biking and simply prefer to drive. Remember, though, that there are no in-town parking lots; parking, although free, is limited to Nantucket's handful of narrow streets, which can be a problem in the busy summer months. Also, gas is much more expensive on Nantucket than it is on the mainland.

Four-wheel drives are your best bet, since many beaches and nature areas are off sandy paths; be sure to reserve at least a month in advance if you're coming in summer. If you plan on doing any four-wheeling in the sand, you need to get an **Over Sand Permit** from the Nantucket Police Department (☎ 508/228-1212). To drive in the Coskata-Coatue nature area, you need a separate permit from the **Trustees of Reservations** (gatehouse ☎ 508/228-0006), which costs about $20 per day for rental vehicles.

Here's a list of rental agencies on the island that offer cars, jeeps, and other four-wheel–drive vehicles: **Affordable Rentals of Nantucket** (6 S. Beach Rd.; ☎ 508/228-3501); **Budget** (at the airport; ☎ 800/527-0700 or 508/228-5666); **Don Allen Auto Service** (24 Polpis Rd.; ☎ 800/258-4970 or 508/228-0134), which specializes in Ford Explorers; **Hertz** (at the airport; ☎ 800/654-3131 or 508/228-9421); **Nantucket Car Rental** (at Steamboat Wharf; ☎ 508/228-1618); **Nantucket Jeep Rental** (across from the airport; ☎ 508/228-1618); **Nantucket Windmill Auto Rental** (at the airport; ☎ 800/228-1227 or 508/228-1227); **National** (at the airport; ☎ 800/227-7368); **Preston's Rent-a-Car** (11 Somerset Rd.; ☎ 508/228-4150); **Thrifty Car Rental** (at the airport; ☎ 508/325-4616); and **Young's 4 X 4 & Car Rental** (Steamboat Wharf; ☎ 508/228-1151).

BY TAXI   You'll find taxis (many are vans that can accommodate large groups or those traveling with bikes) waiting at the airport and at all ferry ports. In addition, in 1998, there may be shuttle bus service from the airport to town. During the busy summer months, I recommend reserving a taxi in advance to avoid a long wait upon arrival. Rates are flat fees, based on one person riding before 1am, with surcharges for additional passengers, bikes, and dogs. A taxi from the airport to Nantucket Town hotels will cost about $8. Recommendable cab companies on the island include: **A-1 Taxi** (☎ 508/228-3330), **Aardvark Cab** (☎ 508/728-9999), **All Point Taxi** (☎ 508/228-5779), and **Peterson's Taxi** (☎ 508/228-9227).

VISITOR INFORMATION

Contact the **Nantucket Island Chamber of Commerce** at 48 Main St., Nantucket, MA 02554 (☎ 508/228-1700). When you arrive, you should also stop by the **Nantucket Visitors Service and Information Bureau** in Nantucket Town at 25 Federal St. (☎ 508/228-0925), which is open daily July through Labor Day; weekdays Labor Day through June. There are also information booths at Steamboat Wharf and Straight Wharf. Always check the island's two newspapers (now owned by the same company), the *Inquirer & Mirror* and the *Nantucket Beacon,* for information on current events and activities around town.

Nantucket Accommodations, Box 217, Nantucket, MA 02554 (☎ 508/228-9559), a 25-year-old private service, arranges advance reservations for inns, cottages, guest houses, bed-and-breakfasts, and hotels. You can call until the day of arrival, and they will arrange a booking based on your preferences. A member of the Chamber of Commerce, Nantucket Accommodations has access to 95% of the island's lodging facilities, in addition to houses and cottages available to rent by the night or week (as opposed to most realtors who will only handle rentals for 2 weeks or more). The charge for the service is $14—a fee assessed only when a reservation is made. The customer pays Nantucket Accommodations by any major credit card or check, and N.A. then pays the inn or hotel. Last-minute travelers should keep in mind that the **Visitor's Center,** 25 Federal St., Nantucket, 02554 (☎ 508/228-0925), a daily referral service for available rooms rather than a booking service, always has the most updated list of accommodations availability and cancellations.

Automated teller machines (ATMs) can be difficult to locate on Nantucket. **Nantucket Bank** (☎ 508/228-0580) has three locations: 2 Orange St., 104 Pleasant St., and the Airport lobby, all open 24 hours. **Pacific National Bank** has four locations: A&P Supermarket (next to the wharves), the Stop & Shop (open 24 hours seasonally), the Steamship Wharf Terminal, and Pacific National Bank lobby (open during bank hours only).

In case of a medical emergency, the **Nantucket Cottage Hospital** (57 Prospect St.; ☎ 508/228-1200) is open 24 hours.

2 Beaches & Outdoor Pursuits

BEACHES   In distinct contrast to Martha's Vineyard, virtually all of Nantucket's 110-mile coastline is open to the public—on purpose. Though the pressure to keep people out is sometimes intense (especially when four-wheel drivers insist on their right to go anywhere, anytime), islanders are proud that they've managed to keep the shoreline in the public domain.

Each of the following areas tends to attract a different crowd.

- **Children's Beach.** This small beach is a protected cove just west of busy Steamship Wharf. Appealing to families, it has a park, playground, rest rooms, lifeguards, snack bar (the beloved Downy Flake, famous for its homemade doughnuts), and even a bandstand for free weekend concerts.

- **Cisco Beach.** About 4 miles from town, in the southwestern quadrant of the island (from Main Street, turn onto Milk Street, which becomes Hummock Pond Road), Cisco enjoys vigorous surf—great for the surfers who flock here, not so great for the waterfront homeowners. Rest rooms and lifeguards are available.
- **Coatue.** This fishhook-shaped barrier beach, on the northeastern side of the island at Wauwinet, is Nantucket's outback, accessible only by four-wheel–drive vehicles, water craft, or the very strong-legged. Swimming is strongly discouraged because of fierce tides.
- **Dionis Beach.** About 3 miles out of town (take the Madaket bike path to Eel Point Road), is Dionis, which enjoys the gentle sound surf and steep, picturesque bluffs. It's a great spot for swimming, picnicking, and shelling, and you'll find fewer children than at Jetties or Children's beaches. Stick to the established paths to prevent further erosion. Lifeguards patrol here and rest rooms are available.
- ✪ **Jetties Beach.** Located about ¹/₂ mile west of Children's Beach on North Beach Street, Jetties is about a 20-minute walk, or even shorter bike ride, shuttle bus ride, or drive, from town (there's a large parking lot, but it fills up early on summer weekends). It's another family favorite, for its mild waves, lifeguards, bathhouse and rest rooms, and relatively affordable restaurant, **The Jetties Cafe & Grille** (☎ 508/325-6347). Facilities include the town tennis courts, volleyball nets, a skate park, and a playground; water-sports equipment and chairs are also available to rent. Every August Jetties hosts an intense sand-castle competition, and the 4th of July fireworks are held here.
- **Madaket Beach.** Accessible by Madaket Road, the 6-mile bike path that runs parallel to it, and by shuttle bus, this westerly beach is narrow and subject to pounding surf and sometimes serious cross-currents. Unless it's a fairly tame day, you might content yourself with wading. It's the best spot on the island for admiring the sunset, and a nearby restaurant, **The Westender** (☎ 508/228-5100), which has an outdoor patio, bar, and take-out window, makes the most of the view. Facilities include rest rooms, lifeguards, and mobile food service.
- **Siasconset Beach.** The easterly coast of 'Sconset is as pretty as the town itself and rarely, if ever, crowded, perhaps because of the water's strong sideways tow. You can reach it by car, shuttle bus, or by a less scenic and somewhat hilly (at least for Nantucket) 7-mile bike path. There are usually lifeguards on duty, but the closest facilities (rest rooms, grocery store, cafe) are back in the center of the village. If you feel like splurging, have lunch at the nearby **Summer House** (see "Where to Stay," below), which includes pool privileges.
- ✪ **Surfside Beach.** Three miles south of town via a popular bike/skate path, broad Surfside—equipped with lifeguards, rest rooms, and a surprisingly accomplished little snack bar—is appropriately named and commensurately popular. It draws thousands of visitors a day in high season from college students to families, but the free-parking lot can only fit about 60 cars—you do the math, or better yet, ride your bike or take the shuttle bus.

BICYCLING   Several lovely, paved bike paths radiate out from the center of town to outlying beaches. The main paths run about 6.2 miles west to Madaket, 3.5 miles south to Surfside, and 8.2 miles east to Siasconset. To avoid backtracking from Siasconset, continue north through the charming village, and return on Polpis Road.

Polpis does not yet have a bike path (it's getting one soon), but traffic is relatively light. Strong riders could do a whole circuit of the island in a day, but most will be content to combine a single route with a few hours at a beach. You'll find picnic benches and water fountains at strategic points along all the paths.

On the way back to town, lighthouse enthusiasts will want to stop by Brant Point Light at the end of Easton Street. Located next to the Coast Guard station, this squat lighthouse is still used by boats maneuvering in and out of the harbor. It's a scenic spot to take a break and enjoy the view; you'll see ferries chugging by, and immense yachts competing for prize berths along the wharves. For newlyweds, a photo at this romantic and picturesque spot is a must.

For a free map of the island's bike paths (it also lists Nantucket's bicycle rules), stop by **Young's Bicycle Shop** (at Steamship Wharf; ☎ 508/228-1151). It's definitely the best place for bike rentals, from basic three-speeds to high-tech suspension models. In operation since 1931—check out the vintage vehicles they have on display—they also deliver door-to-door. See "Getting Around," above for more bike-rental shops.

FISHING   For shellfishing, you'll need a permit from the **harbormaster's office** at 38 Washington St. (☎ **508/228-7260**). You'll see surf casters all over the island (no permit is required); for a guided trip, try Mike Mont of **Surf & Fly Fishing Trips** (☎ **508/228-0529**). Deep-sea charters heading out of Straight Wharf include Captain Robert DeCosta's *The Albacore* (☎ **508/228-5074**) and Captain Josh Eldridge's *Monomoy* (☎ **508/228-6867**).

FITNESS   Just can't get the heart pumping outdoors? You definitely haven't looked hard enough. But if you're simply desperate for some hardware, try **Club N.E.W.** at 10 Youngs Way (☎ **508/228-4750**), which offers all the usual equipment and classes.

GOLF   Two pretty 9-hole courses are open to the public: **Miacomet Golf Club** at 12 W. Miacomet Rd. (☎ **508/325-0333**) and the **Siasconset Golf Club,** off Milestone Road (☎ **508/257-6596**).

IN-LINE SKATING   Cyclists share the island's paved paths with in-line skaters, who can gear up at **Nantucket Sports Locker on Wheels,** 14 Cambridge St. (☎ **508/228-6610**).

NATURE TRAILS   Through preservationist foresight, about one-third of Nantucket's 42 square miles are protected from development. Contact the **Nantucket Conservation Foundation** at 118 Cliff Rd. (☎ **508/228-2884**) for a map of their holdings ($3), which include the 205-acre **Windswept Cranberry Bog** (off Polpis Road), where bogs are interspersed amid hardwood forests, and a portion of the 1,100-acre ✪ **Coskata-Coatue Wildlife Refuge,** comprising the barrier beaches beyond Wauwinet. **The Trustees of the Reservations** (☎ **508/228-6799**), who oversee the bulk of this tract, offer 3-hour naturalist-guided tours via Ford Expedition out to the **Great Point Lighthouse,** a partly solar-powered replica of the 1818 original. Those interested can also tour the inside of the light. The Maria Mitchell Association (see "Museums & Historic Landmarks," below) also sponsors guided birding and wildflower walks in season.

TENNIS   The town courts are located next to Jetties Beach, a short walk west of town; call the **Nantucket Park and Recreation Commission** (☎ **508/325-5334**) for information. Nine clay courts are available for rent nearby at the **Brant Point Racquet Club,** on North Beach Street (☎ **508/228-3700**). Though it's not generally open to the public, the grand, turn-of-the-century **Siasconset Casino,** New

It's a Dog's Life on Nantucket

Everywhere you go in this region you'll see dogs—usually retrievers—hanging out of car and truck windows. Cape Codders and Islanders love to bring their canine companions along for the ride. Although "The Black Dog" (of the famous Black Dog Tavern) has become a world-famous symbol of Martha's Vineyard, Nantucket may well be the most dog-friendly location in these parts. Dogs on leashes are allowed on ferries (though not in the first-class section on Hy-Line), but you may want to consider a 12-minute plane flight over instead. Both Island Air and Nantucket Air (see "Getting There," earlier in this chapter) allow dogs to fly in the back of their tiny planes. You'll sit in the last row for comfort and supervision.

Best of all, dogs are allowed on beaches here. (A certain local pooch has been known to surf in Madaket.) Be considerate and stay clear of sunbathers and volleyball players. Your dog would probably prefer a less-crowded beach like Dionis or Steps Beach to popular Jetties Beach. To get to and from the beach, you can bring your clean, dry dog—as well as bikes and surfboards—on the shuttle buses. Also, always remember to pick up after your furry friend.

There are a number of prime conservation areas for walking on Nantucket. You're likely to meet plenty of other dogs at **Sanford Farm,** a scenic 6-mile loop through conservation land that ends at the beach. The parking lot for Sanford Farm is on Madaket Road. There are many different trails here, including beautiful Ram Pasture; you can take a short half-hour jaunt or spend a couple of hours exploring the area. Keep your eyes peeled for osprey nests, and, on the saltwater pond, swans, ducks, herons, and egrets.

For such a small island, Nantucket has a good number of lodging establishments that allow dogs. The **Jared Coffin House** (☎ 800/248-2405 or 508/228-2400) in the center of town and the **Nantucket Inn** (☎ 800/321-8484 or 508/228-6900), a resort near the airport, are both prominent hotels with restaurants on the premises. **The Safe Harbor Guest House** (☎ 508/228-3222) is located on the harbor at Children's Beach. **The Grey Lady** (☎ 800/245-9552 or 508/228-9552) and **Danforth House** (☎ 800/484-4247, ext. 0136, or 508/228-0136) offer rooms in the center of town. There are a handful of other cottages that allow dogs; the chamber of commerce will provide a list.

In town, you'll want to sit on the garden patio of the **White Dog Cafe** (North Union Street; ☎ 508/228-4479) for a cup of quahog chowder, while your pup rests from a busy day at the beach. Actually, there aren't that many places with sidewalk tables who allow dogs, but you can try **The Boarding House** (☎ 508/228-9622), where you can make a reservation to dine alfresco and your four-legged buddy will be welcome.

Street, Siasconset (☎ 508/257-6661), occasionally has courts available for rent around lunchtime.

WATER SPORTS   Force 5, with its office at 37 Main St. (☎ 508/228-0700) and a seasonal satellite at **Jetties Beach** (☎ 508/228-5358), offers lessons and rents out kayaks, sailboards, sailboats, and more. **Sea Nantucket,** on tiny Francis Street Beach off Washington Street (☎ 508/228-7499), also rents kayaks; it's a quick sprint across the harbor to beautiful Coatue. **Nantucket Island Community Sailing** (☎ 508/228-6600) gives relatively low-cost lessons for adults (16 and up) and families; a seasonal adult membership covering open-sail privileges costs $150.

Scuba diving gear and lessons are readily available at the souvenir shop **Sunken Ship** on South Water and Broad streets near the Steamship Wharf (☎ **508/228-9226**).

3   Museums & Historic Landmarks

Fire Hose Cart House. 8 Gardner St. (about ¹/₄ mile W of town center). ☎ **508/228-1894.** Free admission. July–Aug daily 10am–5pm; call for off-season hrs.

Nantucketers got extra cautious after the fire of 1846 and built many small local firehouses like this 1886 example; the pumper-in-residence, the ornate Siasconset, is of the same vintage.

Jethro Coffin House. Sunset Hill Rd. (off W. Chester Rd., about ¹/₂ mile NW of town center). ☎ **508/228-1894.** Admission $3 adults, $2 children 5–14; also included in Nantucket Historical Association pass ($8 adults, $5 children). July–Aug daily 10am–5pm; call for off-season hrs. Closed mid-Oct to Apr.

Built around 1696, this saltbox is the oldest building left on the island. A National Historical Landmark, the brick design on its central chimney has earned it the nickname "The Horseshoe House." It was struck by lightning and severely damaged (in fact, nearly cut in two) in 1987, prompting a long-overdue restoration. Dimly lit by leaded glass diamond-pane windows, it's filled with period furniture such as lathed ladder-back chairs and a clever trundle bed on wooden wheels. Nantucket Historical Association docents will fill you in on all the related lore.

The Maria Mitchell Science Center. 2 Vestal St. (at Milk St., about ¹/₂ mile SW of town center). ☎ **508/228-9198.** Admission $5 adults, $3 children under 12, $2 seniors. Early June to late Aug Tues–Sat 10am–4pm; call for off-season hrs.

This is a group of buildings organized and maintained in honor of distinguished astronomer and Nantucket native Maria Mitchell (181–89). The science center consists of astronomical observatories, with a lecture series, children's science seminars, and stellar observation opportunities (when the sky is clear).

The **Hinchman House** at 7 Milk St. is home to the Museum of Natural Science, and offers evening lectures, bird watching, wildflower and nature walks, and children's nature classes. The **Mitchell House** at 1 Vestal St., the astronomer's birthplace, features a children's history series and adult-artisan seminars, and has wildflower and herb gardens. The **Science Library** is at 2 Vestal St. and the tiny, child-oriented aquarium at 28 Washington St.

Nantucket Lifesaving Museum. Polpis Rd. ☎ **508/228-1855.** Admission $3 adults, $2 children. Mid-June to mid-Oct daily 9:30am–4:30pm.

Housed in a replica of the Nantucket Lifesaving station (the original serves as a youth hostel), the museum has loads of interesting exhibits, including historic photos and newspaper clippings, as well as one of the last remaining Massachusetts Humane Society surfboats and its horse-drawn carriage.

Old Mill. S. Mill and Prospect sts. (about ¹/₂ mile S of town center). ☎ **508/228-1894.** Admission $2 adults, $1 children 5–14; also included in the Nantucket Historical Association pass ($8 adults, $5 children). July–Aug daily 10am–5pm; call for off-season hrs. Closed mid-Oct to Apr.

Four windmills once stood on the hills west of town; this 1746 structure is the only one remaining. A 50-foot Douglas fir pole (the original was a mast) turns the 30-by-6-foot sailcloth-covered arms into the wind, setting in motion a wooden gear train that grinds corn between millstones weighing more than a ton apiece. You can buy fresh meal after watching it (wind permitting) being made.

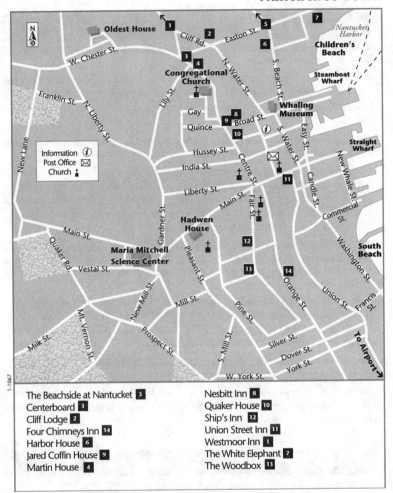

The Beachside at Nantucket **5**
Centerboard **3**
Cliff Lodge **2**
Four Chimneys Inn **14**
Harbor House **6**
Jared Coffin House **9**
Martin House **4**

Nesbitt Inn **8**
Quaker House **10**
Ship's Inn **12**
Union Street Inn **11**
Westmoor Inn **1**
The White Elephant **7**
The Woodbox **13**

🟢 **Whaling Museum.** 13 Broad St. (in the center of town). ☎ **508/228-1736.** Admission $5 adults, $3 children 5–14; also included in the Nantucket Historical Association pass ($8 adults, $5 children). Late May to mid-Oct daily 10am–5pm; call for off-season hrs. Closed early Dec to mid-Apr.

Housed in a former spermaceti-candle factory (candles are made from a waxy fluid that's extracted from sperm whales), this museum is a must-visit; if not for the awe-inspiring skeleton of a 43-foot finback whale (stranded in the 1960s), then for the exceptional collections of scrimshaw and nautical art (check out the action painting, *Ship Spermo of Nantucket in a Heavy Thunder-Squall on the Coast of California 1876,* executed by a captain who survived the storm). A wall-size map depicts the round-the-world meanderings of the *Alpha,* accompanied by related journal entries. The price of admission includes daily lectures on the brief and colorful history of the industry, like the beachside "whalebecue" feasts that natives and settlers once enjoyed. Pursued to its logical conclusion, this booming business unfortunately led to the near-extinction of some extraordinary species, but that story must await its own museum; this one is full of the glories of the hunt. Don't miss the gift shop on the way out.

4 Organized Tours

Carried Away. Pickup sites individually arranged. ☎ **508/228-0218.** Rates $80 and up; call for reservations. Open year-round.

In most tourist haunts, you might feel like a yahoo taking a carriage ride, but here you'll blend in with the prevalent aesthetic and perhaps get a better feel for 19th-century life. The ride comes with historical and architectural commentary, if desired.

✪ *The Endeavor*/Nantucket Whaleboat Adventures.** Slip 15, Straight Wharf. ☎ **508/228-5585.** Rates start at $15 for a 1-hr. sail; reservations recommended. Closed Nov–Apr.

The Endeavor is a spirited 31-foot replica Friendship sloop, ideal for jaunts across the harbor into Nantucket Sound. Skipper James Genthner will gladly drop you off for a bit of sunbathing or beachcombing. New to his fleet is a faithfully re-created whaleboat, *The Wanderer,* in which crews of six can recapture the arduous experience of chasing a whale—minus the target, of course.

Gail's Tours. Departs from the Nantucket Information Bureau, 25 Federal St. and from pre-arranged pickup sites. ☎ **508/257-6557.** Fax 508/325-5526. Reservations required. Rates $10 adults, free for children 3 and under. July–Aug departures at 10am, 1pm, and 3pm; call for off-season hrs.

If you want to get some dirt on the island's colorful residents, Gail Nickerson Johnson—a seventh-generation native whose mother started a tour business back in the 1940s—has the inside track, and the charm, to keep a captive van-load rapt throughout a 1¹/₂-hour circuit of Island highlights.

Nantucket Harbor Cruises. Slip 11, Straight Wharf. ☎ **508/228-1444.** Rates $22.50 adults, $17.50 for children 4–12; call for reservations. MC, V. Closed May.

Adapting to the season, the *Anna W. II,* a lobster-boat-turned-pleasure-barge, offers lobstering demos in summer (passengers sometimes get to take home the proceeds) and seal-sighting cruises along the jetty in winter (no stowaways allowed). In between, Capt. Bruce Cowan takes groups out just to view the lovely shoreline.

5 Kid Stuff

The **Nantucket Park and Recreation Commission** (☎ 508/228-7213) organizes various free and low-cost activities for kids, from tennis clinics to tie-dye workshops (it's a bring-your-own-T-shirt proposition). The **Artists' Association of Nantucket** (☎ 508/228-0722) sponsors "creative days," and the **Nantucket Island School of Design and the Arts** (☎ 508/228-9248) offers all sorts of courses. The **Nantucket Atheneum** (☎ 508/228-1110) holds readings in its spiffy new children's wing, and the **Nantucket Historical Association** (☎ 508/228-1894) sponsors 2-hour adventures for children ages 6 to 10, which include grinding flour at the Old Mill, baking bread at the Oldest House, and trying your hand at knots and sailors' valentines.

The **Actor's Theatre of Nantucket** at the Methodist Church, 2 Centre St. (☎ 508/228-6325), puts on theater for children by children late-July to mid-August Tuesdays through Saturdays at 5pm; tickets are $10. **Nobadeer Minigolf,** at 12 Nobadeer Farm Rd., near the airport (☎ 508/228-8977), offers 18 fancily landscaped holes laced with lagoons; there's a great little Mexican restaurant, **Patio J,** on the premises. Little kids might like to get their hands on (and into) the touch tanks at the modest little **Maria Mitchell Aquarium** at 28 Washington St. (☎ 508/228-5387), which overlooks the harbor from whence the creatures came; the cost is only $1, but hours are limited, so call ahead. For a real seafaring adventure, consider embarking on a treasure hunt aboard *The Endeavor* or signing on as crew with **Nantucket Whaleboat Adventures** (☎ **508/228-5585**).

6 Shopping

The shopping is so phenomenal you'll be tempted to rent a U-Haul. It's as if all the best big-city buyers, from Bendel's to Brooks Brothers, got together and gathered up their favorite stuff. True, some tourist dreck has managed to drift in, but most of what you'll find for sale is as high in quality as it is in price—everything from $6 boxes of chocolate-covered dried cranberries to $900 cashmere sweaters.

ANTIQUES/COLLECTIBLES Most tourists aren't looking to return home with a new living-room set, but ✪ **Lynda Willauer Antiques,** at 2 India St., between Federal and Centre streets (☎ **508/228-3631**), has such an exquisite selection of American and English furniture that it's worth stopping by just to gawk. All pieces are painstakingly tagged as to provenance and state-of-repair, and most are quite pricey. Most impressive are the slant-front desks, but the shop also stocks paintings, quilts, Chinese export porcelain, samplers, majolica, and brass and tortoise-shell accessories.

An island fixture since 1971, **Tonkin of Nantucket,** 33 Main St. (☎ **508/228-9697**), is a perennially well-stocked antique store specializing in brass and silver knickknacks. Many of the rarefied trappings, like a 16th-century carved English oak coffer, are imports, but there are a few native artifacts on hand, including a carefully vetted selection of antique Nantucket lightship baskets—those peculiar woven purses you see dangling from tanned, moneyed arms that are also known (somewhat disrespectfully) as "Nantucket minks." These handbags are descendants of crude baskets fashioned by sailors on lonely "lightship" duty (warning boats off the shoals of the island) in the mid-18th century. Back on shore, they refined the craft, and a cottage industry catering to visitors was soon spawned. Prices ascend into the thousands, and collectibility status is virtually assured. In summer, the shop offers a free shuttle over to its warehouse, where all the big stuff is stored.

ART & CRAFTS **The Artists' Association of Nantucket** has the widest selection of work by locals, and their brand new gallery at 19 Washington St. (☎ **508/228-0294**) is quite impressive.

Visit **The Golden Basket,** 44 Main St. (☎ **800/582-8205** or 508/228-4344), also known as **The Golden Nugget** at Straight Wharf (☎ **508/228-1019**), and two locations on Martha's Vineyard (☎ **508/627-4459**). Widely copied, miniaturized jewelry versions of Nantucket's trademark lightship baskets were introduced here, and artisan Glenaan Elliot Robbins's rendition is still the finest. The baskets, complete with gold penny, represent a small portion of the inventory, all of which is exquisite.

The celebrated sculptor **David L. Hostetler** exhibits his work in one of the little galleries along Old South Wharf (2 Old South Wharf; ☎ **508/228-5152**). His work in various media, including wood and bronze, appear as spiritual icons expressed in the female form. In 1997, *Duo,* one of his monumental sculptures from *The Goddess Series,* was installed at the Trump International Hotel and Tower at One Central Park West in New York City.

Paul LaPaglia Antique Prints, 38 Centre St. (☎ **508/228-8760**), offers superb mounting and framing services, and LaPaglia—an artist himself—collects appealing vintage prints, plus the occasional painting.

Like many seaside resort communities, Nantucket tends to foster pretty imagery more than serious art; however, ✪ **Main Street Gallery,** 2 S. Water St. (☎ **508/228-2252**), offers more substantial work to savor. Look for Will Berry's colorist landscapes and figures, which invite the viewer to fill in from memory or desire.

You'll definitely want to poke your head in **Sailor's Valentine** in the Macy Warehouse on lower Main Street (☎ **508/228-2011**) for a surprising mix of "outsider art" and new versions of the namesake craft, a boxed design of colorful shells, which 19th-century sailors used to bring back from the Caribbean for their sweethearts at home.

In 1966, two grads of the Rhode Island School of Design opened **The Spectrum** in a country schoolhouse, 26 Main St. (☎ **800/221-2472** or 508/228-4606), and it quickly developed into a premier purveyor of crafts. The split-level store is very late-sixties, with its sculpture gardens and expanses of plate glass. The stock is accessible and appealing, from Josh Simpson's glass-marble "planets" to Thomas Mann's totemic "techno-romantic" jewelry.

BOOKS   At ✪ **Mitchell's Book Corner,** 54 Main St. (☎ **508/228-1080**), Mimi Beman handpicks her stock and caters to each customer, with an astute sampling of general-interest books and an entire room dedicated to regional and maritime titles.

DISCOUNT SHOPPING   **Murray's Warehouse,** 7 New St., off Orange Street (☎ **508/228-3584**), has all of last year's (and sometimes this season's) tireless preppie fashions. The ultrarich tend to cast off the eclectic treasures carried at the **Hospital Thrift Shop,** 17 India St. (☎ **508/228-1125**), but a quick visit might be worth your while if you're into secondhand stores.

FASHION   **Force 5 Watersports,** 37 Main St. (☎ **508/228-0700**), rides the surfer mystique, with up-to-the-minute music to browse by and a full line of wet suits, Windsurfers, boogie boards, and surfboards for sale or rent; kayaks, Sunfish, and Daysailers are also available, as are lessons. The bathing-suit selection is the best in town, and for off-water, off-season wandering, there are plenty of Patagonia cover-ups. For kids, they offer minuscule Aqua Socks starting at size 3 and plenty of fleece for brisk days at the beach.

An offshoot of Force 5, **The Haulover,** 51 Main St. (☎ **508/228-8484**), features adventurous fashions—in the functional rather than shocking sense. The men's, women's, and children's clothing here ranges from outerwear to evening wear.

Martha's Vineyard may have spawned "Black Dog" fever, but this island boasts the inimitable "Nantucket reds"—cotton clothing that starts out tomato-red and washes out to salmon-pink. The fashion originated at **Murray's Toggery Shop,** 62 Main St. (☎ **800/368-2134** or 508/228-0437). Legend has it that the original duds were colored with an inferior dye that washed out almost immediately, but that customers so liked the thick cottons and instant aged look that the proprietor was forced to search high and low for more of the same fabric. Roland Hussey Macy, founder of Macy's, got his start here in the 1830s—his shop shows no signs of fading (no pun intended)—although today's management also manages to keep up with current trends. There's a bargain outlet on New Street (see "Discount Shopping," above).

Lilly's back! The latest from **Lilly Pulitzer**—including sensational minidresses—is available at 5 S. Water St. (☎ **508/228-0569**); this is not just grandmother golf skirts anymore.

GIFTS/HOME DECOR   A casual counterpart to its Madison Avenue boutique, ✪ **Erica Wilson Needle Works,** 25—27 Main St.(☎ **508/228-9881**), features the designs of its namesake, an Islander since 1958 and author of more than 2 dozen books on needlepoint. The shop offers hands-on guidance for hundreds of grateful adepts, as well as kits and handiwork of other noteworthy designers. It's worth a stop just to admire the richly textured sweaters, sweet-smocked baby clothes, and home accessories, both silly and refined.

The also eponymous **Claire Murray,** 11 S. Water St. (☎ **800/252-4733** or 508/ 228-1913), is famous for its elaborate hand-hooked rugs. As a New York transplant running a Nantucket B&B in the late 1970s, Murray took up the traditional art of hooking rugs to see her through the slow season. She now runs a retail company grossing millions a year and is so busy creating new collections that she has hundreds of "hookers" (probably an old profession, but not the oldest) working for her around the world. Do-it-yourself kits ($100 to $500) are sold in the shop here for about two-thirds the price of the finished rugs and come with complimentary lessons.

Resembling an old-fashioned pharmacy, **The Fragrance Bar,** 5 Centre St. (☎ **800/223-8660** or 508/325-4740), is run by a colorful fellow who goes by the solo sobriquet of Harpo. A self-professed "nose," he has assembled some 400 essential oils with which he can duplicate designer scents or customize blends. Uncut by alcohol (unlike their commercial counterparts, which typically consist of 94% alcohol), these perfumes linger on the skin and do not cause associated problems such as allergies and headaches. Harpo won't discuss his clientele but admits to creating a custom scent for a certain recording megastar who also goes by a single name, starting with an "M."

Modern Arts, 67 Old South Rd. (☎ **508/228-6711**), is a snazzy store with Tribeca influences, selling everything from deco drinking sets to top-of-the-line mattresses. Stop here for funky decorating ideas and furniture of all stripes. Centrally located **Nantucket Looms,** 16 Main St. (☎ **508/228-1908**), is an elegant shop featuring beautifully textured woven items as well as fine furniture and gifts.

Although certain influences are evident (from Queen Anne to Shaker), the hand-fashioned furniture at **Stephen Swift,** 34 Main St. (☎ **508/228-0255**), is far too individualized to pass as reproduction. Such is its classicism, though, that Swift's work would blend in at the most traditional of homes, or just as easily adapt to a modern setting. Among his signature pieces are wavy-backed Windsor chairs and benches (as sturdy as the original but more comfortable) and delicate, pared-down four-poster beds. At the line's upper reaches (over $4,000) is a "scallop" bed with a hand-carved headboard. Also appealing are his dressers with graduated drawers, and "huntboards" that conjure visions of lavish breakfast buffets. You can wander about this spare and roomy second-floor space, mentally furnishing your dream house.

SEAFOOD ✪ **Sayle's Seafood,** Washington Street Extension (☎ **508/228-4599**), sells fresh seafood from Nantucket waters and a new menu of take-out seafood platters. This is a great place to get a huge steaming plate of fried clams to go.

TOYS **The Toy Boat,** Straight Wharf (☎ **508/228-4552**), is keen on creative toys that are also educational (delighted recipients will never suspect the ulterior motive). In addition to the top commercial lines, owner Loren Brock stocks lots of locally crafted, hand-carved playthings, such as "rainbow fleet" sailboats, part of the Harbor Series which include docks, lighthouse, boats, and everything your child needs to create his or her own Nantucket Harbor.

7 Where to Stay

Most visitors to Nantucket will wish to stay in the center of town. There's no need for a car here; in fact, parking can be a real problem in season. Everything is within walking distance, including beaches, restaurants, and the finest shopping in the region.

VERY EXPENSIVE

Harbor House. S. Beach St. (in the center of town), Nantucket, MA 02554. ☎ **800/475-2637** or 508/228-1500. Fax 508/228-7639. 113 rms. A/C TV TEL. Summer $225–$275 double. AE, CB, DC, DISC, MC, V. Closed Jan–Mar.

Close to the placid harbor cove at Children's Beach, the Harbor House, built in 1886, is a venerable grand hotel encircled by standard-issue, gray-shingled town houses. The larger, more luxurious rooms, which have country-pine furniture and private patios and decks, are located in six town houses, linked to one another and to an outdoor heated pool by nicely landscaped brick walkways. It's a pleasant place to stay, but you could probably find more enticing quarters for these prices.

✪ **Summer House.** 17 Ocean Ave., Siasconset, MA 02564. ☎ **508/257-4577.** Fax 508/257-4590. 10 rms. A/C TEL. Summer (including continental breakfast) $300–$425 double. AE, MC, V. Closed Nov–Apr.

These former fishing shacks, hugging a bluff overlooking the sea and entwined with roses, fragrant honeysuckle, and ivy, are romance incarnate. Of course, this kind of style costs money. The cottages encircle a lush, shady lawn, dotted with Adirondack chairs. At the bottom of the bluff is a small, sparkling pool, where lunch is served; beyond it are miles of scarcely populated beach. The cottages are outfitted with charming English country antiques and luxurious linens, and baths in all but 1 of the 10 rooms have a marble Jacuzzi. On the premises is a celebrated restaurant of the same name serving cutting-edge cuisine (see "Where to Dine," below).

✪ **The Wauwinet.** 120 Wauwinet Rd. (about 8 miles E of Nantucket center), Wauwinet, MA 02554. ☎ **800/426-8718** or 508/228-0145. Fax 508/228-6712. 25 rms, 5 cottages. A/C TV TEL. Summer (including full breakfast and afternoon port) $270–$760 double; $610–$1,290 cottage. AE, DC, MC, V. Closed Nov to mid-Apr.

In 1988, Stephen and Jill Karp renovated this ultradeluxe retreat (to the tune of $3 million), which has since earned several nicknames, including "The Ultimate," or, as the staff has been known to joke, the "We Want It." With 25 rooms in the main building (which started out as a restaurant in 1850) and 10 more in 5 modest-looking shingled cottages, the complex can only hold about 80 decorously spoiled guests, outnumbered by 100 staffers. Each of the lovely rooms—all provided with a cozy nook from which to gaze out across the water—has a unique decorating scheme, with pine armoires, plenty of wicker, exquisite Audubon prints, handsome fabrics, and a lovely array of antique accessories.

Dining/Entertainment: Guests can dine in the highly acclaimed Topper's restaurant on the premises (see "Where to Dine," below).

Services: The staff goes to great lengths to please, ferrying you into town, for instance, in a 1936 "Woody," or dispatching you on a 21-foot launch across the bay to your own private strip of beach.

Facilities: The inn is the last stop on an 8-mile road to nowhere (actually, a wildlife sanctuary), and it boasts several clay tennis courts with a pro shop and teaching pro, a croquet lawn, a platform for nearly life-size "beach chess," and plenty of boats and bikes to borrow.

White Elephant Hotel. Easton and Willard sts., Nantucket, MA 02554. ☎ **800/475-2637** or 508/228-2500. Fax 508/325-1195. 49 rms, 31 cottages. A/C TV TEL. Summer $325–$575 double; $325–$700 cottage. AE, CB, DC, DISC, MC, V. Closed Nov–Apr.

Belying its name, this luxury property, right on the harbor, is the ultimate in-town lodging. Rooms (distributed among 2 buildings and 18 cottages) are big and airy, with picturesque views and country-chic decor. Every space is fresh and breezy, and none more so than the outdoor heated pool and hot tub surrounded by tasteful gray arbors. The hotel's location welcomes "sail-in" guests.

Dining/Entertainment: The new Brant Point Grill has been entirely renovated and re-staffed. The view couldn't be better, but the quality of the service and food (main courses $22 to $32) remains to be seen. In season, there's live music in the bar area every night.

Services: This full-service hotel provides concierge, limited room service, newspapers, and currency exchange. Laundry and dry cleaning service are available for a fee.

Facilities: Guests will enjoy the outdoor heated pool.

EXPENSIVE

Beachside at Nantucket. 30 N. Beach St. (about ³/₄ mile W of town center), Nantucket, MA 02554. ☎ **800/322-4433** or 508/228-2241. Fax 508/228-8901. 90 rms. A/C TV TEL. Summer $185–$225 double. AE, DC, DISC, MC, V. Closed mid-Oct to mid-Apr.

Emphatically not an ordinary motel, the Beachside's 90 air-conditioned bedrooms and lobby have been lavished with Provençal prints and handsome rattan and wicker furniture; the patios and decks overlooking the central courtyard with its heated pool have been prettified with French doors and latticework. If you prefer the laissez-faire lifestyle of a motel to the sometimes constricting rituals of a B&B, you might find this the ideal base.

Centerboard. 8 Chester St. (in the center of town), Nantucket, MA 02554. ☎ **508/228-9696.** Fax 508/228-1963. 4 rms, 1 suite, 1 studio. A/C TV TEL. Summer (including continental breakfast) $165 studio or double; $285 suite. AE, MC, V.

Nantucket actually has very little in Victorian housing: The island was just too poor (and underpopulated) to build much in those days. The few to be found tend to get dolled up like this updated 1890s home, replete with parquet floors, Oriental rugs, lavish fabrics, and lace-trimmed linens. The overall look is lighter and less cluttered than the original, however, and thus more in line with modern tastes. Of the six bedrooms, the first-floor suite is perhaps the most romantic, with a green-marble Jacuzzi and a private living room with fireplace. Other rooms and bathrooms are quite small.

✪ **Four Chimneys.** 38 Orange St. (about ¹/₄ mile E of Main St.), Nantucket, MA 02554. ☎ **508/228-1912.** Fax 508/325-4864. 10 rms. A/C. Summer (including continental breakfast) $150–$250 double. AE, DC, MC, V. Closed Nov to mid-May.

The Four Chimneys is a bed-and-breakfast of rare charm, stylishly outfitted with a grand piano in the front parlor and a crystal-chandelier dining room. For privacy-seekers, there's a beautiful little Japanese garden in back. Authentic antiques, including some stunning colonial chests, adorn the bedrooms, where beds have down comforters. Some rooms have fireplaces and/or terraces.

Jared Coffin House. 29 Broad St. (at Centre St.), Nantucket, MA 02554. ☎ **800/248-2405** or 508/228-2405. Fax 508/228-8549. 60 rms. TV TEL. Summer (including full breakfast) $150–$200 double. AE, DC, DISC, MC, V.

This grand brick manse was built in 1845 to the specs of the social-climbing Mrs. Coffin, who abandoned it for the big city after 2 years and left it to take in boarders. Lovingly renovated to its original splendor by the Nantucket Historical Trust, it is the social center of town, as well as a mecca for visitors. Accommodations range from well-priced singles (rare in these parts) to roomy suites. Rooms in the neighboring annex houses are equally grand. The concierge, Mrs. K., can't do enough to help, and refuses tips! The front rooms can be quite noisy. Twenty-minute waits for breakfast are not unusual—though the cranberry pancakes are worth the wait. It's a good idea to call down and put your name on the list, so you don't wait long.

Union Street Inn. 7 Union St. (in the center of town), Nantucket, MA 02554. ☎ **800/225-5116** or 508/228-9222. 11 rms, 1 suite. A/C TV. Summer (including full breakfast) $140–$200 double; $240 suite. AE, MC, V. Open year-round.

Sophisticated innkeepers Deborah & Ken Withrow have a terrific location for their historic property, just steps from Main Street but in a quiet, residential section of town. Ken's experience in big hotels shows in the amenities and full concierge service offered here. Within the past 5 years, the Union Street Inn has been completely restored, highlighting its period charms and updating all systems. Many rooms have canopied or four-poster beds; some have working fireplaces. Unlike many Nantucket inns that are forbidden by zoning laws to serve a full breakfast, this inn's location allows a superb complete breakfast on the garden patio. If you are hanging around in the afternoon, there are usually home-baked cookies or other goodies to sample as well.

Westmoor Inn. Westmoor Lane (off Cliff Rd., about 1 mile W of town center), Nantucket, MA 02554. ☎ **508/228-0877.** 14 rms. Summer (including full breakfast) $140–$225 double. AE, MC, V. Closed early Dec to Mar.

This yellow 1917 Federal-style mansion has all its original detailing—from the grand portico to the widow's walk—plus a new interior design that maximizes the effect of the mansion's light-suffused hilltop setting. The spacious living room is full of thoughtful touches, perhaps a vase of magnificent gladiola on the baby grand, and a 1,000-piece puzzle of Nantucket arrayed as a work in progress. There's even a cozy little TV room (anathema at most B&Bs) with wicker couches and framed architectural blueprints.

The 14 bedrooms, including a ground-floor suite equipped with a full-size Jacuzzi and French doors that lead to the lawn, are as romantic as one would expect. After breakfasting to classical music in the conservatory, one can head off down a sandy lane to a quiet stretch of bay beach or hop on a bike and explore the island.

MODERATE

✪ **Cliff Lodge.** 9 Cliff Rd. (a few blocks from the center of town), Nantucket, MA 02554. ☎ **508/228-9480.** Fax 508/228-6308. 11 rms, 1 apt. A/C TV TEL. Summer (including continental breakfast) $130–$170 double; $255 apt. MC, V. Open year-round.

In 1995, Debby and John Bennett purchased this popular inn and freshened it up with their own countrified style. The result is a charmer: sunny, cheerful rooms with colorful quilts and splatter-painted floors. Though the inn is vintage 18th century, there is not a cobweb to be found in this immaculate setting. The continental breakfast, serving home-baked breads and muffins in the sunny garden, is congenial. Chat with Debby for a wealth of island info and the latest goings-on, then climb up to the roof walk for a bird's-eye view of the town and harbor.

Martin House Inn. 61 Centre St. (between Broad and Chester sts.), Nantucket, MA 02554. ☎ **508/228-0678.** 13 rms (4 with shared bath). Summer (including continental breakfast) $85–$150. AE, MC, V.

This is one of the lower-priced B&Bs in town, but also one of the most stylish, with a formal parlor and dining rooms and a spacious side porch, complete with hammock. The garret single rooms with a shared bath are a real deal. Other higher priced rooms have four-posters and fireplaces. The extensive continental breakfast includes Martin's famous granola, as well as home-baked breads, muffins, and fresh fruits.

The Quaker House. 5 Chestnut St. (in the center of town), Nantucket, MA 02554. ☎ **508/228-0400** or 508/228-9156. 8 rms. Summer (including continental breakfast) $120–$170. AE, MC, V. Closed Jan to late Apr.

This pretty eight-room B&B, built in 1847, is right in the center of town—a plus for those who like to be centrally located, maybe a minus for those who prefer to retire early. It's not that the street life is rowdy, but people do tend to stroll and socialize till all hours, and the houses are closely packed. All but one of the comfortable rooms have queen-size beds (most canopied), and all are simply but tastefully decorated. Most rooms are air-conditioned. A fine restaurant, Kendrick's, is downstairs (see "Where to Dine," below).

The Ship's Inn. 13 Fair St., Nantucket, MA 02554. ☎ **508/228-0040.** 12 rms (2 with shared bath). TV TEL. A/C upon request. Summer (including continental breakfast) $75 single with shared bath; $125–$150 double. AE, MC, V.

This pretty historic inn is on a quiet side street, just slightly removed—only 1 block—from Nantucket's center. Rooms are comfortable, spacious, and charming. There is also a good variety of bedding situations here, like single rooms and twin beds. The restaurant downstairs holds its own (see "Where to Dine," below).

The Woodbox Inn. 29 Fair St. (about a 5-min. walk E of town center), Nantucket, MA 02554. ☎ **508/228-0587.** 3 rms, 6 suites. Summer $130 double; $170–$220 suite. No credit cards. Closed Jan–Apr.

The oldest inn on the island, this shingled 1709 house is easily the most evocative. The sleeping quarters include nine rooms with queen beds, and most have fireplaces. Breakfasts in the restaurant on the main floor (for an extra fee) feature delicious egg dishes and the inn's famous popovers. The restaurant also serves dinner and is open to the public.

INEXPENSIVE

The Nesbitt Inn. 21 Broad St., Box 1019, Nantucket, MA 02554. ☎ **508/228-0156** or 508/228-2446. 13 rms (all with shared bath), 2 apts. Summer (including continental breakfast) $50 single; $70–$100 double; apts $950 weekly. MC, V.

This Victorian-style inn in the center of town has been run by the same family for 95 years. Though a bit tired, this place is certainly a bargain for Nantucket. Rooms have sinks, while common bathrooms are in the hall. There's a friendly, family-oriented atmosphere to the inn, and beloved innkeepers Dolly and Nobby Noblit are salt-of-the-earth Nantucketers, who will cheerfully fill you in on Island lore.

Robert B. Johnson HI-AYH Hostel. 31 Western Ave. (on Surfside Beach, about 3 miles S of Nantucket town), Surfside, MA 02554. ☎ **508/228-0433.** Fax 508/228-5672. 49 beds. $12 for members, $15 for nonmembers. MC, V. Closed mid-Oct to mid-Apr.

This youth hostel enjoys an almost perfect location. Set right beside Surfside Beach, the former "Star of the Sea" is an authentic 1873 lifesaving station, Nantucket's first. Where seven Surfmen once stood ready to fish out shipwreck victims (preferably still alive), 49 backpackers now enjoy gender-segregated bunk rooms; the women's quarters, upstairs, still contain a climb-up lookout post. The usual lockout (9:30am to 5pm) and curfew (10:30pm) rules prevail.

8 Where to Dine

Nantucket is filled with outrageously priced restaurants, in which star chefs create dazzling meals served in high style. Obviously, you don't need this kind of treatment every night, but you'll probably want to try at least one deluxe place here. Many of the best restaurants serve terrific lunches at half the price of their dinner menus. Thankfully, there are also a number of cafes scattered around town that serve reasonably priced lunches and dinners. Nantucket also has two old-fashioned drugstore soda fountains serving breakfast and lunch right next to each other on Main Street. If you dine in town, you may enjoy an evening stroll afterwards, since many stores stay open late. The supreme experience, though, may be to cruise on *The Wauwinet Lady,* a motor launch, over to Topper's, the fine restaurant at the Wauwinet Inn. After dinner you can stroll along the beach, reveling in your extravagance.

VERY EXPENSIVE

✪ Chanticleer Inn. 9 New St., Siasconset. ☎ **508/257-6231** or 508/257-9756. Reservations recommended. Jacket required. Main courses $28–$35; fixed-price dinner $65. AE, MC, V. Mid-May to mid-Oct Tues–Sun noon–2:30pm and 6:30–9:30pm. Closed mid-Oct to mid-May. FRENCH.

A contender for the priciest restaurant on the Cape and Islands, this rose-covered cottage-turned-French-auberge has fans who don't begrudge a penny and who insist they'd have to cross an ocean to savor the likes of the classic cuisine that has been served here since the mid-1970s. Just to highlight a few glamorous options on the prix-fixe menu: *gateau de grenouilles aux pommes de terre* (a frogs' legs "cake" in a potato crust); *tournedos de lotte marinée au gingembre, sauce au rhum, croquettes d'ail* (a gingered monkfish scaloppini with a lemon-rum sauce and sweet garlic fritters); and *pain perdu, glace au chocolat blanc, coulis d'abricots secs* (a very classy bread pudding with white-chocolate ice cream and apricot sauce). The restaurant also has a stellar wine cellar stocked with 38,000 bottles.

Club Car. 1 Main St. ☎ **508/228-1101.** Reservations recommended. Main courses $27–$36. MC, V. July–Aug daily 11am–3pm and 6–10pm; call for off-season hrs. Closed Jan–May. CONTINENTAL.

For decades one of the top restaurants on Nantucket, this posh venue is also popular with locals, many of whom particularly enjoy beef-Wellington night on autumn Sundays. Executive chef Michael Shannon is chummy with Julia Child, and the menu has classic French influences. Interesting offerings include a first course of Japanese octopus in the style of Bangkok (with mixed hot peppers, tiparos fish sauce, mint, cilantro, lime, and tomato concassee) and an entree of roast rack of lamb Club Car (with fresh herbs, honey mustard glaze, minted Madeira sauce). Some nights, seven-course tasting menus are available at a fixed price of $65 per person. The lounge area is within an antique first-class car from the old Nantucket railroad; you'll want to have a drink while cuddled in the red leather banquets before or after dinner. Lunch at the Club Car is a great deal for those on a budget; all that atmosphere and hearty food arrive without the soaring prices.

✪ The Summer House. 17 Ocean Ave., Siasconset. ☎ **508/257-9976.** Reservations recommended. Main courses $28–$42. AE, MC, V. July–Aug daily 12:30–3:30pm and 6–10pm; Closed mid-Oct to Apr. NEW AMERICAN.

Ruth and Timothy Pitts are considered top chefs on Nantucket, an island with more than its share of culinary talent. Specialties of the house include fresh, locally caught seafood with island vegetables delicately prepared and stylishly presented. Tempting appetizers include the warm goat-cheese tart with salad of *haricot vert* (string bean) and baby tomato; and the duck spring roll with peach compote and spiced pistachios. The most popular main courses are grilled duck breast with wild-mushroom sauce and ricotta gnocchi; the lobster and creamy potatoes, served with a sauce of sweet corn, tomato, and summer truffles; and the grilled veal porterhouse with roast shallot and aged balsamic sauce, creamy porcini potatoes, and oven-fried beets. The atmosphere is classic Nantucket, 'Sconset-style: wicker and wrought iron, roses and honeysuckle. A pianist plays nightly—often Gershwin standards. The pounding Atlantic Ocean is just over the bluff. Prices are high here, but be content that you're paying for some of the best food, atmosphere, and service that Nantucket has to offer.

✪ Topper's. The Wauwinet, 120 Wauwinet Rd. (off Squam Rd.), Wauwinet. ☎ **508/228-8768.** Reservations recommended. Jacket requested. Main courses $29–$42. AE, DC,

MC, V. May–Oct Mon–Sat noon–2pm and 6–9:30pm, Sun 11am–2pm and 6–9:30pm. Closed Nov–Apr. REGIONAL/NEW AMERICAN.

The beneficiary of a multimillion-dollar makeover, this 1850 restaurant—part of a secluded resort—is a tastefully subdued knockout, with wicker armchairs, splashes of chintz, and a two-tailed mermaid to oversee a chill-chasing fire. New chef Chris Freeman continues a tradition of the finest regional cuisine: In his hands, lobster becomes a major event (it's often sautéed with champagne beurre blanc), and he also has a knack for unusual delicacies such as arctic char. Desserts are fanciful and fabulous: Consider the toasted brioche with poached pears and caramel sauce. The Wauwinet runs a complimentary launch service to the restaurant for lunch and dinner; it leaves from Straight Wharf at 11am and 5pm, takes 1 hour, and also makes the return trip.

EXPENSIVE

The Boarding House. 12 Federal St. ☎ **508/228-9622.** Reservations recommended. Main courses $24–$34. AE, MC, V. July–Aug daily 6–10pm; call for off-season hrs. INTERNATIONAL.

This is one of the most popular places in town. Though you can dine by candlelight in this romantic restaurant or on the patio in season, the prime people-watching may distract you from your meal. Chef Seth Raynor's dishes tend to have Asian and Mediterranean accents, like the rare yellowfin tuna with wasabi aioli and soy ginger glaze, but his trademark dish is the grilled native lobster tails with mashed potatoes and champagne beurre blanc.

DeMarco. 9 India St. (between Federal and Centre sts.). ☎ **508/228-1836.** Reservations recommended. Main courses $18–$30. AE, MC, V. June to mid-Sept daily 6–10pm; call for off-season hrs. Closed Dec–Mar. NORTHERN ITALIAN.

Haute northern Italian cuisine hasn't quite swept Nantucket—so far, this frame house carved into a cafe/bar and loft is the only place you'll find it. A forward-thinking menu and attentive service ensure a superior meal, which might include *antipasto di salmone* (house smoked salmon rollantini, lemon herb cream cheese, cucumber and endive salad with chive vinaigrette) and the delicate *capellini con scampi* (capellini with rock shrimp, tomato, black olives, capers, and hot pepper).

✪ **India House Restaurant.** 37 India St. (about ¹/₈ mile W of Centre St.). ☎ **508/228-9043.** Reservations recommended. Main courses $17–$35. AE, DISC, MC, V. Late May to Nov, daily seatings at 6:30 and 9:30pm; call for off-season hrs. Closed Jan–Mar. NEW AMERICAN.

Three small dining rooms, with listing floors and low-slung ceilings, make a lovely, intimate setting for superb candlelit dinners. A longtime favorite dish is lamb India House, enrobed in rosemary-studded breading and cloaked in béarnaise sauce. However, new influences have recently surfaced: for example, Asian (as demonstrated in the 12-spice salmon sashimi with garlic and mint soy oil) and Southwestern (Texas wild-boar ribs with grilled pineapple barbecue sauce). The menu changes biweekly, so you can be sure that this wonderful restaurant won't be resting on its well-deserved laurels.

Kendrick's. 5 Chestnut St. ☎ **508/228-9156.** Reservations recommended. Main courses $16–$29. AE, MC, V. June–Sept Mon–Fri 11:30am–3pm, Sat–Sun 8am–2pm; daily 6–10pm. Closed Jan to late Apr. NEW AMERICAN.

New owners Kendrick Anderson and Stephanie Silva have designed their restaurant to be a little less expensive (meaning entrees are under $30) than others; it concentrates on high quality, fresh ingredients, simple preparations, and ample portions. The menu is small but diverse; a mixed vegetarian-carnivore couple will be satisfied here. Every night there is a tofu vegetarian dish, a steak dish, and a few fish specials, in addition to other choices. Dishes tend to have strong international influences: Grilled rare tuna is served with bok choy and udon noodle cake, and rack of lamb comes with eggplant turbans, feta, and couscous. Set in one of Nantucket's shingled historic inns in the center of town, Kendrick's has three small dining rooms, one lined with banquettes. Intriguing contemporary art, locally produced, is displayed. The bar menu served till 11pm (with prices under $15) is popular with the late-night crowd.

✪ **Òran Mór.** 2 S. Beach St. (in the center of town). ☎ **508/228-8655.** Reservations recommended. Main courses $18–$30. MC, V. May–Oct daily 6–10pm; call for off-season hrs. NEW AMERICAN.

Chef Peter Wallace, formerly of Topper's at the Wauwinet, has taken over at this second-floor waterfront venue, long a beloved neighborhood restaurant. The unusual name is Gaelic and means "great song," which is the name of Wallace's favorite single-malt scotch. Climb up the stairs of this historic building and prepare yourself for a somewhat extravagant dining experience. (There's a seven-course tasting menu here: $50 fixed-price $80 with wine.) Appetizer choices like carpaccio and tartare of beef with truffle oil are fancy even by Nantucket standards. Some winning entrees are grilled yellowfin tuna with a chipotle tomato broth; and grilled breast and long cooked leg of duck with black barley, which some say is the best duck dish on the island. An excellent sommelier is on hand to assist wine lovers.

Straight Wharf. On Straight Wharf. ☎ **508/228-4499.** Reservations recommended. Main courses $22–$34. AE, MC, V. July–Aug Tues–Sun 6–10pm; call for off-season hrs. Closed Oct–May.

Make your reservations for the 8pm seating so you can watch the sun set over the harbor. This is one of the few places you can go to dine right on the water in Nantucket. As befits the location, you'll want to order seafood here. Try the pan-seared tuna with sunflower seed, pepper crust, organic barley, and beef glaze; or the braised halibut with Oregon morels, crayfish, fava beans, and spaetzle. The bar scene hops nightly.

MODERATE

Black Eyed Susans. 10 India St. (in the center of town). No phone. Reservations not accepted. Main courses $14–$19. No credit cards. April to Nov daily 8–11am and 6–10pm. ETHNIC ECLECTIC.

This is supremely exciting food in a funky bistro atmosphere. It's a small venue, popular with locals, so the line for dinner is likely to be out the door in season (reservations not accepted). Inside, it may seem a bit overly cozy, but that's all part of the charm. If you choose to sit at the counter in front of the open kitchen and watch adventurous Chef Jeff Worster, beware of flying spices. Once seated, get ready for some excellent options. The menu is in constant flux, as the chef's mood and influences change biweekly. I was last there during a Thai and Southern–inspired moment, and we relished tandoori chicken on khichuri with pineapple mint raita; and Dos Equis beer–battered catfish quesadilla with mango slaw, hoppin' johns, and jalapeno. We mopped it up with the delectable organic sourdough bread. Black Eyed Susans has no liquor license, so you must BYOB. If you'd rather not wait in line in the evening, come for breakfast; you won't be disappointed.

Le Languedoc Cafe. 24 Broad St. ☎ **508/228-2552.** Reservations not accepted for cafe; reservations recommended for main dining room. Main courses $9–$19. AE, MC, V. Daily 6–10pm; Tues–Sun noon–2pm. Closed Jan–Mar. NEW AMERICAN.

There's also an expensive dining room upstairs but locals prefer the casual bistro atmosphere downstairs and out on the terrace. There's a clubby feel here as locals come and go, greeting each other and enjoying themselves. Soups are superb, as are Angus-steak burgers. More elaborate dishes include the roasted tenderloin of pork stuffed with figs and pancetta, berlotti bean stew, and the napoleon of grilled tuna, tapenade, and roasted vegetables, with pesto sauce.

Obadiah's. 21 India St. (between Federal and Centre sts.). ☎ **508/228-4430.** Main courses $14–$22. AE, MC, V. Mid-June to mid-Oct Mon–Sat noon–3pm; daily 5:30–10pm. Closed mid-Oct to mid-June. REGIONAL AMERICAN.

Finding a reasonably priced restaurant in Nantucket is no mean feat. But this one is a gem. You can eat outdoors, on a lantern-lit patio, or in the atmospheric brick-walled basement of the 1840s house. The cuisine is not all that daring, but reliably and substantially good. Portions are generous; service is swift and friendly. Favorites on the menu include the unique lobster chowder, Jonah crab cakes, and native lobster stuffed with shrimp, scallops, and served with a white-wine cream sauce. For the finale, try Obadiah's big, bad dessert, a sinful dark-chocolate cake with mocha frosting topped with walnuts, coconut, and whipped cream.

'Sconset Cafe. Post Office Sq. (in the village center), Siasconset. ☎ **508/257-4008.** Reservations recommended. Main courses $17–$22. No credit cards. Mid-May to mid-Sept daily 8:30am–9:30pm. Closed mid-Sept to mid-May. NEW AMERICAN.

One of only a handful of 'Sconset businesses, this cute little bistro offers surprisingly sophisticated fare. The decor is simple: an open kitchen, fresh flowers, and Nantucket-themed artwork (for sale) lining the walls. Because there are so few tables, this place can get quite crowded at the height of the season. The kitchen turns out three great meals a day, starting with hearty waffles and ending, perhaps, with fork-tender veal or duck confit. Seafood is also a forte.

✪ **Ship's Inn.** 13 Fair St. (2 blocks SE of Main St.). ☎ **508/228-0040.** Fax 508/228-6524. Reservations recommended. Main courses $15–$24. AE, DISC, MC, V. Late May to mid-Oct Wed–Mon 5:30–9:30pm. Closed mid-Oct to late May. CALIFORNIA/FRENCH.

Within the peach walls of this bistro, the chef finesses a flavorful hybrid of French and Californian cuisines. The island's homegrown produce is put to good use in the intensely flavored chilled soup of pureed vegetables.

21 Federal. 21 Federal St. (in the center of town). ☎ **508/228-2121.** Reservations recommended. Main courses $19–$27. MC, V. June–Oct daily 11:30am–2pm and 6–10pm; call for off-season hrs. Closed Jan–Mar. NEW AMERICAN.

Your agreeable host Chick Walsh has created an institution popular with locals, particularly for the happening bar scene. With 4 years of *Wine Spectator* awards to their credit, each night about 11 carefully selected wines available by the glass are featured. Chef Russell Jaehnig seems to get better and more refined every year. Don't fill up on the cheddar-cheese bread sticks: There's a lot of good food to come. For melt-in-your-mouth pleasure, try the appetizer tuna tartare with wasabi crackers and cilantro aioli. Order a side of mashed potatoes if they don't come with your entree. Not that you'll need more food; portions are generous. The fish entrees are most popular here, although you might opt for the fine breast of duck accompanied by pecan wild rice and shiitake mushrooms. I prefer the pan-crisped salmon with champagne cabbage and beet butter sauce or the pepper-seared yellowfin tuna with cucumber and tamari butter, which have been staples on the menu for years. The small selection of desserts are tantalizing and sinful.

INEXPENSIVE

Arno's. 41 Main St. ☎ **508/228-7001.** Reservations recommended. Main courses $9–$18. AE, DISC, MC, V. Apr–Dec 8am–9pm; call for off-season hrs. Closed Jan. ECLECTIC.

A storefront facing the passing parade of Main Street, this institution packs surprising style between its bare-brick walls (Molly Dee's mostly monochrome paintings, like vintage photographs, are especially nice). The internationally influenced menu yields tasty, bountiful platters for breakfast, lunch, and dinner. Specialties include grilled sirloin steaks and fresh grilled fish, such as swordfish Sedona with corn and green chili relish. Generous servings of specialty pasta dishes like chicken and *linguica radditore* are featured nightly.

✪ **The Brotherhood of Thieves.** 23 Broad St. (at Federal St.). No phone. Reservations not accepted. Main courses $8–$15. No credit cards. June–Sept daily 11:30am–12:30pm; apt to close early off-season. Closed Feb. AMERICAN.

An authentic 1840s whaling bar, this candlelit boîte positively exudes ambiance. But what keeps would-be patrons lining up is the well-priced, down-home food. The curly fries are addictive, and the warm soups, mulled ciders, and abundant camaraderie help locals get through the off-season. Best bets here are the burgers, charbroiled and served on a whole-grain poppy-seed bun: The "New Yorker" is topped with Swiss cheese and bacon; "the Bostonian," with aged bleu cheese.

✪ **Espresso Cafe.** 40 Main St. ☎ **508/228-6933.** Most items under $7. No credit cards. Late May to Nov daily 7:30am–11pm; call for off-season hrs. INTERNATIONAL.

This reliable self-service cafe is in the heart of town. Pastries, sandwiches, and international dishes are affordably priced and delicious, and the cafe has some of the best coffee in town (the "Nantucket" and "Harvard" blends are perennial favorites). In good weather, enjoy a leisurely snack on the sunny patio out back.

Fog Island Cafe. 7 S. Water St. ☎ **508/228-1818.** Most items under $8. MC, V. Mon–Sat 7am–2pm, Sun 7am–1pm. Open year-round. NEW AMERICAN.

You'll be wowed by the creative breakfasts and lunches at this sassy cafe; they're reasonably priced, with superfresh ingredients. Homemade soups and salads are healthy and yummy. This local joint also has their cookbook for sale on site.

Sushi by Yoshi. 2 E. Chestnut St. ☎ **508/228-1801.** Most dishes under $25. No credit cards. Apr to mid-Dec daily 11:30am–10pm. Closed mid-Dec to Mar. JAPANESE.

This place is Nantucket's best source for great sushi. The incredibly fresh local fish is artfully presented by Chef Yoshihisa Mabuchi, who also dishes up such healthy, affordable staples as miso or udon (noodle) soup. It's tempting to order a raft of Rhoda rolls (with tuna, avocado, and caviar), especially when a portion of the proceeds goes toward AIDS support. Be prepared for spotty service during the high season, however.

TAKE-OUT & PICNIC FARE

Bartlett's Ocean View Farm. 33 Bartlett Farm Rd. ☎ **508/228-9403.** Fax 508/228-5340. MC, V. Truck parked on Main St. in season.

You can get fresh-picked produce right in town from Bartlett's traveling market, or head out to this seventh-generation farm where, in June, you might get to pick your own strawberries.

Claudette's. Post Office Sq. (in the village center), Siasconset. ☎ **508/257-6622.** Closed mid-Oct to mid-May.

Home-baked goodies spruce up the breakfasts and lunches prepared here, which can be enjoyed on the small terrace or carted straight to the beach.

Provisions. Harbor Sq., Straight Wharf. ☎ **508/228-3258.** Open daily year-round 8am–5:30pm.

Before you bike out of town to the beach, stop by this gourmet sandwich shop for picnic staples like sandwiches, salads, soups, and muffins.

SWEETS

✪ **The Juice Bar**. 12 Broad St. ☎ **508/228-5799**. Closed mid-Oct to Mar.

This humble hole-in-the-wall scoops up some of the best ice cream around, complemented by superb homemade hot fudge. The pastries are also excellent, and yes, you can also get juice—from refreshing lime rickeys to healthful carrot cocktails.

9 Nantucket After Dark

The Nantucket Arts Alliance (☎ 800/228-8118 or 508/228-8118) operates Box Office Nantucket, offering tickets for all sorts of cultural events around town. They operate out of the Macy Warehouse on Straight Wharf in season, Monday through Saturday from 9am to 1pm and Sunday from 11am to 3pm.

Nantucket usually has an attractive crowd of bar-hoppers making the scene around town. The best part is, everything is within walking distance, so you don't have to worry about driving back to your inn. You'll find good bar scenes at **The Boarding House, 21 Federal,** or the ✪ **Club Car.** Live music comes in many guises on Nantucket, and there are a number of good itinerant performers who play at different venues. For instance, the talented P. J. Moody sings all your favorite James Taylor, Cat Stevens, and Van Morrison tunes; he can be found at the **Jared Coffin House's Tap Room, The Hearth at the Harbor House,** or **The White Elephant.** Meanwhile, it may be Reggae Night at **The Chicken Box,** when the median age of this rocking venue rises by a decade or two.

LIVE MUSIC, BARS & DANCE CLUBS

The Brotherhood of Thieves. 23 Broad St. (in the center of town). No phone. Closed Feb. No cover.

Acoustic performers from all over the country hold forth in this atmospheric boîte (see "Where to Dine," above). There's live folk music just about every night in season, when lines tend to form out the door.

The Chicken Box. 12 Dave St. ☎ **508/228-9717**. Cover varies.

The Box is the rocking spot for the twentysomething crowd, but depending on the band or theme (disco nights rule), sometimes it seems like the whole island is shoving their way in here.

The Hearth Pub and Patio. Harbor House (see "Where to Stay," above), 23 S. Water St. ☎ **508/228-1500.** No cover.

In this handsome, beamed hall with elegant appointments, there's live music most nights in season. The performers range from P. J. Moody on acoustic guitar to jazz by Richard Sylvester and Friends. The Smitty Trio, a premier jazz and cabaret act, plays in July and August.

The Muse. 44 Atlantic Ave. (about 1¹/₂ miles S of town center). ☎ **508/228-6873.** Cover varies; call for schedule. Closed Oct–Apr.

Midway to Surfside Beach, this club with salvage-yard decor and late-night pizza attracts hard-rocking bands and reggae.

The Regatta. At the White Elephant (see "Where to Stay," above), Easton and Willard sts. ☎ **800/475-2637** or 508/228-5500. No cover. Closed Oct–Apr.

At the Regatta, a pianist regales well-heeled guests and well-dressed visitors with low-key show tunes.

RopeWalk. At Straight Wharf. ☎ **508/228-8886.** No cover.

This restaurant/bar right on the harbor is where the rich and famous yachting crowd meets for drinks after docking, and it's a major social scene in July and August. In addition, it's one of the only outdoor raw bars on the island (serves till 10pm).

The Rose & Crown. 23 S. Water St. ☎ **508/228-2595.** Closed Jan–Mar.

This bar features live, loud music for dancing, and all ages show up for the fun.

THEATER

Actors' Theatre of Nantucket. Methodist Church, 2 Centre St. ☎ **508/228-6325.** Tickets $15. Late May to mid-Sept Tues–Sun at 8:30pm; call for off-season hrs. Children's production (tickets $10) mid-July to mid-Aug Tues–Sat at 5pm. Closed Nov–Apr.

Drawing on some considerable local talent of all ages, this shoe-box theater assays thought-provoking plays as readily as summery farces.

MOVIES

Nantucket has two first-run movie theaters: **Dreamland Theatre** (19 S. Water St.; ☎ **508/228-5356**) and **Gaslight Theatre** (1 N. Union St.; ☎ **508/228-4435**). The **Siasconset Casino** (New St., Siasconset; ☎ **508/257-6661**) also shows films in season.

NANTUCKET LITERATI

✪ **Nantucket Atheneum.** Lower India St. ☎ **508/228-1110.** Fax 508/228-1973. Free admission. Call for schedule.

Continuing a 160-year tradition, the Nantucket Atheneum offers readings and lectures for general edification year-round, with such local literati as David Halberstam and Frank Conroy filling in for the likes of Henry David Thoreau and Herman Melville. The summer events are often followed by a charming garden reception.

Index

RESTAURANTS

FROMMER'S® COMPLETE TRAVEL GUIDES

(Comprehensive guides to destinations around the world, with selections in all price ranges—from deluxe to budget)

Acapulco, Ixtapa & Zihuatenejo
Alaska
Amsterdam
Arizona
Atlanta
Australia
Austria
Bahamas
Barcelona, Madrid & Seville
Belgium, Holland & Luxembourg
Bermuda
Boston
Budapest & the Best of Hungary
California
Canada
Cancún, Cozumel & the Yucatán
Cape Cod, Nantucket & Martha's Vineyard
Caribbean
Caribbean Cruises & Ports of Call
Caribbean Ports of Call
Carolinas & Georgia
Chicago
China
Colorado
Costa Rica
Denver, Boulder & Colorado Springs
England

Europe
Florida
France
Germany
Greece
Hawaii
Hong Kong
Honolulu, Waikiki & Oahu
Ireland
Israel
Italy
Jamaica & Barbados
Japan
Las Vegas
London
Los Angeles
Maryland & Delaware
Maui
Mexico
Miami & the Keys
Montana & Wyoming
Montréal & Québec City
Munich & the Bavarian Alps
Nashville & Memphis
Nepal
New England
New Mexico
New Orleans
New York City
Northern New England
Nova Scotia, New Brunswick & Prince Edward Island
Oregon
Paris

Philadelphia & the Amish Country
Portugal
Prague & the Best of the Czech Republic
Provence & the Riviera
Puerto Rico
Rome
San Antonio & Austin
San Diego
San Francisco
Santa Fe, Taos & Albuquerque
Scandinavia
Scotland
Seattle & Portland
Singapore & Malaysia
South Pacific
Spain
Switzerland
Thailand
Tokyo
Toronto
Tuscany & Umbria
USA
Utah
Vancouver & Victoria
Vienna & the Danube Valley
Virgin Islands
Virginia
Walt Disney World & Orlando
Washington, D.C.
Washington State

FROMMER'S® DOLLAR-A-DAY GUIDES

(The ultimate guides to comfortable low-cost travel)

Australia from $50 a Day
California from $60 a Day
Caribbean from $60 a Day
Costa Rica & Belize from $35 a Day
England from $60 a Day
Europe from $50 a Day
Florida from $50 a Day
Greece from $50 a Day
Hawaii from $60 a Day
India from $40 a Day

Ireland from $50 a Day
Israel from $45 a Day
Italy from $50 a Day
London from $60 a Day
Mexico from $35 a Day
New York from $75 a Day
New Zealand from $50 a Day
Paris from $70 a Day
San Francisco from $60 a Day
Washington, D.C., from $60 a Day

FROMMER'S® PORTABLE GUIDES

(Pocket-size guides for travelers who want everything in a nutshell)

Bahamas	Dublin	Puerto Vallarta, Manzanillo
California Wine Country	Las Vegas	& Guadalajara
Charleston & Savannah	London	San Francisco
Chicago	Maine Coast	Venice
	New Orleans	Washington, D.C.

FROMMER'S® NATIONAL PARK GUIDES

(Everything you need for the perfect park vacation)

Grand Canyon	Yosemite & Sequoia/
National Parks of the American West	Kings Canyon
Yellowstone & Grand Teton	Zion & Bryce Canyon

FROMMER'S® IRREVERENT GUIDES

(Wickedly honest guides for sophisticated travelers)

Amsterdam	Manhattan	San Francisco	Walt Disney World
Chicago	New Orleans	Santa Fe	Washington, D.C.
London	Paris		

FROMMER'S® BY NIGHT GUIDES

(The series for those who know that life begins after dark)

Amsterdam	Los Angeles	Miami	Prague
Chicago	Madrid	New Orleans	San Francisco
Las Vegas	& Barcelona	Paris	Washington, D.C.
London	Manhattan		

THE COMPLETE IDIOT'S TRAVEL GUIDES

(The ultimate user-friendly trip planners)

Cruise Vacations	New York City	San Francisco
Las Vegas	Planning Your Trip	Walt Disney World
New Orleans	to Europe	

SPECIAL-INTEREST TITLES

Arthur Fommer's New World of Travel	Outside Magazine's Adventure Guide
The Civil War Trust's Official Guide to	to New England
the Civil War Discovery Trail	Outside Magazine's Adventure Guide
Frommer's Caribbean Hideaways	to Northern California
Frommer's Complete Hostel Vacation	Outside Magazine's Adventure Guide
Guide to England, Scotland & Wales	to the Pacific Northwest
Frommer's Europe's Greatest	Outside Magazine's Adventure Guide
Driving Tours	to Southern California & Baja
Frommer's Food Lover's Companion	Outside Magazine's Guide to Family Vacations
to France	Places Rated Almanac
Frommer's Food Lover's Companion to	Retirement Places Rated
Italy	Washington, D.C., with Kids
Israel Past & Present	Wonderful Weekends from New York City
New York City with Kids	Wonderful Weekends from San Francisco
New York Times Weekends	Wonderful Weekends from Los Angeles

WHEREVER YOU TRAVEL, *H*ELP IS NEVER FAR AWAY.

From planning your trip to

providing travel assistance along

the way, American Express®

Travel Service Offices are always

there to help you do more.

For the office nearest you in Cape Cod,
Martha's Vineyard and Nantucket, call
1-800-AXP-3429.

do more **AMERICAN EXPRESS**
Travel

http://www.americanexpress.com/travel